한국학과 우랄·알타이학 2
관련자료·연구총서

만주어 관계 문헌의 『百排』에 관한 고찰 (상) - 고찰편

박 상 규

책을 쓰면서

"항상 희생을 미덕이라고 생각할 수밖에 없었던 한 女人의 기구한 꽃망울을 생각하면서 이 저서를 시작했지만 이젠 사립문 밖 저 세상에서 미소만 보내오는구나 人生에 첫 女人으로 만나 가고 오는 것이 다 인연인데 무엇을 탓하고 미련에 머물겠는가 다 순간의 바람인 것을 바람개비 소리인 것을"

2007. 헛바람 무덤에서

발간사

오늘 해방 62주년 광복절을 맞아 본 출판사에서 <한국학과 우랄·알타이학>(관련자료·연구총서)을 24책이나 간행하게 되니 무척이나 감회가 새롭다. 民昌文化史에서 거의 15년 전에도 박상규 교수의 <알타이 언어 민속학 총서 1집> 15책을 이미 간행한 바 있었다. 물론 그 당시 있어서도 전체적인 내용은 알타이 전반에 걸친 자료 및 알타이어족의 부분적인 언어와 더불어서 민속학적인 측면에서 일부는 자료 그리고 기타 민속적인 여러 행위들을 필자 나름으로 서술한 바 있었다. 아마도 그러한 작업들은 해방 이후 처음 시도되었던 것으로 학계에서는 진단한 바 있었다. 그런데 또다시 박교수가 이번에는 본 출판사를 통해서 <한국학과 우랄·알타이학>(관련자료·연구총서)을 24책이나 방대한 분량으로 관련 자료와 더불어 연구 총서 전집을 내놓게 된 것은 박교수 자신의 업적과 경사일 뿐만 아니라 우리 한국학계의 눈부신 북방학에 대한 관심의 일원으로 볼 수도 있다. 이러한 방대한 작업을 한 박교수의 노고에 본 출판사는 심심한 사의를 표하는 바이다.

생각해보면 오늘 이 광복절에 만감회가 깊은 것은 과거 우리 조상은 비록 한때지만 중국 대륙의 수나라 대군을 을지문덕 장군께서 살수대첩에서 크게 전승한 바 있었으며 또한 안시성의 양만춘 장군께서는 수많은 당나라 대군을 격퇴한 바 있었다. 그리고 광개토대왕과 장수왕은 우리 역사상 가장 거대한 영토를 우리 후손들에게 물려 주었던 영웅들이다. 또한 백제 역시 왕인과 아직기를 비롯하여 많은 백제 유민들은 일본에다 우리의 찬란한 문화를 꽃피웠던 것도 사실이다. 이토록 우리 선인들의 강렬하고 대륙적이며 용맹스런 기상들은 지금 다 어디에서 찾을 수 있을까? 이제 우리 학계는 위와 같은 사실에 주목하여 과거 융성했던 그 시절로 다시 돌아가 그들의 문화를 연구하고 고찰하고 그리하여 어떠한 새로운 인식의 전환점을 맞을 계기가 되어야 한다고 본다. 이러한 사실들을 종합해 볼 때에 학문적인 측면에서는 <거시적 한국학> 또는 <광의의 한국학>이 이 땅에 뿌리를 내려야 한다고 본다. 말하자면 오늘날 알타이 어족을 포용하는 한국학으로 변모되어야 한다는 것이다. 그래야 과거 북방민족의 기질을 다시 재조명할 수 있지 않겠는가? 어느 민족이나 자기 민족의 우월성 내지 神의 선택성을 표방하고 있다. 그래서 대다수의 민족에게는 이와 상응하는 신화 등이 오늘날 전승되고 있지 않은가? 이런 측면에서 본다면 우리의 신화인 곰과 호랑이의 상징은 어느 측면에서 볼 때에 북방민족과 농경민족과의 결합 또는 북방민족의 농경민족화라고 추론을 내릴 수 있을 것이다. 이제 새삼 그 옛날 대륙적이고 기마적이며 유목적인 생활로 돌아가자는 것은 결코 아니다. 이러한 사실들을 통해서 우리가 주장하고자 하는 바는 현재 우리사회가 안고 있는 여러 가지 병폐적인 생각과 행동을 없애는 방법은 법과 통치로서만 가능한 것이 아니다. 과거 우리 조상들이 가졌던 참신한 기상을 새롭게 인식한다면 새천년을 맞아 새로운 민족사를 바꾸는 데 위와 같은 사실들이 크게 기여할 것이라고 본 출판사는 생각하는 바이다. 이러한 본 출판사의 기획과 의도에 부합되게 금번 경원대학교에 재직 중인 박상규 교수가 <거시적인 한국학> <포괄적인 한국학> <광의의 한국학>이라는 간판을 내걸고서 저 끝없는 우랄·알타이 영역까지 포용하여 여기에 관한 기초적인 자료와 연구서를 내놓게 된 것은 한 개인의 성과일 뿐만 아니라 본 출판사의 업적이기도 하다. 그리고 본 자료와 연구 저서에는 알타이어족에 해당되는 Korea, Manchuria, Mongolia, Inner Mongolia, Yakut, Turkey people, Kazak, Chukchee, Afghanistan 그리고 우랄의 가장 대표적 어족인 Samoyed, Lapp 그리고 아주 상고대로 거슬러 올라갔을 때에 아마도 Iban, Cuna, Inca, Iroquois, Klamath, Ona, Papago, Pomo, Ponca, Tlingit, Seri, Maori, Zuni 이러한 어족 등도 전혀 알타이와 우랄어족에 무관하지 않을 것이라고 필자와 더불어 본 출판사에서도 그렇게 인식하는 바이다. 사실 한국학이란 고구려·백제·신라·가야·고려·조선만을 포용해서는 안 될 것이다. 우리가 새천년을 맞이한 이 시점에서 세계화를 받아들이기 전에 우리 스스로가 세계화 속에서 중추적인 위치를 차지해야 한다는 것이다. 그러기 위해서는 적어도 앞에 나열하였던 이러한 어족들의 문화 등을 개별 종합적으로 연구, 분석, 검토하여 한국학의 기반을 다져야 할 것이다. 바로 그것이 전제된 세계화는 한국을 세계적인 문화의 강대국으로 향상 발전시킬 것이며 그렇지 못할 경우는 우리가 세계화의 주역은커녕 그들의 뒤꽁무니에서 늘 헤매다가 지쳐 쓰러질 것이다. 말하자면 우리는 우리 스스로 세계문화의 주체자로서 한국학을 연구하여야지 추종자로서 한국학을 연구해서는 안 될 것이다. 이러한 종합적인 결과로써 본 출판사와 박교수가 손을 잡고 방대한 자료와 연구 저서를 이번에 선보이게 된 것이다. 이제 우리도 저 넓은 시베리아의 북쪽 대륙에 눈을 돌려야 할 것이며 그러기 위해서는 가장 기초가 되는 작업을 하나하나 차근차근 쌓는 기분으로 연구를 진행해야 한다. 본 출판사가 이번에 <거시적인 한국학> 정립에 보다 박차를 가하는 작업의 일환으로 <학국학과 우랄·알타이학>(관련자료·연구총서) 24책을 내놓게 되니 우리 학계의 경사라 아니할 수 없다. 부탁하건대 박상규 교수는 본 출판사에서 24권의 자료와 연구 저서를 내놓은 셈인데 앞으로도 이제는 보다 세부적인 계획을 수립하여 개별적인 연구가 이루어지길 빈다. 끝으로 이러한 방대한 작업을 본 출판사를 통해서 선보여 주신 박교수에게 고마움을 이 글로 대신하며 많은 국내·외 학자들의 조언과 충고를 본 출판사는 바라는 바이다.

2007년 8월 15일

본 출판사 임직원 일동 드림

序文 〈自序〉

<한국학과 우랄·알타이학>(관련자료·연구총서·24책)이 출간될 쯤에는 필자가 이 분야에 입문한 지 삼십 오년이 되는 해이다. 스물여섯부터 이 분야에 들어와 해매인지 언 삼십 오년… 이제는 검은 머리에서 흰 머리로 내 자신도 변화하였다. 그러나 모양이 변한 만큼 학문은 아직도 초보의 미천을 겨우 벗어난 것이 현 실정이다. 그 동안 필자는 그 무덥고 추웠던 방학 때마다 좁은 공간 연구실과 빈 강의실 한 칸을 얻어 모아놓은 자료들을 맞추고 더하고 빼고 그리고 일부를 수정하였다. 또한 부분적이기는 하나 일부는 번역하고 또한 전체에 대한 줄거리를 매기고 연결하여 이번에 <한국학과 우랄·알타이학>이라는 제목으로 24책을 세상에 내놓게 되었다. 비록 자료와 부분적인 연구 총서집이지만 필자 나름으로 이십년의 각고의 세월을 보낸 것만은 사실이다. 사실 한국학을 연구한다고 하는 것은 그리 용이한 일은 결코 아니다. 그리고 한국학을 제대로 수립하기란 그렇게도 어렵고 방대한 작업이라고 하는 것을 필자가 이 분야에 입문해서 삼십년이 지난 요즘에서야 겨우 알게 된 셈이다. 그러고 보면 처음은 한국학이 고구려·백제·신라·가야·고려·조선을 연결하는 작업인 줄만 알았다. 그래서 필자는 고구려어·백제어·신라어 그리고 계림유사를 통한 고려어 또한 훈민정음 및 용비어천가를 통한 중세국어 그리고 현대국어를 섭렵하는 길이 한국어 형성사 및 국어사를 정립하는 것으로 알았다. 또한 한국의 세시풍속이나 지금까지 일반적

으로 전해 내려온 한국의 신화·전설·민담 등 민속학 개론에서 볼 수 있는 분야를 아는 것만이 전부인 줄 알았다. 그런데 한국학을 깊이 연구하다 보니 많은 부분에서 엉켜지고 섞여지고 혼합되어 빠져 들면 빠져 들수록 우리 한국의 문화적 원류를 찾아내는 데 어려움을 실질적으로 느끼게 되었다. 그래서 어쩔 수 없이 얽히고 설킨 실타래를 풀자니 주변의 여러 언어들 및 문화의 현상을 알아야 한다는 절박한 상황에 필자는 봉착하게 되었던 것이다. 그래서 처음부터 다시 제자리에서 시작하였다. 바로 그 시작은 우랄·알타이학과 그에 관련된 여러 문화에 대하여 알아야 한다는 사실이었다. 그래서 필자는 우랄·알타이학과 여기에 관련된 문헌인 인류학, 고고학, 역사학, 민속학, 언어학 등을 모으기 시작하였다. 그리고 이 엄청나고 방대한 자료를 일관된 맥을 통해서 연결시키는 작업이 시작되었던 것이다. 바로 이러한 작업의 일환으로 필자는 십오 년 전에 '민창문화사'를 통해서 <알타이언어 민속학 총서> 15책, 그리고 이십 삼 년 전에는 '아세아 문화사'를 통해서 <우랄·알타이 인문총서> 10책을 세상에 내놓게 되었다. 그리고 이번에는 한국학과 우랄·알타이학 그리고 아마도 고대의 어느 시점에서는 부분적이나마 한국학과 우랄·알타이학과 관련되었을 것이라고 추정할 수 있는 여러 부족 중에서 필자는 앞으로의 韓國學의 硏究는 다음과 같은 어족인 Iban, Cuna, Inca, Iroquois, Klamath, Ona, Papago, Pomo, Ponca, Tlingit, Seri, Maori, Zuni를 여기에 포함시켜야 한다고 생각된다. 물론 현상적으로는 이러한 Iban, Cuna, Inca, Iroquois, Klamath, Ona, Papago, Pomo, Ponca, Tlingit, Seri, Maori, Zuni 부족들이 한국학과 우랄·알타이학에 얼마만큼 관련되었는지는 모르지만 아마도 보편적으로 이야기할 수 있는 Inca문명이나 Tlingit와 같은 아메리칸 인디언 문명들이 대륙 북방적인 문화와 전혀 무관하지만은 않을 것이다.

돌이켜 보면 필자가 이 분야에 들어섰을 때에는 어디서부터 시작해야 하고 어떻게 해야 할지 몸도 마음도 설어서 마음만 급했지 전혀 학문적인 진척은 없었다. 지금도 이러한 현상은 늘 반복되지만 아마도 나뿐만 아니라 우리 학계 현실도 이러한 실정일 것이다. 그러면서도 필자는 거시적인 한국학, 광의의 한국학을 이 땅에 정립하고자 많은 시행착오 속에서 오늘에 이르게 된 셈이다. 우리는 이 거시적인 한국학을 앞세워 우리의 민족의 기질도 대륙적이며 기마적이고 거시적으로 변모해야만 새천년 세계의 주역이 될 것으로 필자는 굳게 믿는 바이다. 민족의 기상이 드높지 못하다면 여기에 수반된 민족과 갈 길도 좁고 짧고 옅은 길을 가게 될 것이 뻔한 이치이다. 그러나 거시적인 한국학을 이 땅에 뿌리내리게 하는 것은 결코 용이한 일이 아니다. 그리고 또한 한 사람의 힘만으로 되는 것도 아니다. 다만 필자는 거시적인 한국학을 위하여 가장 기초가 되고 뿌리가 되는 자료와 일반적인 개념을 도출하는 데만 삼십 오 년의 세월을 보냈다. 이 길이 이토록 어렵고 고통스럽고 바보스러운 외길일 줄 처음부터 꿈엔들 알았으랴. 사실 한국학과 우랄·알타이학 그리고 여기에 관련되어졌다고 보이는 고대 여러 종족의 언어와 민속을 동시에 연구한다고 하는 것은 한 개인의 문제는 결코 아니다. 아마도 국가적인 차원에서 이 문제를 보다 적극적으로 검토하고 분석하여 민족사를 정립하는 데 앞장서야 할 것이다. 그럼에도 불구하고 해방된 지 반세기가 되었지만 어느 누구 하나 거시적인 한국학을 표면으로 내세워 방대한 자료 수집과 연구를 해놓은 학자는 없었다. 그리고 어느 의미에서는 지금도 할 생각이 한국 학계에서는 어떤 의미에서는 거의 없는 것처럼 보여 지고 있다. 필자가 97년도 중국의 俗文學會, 북경대학 한국문화 연구중심, 북경대학 사회과학처(북경대학 白化文 교수, 王文寶 교수)와 그리고 楊通方(북경대학 한국학 연구중심 주임)교수 초청을 받아 북경대학에서 '한·중의 巫俗考'를 한국인으로서 처음 발표하였다. 그리고 이 발표기간 동안 북경대학의 도서관부관장 高倬賢 교수와 도서관 사서주임인 李仙竹선생의 초청을 받고 북경대학 도서관 전체 서고를 관람할 기회가 있었다. 약 1000만 권의 장서 속에서 필자가 느낀 것은 중국의 위대한 유산의 산물인 것이다. 그리고 필자는 98년 북경대학 개교 100주년(북경대학 한국학 연구중심 주임 楊通方교수 초청) 국제 학술 심포지엄에 또다시 초청을 받은 바 있었다. 이 때 <대청황제 숭덕비문의 어학적 연구>를 제목으로 발표한 바 있었는데, 이때 필자의 토론자로는 趙杰

(북경대학 교수) 박사였다. 과거 김일성종합대학의 출신이었으며 전 북경 민족대학 교수(조선 언어문화계, 중국 조선 언어학회 부이사장)이며 북경대학 한국학 연구위원인 徐永燮 교수와도 북방 유목 기마 민족에 대한 종합토론을 한 바 있었다. 결국 여기에서도 느낀 것은 중국 북경대학에서는 중국의 거대한 문화유산을 연구할 뿐만 아니라 유목민족의 우랄·알타이어족에 대한 전반적인 연구도 부분적으로 이루어지고 있었다는 사실이다. 그런데 막상 우리가 기마 유목민족이라고 자랑하고 고구려의 기상이 드높고 장대하다고 말들은 하면서도 실질적, 현상적으로 연구 성과는 거의 없는 상태이며 만약 더러 있다고 한다면 발해지역을 겨우 답사할 정도에 머무르고 있는 것이 우리 학계의 현실정이라고 하여도 과언이 아닐 것이다(1990년을 기준으로 한다면 그렇다).

필자는 여러 사실을 생각해 보면 새천년의 과제 중의 가장 막중하다고 생각되는 것은 우리 민족사를 거시적인 측면에서 보아야 한다는 사실이며, 이러한 사실 속에서 전체적인 윤곽을 잡는 데 심혈을 기울여야 할 뿐만 아니라 개별적인 연구도 병행되어야 한다는 사실이다. 그러자면 이 방대한 거시적인 한국학을 위하여 한국학과 관련될 수 있는 모든 자료들을 방대하게 먼저 집대성하는 작업이 선행되어야 한다. 필자 생각으로는 현재의 한국학 그리고 우랄·알타이학을 연구하기 위해서 여기에 상응하는 고대 유목민족과 관련된 원시 여러 종족들의 인류학, 고고학, 민속학, 언어학 연구도 포함되어야 할 것이다. 이러한 계획의 일환으로 먼저 자료 연구 총서 24책을 역락출판사를 통해서 내놓게 된 셈이다. 이 자료를 이십여 년 동안 모으는 데 있어서 서울대학교 도서관에 계셨던 이황산, 김영애 그리고 조주임 선생님의 고마움을 잊을 수 없어 이 책을 통해서 감사의 마음을 전하며 그리고 하바드대학 연경연구소, 모스크대학 도서, 북경대학 및 북경민족대학의 도서, 몽골 국립대학에서 얻은 자료 및 그 밖의 세계 우수한 대학 도서관에서 자료를 복사할 수 있었던 행운은 필자가 이 방대한 자료를 내놓게 된 결정적인 동기였다고 할 수 있을 것이다. 또한 오늘날 학술서적의 부진한 상황 속에서도 이러한 연구총서 24책을 세상에 선보이게 해주신 역락출판사 이대현 사장과 본 출판사 편집부 직원에게도 고마움을 표하는 바이다. 또한 평소부터 필자가 이 방면에 많은 공부를 하도록 권하여 주신 마음의 스승이며 학계의 스승이신 임동권, 황패강, 김청하님의 후의에 늘 고마움을 표하고 지금은 고인이 되신 故 원계 김동석(경원대학교 설립자) 박사님의 살아 생전의 따뜻한 격려의 말씀도 늘 잊을 수가 없다. 또한 처음 필자가 대학원 석사과정에 입학하였을 때 무애 양주동 선생님의 비교언어학적 선견지명은 지금도 마음속에 자리 잡고 있다. 그리고 자료를 수집 정리하는 데 있어서 동행해 준 본교 김정아, 김이주도 고마웠고, 방학동안 옆에서 기록을 정리해 준 본교 대학원 김희지 선생과 김성희 양 그리고 컴퓨터 작업에 처음부터 동참했던 황창식 군과 박선영 양에게도 고마움을 표한다. 그리고 이 방대한 작업에 많은 도움을 주신 북경대 교수와 본교 박찬식 선생도 고맙구나.

2007년 2월 어느 춥고 지루한 K동 301호 강의실에서 한국의 거시적인 한국학이 언젠가 정립되기를 바라면서, 그리고 설립자였던 故 경원대 총장이셨던 김동석 선생님께 이 책을 드리고 싶다는 생각을 하면서……

2007년 설날에 편, 역, 저자
일산 박상규 근직
(한국학의 미래를 걱정하면서……)

목차

『Tanggu Meyen에 대하여』

—≪百排≫—

and other

Manchu Reading Lessions.

Romanised Text and English Translation

side by side

by

M. Forbes A. Fraser, F,R.G.S.

暻園大學校 國語國文學科

教授 朴相圭

—(文博, Altai 言語民俗學)—

만주어 관계 문헌의 『百排』에 관한 고찰

본 文獻은 冊名이 'Tanggu Meyen'으로서 意味는 '百排'라는 뜻의 滿洲語이다. 表題에서 볼 수 있었듯이 主題目은 滿洲語인 'Tanggu Meyen'이며 더불어서 'and other Manchu Reading Lessions'는 위에 붙은 小題目이다. 그리고 表題에도 있듯이 'Romanised Text and English Translation side by side'에서 우리가 알 수 있는 것은 이 冊의 體系가 'Tanggu Meyen'인 것처럼 '왼쪽'에는 Manchu 語의 文獻語의 Romanization(轉寫)인 Alphabet이 쓰여 있으며 그 文章의 '오른쪽'에는 이 Manchu語에 대한 英語 解析이 쓰여 있다. 또한 'Tanggu Meyen'의 題目처럼 그 意味인 '百排' '百段' '百伙'와 같이 全體的인 內容 역시도 'chapter I'에서 始作하여 마지막에는 'chapter XCVIII'로 끝을 내며 그 뒤에 있어서는 몇몇 Manchu에 關한 諸事項等이 紹介된다. 例를 들면,

① 'Mr. Burlingame's Letters of Credence'
 －(31st December, 1867)－
② Khan-i Arakha Manju Gisun-i Buleku Bitkhe-i Shutuchin.
 －(Preface to the 'Imperial Mirror-Book of the Manchu-Language')－
 －(Manchu-chinese Dictionary)－
③ Preface to the second Edition of the Great Manchu-chinese Dictionary, 1771.
④ The Manchu part of a Monumental Inscription in Corea in Chinese, Manchu, and Mongol.

등에 대해 說明하였다.

그리고 本 冊에서 가장 重要한 것으로 볼 수 있는 것은,

① Tanggu Meyen에서의 体制上은 왼쪽에 Tanggu Meyen Shutuchin으로서 그 意味는 '百排序'이다. 여기에서 'Tanggu'는 滿洲語로서 '百'이며 'Meyen'은 滿洲語로서 '排'이고 'Shutuchin'은 滿洲語로서 '序'이다. 여기에서 'Shutuchin'은 原 文獻語로는 'Šutucin'으로서 滿洲文字로는 이다. 그런데 'Shutuchin'으로 本 冊에서 인쇄된 이유는 'Š' 文字 대신으로 'Sh'로 'c' 대신 'ch'로 옮겨 적었기 때문이다. 우리는 일반적으로 오늘날에도 '샤만'인 '巫師(巫堂)'를 滿洲語에 있어서는 'šaman'이라고 하며 滿洲文字로는 이다. 그리고 英語에 있어서도 'shaman'인 이유도 위의 例와 같은 경우이다. 말하자면 'shaman'인 '巫堂'은 英語가 아니고 滿洲語인데 이 滿洲語를 音借하여 'shaman'이라고 表記하였을 뿐이다.

② 'Tanggu Meyen Shutuchin'에서는 滿洲文을 Romanization(音寫)하여 적었으며 이 滿洲文에 대한 解析을 'The Hundred Chapters Preface'에 해 놓았다. 그리고 단지 여기에서도 매우 중요한 것은 滿洲語의 重要한 語彙的인 諸事實을 다시 'The Hundred Chapters Preface'에서는 分析하였다는 점이다.

例를 들면,

① Tanggu Meyen에서 ;

왼쪽, Tanggu Meyen Shtuchin의 文章에서 'Manju gisun serengge, Manju niyalmai fulekhe da.'를 볼 수 있는데 이 文章은 Manju語의 文字를 Romanization한 것이다. 위의 轉寫法은 Möllendorff式이 아니고 佛蘭西式의 轉寫法인 듯하다.

그리고 上記의 文章에 대한 解析은 오른쪽, The hundred chapters preface에서는 'what the Manchu language is, that is the root and foundation of {us} Manchus. ((Da, 'root', also 'chief' ; orkha-da, 'king of plants', is the ginseng, panax quinque-folium.))'라고 하였는데 여기에서 우리가 알 수 있는 것은,

㉠ 'Manju'는 '滿洲' 滿洲語의 文獻語이다. 그러나 이 冊이 나올 當時만 하여도 England에서는 'Manju' 대신 'Manchu'로 使用한 듯하다.

㉡ 'gisun'은 '句' '活' '言語'라는 滿洲語이며, 예를 들면 의 문자이다.

㉢ 'serengge'는 '所言者'의 滿洲語이며

㉣ 'niyalma'는 '사람'이라는 滿洲語이며

㉤ 'fulekhe'는 '根'의 뜻이며

㉥ 'da'는 '長' '本' '始' '根' '原'의 뜻인 滿洲語이다.

따라서 上記에서 記述하였던 것처럼 滿洲語 'Manju gisun serengge, Manchu niyalmai fulekhe da'의 뜻은 'what the Manchu language is, that is the root and foundation of Manchus'이다. 그리고 여기에서 滿洲語의 語學的인 分析은 本 冊에서도 위와 같이 밝혔듯이,

㉠ 'da'는 '長' '本' '始' '根' '原'의 뜻이기 때문에 本 冊에서도 'da'의 解析을 "da, 'root', also 'chief' ; orkha-da, 'king of plants,' is the ginseng, panax quinque-folium"라고 하였던 것이다.

㉡ 그리고 위의 文章에서,
fulekhe도 名詞, 그리고 意味 역시 '根' da도 名詞, 그리고 意味 역시 '長' '根' '原' '本' '始'이기 때문에 위의 文章에서 'fulekhe da'의 解讀을 'that is the root and foundation of Manchus'라 하였다.

㉢ 또한, Manju gisun serengge, 에서도 'gisun'은 '活'이며 이와 비슷한 어휘는 'bithe'인데 이 意味는 '文' '冊' '文獻'이다. 그리고 'serengge'는 '所言者'로서 'speaker'에 해당이 된다. 따라서 'Manju gisun serengge'의 解讀은 'what the Manchu Language'가 되는 셈이다.

② Tanggu Meyen에서 ;

왼쪽, Tanggu Meyen Shutuchin의 文章에서

ⅰ. 'Manju-be ayan suwayan ofi'

ⅱ. 'Beye ubu-de inu valiyabumbi-kai, khairakan aku semeo?'

ⅲ. 'Nikan bitkhe-de ai khachin-i mangga okini! Fi nikebukhe manggi, gisun eden dadun'

上記의 滿洲文獻語의 轉寫된 解析을

i 의 경우는, 'Considering what is Manchu to be great and precious.(suwayan, 'costly' literally 'yellow.')'이라 하였으며

ii 의 경우는, 'One's proper person is cast away (one loses face), is that not (not to be called) a pity?'라고 하였으며

iii의 경우는, 'Chinese books to whatever degree ripe (mangga) scholars, well! On laying down the pen, their speech is faltering'이다.

위의 i, ii, iii의 해석에서 우리가 알 수 있는 사실은 다음과 같다.

첫째, i 에서 滿洲語 'suwayan'을 本 冊에서의 'costly' 'yellow'라고 하였는데 辭典에서는 'suwayan'은 形容詞로는 '黃色'이고 名詞로는 '戊'(天干)이다. 그러나 위 冊의 解析에 있어서는 '黃色'이나 '戊'이나 'yellow'의 英語 解析보다는 'costly'로서 'precious'로서 해석이 된 듯하다.

둘째, ii에서 滿洲語 'Beye'는 '身體' '本身' '自己'이며 'ube'는 '(旗)分' '分數' '執掌' '倍'이다. 그리고 古代 韓國에서나 그리고 現代 韓國語에서 보았을 때에 滿洲語 'Beye'는 '-베이' '-방이' '-벵이' '-방'과 相關性이 있다. 말하자면 오늘날에 있어서 '-벵이' '-방이' '-방' 等은 虛辭로서 앞에 實辭인 '가난-' '거렁-' '앉은-' 等이 와야 '간난벵이' '거렁뱅이' '앉은뱅이' 等의 語彙가 된다. 그러나 古代 韓國語에 있어서는 '-벵이' 以前의 '-베이' '-바이' '-보' 등은 'Beye'인 Manchu-Tungus語처럼 '本身' '身體' '사람' 等의 意味로 쓰였던 것이나 言語의 歷史性과 恣意性에 의하여 實辭의 虛辭化에 의해서 오늘날은 虛辭로서 free morpheme였던 것이 bound morpheme化 하였다고 보겠다. 그리고 現在 咸鏡道方言에서도 '-보이' '-베이' '-바이' '-배이'라고 하는 것은 원래 '배이' '베이' '바이' '보이'의 語形態였을 때에는 實辭인 free morpheme이였고 뜻은 '사람'과 關聯된 '사람' 關係語彙였다. 그러나 'ᄯᅡ'가 'ㆁ' 添加現象에 의해서 'ᄯᅡ>ᄯᅡᆼ>땅(土, 地)'가 되었듯이 '배이' '베이' '바이' '보이' 等의 free morpheme이 'ㆁ' 添加現象에 의하여 '뱅이' '벵이' '방이' '보이>봉이>봉이~벙이<봉이~벙이間은 相互 間에 異形態로 봄도 괜찮을 듯 하다>'로 變化하였을 때에는 實辭가

아닌 虛辭로서 bound morpheme 역할로 轉異되었다고 보겠다. 말하자면 어느 意味에 있어서는 古代에 있어서의 우리 韓國語의 特徵 중의 몇 가지는 간단하게 말하면 다음과 같다.

첫째로는, 現代에 있어서의 言語 槪念인 signifié와 signifiant의 二元的인 恣意性이나 어떤 言語의 生産性이나 또한 言語를 synchronic的인 水平的 次元에서 보는 것이 아니고 '言語를 呪術的인 次元'에서 보았다는 점이며

둘째로는, 言語라고 하는 것은 매우 神聖스러운 것이어서 言語는 神과 人間과의 相互關係를 聯關, 戀結해 주는 媒介體라고 생각하면서 따라서 古代 初期에 있어서는 아마도 神 關聯語系 등이 發達 내지 生成하였을 것으로 추측할 수 있으리라. 이런 생각의 基底에서 본다면 古代의 韓國語에서는 巫俗 聯關語系 등이 韓國의 初期言語였을 것은 자연스러운 것이며

셋째로는, 古代의 初期에 言語에 있어서는 言語의 未分化性에 의해서 오늘날처럼 數 많은 語彙들이 發達하지 못했을 것이다. 따라서 둘째에서도 언급하였듯이 '巫俗語系'를 비롯한 '身體語系' '地名語系' '天體語系' '官職語系' 等의 語彙들이 발달하였을 텐데 오늘날처럼 이런 어휘들도 細分化되지 못하고 未分化的인 狀態의 語彙로 머물러 있었지만 意味面에 있어서는 한 個의 單語가 여러 意味를 包括하였던 것이다. 말하자면 어떤 의미에 있어서는 人間의 생각은 古代나 現代나 크게 變化된 것은 없었을 것이나 周邊에 諸事項에 의하여 變化됨에 따라서 여기에 隨伴되어 여기에 關한 單語들이 生成되기 시작하였을 것이다. 이 때 生成된 單語들은 대체적으로 原來 未分化的 상태에 있었던 語彙 중에서 分離되어 각각 獨立되어 原來 있었던 語彙와 相關되어 近接된 單語로 發展하였던가 또는 原來 없었던 單語가 生成되어 發展되던가 할 것이다. 말하자면 古代 初期의 言語들은 아마도 커다란 單語族 내지 語彙集團體族으로 묶여 있었을 것인데 이것이 바로 언어의 未分化性으로 볼 수 있는 증거일 것이다.

例를 들면, 다음에서 神, 天, 父와의 關係를 古代語的인 측면에서는 다음과 같다. 巫俗語係 單語인 'kam(ᄀᆞᆷ)'은 '神聖스러운 語彙'와 關聯이 많기 때문에 처음은 '神語系'이거나 '神語族' 또는 '神關聯單語族'이었을 것이다. 그래서 아

마도 이때의 單語族의 意味는 '天과 關聯된 神聖스러운 어떤 存在'였을 것이다. 그러나 이 당시에는 文獻上 어떤 記錄이라도 이러한 說明을 할 수 없었을 것이다. 물론 文字도 없었기 때문에 더더욱 그렇다. 따라서 文字로 定着하기 以前 口碑傳承된 意味에서의 '감(kam)'은 '天과 關聯된 神聖스러운 어떤 存在'라는 單語族으로서의 語彙였을 것이다. 따라서 이러한 單語族이 基底에 있는 것으로서는 '天·神 語係'였을 것이다. 때문에 오늘날 'kam(감)'의 意味를 '神' '巫堂' '巫師' 그리고 '朱蒙' 等과 同一視하는 것은 위의 사실을 토대로 하였기 때문이다.

따라서 위와 같은 관점에서 본다면 古代言語에서는 위와 같이 '天과 關聯된 神聖스러운 어떤 存在'라는 單語族 의 '감(kam)'은 時間의 흐름에 따라 점점 未分化的 意味에서 分化的인 意味로 轉異되면서 單語族의 未分化性에서 語彙의 分化性으로 意味가 分化된다. 때문에 '감(kam)'은 처음 原初的인 意味인 單語族에 있어서는 '神'의 意味 뿐만 아니라 아마도 '天' '巫師' '스승' '王' 等의 意味가 象徵的으로 包括되었을 蓋然性이 크다고 하겠다. 그러다가 文化의 發達에 의해서 單語들이 單語族에서 分離 分派되었을 可能性이 推論되며 또한 分派되어진 單語에서 또다시 派生되어 現代에 이르게 되었을 것이리라. 이런 意味的인 측면에서 본다면 '감(kam)'은 初期의 意味에 있어서는 앞에서도 언급했던 것처럼 '天' '巫師' '스승' '王' 等의 結集體的 象徵意味가 包括的으로 內包되어 있는 '神(god)'였을 것이다. 이러한 未分的인 性格을 띈 複合的인 意味인 '감(kam)'은 時間이 흐름에 따라서 점점 分化的 意味로 分化 變貌해지면서 그 意味도 '神'의 意味는 象徵的으로는 그 속 깊이 남아 있겠지만 겉에 나오는 意味는 '天' 그리고 여기에서 滿洲語의 'abka'와 相關해서 考察할 수도 있을 것이나 여기에서는 한 가지 例만 든다면 우리 韓國語의 '아버지' '아바지' '아바디' '앗지' '아치' '애비' '아비'의 뜻인 '父' 形態論的인 측면에서 본다면 물론, 標準語와 方言의 差異는 現代 韓國語의 경우에서는 相異하겠지만 古代 韓國語의 경우에서는 現代國語와 이런 面에서는 無關하기 때문에'아버지' '아바지' '아바디' '앗지' '아치' '애비' '아비'는 몇 가지 形態로 區分해서 생각할 수 있을 것이다.

㉮ '아버지' '아바지' '아바디' '애비' '아비'의 形態의 祖語形態는,

① 'aba +či > abači'의 形態에서는 '아버지, 아바지, 아바디, 애비, 아비' 等의 形態로 變化하였을 것이다. 그리고 이 語形態인 '아버지, 아바지, 아바디, 애비, 아비'의 意味는 原來는 '天者' '天人'의 意味였을 것이다. 그 이유 중의 하나는, 滿洲語 'abka'는 '天'의 뜻인데 이 'abka'는 原來 'aba + kan'의 合成語로 볼 수 있을 것이다. 말하자면 'aba + kan'에서 볼 때 'kan'에서 Altai 祖語에서는 語尾 '-n'이 脫落 내지 唯持되나 上記의 경우에는 脫落되며 또한 'aba'와 'kan'에서 'aba'에서 '-b-'와 'kan'에서 'k-'는 相互 子音이기에 충돌을 피하기 위해서 삽입 母音인 '-a'가 들어가게 되었을 것이다. 따라서 'abakan > abka'가 되었을 것이기에 意味는 'abakan'과 'abka'가 同一하게 되었을 것이리라. 그러기에 'abači'와 'abkan' 'abka'는 모두 '天'을 지칭하는 것이며 여기에다 '-ci'는 '사람'즉 '者'이기에 '天者'뜻으로 해석이 됨을 증명하게 되는 셈이다.

② 따라서 '아버지' '아바지' '아바디' '애비' '아비'의 原始祖語形態는 'abči' 語系인 'ac'이다.(여기에서 'c'는 consonant이다.) 그리고 後代에 들어와서 'abka'의 'abakan'에 比較 相互 關係가 있듯이 'ac'에 'kan'에 해당이 버금되는 語彙인 'či'인 '者'가 添加 되었던 것이다. 이 'či' 역시 初期에 있어서는 free morpheme으로서 實辭로서 名詞類에 해당되는 '사람' '者'였지만 後代에 와서는 '사람語系類'에서 '虛辭'로서의 bound morpheme에 해당되는 그래서 앞에 實辭의 뒤에 붙어서 意味를 確正지어 주는 역할로 轉移되었다.

㉯ '앗지' '앗치'形態의 祖語形態는 다음과 같다.

① 'ač +ci' 'ač +či'에서 볼 때에 '-ci' '-či'는 '知' '智'로서 同音同意語이며 表記만 '-ci' '-či'로 할 뿐이다.

② 이 'ačci'와 'ačči'는 Altai 語系 가운데에서 滿洲語와 相關하여 문제를 認識한다면 다음과 같다.

첫째, 'ačči'와 滿洲語 'ama'인 父親과 同一하다. 또한 'ama'는 'am +a > ama'로서 'am'은 '大'의 의미도 포함되어 있다고 하겠다. 滿洲語에서 'amaka'는 '公公' '翁'의 뜻인데 이 'amaka'역시 'ama +kan > amakan'에서 語尾 '-n'이 脫落되었을 可能性이 크다고 보겠다.

둘째, 滿洲語에서 'am-'과 關聯된 語彙를 살펴본다면 다음과 같다.

○ ama : (名) 父親

○ amaka : (名) 公公, 翁

○ amba : (形) 大, 弘, 巨

○ amban : (名) 臣

○ ambula : (副)(形) 大, 最

○ amji : (名) 伯父

○ ambu : (名) 大姨母

○ ambuma : (名) 大姨父

○ ambarame : (副) 大

以上의 'am-'과 關聯된 語彙 중에서 'ačči'와의 關聯된 語彙를 생각해본다면 'ačči'와 'amji'는 同音同意語일 蓋然性이 古代 言語的인 측면에서 볼 때는 크다고 할 수 있을 것이다.

그 이유 중의 몇 가지를 例를 들면 다음과 같다.

㉠ 아마도 'ačči'와 'amji'는 'atti'에서 變化되었을 蓋然性이 크다고 할 수 있으니 그 이유는 '-t > -č'와 '-t > -m,n'에 의해서 생각해 본다면 'atti'가 最初의 形態였을 것이다. 말하자면 'at' 語形態가 'ačči'와 'amji'의 祖語形이었을 것이다.

㉡ 따라서 이들 사이의 語形態의 變化는

at > { at>ač
at>am }

으로 되었으며 또한 'ač'과 'am'에 '사람 關係諸語'인 'či(支, 知, 智)'가 添加되어서 아래와 같은 形態가 되었다.

at > {at>ač+či>ačči,

at>am+či~ji>amči~

amji

위에서 'či'와 'ji'는 漢字語인 '知, 支, 智'의 音譯일 것이며 意味는 '者' '사람'으로서의 尊稱語인데 古代語에서는 '人稱에 관한 名詞類'의 單語는 貴族에 해당되는 上流層에나 붙여서 使用하였을 것이다. 말하자면 官職에 해당되는 名稱에만 이러한 'či' 'ji'인 '知' '支' '智' 등이 添加되었다. 이러한 言語的 現像이 古代 韓國語의 特徵이라고 보겠다. 例를 들면, 乙支文德에서 '乙支' 또는 '莫離支' 등은 '-支'가 '-či'를 가리키며 意味는 '者'로서 梁柱東 敎授는 그의 著書인 '古歌硏究'나 '國學硏究論攷'에서도 高句麗의 관직명칭을 예를 들면서 '乙支文德'을 '上者文德'이라 하면서 '웃치文德'이라고 하였다. 말하자면 '벼슬'이 '웃'에 해당되는 '者'인 이름이 '文德'이라고 하였다. 말하자면 '乙支文德'이 사람 이름이 아니라 '乙支'는 官職名稱이며 '文德'에서 姓氏는 '文 '氏 이며 이름이 '德 '이라는 뜻이다. 또한 '莫離支淵蓋蘇文'의 경우에 있어서도 마찬가지 경우가 되겠는데 이 意味는 '宗者 淵蓋蘇文'으로서 다시 우리말로 고쳐 쓰게 되면 'ᄆᆞᄅᆞ치 淵蓋蘇文'이니 말하자면 '벼슬'이 'ᄆᆞᄅᆞ'(宗)에 해당되는 '者'인 이름이 '淵蓋蘇文'이라고 하였다. 말하자면 '莫離支 淵蓋蘇文'이 사람 이름이 아니라 '莫離支'는 官職名稱이며 '淵蓋蘇文'에서 姓氏는 '淵'氏이며 이름이 '蓋蘇文'이라는 뜻이다. 즉 '乙支文德'이나 '莫離支 淵蓋蘇文' 모두가 '웃치' '마라치(ᄆᆞᄅᆞ치)'인 '上者' '宗者'로서 요즈음 같으면 '官職이 높으신 분' 즉 '어른'에 해당되는 사람이다. 말하자면 '莫離支'의 '-支'와 '乙支'의 '-支' 그리고 百濟時代 王의 官職名稱인 '健吉支'의 '-支' 모두가 다 '上에 관한 官職名稱에 붙은 人稱 接尾語'이다. 결국 古代社會에 있어서는 오늘날처럼 누구에게나 人稱 接尾語를 붙여 주는 것이 아니라 上流層이나 붙으며 이 接尾語 역시도 後代에 와서는 虛辭로 變化 되었음을 우리는 앞에서 알 수 있었다.

以上의 ㉮㉯에서 살펴 보았듯이

㉮의 '아버지' '아바지' '아바디' '애비' '아비'의 祖語形態는 'Ac'이며 이 祖

語形態는 'At'의 形態와도 결코 無關하지만은 않은 까닭은 아마도 'AT'形態에서 'Ac'으로 變化하였을 可能性에 대한 蓋然性이 크기 때문이다. 말하자면 '아버지' '아바지' '아바디' '애비' '아비'라고 하는 形態는 오늘날 우리가 그 意味로 '父' '父親'로만 쓰이고는 있지만 원래부터 그러한 것은 아니였던 것 같다. 그리고 祖語形態로 보았을 때에,

at

① at>ač(ac)+či>ačči<앗지, 앗치>의 形態로서 意味는 '父' '大' '巨' 였지만 현재에는 '父'의 意味로 限定된 바처럼 쓰이고 있다.

② at>am+či>amči~amci(amji)의 形態로서 韓國에서의 경우와 滿洲語 경우와 그 變化의 과정에서 相似와 相異點이 있다고 하겠다. 語學的 觀點에서 먼저 滿洲語 경우에서는 'at'의 祖語形態에서 다음 變化形態인 'am'에 人稱接尾辭인 '-či~ci'가 添加되었다고 보겠다. 그리고 여기에서의 '-ji' 역시도 同一 形態로 보아야 할 것이다. 그리고 韓國語 경우에 있어서는, 'at'의 祖語形態에서 바로 '-či~ci'가 添加되어 'atči>ačči'의 形態로 變化되어서 'ačči~ačci' 가 되었다고 볼 수 있을 것이다.

③ at~ap의 祖語形態를 생각할 수 있겠는데 여기에 대한 것은 간단하게 다음과 같이 할 수 있을 것이다.

AC : at~ap〉

① at>at+či>atci>ačči

② ap>apa(開音節化現象)>apa~aba+či>apači~abači 여기에서 우리가 알 수 있는 것은 'Ac'라는 原始 共通祖語形態에서 at~ap로 區分하여 생각할 수 있는 것은 'Ac'에서 '-c'는 consonant를 말함인데 이 consonant인 '-c'가 바로 '~t,~p'인 것이다. 그리하여 'at'인 경우에 있어서는 여기에 人稱接尾辭에 오늘날 해당되는 '-či'가 첨가되어 'ačči~ačci' 등의 語彙로 되어 그 意味는 '大' '父' '巨' 등과 類似하며 'ap'인 경우에 있어서는 'ap+či'에 있어서는 'ap'의 '-p'와 '-či'

의 '-č'에서 同一한 子音끼리 충돌을 피하기 위하여 위에서 媒介母音 '-a-'가 '삽입'되어서 'apači'가 된 것이다. 그리고 'apači'와 'abadi' 'abati' 'abači'와의 關係는 'apači'와 'abači'는 '-p-'와 '-b-'와의 關係인데 子音 '-p-'와 '-b-'는 Ferdinand de Saussure에 의한 開口度 7단계 分類에 의하면 모두 'p'와 'b'는 '0度'이며 Otto Jespersen에 의한 可聽度 8단계 分類에 의하면 'p'는 1度이며 'b'는 '2度'이다. 따라서 子(자)音 'p'와 'b'는 語學的으로 큰 辨別性이 있는 것은 결코 아닌 것 같다. 特히 古代에 있어서의 言語的인 諸現象이란 現代人이 생각하는 細分化的이고 音聲學的인 高度의 言語的인 性格이 내포되어 있는 것이 아닌 原初的인 그러면서도 未分化的인 그런 性格이 內包되어 있을 것이며 音韻的인 어떤 法則 보다는 民間語源 또는 民間의 어떤 發音上 經濟性 등에 의해 變化 내지 異化現象이 發生되기 때문에 'apači' 'abadi' 'abati' 'abači' 等은 어느 측면에 있어서는 文獻上에서의 論理的 측면에서는 辨別的이면서도 通時的인 變遷過程을 理論的으로 생각할 수 있을 것이다. 그러나 古代人들은 이런 科學的인 知識을 通해서 얼마나 語學的인 思考力을 가졌을까 하는 점은 사실상 筆者로서는 의문의 여지로 남겨두기로 한다.

㉯의 '앗지' '앗치' 의 祖語形態 역시도 'Ac'였을 것이다. 그리고 아무래도 ㉮의 '아버지' '아바지' '아바디' '애비' '아비' 보다는 '앗지' '앗치'가 보다 더 祖語形態에 가깝고 보다 原始語形態에 속한다고 볼 수 있을 것이다. 결국 ㉮㉯에서 알 수 있는 것은 오늘날 아버지에 해당되는 '父'의 形態는 'Ac'의 祖語形態에서 發達하여 한 쪽으로는 'ač'形으로 또 하나는 'am'形으로 그리고 다른 하나는 'ap~ab'形으로 分離 발전하여 왔음을 알 수 있을 것이다.

셋째, (iii)에서 滿洲語 'Nikan'은 '中國'을 指稱하는데 앞에서 언급했던 바를 다시 보면,

'Nikan bitkhe-de ai Khachin-i mangga okini! Fi nikebukhe manggi, gisun eden dadun' 에서 'Chinese books to whatever degree ripe(mangga) scholars, well! on laying down the pen, their speech is faltering'라고 解析한 것을 보면 'Nikan'은 'Chinese'이다.

또한 閔泳珪는 1964년 延世大 人文科學 第 11집에서 '老乞大 辨疑'에서 '예

나 이제나 女眞 또는 滿洲 말로 Nikan, 蒙古말로 Kita(i)는 모두 中國을 가르켜 서 쓰여 오던 말들이다'라고 하였다. '元朝秘史나 華夷譯語 등, 明·清의 이 方面 譯書에 보이는 乞塔·乞塔惕·起炭·古代 등은 모두 이 kita(i)가 漢譯된 例이며 가다가 契塔特 등은 그 複數形 Kitat의 -t음이 정직하게 寫音된 때문이다. 老乞大의 -乞大는 그러므로 中國을 가리키는 蒙古 말 Kita(i) 일시 분명하며 老乞大란 곧 '老漢兒' 다시 말해서 時際 中國의 俗語를 엮은 教材에 붙여진 이름으로서 조금도 이상할 것이 없다'라고 閔泳珪는 덧붙였다. 또한 李承旭은 1983년 西江大의 人文科學研究所의 '蒙語老乞大'解題에서 '蒙語老乞大'라는 冊名은 (清語老乞大)의 경우도 포함하여 이 책의 성격에 걸맞지 않은 異例性이 엿보여 우리를 當惑케 한다.'라고 지적을 하면서 '아직도 그 語源의 定說을 얻었다고 할 수는 없으며……'라고 하였던 점을 본다면 '老乞大'의 語源에 대한 생각이 아직도 제각각이라는 생각을 할 수 밖에 없을 것이다.

'老乞大'의 解讀은 일찍이 渡邊薰太郎은 1935년 '女眞語の新研究' <亞細亞研究> 等 12號 大阪, 出版에서 비롯되었는바 '乞大'를 Kitat 또는 Kitai로 읽고 이것을 '中國'을 가리키는 蒙古語 單語라고 하였다. 그리고 '老乞大' 즉 '大中國'의 對應으로 해독하였는데 문제의 '老'가 어떻게 중국어 '大'에 해당하였는지는 확실한 해명이 없다. 그리고 閔泳珪는 1964년 '老乞大 辨疑'<延世大 人文科學 12집>에서 역시 '老乞'을 蒙古語 Kita(i)로, 그리고 이것을 '漢兒'로 해석하는 점은 日本學者 渡邊薰太郎과 크게 다를 바는 없다고 할 수 있을 것이다. 그리고 李基文은 1967년 '蒙學書研究의 基本問題'<震檀學報 제31號 p109>에서 '乞大'를 kida, '中國' 또는 '中國人'을 가리킨 中世蒙古語 단어의 한 語形이라 하였으니, 앞의 것들과 크게 다르지 않으나 '老'의 讀法은 아주 다르다. 즉, '老'에 대한 既往의 독법을 비판하면서 '乞大'가 蒙古語인 限, '老'도 마땅히 蒙古語였을 當爲性을 강조하여 '老'는 다름 아닌 中世 蒙古語의 lab이라고 推定하였다. 그리하여 '老乞大', 즉 lab kida로 보고, 이것은 '참된 中國' 또는 '참된 中國人'을 뜻한다고 하였다.

以上을 통해서 볼 때,

滿洲文獻인 ‘Tanggu Meyen’에서도 ‘Nikan’을 ‘中國人’으로 보았듯이 우리 文獻에서는 ‘乞大’ ‘老乞大’ 등은 모두가 學者에 따라서 見解의 差異가 있기는 하지만 모두가 ‘中國’을 指稱하는 것으로 보는 데는 일치되는 것 같다.

그러나 끝으로 問題를 하나 생각할 수 있는 것은 蒙古語로 ‘中國’을 ‘domdatu olos’라고 하는 점에 대해서는 아무도 언급한 바는 없는 것 같다.

결국 滿洲語에서는 中國人을 ‘Nikan’이라고 한 것은 中國의 河南大學 出版部에서 出刊된 ‘簡明滿漢辭典’(1988年度)에서 보면 ‘Nikan’은 ‘名詞’로서 ‘尼堪’의 音譯이며 意味 ‘漢人’이다. 따라서 이 ‘辭典’에서는 ‘nikan bithei kunggari boo’의 意味 역시 ‘漢科房’이라고 하였다.

그리고 ‘A concise English-Mongolian Dictionary(1986)’ <內蒙古教育出版社>에서 보면,

(1) ‘chin’은 몽고어로 ‘erao’이며

(2) ‘china’은 몽고어로 ‘šajang’ ‘šejen’

(3) ‘china’는 또한 몽고어로 ‘Kitan’ 또는 ‘Kitat’이며

(4) 또한 ‘china’는 몽고어로 ‘Kitan ulus’ 또는 ‘Kitat ulus’이다.

(5) 그리고 ‘china’는 ‘domdatu olos’라고도 몽고어로 말하며

(6) 또한 ‘chinese’는 ‘kitat kümün’ ‘kitan kümün’라고 몽고어로 말한다.

以上을 통해서 알 수 있는 것은 ;

첫째는, 滿洲族은 中國人을 ‘Nikan’이라고 하였으며 이것은 ‘尼堪’의 音譯이며 意味 역시 當時로서는 ‘漢人’이였으며

둘째는, 蒙古人들은 中國을,

‘① erao ② šajang(šejeng) ③ kitat ④ kitan ⑤ kitat ulus ⑥ kitan ulus ⑦ domdatu olos’ 라고 하며 中國人들을 蒙古人들은 ‘kitat kümün’ ‘kitan kümün’이라고 한다.

따라서 ‘老乞大’와 ‘漢人’ ‘中國’과의 相關關係는 더 깊은 속을 캐 봐야 할 것이 아닌가 한다. 以上에서처럼 필자는 諸 사실을 통해서 어학적으로 접근하였지만 만주어, 여진어, 몽고어 등의 상관성을 이해한다는 것이 그렇게 쉬운 일만은 아니기 때문에 보다 이 분야의 노력이 절실하게 필요하기는 하나

한국의 學界 현실로는 이 이상 밝히는 문제는 시기상조인 듯 보이는 것은 필자만의 생각은 아닐 것이다.

그리고 'Tanggu Meyen'의 文獻의 体系는 各 章마다 '왼쪽'에는 滿洲 文獻語의 音譯을 적어 놓고서 '오른쪽'에는 이 滿洲 文獻語에 대한 意味를 英語로 번역하였다. 앞에서도 필자가 언급하였듯이 이 책은 1924년 영국의 London에서 發刊하였다. 그러고 보면 淸나라인 滿洲族이 멸망한 지 거의 10여 년이 된 셈이다. 따라서 이 문헌은 이러한 점에서 매우 귀중한 문헌적 가치가 있다고 볼 수 있으니 앞으로는, 筆者의 계기를 통해서 本 文獻의 語彙를 分析할 수 있는 기회를 필자는 가져볼 생각을 하고 있다.

TANGGU MEYEN

and other Manchu Reading Lessons.

ROMANISED TEXT AND ENGLISH TRANSLATION SIDE BY SIDE.

by

M. FORBES A. FRASER, F.R.G.S.
Ex China Consular Service.
Member of the North China Branch of the Royal Asiatic Society.

LUZAC & Co.,
46, GREAT RUSSELL STREET, LONDON, W.C.1.
(Opposite the British Museum).
1924.

TANGGU MEYEN

and other
Manchu Reading Lessons.

ROMANISED TEXT AND ENGLISH TRANSLATION
SIDE BY SIDE.

by

M. FORBES A. FRASER, F.R.G.S.
Ex China Consular Service.
Member of the North China Branch of the Royal Asiatic Society.

LUZAC & Co.,
46, GREAT RUSSELL STREET, LONDON, W.C.1.
(Opposite the British Museum).
1924.

PREFACE.

WHEN Schliemann, the German explorer, resolved to set out to discover historical treasures in the Plain of Troy—an expedition which reaped a rich reward—he set to work to learn Greek, not from a grammar, which would give him the various moods, tenses, numbers, persons, and genders pertaining to the verb *typto*, "I strike," but from all the Greek writings and "cribs," *i.e.*, easy and exact translations of them which he could lay his hands on.

The ingenious person, probably a Chinese, who composed the *Tanggu Meyen*, probably about the time of our Queen Anne, had evidently the same idea as Schliemann, the projectors of the Loeb series, and various talented French *arabisants*, of the efficacy of the "crib." These pieces, most of them dialogues, a few monologues, were the result. Half-a-century ago European students were learning Chinese from them at Peking, where they appeared, in Chinese, in Wade's Course, with a correct English translation by Wade Before that, no doubt, Chinese had learned Manchu from them, and Manchus had learned Chinese from them for many years. Some of those which are given here are totally different from those given in Wade's Course.

漢軍

The book being hard to buy, I engaged a friendly *Han Kün* to make me a manuscript copy, for fair payment in money. He executed the work conscientiously, with Chinese and Manchu side by side, each in its own script, in flowing handwriting as plain as print, done with a Chinese brush dipped in the beautiful China ink ("Indian ink"). A *Han Kün* is "a descendant of those natives of Northern China who joined the Manchu invaders during the period of their contest with the Ming dynasty in the early part of the seventeenth century"—(Mayers). I corrected a few *lapsus calami*, after study. A few others baffled me long.

The occasional references to the extremes of the Peking climate are not exaggerated. For any one who has lived at Peking, there is an atmosphere of that grand old city about the whole book, especially for those who lived there long before the arrival of railways in China. Some of the dialogues are prosy and didactic, but amusing and interesting ones, also, are not few, as for instance the Archery scenes, the Haunted House, the disparaging opinion about Doctors, the Hunting Story, the Betrothal and New Year visits, the trip to the charming Western Hills.

INTRODUCTION.

The Manchu character, improved from the Mongol (and that again founded on the Syriac, through the influence of Nestorian Christian Missionaries), is not used here. Using our Roman characters instead of Arabic letters has been tried successfully with Urdú, and with Malay, and might prove as convenient with Persian and with Turkish. It is "religious" and national feeling that has imposed the Arabic letters on these mutually unrelated four languages.

The main system of transliteration is that in greatest vogue, the Russian, both for the Manchu, and often for such Chinese words as are quoted: (1) The frequently recurring *kh* is the Russian X, the modern Spanish J, formerly written as X, the guttural (خ) *kha*, which forms the seventh letter in the Arabic Alphabet, and the Chinese 哈. This information is derived in the main from the great Manchu-Chinese Dictionary, and from a Manual, which a Chinese *haji* once showed and lent to me, to teach Chinese Moslems the language of the Prophet. What follows is from the same two authentic sources, mainly.

(2) The sound written, in Russian transliteration of Chinese and Manchu, as G, is no true sonant, though it is softer than our K; and has no trace of H following it 噶. For Irish people it must be especially difficult. Some English travellers, I have heard, get over the difficulty by boldly pronouncing the name of the Chinese province *Kansuh* in the Russian way "Gansuh." The equivalent Arabic Sound is the 21st Arabic letter, now usually by English-writing Orientalists written Q (ق).

(3) The sound written, *à la russe*, as K, is the aspirated K which begins the name *K'ang* Hi, or K-hang Hi, the name of the reign of a Manchu Emperor which ended just 200 years ago, in 1723 喀. It corresponds to the Arabic 22nd letter, "Kàf (ك). The German form CH for KH has no place here. Our CH is "tsh" in "*chain*," and our J is the J of "*jam*," "*jury*."

The letter H would have been used for the first of these sounds, the Russian X, but for the occurrence of such words as *iskhun-de*, which if written *ishun-de*, might lead to mistakes, such as are made by English and French-speaking tourists who pronounce *Scheveningen* incorrectly, little knowing that the Dutch pronounce the initial S apart from the guttural *CH* (Kh) which follows the S.

Mutatis mutandis, the above remarks apply to T, D, and to P, B, and to CH, J.

The vowels are, of course, to be pronounced as in Italian, in every combination that occurs, giving each its full value, *oo* as in "oölite," "Zoölogy," not as popularly pronounced in the contraction "Zoo" for the Zoological Gardens.

The Sibilants:—In Chinese the sound of the name of the 12th Arabic letter س **which is called "sin," is represented either by one Chinese** character, *sin* 心 ("the heart"), or by the combination of two characters (or monosyllabic words) *si-in* 西音 ("Western sound"). The regrettable *hs* introduced by Wade, on a supposed phonetic principle, is used nowadays (as he surely never foresaw) indiscriminately for Chinese words beginning with h, as transliterated by other Orientals, such as Japanese, Manchus, etc., and the words beginning with s, as transliterated by these peoples, whose intimate knowledge of China and the Chinese language entitles their views on the subject to respect. Eminent Sinologues, including W. F. Mayers, S. Wells Williams, E. H. Parker, disapproved of the "revolutionary changes" of Wade; and Kingsmill, President of the North China Branch of the Royal Asiatic Society, said "it may be a question which is the best system, but there can be no question about Wade's being the worst." By this system the Province of Kiang-si appears as *Chiang-hsi*, with other absurdities too numerous to mention, amongst them being the identifying of the name of the Tsin Dynasty (A.D. 265—420), with that of the Kin (Aisin, in Manchu, "gold" in English) Dynasty (A.D. 1115—1234), by lumping them together as *Chin*. On the official seal of the Shanghai District Magistrate were engraved, in Manchu characters to the left, in Chinese to the right, the words, *Shanghai Hien*-(or *Khiyan*)-*i Doron*, in Manchu—*Shanghai Hien Yin*, in Chinese. These words, in Japanese, would be *Jō-kāi Ken*. Here there is no trace of HS. The Wade system spells Hien, "a district magistrate," and SIEN, "a fairy," alike, "*Hsien*," which is obviously absurd. In Japanese *senjō* is "a fairy lady," while *kenjō* would mean "a district castle." The Japanese know better than to write them both as "*hsien-jō*," even if their meagre syllabary permitted it.

Therefore, let Orientalists learn from Orientals, and in transliterating the Chinese for "Filial Piety" write *hiao*, and for "small" write *siao*, and by no means write *hsiao* for either of them! This will greatly facilitate their studies, if they go in for enquiry into Chinese dialects, or go further afield, and, starting from Chinese, go on to Japanese, Corean, Manchu, etc.

All Chinese words quoted here are "romanized" according to the good old Oriental systems, before the invasion of *hs* and *ch*; and the final *h* is only placed after vowels which are in the abrupt, or "entering" tone, not after others. The Manchus, of course, learned nothing of this Southern tone; the Southerners have eight tones, the Pekinese are content with four. Their Pekinese language was easily acquired by the Manchus. It is softer than the Southern, and the Southerners call it "oily"—as, not having the abrupt tone, it runs more smoothly.

Zakharoff's Russian Translation of the Manchu-Chinese Dictionary has helped me greatly, as it is much easier to read the explanations of words in Russian, than in the Manchu from which he translated them. The grammar of Gabelentz, written in French in 1832 (good pioneer work), is in a language much more accessible to most readers than either Manchu or Russian. Kaulen, another German, wrote on the subject in 1856 (published at Ratisbon). But the pioneer seems to have been Rev. Père Amyot (Paris, 1790), who, says Zakharoff, was as yet lacking in the full knowledge of *Chinese* necessary for a compiler of a good *Manchu* Dictionary. Zakharoff's Preface to his Dictionary, 1875, is a great and interesting historical work of thirty large pages. The latest work, by the German, Möllendorff, in English, is highly spoken of.

NOTES ON GRAMMAR.

The translation places the English words, as far as possible, in the order of the Manchu words, and each line corresponds to each line of Manchu words on each page. The construction of a Manchu sentence will be found very like that of a Japanese sentence, "pushing to the extreme," as B. H. Chamberlain says in his Japanese Handbook, "the synthetic tendency in the structure of sentences . . . when the verbs of several clauses express the same tense or mood, only the last verb takes the suffix indicating that tense or mood, the previous verbs all taking the ***gerundial*** form."

The gerund forms are *me* (which Gabelentz calls an Infinitive, Zakharoff denying the existence of an Infinitive) *re ndere, tere;* thus ***gamambi***, "I fetch," root *gama*, gerundial form *gamame; **gamame genekhe***, "went to bring"; *ombi-me*, "though it is possible"; *chookha-de **ome***, "having become a soldier" (lit. "in the army"); *ukherileme **bodochi***, "generalizing if one considers," ***i.e.***, considering in a general way.

An auxiliary verb, *sembi*, means both "to be" and "to say." ***Sere***, its present participle, sometimes means "as regards" (so-and-so, of whom, or of which, I wish to speak)—like the Japanese suffix *ga*, or *wa*. ***Sere*** is used when the opinion, design, or words of another are quoted (***oratio** obliqua*). *Serengge*, verbal adjective, or participial adjective, or adjectival participle, is also from ***sembi***.

Nenembi, "I anticipate," "I do first"; preterite, ***nenekhe;*** gerund, *neneme*. *Nenekhe aniya* "last year," ***nenekha*** *ama*, "my father before me," *nenekhe Ejen*, "the late Sovereign"; ***neneme*** *amala*, "before and after," "the former and the later" (times).

Present participle *re;* ***bimbi***, to be, exist; *bisire ele **jaka***, "all things existing." Future tense, ***ra***, ***re***, ***ro***, also expressed by optative suffix ***ki;*** *alaki sembi*, I wish to tell, mean to tell. *Alaki* also means "please tell!"

Past tense—*kha*, past iterative tense—*khai*. *Bikhe* after a verb in the past tense, expresses time long past.

Concessive forms, udu...bichibe, udu...ochibe; although, granting (all that).

Other notes will be found in abundance, further on; *passim*.

vii.

TANGGU MEYEN

TANGGU MEYEN SHUTUCHIN	THE HUNDRED CHAPTERS. PREFACE
Manju gisun serengge, Manju niyalmai fulekhe da.	What the Manchu language is, that is the root and foundation of [us] Manchus. (*Da*, "root," also "chief"; *orkha-da*, "king of plants," is the *ginseng*, *panax quinquefolium*.)
Yaya ve bakhanar*aku*chi ojor*aku*ngge kai.	Every person should not be not knowing it. (All should know it. *Aku* means "not.")
Adarame sechi? muse jabshan-de vesikhun jalan-de banjime.	How (indeed)? We, by good fortune, born into a noble race. (*Muse* for "we," includes the person addressed, like Chinese *tsa-men*.)
Manju-be ayan suwayan ofi.	Considering what is Manchu to be great and precious. (*Suwayan*, "costly," literally "yellow.")
Aika Manju gisun-be bakhanaraku ochi.	If we do not know the Manchu language.
Niyalma-be achakha-dari, angga gakhushara, yasa sharinjara, dabala.	Whenever we meet a man, with gaping mouth and goggling eyes, that is it.
Ere-chi gichukhengge bio? ere-chi fanchachukangge geli bio?	Than this is aught (more) shameful? Than this is anything, moreover (more) exasperating?
Ede (*i.e.*, ere-de) niyalma-be chokhome yekershere basure vaka.	By this not specially (*i.e.*, only) one gets satirical and mordant talk from people.
Beye ubu-de inu valiyabumbi-kai, khairakan aku semeo?	One's proper person is cast away (one loses face), is that not (not to be called) a pity?
Kemuni tuvachi ememu urse, Manju gisun-de.	One often sees various people, in (the matter of) the Manchu language.
Iletu bakhanara gisun bime, lak seme bakhanaraku, deng seme ilinjakhangge bi.	Though understanding plainly, cannot be fluent in speech, but stutter and hesitate.

In the first few pages of the Manchu text the letter V is used, afterwards invariably W. Zakharoff uses the v, which is orthographically correct; but as Gabelentz and others use the *w*, and as, moreover the Manchus use the combination *hv* to represent the *hw* which appears so frequently in Chinese, I decided to use the *w* instead of the *v*, as more and more instances occurred justifying the change. I think the *v* and *w* sounds are rather blended, as in Spanish the *v* and the *b*.

B

Aichi jing gisurere siden-de, dere dukseme fularakangge bi.

Maybe also some, in the act of speaking, whose faces flush and turn red.

Ere umai guva aku, gemu an-i uchuri kicheme tachikhaku urebume giyangname gisureraku ofi.

This is nothing else but from not habitually striving for ripe practice in speaking.

Geli injechukengge, Manju gisun oron unde-de, utkhai ubaliyambure-be tachirengge bi.

Still more) ridiculously, without (having any Manchu speech yet, forthwith studying to be interpreters there are (such).

Enteke niyalma, michume bakhanara onggolo, sujure-be tachire-chi, ai enchu?

Such people, what is the difference between them and those who before they can crawl (would), learn to run?

Note the *postpositions* (instead of *prepositions*) as in Japanese, Turkish, and other "agglutinative" languages. The suffix *be* marks the accusative case, like *wo* in Japanese: *i*, genitive, *Chi*, "from": *de*, "in" or "by": *onggolo*, "before": *manggi*, "after." The idiom of using "from" to mean "than" occurs in Japanese (*yori*), in Arabic (*min*), in Latin the ablative case. Doubtless in other languages, besides in these and in Hindustani (*se*), which much agrees with Manchu in the use of postpositions for prepositions.

Nikan bitkhe-de ai khachin-i mangga, okini! Fi nikebukhe manggi, gisun eden dadun.

Chinese books to whatever degree ripe (mangga) scholars, well! On laying down the pen, their speech is faltering.

Tamin achaburaku, yokhi banjiraraku be, ainara? udu sakda-tala tachikha seme.

Not smooth, incomplete, how is it. If (such) learn till they are grown old.

Eden baksi sere gebu-chi guweme mutembio? muwashame duibulechi

Can they be freed from the name of being bad scholars? In a rough (popular) way to compare.

utkhai boo arara adali, taibu ture wase faise i jergi khachingga jaka

Then, as in building a house [if] beams, posts, tiles, bricks, all sorts of similar things.

aku ochi, faksisa-be teile gajikha seme ai weilebumbini? Gala joolafi tuwara dabala!

If they be lacking, simply hiring workmen, what will that get done? You may fold your arms and look on!

boo shanggara kooli aku kai. Ere-be tuwakha-de, ubaliyambure-be tachire onggolo-

There is no sense in trying to get a house finished so. Looking at the matter so, before learning to interpret (or translate).

geli neneme Manju gisun tachire-be oyonggo obuchi achambi.

It is proper, also, before that, to account important the learning of Manchu speech.

Damu Manju bitkhe umesi labdu geren; teni tachire urse wachikhiyame khulachi.

But Manchu books are many and various; for people just learning to read all of these (aloud).

Atanggi dube da bi? Tutti ofi, bi dolo yabure sholo de.	When can they achieve that? That being the case, I, in such leisure as my Court duties [allowed me].
Yaya sakdasa-i u l a n d u m e gisurekhe, mini tachifi ejekherengge be.	Each phrase that old people speak to each other, and what I have learnt and noted down.
Emu gisun emu gisun-i amchanja-khai ukheri "TANGGU MEYEN" iktembufi	Fitting phrase and phrase together, I have collected the whole "HUNDRED CHAPTERS"
mini mukun-i deote juse-be tachi-bukha. Geren deote juse mini-de baime khendukhe:	[and] taught the juniors and children of my clan. All these juniors and sons besought me, saying:
Ere bitkhe-i dorgi-i washinara ichi tukhenere kemun, yaya Manju khergen-i fakjin-be.	"In this book with its inevitable omissions, for every Manchu word (to give) a handle
Udu akumbume yongkiyakhaku bichibe, amba muru	although it has not exhaustively accomplished, yet [taking], a general view,
oyonggo-i oyonggongge be tuki-yeme, gemu jorime tuchibukhe khamika.	raising [to notice] the principal of the important words, it points them out nearly (approximately "pointing at them, *faire ressortir*, fetched, made them come, out," as perfectly as was feasible).
Manju gisun-i jorin-oyonggo sechi ombikai. Tachire urse	It may be said to indicate the main points of Manchu conversation (speech). The learners,
unenggi ede gunin girkufi, khing fukhashame urebuchi	if applying their minds honestly to this, they zealously grind at it till they become "ripe" (expert).
goidakha manggi, ini chisui, gunin ichi, forgoshome-gamame mutembi	After some time has passed, spontaneously, as they will, they can change (*i.e.*, manipulate) it.
gisurechibe gisun, bakhanarakungge aku be dakhame.	Say what words they may, since there is nothing in which they do not succeed,
Bakhanaraku geli ai joboro? Damu ere bitkhe khergen jachi labdu	what difficulty then can they not meet? Still, the written words in this book are exceedingly many,
geli khulara urse arara khusun baiburakhu seme. Tuttu	also the readers (aloud) in forming these (writing) would have hard work. Therefore

Khusun, strength, effort, *baiburakhu*, it is to be feared they must use, exert,—the first instance of the Deprecative Mood in *-rakhu*, the reverse of the Optative in *-ki*.

faksi-de afabufi folobufi, Manju gisun-be adali-de amuran guchese	I engaged artificers to print it, [and] with like-[thinking] friends who love the Manchu tongue
ukheleki sembi! Udu khafungga saisa-de nonggibure-be aku bichibe	I would share it! Though to perfected *virtuosi* (*saisa*), it may add nothing of new [knowledge].
Tuktan tachire urse de, niyechebun akungge aku sembi	To people who have just begun to learn, it will not be without profit.

CHAPTER I.

A. Donjichi si te Manchu bitkhe tachimbi sembi; umesi sain! Manju gisun serengge

A. I hear, you are studying Manchu books. Very good! As for the Manchu language

musei uju uju-i oyonggo baita; utkhai Nikasai meni meni ba-i gisun adali

(is) the head and chiefly important concern for us Manchus; like as the various local languages of the Chinese.

Bakhanarakuchi ombio?

If one did not understand them would that do? (be possible).

B. Inu, waka ochi ai? Bi juwan aniya funcheme

B. Yes indeed! How not so? For two years and more I

Nikan bitkhe tachikha, tetele umai dube-da tuchikeku; jai aikabade

have studied Chinese books, as yet I have found no end to it (imperfect): now if also

Manju bitkhe khularaku, ubaliyambure-be tachiraku ochi, juwe-de gemu

I do not read Manchu, unable to learn interpreting, then in both (attempts) entirely

Sartabure-de isinambi. Uttu ofi, bi emu-de ochi Age-be tuwanjikha, jai-de

I shall come to a deadlock. That being so, I have come, firstly, to see you, Sir; and secondly,

ochi, geli sakda Akhun de baire-ba bi, damu baibi angga juwara-de mangga.

also there is something I would ask of you, venerable Elder-brother, but [I find it] hard to open my mouth.

A. Ede baibi gisun bichi, utkhai gisurere; mini mutere baita ochi, *sinde* bi geli

A. As for that, if you have a word to say, then say it; if it is anything I can do, for *you*, could I

marambi-o? *B.* Mini bairengge, Age gosichi, shadambi seme

cry off from doing it? *B.* My request is, from your interest with which you honour me, Sir, though it may be wearying you,

ainara? Sholo sholo de udu Meyen Manju gisun banjibufi, minde khulaburu;

how (shall I say it)? In any spare times you have, to compose some pieces of Manchu talk for me to read;

deo bi bakhafi hwashachi, gemu Age-i kesi kai, ainakha seme

if I, your younger brother, gain any success, all, Sir, will be by favour from you, and however things may be,

baili-be onggoraku, urunaku ujeleme karulaki. *A.* Aina uttu gisurembi?	I'll not forget the kindness, will certainly repay a heavy debt [of gratitude]. *A.* Why do you speak so?
Si aika niyalma guwa-o? Damu sini tachiraku be khendumbi dere!	Are you a stranger? Just say you will not learn!
tachiki sechi tetendere, bi nekuleme simbe niyalma okini sembikai	As soon as you say you wish to learn, I joyfully say, become a man (of education).
karulaki serengge ai gisun? musei dolo gisurechi ombio?	This about wishing to requite me, what talk is this? Between us, is it possible to speak so?
B. Tuttu seme, bi khuksheme gunikha seme wajiraku	*B.* Even when that is said (is so), I feel infinitely grateful.
Damu khengkileme baikha bure dabala.	It only remains for me to make you my reverence (a "kotow"), and to thank you.

CHAPTER II.

A. Age, sini Manchu gisun, ai sholo-de tachikha? Mudan sain bime	*A*. Sir, where did you find time for (leisure for) the Manchu conversation you have learned? Accent is good,
tomorokhon. *B*. Mini Manju gisunbe, ai dabufi gisurere ba-bi. Age	distinct. *B*. My Manchu talk, what is there about it worth mentioning? You, Sir,
gosime uttu dabali maktambi. Mini emu guchu Manju gisun sain. Getuken	by favour for me praise it excessively. (Now) a friend of mine has good Manchu. Clear
bime dachun. Majige Nikan mudan aku. Umesi urekhebi Tuttu bime	it is and nimble (fluent). A little (trace) of Chinese accent is there none. Very perfected. Moreover

Nikan mudan, Chinese accent. The Chinese text gives ***Man-yin***, **South-China accent,—the *Mantsze*, Chinese of the South, are Marco Polo's *Manzi*.**

shan geli fe gisun labdu donjichi, tere teni mangga sechi ombi.	his ear has heard many old phrases; that, when one comes to it, may be called real (knowledge).
A. Tere sinchi antaka? *B*. Bi adarame inde duebulechi ombi? Fukhali	*A*. How is he (compared) with you? *B*. How can I be compared (classed) with him? Altogether
terei bakchin waka. Abkai na-i gese giyalabukhabi. *A*. Ai turgun sechi?	he has no rival (in me). As distant as Heaven from earth, like. *A*. What is the reason?
B. Ini tachikhangge shumin, bakhanarangge labdu, bitkhe-de amuran; tetele khono	*B*. He has studied deeply, acquired many things, is devoted to books; ever up to now
angga-chi khokoburaku khulambi; gala-chi aljaburaku tuwambi.	without resting from (resting) his mouth he is reading (aloud); without taking from his hand, he looks (reads)
imbe amchaki sechi yargivan-i mangga. *A*. Age sini ere gisun majige tasharabukhaku semeo	if one wishes to catch him up, it is indeed difficult. *A*. Is not what you say a little mistaken, Sir?
"khing sere ochi, alin-be khafabuchi ojoro" gisun bikhe. Tere inu tachifi bakhanakhangge dabala!	"When there is resolution one can pierce a mountain," the saying is. He, too, has acquired what he has because he studied it!
umai banitai bakhanakhangge waka kai! Muse tere isirekhungge ya bi?	He by no means got it by being born with it! Why should not we (you and I) catch him up?

8 *TANGGU MEYEN:*

I ai khachin i urekhe bakhana-khangge okini, muse damu mujilen gunin-be	Let him be advanced to what degree of attainments he may, if we only, heart and soul
teng-seme jafafi, gunin girkifi tachi-chi udu tere ten-de isiname	resolutely taking, concentrating our intellects, learn, though attaining to that pitch
muteraku bichibe, inu urunaku khaminambi dere!	may be impossible, yet we shall surely arrive near to it!

CHAPTER III.

A. Si Nikan bitkhe bakhanara niyalma kai, ubaliyambure-be tachichi	*A*. You are a man who is acquiring Chinese literary learning, if you learn translating
nokai ja dabala. Gunin girkufi, giyalan lakchan aku, jergi anara tachime okhode	it will be very easy. By giving special attention, without interruption, learning in regular stages,
juwe ilan aniya i siden-de, ini chisui, dube-da tuchimbi. Aika emu inenggi	in two or three years, automatically, success will emerge. (But) if "on one day
fiyakiyara, juwan inenggi shakhurara adaii tachichi, orin aniya bitkhe	you heat it, and ten days cool it," learning it that way, in twenty years of book-
khulakha-seme, inu mangga-kai. *B*. Age, mini ubaliyabukhangge-be tuwafi,	learning, it will still be hard. *B*. Sir, (will you) look at my translation, (and)
majige dasatareo? *A*. Si tachikhangge ambula nonggibukha.	will you correct a little? *A*. Your studies have made great progress (additions)
gisun tome ijiskhun, khergen tome tomorokhon, majige chilchin fukhai aku	wording all runs smoothly, characters all distinctly (written), there is not even a slight error,
simnechi, seferekhei bakhachi ombi. Ere mudan ubaliyambure-be simnerede	if you go to the examinations, you will win as easily as closing the fist. This time, for the Interpreter's Examination,
gebu alibukhao akun? *B*. Simnechi bakhafi esi sain; Damu bitkhei shusai	have you given in your name or not? *B*. Yes, 'twould be good to pass the Examinations, but as a *siu-tsai*
ainakhai ombini? *A*. We-i kooli? Sini gesengge jakun gusa gemu simnechi ombime	how could I possibly try for it? *A*. Whose rule (stands against that)? Your sort, from the Eight Banners, are able all to be examined (for that Degree).
sim-be teile simeburaku doro bi-o? Tere anggala, jurgangga tachiku-i	Would there be justice in not allowing you alone, to be examined? Moreover, the Patriotic Schools'
juse gemu ojoro de, Shusai-be aikhendure? Simnechi ome ofi, sini deo	boys all can do so, so what shall we say of a *siu-tsai*? Just because they can be examined, your younger brother,
ere sidende teni khachikhiyame, Manju bitkhe khulambi. Khudun gebu yabubu	is at this time working diligently at reading Manchu books. Hurry up, and pass your name in,
naskhun-be ume ufarabure!	do not lose the opportunity!

CHAPTER IV.

A. Sini Manjurarangge majige muru tuchike-bi. *B.* Aika-bi? Niyalmai gisurere-be	*A.* Your Manchu talking has grown into some shape. *B.* How can that be? People's speaking
ulkhime gojime, mini beye gisureme okhode oron unde. Guwa-i adali	though I understand, I myself am not in the least able to speak yet. Compared with others,
fiyelen fiyelen-i gisureme muteraku sere anggala emu siran-i duin sunja gisun	fluent speaking is (for me) impossible, and in addition to that, one series of four or five words,
gemu sirabume muteraku. Tere anggala, khono emu aldungga ba-bi. Damu gisureme onggolo,	even that I cannot connect. Besides that, there is yet an (other) queer thing. Even before I speak,
baibi tasharaburakhu chalaburakhu seme, tatkhunjame gelkhun aku, kengse laskha,	merely from thinking I may go wrong, or be incorrect, I boggle at it, so that fearlessly and decidedly

Note 2 instances of Deprecative Mood in *-rakhu.*

gisureraku. Uttu adali, mimbe adarame gisureme sembi? Bi inu usaka, gunichi,	I cannot speak. As things are so, how can I hope to speak? I feel really mortified, when I think
adarame tachinambi? Damu ere bengse dabala, nonggibure ai-bi?	how am I going to learn? With only this much ability (talent), what chance of improvement?
A. Ere gemu sini urekheku-i kharan. Bi sin-de tachibure. We-be seme, ume bodoro!	*A.* That is all because you do not practise. I will teach you (a plan), whoever it may be, do not consider,
damu yaya ucharakha-be utkhai amchadame gisure! Jai bitkhe-de khafu *sefu*-be baifi	*but* whomever you meet, hasten to talk with! Then, also, a *Teacher* versed in books, look for (such a one),
bitkhe khula; Manju gisun-de mangga guchuse-de adanafi gisure; inenggi-deri	(and) read books; and form a *côterie* of friends, "pucka" Manchu talkers; and, every day,
khulakha gisun utkhai ejekhebi, erindari gisurechi, ilenggu utkhai urekhebi	the words, once read aloud, forthwith note down; speaking every day, the tongue gets practised.
uttu tachire okho-de, mangga-i emu juwe aniya siden-de, ini chisu-i gunin-i chikhai-	thus learning, in the space of one or two years at most, spontaneously, according to your wish,
angga ichi tang-seme gisurembi. Muteraku jalin geli ai jobombi-ni?	following your tongue, you will be speaking freely. What reason for anxiety lest you can not?

CHAPTER V.

A. Absi yabukha bikhe? *B*. Bi ergi emu niyamangga niyalma-i boo-de, genekhe bikhe?	*A*. Where are you walking to? *B*. I was going to (towards) a relation's house.
A. Ere ildun-de mini boo-de isinafi majige teki. *B*. Age, si uba-de tekhe-bi-o?	*A*. This occasion (lit. this journey) I hope you will come and sit in my house a little. *B*. Do you live here, Sir?
A. Inu, jakan gurinjikha. *B*. Uttu ochi, muse tekhengge giyanaku udu goro?	*A*. Yes, just moved in. *B*. That being the case, we cannot be living far apart (lit. now far apart?).
Sakha ochi, aifini simbe tuwanjiraku bikhe-o? *A*. Age yabu. *B*. Ai ere giyan bi-ni?	If I'd known, would not I have come to see you a long time ago? *A*. Step in, Sir! *B*. How'd that be polite?
A. Mini boo, inu. Age wesifi teki. *B*. Uba-de ichangga. *A*. Si tuttu tekhe-de bi absi	*A*. Yes, indeed, it's my house. Go up and take a seat, p'ease. *B*. I'm comfortable here. *A*. If you sit so, where am I
tembi? *B*. Sain, teme jabdukha. Uba-de emu nikere ba-bi. *A*. Boo-i urse, aba?	sitting (to sit?). *B*. Good, I sat down first, there is a back rest here. *A*. Where are the house servants?

Teme jabdukha, literally "sitting, anticipated (you)."

Tuwa gaju! *B*. Age, bi dambaku jeteraku. Angga furunakha-bi. *A*. Uttu ochi-	Bring a light (fire)! *B*. I cannot smoke (eat tobacco), Sir. My mouth is sore. *A*. If that is so,
chai jafame (?) gene! Age, chai gaisu. Ke! Chai absi khalkhun! *B*. Khalkhun ochi,	bring tea! Have some tea, Sir. Oh! how hot this tea is! *B*. When it is hot,
majige tukiyechebu khwanggiyaraku, mukiyekini. *A*. Je! buda-be tuwara!	stirring it a little does it no harm, to let it cool (optative mood). *A*. Yes! See [and get] some rice?
beleni bisurengge be khudun banju, se. *B*. Aku! Age ume! Bi kemuni	tell them to send in what (ever) is ready. *B*. No, Sir, do not (do that)! I have still
guwa ba-de geneki sembi. *A*. Ainakha-bi? Beleni bisirengge,	other places to go to (optative mood). *A*. How so? These things are all ready,
sini jalin dagilakhangge geli waka, majige jefi genechi-na!	and not at all prepared on account of you, won't you eat a little before you go (lit. "having eaten, go")?
B. Joo! Emgeri sini boo-be takakha kai, enchu inenggi jai chokhome jifi	*B*. Hold hard! Now that I have once located (recognize) your house, another day I will come again on purpose
gulkhun emu inenggi gisureme techeki.	as I would like to sit a whole day and talk!

CHAPTER VI.

A. Age, si inenggidari erechi yaburengge, gemu aibi-de genembi?	*A*. Sir, when you walk past here every day, where are you always going to?
B. Bitkhe khulaname genembi. *A*. Manju bitkhe khulanambi waka-o?	*B*. I go to read books. *A*. Manchu books, you go to read, is it not so?
B. Inu. *A*. Ne ai jergi bitkhe khulambi? *B*. Guwa bitkhe aku, damu	*B*. Yes. *A*. What class of books are you reading now? *B*. No other books, only
yasa-i juleri buyarame gisun. Jai Manju Nikan-i oyonggo jorin-i bitkhe-i	every-day (before one's eyes) miscellaneous phrases, also a Guide-book to the Chief Subjects, Manchu-Chinese,
teile. *A*. Kemuni, suwe-de Manju-i ginggulere Khergen tachibumbi-o, akun? *B*. Te	only (that). *A*. Besides that, do they teach you Manchu ceremonial writing, or not. *B*. Now
inenggi fokholon, khergen arara sholo aku; ere-chi inenggi saniyakha manggi.	the days are short, with no time for writing the characters; from now on, when the days have got longer,
Khergen arabumbi sere anggala, khono ubaliyambure-be tachibumbi.	besides setting us to write the characters (letters), they will teach us interpreting (translating) too.

CHAPTER VII.

A. Age, bi bitkhe khulara jalin yala uju silgime, aibi-de baikhana-khaku?	*A.* Sir, I have to get some reading been truly pushing my head (everywhere); where have I not been to search?
Musei ubai shurdeme fukhali Manju tachiku-i aku. Gunichi sini tachire ba	All round our neighbourhood here there is absolutely no Manchu School. I am thinking, your place of learning,
ai khendure? atanggi seme? Bi inu bitkhe khulaki sechina. Mini funde,	what is it called? when is it? I, too, am wishful to read books there (study). On my behalf,
majige gisurechi ojoro. *B.* Age, si minde tachibure niyalma-be we sembi?	you might say a word (a little). *B.* Sir, whom do you say the man who teaches me to be?
Sefu sembio? Waka kai! Mini emu mukun-i akhun. Tachibure urse, gemu	*A.* *Professor?* (Instructor). No, indeed! An elder brother in our clan. The men he teaches, are all
mini emu boo-i juse deote. Jai niyaman khunchikhin; umai guwa niyalma aku.	juniors (sons and younger brothers) of my own, the one, house. Then, kindred and connections; no outsider at all.
A. Adarame sechi? *B.* Mini Age inenggidari *yamulambi*,	*A.* How does that happen? *B.* My Senior goes every day to the *yamun* (public office),
jabduraku. inu mini erde yamji nandame genere jakade, arga aku,	has not leisure, indeed, in consequence of my going to importune him early and late, having no resource
sholo-be jalgiyanjafi, mimbe tachibumbi. Waka ochi,	he manages to find some leisure (apportions leisure) and teaches me. Even if it were not so,
Age bitkhe khulame geneki sekhengge, sain baita dabala. Sini funde	Sir, your wishing to go and study, is a praiseworthy (good) thing. On your behalf
majige gisurechi, minde geli ai fayakha kai?	to say a word (speak a little), how does that inconvenience (trouble) me, too?

CHAPTER VIII.

A. Tere age, musei fe adaki kai; shame tuwame mutukha juse; giyalafi

A. That gentleman is an old neighbour of ours, a lad grown up under our eyes; after an interval

giyanaku udu aniya goidakha, te donjichi mujaku huwashafi, khafan tekhe sere,

of how few years past can it be? now we hear he has progressed greatly, has an official position.

Suchungga, bi khono akdara dulin, kenekhunjere dulin bikhe, amala

At first, I still half believed, half doubted it, (but) afterwards

guchuse de fonjichi, mujangga. Erebe tuwachi, "mujilen bisurengge, baita

enquiring of friends, [I found it was] really thus. Looking at this, "where is courage, the business

jiduji mutebumbi, se de aku" sere gisun tashan aku ni? *B.* Age-i gisun

can be accomplished, not (only) by one's years," the saying is no lie, eh? *B.* Sir, your words

inu, tuttu seme inu terei sakdasa wajiraku sain-be bifi, teni ere gese

are true (so), but even so his parents (old folk) must have had unexhausted merit, when such a

dekjingge juse banjikha, nomkhon bime sain, tachin fonjin-de amuran.

successful son they produced, kind and honourable, fond of learning and enquiring.

Gabtara niyamniyara, yaya khakha-i erdemu, se-de teisu aku, ambula tachikhabi.

In foot and horse archery, (and) every manly prowess, beyond his years, he is well versed.

An-i uchuri, boo-de bichi, bitkhe tuwara dabala; balai ba-de emu okson

Habitually, when indoors, he is looking at his books, and that only; to scenes of folly, one step

seme, inu, feliyeraku. Tere anggala, siden-i baita-de ochi, ginggun olkhoba,

let it be (being) even, he will not step. Besides this, when he is on public service, attentive and careful,

bakhara sara ba-de ochi kheni majige icheraku. Tere tob sere

whatever place he gets to be in, he is never guilty of corruption. The case is exactly this:

Sara, not *sere*: from *sambi*, to know, to know how.

"Sain-be iktambukha boo-de, urunaku funchetele khuturi bi" sekhe gisunde

"To the house that accumulates merit (virtue) there will without doubt be abundant happiness." To the word (proverb) that said so

achanakha.

(the facts) have come to agree.

CHAPTER IX.

A. Age yalu! Bi sinde jailakha kai! Shadame geli; aise ebumbi?	*A.* Keep your seat on your horse (ride), Sir. (Do not dismount.) I feigned not to see you! You are tired, too; why get down?

Aise, why; not *aisi*, which means "a profit."

B. Ai gisurembi? Sabukhaku ochi, ainara? Bi kejine aldangga-chi utkhai simbe sabukha,	What do you say? Had I not seen you, what could I have done? But as I had seen you from afar this long time,
yalulakha-i dulere kooli bi-o? *A.* Age, boo-de dosifi terakun? *B.* Inu kai!	would it be manners (reasonable) to pass you still riding? *A.* Won't you come into the house and sit down, Sir? *B.* Of course
Muse achakhakungge kejine goidakha, bi dosifi majige teki. Ara!	(yes, indeed!). We have not met for a long time. I'd like to come in and sit a little. Hullo! (Chinese "*Ai-ya!*")
Utala khachingga moo ilkha tebukhebi-o! geli utala bochonggo nimakha ujikhe-bi.	All these different (lit. so many) kinds of trees and flowers planted? and so many coloured fish (gold-fish) reared!
Wekhe-be jibsime sakhakhangge inu sain! Gunin isinakha ba umesi faksi!	The stones (rockery) are piled up in layers all very prettily indeed. The idea attained, quite artistic.
Jergi jergi-de gemu durun *yangse* bi.	Each layer has style and *chic*.

[*Yangse*, rendered "*chic*," is a word borrowed from Chinese.]

Ere bitkhe boo yala bolgo; absi tuwachi absi ichangga.	This library (book-house) is really neat (clean); wherever one looks, it is comfortable.
A. Tob seme musei bitkhe khulachi achara ba. Damu, korsorongge	*A.* It is exactly the fit place for us (you and me) to read books in. But, unfortunately, placed (as I am)
minde asuru guchu gargan aku, Emkhun bitkhe tachichi dembei simoli.	I have not very many friends or companions, alone book-studying (is) very lonely (work).
B. Ere ai mangga? Si ekseraku ochi, bi sinde guchu arame jichi antaka?	*B.* What difficulty is that? If it were not distasteful to you, how if I came and made myself your friend? (companion?)
A. Tuttu ochi, minde tusa okho; solichi khono jideraku j a l i n *joboshombi* kai,	*A.* If it were so, it would be a gain to me; one often *is vexed* because even when one invites, the person does not come.

Frequentative form of verb *jobombi*.

Yala jichi, minde jabshan dabala, eksere doro bi-o?	If you really come, it will my good fortune, just that (*dabala*), is there any reason for it being disagreeable (distasteful) to me?

CHAPTER X.

Niyalma jalan-de banjifi, uju uiu-i tachirengge oyongo, bitkhe khula-ranggc-

When a man is born into t| world, the chief thing of importan is to learn, to read books.

Khularangge, not *khularengge*: "reading (aloud)."

chokhome jurgan giyan-be getukelere jalin. Tachifi jurgan giyan-be getulekhe sekhe-de

Specially for the sake of clear vie of justice and reason. When learning, he has got these clear vie of justice and reason

boo-de bichi niyaman *khiyooshulara*

being in the home (house) he w practise *filial deference* to parents,

Chinese compound *Hiao-shun*. "filial obedience."

hafan techi gurun boo-de khushun bure. Eiten baita-be ini chisui mutebumbi.

holding posts as "mandar: (official), he will give his strength the country and the (reigning) hou In each affair (thing he does), of own accord (spontaneously) he w succeed (be able).

Te bichi unenggi tachikha erdemu

If (supposing, now, it be tl

Erdumn, lit. virtue, valour, merit.

bichi, ya ba-de isinakha manggi,

he has really learned solid acc plishments then whatever place has gone to

Lit. "is after having gone to," as in Welsh and Gaelic.

niyalma kungdulere ginggulere teile aku, beye yabure-de inu

not only will people honour respect him, but even in his body walk (bearing, deportment)

hoo-hiyo sembi. Ememu urse bitkhe-khularaku, yabun-be dasaraku,

there is a noble air. There are s men who do not study, do not att to (right) conduct.

baibi gulldurame enchekhesheme sikhesheme yabure-be "*bengse*" oburengge.

By sheerly worming and wrigg their way in, by adulation (wagging) they progress (walk), this they make (out to themselve be "cleverness" (*bengse*, Chinese for "talent").

Terei gunin-de absi ojoro-be saraku! Bi yargiyan-i ini fun-de girume! Korsombi!

I do not know how these mus (feeling) at heart! I really (ashamed on their account! (and angry (too)!

Absi, not *ebsi*. *Absi* = "how?" but *ebsi* = "hither."

Entekengge beye fusikhushabure yabun efujere-be khono aisembi?

People of that sort, how can on they only despise themselves self-respect) and spoil their wa life)?

weri ini ama eme-be suwaliyame gemu toombikai. Age, si bai

Also one is reviling their very father and mother as well. Sir, just you

gunime tuwa, ama eme-i baili, jui okho niyalma ainakhai, tu men-de emu,

consider and look at it, a father's and mother's kindnesses, how can a son (even) of ten thousand, one, part

karulame mutembi-o? Derengge iletu nongime eldeme muteraku ochi joo dere!

be able to repay? To gain distinction for, to add fame to them, may be impossible; never mind!

fudarame niyalma-i firume tooburede isibuchi, utkhai huwasharakungge dabala!

to do the reverse, and make them incur the curses and abuse of mankind, that is being incorrigible!

ere-bi kimchime gunikha de, niyalma ofi bitkhe-khularaku-chi ombio?

Thinking and pondering on this, can a man be a man without studying?

yabun-be dasaraku-chi ombio?

can he do without regulating his conduct?

CHAPTER XI.

A. Sikse wei boo-de genekhe, tuttu goidafi teni jikhe? *B.* Mini guchu-de	*A.* Yesterday whose house did you go to, that so long time passed ere you came? *B.* It was at a friend of mine's
tuwanakha bikhe, cheni tekhengge goro. Wargi Khechen khenchekhen-de bi.	that I had gone to see, they are living a long way off, it is at the foot of the Western City-wall.
Ere da-be, geli yamji buda ulebure jakade, majige sitabukha. *A.* Bi	Besides that, as they made me have supper (evening rice) I was a little delayed. *A.* I
sin-de emu gisun khebdeki seme sechi, ududu mudan niyalma takurafi	was wishing to have a word of consultation with you; several times. I sent off men
solinachi, sini boo-i urse simbe sejen teme tuchike, aibide	to invite you (ask you to come), your house people (said) you had gone out in a cart, whither
genekhe seme, gisun werikheku. Bodochi sini feliyere ba umesi	gone, word had not been left. Considering, that the places you go to, are very
komso kai, damu muse ere udu guchu boo-de dabala, toktofi	few indeed, only these few friends of ours, and that is all, I made sure that
mini uba-de darimbi, fukhali shun dabsitala umai jikhaku. Mekele	you would look in at my (house) here, but quite till sunset you had not come. In vain
emu inenggi aliyakha sechi-na. *B.* Inu! Age-i boo-i niyalma	we had been waiting a (whole) day. *B.* Yes! before your house-people
isinara onggolo (onggolo = "before") bi aifini duka tuchike; amasi	arrived, I had long gone out at the door; afterwards
jifi boo-i urse alakhangge Age niyalma unggifi emu siran-i	when I came (back) my domestics informed me that you, Sir, had sent men in (one) succession
juwe ilan mudan "jio" sekhe. Tere nergin-de utkhai jiki sembikhe	two or three times and said "come along!" Then I was just wishing to come
abka yamjikha, geli khiyatari yaksirakhu sembi, tuttu	the day (sky) was late, also the barrier was likely to be closed, so
bi enenggi jikhe.	I came to-day.

CHAPTER XII.

A. Alban kame yabure niyalma, damu meni-meni naskhun uchara-be tuwambi.

A. A man engaged in official duties, has only to watch all occasions as they present themselves.

Forgon juk en ochi, baibai achun-de chachun, yaya baita t u w a k h a tuwakhai mutebure khamika

In ordinary times, it is only because (officials) are at loggerheads, that any affair that is about to (could easily) be managed pretty well (nearly right)

urui niyalma-de sikhelefi fasilan tuchinjimbi. Ememu

only through thwarting by people (people's marring), gets to producing complications. Some

mayan-sain forgon-sain-i niyalma, yala ini gunime ini bodokho songkoi, lak seme

men, lucky in their lot and their time, verily according to their wish and calculation, swimmingly,

gunin-de achanarakungge aku, yasa tuwakhai dabali wesimbi.

with nothing not suiting their intentions, under one's eyes, rise (are advanced) extraordinarily.

B. Age, si uttu gisurembi, waka-o? Mini gunin-de tuttu aku. Damu

B. So you say, Sir, do not you? To my mind it is not so. It is only that

fashshara fasharaku-be, khendure dabala. Aika, uren-i gese, baibi

some are active, (others) not active, that is all we need discuss. If (inactive) as a lifeless body, one merely

fulun jeme, aniya khusime yaburaku ochi, khono nakabuchi achara dabala,

eating one's salary, all (round) the year does nothing (takes no step), one should, appropriately, even be made to retire,

wesire-be ere-chi ombi-o? Damu alban kicheme ginggun, guchuse-de

promotion (indeed) from this, is it possible? Only in affairs be zealous and cautious, with one's colleagues

khuwaliyasun dele, ume ichi kaniaku ojoro; baita bichi, niyalma-be guchikhiyereraku!

place concord highest, do not be intractable (obstinate); into any affair there is, do not drag people!

teisulebukhe-be sabume, beye sisafi ichikhiyara, fafurshame j u l e s i yabure okho-de,

Whatsoever you take cognisance of, lavish yourself (do your best) in dealing with it, go fearlessly forward! if you do

toktofi sain ba bi; wesiraku-i doro bi-o?

benefit will surely follow (be); is it reasonable to think you will have no promotion?

CHAPTER XIII.

A. Age, si aine-o teni jikhe? Bi suwembe aliyakhai, elei elei amu shaburakha!	*A*. Sir, how is it only now you have come? I kept waiting for you (plural) till I nearly dozed off.
B. Bi sinde alara:—mini teni ashshafi, sini beo-de jiderengge, gaitai	*B*. I will tell you:—just after my starting, about to come to your house, unexpectedly
emu eimebure nivakha yali-be ucharakha. Gisun dalkhun bime oyomburaku,	I met a tedious (disgusting) rotter (lit. decayed flesh). His talk is tiresome, and insignificant,
uttu sere, tuttu sere, ja ja-de bakhafi wajiraku. Baita aku-de, lolo-sere	touching now here, now there, not easiy coming to an end. If one has no business in train, the gabbling
khuwanggiyaraku urui chikhai alakini dere. Geli simbe aliyarakhu seme.	does no harm, let him just say on as he will. But (but also) I was wishing you not to (have to) wait.
Tede arga aku, minde baita bikhe seme, chimari jai gisureki seme. Ini	For this I had no resource (scheme), (but) to say I had business, would like to talk again to-morrow. His
gisun-be meitefi jikhe, sechi-na? aku-chi aifini-chi jifi, teme shadambikhe.	talk I just cut short, did not I? If it had not been (for him), I should have arrived a long time ago, we would (by now) be tired of sitting (here).
A. We-be aba? Khudun dere-be sinda! Gunichi *looyese* gemu yadakhushakha.	*A*. Who's (there)? Where (are you)? Lay the table quickly. (To servants.) I suppose the gentlemen are all hungry.
Buda, ai-be, gemu lak se! *B*. Age, sini ere absi?	Rice what (not), say (*se*) be quick with it all! *B*. Sir, what is that (you are saying)?
Faitakha yali bichi, utkhai wajikha kai, geli utala bookha saiku-be	If there is a slice of meat, that's enough (finished), in addition so many vegetable dishes
ainambi? Mimbe antakha doro-i tuwambio? *A*. Bai emu gunin oki-ni	how can I deal with them? Would you look on me as a ceremonious guest? *A*. It's merely a snack,
giyanaku ai sain jaka bi? Age, si bookhalame machige jedu!	what good things can these be? Sir, you just taste a little of them (tasting, eat!).

B. Si uttu ambarame dagilakhabi-kai, mini esi jechi, ebiraku ochi inu *sabka* be sindaraku. *A.* Uttu ochi, ai khendure, deo-be gosikha kai.

B. You have made such grand festal preparations. I must eat, of course (*esi*) and till well-filled (being unsatisfied) indeed I won't lay down my "*chop-sticks.*" *A.* Then what can I say, (but) that your are showing a great favour (lit. affection) to your very humble servant (lit. younger brother).

CHAPTER XIV.

ON ARCHERY.

A. Gabtambi serengge, muse Manjuse-i oyongo baita, tuwara de ja,

A. Archery, is an important thing (business) for us Manchus,—to look at, easy,

gojime; fakjin bakhara-de mangga. Te bichi, inenggi dobori aku

it may be; but hard to get the hang (lit, handle) of. For instance, day and night (without distinction)

tatashame beri-be tebeliyekhei amgarangge gemu bi-kai. Cholgoroko

drawing at it, going to sleep hugging the bow, even (such enthusiasts) there are. (But) outstanding

sain-de isinafi, gebu tuchikengge, giyanaku udu?

good shooting who have attained to, and have grown a name for themselves, how many can there be?

B. Mangga ba ai-de sechi? *A.* Beye tob, khachin demun aku,

B. Where are the difficult points? *A.* The body must be straight, without any failing (in this),

meiren nechin, umesi elkhe sulfa. Ere da-de beri mangga, kachilan

shoulders even, very easy and unconstrained. Then the bow (held) stiffly, the arrows

tuchiburengge khushungge, jai da tolome goibure ochi. Teni

discharged with force, then each stick of them you count, aimed straight. Then (only)

mangga sechi ombi. *B.* Age, si mini gabtara-be tuwa

you can be called expert. *B.* Sir, you watch me shooting!

nenekhe-chi, khuwashakha-o akun? Aika ichaku ba bichi.

Compared with the past, have I improved or not? If there be points (wherein I) am not fit,

majige jorishame tuwanchikhiya! *A.* Sini gabtarangge ai khendumbi?

point out and correct them a little (*majige*). *A.* Your archery what am I to say about it?

yamji chimari ferkhe-de akdafi funggala khadambi! Durun sain,

late and early trust to (that) thumb (of yours), and you'll sport the peacock's feather. Style good,

umesi urekhebi. Uksalarangge geli bolgo. Niyalma gemu sini adali ome mutere,

extremely well-practised. The sending off too, is clean. If everyone could be like you

geli ai [illegible]? Damu beri kemuni majige [illegible] gunirembi, khefelibe	what more to ask for? Still, the bow is a trifle weak and slack, the (archer's) belly
majige [illegible] bume muteraku. Ere udu ba-[illegible] [illegible] khalakha sekhe-de, yaya [illegible]	a little unable to keep still. These few points if you note, and alter, to whatever place
isinafi, [illegible]chi toktofi geren-chi tuchire, [illegible]! gidabure ai-bi?	you go (arrive) to shoot, you will surely stand out (come out) from the ruck. How can you be held down (crushed)?

CHAPTER XV.

A. Si serengge wajiraku sere sain niyalma, dolo majige khede da aku [another rendering is "a man of (inherited) merit not exhausted yet"].

A. You are a man of no end of good qualities, with no dross in your composition (lit. interior).

Damu angga jachi sijirkhun. Niyalmai uru waka be sakha-de,

But your mouth is too stiff (straight, plain-speaking). When you have seen a man's truth or untruth,

majige ba acharaku, utkhai kangseme gisurembi. Guchuse-de

you do not in the least regard expedience, you just speak out loudly. With friends,

endebuku-tuwanchiyara doro bichibe, inu guchulere sain, sain aku-be

error-reproving is, indeed, proper (doro), but still, whether they are good friends, or not, that

bodome tafulambi dere! Damu guchu sere-de emu adali sechi,

one must consider (reckon, and then) admonish, indeed. Only to say all that are friends are alike,

tere ainakhai ojoro. Teike ere emu meyen gisun-be, si

how would that ever do, possibly? Just now that bit of talk, you

sain gunin sefi, waka-o? Ini gunin-de labdu ichaku (not fitted)

said it with good intentions, did not you? In his mind he was very uneasy (indignant),

buling bulingjame, "ara. guwelke! mimbe tukhebukhe boljon aku seme kenekhunjembi-kai."

(his eyes) stared, "oho! beware, he would injure me without giving warning, I doubt!".

Boljon-aku, without waves, without commotion.

B. Age-i gisun fukhali mimbe dasara sain okto, bi gunin-de umesi

B. Your words are quite good medicine to cure me, in my mind I heartily (very much)

dakhambi. Ere teni mini emu jadakha ba, bi saraku ainakha? Damu,

accept it. That unsound *trait* (sick spot) of mine, how should I not know of it? Only,

ere gese baita-de teisulebukhe manggi, chikhaku anga yojokhoshombi,

this sort of business! every time, as soon as I have met with it, involuntarily my mouth begins itching,

"gisurechi ojorakungge-de gisurechi gisun-be ufarakha" sekhebi.

"when one speaks to whom one may not speak, one wastes one's speech," (as) the saying is.

Enenggi-chi bi umesileme khalaki (optative form). Jai uttu ochi—fulu aisembi?—

From to-day, I wish thoroughly to change. If I am that way again,—why should I say much?—

Age utkhai dere-be baime chifele, bi chikhanggai janchukhun-i alime gaimbi!

Sir, you may then aim and spit at my face I will take it willingly and cheerfully!

CHAPTER XVI.

A. Suwe umesi banjire sain kai, te ainakha ? fukhali sini duka i bokson-de	*A*. You were very good friends, why is it, now, absolutely (quite), over the threshold of your door
fekhunjiraku okho-ni ? *B*. Saraku	he never comes and steps, is it not so ? *B*. I know not

The middle syllable of the five, *ji*, means "comes."

We aika inde waka sabubukha ba bichi. Gemu emu gisurere-ba bi.	if there was anything (place, point) that seemed offensive (wrong) to him. Also there is another thing to mention,
Umesi aku ba-de khochikosaka yabumbikhenge, gaitai ya emu gisun ofi	when there has been no fine great intercourse at all between people, then suddenly (because) there has been one word
endebuku ufaran, fuchekhe laskha feliyeraku okhobi !	to offend, or amiss, one flares up in a rage, and positively will not come near a person !
feliyeraku ochi, inu dabala ; enggichi ba-de aibi	Not coming near a person (associating) does not matter, indeed ; but behind my back why (does he)
mimbe uttu ekhe sere, tuttu nimechuke sere ? mini takara ele guchusebe achakha-deri.	say I am so wicked here, so dangerous there ? With each of the friends I know, whenever he meets (lit. met) them
gisun fesin obome jubeshekhengge, adarame ? Jaka mini jui-de urun isibure-de	he makes out some handle for slandering me ; how is this ? Lately bringing in a daughter-in-law, (wife) for my son.
bi khono dere-de ainara seme,	I, again, thinking to preserve appearances at least,

The verb ainambi, "how am I ?" is conjugated like any other verb, *e.g.*, *ainakha*, what kind, lit. how was that done, made? Literally saying, "how would it be as regards face."

imbe soliname bikhe, intakhun emke inu takurakha ba aku.	I sent to invite him, he did not send me one messenger, even a dog.
Mini ucharakha gemu ere gese guchu kai ! mimbe jai adarame guchule sembi ?	If those I meet are all friends of that sort, how do you say I am to live in friendship ?
Tere niyalma gisun yabun kholo kukduri akdachi ojoraku seme	That man is a lying braggart who cannot be trusted,

bi aika khendukhakun? Tere fonde si geli khersembio? Khono mujaku	did not I say so? At that time did you notice it, even? Moreover, really
mimbe ichakuliyan-i b i k h e. Niyalma-i chira-be takara gojime,	he was (always) rather antipathetic to me. Even when you know a man's face,
gunin-de adarame shuwe khafu sambi-ni? Sain ekhe-be ilgaraku	his mind how can you right through penetrate and know? Good, bad, indiscriminately
bireme gemu umesi khaji guchu sechi, ombio?	lumping together, to say all are very close friends, is that possible?

CHAPTER XVII.

A. Ere uchuri si geli aibide shodonokho (bikhe)? mudan mudan-i	*A.* This long spell, where have you been running to, again? From time to time
mini jakade inu majige feliyechi-na! Ainu sini dere y a s a - b e o r o n saburaku?	could not you just step over to my place? Why is it one never sees your face (face and eyes)?
B. Bi aifini Age-be tuwanjiki sembikhe, gunikhaku emu daljaku kheturi	*B.* I have long been wishing to come and see you, Sir; unexpectedly an outside, unrelated
baita-de siderebu, fukhali lakhin takha, inenggidari fu su-fasa,	affair in (which) I got involved, quite embarrassingly implicated, every day I was worried,
sholo-de khono-bio? akuchi enenggi, bakhafi ukchame muteraku bikhe,	(what) leisure had I still? (was there yet leisure?) But for to-day, I could not have escaped,
"minde khakhi oyonggo baita bi" seme, kanagan arame, gisurekhe-i arkan teni	"I have pressing important business," making (that) excuse, a *ruse* (*arkan*) of saying that, then only (*teni*)
mimbe sindakha. *A.* Jikhengge umesi sain, jing alishame ede bi,	they let me go. *A.* You are most welcome (well come). I was (am) just feeling (so) bored here,
gunichi sinde inu asuru oyonggo baita aku, muse emu inenggi gisureme teki	I am thinking, too, if you have no very important business, how pleasant if we sat a day and conversed

Teki, optative, I would be pleased to sit.

beleni buda jefi gene. Bi inu enchu	and eat a pot-luck meal (ready rice) before you go. Indeed (*inu*) I am

Lit. rice, having eaten, go.

bookha dagilaraku.	not offering dishes specially prepared.
B. Damu jikhedari baibai, Age, simbe gajikhiyaburengge, mini gunin-de elkhe aku.	*B.* But giving you trouble, Sir, every time I come, I am uneasy in my mind,
Tuttu ofi, gelkhun-aku-de seme an-i jideraku.	and so with this apprehension, I do not make bold to come often.
A. Si aineo tulgiyen obofi gunimbi? muse atanggi "si," "bi," seme ilgambikhe?	*A.* Why made a fuss about me specially (think to put me outside)? we two (you and I), when were we estranged into "you" and "I" (differentiated)?

Jai udu inenggi giyalafi jideraku ochi, bi khono majige jaka belkhefi, chokhome	If you don't come again in a few days, I will even be inclined to prepare a few things (a feast) and specially
simbe solinaki sere? Emu erin i balai untukhun buda, be, geli aiseme	to be inviting you! One meal (literally *time*) of plain ("empty") rice, now how can you call
dabufi gisurembi? Tere anggala, sininggc-be jaka, bi ai	that worth (reckonable in) speaking of? Besides, your things (dinners) which have I
jekaku? Ere-be tuwachi, iletu mimbe suweni boo-de jai ume genere serengge kai!	not eaten? Looking at that (at it so) you are plainly telling me not to go to your house again!

CHAPTER XVIII.

A. Age, bi gunichi, niyalma-i boo-de jui banjichi, tachiburengge umesi oyonggo,	*A*. Sir, I think, when a man is rearing a son in his house, discipline (teaching) is most important,
achige-de kadalaraku ochi, khak-hardakha manggi, utkhai mentukhun albatu ombi.	if when little he is not controlled (governed), when he has grown a man, he is foolish and awkward.
B. Age-i gisun umesi inu. *A*. Si udu inu seme jabukha gojime,	*B*. Sir, your words are very true. *A*. Though your answer is that they are true (that it is so)
ere gisun-i tusa bakhara ba-be, kemuni shumilame saraku ni!	what these words hold of profitableness, do you profoundly realize (deeply know)?
Duibulechi mini beye, asikhan-chi ama eme-i kadalaburangge chira bime,	For instance, I myself, from infancy, was strictly tutored by parents,
bitkhe khulakha manggi, *sefu*-i kadalarangge geli chira,	and after I had learnt reading, was also strictly tutored by my *school-master*,
tetele udu asuru sain ba aku bichibe, yaya baita yabure-de	until now, although I am not perfect (perfectly good), in any affair I am concerned (I move) in
asuru tasharara usharara de isinaraku. Ere, utkhai,	I do not go so far as to go perfectly wrong, or be quite in error. This, then
tachibure kadalara tusa ba okhobi.	is the profitableness of education with discipline.

CHAPTER XIX.

A. Age, ume jilidara! ere "kiribe"-i khergen-be gunime kimchichi,

A. Sir, do not give way to anger (passion)! consider that word "forbearance,"

absi emu sebjeleme arga! *B.* Age, uttu gisurengge waka!

what a delightful plan it is! *B.* Sir, do not be talking like that! (there is no talking like that!)

tere-i baili-be urgedeme gutubukhe khulkha!

That, ungrateful for benefits, degraded thief (of a fellow)!

I suchungga yadakha fon-de, bi adarame imbe tuwashakha bikhe!

At first, in the days (time) when he was poor, how was I always looking after him!

Tetele i teni nikere ba bakhara-de, utkhai niyalma-be kherseraku okho!

But now (till now) he has got something to rely on (lean on), at once he does not notice a man!

Ere gese fusi geli bi-ni? *A.* Si mini tafulara be donji!

Do wretches of that sort too exist? *A.* You listen to what I advise you!

Dekden-i khendukhengge: "niyalma-de anabuchi menen aku; duleke manggi,

There is a common proverb, "To yield to a person, need not be weak-mindedness; when (time) has passed

jabshun-be bakhambi," sekhe-bi.

you gain advantage," it says.

CHAPTER XX.

A. Sini sain gunin-be, Abka saki-ni sere dabala. Tere-be g i s u r e fi ainambi?

A. Your good intentions, may Heaven know them indeed! What good is there in speaking about them.

bi da-chi sini ere baita-be, tede gisurechi nokai ja sembikhe

I used to say (think) that affair of yours was a very easy one to say to him;

eimede tuttu jayan chira fangnai ojoraku-be, we gunikha?

(one so) unpleasant, so obstinately unwilling to agree, who thought of?

Ede, umesi, gunin baibukha sechina, musei khebdekhe ba-de inde alakha-de

For that, it was a case of using up much mental (effort), and on my telling him the points of our consultation,

dere efulefi, mini gisun-be fiyokorome sembi. Tuttu, bi khur sekhe,

his face fell, and he said my words were lying nonsense. So, I was furious,

jili monggon i da deri okho, "ainachi utkhai ainakini, dabala" seme.

rage was up to the head of my throat, (my gorge rose, choking with anger), "if he wants to do anything, then let him do whatever he wants to do, and that is all," said I.

Imbe nechiki sere gunin-de jalu jafakha bikhe.

The wish to defy (provoke) him, my mind was full of that.

Amala, gunifi, beye-de beye-be fonjime, "si tasharabu khabi!

Afterwards, on reflecting, I myself asked myself, (and answered) "You are wrong!

ere jikhengge beyei baita waka, guchu-i, jalin kai.

Thus coming here of yours, is not your own affair, but for the sake of friends.

imbe majige baktambure-de, geli ai fayambi?" seme.

By conceding a little to him, again, what does that cost you?" I said (to myself)

Ini elere, ebsikhe akshalame bechere-be kirime, emu jilgan tuchikaku.

To his heart's content, exhaustively, with insults, to scold me, I endured, not uttering a sound,

ijiskhun-i alime gaime. Geli kejine goidame tefi, terai arbun-be tuwachi,

without opposing him, I received it. Again I sat a good long while, observing his looks,

ichi achambume, elkheken-i bairejakade, jakan teni uju gekheshekhe.

humouring him, (till) when I gradually put the request, then at last he nodded his head.

Si gunime tuwa, mini jili majige khakhi ochi, sini baita faijuma bikhe, waka-o?

You look at this reflectively, if my temper had been a little quick, your business was in a bad way, is it not so?

CHAPTER XXI.

Sikse, erde, ilikha manggi, boo-i dolo dembei farkhun. Bi	Yesterday, early, after I rose, inside the house it was very dark. I
"ainchi kemuni gekhun genere unde" seme, khuwa-de tuchifi tuwachi,	said, "perhaps it has not yet got very light yet," went out into the court-yard to look,
Dule, lok-seme tulkhushekhe; dere obofi, teni	lo and behold! suddenly it grew darker; I washed my face, and then, finally, just
yamulaki serede, sebe-saba aga-i sabdan tukhenjikhe	when I wished to start for the *yamun*, a gentle rain's drops came dripping down
kejine aliyara, siden-de, "shor"-seme, asuki tuchikebi. Geli te manggi	after waiting some time, (I heard) a sound "*sho-r-r-r!*" (thundered) out. Again, after sitting
emu khuntakhan chai omikha bichi, gaitai "kiyatar" seme emgeri akjan akjame,	(and) drinking a cup of tea, suddenly "*kiya-tar-r-r*," once, the thunder thundered,
khuwanggar seme agame deribukha. Bi; "ere emu burgin khuksidere dabala,	torrent-like the rain (*agame* = raining) began. (Said) I, "this is just a a sudden squall,
duleke manggi, jai yabuki," sechi. Aibide, yamji-tala khungkerekhe bime	after it has passed, I'll walk," said I How (could I foresee), till evening it was flooding down,
dobonio, gere-tele, umai nakakhaku, enenggi buda-i erin otolo, teni	all night, till dawn, it never ceased, up to dinner-time (rice-time) to-day, then, at last,

"*Until*" is represented by "*otolo*," variations of which for euphony, are "*tala*" and "*tele*."

buru-bara shun-i elden-be sabukha. Yala erin-de achabure sain aga,	mistily the sun's light was seen. In truth a season-befitting good rain.
gunichi ba-ba-i usin khafunakungge aku kai,	I think (among) the cultivated fields in every district there are none not soaked through
bolori jeku elgiyen tumin-i bargiyar-aku ainakha?	How (*ainakha*) should the autumn grain not have a rich abundant harvest?

CHAPTER XXII.

Sini dachilarangge tere Age waka-o? Tere serengge, "fulkhu-i dorgi suifun" kai!	Is that gentleman the person you ask about? As for him, he is "an awl in a corn-sack"!
atanggi bichibe urunaku dube tuchimbi. Turgun ai sechi?	at some time or other (whenever it may be) sure to get its end out. What is the reason?
Banitai ujen, jinji; ambula tachime; yabuchi doron, ashshachi kemun;	By nature grave, serious; deeply learned; in his walks, decorous, in his actions correct (measured).
alban-de ochi, emu julekhen-i yabumbi; boo-de ochi, emu suikhen-i banjimbi.	When on official duty, doing it with singleness of aim; when at home, only caring to live;
yargiyan-i majige khachin demun aku. Ama eme-de *hiyoo-shungga*,	Veritably without the smallest vice. *Dutiful* to his father and mother,
akhun deo-de khaji. Ere da de guchu gargan-de umesi karaba,	kind to his elder and younger brothers. Besides this, to his friends most obliging.

Full of *esprit de corps* or good fellowship—*karaba*—with his friends.

yaya we inde emu baita yandure de, alime gaijaraku ochi, wajikha!	If any one, no matter who, charges him with something, if he cannot accept, there is an end to it.
uju gekhcshekhe sekhede, urunaku beye sisafi sini fun-de fachikhiyashambi-	When he has said assent (nodded his head), assuredly he will spend all his energy to hasten its accomplishment,
mutebureku ochi, nakara kooli aku. Uttu ofi, we imbe kunduleraku? We	so long as he does not succeed, to give up is not his rule. Thus, who does not respect him? Who
khanchi oki seraku? "Sain niyalma, Abka kharshambi," sekhebi.	does not wish to be drawn near to him? "A good man, Heaven will care for him," the saying is.
Enteke niyalma, mekele banjifi untakhuri wajire, ai-bi? Abka urunaku	Such a man, to be born in vain and die ineffectively (emptily) can that be? Heaven assuredly
khuturi isibure dabala!	will make its blessing reach him, indeed!

CHAPTER XXIII.

A. Age, sini beye gemu nure-de beshembukhe, jai targaraku ochi	*A.* Sir, your body is all soaked (sodden) with drink (wine), if you still (again) will not eschew it,
ergen-be guweke! *B.* Age, si nure-be ergen kokiran jaka sembi, bi	look out for your life! *B.* Sir, you say wine ("samshoo," *saké*) is a thing hurtful to life; I
yargiyan-i nure-be ergen ujire okto obumbi, emu erin seme, inu,	truly hold wine to be a life-nourishing medicine; for a time even,
aljachi ojoraku, ainara? *A.* Ere ai mangga ba bi? Duibulechi, si emu inenggi	I can't be without it, how's that? *A.* What difficulty is there? Suppose, for instance, you in one day
juwe tampin omichi, damu emu tampin omiki, elkheken-i eberembufi,	drink two bottles, you want to (should) drink one bottle; gradually when you have lessened the quantity,
komsokon-i omire okhode, beye ini chisui etukhun okhobi. *B.* Age-i	and have got to drinking less, your body will, naturally (automatically) have grown robust. *B.* Sir, your
tachibure-be gingguleme dakhara dabala.	instructions I shall regardfully follow (obey), indeed.

Elkheken, "gradually," gently, diminutive of elkhe, "peaceful, peacefully." *Komsokon*, "less," rather little, dimin. of *komso*, "few, little" (*saikan*, "pretty," is the diminutive of *sain*, "good," as in Spanish *bonita*, "pretty, bonny," is the diminutive of *buena*, "good").

CHAPTER XXIV.

Tuktan. bi abalame genekhe-de emu morin yalumbi-khebi, katarar-angge	Formerly (once upon a time), when I was going hunting, I was riding a horse that trotted
nechin, faksirengge khudun. Jebele askhakhai, teni aba sarafi genere de,	evenly (smoothly), galloped fast. Quiver I had slung (girt) around me, just as the game was beaten up,
orkho-i dorgi-chi emu jeren feksime	from inside the bushes an antelope

Jeren, in Siberia, "zeren," Mongolia, the same, an antelope of Mongolia. Antelope, at Peking, known as "hwang-yang," "yellow sheep," or "yellow goat.")

tuchifi.	galloping came forth.
Bi utkhai morin-be dabkime, beri darafi, emgeri gabtachi. Majige	So I at once whipped up my horse, drew my bow, and once shot (shot one arrow). Slightly
amarilakha. Gala marifi niru gaire siden-de,	it fell short (lit. behind). By the time (*siden-de*) I had passed my hand back to take an arrow,
jeren-i unchekhen dube ashshame. Dartai andan-de, emu meifekhe be dulefi,	(I just saw) the antelope's tail's end bobbing (moving). (Then), in a moment, passing over a spur of the hill (*alin*)
alin-i antu ergi-be baime wesikhun ichi genekhe. Unchekhen	he sought the south side of it, taking his course upwards. His tail
dakhalakhai, amchanakha bichi, geli alin-be dabame, boso ergi-de	I still pursued, and was overtaking, again crossing the hill, towards the North,
wasime genekhebi. Tede bi morin-be khachikhiyakhai khanchi amchan-ifi	he was going downwards. Thereupon I pressed my horse all the time till I drew closer up,
emgeri gabtachi, geli uju-be dabame duleke. Gunikhaku, chargichi emu	shot off one arrow (once shot), again it passed over his head. Unexpectedly, from that side a
bukhu feksin ebsi jikhe. Teni, alin-be dabame	deer bounding along in this direction (hitherwards) came. Just as, passing the hill,
iskhun jiderengge, tob-seme mini gabtara niru-de goibufi, "kub"-eme	meeting me, he was coming along, he exactly lighted on the arrow I had shot off, "whop"
tukheke. Yala injeku mayan sain. Amchabukhangge,	down he fell. Truly a ridiculous (case of) luck good. What I was pursuing,
turibukhe; muterakungge, lemangga, nambukha.	I let slip; what was (seemingly) impossible, reversely, I captured.
Saraku urse de alachi, aimaka yasa-tkhun kholtoro adali?	Telling it to people who do not know (me) how could I but resemble (*adali*) a (stark) staring liar?

CHAPTER XXV.

A. Ara! Si ainambi? Muse giyanaku udu biya acharaku,

A. Halloo! what is up with you? Since we met (lit. have not met) how many months can it be,

ai khudun de salu sharampi? Sakda fiyan gaikha! Age, si

how (so) suddenly your beard has turned white? An old look your face has taken! Sir, you

mimbe angga sijirkhun seme ume wakashara! Urakhilame donjichi

will (please do) not be offended at my mouth being straight (candid)! By report I hear

si te jikha efire-de dosifi, tatala bekdun arakha sembi.

you now have gone into gambling for money, and have made (ever) so many debts

Yala ochi efiku waka kai! Majige bargiyakha-de sain!

If that is true, it is no joke (lit. game), indeed! A little retrenchment would be good!

B. Ere gemu oron-aku gisun, niyalma-i banjibukhangge! Si Akdaraku ochi,

B. That (is) all baseless talk, people's fabrications! If you do not believe (me)

narkhushame fujurulachi-na! *A.* Ai gisun?

just narrowly (minutely) enquire! *A.* What talk is this?

Beye-i yabukhangge be, beye endembi-o? Guchuse gemu simbe leolekhe-be,

One's own ways, does not oneself know? Your friends all talking about you,

tuwachi, sinde majige bifi dere. Jikha efire-de, ai dube?

looking at (them), so you have a bit of that (gambling). In gambling for money, where is the end?

lifa dosika sekhe-de, ai bikhe-seme taksimbi? Wajime dube-de

When one is deeply involved in (entered into) it, what existing thing is retained. At the last end,

weile daksa araraku ochi, utkhai majige khede funcheburaku. Boo

(even) if one does not incur (make) criminal guilt, then one has not a bit (of anything) left. House,

boigon, fulakhun wajifi, teni nakambi! Ere gesengge, muse

land, clean gone (stripped off) finally, then at last one stops! That sort, we (*muse* = you and I)

shan-de donjikha, yasa-de sabukhangge. Labdu-aku bichibe, absi-aku

with our ears have heard of, with our eyes, have seen. Not many, though there be, yet anyhow .

tanggu juwan, funchembi. Si bi muse sakha tuwakha guchu kai. Safi

(in) a hundred, ten, and more. We, you and I, are friends who know (each other). Knowing,

tafularaku, "ai dalji?" sechi,—banjire sain serengge aide? ainame aku ochi

not to admonish, to say "what matters it?"—how is that being good friends? To be nothing at all

sain dabala! Bi fujurulafi ainambi?

would be better (lit. good, *i.e.*, compared to that), indeed! What use would my "enquiring" be?

CHAPTER XXVI.

Sikse, umai edunaku, abka khochikosaka bikhengge. Gaitai ekherefi,	Yesterday, there was no wind (*edun*) at all, the sky was (being) lovely. Suddenly came a change,
sokhon, shun-i elden gemu fundekhun okhobi. Tede bi "faijume! amba edun	pale yellow, the sun's light was all lurid (pallid). Then I (said): "It looks bad! A great wind
daran isika; edun tekdere onggolo, muse yoki!" sefi.	it is coming on (*isika*) to blow. Before the wind rises, we should move (walk)," I said.
Beri-beri fachafi, boo-de isinarangge. "Kho-o!" seme, amba edun dame deribukhe.	Each his own way, dispersing, they got to their houses. "Khoo!" (bellowing) the great wind began to blow.
Moo-i subekhe, edun-de febume lasibure, asuki absi ersun!	The twigs of the trees blown back and torn off by the wind, the sound how hideous!
khujime dakhai dobori dulin otolo, teni majige toroko.	Howling, it kept on blowing (*dakha-i*) till mid-night, and then (*teni*) calmed down a little.

Dakha, "blew," *dakha-i*, "kept on blowing" (*iterative* form of verb.)

CHAPTER XXVII.

Chimari, ebsi jidere-de, jugun *giyai*-de yabure urse gemu ilime toktoraku,	In the morning, when I was coming hitherwards, in the roads and streets the

Giyai, "street," is the Chinese word *kiyai*, pronounced *chiè* in Peking.

"kho-kha!" seme sujumbi.	pedestrians were all unable to stand still, running along with "ho-ha!" (shivering).
Bi aika edun-i chaskhun feliyechi, khono yebe bikhe,	Whilst I stepped along with the wind following, it was still tolerable (better, *i.e.*, "not so bad")
geli eduni iskhun ojoro jakade, dere uleme tokshoro adali,	but when it had become a head wind again, my face was as if pricked with needles,
chik-chik-seme nimembi. Gala simkhun beberefi	suddenly smarting. My hands and fingers were so numbed,
shusikha jafara-de gemu fakjin bakharaku okhobi.	my whip, to hold it, even, (*gemu*, lit, all) they were not possessing the power,

Fakjin, liter. "the handle," the wherewithal.

chifelekhe chifenggu, na-de isinara onggolo, utkhai jukhene	the saliva that one spat out, before reaching the ground, at once turned into ice (froze)
"katak" seme meyen meyen-i lakchambi.	and (fell) "patter-patter," sundered into fragments.
a-da-da! banjikha-chi ebsi, ere gese beiguwe we dulembukhe-ni?	Br-r-r-r! From the time I was born till now, such cold as this who has passed through?

CHAPTER XXVIII.

Si saraku. Ere gemu se asikhan, senggi sukdun etukhun-i kharan. | You do not know. That is all because (*kharan* = "cause") their age is young, blood and breath sturdy

i.e., constitution, *physique*.

udu mudan koro bakha manggi, | after a few times of getting hurt

Getting the worst of it; *bakha* "got," is shortened from the old *bakhakha*. from *bakhambi*, "I get."

ini chisui amtan tukhembi-kai. "Ai-de sakha?" sechi, | of course they lose their taste (for it). "How do you know that?" if you say (ask me),

Bi da-chi utkhai, bashilara-de mujaku amuran. | I, from the beginning, then, for boxing (*bashilara*) was greatly inclined (a great amateur),

mini emu mukun-i akhun-i emgi, inenggidari urebumbikhe. | with one elder relation of my clan, daily I practised (lit. made myself riper).

Mini akhun-i gidalarangge umesi mangga | My senior (lit. elder brother)'s play with the spear was very expert (ripe; tough)

juwan udu niyalma seme, inu beye-de khanchi fimechi ojoraku. | ten, or so, of men, though there were, could not get near to his body.

uttu bime, amala, khono, emu mangga bata-be ucharakha-bi, | Though it was thus, afterwards, nevertheless, he met a tough antagonist;

nakchu-i boo-de jikhe emu tokso-i niyalma, betkhe dokholon, | from my mother's brother's house (*nakchu*, "maternal uncle, Chinese *kiu-kiu*) came a peasant, lame in the leg,

lokho maksime bakhanambi sembi. Juwe niyalma | in sword (*lokho*) play (*maksime* = dancing) an expert, it was said. The two men

emu ba-de ucharafi, erdemu-be chendeki semi, | at a place met together, desiring to try (optative mood) their valour

Skill; *erdemu-be* = *virtutem*.

teisu teisu agura-be gaikha manggi, mini Age yasa-de geli imbe dabumbi-o? | After each man had taken his weapon, did my kinsman (elder brother) even take him into his eyes? (think him worth regarding)?

anakhunjara be inu aku, utkhai gida-be dargiyafi,	not even recoiling, at once (forthwith), he brandished his *gida* (spear)
niyaman-i baru emgeri gidalakha. Tere dokholon majige eksheraku,	towards the heart made a spear-thrust. That lame one, a little (even) not hurrying himself,
elkhe nukhan-i jeyen-i esheme emgeri jailabume sachire, jakade	composedly, with the edge sideways gave one (once) parrying slash, after which (*jakade*)
gida-i dube utkhai mokso emu meyen genekhe	the spear's end (point) forthwith, chopped off, went off a separate piece (lit one piece)
gida-be gochime jabduraku, lokho aifini monggo-de sindakha	the spear he had no time to draw back (*gochime*), the sword already (a long time) was placed at his throat.
teni jailaki sere-de, monggo-be khakhara okho, lasikhime	then when he would have dodged, his throat was gripped, with a wrench (the lame man)
emgeri fakhara jakade, ududu okson-i, dubede, maktafi,	with one throw immediately, a good many feet, finally, flung him,
kub-seme tukheke	prostrate he fell down.

The Chinese renders "kub" seme, "*putung!*" as an onomatopoetic word, like "thump," but Zakharoff says *kub* means relaxed, powerless; from fatigue or somnolence; and renders this very phrase *kub-seme tukheke* "*vdruk pavalilsya ot ustalosti,*" "suddenly fell down through fatigue" (Dict., p. 290).

Tere-chi, niyanchan bijafi, jai-jai tachiraku okho.	After that, he was discouraged (lit. his starch was crushed), so that he was not learning any more.
Ere-be tuwachi, abkai-fejergi amba kai, mangga urse komso aku.	Looking at this, (one exclaims), the Empire is great indeed, skilled (tough, *mangga*) men not few.

Abka-i fejergi exactly signifies the Chinese *Thien-hia*—"under Heaven," or "under the Sky"—the Empire.

CHAPTER XXIX.

Chananggi, be Wargi Alin-de ambula sebjelekhe bikhe. Inenggi, shun-de,	Yesterday, we greatly enjoyed ourselves at the Western Hills (near Peking). By day, in the sun,
sargashara efire-be khono aisembi? Dobori okho manggi, elen	excursions, amusements, need we say more (than mention them)? After night is (there), in fuller measure
se salakha. Mini udu ofi yamji buda jefi,	it (*i.e.*, the pleasure of such trips) is participated in. Some of us, after dinner ("evening rice"),
jakhudai-de tekhe manggi, goida-khaku biya mukdefi	after seating ourselves in a boat, without waiting long (saw) the moon rose

Mukdefi, "rose," cf. Mukden (elevation, elation), the capital of Manchuria, in Chinese Shing-king—*King*, of course=capital city, as in *Peking*, *Nanking*, Tonking; and Japanese Tōkyō, a corruption of Tungking.

gekhun elden fosokongge, utkhai inenggi shun-i adali	so lustrously pouring her beams, that it was just like daylight (day and sun).
elkhei shurubume, edun-i ichi, wasikhun genekhei	We got them to pole slowly, and with the breeze, went dropping down (stream)
alin-i oforo-be murime dulefi, tuwachi: abka, bira,	winding round a projection (lit. "nose,"—*oforo*) of hill we passed, and looking: sky, river,
bocho fukhali ilgaburaku, hwai sembi. Yala, "alin gengiyen	their colour was absolutely indistinguishable, (one) vast expanse it was. Verily, "Hills bright
muke bolgo," sechi, ombi.	and waters clear," one might (*ombi* = can) say.
Selbikhei ulkhu shumin ba-de isinakha bichi; kholkon-de	We rowed (were rowed) into a place where the reeds grew thickly; suddenly
jungken-i jilgan, "yang"-seme, edun-i ichi, shan-de bakhabure, jakade,	a bell's voice, (solemnly) booming, down the wind, reached our ears, and then
tumen khachin-i gunin seolen, ede isinjifi, utkhai muke obokho adali,	the myriad mental cares, when we reached that (moment), were at once washed away as with water.

geterembukhekungge aku.	there was none but was purged clean away.

The root of the heptasyllabic word is *getere.*

Udu jalan-chi cholgorome tuchike enduri sekhe seme	Although one speak (*i.e.*, whatever one may say) of sacred beings (*enduri*) leaving beneath them (lit. "coming out from," *tuchike*, came out) the world which they surpass (*cholgorome*)
changgi tuttu sebjelere dabala.	only so far and no more (*tuttu* = "so, thus") will they easily, *i.e.*, likely rejoice, indeed (*dabala*="and that is all").
Tuttu ofi, iskhun-de amtanggai omichakhai.	And so, mutually, with *gusto* (*amtan* = taste), we kept drinking together

Note: *Omimbi* means simply "I drink"; *omibumbi*, "cause to drink"; and *omichambi*, "to drink together"; *omichakha*, "drank together"; *omichakhai*, "kept on drinking together."

Kherchun aku adarame gerekhe-be saraku bikhe-bi.	Without our noticing it, how the dawn came (*gerekhe; geren* = light) we did not know.
Niyalma jalan-de banchifi, enteke genggiyen biya sain arbun	Men born in this world, such bright moons and lovely scenes
giyanaku udu untukhuri dulembichi! Khairan aku seme-o?	how many can they let pass unheeded (literally, "empty")! Can we say it is not pitiable?

CHAPTER XXX.

A. Si ainakha-bi! chira biyabiya-khun, kob-seme wasifi, ere durun-de	What a state you have got into! your face pallid, quite fallen, to that appearance
isinakhabi! *B.* Age, si saraku. Ere udu inenggi, ulan fetere-de, wa amtan	you have come (arrived)! *B.* Sir, you do not know. These few days, owing to digging drains, the stench
umesi ekhe. Tere da-de geli gaitai shakhurun gaitai khalkhun, tokto-khon aku.	(has been) very bad. In addition to that, also it has been suddenly cold, suddenly hot, with no fixed (weather).

There being no such distinction between adjectives and nouns as in many European languages, *toktokhon* might with equal correctness have been rendered "fixity."

Tuttu ofi, niyalma gemu beye-de ujire an kemun bakharaku.	Things being so, people all could not get their normal (usual) rules to lead their lives (literally, to nourish, or rear, their bodies).
Chananggi, b u d a - i e r i n - d e shakhurusaka bikhengge	The day before yesterday at dinner-time it had been cool,

Diminutive of *shakhurun*, "cold," or "the cold."
Chananggi, short for *chara-inenggi*.

gaitai khalkhun ofi, niyalma alime muteraku fetkhashambi.	it suddenly was hot, people were unable to endure it and became run down (made tremble)

Or, a person could not stand it, and was made sickly.

Beye gubchi khumbur-seme nei tuchire, jakade, majige serguwesheki seme,	My whole body perspired (*nei*= "sweat") copiously, and then, being desirous of cooling myself a little,
sijikhiyan-be sukhe, emu moro shak-hurun chai omikha. Ilikhai	I took off my upper garment, and drank a cup of cold tea. *Instanter* (or, immediately)
utkhai uju nimeme deribukhe, oforo, inu, wanggiyanakha, bilkha	then my head began to ache, my nose, also, had a cold (*i.e.* catarrh), my throat,
inu, sibukha, beye tugi tekhe adali, huwi sembi.	also, was obstructed, my body as if riding on the clouds, (so) giddy I was.
A. Sini teile tuttu waka. Mini beye inu asuru chikhaku,	*A.* (Was) your (case), alone, like that (?) no. My body, also, was quite listless (*i.e.* languid),

ashshara buyeraku. Jabshan-de sikse jeke omikhangge wachikhiyame oksikha	not liking to move. Luckily (by good luck), I vomited out everything which I ate and drank yesterday,
akuchi, enenggi inu katunjachi ojoraku okho.	had it not been so, to-day it had been impossible for me to stand firmly.
Bi sinde emu sain arga tachibure, damu khefeli-be omikholobu,	I will teach you a good plan, simply starve the stomach,
komsokon-i jefu, ume labdulara. Tuttu okho-de	eat a little less, do not make it more. If you can do like that

Komsokon, diminutive of *komso*, "few"; *labdu*, much, *labdulambi*, the verb thence formed, "to augment."

utkhai majige shakhurakan seme, inu ainakha-seme, khuwanggiyaraku.	then even if you get a little chilled, still, anyhow, you will take no hurt.

CHAPTER XXXI.

THE HAUNTED HOUSE.

A. Suwe-ni bakchin-de bisire tere emu falga boo, antaka?

A. That house that is opposite to yours, what sort (of a house) is it?

Falga is the numerative of houses, as are, in Chinese, *so'*, in Japanese, *ken*, in Malay, *buah*. In English such numeratives are few: "sail" of ships, "head" of cattle, seem the only ones. These exist in Burmese and Siamese, and also in Persian, where they are numerous.

B. Si tere-be fonjifi ainambi? *A*. Mini emu tara akhun udaki sembi.

B. Why (for what purpose) do you ask about that? *A*. A cousin (father's sister's son older than I) of mine is wishing to buy it.

B. Tere boo techi ojoraku. Umesi doksin! Tuktan-de

B. It is impossible to inhabit that house. Most uncanny! Originally

mini emu akhun-i udakhangge. Girin-i boo nadan giyalan

it was purchased by an elder brother of mine. Seven (front) rooms in a row,

Numerative of *boo*.

fere-de isitala, sunja jergi, umesi ichangga bolgo sain, bikhe.

up to the rear end, five suites (divided by courts), very comfortable, clean and good, there are.

Mini akhun i jui-i gala-de isinakha, manggi juwe ergi khetu boo-be, sangsaraka seme

After they came into my brother's son's hands, the side buildings on two sides, being in a ruinous state,

efujefi dasame weilekhe turgun-de. Kholkon-de

he pulled down, with the object of making repairs. Suddenly

khetu d a k h a m e deribukhe. Suchungga daishakhangge kemuni yebe.

spooks began to play up. At first their rioting was still not so bad.

Yebe means, literally, "was a little better."

Bikhe bikhe-i inenggi shun-de asuki tuchibume, arbun sabubakha

At last, by daylight, they emitted sounds, and made shapes to be seen.

We should say: "Sounds were heard, shapes were seen," which is, in fact, what the Manchu means; but Manchu, like Japanese, prefers Active constructions to Passive, as Malay (like Sanscrit) prefers Passive to Active.

Boo-i khekhesi jachi okhode utkhai "bucheli-be ucharakha," seme

The women of the household were saying at any time (again and again) "I've met a Ghost!"

golofi ergen jochibukhangge gemu bi. Samashachi

(some) frightened out of their lives (losing their lives) even, there were. *Shaman* dances

Saman ("*shaman*"), a magician, from *sambi*, "to know."

mekele, fudeshechi baitaku.

all in vain, *shaman* rites without avail.

Tuttu ojoro jakade, arga aku, ja khuda-de unchakha.	When it had come to be so, having no resource, he sold it at any easy price (cheap).

Ja, "easy," hence "cheap." Similarly, in Japanese, "*yasui*" means both "easy" and "cheap."

A. Age, si sambi-o? Ere gemu forgon ekhe-i kharan.	*A.* Sir, do you know (what)? That is all because of his fortune being bad.

Forgon means a revolution, a turn (as of "Fortune's wheel").

Yaya boo-de umai kharan aku. Forgon sain ochi, udu bushuku yemji	In every house,—there is not one without its luck. If the luck be good, how many (soever) goblins (and) sprites
bikhe seme, inu jailatame burulara, dabala.	there may be, they will flee in retreat (from it), indeed (they will).
Niyalma-be nunggeme mutembi-o? Tuttu seme, mini akhun	(How) can they annoy people? Though it is so, my elder brother
umesi fakhun-ajige. Bi dachilakha yargiyan-i ba-be inde alachi	(is) very small-livered (timorous). I will tell him the true things I have learnt by enquiring,
wajikha. Udachibe, u d a r a k u ochibe ini chikha-i gamakini!	and that ends it (that is all I will do). Whether he buys, or does not buy, according to his wish let him decide!

CHAPTER XXXII.

THE FORTUNE TELLER.

A. Age, si donjikhaku? Jaka khoton-i tule emu *jakun khergen* tuwara niyalma jikhe-bi	*A*. Sir, have you not heard? Lately outside the City a man who looks at one's *Eight Characters* has arrived.

"The eight characters (or words), the eight cyclical characters appertaining to the hour of a person's birth, viz., those of the year, month, day, hour. These are communicated between the parties to a betrothal" (Mayers). The cycle of the Far East comprises 60 years.

Umesi ferguwechuke mangga, sembi. Niyalma-i alara-be donjichi,	Very wonderful (clever) and skilful, they say. (From what) people have told, that I have heard,
tere n i y a l m a fukhali enduri suwaliyame banjikhabi. Yaya muse	that man quite has an admixture of deity (the supernatural) in his nature. Each (thing) we
d u l e k e l e (*duleke-ele*) baita-be, aimaka-we in-de alakha adali,	have ever e x p e r i e n c e d (gone through), as if (*adali*) some one or other had told him,
jafakha sindakha gese, bodome *bakhanambi*. Muse niyalma	taking and laying out, like (*gese*), he can map (figure) it out. Of our people
genekhengge umesi labdu, siran siran-i, lakcharaku.	there have gone very many, in a stream (row, or series, upon row) without intermission,
jalu jikheke-bi. Ere gese shengge niyalma bini?	they arrived in crowds (*jalu* = "full"). Such sort of prophetic man (diviner) exists?
atanggi muse akhun deo inde inu tuwabunaki? *B*. Bi, aifini,	When should we, brothers elder and younger, go and get him to come and look. *B*. I, some time back,
sakha; mini guchu, ere udu inenggi, feniyen genere jakade,	knew; my friends, these few days, had been going, in flocks, and then
chananggi bi inu tuba-de isinakha. Mini *jakun khergen*-be	the day before yesterday I also went thither. My *Eight Characters*
inde tuwa bukha-de: ama eme ai aniya? akhun deo udu ofi?	I got him to look at. Father, mother, what year? elder, younger brothers, how many are there?

Causative form, from *tuwambi*, "I look."

sargan-i khala, ai? atanggi khafan bakhangge? khachin khachin-i baita	Wife's surname, what? when official rank obtained? Every sort of thing (affairs)

gemu achanakha, kheni agige tasharaburaku — all came right (lit. matched, fitted), not a bit the least did he have wrong.

Causative form of verb.

A. Dulekengge udu achanakha bichibe, damu jidara unde baita — *A*. Although the past came right, still, things that have not come yet.

ainakhai ini khendukhe songkoi ombi-ni? *B*. Tuttu seme, — how can these be in accordance with his pronouncements? *B*. (Granting) it is so,

muse yamaka ba-de tere udu jikha mayaraku? Eichi-be, si, geli, — why ever should not we spend these few "*cash*" (farthings)? Anyhow, you, also,

baita aku; boo-de bai tere anggala, sargashara gese, genechi, — have nothing to do; rather than sitting (*tere*) idly at home, for an outing, like, to go,

ai urunaku sere ba-bi? Alishara-be tookabure ton oki-ni! — what is there wrong about that? Let us just put it in the list (number) of our recreations (lit. preventing melancholy).

CHAPTER XXXIII.

A. Ini tere arbusharangge, absi yabsi? Neneme tuktan

A. That behaviour of his, of what sort is it? Before, (when) first

Verb, from *arbun*, "form," "mien."

imbe achakha-de, nomkhon ergi-debi sembikhe; te, tuwachi

I met him, I said he seemed on the simpleton side, now, looking at him,

fukhali niyalma-de eleburaku; albatu ten-de isinakhabi niyalma-i juleri

a man is quite dissatisfied; he has attained to the acme of clownishness; in people's presence

"bu-bu ba-ba," absi fonjire jabure ba-be gemu saraku. Chichi gochi,

"bu-bu, ba-ba!" of how to ask and how to answer he is totally ignorant. Fidgetting,

adarame ibere adarame bederere-be gemu ulkhiraku. Getechi-be

how to come in, how to go out, he quite fails to understand (knows not). Though awake,

weri amgara adali. Bai niyalma-i ton, dabala. Khulkhi lampa-i

like somebody asleep. A mere cipher of a man, that is all. Stupid, muddle-headed

Lampa, literally "primeval chaos," chaotic, *khulkhi*, "foolish."

adarame banjikhabi! Suwe banjire sain kai. Tede majige

why was he born! You are on good terms. To him a little

jorishachi achambi, dere. *B*. Age, suwe

guidance (from you) would be appropriate, perhaps. *B*. Sir, you

Jorimbi, to guide, has *jorishambi* as its Frequentative Form.
Suwe, plural of *Si*.

emu ba-de goidame guchulekheku ofi, khono tengkime sara unde.

have not been associated (with him) long in one place, as yet you have no profound knowledge of him.

Ere-chi injechuke baita geli bi-kai. Iskhun-de techechi gisurembikhe-de,

There are also things more ridiculous than this. When sitting face-to-face (mutually) talking,

ere-be gisureme bikhengge, kholkon-de tere-be gunifi leolembi. Akuchi,

while talking of this, suddenly he has thought of that (and) discusses it. When not so,

angga labdakhun-i, ergen sukdun aku, yasa fakha guriburaku

with mouth dropping, inanimate, without ever averting the pupils of his eyes,

simbe tuwambi. Gaitai geli emu uju unchekhen aku baliyen gisun tuchike-de

he looks at you. Suddenly, again, when some silly words without head or tail come out, niyalma-be dukha lakcha-tala fashame injebumbi! — it makes a man laugh till he splits (liter. sunders) his vitals (entrails) asunder!

Chananggi imbe tuwaname genekhe (lit. I went, going in order to see him) — The day before yesterday (or, a day or two ago), I went to see him.

Amasi marire-de, shuwe yaburaku, fiyan forofi (the Chinese renders "his back") — On returning back, he did not walk straight, turning his face (*i.e.*, backwards),

sosorome tuchimbi. Tede bi: "Age, bokson-de guweleke!" — he went out recoiling. Thereupon I: "Sir, beware of the door-frame!"

gisun *wajinggala* (*i.e.*, *wajire-onggolo*, before finishing), i, betkhe tafi, — before I could finish the words, he, getting his feet entangled,

saksari-onchokhon-i tukhenere. Bi eksheme amchanafi — went tumbling backwards, face upwards. I hurriedly chased up (to him).

khusun-i mutere, ebsikhe, tatame jafara jakade — with what my strength could,—I used it all (*ebsikhe*) I took (*jafara*) and set him upright, and then

arkan tamalibukha. Neneme, bi khono imbe ton-aku tafulambikhe — he was hardly able to stand up. Before even, I had lectured him (times) without number,

amala, dasara khalara muru-aku-be tuwachi, khwashara tetun waka kai — afterwards, seeing no signs of mending or of change, (I say) he is no improvable vessel,

aiseme angga shadabume gisurembi? — why make my mouth tired by talking to him?

Shadambi, "to be tired"; causative form, *shadabumbi*, "make to be tired."

CHAPTER XXXIV.

A. Age, si tuwa! Te, geli, isika! lalanji omifi	*A.* Sir, you look! Now, again, he has had enough! he is limp (sodden) with drinking,
ilime toktoraku okho-bi. Bi: "tere baita-be, si tede alakha-o akun?	he cannot stand straight. I (asked): "That business, did you tell him, or not?"
seme fonjichi. Kheikhedeme, yasa durakhun-i, mini baru gala alibumbi.	I said, asking him. Reeling drunk, eyes staring, he held out his hand towards me.
Udu khele waka, jaburakungge aineo?	He is not at all dumb, why did not he answer?
Ere gese niyalma-be fanchaburangge geli bi-ni? Enenggi (ere-inenggi)	Has he that way, too, of exasperating people? To-day (this very day)
fiyara-tala tantaraku ochi, — bi utkhai gaskhukini!	if I do not beat him till he is half dead,—I, would take my oath, then!
B. Age, si joo! ume! I ainchi onggofi genekheku.	*B.* Sir, you stop! do not! He maybe forgot and (so) did not go.
Ini waka ba-be, ai saraku sembio? Uttu ofi, olkhome, jabure	His faults, how can he not know them? It being so, through fearing, an answering
gisun bakharaku okho-bi. Enenggi, bi ubade bisire-be dakhame,	word he could not find (lit. get). To-day, as I am here, in consideration of that (lit. accordingly)
mini dere-be tuwa, ere emgeri onchodafi, (*oncho* = wide, broad)	have regard for my face, (when) you have for this once shown lenience (literally *latitude*)
ere-chi julesi, nure omire-be eteme laskhalangkini!	from now forward, wine-bibbing let him resolutely cut off!

Japanese *kore-kara* = *ere-chi*.

Khendure balame, "kangnachi ulkhen ja, bungnachi akha ja," sekhe.	One says, jocosely (*balame*), "to ride bare-backed, a donkey is easy, to oppress, a slave is easy."

In the Chinese, the *proverbs* quoted are in *rhyme*, which, in the Manchu, is lost.

Si jingkini sonchokho jafakha ejen kai, aibi-de ukchambi?	You are effectively his lord (*ejen*) who holds him by the "pigtail" (tress), whither should he escape?
Khalachi khalakha, aikabade khalaraku, kemuni uttu	If he changes (reforms) he changes, if by any chance he does not change, but still so

suikhume omichi, Age, chikhai isebu! Bi udu jai ucharakha seme,

drunkenly imbibes, Sir, however you please, chastise him! Though I happen to be here again,

inu baire-de mangga! *A.* Age, si ainambakhafi sere?

yet I shall be hard to entreat! *A.* Sir, on what grounds do you say that?

Ainambakhafi, from *ainame bakhafi* (*adarame bakhafi*, what have you to go on, what data, what information?)

banitai, emu guskheraku fayangga! Arki omimbi sere-de

from his birth, a ne'er-do-well (incorrigible) imp! Arrack-drinking, talk of that,

utkhai buchetei amuran! Ini ama-i senggi-chi khono khaji!

then to the very death he loves it! Than his father's blood is it (more) near (and dear) to him!

ere mudan guwebekhede, utkhai khalaki sembio? Manggi ochi,

If he is let off this time, then he will wish to reform, say you? At the most,

Manggi-ochi also appears contracted into *manggichi*.

emu juwe inenggi subukhun dabala. Duleke manggi, geli fe an-i omimbi.

one (or) two days sober, and that is all (*dabala*). After these have passed, he will drink in his old fashion.

Arki, "arrack," Zakharoff calls "*vodka*," in his Dictionary, Chinese *shao-tsiu*, Mongol *arikh*, Arabic *'araq*, Malay *'araq*. The origin of the word appears to be Arabic, meaning "essence, spirit, basis."

CHAPTER XXXV.

A. Age, ere jui uduchingge? *B*. Ere mini fiyanggu.

A. Sir, this son (of yours) is number what? *B*. That is my youngest (smallest).

Udu, how many? *uduchi*, number what? *uduchingge*, *a gerandial* form of the same meaning. (*Fiyanggu simkhun* means the last finger, the little finger.)

A. Mama ershekhebi? *B*. Unde. Ne gemu ikiri akhun deo. Uyun

A. Has he had small-pox? *B*. Not yet. They are all a regular series of brothers. Nine

Mama ershekhebi: literally, "has *grandmother*,—or, *an old woman, nursed* him?" *Ikiri*, a pair, twins; also, a series, used for *elder* and *younger brothers* (*akhun deo*), with one year between them.

banjifi, uyun gemu taksikha. *A*. Age, bi yobodorongge waka,

were born, all nine are living (literally, "were kept"). *A*. Sir, I (say it) not joking,

asha mergen kai, juwe banjire-de singgebukhabi.

your ***good lady*** is a ***genius***, experienced (skilled) in bearing sons.

asha, "my elder brother's wife," hence "your wife,"—as the person addressed is complimented as "elder brother" of the speaker. The word has passed from Manchu into Chinese, at Peking.

Mergen, in Manchu as in Mongol, means skilful,—a good shot, a good marksman. For small-pox the Chinese say, euphemistically, "putting forth flowers."

"Omosi mama" sechi ombi. Si yala khuturi yong-kiyakha niyalma.

"The grandmother of grandchildren" one might call her. You indeed are a man whose happiness is complete.

Omosi-mama is in Chinese *Fuh-shin*, the "Goddess of Happiness," the patroness or protectress of children and posterity.

B. Ainakha khuturi! gajikha sui kai! amba-ningge okho, yebe;

B. What kind of happiness! Punishment brought (into the world) with me! the bigger ones are not so bad

Literally, *yebe*, means "slightly better."

ajigesi ningge, inenggi-deri "gar, miyar!" sekhei banjimbi.

the smaller ones, the whole day they are bawling and squalling!

alimbakharaku yang-shan! Dolo gemu urekhebi!

unbearable their whimpering and whining! My heart (interior) feels thoroughly bored!

A. Jalan-i niyalma utkhai uttu: juse elgiyen urse, geli

A. The world's people are just so: folk with plenty of children, again,

cimeme gasambi; mini gese juse khaji niyalma de,

are surfeited and discontented with them; for my like, the men poor in sons,

emke bichina sechi, aba? Abka inu mangga kai.	to speak of their being even one, where is he? Heaven indeed has a hard task (to please all).

Aba for *ai-ba*, "where."

B. Sini tere jui walivakhaku bichi, inu uyun juwan se okho-bi,	*B.* That son whom you lost, just (about) nine or ten years (old) he was,
yala emu sain jui. Tetele jongko-dari, bi	that truly was a fine son. Even now whenever I mention him, I,

Te-tele. "up till now"; *jongko*, past tense of jompi, "I mention."

sini funde, nasame gunimbi. Tere banin-wen, gisun-khese,	for your sake, feel sorrowful. That look he was born with, that speech,
guwa juse-chi ching-kai enchu. Alkha bulkha etufi,	from other boys (sons) far different. When dressed in his festal clothes,
niyalma-be sabumbi khede, beye-be tob-seme obufi,	he was introduced to people, (made acquainted), he held his figure erect,
elkhei ibefi, "sain"-be fonjimbi.	and came forward calmly and asked "are you well?"

Saiyun? the interrogative form of *sain*, "good, well," means "are you well?" between equals. Superiors are asked "elkhe-o?" "Are you in peace?" These are exact counterparts, *saiyun*, of the Chinese "*hao-mo?*" and *elkhe-o*, of the Chinese "*Ngan-mo?*" the Arabic *salam*.

jilakan manggi! tere ajige angga, ai gisun bakhanaraku?	Poor child! that little mouth, what words did not it know?

Jilakan is a diminutive form connected with *jilan* "pity." *Manggi*, "only, merely."

Tede emu baita fonjikha-de, aimaka we inde tachibukha adali,	If one asked him a thing, as if (*adali*) some one or other had taught him,
da-chi dube-de isitala, khachingga demun-i akumbume alame mutembi.	from beginning to end, he was able (*mutembi*) to tell all the particulars perfectly (*akumbume*).
Tentekengge emge bichi, juwan-de tekherembi-kai.	Of that sort a single one, even (*bichi*) is worth as much as ten.
Utala baitarakungge-be ujifi, ainambi?	When one has reared all these useless ones, to what end? (what does one gain?)

CHAPTER XXXVI.

A. Ere seke kurume, puse-li-de udakhangge-o?

A. That mantle of sable-fur (*seke*, "sable"), did you buy it in a shop?

Puseli is Chinese for "in the shop, in a shop," here used in Manchu to mean "a shop."

B. Puseli ningge waka, juktekhen-de udakhangge.

A. (No) it was not in a shop, it was bought in a temple (or, monastery).

A. Khudai menggun udu? *B.* Si tubisheme tuwa!

A. Price how much silver (how many Taels?). *B.* You look, and guess!

A. Ere absi-aku ninju yan menggun salimbi dere!

A. This must be (literally, "how not?") worth sixty Taels (*yan*, in Chinese *liang*, ounce).

B. Gusin yan menggun-chi nonggikhai dekhi yan menggun-de isinafi,

B. Starting from thirty Taels, I kept on adding till we reached forty Taels,

utkhai unchakha. *A.* Khuda ai uttu wasikabi?

and then he sold it. *A.* Why was the price down so low?

Note that *yan*, silver "Tael," has nothing to do with the Japanese *yen*, "Dollar," which is from the Chinese word *Yüan*. *Liang*, Chinese for Tael, becomes in Japanese *riyo*. The Japanese is very poor in sounds.

Nenekhe forgon-de, ere gesengge, juken, jakunju yan menggun

In past times, this sort, usually, Eighty Silver Taels,

unchachi bakhambi. Bocho *sakhaliyan*, funiyekhe luku.

it could be sold for (that price). Colour *black*, pile (hair) luxuriant,

weilekhengge, inu, bokshokon. Fuserekengge inu teksin.

the making-up, too, neat-and-smooth. The bordering is beautifully-even also.

Uttu bime, tuku-i suju jiramin. Iche ilkhangga

(Besides) its being so, the satin (*suju*) of the facing is thick. New flowery (pattern),

erin-i doron. Yargiyan-i umesi, salimbi. *B.* Mini ejekhengge,

the style of the time. Really very valuable. *B.* I remember (am calling to mind)

Ejekhengge refers more to records, or memoirs noted down in writing.

sin-de inu emke bikhe. *A.* Mini tere ai ton? Bai "emu kurame" dabala.

you had one, too. *A.* That of mine, how can we count it? Simply "one mantle!"

funiyekhe manakha, simen wajikha, tulesi etuchi ojoraku okho.

Hair ragged, gloss (lit. vital spirit) finished, impossible to wear inside-out (lit. wear outwards).

B. Fulun bokha manggi, giyan-i emu sain-ningge udachi achambi-kai.

B. After you get your *salary*, it would be appropriate (*achambi*) to buy a good one.

A. Suweni se-asikhata jing *wesikhun* ichi genere niyalma,

A. You young people, exactly, the men who go in the direction of the *Court*,

yamulara isara ba-de, etuchi giyan ningge. Min-de geli ai *yangse?*

or flock to the *yamuns*, are who should wear (such). What elegant *style* is there about me?

Yamulambi, verb formed from *yamun*, Chinese for a Public Officer, or Court of Justice. *Wesikhun* means superior, upper; *wasikhun*, lower, inferior; *wasikha*, fallen lower, *e.g.*, come down in price, come down in the world. *Sakhaliyan*, "black," appears on Maps as "Saghalien"; the Saghalien Ula is the River Amur, in Chinese Heh-lung Kiang, "Black Dragon River."

Erin dulekebi. Damu khal ukan ochi joo kai.

The time has passed. Only let it be warm, that will do!

Joo means "hold, enough!"

Sain ningge etuchi, fiyan tuchiraku bime; elemangga kushun.

If I wear fine ones, I do not excel in smartness; on the contrary, I am awkward (in them).

Tere anggala, mini ere khitkhun *alban*-de inu teisu aku.

Besides, this finger-nail (tiny) "*billet*" of mine, moreover, does not tally with them.

Ine-mene fereke manakhangge elemangga minde fitkheme achambi.

Anyhow, old worn-shabby ones, on the contrary, suit me perfectly.

Alban means *official position, State employment.*

CHAPTER XXXVII.

A. Cheni boo-de we aku okho? chananggi bi tederi (terei-deri)

A. In their house who is dead (*non est*)? The other day I through that way,

dulere-de, tuwachi, boo-i urse shakhun sinakhi khuwaitakhab-i,

passing by, I saw that the house were in white, in mourning attire, (girdles)

bi eksheme *idu* gaime jidere, jakade, *bakhafi fonjikhaku*.

I was in a hurry, going to do my *turn of duty* (*idu*), and so *had not time to enquire*.

B. Jaka ini echike ufarakha. *A*. Banjikha echike waka-o?

B. He has just lost his father's younger brother. *A*. His own born uncle?

B. Inu. *A*. Si jobolon-de achanakha-de? akun?

B. Yes. *A*. Have you been to visit the (house of) mourning? (or) have not you?

B. Sikse *Nomun* khulara-de. Bi gulkhun emu inenggi tubade bikhe.

B. Yesterday they were to read the *sûtra* (Buddhist Service). I was there all day.

A. Atanggi giran tuchibumbi? *B*. Donjichi, biyai manaskhun-de.

A. When is the funeral (lit. do they carry out the corpse?) *B*. I heard after the 20th.

"After the 20th": literally "in the waning (or aging) of the moon." Of lunar months, the 15th day is always when the Moon is full.

A. Cheni *yafan* ya ergi-de bi? *B*. Mini yafan-de khanchi.

A. Where is their *burial-place?* *B*. Close to ours (literally, to mine).

Yafan, Chinese *yüan*, means, primarily, "a garden."

A. Uttu ochi, jugun goro kai. Dekhi *ba* isimbi-dere.

A. If it is so, the way is long (*goro* = "distant"). (If so) then 40 *li* approximately.

Ba is Manchu for the Chinese *li*, a third of a mile. In Japan, the Chinese word *li* is corrupted to *ri*, and means a Japanese league, nearly 2½ miles.

Ere siden-de, jai imbe achafi gunin-seki

In the meantime, I am going to see him, to express my sympathy (condole).

B. Bi idu-chi khekokho manggi, simbe guilefi sasa achaname genere.

B. When I leave duty, I will accompany you when you go to see him.

A. Giran tuchibure onggolo, minde emu majige isibufi. Bi utkhai

A. Before the funeral, send me some intimation. Although I, indeed,

ten-i ba-de isiname muteraku okini, khoton-i tule isibure beneki.	cannot escort it to the end, I should like to go with it as far as outside the city.
An-i uchuri be, udu taskhume feliyeraku bichibe, sabukha-dari,	Usually, though we were not constant companions, whenever I saw him,
mini baru dembei gabsi-khiyan. Niyalma seme, jalan de banjifi,	he was very cordial towards me. Of men, born into the world,

Gabsikhiyan means *eager*; here "pleased to see."

ya gemu guchu waka? Weri ere gese baita-de, muse beye-de	who is entirely not a friend? When people have this sort of affair, if we personally
isinachi, gunichi acharaku-seme leorere niyalma aku dere!	attend (are present). I should think there would be no one to talk about it being improper. .

CHAPTER XXXVIII.

A. Ere khojikhon-de bure etuku waka-o?	*A.* Is not that the costume to give your son-in-law?
B. Inu! *A.* Ese ainarangge? *B.* Turifi gâjikha faksisa.	*B.* Yes! *A.* What are these doing? *B.* Workpeople brought here for hire.
A. Ai musei fe kaoli gemu wajikha! Sakdasa-i forgon-de,	*A.* How old customs have quite died out! In the old people's time,
juwan udu se-i juse gemu etuku shanggabume mutembikhe.	children (girls) about ten years old, were all capable of making costumes completely.
Kubun sektefi, tuku doko achabufi; ubaliyambukha manggi,	They spread the cotton, fitted facing to lining; after they had turned it,
"si adasun-be, ifichi, bi utkhai jurgan gochimbi,"	"you hem the skirt, and then I will do the back-stitching,"
ere okho-be jafachi, tere monggon hajambi.	one settling the armpits, another hemming the neck.
Khetkhe khuweshengge khetkhe khuwesheme, tokhon khadarangge tokhon khadame.	The sleeve-ironers ironed the sleeves, the button-fixers fixed the buttons.
Manggi, emu juwe inenggi siden-de, utkhai wachikhyabumbi.	At most, within one or two days, and then it was finished.
Tere anggala, makhala-chi aname gemu boo-de weilebumbikhe,	Besides that, even the very caps were all finished in the home,
basa bume turifi weilebure, jikha menggun-i udafi eture ochi,—	to give wages (*basa*), and hire people to set them to work, to be buying with money the wherewithal to wear,—
niyalma oforo-deri "suk"-seme injembi kai!	people would snigger (laugh, "*suk!*" from their noses)!
B. Age-i gisun giyangga bichibe, si damu emke-be sakha gojime.	*B.* Sir, though your words are right, you only know one thing.
juwe-be sakhaku-bi. Tere erin, ere erin, emu-adali obofi gisurechi ombio?	You do not know the second. That time, this time, can one make them alike, in speaking of them?
jai gaire inenggi geli umesi khanchi okho. Simkhun fatame bodochi,	Also, the fetching-day (marriage-day), also, is very near. Reckoning by crooking down the fingers,

arkan-karkan ude inenggi *sholo* bi. Ere siden-de,	hardly any days are left free (*sholo*, leisure, free time). In that space of time,
majige sholo tuchiburaku. Dobori dulime, khachikhiyame weilechi,	even a little spare time cannot be seen (coming out). Nights awake, bustling at the work,
amchabure, amchaburakungge, khono juwe siden-de bi-kai.	and still (*khono*) it is doubtful (lit. between two) if we catch up, or do not catch up.
Aika memereme fe kooli sekhe-i "giru-silten fejile, chulgan-be sartafi,"	If we insisted on the old custom, "under the flag-staff, but late for the parade" (review)
yasa gekhun tookabure de isibuchi Al yokto!	with eyes wide open we should be brought to failure (obstruction). What an idea! (Also rendered, "what pleasure could that be?")

CHAPTER XXXIX.

Niyalma ofi, tanggu se banjirengge umesi komso. Ere

Being a human being, even if one lives a hundred years, one lives very few. This (body)

taka banjire beye, yaya tolgin-i gese, sebjelere-ba giyanaku udu?

Fleeting the time this body exists, much like what dreams are made of, chances of enjoyment how few!

The above are Buddhist phrases. Literally, how many can there be?

Shun biya khomso maktara adali. Geri-fari uju-i funiyekhe

Days and months (pass) like the shuttle thrown. Suddenly, the hair of one's head

shakhun-de isinafi. Eiten baita baitaku okho manggi,

has got to white. After one has become incapable of doing anything,

elemangga juse amosi-i senchekhe-be tuwame shame banjire dabala,

on the contrary, one is just watching the chins of children and grandchildren,

ai amtan? Jai sube giranggi mangga okho sekhe-de,

what treat is there in that? Also, with muscles and bones become stiff,

etuchi fiyan tuchiraku, jechi amtan bakharaku.

one's dress displays no elegance (grace), one's food gives no savour.

Bikhe seme ai baitalan? Te sakdara unde-be amchame

When things have come to this pass, what use has one? Now, seizing the time before old age,

Amchame, literally "overtaking," *i.e.*, not letting it go past one; *sakdara unde*, literally "when one is *not yet* (*unde*) old."

eturaku jeteraku ochi, jikha menggun-be fata seferefi ainambi?

if one is not dressing and is not eating, but pinching and grabbing money, to what end?

Si dababume mamgiyaraku dere bakhara ufukhi-be bodome.

you go to excess in avoiding extravagance, reckoning just your right expenditure.

Bakhara ufukhi means "one's quota," "the amount one should get as one's portion, share."

Majige sebjelechi *kheo* sembi, dabala, mamgiyame sechi ojoraku.

A little enjoyment is *rather a good thing* (*kheo*) in sooth; that cannot be called extravagance.

B. Sini ere gisun mimbe *same* gisurekhengge-o? Eichi

B. Are you saying these words of yours *knowing* me? Or perhaps mimbe *saraku* tubishame gisurekhengge-o? Minde ele mile bichi,

you say them *not knowing* me, conjecturing? If I were independent (in easy circumstances)

sebjelerengge inu giyan. Umai inguwa gese funche daba-i bakhara ba aku ba-de,

to go in for pleasure would be, indeed, reasonable. As I have no balance over, like some others,

Gese, a suffix like the Japanese *gotoku*, meaning "like to"; *funche*, "superfluity"; *daba*, "in excess"; *cf. supra, dababume*, "go to excess."

mimbe adarame sebjeleme sembi? Bekdun arafi ebu sembi-o?

how can you speak of my enjoying myself? Debts, should I make, to dress, do you say?

eichi boigon fayafi jetu sembi-o? Sini gisun songko okho-de,

or perhaps waste my household substance, to eat, do you say? If I did as you say,

jikha ulin wajifi, utkhai "giyok"-seme beye wajifi, teni sain!

money, goods, finished, and so with a "thud!" I would make an end of myself; then, at last, all right!

aikabade beye wajiraku ochi, kemuni ergen tafi banjichi,

If by any chance, my body (*i.e.*, life), were not finished, if I still drew breath (and) existed,

tere erin-de ainachi ojoro? Falanggu alibume sinde baichi,

by that time in what condition should I be? Begging from you with outstretched palms,

Si ainakhai achabumbi-ni?

how would you be likely to look after me?

CHAPTER XL.

Yaya niyalma damu akdun bichi, niyalma teni gumin dakhambi.

A. If any man only is trustworthy, *then, not else* (*teni*), people's hearts will be with him.

Enenggi ochi "chimari" sere, chimari okho manggi, geli "choro" sere,

When it is to-day to say "to-morrow," when to-morrow has come, again to say "the day after to-morrow,"

erken terken-i inenggi anatakhai, atanggi dube da?

backing and filling, putting off from day to day, when will (such goings on show) anything definite?

alime gaisu manggi, geli angga khalara ochi, niyalma jai adarame,

after undertaking (*gaisu*) to answer for it (guarantee), then to be changing your mouth, how can people again

sini gisun-be akdambi? Ere doron-i ushan-fashan kengse laskha-aku ojoro anggala

trust your words? Besides this style of nonsensical absence of smart decision,

doigon-de emu yargiyan ba-de inde ulkhibuchi,

[there is this other way:] in the first place (at first) to let him know something true,

niyalya inu gunin usafi, jai ere gunirakhu okho-bi.

then the man would be discouraged, and would not have these expectations.

B. Waka! Bi yamaka ba-de akdun-be ufarabukha-ba-bi-o?

B. No (it is not so). Where did I ever go so far as to break faith?

Si te jorime tuchibu. Umainara onggolo, utkhai uttu,

Point it out, now, will you? Before there is anything (real), then such a

algingga jubengge-i gisurerengge! Baita oron unde kai! Ini funde

report. scandalous talking! Before the affair has any shape! On his account

fachikhiyashafi. ainambi? Eiten baita tunggalakha-dari,

this eager zeal. to what purpose is it? Whatsoever affair one meets with,

The suffix *Dari*, means "as often as," "every time that."

kimchikha da-de kimchifi, fakjin bakhe manggi

examine and examine again; after you have gotten some handle,

jai niyalma-be wakashachi! niyalma inu dakhame.

then complain of people's faults (*waka*)! People then will agree (submit).

Si umai getuken-i saraku ba-de baibi mimbe wakashachi ombi-o?	You, knowing nothing clearly, can you be idly reproaching me for my failings (*waka*).
Tere anggala, yabuchi mini chikha, yaburaku inu mini chikha!	Besides, taking steps is in my option, and taking no steps is also in my option.
Si shorgifi ainambi? Bi banitai utkhai uttu cha mangga,	What good your pressing me? I am naturally of just that sort, dour to compel,
baita-be yargiyalakhaku-de, gidame jafafi mimbe "uttu oso!" sechi	In a thing that I have not ascertained the truth about, to take and press me, saying "Act so!"
bi ainakha-seme yabure ba aku! Adarame sechi? Tenteke basuchun	I will by no means move at all! How do you mean? Such-like ridiculous
werifi, gisun anaku ojoro, baita-be (*anaku* means a key,—an opening for)	(ridicule-bequeathing,—*werifi* = leaving behind) affairs, that serve as a pretext for tittle-tattle
ajige-chi yabure tachikhaku kai. I akdachi, "aliya!" se,	since I was little I have not learnt to move in them. If he trusts me tell him "wait!"
akdaraku ochi, chikhai, gwa ba-de genefi, enchu niyalma-de yandukini dere!	if he does not trust me, at his option, let him go elsewhere and ask someone else to do it.

Genefi; the *fi* indicates past tense, "having gone" elsewhere; yandu*ki*-ni; the *ki* is the Optative sign, "I wish he would" engage.

We imbe aliyakhabi?	Who waits for him?

CHAPTER XLI.

A SHAM GHOST.

Ere udu inenggi, gungkame khalkhun ojoro jakade,	For these some days past, as the heat has been stifling
fa-be sujekhai, tulergi giyalan boo-de amgakha bikhe	with window propped up, I have been sleeping in an outer room (verandah).
Sunjachi ging-ni erin-de isinafi, deri dosi forofi,	When it came to the time of the fifth watch, with face turned towards inside (the house)

Ging, the Chinese word *King*, "a watch of the night"; "the 5th Watch" is from 3 to 5 o'clock in the morning.

jing amgame bisire-de, shan-de asuki donjibumbi. Amu suwaliyame,	I was just asleep, (when) a sound (*asuki*), made itself audible to my ears. Half-asleep

Suwaliyame means, "with an admixture of,"—"coupled with," literally.

yasa neifi tuwachi, uju-i juleri emu aldungga jaka ilikhabi,	I opened my eyes and looked, before my head a weird being was standing,
dere shanyan khooshan-i adali, yasa-chi senggi eyembi!	face like white paper,—from the eyes blood oozing!
Beye-i gubchi shakhun. Uju-i funiyekhe labdakhun.	All the body *bright white* (*shakhun*). The hair of the head dishevelled.
Na-de fekuchere de. Bi sabure jakade, bi ambula	It was hopping along the ground (floor). As soon as I saw it, I was greatly
guwachikhiyalakha. Ara! Ere utkhai khutu serengge inu dere!	shaking with fright. "Oh, dear! So this is what a devil (ghost) is, in very truth!"
Mini ainara be tuwaki seme. Yasa-be jiberefi tuwachi; guninakhaku,	I said, "I would fain seen what it will do (*ainara*). With eyes half-closed, I looked. Unexpectedly,
fekuchekhe-i khorokho-be neifi; etuku-adu-be kejine tuchibufi,	it still hopping along, opened a wardrobe, and having taken out many garments,
okho-de khafira, fa-deri tuchifi genekhe. Tede bi gaikhari	clutched them under its armpit, got out through the window. Thereupon I suddenly,

ulkhifi, dolori gunime: khutu ochi, etuku-be gamara kooli bi-o?

fullv awake (intelligent) inwardly reflected: If it is a ghost, can there be any reason in its taking away clothing?

Ilifi, lokha-be tuchibu, jabduburaku inde lasikhime emgeri genchekhelere jakade.

I rose, drew a sword, and giving him no time to get out, gave a sword-fiat's swipe at him and then

"Ara!" emu jilgan, na-de sarbatala tukheke. Boo-i niyalma be khulame; gaifi

with a cry of "Oh, dear!" he fell to earth flat on his back. I called, and collected the domestics,

tenjan dabufi tuwachi. Umesi injeku! Da-chi emu butu khulkha,

and lit a lamp to see. Very laughable! The origin of the affair (lit. originally) was a nocturnal thief.

jortai khutu arafi niyalma-be gelebumbi.

who made (himself) a ghost purposely (*jortai*) to frighten people.

CHAPTER XLII.

A BETROTHAL VISIT.

A. Feten achafi be muse niyaman jafaki-sere-be baime jikhe.

A. As the destinies (horoscopes) agree, we would take kinsmanship, have come to seek it.

Mini ere jui, udu cholgoraku erdemu, ferguwechuke *bengse* aku bichibe,

This our son, although excelling in merits, and wonderful in accomplishments he be not,

Bengse is from the Chinese, and means "talents, accomplishments."

damu nure omire, jikha efire, ekhe fachukhun urse-de dayanafi,

still, wine-bibbing, money-gambling, resorting to the company of bad disorderly men,

balai sargashara jergi baita, inde kheni majige aku.

idle amusements, all such (*jergi*) things (faults) he has not even a particle of them,

khatame waliyaraku ochi, Lao-yé emu gosire gisun bure-o.

if you do not dislike and reject him, Sir will you give him a kind (affectionate) word.

Lao-ye is the Chinese word *Lao-yé:* Zakharoff renders it "*Gospodin.*" It is applied to Magistrates.

B. Age, si julesiken jio! *A*. Muse Lao-ye-de khengkileme baiki.

B. Sir, come forward a little. *A*. We wish to make our request *kowtowing* to you, Sir!

Khengkileme, "knocking head," making the ceremonial prostrate reverence.

Techefi mini emu gisun donjire:—

[He rises, and continues speaking.] Will you sit and listen to a word from me?

Muse gemu fe niyaman, gese-gese giranggi yali.

You and I are quite old relations, alike in bone and flesh (*i.e.*, same flesh and blood).

We we-be saraku? Damu, eiken sargan serengge, gemu

Who does not know whom? But, the being husband and wife, all (that)

nenekhe jalan-i toktokhon salgabun; niyalma-i chikha bakharaku.

is in a former world (life) fixed and fated (decreed); it is not man's will (choice) that will obtain it.

Juse-be ujifi, shame tuwame sain-i juru achabuchi, ama eme okho niyalma,

When they have reared children, under their own eyes to arrange a good match (couple), people who are in the position of (*okho*) father and mother

jobokho suilakha gunin inu wajimbi.	(that) indeed (they find makes) the anxiety and labour of mind cease.
B. Tuttu sekhe seme, emu-de ochi, minde ungga jalan bi	*B*. Although it is as you say, in the first place, I have relatives of an elder generation,
ere Age-be sabure unde; jai de ochi, jikhe tai-tai-se	who have not yet seen this gentleman; in the second place, the ladies who have come

Tai-tai, Chinese for "lady."

mini mentukhun sargan jui-be inu majige tuwachi.	(might like) to have a little look at our stupid daughter.

Mentukhun, "stupid," meant in polite depreciation of the speaker himself, rather than of the daughter.

A. Inu. Looye-i gisun umesi ferguwechuke giyangga kai.	*A*. Yes, indeed. There is wonderfully good reason in what you say, Sir.
Ere gisun-be utkhai muse jikhe taitai-sa-de khafumbi;	So we will take your words through (*khafumbi*) to our ladies who have come;
B. Gege-be tuwakha manggi, inu Age-be dosimbufi	*B*. After they have seen the damsel, let the (young) gentleman be sent in, too,
uba-i tai-tai-sa-de tuwabuki.	it will be well that the ladies here be allowed to have a sight of him.

Tuwambi, "to see," *tuwabumbi*, "to make to see," *tuwabuki*, optative, also used as imperative of *tuwabumbi*.

A. Iskhun-de gemu gunin achakha sekhe-de, jai khengkilechi inu goidaraku kai.	*A*. When we are all mutually satisfied (suited), to salute again with a "kowtow" will not be too late.

CHAPTER XLIII.

A QUEER COUPLE.

Cheni eiken sargan-be si bachikhi sembio? sirame gaikhangge.

These, husband and wife, do you say (think) betrothed from childhood? It was a second marriage (literally, "married consecutively").

Ere khekhe ududu anakhabi Beye giru sain, gala-weile inu ombi.

That woman had faults Face, figure, handsome,—hand-work, also, she was in (occupied herself in work with her hands).

Damu emu-ba eden: jushun-jedere mangga. Eigen

But she had one defect: she was customarily jealous. The husband

Jushun is "vinegar." "Eating vinegar," as here, is a Chinese idiom for being jealous. Manchu has also the phrase "*yasa niowanggiyan*," "green-eyed" for "jealous" (which Shakespeare used).

susai se tulitele, umai juse enen aku bime.

till he had passed 50 years (his fiftieth year), he had no son and heir at all,

emu sula khekhe takuraki sere-de khetu dedufi ojoraku.

he wished to engage (employ) a secondary wife, but she (the first wife) obstinately opposed it.

Sula khekhe, lit. "a free woman"; *sula* means loose, or at large. *Sula* was "a Manchu of one of the Eight Banners at large, without position or pay"—Mayers. *Sula boikhon* "loose earth," *sula inenggi*, "holidays," *sula bitkhe*, "idle books," novels. *Khetu dedufi*, "transversely lying down,"—she lay down and barred the door against ingress.

fasime bucheki, sere, beye-be beye saraki sere,

she wanted to hang her and thus kill her, she said; she wanted her to rip her own body open;

khachingga-i gelebume daishambi. Fisika menen, geli eberi ten,

all manner of intimidation (she tried) in her fury. Dull, stupid, and feeble in the extreme,

sargan-de ergelebufi, fukhali khoron gaibukha imbe umainame muteraku bime,

bullied by the wife, quite beaten by terrorism (*khoron*), unable to get on with her in any way,

Umai, "nothing at all"; *umainame muteraku*, "cannot be done in any way"; *umainachi ojoraku*, "absolutely impossible"; *umainakhaku*, or *umainaraku*, "no matter at all"—compare with *ainame*, &c.

niyokhon jili banjikhai ergen susaka.

after living a long time green with anger, she died (or, "of jealous rage.")

B. Ere-be tuwachi, jalan-i baita taksin aku bime, mujangga.

B. Looking at that, the world's affairs are out of order, that is true.

Mini tuba-i emu Age, jaka, utala yan-i menggun, emu khekhe udafi,	Where we live (of ours, there) a gentleman lately, for so many ounces of silver, bought a woman,
asikhan sargan arakha. Fukhali nichukhe boo-bai obokhobi.	(and) made her his petty (or junior) wife. Altogether like a pearl jewel he treated her,

Bao-be (*pao-pei*) is a Chinese word for precious things, *e.g.*, jewels.

aika gelere adali gosime, ai sechi jai, gelkhun-aku majige jurcheraku.	as if in dread (of losing her) he cherished her; what she said, he did not dare in the slightest to disobey (oppose).

Gelkhun, "fear," from *gelembi*, "I fear"; *gelkhun-aku-ojoraku*, lit. "fearlessly cannot," means "I do not dare to."

Ere *khachin-i* akha-be, uju-de khuksheme	That kind of slave! to exalt and respect (lit. to carry on one's head)

"To carry on one's head," in Chinese *ting-tai*; in Japanese, corrupted into *cho-dai*, with the meaning of "respectfully receive," it means "please give me."

elemangga jingkini sargan-be akhanekhu de isiburaku, adunggiyambi,	on the other hand, one's proper wife, not even assimilating her to a slave, to oppress!
inenggi-dari tantakhai, fasime buchere-de isibukha. Danchan-i urse	every day he was beating her, he even came to hanging her. The wife's people
khabshakha; tetele umai wajire unde. Ere felekhun khekhe,	appealed to the law; up till now it is by no means finished. Here, a savage woman,
tere doksin khakha, jing emu juru! Abka aineo	there, a cruel male, just make a pair of them! How is it that Heaven
cigen sargan obome, kholboburaku ni?	did not link them together (couple them) by making them husband and wife?

CHAPTER XLIV.

THE SIX BOARDS, OR DEPARTMENTS OF STATE.

A. Age-de fonjiki adarame "Ninggun Jurgan"-be sembi?	*A*. I wish to ask you, Sir, what do people call "the Six Boards?"
B. Khafan-i Jurgan, Boikhon-i Jurgan, Dorolon-i Jurgan,	*B*. Board of the Civil Service, Board of Revenue, Board of Education,
Chookha-i Jurgan, Beidere Jurgan Weilere Jurgan, inu.	Board of War, Board of Justice, (and) Board of Works, these are they.

Board of Education: literally, "of Ceremonies," one of whose functions was to deal with ecclesiastical matters, Buddhist and Taoist.

Khafan-i Jurgan serengge, Abka-i fejergi Bitkhei khafasa-be kadalarangge,	The Board [Ministry] of Civil Service: this controls the Civilian Officials of the Empire (lit. of under Heaven).
Ninggun Jurgan-i uju obombime. Geli "tiyan gwan dai chung tsai" sembi.	it is held to be the chief of the Six Departments of State, also called, "Great Ministers, Officers of Heaven."
Boi khon-i Jurgan serengge: Abkai-fejergi chaliyan-jeku-be ichikhiyarangge	The Board of Revenue (Treasury): it manages the Empire's Accounts in money and grain,

Firstly, imposts collected in money and grain; secondly, money paid out in salaries, wages, etc., and rice, etc., as rations.

tumen irgen-i ergen-be kadalambime. geli *Di Gwan Dai Sze Tu*	it controls the living of the myriads of subjects. It is also called "Earth's rulers' Great Inspectorate.

Tumen, "ten thousand." This word mean "a cloud," in Russian *tyma*: in Persian from the Mongol domination, *tuman, tomaun*, "10,000 men"; a gold coin. *Di Gwan*, etc., are pure Chinese words, in Manchu letters.

Dorolon-i Jurgan serengge: Abkai-fejergi dorolon kumun-be yendembime.	The Ministry of Education (or, Religion): this promotes the Empire's Ceremonies and Music.
Geli *Chun Gwan Dai Jung Be(h)* sembi.	It is also called "Spring Officials' Great Tribal Ruler."
Chookha-i jurgan serengge: Abkai-fejergi chooka morin-be dasambime.	The War Department: the Empire's armies and horses it directs.
Geli *khiya (hia) gwan Dai sze-ma* sembi.	It is also called "Summer Officials' Great Marshal."

Beidere Jurgan serengge: Abkai-fejergi fafun shajin-be alifi ichikhiyambime.	The Board of Justice: it has charge of the Empire's judicial administration and laws (*shajin* = "prohibitions").
Geli *Chiu* (*Tsiu*) *Gwan Dai Sze-kco* sembi.	It is also called "Autumn Officials' Great Judge."
Weilere Jurgan Serengge: Abkai-fejergi weile kichen be ukherileme ichikhiyambime.	The Office of Works: it has supreme control of the Works department of the Empire.
Geli Dung *Gwan Dai Sze-kung*, sembi.	It is also called "Winter Officials' Great Overseer."

The above Chinese names are very recondite and unusual.

CHAPTER XLV.

A. Age, bi tachibure-be baire-ba bi. Manju Chookha-i kuwaran-de	*A.* Sir, I have something on which I ask for instruction. In the camps of the Manchu armies

Ba means a place, a topic, and an abstract quality: it thus corresponds to the Chinese *so* and the Japanese *tokoro*,—more exactly to the latter, as it is a suffix.

jingkini ton-i toktobure ilibukha, khafasa udu?	how many officers (*khafasa*) are stationed, according to the fixed number?
B. Jiyanggiyun (Chinese *Kiang-kün*) amban, meiren *i janggin*-chi tulgiyen	*B.* Besides Their Excellencies (*amban*) the Commander-in-Chief (Military Governor or Captain General) and the Military Lieutenant-Governor.

Meiren means shoulder, or wing. *Janggin*, from the Chinese *chang-yin*, "keeper of the seal," is a head of a department in a Public Office; a common address of Staff Officers, corresponding, Zakharoff says, to *Vashe Vysoko-blagorodie*,—Colonels down to Majors.

Jakun gusabi. Jakun gusa-i dorgi-de, juwe gala delkhembi.	There are Eight Banners. Within the Eight Banners, there is division into Two Wings.
Daskhuwan gala duin gusa: kubukhe suwayan gulu shanyan, kubukhe shanyan,	Left wing, four banners; bordered yellow, plain white, bordered white,

Daskhuwan, left, or East, to one facing South: *Jebele*, right, or West. Among the *Mongol* tribes, also, the left wing means the Eastern wing of the tribe, hence the name "Sungaria," from the Mongol (ZEGUN), Dzun, or Zun, "left," and GHAR "hand." The Hindus faced East, their *Deccan* (*Dakshina*) means "right," also South. The Arabs, also, faced East in naming the cardinal points, hence *Yemen* means "right," also South; the Hebrews also, whose *yamin* means South as well as Right,—*Ben-yamin*, "Benjamin," "son of the right hand." The Gaelic *Deas* means "South," also "proper," "comely." Last, but not least; the Chinese faced South, and their word for "North" is obviously connected with their word for "back," both in writing and in speech, and perhaps with our word "back," which it resembles in sound. (*Pek, pei*)

gulu lamun. Jebele gala, duin gusa; gulu, suwayan, gulu fulgiyan	plain blue. The right wing, four banners: plain yellow, plain red
kubukhe fulgiyan, kubu-khe lamun. Emu gusa-de, Gusa-i Da, Emke,	bordered red, bordered blue. To one Banner, one Colonel,
nirui janggin, emke, tuwakiyara Khafan-i jergi janggin emke,	one Lieutenant-Colonel, one Major,
fun-de boshoku juwe, amba ajige khafan ukheri dekhi.	two Captains, greater and lesser officers, altogether, forty.

Ilan gusai bayarai ("les boyards") *Kwaran*: in the Palace, Yüan Ming Yüan, staff of the guards, from three (*ilan*) regiments, Bordered Yellow, Yellow, and White Banners.

CHAPTER XLVI.

A. Age, niyowanggiyan turun kuwaran, jingkini ton-i toktobume,

A. Sir, about the Green Flag Camp, the regular number fixed

Turun, a flag, ordinarily square, but for the Guards long and serrated. The Green Flag is the Chinese Territorial Army.

ilibukha khafan, adarame? *B.* Ukheri kadalara amban fejergi-de

for Officers appointed, how is it? *B.* Under his Excellency the Commander-in-Chief

dulimbe, Khaskhu, ichi ergi, ilan kuwaran bi. Dulimbe

there are Central, Left and Right Sides, three Camps. The Central

Khaskhu, "Left," also "East." *Ichi*, "Right," also "West." *Ichi*, in Mongol, means the samo as in Manchu. The Greeks and Romans, like the Manchus, had several names for "Left." *Dexios; dexter;* for "Right"; but *skaios, scævus; sinister; lævus, laios, aristeros,* for "Left."

Kuwaran-de: Jung-giyun aisilame kadalara da emke

Camp:—"jung-giyun" Colonel, one (lit. Adjutant).

Chinese *Chung-kün*, Central Force.

tuwakiyara Khafan, emke. Minggatu, duin. Baksatu, jakun.

Major, one. Captains, four. Lieutenants, eight.

Minggatu, literally *chiliarchs*, from *minggan*, "a thousand." *Baksatu* exactly corresponds with the Turkish *yüz-bashi;* and *Minggatu*, with the Turkish *bim-bashi*, from *bin*, a thousand. (See Marco Polo, Chapter XLIX., "on the Tatar Armies.)

Khaskhu, Ichi-ergi juwe Kuwaran-de, Adakha Kadalara Da, juwe;

In the camps of the Left and Right (two Camps), Lieutenant-Colonels, two;

tuwakiyara Khafan, juwe; Minggatu, jakun; Baksatu, juwan ninggun.

Majors, two; Captains, eight; Lieutenants, sixteen.

MARINE BRANCH.

Bira-be ukheri-kadalara Amban-i fejergi,

Under His Excellency the Director-General of the (Yellow) River (Hoang Ho), (and)

jeku-be ukheri kadalara Amban-i fejergi,

under His Excellency the Director-General of the Grain Transport Service,

gemu uttu.

are all so (as above).

CHAPTER XLVII.

Giyarime dasara Amban-i fejergi, jingkini ton-i toktobume:

Under His Excellency (*Amban*) the Provincial Governor, the regular fixed number

alibukha Khafan, Ukheri Kadalara Amban-i fejergi-chi inu adali-o?

of Officers appointed, is it also the same as that under the Commander-in-Chief (Governor-General)?

Adali aku. Damu Khaskhu Ichi ergi juwe kuwaran bi. Khaskhu-ergi

Not the same. Only two (*juwe*) Camps, Left and Right. Left-side

Kwaran de: Jung-giyun Adakha Kadalara D'a, emke. Tuwakhiyara Khafan,

Camp; in (this are): Adjutant, (or Military Secretary, a Brigadier-General) one. Major,

emke. Inu minggatu duin, baksatu, jakun. Ichi-ergi Kuwaran-de,

one. Also, Captains, four,—Lieutenants, eight. In the Right-hand Camp,

Dasikhire Khafan, emke, Tuwakiyara Khafan, emke.

Colonel, one; Major, one.

Dasikhire, exactly representing the Chinese by *Yu-kih*, "soaring and swooping,"—a picturesque name indicating quick attack on, and rout of, an enemy force.

Inu, minggatu, duin, baksatu, jakun.

Also, Captains, four, Lieutenants, eight.

CHAPTER XLVIII.

A. Ukheri Kadalara Da fejergi-i, jingkini ton-i toktobume ilibukha Khafan,	*A.* Under the Brigade General, the regular fixed number of Officers appointed,
geli adarame? *B.* Ukheri Kadalara Da-i fejergi ochi, ele enchu okho.	How is that, too? *B.* As for those under the Brigade General, the difference is still greater,
eichi ilan Kuwaran ojoro eichi juwe Kuwaran ojoro, toktokhon aku.	where there shall be three Camps, or shall be two Camps, there is no fixed rule.
Duibulechi, dulimbe khaskhu ichi-ergi ilan kuwaran ochi:—	For example, where there are the three Camps, Central, Left, and Right:—
Dulimbe Kuwaran-de jung-giyun dasikhire Khafan emke.	In the Central Camp, General's Adjutant, a Colonel, one.
tuwakiyara Khafan, emke, minggatu juwe, baksatu duin. Khaskhu, Ichi-ergi	Major, one; Captains, two; Lieutenants, four. Left Side, Right Side
juwe Kuwaran-de, emu Kuwaran-de dasikhire Khafan emke.	of these two Camps, each Camp has one Colonel ("*Eagle-like*" *Dasikhire*)
tuwakiyara Khafan, minggatu, baksatu, emu adali.	(and) as regards Major, Captains, Lieutenants, similarly (to the foregoing).

CHAPTER XLIX.

B. Kemuni, Muke-i Chookha-i fideme kadalara Amban-i fejergi,	*B.* Now further, under His Excellency the General in charge of the Marine Force,
Olkhon jugun-i Chookha-i fideme kadarara Amban-i fejergi bisire-be	(and) His Excellency the General in command of the Land Force (literally Dry Road) what there are
si sambio? *A.* Saraku. *B.* Muke-i Chookha-i	do you know? *A.* I do not know. *B.* Of the Marine force,
fideme kadalara Amban-i fejergi serengge: Dulimbe, khaskhu, Ichi-ergi	under His Excellency the General in charge there are: Central, left (east) right (west)
julergi, amargi, sunja Kuwaran. Dulimbe Kuwaran-de,	vanguard (front, or South) rearguard (back, or North),—five Camps. In the Central Camp,

"Front," *julergi*, contracted from *juleri*, "before," *ergi*, side. "Back," *amargi*, contracted from *amala*, "behind," *ergi*, "side." *Amargi Gemun*, Peking, "Northern Capital," an exact equivalent of the Chinese "Peh-King"; by Manchus who write Chinese words in Manchu script, this is written as *Pé-king*, but pronounced in the North-China way "*Pé-ching*."

Jung-giyun adakha kadalara Da, emke; Tuwakiyara khafan, emke;	there is one Lieut.-Colonel; one Major;

Jung-giyun is the Chinese word Chung Kün; "Adjutant or Military Secretary," according to W. F. Mayers, a great authority.

Minggatu duin; Baksatu jakun. Tere duin Kuwaran-de:	four Captains; eight Lieutenants. In those (*i.e.*, the other) four Camps:
emu Kuwaran-de, Dasikhire khafan emke; tuwakiyara khafan,	to one Camp (each Camp) one Colonel; as for Majors,
Minggatu, Baksatu, gemu Dulimbe Kuwaran-chi emu adali.	Captains, Lieutenants, all just the same as in the Central Camp.

The postposition, the suffix *chi*, "from," signifies "compared with," like *yori* in Japanese; compare *min* in Arabic, and the Ablative case in Latin.

Olkhon jugun-i fideme kadalara Amban-i fejergi serengge,	As regards those who are under His Excellency in command of the Land Force
Muke-i chookha-i fideme kadalare Amban-i fejergi-chi enchu aku.	there is no difference from those under His Excellency in charge of the Marine Force.

Fejergi, "under," contracted from *fejile*, "below, down," and *ergi*, "side." *Amban*, "His Excellency, from *amba*, "great"; the Chinese is *Ta-jen*, from *ta*, great, or still more correctly *Ta-ch'en*, "high officer of State."

CHAPTER L.

Enenggi erde, cheni bitkhe shejilebufi, emke emke-chi eskhun

This morning, early, when I made them recite their lessons, one was rawer than another,

Shejilebufi, "make to recite," is in Chinese, *kiao pei shu,* "make turn their backs (and recite) their books": *eskhun,* raw, unripe, untaught, the reverse of *mangga,* ripe, well-taught.

"Eng-eng"-seme, angga gakhushame, deng-deng-seme ilinjambi.

"er, er," they went, with mouths a-gape, speechlessly they stood, tottering, there.

Ilimbi, simply "to stand," or "to rest." *Ilinjimbi,* "to come and stand." *Ilinambi,* "to go and stand." *Ilinjambi* is said of babes, "just learning to stand on their feet."

Tede bi: Takasu, mini gisun-be donji! Suwe,

Then I: You just wait a bit, listen to my words! You,

Takasu for *taka-oso, taka* "for a short time," or "wait a short time," *oso,* Imperative of *ombi,* "be!" As Europeans say "one moment!" or "un moment!" *Tede bi, then I,* followed by my speech to the pupils, without the preliminary word "said." This idiom is the same in Manchu and in Japanese. The Chinese always has the word for "said," *i.e., shuo.*

Manju bitkhe-be khulachi tetendere, utkhai emu julekhen-i tachichi-na.

since you really wish to read Manchu books then go on evenly, steadily, studying.

Tetendere, "as soon as," "since," as the French *dès que, du moment que.* Tach'ki sechi tetendere, "since you say you are,"—or "since you are—wishing to learn."
Khulambi means "to read aloud," and also "to call, to shout to."

Ere gese, ton arame, untukhun gebu gaichi, atanggi dube-da tuchimbi?

This way of making a number (*ton,* a mere cipher), acquiring an empty name, when can anything definite (*dube,* "end," *da,* "root, head") grow out of it?

Suwe inenggi biya-be untukhuri anabukha sere anggala, bi inu mekele.

You, days and months idly procrastinating, nor is that all (*anggala,* in addition) I also fruitlessly

Khusun baibukha sechina. Aichi suwe-ni beye-be sartabukha sembio?

am using my strength (efforts). (*Aichi,* whether) is it your keeping yourselves back?

Aichi bi suwe-mbe sartabukha sembio? Chiksika,

Or is it my keeping you back? Grown up,

amba khakha oso naku, khendutele geli uttu

great fellows (men) as you have lately become and thus, all the time I tell you things,

Tele, until, same as *otolo.*

shan-de donjire gojime, gunin-de teburakungge,

though you hear with your ears, not implanting them in your minds;

Gojime, although, same as *sechi-be.*

dere jachi silemin bi. Mini ere gosikhon-i gisurere-be,	it is quite too much effrontery. This bitter speaking of mine,

Dere, silemin, or *dere mangga*, means "brazen-faced," lit. "face-tough"; in the Chinese "face-skin tough."

Suwe ume gejinggi sere, ume fiktu baimbi sere. Te bichi-be	do not take it to be wrangling, nor for seeking defects (in you). Now, supposing
mini beye alban-kame funchekhe sholo-de, majige ergeçhi oikhori?	in the spare time left to myself as an official, I simply (*oikhori*), took a little rest?
Baibi suwembe changgi ere tere serengge, ainu-ni? Ineku,	Doing nothing but only getting you to do this and that, why so? Just this,
giranggi yali ofi, suwe-mbe khwashaki-ni niyalma okini sere gunin kai.	you are my own bones and flesh (kindred), my mind is set on your being enlightened, on your becoming men.

(The desiderative or optative verbal form), *ki* occurs in Khwasa*ki* and *oki*, "wishing you to *become educated* men."

Ainara? Bi gunin akumbume tachibure-de, giyan-be dakhame tachibuchi,	What am I to do? If I teach you, using all my mind, teaching you according to what is right,
wajikha. Donjire donjirakungge suweni chikha. Mimbe aina sembi?	there is the end of it. To listen, or not to listen, is at your choice. How can you say it is I?

CHAPTER LI.

Waka! Sini ere absi serengge? Inenggidari ebitele jefu manggi,	No, indeed! What (ways) are these of yours? Every day, after eating your fill,
fifan tenggeri-be tebeliyekhe fitkherengge, aika alban seme-o?	hugging and strumming your guitar or your *balalaika*, what Government work is that?

Fifan, from the Chinese *pi-pa*—Japanese *bi-wa*—with four strings. *Tenggeri* with three strings, in Japan *samisen*, which means three strings, Zakharoff calls a *balalaika*.

Gebu gaichi sembio? Aichi ede akdafi banjiki sembio?	Is a name to be made so? Or relying on this, do you wish to live?
Muse jabshan-de Manju ofi. Jeterengge alban-i bele. Baitalarangge	We, by our good fortune, are Manchus. We eat the Government rice. We use (what we use is)
chaliyang-i menggun. Boo-i gubchi	(Government) money. The whole of our families,

Cha-liyang, from Chinese *tsien-liang*, *tsien*, "money," *liang*, "rice, grain"; money and rations; *menggun*, "silver."

ujui khukshengge, betkhei fekhukhenge, gemu Ejen-i	to have this (sky) above their heads, to tread this (ground) under their feet, is all our Sovereign Lord's
gesi-de bakhangge. Erdemu-be tachiraku,—.	grace, by which we obtained it. Not to study (to develop) our abilities,—
alban-de fashshame yaburaku oso naku, baibi ede gunin girkufi tachichi,	merely (*oso naku*) to avoid hard work at our official duties, idly to devote one's special attention to learning (a thing like) that,
Manju-be gutubukha-ni dabala! Baitangga gunin-be	is disgracing the [name of] Manchu, indeed! A useful intelligence,
baitaku ba-de fayabure anggala,—	to waste it in useless ways! rather than that (*anggala*), (instead of that)
bitkhe tachire-de isiraku. "Uchun-be tachikhangge	nothing comes up to study. "They who learn songs,
uche-i amala ilinambi; baksi be tachikhangge	go and stand up behind the house-door (beg at the back-door); those who learn to be scholars,
bakchin-de tembi" sekhe-bi. Utkhai ai khachin-i	sit face to face" (as equals) the saying is. So, to whatever degree (class)
ferguwechuke mangga-de isinakha seme, niyalma de	of wonderful skill you may attain, for people (people's diversion)

G.

efiku injechi arara dabala. Mentukhun	you will be making sport and laughter, that is all. A dirty
fusikhun-sere gebu-chi guweme muteraku kai.	and low name (reputation) you would not be able to avoid (escape).
Jingkini siden-i ba-de isinakha manggi, fitkhere khachin-be,	After you have come to a regular public (lit. central) position, strumming and the like,
bengse obuchi ombio? Mini gisun-be temgetu aku, akdachi ojoraku sechi,	will you be able to count these as talents? If you say my words are unwarranted, incredible.

Temgetu, a seal, *sigillum*, a warrant, a proof.

amban khafasa-i dorgi-de, ya emkhe fitkhere, uchulere-chi	Among the high officials (*amban*), which one by guitar-playing, or by singing,
beye tuchikhengge be, si te seme tuchibu!	has brought himself forward, you now tell me!

Seme tuchibu, "speaking, bring out," *i.e.*, "utter."

CHAPTER LII.

A. Age, urgun kai, jangkin sindara-de tomilakha sembi!

A. Sir, I wish you joy, it is said (*sembi*) you are designated for a post of Chief Staff Officer.

Jangkin, Mayers took this for a Manchu word: but Zakharoff says it is Chinese, *chang-yin*, "keeper of the seal." It means the head of a Department, Civil: a Staff Officer, Military.

B. Inu, sikse ilgame sonjoro-de, mimbe chokhokho.

B. Yes, yesterday at the classing and selecting, they nominated me as first.

A. Adabukhangge we? *B.* Bi takaraku.

A. Who is appointed adjunct. *B.* (Some one) I do not know personally.

Emu gabsikhiyan juwan-da inu.

A lieutenant of the Vanguard. (First Guards).

Juwan-da, Chinese *shih chang*.
Juwan-da, liter. "a decurion."

A. Inde chookha bio? Akun? *B.* Aku. Aba-i teile.

Has he war-service (lit. war)? Or none? *B.* None. Hunting Service only.

"Hunting service," practically Review service, as at the annual *battues* whole armies, employed as beaters, were trained for campaigning.

A. Bi sini funde ureme bodokho, tojin funggala khadambi seme, belkhe!

A. For your affair, I am quite anticipating your sticking the *Peacock's Feather* on,—get ready!

Peacock's feather, attached to the cap, hanging down behind, of three grades: with three eyes, two eyes, or one eye.

B. Bi ai ferguwechuke? Min-chi sain-ningge ai yadara?

B. What is there wonderful about me? Better men than I, how are they lacking?

Urunaku bakhambi seme erechi ombio? Ama mafari

Can I (*ombio*) hope (expect, *erechi*) with certainty to get it? By father's and ancestor's

kesi-de, jabshan-de kherebure-be boljochi ojoraku.

luck (or grace) by good fortune to fish it out, to fix this is impossible.

Boljochi, appoint, fix, settle.

A. Ai gisurembi? Si ai erin-i niyalma?

A. What are you talking about? You are a man of what period (seniority)?

aniya goidakha, fe-be bodochi, sini emgi yabukha guchuse

years have passed, reckoning seniority (*fe*, "old"), your friends who started with you

Goidakha means being "late," you are *late* in getting promotion; *yabukha*, "walking," meaning performing public duties, being in the service.

gemu amban okho. Jai, sini amala gajikha isikhata, yooni	are all *ambans* (Excellencies). Then, the men selected and taken, who were later than you all
sinchi enggelekhebi. Yabukha feliyekhe-be bodochi,	worked themselves up more than you (higher). Reckoning service and movement,
chooka-de fashshakha, feye bakha. Tuttu bime, ne	you have striven in war, got wounded. And with all that, now

Feye, a nest; a den; a stab or other wound.

tofokhon mangga [mergen]. Si khendu, gusa-de sinchi duleterengge	a "fifteen skilled" (a crack shot). Say, you, (if) there be in the Banner Force one who surpasses you,
inu we?	truly, who is it?
Bi sakha, ainchi sini urgun nure-be omime *jiderakhu-seme*	I know, perhaps you *do not wish me to come* in order to drink the festive wine

Urgun, **joy, congratulation. The form *rakhu*, in *jiderakhu*: this negative form, made up of *khu* added to the present participle *ra*, means just the reverse of the optative; Zakharoff calls it "peculiar to Manchu." The simple negative is *raku*, *khaku*. *Vide supra, passim.* It may just as well be said, "perhaps you *are afraid I* have come merely to drink the arrack of congratulation."**

jortanggi uttu gisurembi dere.	(you suspect) I am purposely (*exprès*) speaking this way, very likely.

Dere, **the usual complement of *ainchi*, the foregoing, or *aise*, both of which mean perhaps.**

B. Ainakhai ere giyan bi-ni? yala bakhachi,	*B*. How would that be reasonable? If I had really got it,
nure-be ai sembi? Sini gunin-de achabume soliki.	wine, why speak of it? I'd like to invite you to whatever you pleased.
A. Bi yobo gisurembi. Bi urgun-urame jichi giyan ningge,	*A*. I was speaking in joke. It was proper that I should come to felicitate you,
fudarame siningge-be jechi, geli ombio?	to do the opposite and eat up your (provisions), is that a thing I could do?

CHAPTER LIII.

A. Enenggi ya jikhe? *B.* Age duka tuchime, dakhandukhai

A. To-day who came? *B.* When you had gone out, Sir, one after the other

juwe niyalma tuwanjikha bikhe. Age-be, wesikhe seme,

two men came to see you. On account of your promotion, Sir,

Tuwanjikha, "came to see," *bikhe*, were.

chokhome urgun-de achanjime sekhe.

they purposely (specially) came to visit you to congratulate, they said.

A. We tuchifi jabukha? *B.* Mini beye

A. Who went out to answer (the call, the knock)? I myself

duka-i tule-de ilikha bikhe. Bi "mini akhun boo-de aku-

was standing outside the gate. I (said): "My Master is not at home,

looyese dosifi teki seme," anakhunjachi. Farshame

gentlemen, please come in and sit down," I invited them. By no means,

Teki, optative, "I hope you will sit down"; *farshame*, "desperately, obstinately."

dosiraku, amasi genekhe. *A.* Ai gese niyalma?

they would not come in, back they went. *A.* What sort of men?

adarame banjikhabi? *B.* Emke yalikhangga

how were they made (physically?) *B.* One was fleshy (corpulent),

Age-chi majige dekdekhun. Beye teksin. Shufangga salu.

a little taller than you, Sir. Body straight (erect). A beard all round,

Shufangga, "in folds"; *salu*, beard, in Turkish, Mongol, and Magyar, *sakal*. *Un collier de barbe.*

Yasa bultakhun, fakhala chira. Tere emke, yala yobu.

eyes prominent, a purplish colour of face. The other one, really comical to behold.

Nantukhun mangga-i fukhali tuwachi ojoraku. Yasa gakda bime

Dirtv so thoroughly that it was quite impossible to see him. One-eyed, and withal

khiyari. Kerkenekhe kerkeri, khuskhuri salu. Tere demun-i,

squinting. Rough pock-marks (*kerkeri*), shaggy beard. That queer-looking one,

mini baru emgeri gisurere jakade, bi eleke-i pos-seme injekhe.

as soon as he had spoken once addressing (*baru*, towards) me, I nearly laughed right out.

A. Tere yalikhangge bi sakha. Ere emke geli we bikhe?

A. That fleshy (corpulent) one I know. But who was (is) that (other) one?

Sakha, "know," have seen; cf. Greek αοϊδ, *oida*. "I've seen; I know."

B. Cheni khala-be fonjime bikhe.	*B*. I asked them their names.
Minde emte justan gebu-jergi-arakha bitkhe werikhebi.	Each left with me a slip (strip) with his name and rank written (*arakha*, worked) on it.

Emte, for *emu-te*, each one, "by ones," by units. *Ningguta*, "by sixes," a Manchurian tribe, and town, from *ninggun*, "six"; *jakuta*, another tribe, "by eights."
Justan, a strip, a label, used as the numerative of ribbons, tickets, stripes, and so on. Literally, a strip of books, or writing, *justan bitkhe*, *i.e.*, a card.

Bi gaifi Age-de tuwabure. *A*. Ara! ere suisinengge,	I will bring them for you to look at, Sir. *A*. Oh! that wretch

Tuwabure, causative form of verb, to make to look, "to let look," have to look.

aibi-chi jikhe? Si tere-be ume yokchin-aku seme ja tuwara. Beye giru	where has he come from? Do not you say he has no good looks and regard him lightly! His bodily form
udu waiku-daiku bichibe fi de sain. dotori bi. Imbe jongko de,	may be crooked; at the pen (with his pen) he is good, he is gifted. When he is mentioned,
We saraku? Aifini gebu bakha. Seibeni ainu oikhori koikashambi kai?	who does not know him? He gained fame a long time back. In past times how many scuffles has he been in?

Oikhori, very greatly. *Koikashambi*, a brawl, fisticuffs.

CHAPTER LIV.

A. Muse juwe ofi, da-chi banjire sain bime, te geli	*A.* We two, were originally good friends, now, in addition,
ududu jergi niyaman nonggibu-khabi. Utala aniya	(linked) by several kinds of kinsmanship added on. For so many years
bakhafi sabukhaku. Bi chookha ba-chi amasi isinjikha-de, utkhai	I had not been able to see him. When I arrived back from the seat of war, (I) at once

A peculiar idiom. This verb, *bakhambi,* to get, to be able to, used as the Auxiliary verb "can," must be put in the past participle form; *bakhafi,* or requires that the verb to which it is Auxiliary, be in the past participle form; *tulefi bakhara-be,* "that which may be set," *bakhafi sekhe,* "could know," "knew"; *bakhafi achakhaku,* "they could not meet"; *jafafi bakha,* "comprehended," "could understand." Similarly, in Greek, φθάνω "to outstrip" (phthano) the action of the outstripper is expressed by the participle agreeing with the subject, φθάνει βλάπτουσα, "she is beforehand in harming," ἔφθησαν ἀπικόμενοι "they arrived first." Also λανθάνω "to lie hid," ἄλλον τινὰ λελήθω μαρνάμενος I fight unseen by others, δουλεύων λέληθας, "you are a slave without knowing it."

imbe baikhanafi, kidukha jongko-be gisureki sembikhe.	went in quest of him, (as) I wished to have a talk of old recollections.
Gunikhaku baita-de siderebu, fukhali sholo bakhaku.	Unexpectedly impeded by business, I could get no leisure at all.
Sikse ildun-de ini boo-de fonjifi, "gurifi kejine goidakha	Yesterday I happened to ask at his house: "he moved out a good long time ago
ne *siao-kiai* dolo, Wargi ergi genchekhen murikha-de tekhi," sembi.	now, in the *siao-kiai* (Chinese for Little Street), Westwards, round the corner, he lives,"—they said.
Alakha songko-i baime genefi tuwachi. Umesi kocho wai (*wai* = "bent")	According to what they told me, I went in search to see him. Very secluded and out of the way.
Duka yaksifi. "Duka nei!" seme khulachi. Umai (*ume-ai,* "not any-one")	The gate was barred; I shouted "Open the gate!" No one whatever,—
jabure niyalma aku. Geli toksime kejine khulakha manggi,	there was no person to answer. After (*manggi*) again tapping and shouting (by me) a long time,
emu sakda mama tame afame jikhe tuchikhe. "Mini ejen boo-de aku,	an old dame dragged herself out (hobbled out). "My master is not at home,
guwa ba-de genekhe," sembi. Bi, "Sini *Lao-yé* umesi jikhe manggi,	he has gone somewhere" (lit. elsewhere) she said. I (said): "When your Gentleman returns,

ala mimbe tuwanjkha" sere-de; shan umesi jigeyen, fukhali donjikhaku.

tell him I came to see him"; when I said (it), her ears were very slow, she heard nothing at all

tuttu ofi, arga aku, cheni adaki achige *puseli* de,

so then, having no (other) means (resource), in a little *putse* (shop) next to them

Puseli, Chinese for "*in* the shop," "*in* a shop," came to mean, in Manchu, "a shop"; *puseli girin-i boo,* "a shop frontage."

fi yuwan baifi, mini genekhe gisunbe bitkhelefi werikhe.

I asked for brush and ink-slab ("pen and ink"), my words about my coming I wrote down, and left (with her).

Fi, the Chinese *pih.*—Northern Chinese, *pi.*—*yuwan,* the Chinese *yen,* ink-slab, on which the China ink,—"Indian ink,"—is rubbed down, having a small well for the water, a depression in the slate. The fine paint brushes used for writing are dipped into this. Not in use, they are carefully cleaned, pointed, and protected by a metal cap or tip.

CHAPTER LV.

A. Age iche aniya amba urgun kai! *B.* Je! iskhun-de urgun okini.

A. Sir, a very Happy New Year to you (lit. "New Year great joy")! *B.* Yes, Sir, the same to you!

Iskhun-de, "reciprocally," *urgun,* "joy," *okini,* "may there be!"

A. Age, teki. *B.* Ainambi? *A.* Age-de aniya doro-i khengkileki.

A. Sir, please sit. *B.* Why should I do that? *A.* I would like to salute you, Sir, with a formal annual *kowtow*.

Teki, optative of *tembi* to sit. "I hope you will sit." *Khengkileki,* optative, I wish to 'kowtow."

B. Ai gisurembi? *A.* Sakda akhun-kai, "khengkilerengge giyan waka" seme-o?

B. What talk is this? *A.* You are old, a senior relative, that "a *kowtow* is not *en règle*," (who) would say?

Je! Khafan-be wesikini! juse-be fusekini! bayan wesikhun banjikini.

Yes! Official promotion to you! Birth of many sons to you! Rich and honoured may you live!

B. Age, ili wesifi te! Beleni bujukha khokho efen, udu-fali jefu! *A.* Bi boo-chi jefi tuchike.

B. Sir, get up (*ili,* stand, *wesifi,* having risen) and sit down. I have ready some boiled pod dumplings, eat some of them! *A.* I ate some at home before I came out.

Fali is a general numerative for things not otherwise classified, and corresponds with *ko* ("piece") in Chinese,—"I from the house, having eaten, came out."

B. Jekengge tuttu e b i k e b i - o? Asikhata, teike jeke seme utkhai yadakhushambi kai.

B. Eaten so full as all that? Young people (like you), immediately they have eaten, then they are hungry.

A. Si ainchi manggashambi dere; Yargiyan! Age-i boo-de bi geli antakharambi-o? gelkhun-aku kholtoraku. *B.* Je, wajikha.

A. You think I feel constrained about it? But it is true! In your house, Sir, would I play the ceremonious guest? I would not dare to tell an untruth. *B.* Yes, indeed. That is all right (literally, finished).

Mangga, hard,—*manggashambi,* to feel difficulty;—*ainchi orin ba yabukhabi dere,* "seems to have gone 20 *li*" (*stades*); *ainchi uttu dere* "probably so."

Chai achabufi benju! *A.* Age, bi omiraku. *B.* Aineo?

Bring tea! (lit. set ready, and hand it). *A.* Sir, I cannot drink. *B.* Why?

A. Bi kemuni guwa ba-de isinaki sembi, genechi achara boo labdu.

A. I still have other places I ought to go to, the houses it is proper to visit are many.

Onggofi, shadafi, jai genere okho-de niyalma gemu guninara-de isinambi.	If I forgot, or were (too) tired, next time I went they would get to thinking about it.
Age, utkhai jefu. Mimbe ume fudere.	Sir, just go on eating (lit. eat). Do not see me off (do not come to the door with me),
amtan gamaraku. *B.* Ai ere giyan bi-ni? Uche-be tuchiraku	not to lose the relish of the food. *B.* What manners would that be? Not to come out of the door,
kooli bi-o? Je, shadakha kai, jifi untukhusaka	would that be polite (*etiquette*)? Yes, indeed, you surely are tired you came here hungry as one may say,

The termination *saka* means *rather;* "hungry-like." It answers to the Russian *khonek*, shenek, vat, ovat, the English-*ish*, thus *ambakan-saka*, "rather big, biggish, *velikonek, velikoshenek, velikovat.*

chai inu omiraku. Boo-de isinakha mangga, "sain-be fonjikha" se.	you do not even drink tea. After you get home say I "asked after their health."

CHAPTER LVI.

A. Muse tere oskhon-ningge amba obolon-be nechikhebi. B. Ainakha-i?

A. That blackguard of ours has brought great trouble on. B. How was it?

i gese niyalma-be tantame ochibukha? Turgun adarame?

what sort of man (meaning simply "whom?") has he beaten and wounded? For what reason?

1. Fili, fiktu-aku kai. Cheni adak i

A. For no reason whatever (lit. "hard, without a crack," *i.e.*, without an opening, a pretext). Their neighbour

Ini duka-i dalba-de sitekhe" seme, onjin gisun inu aku

"urinated beside their gate," it was said: without even (*inu*) a word of enquiry,

akhame, tukhebukhe; beye-be alufi, dere yasa-be baime tantame leribukhe.

he threw himself on him, felled him, straddled across his body, began hitting, aiming at his face and eyes.

suchungga tantara de, khono toome urembikhe, amala gudeshekhe-i

At first when he was beating him, he was still reviling and yelling, afterwards through (long) hammering

idure jilgan gemu aku okho. Borkhome tuwara niyalma

he had not even (*gemu*) a voice (jilgan) to groan, he was in that state (*okho*). People collected to see,

irbun faijume okho-be safi, tantara nakabufi, tuwachi,

the aspect (of things) was boding ill (*faijume*), when they saw this (*safi*), they made him cease beating, looked,

ifini ergen yadakhabi. Ede yafakha uksin imbe jafafi gamakha.

for a long time life had departed (lit. was exhausted, tired out). Thereupon the police seized him and took him away.

Yafakha means "pedestrian," "man on foot"; ***uksin***, man in armour; in Chinese *u kiah* is the exact translation given.

Buchekhe niyalma-i boo-i gubchi gemu jifi, ini boo nakhan-be susubukha.

The slain man's household came, all together, and destroyed his (the assailant's) house and bed-stove.

Nakhan, the brick *kang*, as the Chinese call it, warmed with charcoal underneath, on which bedding is spread. By day it serves as a sofa to sit on.

Agura tetun-be khuwalame, *wa-se-chi* aname yooni kolakha.

The furniture and crockery they smashed up, even stripped off all the tiles.

Wa-se, "tiles," is Chinese. *Wase-chi aname*, "going backwards from the tiles," means "comprising even the very tiles."

Kaichara jilgan juwe ilan ba-i gemu donjikhabi.	Their yelling voices were heard even two or three *li* away (three *li* = 1 mile).
Sikse jurgan-de isinakha, inenggi erun nikebukhe sembi.	Yesterday it came to the Court, today the punishment (torture, question) is applied, they say.

Jurgan, or *jurgan-yamun*, in Chinese the *yamun*, the Court of Justice.

B. Age, si donjikhakun? "Ekhe niyalma-de ekhe karulan bi," sekhebi.	*B*. Sir, have not you heard (this)? "For the bad man is the bad retribution," it has been said.
Ere ini beye baikhangga dabala. We-de ai dalji?	This was what he himself was asking for, in fact. What concern is it of anyone (else)?

CHAPTER LVII.

Guchuleki sechi, juleri Gwan-Jung Boo-Shu-be alkhudan.	If people would live as friends, let them take as their example (model) Kwan Chung and Pao Shuh of old.

Two Chinese worthies.

Ere juwe nofi, emu inenggi, shekhun bigan-de yabure-de,	These two gentlemen (*nofi*), one day, while walking in the open (bare) plain,
tuwachi jugun-i dalba-de emu aisin-i shoge makatafi	espied by the side of the road a gold bar left lying (thrown down)

Shoge, a mass of gold of 5 to 10 ounces (Taels); *amba shoge,* "a big bar," of 50 ounces.

Iskhun-de anakhunjakhai, gemu gaijaraku. Waliyafi genere-de	Mutually they kept declining it, neither would take it. They rejected it, and as they went on,
emu usin-i khakha-be ucharafi, jorime khendume "Tuba-de	they met a rustic (man of the *usin,* ploughed fields), they pointed, and said, "Yonder
emu aisin shoge bi. Si genefi gaisu!" Sere-de, tere usin-i khakha	is a bar of gold, you go and take it." When they said this, the peasant
eksheme genefi baichi. Aisin be sabūraku, juwe-ujungga meikhe-be	hastily went off to look for it. He saw no gold; a two-headed serpent
sabukha. Ambula golofi, khomin-i meikhe be juwe meyen obume laskha sachikha.	he saw. Greatly terrified, with his weeding-hoe he slashed the snake into two pieces,

Meyen, pieces. These Dialogues are called the *Tanggu Meyen,* "Hundred Pieces." *Laskha,* adverb, "asunder," *laskhalambi,* "to sunder." *Sachikha,* "cut in two." *Obume,* "causing to be."

Amchafi, jamarame khendume: "Bi suwe-de aika kimun bio?	hurried in pursuit (of his informants), and clamorously addressing them: "What quarrel have I with you?

Kimun, hatred, feud, *vendetta.*

juwe-ujungga meikhe be, ainu minde aisin-i shoge seme, kholtome alambi?	a two-headed snake, why did you say a bar of gold to me, telling me (such) a lie?
elei mini ergen-be jochibukha!" sere jakade, juwe nofi akdaraku	it nearly destroyed my life," said he: thereupon (*jakade*) the two gentleman, incredulous,
emgi-i sasa genefi tuwachi, da-an-i aisin-i shoge-be sachibufi	went together with him to look; just as originally, (they saw) a bar of gold severed

juwe farsi ofi na-de bisire-be. Gwan-Jung Boo-Shu emte dulin gajikha,

made into two pieces, on the ground. Kwan Chung and Pao Shuh each took a half,

Bimbi, "to be," *bikhe*, "was," *bisire*, "being, existing."

Dulin, "half," *Dulimbe*, "central," *Dulimbe Gurun*, "The Middle Country," China. There is the same connection between *dulin* and *dulimbe* as between *dimidium*, demi, half, and *medium*, "middle."

tere usin-i khakha kemun-i untukhun gala-i genekhe. Julge-i niyalma-i

that rustic went off with his hands empty as before (kemuni). The men of old times, their

guchulere doro uttu. Ere udu julen-i gisun-de khanchi bichibe,

rules of friendship were like that (so). This, though it may be near to a (romantic) old tale,

yargiyan-i ere forgon-i aisi temshere urse-de durun tuwaku obuchi achambi.

in truth, is fit for a model and pattern for the people of this age who strive with each other for gain (*aisi*).

CHAPTER LVIII.

Waka! Bi simbe gisureraku ochi, baibi, dosoraku,	No, no! If I leave you without speaking (about it), it will be simply unbearable.
Khairaka, niyalma-i suku adarame sinde nerebukhe.	What a pity it is! how is it you have donned the skin of a man?
Ninju se fereme genere niyalma kai! Aika achige semeo?	Of sixty years, grown an old (*fe* "old") man, you are! Is that a small (age?)
Boikhon monggon-deri isinjifi, saliyan-i uju koika funchekhe-bi,	You have got into the ground past your throat, scarcely is the scalp of your head left out,

Meaning, "you have two feet in the grave," "you have not much longer life to expect." —

yasa kaikara urui khekhesi feniyende guwelecheme, gokhodorongge	with eyes asquint, you just dart glances in a crowd of women, and act the fop.
adurame? Duebulechi, niyalma enggichi ba-de sini sargan-be	Why do you do so? Say, for instance, a man, behind your back, about your wife

Engichi ba-de, is a place of secrecy.

uttu tuttu seme leolechi, sini günin-de ai sembi?	were to talk, saying this and that, how would you think (feel) in your heart?
"Emu karu-be emu karu gaire" gisun, sain ekhe-i karulan khelmen beye-de dakhara adali.	The saying, a "turn brings a return," reward for good and evil follows like the shadow after the body
Utala se, majige butu-i erdemu-be isaburaku,	So many years (old), not getting stored up (accumulated) a little hidden merit

Hidden merit (cf. Matthew VI, actions performed ἐν τῷ κρυπτῷ, rewarded ἐν τῷ φανερῷ.). The idea here is the Buddhistic:— *Karma*, the moral actions which alone survive.

Baibi ere gese oyomburaku, ekhe, baita-be yabuchi, te forgon-i Abka fangkala, kai	idly walking in this frivolous way, acting ill at this time when Heaven is low, indeed

When going to your account is no longer far away.

Absi sini funde joboshombi!	how troubled (anxious) one feels on your account!

CHAPTER LIX.

Ere niyengniyeri *dubesilekhe*, erin-de boo-de norokho bichi

This (time of the) *ending* of Spring, to remain stuck in the house,

Dube means "end."

absi alishachuka! Sikse mini deo "khoton-i tule

how tiresome! Yesterday my younger brother (said) "Outside the City

sargashachi achambi" seme. Mimbe guilefi

for a pleasure saunter, that is the thing," he said. So he accompanied me,

ildungga duka-i tule genekhe. Shekhun bigan-de isinafi, tuwachi,

(and) we went outside the Side Gate (*Pien Men*). Arrived at the open country, we saw

niyengniyeri arbun absi buyechuke! Toro ilkha fularambi, fodokho

spring scenes, how enchanting! Peach blossoms rosy-red, willow

gargan sunggeljembi, chekike-i jilgan jingjing-jangjang,

branches waving, the twittering and chirping of bird's voices,

moo-i abdakha nioweri-nioweri. Niyengniyeri edun

the bright green of the leaves on the trees. The Spring breeze,

falga-falga, orkho-i wa guksen-guksen.

blowing from time to time, the sweet smell of the grasses in occasional gusts.

Bira-de jakhudai bi, daling-de moo bi.

On the river there are boats, on the high banks are the trees.

Jakhudai-de fitkhere uchulurengge, siran-siran-i lakcharaka.

On the boats they are strumming and singing, turn after turn without a pause.

Moi fejile sargashame yaburengge, ilan sunja feniyelekhebi.

Under the trees they are strolling about, in companies of threes and fives.

In companies of three and fives; *san wu ch'eng k'ün* in Chinese: the Manchu seems a slavish rendering of this quaint idiom.

Tere da-de yen jugun-chi birgan-be baime, nimakha-be welmiyembi;

Also by the ravine paths, seeking rivulets for angling for fish;

yala sain; shumin bujan-i dolo sebderi-de serguwesheme, nure omichi umesi

it was very nice; to cool oneself in the shade of a deep wood, to drink wine, very

amtangga. Jai tere shurdeme emu bade ilkha-yafan yargiyan-i gemu sain

grateful it was. Besides, round about there the flower-gardens are all really fine,

amba juktekhen inu bolgo. Tuttu ofi, muse e l e t e l e emu inenggi sargashakha.	the great temples, also, clean. And so, we took our fill with a whole day's strolling about.
Giyan simbe guilechi achambikhe; sinde mejige isibukhakungge turgun	By rights you should have been asked to join; the reason (*turgan*) for not sending you news (of it),
umai gumin bifi simbe goboloki serengge, waka; erei dorgi-de	was not that there was a wish to leave you out, no! amongst that (crowd),
sinde acharaku niyalma bifi kai.	there were people you do not get on well with, that was it.

CHAPTER LX.

A. Donjichi muse tere gabula gachilabufi umesi oitobukha,	*A.* I hear that glutton (friend) of ours is hard up, and in great straits,
kheshenekhe, giokhoto-i adali; dardan-seme, i l b a n nakhan-de shoyokhoi	reduced to rags, like a beggar, shivering, cowering (*shoyokhoi*) on a bare stove-bed
emu farsi m a n a k h a jibekhun nerekhebi, sembi. Ainchi	with one scrap of worn-out quilt thrown over him, they say. Probably
wasikhun betkhe gaikha, ai-se? Dulekhe aniya, ai sui tuwakhaku?	he takes a (more) humble footing, now, eh? In (these) past years, what misery has he not seen?
ai gosikhon dulembikheku? Majige niyalma-i gunin bichi, inu	what bitterness has he not passed through? If he had a little of manly spirit, indeed
khalame aliyame gunifi. Dekdeni gisun: "yadakhun-ningge	I thought he would change and reform. There is a common proverb:
bayan-ningge-be amchambi sekhebi, betkhe niyokhushun okhobi,"	"If the poor man will be for keeping up with the rich, his legs will be bare,"
sekhebi. Akaburengge ai gunin bifi: "Ubai nure tumin,"—"tubai	it says. It is distressing (to think) what ideas he had: "Here the wine is rich," "there

Ubai, from *ere-ba-i*, "of this place"; *tubai*, from *tere-ba-i*, "of that place."

bookha amtangga" seme. Bayan u r s e-i g e s e s a s a ba-ba-de sargashambi	the snacks are tasty," he would say. Classing himself (*gese*) with the rich, went pleasuring with them everywhere.
Tede bi: "Gechukhun-i erin-de isinafi, jai tuwara dabala," sechi.	Then I (said): "When it gets to the frosty weather, then we shall see," I said.
B. Te yala yuyukhe khangkakha, uttu khenduchibe, ainchi ainara	*B.* Now in truth he is hungry and thirsty. Though we may say this, perhaps something might be done,
yargiyan-i yasa tuwame buchebumbio? Mini gunin-de, muse, ukhei,	could we really let him die and look on? In my opinion, we, jointly,
majige shufafi inde aisilafi teni sain. Menggun khono tusa aku	should collect a little to help him, then it will be right. Money, indeed, will be no gain.

A. Adarame sechi? *B*. Ini banin-be si sarku aibi? Gunichi	*A*. How so? *B*. His disposition, do not you know what it is? I think that
gala-de isiname jeke yadakhai wajifi. Da-an-i	as soon as it reaches his hands it will be eaten, consumed and finished. Just as before
fulakhun ojoro dabala. Ai funchembi? Ine mene emu jergi etuku	he will be naked, surely (*dabala*). What will remain? Anyhow, a suit of clothes
udafi buki. Inde khono tusangga, dere.	we should buy and give him. That, indeed, will be a benefit to him, that will be it.

CHAPTER LXI.

Bi sinde injeku alara. Teike mini emkhun uba-de tere-de,

I will tell you something amusing. Just now when I was sitting (*tere*) there alone,

fa dutkhe-de emu chechike dokhobi, shun-i elden-de khelmesheme

on the window-sill a bird alighted, shining in the sun-light,

emgeri chongki emgeri fekuchembi, ede bi asuki tuchiburaku,

giving now a peck and now a hop. Thereupon I, without uttering a sound,

elkhe-i oksome isiname, lep-seme emgeri jafara jakade,

silently stepping, reached it, (and) suddenly with one move caught at it, so that

fa-i khooshan be fondo khuwajafi, lakdari nambukha.

the window-paper (used instead of glass) was broken right through, I luckily caught it.

tuwachi emu fiyaskha-chechike. Gala guribume

I looked at it, it was a sparrow (lit. "wall-bird"). As soon as taken into my hand

"pur"! seme deyekhe. Eksheme uche dasifi,

"whirr," off it flew. I hurriedly lowered the curtain over the door (*uche* "door")

jafafi namburalame, geli turibukhe. Jing uba tuba

and had very nearly caught it, (when) it escaped again. Just (when), now here, now there,

amchame jafara siden-de, buye juse "chechike bakha" sere-be donjire

while I was pursuing to capture it, the small children hearing it said "got a bird"

jakade, kaichaka kiru-i gese, tukhere, afara, sujume jifi

thereupon shouting (with) flags and the like, tumbling, fighting, came in, in a crowd,

bur-seme amchangga amchame, jafarangge jafame, makhala gaifi emu ungkefi bakha.

eagerly chasing and catching at it, one took his cap and, with one swoop down, got it.

Makhala, "a fur cap," in Russian *malakhai*. *Ungkembi*, to turn anything upside down, as a dish; to knock head to ground, to "kowtow."

Amala, bi: "Niyalma khono erengge jaka-be udafi sindambi,

After that I (said): "People even buy them (birds) to set free as living creatures,

fili fiktu-aku muse erebe jafafi ainambi? sindaki" sembi

why should we catch this one for no reason whatever? We had better let it go" (set it free), said I.

bucheme susangga ojoraku, lakdakhun farshatai temshen "gaji!" sembi.

To save their lives they would not have given in, desperately they wrangled, saying "give it to me!"

Jiduji bukhe manggi, teni urgunjefi fekunchekhe genekhe.

Finally I gave it to them, and then, rejoicing and skipping, they went off.

CHAPTER LXII.

A. Ara! muse fachakha-chi ebsi, giyanaku udu aniya bikhe-ni?	*A*. Oh dear! since we parted, how many years can it be?
ai khudun-de sini salu sharapi! Sakda fiyan gaikha.	how quickly your beard has turned white? You have gotten an old face.
B. Age, si saraku ainakha? Ajigan-chi boo-de yadakhun ofi,	*B*. Sir, how is it that you do not know? At home, from a youth. I was poor,
tuttu gunin sitkhufi bitkhe khularangge, chokhome gungge gebu shanggafi,	and so I fixed my thoughts on study, intent on succeeding in gaining merit and fame.

Bitkhe khularangge, "intoning books aloud,"—study.

"Bayan wesikhun-i inenggi bisire"-be, gunikha erekhe bikhe.	"Riches and exalted station, the day of those will some time be," I thought and hoped.
Te uju sharatala, gebu aisi-be fukhali mutebure ba aku.	Now, till my head has grown white, fame (name) and gain are all impossibilities for me.
Jai-de ochi, boo-de yadakha ten, eiten baita gemu mujilen-de ichaku.	And furthermore, at home extreme poverty, all sorts of things happen distasteful to my feelings,
udu "khesibukhengge" sechibe, inu mini nenekhe jalan-de gajikha erun sui,	though one say "it was fated," yet, verily,—my punishment of sin brought with me from a former life!
ele gunichi, ele fanchakha! Si mimbe adarame sakdaraku sembi-ni?	the more I think that, the more I grieve. How can you say I ought not to have aged so?

CHAPTER LXIII.

A. Age, sini ere emu falga boo yargiyan-i sain kai. Girin boo, nadan	*A.* Sir, that is a very fine house of yours. The house front (presents) seven
giyalan a d a k h a, juwe ergi-de eshengge fu bi. Chin-i duka-chi dosifi,	apartments *en suite* (adjoining); on two sides are diagonal walls. Going in by the main gate,

A diagonal wall, or uneven, oblique, or slanting wall, for vehicles to draw up alongside in its shelter.

emgeri tuwachi, fere-de isitala sunja jergi, shurdeme fiyaskha.	if one has a look one sees at once, looking through to the end, five blocks, with an outer wall (*fiyaskha*) surrounding (the whole).
Tanggin shekhun bime, dergi wargi geli khetu boo. Khafungga,	The large hall spacious, left and right (East and West), also, side-buildings. Right through,
boo-i duin ergi-de gemu durun bifi. Tangguli amala, utkhai	the buildings all four sides there is symmetry. Behind the reception-room, next (comes)
chin-i boo kai. Tere funchskhe dalba-i boo khasha-be tolokho wajiraku.	the room of ceremony, The remaining side rooms, store-rooms, are innumerable.
Sikhin-de muke-i eyebuku inu bi. Wase irun-de yabi inu bi.	For the water of the eaves there is also guttering. The courses between the tiles have laths, too.
Jai khafungga talu duka-chi tuchifi, geli emu amba	Besides, when you go out at a gate in the side road that goes right through, again (there is) a large
huwa bi, dasame emu ilkha yafan-be jibseme mukhaliyambi.	courtyard (*patio*), and there installed a flower-garden, terraced up in steps,
utala moo ilkha tebukhebi, udu gaskha chekike ujikhebi.	with so many (*i.e.* very many) shrubs and flowers set in, so many birds, large and small, reared.
J e r g i jergi-de g e m u d u r u n yangsangga bi. Dulimba-de, geli,	Every terrace is designed gracefully. In the centre, again (yet another point)

emu giyalan-i bitkhe-i boo bi, erei dorgi-de faidakha kitukhan, tonio,

there is a book-room, inside this are arranged a psaltery, playing-chess set,

Kitukhun, a seven-stringed Chinese *k'in,* called by Zakharoff a "*gusla.*" J. A. van Aalst calls it "one of the most ancient" (Chinese) "instruments, and certainly the most poetical of all." In Japan it is called *Koto.*

bitkhe nirugan.

and picture books,

khachin khachin-i gemu yongkiyakha, yala bitkhe khulachi ombi. Udu

each kind all complete, truly one could study well there. How much

tanggu yan-i menggun udakhangge? *B.* Jakun tanggu yan-i menggun

money in hundreds of Taels did you buy it for? *B.* For Eight Hundred Taels

udakhangge. *A.* Yargiyan-i salirengge ten-de isinakhabi. Age,

I bought it. *A.* Indeed it was extremely well worth it. (When you,) Sir,

ere boo-de techi, boo-be dejimbi sere anggala, juse omosi

live in that house, not only will your household have distinction,—your sons and grandsons

urunaku khafan wesimbi. *B.* Ai geli bi?

will surely rise to high official position. *B.* Oh, how could that be so?

In Chinese *k'i-kan,* "how could I dare."

Bi adarame alime gaichi ombini?

How could I possibly accept that (meaning, such a flattering prophecy)?

CHAPTER LXIV.

A. Sain niyalma sinchi chala jai aku sechi-na! Kemuni angga tukheburaku

A. Say there does not exist a man better than yourself! Still, without letting your mouth rest, (be relaxed)

sini guchu-be jondorongge, jachi nomkhon dabanakhabi.

to be always reminding of your friends, such simplicity is too excessive.

Jondombi, frequentative of *jompi*, to mention: to remember: to remind.

B. Tere nantukhun ai ton-seme jing dabufi-gisurembi?

B. That low (dirty) fellow, how is he an item (*ton*) worth speaking about?

niyalma-de baire yandure erin ochi, muse ai-sechi, i utkhai ai gese

when it was his time to seek favours of people, whatever we said, he then in that way

Muse ai sechi, "if we said *what*,"—anything, *ai gese*, then that was "*what sort of thing*" he would do.

dakhame yabumbi. Jai, baita wajime,

obediently would walk (or act). But then, when the business was done,

dere-be emgeri makhula, yaya webe seme kherseraku

with one smear of the face, whoever you may be, he takes no notice of you.

He erases a benefactor from the tablets of his memory.

Duleke aniya, i khafirakha nergin-de, we inde aika "gaji" sembikhe

Some years ago, at the time he was in straits (pinched), who asked for anything from him?

"*Saji*," *sembikhe*, "said, 'give.'"

Ini chisui, inde sain bitkhe-be seme, "Age tuwaki sechi, benebure."

Of his own accord, he said he had a fine book, "if you, Sir, would care to see it, I will have it sent."

Ai golmin ai fokholon-i inde angga aljakha. Amala,

Without qualifying it, he made me an oral promise. Afterwards,

Literally, "how long, how short, by him through his lips it was promised"; the Chinese idiom is the same as the Manchu, and perhaps the origin of the latter. Perhaps it might be rendered "the long and the short of it is, he promised,"—which comes to much the same thing.

baita wajikha manggi, jondoro ba inu aku okho.

after the affair was concluded, then indeed he was not always reminding of it,

tuttu ofi, jakan, bi dere, tokome

and therefore, just lately, I face to face, nailing him down to it (*tokome*)

"Age, si minde bumbi sekhe bitkhe absi okho?" seme fonjire,

(said) "Sir, how about that book you said you would lend me?" I asked,

jakade, ini dere emu jergi shakhun, emu jergi fulkhun,	and then, his face turned white and red by turns,
damu khetu gisun andubume guwa-be gisurere dabala.	merely sidelong talk, to distract, and to evade, he talked, and that was all.
Fukhali jabure gisun aku okho-bi. Te bichibe, emu yokhi bitkhe,	He had no answer at all to say. Now, a book

Yokhi, the Chinese *pu*, is the Numerative of books, and is applied to important works in several volumes, not small books.

giyanaku ai *khikhan?* Bukhe-de, ainambi?	what is there so *recherché* about that? If he gave it, what about it?

"*Khi-khan*" is pure Chinese for "rare and valuable."

buraku okho-de geli ainambi? Damu tur gun aku	If he did not give it, also, what about it? But without any reason
niyalma be kholtorongge, jachi (jai-ochi) ubiyada.	to lie to a person, that is more than (repeatedly) hateful conduct.

CHAPTER LXV.

A. Sini ere absi? Weri gingguleme sinde baire de, sachi,	*A*. What is this (way) of yours? If a stranger politely enquires of you, if you know,
"sambi," se. Saraku ochi, "saraku" sechi, wajikha.	say "I know." If you do not know, and say "I do not know," that finishes it.

Some good examples of the suffix *chi* meaning "if": *Sa-chi*, "if you know"; *saraku ochi*, if you are in a state of not know; *se-chi*, if you say.

Kholtofi ainambi? Talu-de ini baita-be tookabukha	Where was the good of saying untruths? By any chance, to have impeded his affairs
aimaka si gunin bifi imbe tukhebukhe adali.	will look somehow like your having intentionally laid a trap for him.
Iaika emu usun seskhun niyalma ochi, bi inu	If he were some repulsive individual, then indeed I
gisureraku bikhe; tere emu nomkhon niyalma, jilaka manggi	would not have spoken; (but) he is a simple soul, quite deserving compassion.
I far-seme banjikha mudan-be tuwachi, endembi-o?	Looking at the liberality of his nature and habits, why, do not you know?
guwa imbe uttu tuwachi, muse giyan-i tafulachi achara ba-de.	if any outsider had regarded him that way, you and I would rightly have had grounds for rebuking.
Si elemangge ere gese keike baita be jabukhangge, ambula	But when it is even you, yourself conversely, who do these mean things, you are greatly
tasharakhabi, vala mini gunin-de dosinaraku. *B*. Age, si dachi	in the wrong, I cannot reconcile it with my conscience. *B*. Sir, you, from the beginning,
imbe saraku, tede eiterebukhe kai. Tere niyalma bai oilorgi	do not know what he is; you have been cheated by him. That man is only outwardly
mentukhun-i gese bichibe dolo ja aku. (Not to be taken lightly).	stupid, and yet (*bichibe*) inwardly very serious (no lightness, frivolity).
Ini ekhe nimechuke ba-be, si chendekheku, inu sakhungge giyan.	His wicked, mischievous ways, you have not made trial of, and that you do not know him, is natural (there is reason for it).

Argan labdu, khubin amba; niyalma yaya baita bichi, afanggala	His tricks are many, his snares extensive; when a man has any affair, first of all
gisun-i yarume, geodeme, niyalma-i gunin-be murusheme bakha manggi	by his talk he leads him on, lures him on till after (*manggi*) he has got the man's general idea,
amala tuwashame aliyakiyame, sini eden ba-be khirachambi,	then (afterwards) he is ever watching you and ambushing you, spying out your weak places,

Tuwashame, "ever watching," frequentative of *tuwame*.

majige jaka bichi, utkhai emgeri ura tebumbi. Age, si gunime tuwa!	if there is anything not complete, at once attacking you from the rear (*ura*). Sir, you look at it reflectingly!

Ura, the back, reverse side; exactly the same word in Japanese, *ura*, with the same meanings as in Manchu. οὐρά (*ura*) in Greek, same meanings.

ere baita minde kholbobukha babikai. Adarame tondoko-saka	This affair has a connection with me. How frankly
da gunin-be inde alachi ombini? Ede mimbe wakashachi,	to tell him the idea how could I do so? When this is made a reproof for me,
bi sui-mangga aku seme-o?	is it not the case that I am harshly treated?

Sui is "guilt," *mangga* "hard" to bear.

CHAPTER LXVI.

A. Udachi, emu sain morin udachina! Khuwaitara ujire-de inu amtangga.

A. If you buy, buy a good horse! Then to have it in the stable will be a pleasure.

Khwaitara, "you will tie it up" (*scilicet* in the stable); "*ujire*, "you will feed," rear it; *amtangga*, affording *amtan*, a pleasant taste.

eichibe, orkho tori waj'mbikai, ere gese alashan morin be khwaitafi

But, anyhow, hay (and) beans are consumed, so, this sort of screw of a horse, keeping it

ainambi? *B*. Age, si saraku. Sikse gajime jaka,

what is the use of it? *B*. Sir, you do not know. Yesterday as soon as it was brought

Gajime, "brought," *i.e.*, led by the rein or a halter,—answers to the Chinese word *na*.

bi utkhai khoton-i tule gajifi chendekhe. Yaluchi ombi.

I at once led it to outside the city wall and tried it. It can be ridden.

Katararangge nechin, feksurengge tondo. Niyam niyachi,

It trots evenly, gallops straight. In archery-on-horseback

ichikhi majige inu aku. Bukhi dakhame, gala-i ichi,

faults, in the slightest degree even, are absent. It obeys the thigh, follows the hand,

jabdumbi. *A*. Uttu ochi, si da-chi takuraku-ni-kai.

makes it easy for me. *A*. If that is the way, you just do not recognise (a good horse).

Sain morin serengge, betkhe akdun, on dosombi. Aba sakha-de

A horse which is a good one, (has) solid legs, endures a long distance. At the grand *battues*

Aba, a grand hunt in which the soldiers, as beaters, practised for warfare. *Abalambi*, "to hunt," *abalanjimbi*, "to come to hunt"; *abalanambi*, "to go hunting"; *abalabumbi*, "to make to hunt"; *abalandumbi*, "to hunt in company." Turkish, *av*, "hunting," *avlamak*, "to hunt."

ureskhun, gurgu-de mangga; giru sain bime, ildamu, yebken.

well-trained, used to wild animals; of good build, with that, nimble and quick,

askhata kiyab-seme jebele askhafi yalumbikhede. Tede

young men will smartly get astride (such), girt with the quiver of arrows. By this (horse)

Jebele means "right hand side" as well as "quiver." Zakharoff says "quiver hung on the right side" *kolchan privazyvayemyi s'pravoi storony*; but the Mongol for arrow is *jebe*.

tukiyebufi, nachin shongkon-i gese ombi. Ere ai?

they can show themselves off, like gerfalcons or hawks. What is this (horse)?

Se-weikhe, senchekhe, gemu labdakhun okho; betkhe ujen,

Its age-teeth, its lower jaw, all hung limply; its legs (feet) heavy,

ıldurire de mangga. Sini beye geli .ju, labdu ichaku.	accustomed to stumbling. Also, your build being corpulent, quite unsuitable (for you).
. Te, ainachi ojoro? Emgeri dakha, ainame okini, dabala!	*B.* Now what can I do? Once bought, it can be as it likes, and nothing more to say!
ichibe minde ujen alban aku, geli oro takuran aku.	Anyhow, I have no heavy official duties, and no distant official missions.
)amu nomkhon ochi, utkhai minde .hafi. Yafakhalara-chi ai dalji!	If only because it is quiet it suits me. How different it is from walking!

Dalji means "connection." *Sin-de ai dalji?* means "what has that to do with you?" [ere the meaning is "*far better* than walking. No comparison!"

CHAPTER LXVII.

A. Weri imbe gisurembi kai, sinde ai dalji? Ele	*A*. When other people are talking to him, what has that to do with you? The more
tafulachi, ele nokchikhangge arbun shosiki bi. Antakha fachakha manggi,	they rebuked him, the more angry you were, with a look of fury. When the company have dispersed,
jai gisurembi dere. Urunaku ere erin-de, getukeleki sembio?	then is (the time) to speak. Must you positively, at the very moment, say you wish for an explanation?
B. Age, sini ere gisun fukhali mini gunin-de dosiraku.	*B*. Sir, what you are saying there I absolutely cannot admit into my mind (accept).
Muse emu jakhudai-i niyalma kai. Ere baita sinde inu lak aku.	You and I are men in one boat. For you also the affair is inconvenient (awkward).
Kheni majige goichuka-ba aku sembio? Imbe leolechi,	Can you say you have not the least concern in it? When they criticise him,
muse-be inu dabukhambi. Si dangname aku ochi, okini dere!	they include us also. If you do not stand up for it, well, so be it!
Fudarame anan shukin-i niyalmai ichi dakhachame gisurerengge	But to do the reverse, to slavishly say things in order just to humour the fancies of others,

***Anan shukin-i*, "following without resistance" *ichi*, "agreeing with, going the same way as"; *dakhachame*, "to say or do what one thinks will flatter others."**

ai gunin? *A*. Bi yala simbe urusheraku tuttu waka.	what intention have you? *A*. Where I disagree with you is really not on that point,
gisun bichi, elkhe nukhan-i giyan-be baire gisure! Shara fanchakha-de	when one has something to say, quietly and calmly, adducing reasons, say it! Getting in a rage,

***Baire*, seeking, looking for; the Chinese is *an-cho li*, according to reason.**

wajimbi-o? Si tuwa ubade sekhe niyalma, gemu	will you settle the matter by that? Consider the men sitting there, every one of them
sini baita-de jikhengge. Chingkai uttu olkhochome jilidachi,	had come on account of your business. If you so unreasonably fly into a fearful passion,
aimaka gunin bifi we-be boshome unggime adali.	it seems in some way as if you had the desire to repel one and send him about his business.

Jikhe niyalma ai yokto? Boo-de yabuki sechi, dere-de eteraku.	How could it be pleasant for those who came here? They wished to go home, but that would have been an intolerable loss of face (affront).

Dere-de eteraku, "unbearable by one's face,"—in Chinese *lieu shang kwo puh k'ü*,—impossible to perform without loss of face, dignity.

ubade teki sechi, si geli ek-tak seme nakaraku, tuchichi dosichi	Thev wished to sit here, but then with you scolding away incessantly, to go out or come in
gemu waka. Techi ilichi gemu mangga kai.	were both wrong. To sit and to stand were both difficult.
Guchuse jai sini boo-de absi feliyembi?	How can friends again resort to your house?

CHAPTER LXVIII.

A. Jalan-i niyalma ejesu akungge, sinche tule jai aku sechina!	*A.* Of all men in this world without memory, you may say nobody goes beyond you!
Chananggi, bi adurame sini baru khendukhe? Ere baita-be	A few days ago, how did I tell you personally (*baru*, confronting)? That affair

Chananggi, from *chara-inenggi*, "a past day."

yaya wede ume serebure sechi. Si naranggi firgebumbi.	to no one whatever was to be made known. You have just precisely let it leak out.
Muse weilume khebeskhekhe gisun,—te algishafi, ba-ba-i niyalma	Our secret discussions,—have now been given (such) publicity, that everywhere people
gemu sakha kai. Che bakhafi donjiraku ainakha?	know them. How should they not have got to hear about them?
Ese muse-de eljeme iselere ochi, saiyun?	If they became antagonistic and strive against us, will that be well?

Saiyun also means "are you well?" or "how are you?" a phrase of greeting.

Khochi kosaka emu baita-be, ondofi ere ten-de isinakha, wachikhiyame si kai!	An affair that was in splendid form, by being fooled with brought to this pitch, entirely by you!
B. Age si mimbe wakashachi, bi yala sui mangga.	*B.* Sir, if you blame me, I am truly submitted to unfair censure.
Damu baita emgeri uttu okho, bi, te,	Only, when the thing has once got into this condition, now, if I
jayan jushutele faksalame gisurekhe seme, si akdambio?	were to keep on explaining and talked my jaw bitter, would you believe me?

Jushu-tele, "till bitter."

Ere gunin-be, damu Abka sakini! Mini beye bikheo waka bikheo,	This heart, let only Heaven know! If it was I, or if it was not I.
goidakha manggi, ini chisui getukeleki.	In course of time, of its own accord let the explanation (light) come!
Mini gunin gunichi, si gasachi ojoraku. Ine-mene saraku gese,	My opinion (is this): I think you have no need to fret about it. Simply feign ignorance,
Cheni ainara-be tuwaki, Ochi, okho; khon ojoraku, dubede,	and you should watch what they do. If they are willing, all right; if they will not agree, finally,
jai achare-be tuwame belkhechi, inu sitakha sere ba aku.	then to prepare with a view to adopting fitting measures, it will still not be too late.

CHAPTER LXIX.

THE ARCHERY LESSON.

A. Age, enenggi baita aka, muse ;iyoq-chang de genefi — *A*. Sir, to-day we have nothing to do, if we went to the Kiao-chang,

The *kiao-chang*, in Chinese, means the "Instruction-ground," *i.e.*, drill-ground or :aining-ground for troops.

;abtanachi, antaka? — if we went there for some archery, how would that be?

Gabtambi, to shoot arrows; gabtanambi, to go in order to shoot arrows.

B. Si gabtaki sekhe-be dakhame, ere ;abtara doro inu shumin — *B*. As you say you would like some archery,—the art of shooting is profound,

:lichi chejen anamaliyan; beri :atachi, julergi amargi — one should stand with the chest protruded a little; in drawing the bow, both forward and back

;ala nechiken. Beri mangga, tuchike :achilan khusungge. — hands must be pretty even. The bow firm, the arrows discharged with force.

Anamaliyan and *nechiken* end in Diminutive forms,—meaning "a little," "rather," d so forth.

Udu kachilan tome goibume nuteraku seme, sunja-de dorgi, oktofi — Although every arrow may not hit, in (every) five, (when) with certainty

juwe ilan-de goibure ochi teni :nangga sechi ombi. — you hit with two or three, then you can be called expert.

Ia-de utkhai gisurechi ombio? *A*. Si tuwa bi gabtame. — Lightly, off-hand, to call one so, can that be done? *A*. You watch me shooting!

B. Sain! Aigan-be tuwane, gabta! 'Chas" sekhe, ereo? — *B*. Good! Keep your eye on the target (and) shoot! That one, that went "whiz"?

Khiskhalame genekhe, dabure)akharaku. — It grazed past, it cannot be counted (a hit).

A. Tonortai fondolome goibu-:hangge-be, geli "khiskhalame — *A*. A dead-straight penetrating hit, and yet "it grazed

;enekhe" sechi, ai gese goibukha, eni dabumbini? — past," say you! what sort of hit must it be and then you will count it in?

B. Si mini gisun donji:—"chas-:his"-seme goibukha be daburaku, — *B*. You listen to me:—Those that hit with a rattling and a rustling do not count.

I

chikten-i lasikhibukhangge-be-daburaku, gungguleme goibukha .	Those that leave the arrow-shaft wagging do not count. High-trajectory down-hits,
soil'eme goibukha, fijirime goibukha-be, inu daburaku,	scaring-arrow hits, ricochetting hits, all these, also, do not count.
" Tas-tis " seme goibukhangge gemu daburaku. Damu	Those that hit, but with a scratching noise, all do not count. Only
tob dulimba goibukhangge, teni dabumbi! *A.* Je! utkhai uttu okini bi!	those, that hit exactly in the centre, count! *A.* Right! so be it!

CHAPTER LXX.

MENTOR DISSUADES FROM A DISREPUTABLE SCHEME OF "BUSINESS."

A. Sini ere baita absi okho? *B.* Bi ede jing gunin baibumbini.

A. That affair of yours, how does it stand? *B.* Here I am just exercised in mind (over it)

Yabuki sechi, majige kholbobukha ba bisire gese.

Though I would like to take a step, there is a little in it of a kind that might involve me.

Te chi yaburaku, aldasi nakachi, ambula khairachuka.

If I do not move now, but halt half way, it seems a great pity.

Ne angga-de isinjikha jaka-be, bakhafi jederaku! Baibi

A thing actually brought up to one's mouth, not to be able to eat it! Gratuitously

niyalma-de anabumbi! Yabuchi, waka; yaburaku ochi, geli waka!

to give it up to people! If I move, I go wrong, if I do not move, I go wrong again!

Yargiyan juwe-de geli mangga okhobi. Adarame okho-de

Truly in either case I am in a difficult position. How to act

emu tumen-de yooni ojoro arga bakhachi, teni sain? Uttu ofi

so as to obtain security in every eventuality, and then I shall be satisfied. For these reasons

Tumen-de, "for ten thousand" contingencies, *yooni,* "perfect, complete," *arga,* "a plan, means, method"; *teni-sain,* "and then at last, it will be well."

chokhome sinde da gunin baime jikhe. *A.* Age, si minde khebeshembi,

I have come specially to ask your opinion. *A.* Sir, as you ask counsel of me,

bi ainame ainame, ichi-achame, jabufi unggichi. Niyaman sere-de

I will, with all frankness, categorically answer you. To be tender about it,

ai tusa? Ere baita getukesaka iletusaka, ai da gunin bakharaku sere ba bi?

what is the advantage of that? The thing is most plain and evident, what difficulty is there about forming (getting) an opinion about it?

Amaga inenggi, urunaku bultakhun tuchimbi. Yaburaku ochi,

On some future day, (the truth) is bound to push its way out. To do nothing in it,

sini jabshan. Yabukha sekhe-de, we angga-be butulechi ombi?

will be good fortune for you. If you have anything to do with it, whose mouth will you be able to stop?

Dur sekhe manggi, tere erin-de teni mangga obumbini!	After it has once been shouted out, that is the time you will be "in a difficult position"!
Imbe ainarangge, Enduringge-niyalma gisun sain:—	Let others do what they may, the words of the Sage are good words:—
"Niyalma goro bodoraku ochi, urunaku khanchi jobolon bi,"	"If a man will not trouble himself about what is far off, certainly trouble will be near him,"
sekhe-bi. Ere yasai juleri agige aisi-be, urgun sechi ombio?	they say. This small (immediate) gain before your eyes, can you call it a pleasure?
Tob-seme amaga inenggi amba jobolon-i ursen, daldaki sekhe-i	It is precisely the bud which will grow to huge trouble at a later date, (when) the more you would conceal it,
ele iletulembi. Jabshaki sekhei, elemangga ufarabumbi.	the more manifest it will be. Try for gain as you may, you will, on the contrary, lose.
Aisi bichi, jobolon aku obume muteraku. Mini gunin okhode,	Where there is gain, it is impossible to have no trouble. In my opinion,
Si ume kenekhunjeme gunire, kafur-seme askhuchi wajikha.	do not think doubtfully about it, but summarily reject the idea and have done with it.
Aika mini gisun be donjiraku, emdubei jechukhunjeme laskharaku ochi,	If you will not listen to my words, but continue to vacillate and not come to a decision,
Takha manggi, "bele bakharaku bime, fulkhu waliyabure be guweme"	after you are well entangled, "if you cannot get the rice, get rid of the rice-bag" (sack),
sekhe. Ai gese buchikhe tuchibure-be gemu boljochi ojoraku.	the saying goes. What sort of ugly thing may come out of this, no one can forecast.
Tere erin-de mimbe shame tuwame tafularaku seme ume gasara!	At that time, do not complain of my looking on and giving you no advice!

CHAPTER LXXI.

A. Te-i a s i k h a t a, teni udu khergen-be takara-de,	*A.* Now-a-days young people, as soon as they know a few written characters,
darukhai julen-i bitkhe-i tugi-chi jidere, talman deri genere gisun-be	are c o n t i n u a l l y (reading) the romancers books' talk, come from the clouds, gone in a fog,
dere j i l e r s h e m e niyalma-de donjibume khulambi. Emu jergi-i	hardening their faces they read such aloud for people to listen to. A class
khulkhi urse, menekesaka amtangga-i donjimbi.	of silly persons, have a most foolish taste for such things and listen.

Menen, "foolish," *menekesaka,* "very foolish." The original meaning of *saka* was Diminutive, not Augmentative. Perhaps the meaning grew from "slightly" to "very" through the same Ironical humour that makes our own popular "not half" pass current for "very much."

B. Age-i gisun be dakhachi, aichi bitkhe khulakha-de sain?	*B.* Following what you say, Sir, what are the books that are good to read?
A. Ai ochibe, Enduringge Saisa-i Nomun Ulabun-chi tuchineraku,	*A.* Whatever you do, do not go and stray away from the Canonical and Historical works of the Sages.
aika Enduringge Saisa-i bitkhe urebume khulame okho-de,	If one has thoroughly studied the books of the Sages (Inspired Worthies)
beye-de tusa bakhambi sere anggala, Kemuni jalan-de baitalachi ombi-ni.	besides gaining benefit for oneself, one may also be of use to the world.
B. Uttu okho-de, Age-i tachirengge-be gingguleme dakhambi.	*B.* Since it is so, I will carefully follow your instructions, Sir.

CHAPTER LXXII.

A. Sikse mini gu-de achanakha de, arkan-seme mini gu-fu boo-de aku.

A. Yesterday when I went to see my aunt, by chance my uncle was not at home.

Gu (or *Ku*), a Chinese word, meaning "father's sister." *Gu-fu*, a Chinese compound word, meaning "father's sister's husband."

Mini gu tara deo i baru khendume, "Sini ama boo-de aku-be dakhame,

My aunt (spoke) to my cousin, and bade him "As your father is not in,

amba giyai-de udu khachin-i bookha-be udanafi, sini tara akhun-de solibu."

go into the great street (*giyai*, in Chinese=street) and buy some eatables, to offer to your cousin,"

Udambi, "I buy"; *udanambi*, as here, "to go and buy"; *udanjimbi*, "to come and buy"; *udanumbi*, "to buy jointly"; *udabumbi*, "to cause to buy." The aunt's son is the younger cousin *deo*, while the visitor is the elder cousin, *akhun*. *Akhun*, elder brother, *tara akhun*, elder cousin, etc.

seme. Mini tara deo majige sitakha-de, utkhai fakhame tukhebume tantambi.

she said. My young cousin, on his being a little late, she at once threw down and was beating.

Ede bi niyakurame khenggilere baichi. Ainakha seme ojoraku

On that, I knelt and *kowtowed*, pleading (for him). In no way could I effect anything.

Amala sakda taitai tuchinjikhe, "gwebu" seme tafulara jaka-de, teni

Later, the old lady came out, enjoined her saying "spare him," and then, at last

gala nakakha! Age! Si guni! mini dere-de yala eteraku!

she gave her hands a rest! Sir! you think! for my face, truly intolerable!

Meaning, "what a humiliating situation for me! it made me blush with shame!"

B. Ere sini gufu gu-i boo-i tachikhiyan kai! Ama eme serengge

B. That is the discipline of your uncle and aunt's household! To be father or mother,

Abka-i adali, jurchechi ombio? Tere-be tantaraku, ochi, we-be tantambi-ni?

is to be like Heaven; can one go counter to them? If she does not beat him, whom is she to beat?

CHAPTER LXXIII.

Cheni juwe ofi scibeni ton-aku yabumbikhe; maka ya niyalma	Those two, in the old days, met as friends numberless times, I do not know what man

Maka, an expression of uncertainty, seems connected with ***aimaka***,—as ***aimaka we***, "some one or other."

ekhechure jakade, te laskha yaburaku. Iskhunde,	acted the slanderer, and consequently (*jakade*) they now definitely meet no longer. Mutually
ekherefi, nememe kimun bata okhobi. Gemu	hating, they have even become vindictive enemies. It (has) all
baktambume muteraku-chi banjinakhangge. Tere anggala,	come to pass from inability to make allowance (to pass over an offence). Besides,
jalan-de niyalma banjifi isara acharangge, gemu emu erin bi;	for men to be born in the world, to meet and consort together, for all these there is a time;
darukhai emu ba-de bisirengge, gemu emu salgabun bi. Gemu	for them to be often in one place, for all that there is an innate predisposition. All
nenekhe jalan-chi salgabukhangge. Oikhorilachi ombio?	is predestined from a former existence. Can this be thought of lightly?
"Yargai bocho oilo, niyalma-i gunin dolo," sekhebi. Chira bocho-be	There is a saw: "The panther's colour is outside, a man's heart is inside." Face and colour
takara dabala; mujile gunin-be ainakhai shuwe khafu-seme mutembi-ni?	one knows, that is all; to heart and soul how can one's knowledge penetrate?
Uttu ofi, guchulembi serengge, ja gisurechi ojoraku. Mentukhun	Therefore, to perform the duties of friendship, cannot be called an easy matter. Foolish
albatu, sure mergen niyalma inu bi. Jalingga koitonggo, serebe	uncouth (men) there are, intelligent, clever men, also, there are. Sly, treacherous,—cautious,
butemji, — ujen jinggi, — buya ambalinggu-i,—niyalma inu bi.	secretive,—solid upright,—small-minded, high-minded men,—of all there are.
Faksi modo, tondo sijirkhun-i niyalma inu bi. Ilgaraku ochi ombio?	Adroit, clumsy men, — honest straightforward men, all exist. How could one get on if one did not discriminate?

CHAPTER LXXIV.

Juwari forgon-de, kemuni katunjachi ombikhe. Goidatala, ulkhiyen-i	For the summer-time, he was still able to keep up. As time went on, gradually
nimeku nonggibufi, fukhali maktabukhabi. Ere-i turgun-de (*turgun* = cause)	as his illness increased, he was quite prostrated (overcome by it. In consequence of this,
boo-i gubchi buran-taran de, gunin bakharaku. Sakdasa yali	the whole household was upset and knew not what to do. As for his old folk, their flesh

Gunin bakharaku, "could not get an idea."

gemu wajikha. Boo-i dolo, fachakha sirge-i gese okho.	was worn off their bones (literally, all finished, consumed). In the house, all was fiurry and flutter.

Fachakha sirge, literally "silk all showing loose ends, silk come unwound."

Imbe tuwachi, gebserefi, giranggi teile funchekhebi. Nakhan de dedume,	To look at him, he had grown so thin, that only bones were left of him. He lay on his stove-bed,
ergen khebteshembi. Tede bi elkhei khanchi ibufi "Si majige ye beo?" seme,	drawing breath with difficulty. So I gently advanced near, and said, "Are you a little better?"
fonjire jakade, yasa neifi mini galabe jafafi. "Ai! ere mini	when I asked him that, he opened his eyes, and took my hand. "Alas! this is my
gajikha erun sui. Nimeku fachukhun ba-de dosifi,	punishment for sin brought with me. The disease has entered my internal vital organs.

Gajikha erun sui, "sin brought with me" into this world from a previous existence.

Absi duleme muteraku-be bi endembio? Nimeku bakha-chi ebsi,	How should I not know that I can never get through this? Since I took this illness,
ya oktosi-de dasabukhaku? Ai okto omikhaku? yebe ojorolame,	what physician have I not been treated by? What medicine not drunk? Just when I was improving a little,
geli busubukhangge. Utkhai khesebun. Bi umai koro-seme baaku, damu	I got worse again. So it is fated ("*Kismet*"). I am not tormented about anything else, only
ama eme se-de okho, deote geli ajige. Jai niyaman khunchikhin	father and mother in their old age; and my younger brothers, who are little, also. Besides, my relatives

giranggi yali mimbe tuwakha-i bikai. Bi mangga mujilen-be	my bones and flesh (flesh and blood), were all looking to me. Could I be so hard-hearted
ya emke-be laskhalame mutere?" Gisun wajire unde,	as to be able to cut off any one of them?" Before he could finish his speech,
yasa-muke far-seme eyekhe. Ai! absi usachuka! Udu	his tears flowed abundantly, Ah! how sad it was! Although
sele wekhe-i gese niyalma seme, terei gisun-de,	a man might be like iron or stone, at these words of his,
mujilen efujerakungge aku.	his heart could not but be touched.

It is curious how like *sele*, "iron" is to the Russian word *zhelézo*, and how unlike the Mongol and Turkish *demir*, *temir*.

CHAPTER LXXV.

Sain jaka-be khairame malkhushachi, teni banjire were niyalma-i doro.	To spare and be careful of good things, such is the reasonable way for any man to live.
Simbe gisureraku ochi, bi aichibe ojoraku. Jeme wajiraku funchekhe buda-be	Not to speak to you would be simply impossible for me. Rice left over uneaten
boo-i urse-de ulebuchi inu sain kai. Gunin chikha-i ko sangga-de doolakha	to give to the domestics to eat, that is the right way. Wantonly rinsing it down into a drain-hole,
aine-o? Gunin-de inu elkhe bakhambi-o? Si damu	what is the use of that? And can peace of mind be got so? You only
buda jetere-be sara, gojime; bele jeku-i mangga suilachun-be sakhakubi.	know how to eat rice, and that is all; you do not know the hard labour for the rice-grain.
Tarire niyalma, juwere urse, ai jergi jobome suilafi,	Those who plant, those who transport it, what degree of trouble and hard work they endure,
teni ubade isinjikha. Emu belge seme, ja de bakhangge seme-o?	before (lit. "and then at last") it arrived here. One grain of it, is it easily obtained?
Tere anggala, muse ai bayan mafa seme dabure-o?	Moreover, how can we be accounted rich men or wealthy proprietors (*mafa*)?
Ere-be jeme, tere-be kidume, yaya gunikha-i utkhai udafi,	eating this, fancying that, anything no sooner thought of, than bought,
waliyame-gemin-i mamgiyambi khairandaraku! Angga-de ai kemun,	with no regret for expenditure in sheer extravagance. What measure for the mouth,
jetere-de ai dube-da? Chingkai uttu ochi, khuturi	what method for its eating? By persisting in this course, prosperity
ekiyembumbi sere anggala ai bikhe seme wajiraku?	is turned into poverty, and not only that, but what thing at all will be left unconsumed?
Sakda-i gisun "khairame jechi, bele jeku-i da, khairame etuchi	The old man's words: "The frugal eater, is lord of rice; the frugal dresser,
etuku-adu i da" sekhebi. Sini khuturi giyanaku udu?	is lord of clothing," so they run. Your wealth (prosperity) how much can it be?

ere durun-i sotachi, beye-de sui arafi,	If you scatter it in this way, you will be the agent of your own chastisement; (and)
Omikhun-de amchambukhe erinde, aliyakha-seme amchaburaku kai.	when you are brought face to face with famine, repentance will come too late for recovery.

CHAPTER LXXVI.

Ai fusi geli bi-ni niyalma-i banjikhangge waka!	What a rascal he is! he was never born of human beings!
Ini ama-i gese urekhe banjikhabi, yala ini ama-i khunchikhin,	His disposition resembles his father's out and out, truly his father's breed,
absi tuwachi absi ubiyada. Yayá ba-de imbe takurshachi,	however one regards him, odious. If one tells him to go anywhere,
yasa nichu-nichu shame, eiten saburaku, balai chunggushambi,	he looks on with eyes blinking, seeing nothing whatever, merely bumping against things,
angga-i dolo ulu-wala, aimaka niyalma-be niyoboro adali.	muttering inside his mouth, in some way or other as if he were mocking a person.
We ini gisun-be ulkhimbi? Jingkini ba-de, umai baitaku bime;	Who is to understand his talk? For doing serious things, he is of no use at all;
efimbi-sere-de jergi, bakchin aku. Ajige sholo buraku,	at saying facetious ones, no one can stand up to him. He gives one no leisure.
khanchi ershebuchi, khono yebe. Majige aljabukha-de,	If I keep him near me in attendance, he is not quite so bad. If I let him get a little away from me,
taji tuwara ba aku. Fukhali abkai ari!	he grows so mischievous, there is no looking at him. A regular incarnate demon!

This phrase, *tuwara-ba-aku*, Zakharoff *renders nyechevó i smotrět', ni na shto nye pakhózhe,*—"like nothing on earth," as we would say. For *abkai ari,* he gives "an incarnate imp," also "a rogue sent by Heaven"; while the Chinese gives *t'ung-t'ien kwei,* and in this book *tsuan-t'ien kwei,* which would seem to mean a little "devil" that, instead of being sent by "Heaven," has managed to "bore his way in" thither.

Tere-be gaisu, erebe sinda, majige andan-de seme ekisaka banjiraku.	Taking up this, putting down that, unable to live quietly for the smallest moment.
Uru-i kuwak-chak seme moniyo adali. Jing jili nergin-de ochi,	Always riotously noisy, like a monkey. Just when I am in a rage with him,

Moniyo, "a monkey"; there is a Cantonese word *malu* for "a monkey," for which the classical Chinese word is *hou*. *Moniyo* curiously resembles the Spanish, and also the Portuguese, word for "a monkey," which is *mono;* in Malay, *Munyit*.

"ere nantukhun-i dukha gemu sarabukha-de, teni kek-sere dabala!"	I say, "I must positively eviscerate the wretch before I can be happy!"

dulcke manggi, geli gunichi "ainara yargiyan-i imbe wambi-o?

then when it (the rage) passes, I think again, "how could I really slay him?

This is not all joking. The *patria potestas* in the Far East was so real, that little account would be taken of the killing of a slave.

uju-de, ochi, "fokholon taimin galachi ai dalji." Jai-de ochi,

In the first place, "Even a short poker is infinitely better than the hand." Secondly,

boo-i ujin jui seme, bakhara jetere ba-de geli esi-sechi jechi ojoraku.

being bred up in the household in childhood, what should he eat but what he gets here?

Bakhara-jetere ba-de, "what he gets to eat." *esi sechi ojoraku,* "*cela va sans dire,*" "needless to say."

imbe fulu majige gosimbi.

all the more (for that very reason) one has a little affection for him.

CHAPTER LXXVII.

Ai, oifo jaka, mimbe weikhukelerengge ja aku!	What, that futile creature, to show such extraordinary contempt for me! (When) I
Sini baru gisurechi teisu aku semeo? Jime okho-de utkhai	speak with you, do I not speak as an equal? As soon as he had come, he at once
faksi gisun-i mimbe kedershererengge. Beye-bi ai dabukhabi?	with his clever sayings took to sarcasm at my expense. In what class does he reckon himself to be?
Oforo yasa emu ba-de fumereme ofi, bi-damu gisureraku dabala.	United as we are like nose and eyes in one place, I simply was not saying anything,
da sekiyen-be gisureme, tuchinjichi, geli mimbe fetereku sembi.	then when I spoke and set forth the whole matter root and branch, he called me a sycophant.
Sini da gashan, mini fe susu, we-be we saraku?	Your original village, my old hamlet, which "of us does not know (what) the other (was there)?"

The speaker refers to the third person, not to the person addressed, and means "*his* original village."

Niyalma monjirshaburaku ofi, giyanaku udu goidakha?	Since he was letting himself be bullied by people (there), how long ago can that be?
Te mini baru ine-mene gisun endebukhe seme, mini dolo khono yebe.	Now if he addressed me and simply say he had spoken under a mistake, I should not feel so badly about it.
Muritai ini gisun-be uru arafi, ainakha-seme waka-be alime gairaku kai.	Now he obstinately makes out he spoke aright, and in no way will he accept and shoulder the blame.
Tede, niyalma ini chisui khur sechi. Mimbe adarame ja tuwakhabi?	By that, a man is naturally incensed. Why does he regard me with such contempt?
We-i fiyanji-de ertufi? Enenggi teile gala elkime mimbe "jio!" sembi.	On whose protection is he relying? Only to-day he waved a hand to me and said "come here!"
Yala we-be we ainambi? We-de we gelembi?	Really now, which of us can do anything against the other? Which is afraid of the other?

Meke cheke chendeki sechi, mini gunin-de kek-sere dabala!	If he wishes to try "back or spoon," I shall be quite pleased!

Meke is the ridge, "the back," Chinese *pei*; *cheke* is the flat side, Chinese *chek*, "spoon"—at the game of *astragalus*, "cockals," "knuckle-bones," or "huckle-bones," a game well known to the ancient Greeks.

Majige tatkhunjachi, inu khakha waka.	He who hesitates about it, indeed he is no (true) man.

CHAPTER LXXVIII.

Utala inenggi, " ta-ti ta-ti " seme sirkedeme agakhai,—

For so many days a soaking rain continued,—" drip-drip ! "—

dolo gemu urekhe. Uba sabdakha, tuba isikhikhe,

one grew heartily weary of it. Leaking here, all wet there,—

amgara-be gemu bakharaku okho-bi. Tere da-de,

sleep was quite unattainable. In addition to that,

wakhun u m i y a k h a, suran, ai shufarangge, fukhali khamiraku.

bed-bugs, fleas, each and all biting (stinging), it was quite unbearable.

Wakhun means " stinking " ; *wakhun umiyakha* corresponds exactly with the Chinese *chow-chung*, " stinking insects " ; *ai*, same as *eiten*, or *yaya*, " each."

kurbushukhei, emu dobori tulitele, amu isinjiraku.

tossing all the time, till the whole night was ended, one could not get to sleep.

The final *i*, in the first word, signifies continued action ; as earlier, *agakhai-i*, " it rained continually," or " continuously."

Yasa eteme nichuku, geli majige kirikha, jaka buru-bara amu shaburakha-

Closing eyes with an effort, I endured for a little, and just when I was drowsily dozing off,

jing sereme amgara-de, gaitai wargi amargi khosho-chi

just when I was (between) awake and asleep, suddenly, from the north-west corner,

utkhai alin ulejekhe, na fakchakha, adali, " konggar " seme

like a mountain collapsing, like the earth being rent open, " cr-ash ! "

emu guwere jaka-de, tar-seme dokdolafi getekhe, kejine,

it sounded, then with a start I jumped up, a long time

ofi beye kemuni shurgime dargime, niyaman " tok " sembi.

it was that my body was still trembling and quaking, my heart audibly thumping (going " pit-a-pat ").

Yasa neifi tuwachi, boo nakhan agura-tetun umainakhaku (ume-ainakhaku)

I opened my eyes and looked, and nothing had happened to the stove-bed, furniture, or crockery.

eksheme niyalma takurafi tuwabuchi, " Adaki boo-i fiaskha,

I sent a man, with all speed, with orders to look ; " A wall of a neighbour's house,

Tuwambi, to look, Causative form, *tuwabumbi*, to cause to look.

Aga-de shekebufi, tukheke," sembi. Tere asuki-be,

saturated by the rain fell," he said. That noise

amu tolgin-de donjire turgun-de, urkin ainu tuttu amba bikhe !

because it was heard in the midst of dreams, somehow, was so loud !

Ainu, " how? " here, " somehow."

CHAPTER LXXIX.

Ere udu inenggi, baita bifi, emu siran-i juwe dobori

These few days, as I was so occupied, for two nights consecutively

yasatabukha turgun-de, beye gubchi fakjin-aku liyar sembi;

I got no sleep, consequently my body was all limp and languid;

Sikse, yamji forgon-de, bi utkhai amgaki sembikhe,

yesterday at evening-time, I would therefore have been glad to sleep.

niyaman khunchikhin yooni ubade bisire jakade, Bi ai

but because my relations were all here, how (could) I

khendume waliyafi amgana-bi? Tuttu ofi katunjafi,

speak of throwing myself down and going off to sleep? So I made an effort,

geli katunjame; beye udu simen arame techechibe, yasa baibi

and again an effort; though my body, simulating vivacity, sat with them, my eyes simply

Simen, vital spirit, good spirits, "vivacity"; *udu*, "although"; *tembi*, "to sit," *techembi*, or *tenumbi*, "to sit together, with others"; *udu*, although, leads on the Concessive termination *chibe*, of the verb *techechibe*; *arame*, "simulating," means more precisely "fabricating," "making."

ojoraku. Debsekhun murkhu farkhun-ome genembi.

could not do it. With drooping lids, with the mind dull and dark, they went dim.

Amala, antakha fachakha-de, bi emu chirku sindafi,

Afterwards, when the visitors separated, I set down a pillow, (and)

etuku nisikhai uju makta khiri amgakha.

fully dressed, I dropped my head on to it and fell into a deep slumber,

Literally, "clothes too," "clothes and all"; Zakharoff cites: *morin-be tede buchi tetendere, enggemu nisikhai yooni buchina.* "If you give him a horse, give him the saddle in, too."

Jai ging otolo teni getekhe. Tede, majige shakhuraka ainakha-be

right till the Second Night-watch, then I woke. Then, having caught a little cold, or how?

The 5 Watches of the Night are of 2 hours each, and the First begins at 7 p.m., the Fifth ends at 5 a.m.; the Second Watch is from 9 p.m. to 11 p.m.

saraku, dolo umesi kushun ping sembi, bey'ei gubchi wenjerengge

I know not, internally I felt much flatulence and distention, my whole body so feverish,

utkhai tuwa-de fiyakubukha adali. Ere dade, shan geli sulkhume ofi

it was just like being roasted at a fire. In addition, my ears felt internally swelled,

K

tatabufi jayan e r g i g e m u suksurekebi. Jechi, omichi,	I had a dragging sensation in my teeth, where (my jaws) were all swollen. What I ate or drank

Jayan ergi; jayan is the visible teeth, *ergi,* the border; in Chinese the phrase is *ya-kwan,* which is just the ἕρκος ὀδόντων of Homer.

amtan, aku. Techibe ilichibe elkhe a k u. B i "ere ainchi j e k u saksalibukha aiyoo" seme. Emu jemin	had no taste. Sitting, standing, no ease. Said I: "I fear this means I may have to bar off my eating." One dose
wasibure okto omire, jaka-de sain ekhe jaka gemu wasinjikha. Teni	of purging medicine I drank, and then it brought down everything, good and bad. Then
majige sulakan okho.	I felt a little relieved.

Sulakan, Diminutive of *sula,* "free."

CHAPTER LXXX.

A. Age, Sini tere erikhe-be, bi gamaki sekhe, jiduji

A. Sir, that rosary of yours, I was wishing to take away, but after all

"Rosary," *erikhe*, of 108 beads of wood, coral, amber, etc., worn by Manchu and Chinese Officials and by Buddhist priests.

bakhafi gamakhaku. "Ai turgun" sechi, jikhe deri si

I did not get to taking it with me. If you ask "why?" every time I came, you

gemu boo-de aku. Simbe achakhaku-de, ai khendume buksuri jaka-be gamambi?

were not at home. Not having met you, how could I without notice take away your property?

Ai khendume? how could I "explain," or justify, or "say" anything? in favour of *gamambi*, taking the rosary away with me. *Buksuri*, privily, without notice.

Uttu ofi, bi enenggi chokhome sinde achafi, alakha manggi, gamaki sembi,

And so, to-day, I came on purpose to meet you, and after telling you, I would like to take it,

tede tekherebume si ai jaka gaji sembi, bi sini gunin-de achabume,

and if you asked me to bring anything in exchange, I, in accordance with your wishes,

udafi khulashaki. Utkhai *puseli-de* unchara sain-ningge aku seme,

would buy that and exchange this for it. So, if there are no good things on sale *in the shops*

bi inu urunaku ba-ba-de forgoshome baifi sinde bure. Sini gunin antaka?

I would not fail to rummage around every place seek one out, and give it you. How think you?

B. Si kemuni jondofi ainambi? Ini-mene gamakha bichi sain bikhe.

B. Why do you keep on mentioning it? If you had simply taken it, it had been well.

Jondombi, "to mention often," *frequentative* form of *jompi*, "to mention."

Ainakhai waliyabumbi-ni, khairakan! Putisu ningge ai yadara? Damu

How would they have been lost? alas! Buddhist beads are not rare at all; only

tede isirengge umesi komso. Tuttu waka ochi ai? Inenggidari

there are very few to come up to those. How could it be otherwise? Every day

jafakhai, damu siberi dakha umesi nilgiyan okho-bi.

by constantly handling they had got very glossy merely by the sweat of the hand penetrating them.

Siberi is "the sweat of the hand, or of the foot"; the *general* term for perspiration is *nei*.

jafasharaku guwabsi genembikhe-de,	As I was not continuing to hold them, on my going elsewhere,

Jafashambi is the Frequentative of *jafambi*, "to hold"; to handle."

tere-be khorkho-de asarambikhe; inu waliyabure giyan ofi;	I stowed them in a bureau; indeed I must have been bound to lose them;
duleke biya-de, bi yafan-de genere-de, onggofi bargiyakhaku,	last-month, when I went into the garden, I forgot, and did not put them by, (and)
amasi jifi baire-de, uba arun-durun saburaku okho.	when I came back and looked for them, there was not a trace or vestige of them to be seen.
We-de khulkhabukha-be inu saraku. Merkime baikha seme, fukhali bakhaku.	By whom they were stolen I do not know, either (*inu*, "also"). Wherever I could think of (*merkime*) I hunted for them, but utterly failed to get them.

CHAPTER LXXXI.

Enenggi absi nimechuke! Juwari dosika-chi ebsi, ujui-uju khalkhun

What awful (weather) to-day! Since Summer came in, the extremest heat of all

Ujui-uju, "head of head," "chief of chief,"—the hottest of all the hot days. "Summer comes in," in China, on 5th May, when the sun enters Taurus. The year is divided into 24 periods, each with an appropriate name. Thus July 23, Great Heat! October 8, Cold Dew; January 21, Great Cold (sun enters Aquarius).

sechi, ombi. Majige edun aku. Ludar sembi.

if one called it, one would be right (" one can call it "). No breeze at all. A clammy heat.

Eiten agura-te tun, gemu gala khalame khalkhun. Ele

Every bit of furniture or vessels, all so hot they scorch the hand. The more

jukhe-muke omichi, ele kangkambi. Arga aku, ebishefi,

one drinks ice-water, the thirstier one is. Having no means (of getting cool) I bathed myself,

moo-i fejile, kejine, sebderilekhe manggi, teni majige tokhoroko.

(and) under the trees, for a long spell. I stayed in the shade, and after that, felt a little easier.

Ere gese khukteme khalkhun-de, weri beye niyokhushun bai tekhe-de,

In this kind of steamy heat, any one merely sitting still, with body stripped,

khono khalkhun chalirakhu sembi-kai. Si ainakhabi

even then feels afraid of catching a heat-stroke (heat apoplexy). How is it that you

Chalirakhu. This Negative form in-*rakhu* is the reverse of the Optative in-*ki*, which means "to wish to do something," or "to hope, or anticipate that something will occur."

Uju gidakhai, khergen ararangge, ai sui? Ergen khaji aku semeo?

keeping your head bent down, forming written characters, what torture is this? Is not your life near (and dear) to you?

Sui is guilt, or the punishment of guilt, the chinese *tsui*, the speaker looking on the other as a sort of *Heautontimoroumenos*. The Chinese dialogue gives *khu*, "bitterness."

Si alban aku, baisin-i jirgeme tachikha dabala!

You have no official business, used to living independently at leisure!.

Duibulechi khudai urse, khaijungsere ujen jaka-be damjalafi,

Now, if you compare the hawkers, carrying, slung on a pole, laboriously, ponderous objects.

Damjalafi, carrying on a carrying pole, a "*dan jang*" ("tan-tan"), a word evidently formed from the Chinese.

monggon sampi, ba-ba-de shodome khulakhai,

with throats stretched out, incessantly shouting as they hurry along from place to place,

nei taran waliyatala arkan-teni tanggu funchekhe jikha butafi,	the sweat dripping down, then barely hunting down a hundred or so of "copper cash,"
ergen khetumbumbi-kai. Mini adali beleningge-be jefi	they scrape together a living. Like me, who eat things found ready for me,

Above there are two words for sweat, *nei*, "sweat," *taran*, "cold sweat." The Chinese version is more forcible, *hich*, *han*, "bloody sweat."

elekhun-i khergen araki sechi, dakhambio?	(and then) placidly, do some writing, if they wished to, could they be like that?

Here, though *araki* is the only verb of Optative *form* ("wish to write"), *jefi*, "to eat" meals got ready for one (*beleningge*, or *beleni-jaka*), is also Optative in intention: what the poor hawkers *would like*, at least as much as the leisurely writing, is the comfortable feeding.

Tere anggala, tuweri beikuwen, juwari khalkhun, julge-chi ebsi,	Moreover, winter is cold, summer is hot, ever since times long gone by,
khalachi ojoraku toktokho doro Ine-mene ekisaka dosobuchi,	by a law which fixed them immutably so. Just calmly to endure it,
embichi serguwen ombi dere. Fatkhashakha-seme, ai baita? Bakhafi guwechi ombio?	perhaps will make you feel cool. Hurrying and bustling, what is the use of them? Can you escape so?

Dere, at the *end* of a phrase, "perhaps," confirms, rather pleonastically, the *aise*, *ainchi*, *eichi*, or *embichi*,—each meaning "perhaps," at the *beginning* of the phrase.

CHAPTER LXXXII.

Ibam forte viâ sacrâ, etc.

I jidere fun-de, bi khono amgakha bikhe. Sek-seme getefi donjichi	At the time he came, I was still asleep. Suddenly I awoke and heard
chin-i boo-de niyalma bifi, ten jilgan-i gisun gisurembi. We jikheni?	at the front door a man, speaking with a loud voice. Who has come?
Ai uttu konggolo ten? Ainchi tere usun dakula jikhe aise seme.	Who has such a jaw on him? It must be that tiresome bore.

The Manchu gives *konggolo ten,* "a bird's crop so high," the Chinese *kaw-lung kao.* "a throat so high,"—not very courteous,—justifying the English being "*such a jaw.*" *Dakula,* belly; compare Titus, I, 12, where St. Paul, writing to a Greek, quotes γαστέρες ἀργαί, "slow *bellies,*" against the Cretans. The Chinese gives "adhesive proser," for *bore,* which seems appropriate to the case.

Genefi tuwachi; waka ochi ai? farangge seme te, jing	I went to see: what else was it? Firmly seated there, just
amtangga-i leoleme bi, jikhe-chi angga majige mimikhaku.	revelling in his eloquence, there he is, from the time he came never having closed his mouth at all.
Uttu, tuttu, sekhe, juwe erin-i buda jefi, gerkhen mukiyetele teni genekhe.	Talked here, talked there, for two meal-times, till twilight was fading, then at last he went.
Khakha niyalma baita aku-de, were-i boo shuntukhuni teme dosombio?	A man, who is a man, with nothing to do, to sit in one's house till sunset, can that be endured?

Khakha, in Chinese *khan-tsze,* means a grown-up man, a man in his full strength, and in his years of discretion,—"no child," "no chicken." *Shun-tukhuni,* for *shun-tukhe-tele,* "till the sun sets," till sunset.

Ai-bi onggokho shadakha baita-be gisurekhei, niyalmai fekhi gemu nimekhe.	He kept on talking of things forgotten, worn-out platitudes, (till) a man's brain felt ill.
Damu uttu ochi ai baire?. Yaya jaka-be khono inde tuwabuchi ojoraku-	If that were even all, why worry? But also, one cannot let him see any of one's things,
emgeri yasalabukha sekhe-de, fonjire gisun aku, nambukha-be deleri gamambi.	if once his eye falls on them, without a word of asking, whatever it is, he unceremoniously annexes it.
Yala damu "gaji" sere be sambi, gaji tuchire-be fukhali saraku sechina.	Indeed he only knows the meaning of "give!" but has no conception of giving anything away.
Enteke niyalma dukha-do absi banjikha-be, bi yargiyan-i saraku.	How such a man may be framed in his interior, I truly do not know.
Ai jabshambio? Ai bakhambio? Abka-de yasa bi kai, ainakhai inde ombi-ni,	What benefit is he? What is to be got out of him? Heaven has eyes, however can it tolerate him?

CHAPTER LXXXIII.

A. Muse tere guchu ainakha-bi? Ere uchuri shenggin khetere	*A.* What has happened to our friend there? Just lately his brow is wrinkled
munakhun joboshorongge, ai turgun bisire-be saraku.	he is morose and melancholy, what is the reason, I do not know.
An-i uchuri, aga labsan inenggi ochi, boo-de bisire dabala!	Usually, if the day was one of rain or sleet he was in his house, indeed!
Tere-chi tulgiyen, mujaku ba-de gemu shodombi-kai,	But with that exception he was bustling everywhere from place to place,
baibi boo-de teme dosombio? Ere uchuri duke uche tuchike-ba aku,	could he endure merely sitting indoors? Lately he has not been outside the door,
boo-de norokhoi tekhe-bi. Sikse bi tuwaname genere de, tuwachi	he has kept sitting in the haven of his home. Yesterday when I went to see him, looking (at him),
chira ai kemuni nenekhe adali sembio? Serebume	(I thought) how is his face like what it used to be in olden times? Visibly
wasika; tuchire, dosire-de, fukhali teme toktoraku. Maka	gone down (fallen in); going out, coming in, quite unable to sit still. I know not
ainaki sechi-na. Tede bi umesi kenekhunjeme, "ere ainakha ni?"	what he wished to be doing. Consequently I was very suspicious "how is this?"
teni fonjiki sere, ini emu niyamangga niyalma jikhe-de khiyakhalabukha.	I was just longing to ask him, but the arrival of a relative of his impeded me.
B. Ara! Bi bodome bakhanakha! Ainchi, tere baita-de lakhin tafi,	*B.* Oho! my lucubrations have led me to guess it! It must be, mixed up as he is, in that affair,
gunin farfabukha, aise? Tuttu seme "Aga-de usikhibukhe niyalma	his mind is distracted, eh? So to speak, "The man who has got wet by the rain
silenggi-de geleraku" sekhe kai. An-i uchuri,	is not scared at the dew" as the proverb says. Habitually,
antaka mangga baita-be i gemu uksa-faksa ichikhiyakha? Ere	whatever sort of difficult affairs he might have, he managed them easily. This one
giyanaku ai kholbobukha seme jing uttu joboshombi?	what great interest for him can be involved in it, that he should be so perpetually worried?

Joboshombi, "to be often, or continually, troubled, anxious," is the Frequentative of the verb *jobombi*.

CHAPTER LXXXIV.

Da-chi ai etukhun beye, tere da-de geli ujire-be saraku,

At first what a wonderful frame he had! But then he knew nothing of how to keep it,

nure bocho-de dosifi, b a l a i kokiraburc jakade, te

he acquired (lit. entered) a passion for drink, foolishly injured himself by it, and now

nimeku-de khusibufi, dembei sirke okho-bi, sikse bi tuwanakha-de

he is imprisoned by illness, enslaved by the habit as he is. Yesterday when I went to see him,

kemuni katunjame chin boo-de jifi, mini baru: "Age jikhengge *jobokho* kai!

he still, with an effort, came to the front room, and addressed me: "Sir, you have *taken great trouble* to come (to see me)!

In Mongol, which has affinities with Manchu and affinities with Turkish, the phrase is *jobolon, jobolon*," "[thanks for] the trouble, the trouble!"

Ere gese khuktame khalkhun-de, taseme tuwanjime, ton-aku jaka banjirengge,

In this sort of steamy heat, often visiting me, bringing me innumerable presents,

ambula shadakha, umesi banikha! Inu niyaman-khunchikhun i dolo,

you have endured much fatigue, I am very grateful! In truth it is between kinsfolk,

tatabume ofi uttu dabala! Khalbadalba ochi, geli mimbe gunire mujanggeo?

that is why you have stuck by me! Would strangers have thought about me, indeed?

Bi labdu khukshembi! Damu khadakhai gunin-de ejefi, yebe okho erin-de,

I am much beholden to you! I can only keep firmly in mind, for the time when I am a little better,

jai khengkileme tuwame!" Angga de uttu gisurechi seme,

to look towards you with a *kowtow!*" Though his lips were uttering these words,

beye serebume katunjame muteraku. Uttu ofi—

his body evidently was unequal to the strain he was putting on it. And so:—

"Age, si sure niyalma kai, mini fulu gisurere-ba baibumbio?

"Sir, you are an intelligent man, so why should I say much to you?

Beye-be sain ujiki-ni, khudan yebe okini. Sholo-de,

If you would take, as is desirable, due care of yourself, you should soon be better. When I have time,

bi jai tuwanjire." Uttu sekhe, amasi jikhe.

I am coming to see you again." So I spoke to him, and then returned home.

CHAPTER LXXXV.

Sikse guwa ba-de genere jaka-de, fatan akhasi utkhai	Yesterday, as soon as I had gone away, those low slaves of mine
chikhai balai emu jergi daishakha. Bi amasi jikhe nergin-de	kicked up a silly disturbance, left to themselves. When I came back,
che jing tubade "ge-ga!" seme churgindu khai. Tede, bi	there they were just at it, all quarrelling and yelling. So, I
"kak"-seme emu jilgan okho, leksei jilgan nakafi, iskhun-de	just gave one cough, with one accord they were silent, one to another
kulisitame yasa arafi: sun-sun-i melerjeme yabukha.	looking with eyes of consternation, they sneaked off in little knots.
Mini jikhengge goidakha, beye inu shadakha, turgunde,—umai sekheku,	Owing to my coming late, and fatigued,—I did not say a word,
kirifi amgakha. Chimari ilifi tuchike nergin-de, waburu-sa	but bore with them and went to bed. To-day when I rose and went out, the rascals

Waburusa, lit. "deserving of death,"—the final *sa* giving the plural,—from *wambi*, or *wabumbi*, "to kill."

gemu jikhe, "akhasi buchere giyan, ambula tasharakha," seme	all came, saying, "We slaves ought to die, we have behaved very wrongly,"
emu teksin godokhon-i niyakurafi, bairengge baire, khengkisherengge khengkishere	simultaneously knelt down stiffly, beseeching, and "kowtowing" repeatedly,

Khengkisherengge is the Frequentative form, from khengkilembi, "I kowtow."

jakade, tuttu ofi mini jili teni majige nitaraka, tede bi:	and then, as my anger was in consequence rather mollified, thereupon I:
"Suwe ainakha-bi? Taifin-i banjiraku? Yali yojokhoshombio?	"What is the matter with you? Cannot you live quietly? Do your hides (flesh) itch so much?

Frequentative of *yojombi*, "to itch."

Urunaku tantabukha-de ai bakhambi? Khala! Erechi julesi,	What will you gain by an inevitable beating? Change those ways! From now onward,
geli ere gese mudan bichi,—yasa fakha guweleke!	if there is any more of this sort of incident,—you be careful as of the apple of your eye!
nishalaraku ochi, gunichi suwe inu iseraku!" sekhe manggi	unless soundly thrashed, I suppose you will not be warned!" When I said this,
gemu "je!" sefi, genekhe.	all said "je!" (a respectful form of assent, expressing obedience) and went away.

CHAPTER LXXXVI.

Tere kesi-akungge-be, si absi tuwakhabi? N i y a l m a i s u k u nerechibe,

' That graceless wretch, how can you look at him? Though cloaked in a man's skin,

ulkha-i dukha, jailame yabukha-de sain.

he has a wild beast's inside (bowels), best to walk keeping at a distance from him.

Fukhali baita-aku d e b a i t a dekdebure, e m u fachukhun-da sechina!

Where there is absolutely no trouble, he raises it, you can call him a regular ringleader in mischief.

G u n i n silkhingge, oforo-dome mangga. Yala,

A malignant heart, an adept at interference and stirring up strife. Verily,

Oforo, "nose"; *oforo-dome,* like the popular English word "nosey," the German *naseweis,* in addition carries the meaning of "stirring up strife" by carrying tales.

sabukha-de saksari, donjikha-de dokdori.

to the eye, fallen on his back, to the ear, getting up.

A curious alliterative phrase which seems to have the general meaning of "fishing in troubled waters" The Chinese is: "Meeting an affair, raise the wind and follow the waves."

Chikhe yerhuwe-i gese majige baita bichi, ini angga-de isinikha sekhe-de

An affair as tiny as a louse or an ant, once getting to be mentioned by his mouth,

jubeshekhei fikatala genembi. Uba-de baita-be, tuba-de ulaname

will go wandering far as a scandal. What happens here, he goes away and tells there.

Ulambi, "to tell"; *ulanambi,* as here, "to go and tell," to carry tattle about; *ulabumbi,* "to cause to tell"; *ulanumbi,* to tell each other.

tuba-de gisun-be, uba-de alanjime. Juwe ergi-de kimun jafabure-de

Of a conversation there, he comes and gives information here. When he has set both sides at enmity,

Alambi, to inform; *alanjimbi* or *alanjambi,* to come and inform.

i dulimba siden-de sain niyalma arambi. Mini gisun-be temgetu-aku sechi,

he in the middle, between the two, plays the honest man. If anyone says I have no proof of these words

Temgetu, literally "seal." It was a word engraved on official seals under the Manchu rule in China. A similar word, *tamga,* exists in Russian, having been adopted bodily from the Mongol, like many other words (in Malay, *tanda*).

si tuwa ini baru guchulere niyalma aku sere anggala,

consider! not only is it that no man regards him with friendly feelings, but

fise jorime tooraku ochi, utkhai ini jabshan okho.	if one there is who does not point at him behind his back and curse him, he is lucky.
Ai nasachuka! Ini ama emu fili-fiktu-aku, ere fusi-de ushabufi	Oh it is pitiable! His father and mother, without any reason, dragged in by this scoundrel
niyalma-de tooburengge, ai sui?	to be cursed by mankind. what harm have they done to deserve it?

CHAPTER LXXXVII.

Buchere giyan-aku ochi, ini ıisui emu naskhun tuchinjimbi.

If one is not (fated) to die, spontaneously a lucky way of escaping will come and crop up (out).

terc emu dobori nimeku ujelekhe, ırapi (farakabi) kejine teni aitukha.

His illness had grown very grave, that night, he swooned for a long time before he came round.

ıgga-de niyalma-be tokhorome ·okhorobume) gisureme "bi ıwanggiyan-aku,

Although he spoke reassuring words to people, "I am all right (nothing hurting me)

ıwe sulakan gunin sindakhai" seme ikhe, yala mafa-i kesi, boo-i gubchi huturi inu.

be easy and do not be anxious" (lit. "relieve your minds"), yet truly it was his ancestors' blessed merit, and the happiness that belongs to his whole family.

ai ineńggi enchu emu oktosi khalafi ıasare jakade, yasa tuwakhai,

Next day another physician was called in to treat him, and then, under one's very eyes,

mu inenggi emu inenggi-chi yebe, ıkho. Chananggi bi genefi tuwachi,

each day he was a little better than on the day before. A few days ago I went to see him,

ıeye da bakhara unde bichi-be, chira nu aitukha, yalı . . .

though his body had not yet got its original state yet, his colour had revived, his flesh

.nu majige nonggikha, jing chirku-de nikeme teni jaka jeme,

even was a little increased, he was just reclining on a pillow, eating something,

tede bi: "Si jabshau kai! Urgun kai! Ere mudan buchekheku bichibe,

so I (said): "You are a lucky one! I congratulate you! Though you did not die, this time

suku-i emu jergi kobchikha seme"! Mini baru injersheme

you peeled off a layer of skin!" Looking at me, with a hearty chuckle

"Peeled off,"—as who should say "escaped by the skin of your teeth."

injembi. Yata nei tuchifi umesi duleke-bi.

he laughed. True it was that the sweating had brought him through grandly.

CHAPTER LXXXVIII.

A. Si ai uttu sofin aku? Doronggo yangsangga-i techi, we	*A.* Why are you so fidgetty? If you sit sedately and nicely there, who
simbe moo sholon sembio? gisun-khese aku ochi, we	will call you a wooden post? if you never say a word, who
simbe khelen khempe aku sembio? Aimaka webe yobo arara adali,	will call you a stuttering tongue-tied dummy? It really seems as if you were making game of people;
erebe nechi manggi, geli terebe nungnerengge, ai sebjen ba-bi?	you irritate one, and then you go and chaff another; what entertainment is there in that?
Si sereraku dere, dalbaki niyalma gemu dosoraku okho-bi.	You do not perceive it, perhaps; but strangers, all, are not inclined to stand it.
Atanggi si emu jekshen kechu niyalma be ucharafi, koro bakha manggi.	Some time or other you will fall in with an abusive, cantankerous individual, and get the worst of it, and then
Si teni: "Ara! da-chi uttu nimechuke-ni!" sembi-kai.	you will be saying: "Oh, dear! can there really be such truculent people as that!"
B. Age, sini akhun-i gisun inu. Khetu daljaku niyalma, ainakhai	*B.* Sir, your senior relative's words are true. Had he been an outsider and no relation, how
uttu gisurembi-ni? Efin serengge bechen-i deribun kai.	would he have spoken so? Indulgence in jesting is the beginning of quarrels,
Bikhe bikhe-i ai sain ba banjinara? *A.* Eiterechibe, ini beye	In the long run, what good will you make out of it? *A.* Well, anyhow, (tho') his form
khakhardakha seme, se isinara unde. Muse ere fon-chi dulembukheku inu.	is manly (well-grown lad), he is not yet of age. You and I, also, did not we pass through that phase?
Jing efin-de amuran erin-de bikai.	It is just the time when one is fond of playing.
esi uttu inu, ere siden-de-uttu. Damu gebungge *sefu* be solifi,	Of course he is like that, at that time of life one is so. Only to engage a tutor of good repute,

Sefu is a Chinese word for "a teacher" or "tutor."

itkhe-be tachibuki-ni. Doro rebuki-ni, inenggi goidakha aanggi,	to teach him letters, that is desirable. Then he can become well-instructed in behaviour, and as the days pass,
hun-chun-i ulkhinjefi, emu chimari ndan-de,	he will by degrees begin to understand, then in one day (one fine day)

Ulkhimbi, "to understand," *ulkhinjembi,* to understand a little, to begin to understand.

alan-i baita-be sakha sekhe-de, itkhai sain okho-bi.	when he knows about the business of life, it will be well.
Khuwasharaku niyalma muteraku jalin ai jobombi-ni?	What cause is there to be anxious lest he be not educated, or not able to be a man?

CHAPTER LXXXIX.

Age, baita dulembukheku, olikha ten. Gisun bichi, aiseme

Sir, you are not experienced in business, timorous to excess. If you have something to say, why

dolo gingkambi? Sijirkhun genefi ini baru getuken-shetukeni neilembi gisurechi-na!

keep fretting silently? Just you go straight to him and speak out a clear account of the matter!

Tere inu emu niyalma dabala. Doro giyan-be baime yaburaku mujangga-o?

He is a man, too, after all. Can it really be (*mujangga*) that he would not try to act with reason and fairness?

turgen-be tuchibume da dube-chi aname, faksalame ilgara-de,

If you show the causes, in due order, from the origin of the affair, and explain each distinctly,

simbe ainaraku sembio? Warakhu sembio? Eichi jederakhu sembio?

what are you afraid he may do to you? Kill you? or eat you?

The ending *rakhu* comes into three verbs here; it expresses just the opposite of the Optative in *ki*, as already explained. See earlier dialogues.

Tere anggala, weri tubade umai asuki aku, geli ainaraku;

Besides, those others there make no sound, have taken no action of any kind;

utkhai goloro-de gunin-aku, uttu tuttu seme tosorongge

so (all) this fear and indecision, this looking out for attack from this side and from that side,

geli khakha-i wa bi? Huwanggiyaraku. Si damu gunin-be sulakan.

are these the spirit that inspires a Man? No harm can come to you. Set your mind at rest.

I unenggi ojoraku, ainaki sechi, khono sinde dere werimbio?

If he should really prove impracticable, and wish to do you some (harm), will that save your face?

Si utkhai uttu tuttu gelekhe, bakhafi bolgosaka (bolgokosaka) ukchara aibi-ni?

So with all your fears of this, and fears of that, how can you get sheer rid of the business?

Bolgo, "pure, clean"; *bolgoko-saka*, sheer rid of, from *bolgombi*, "to wash clean," also "to decide between winning or losing."

Tetele umai mejige aku-be tuwachi, gunichi aifini

Looking at the absence of news from him up till now, I am thinking it is long since

monggon-i amala mak-tafi onggokho-bi. Khon akdaraku ochi

he has thrown the matter behind his back (neck) and forgotten it. If you are obdurate in not believing me

jenduken-i mejigeshe, bi akdulafi khwanggiyaraku!

make some enquiries secretly. I warrant you will have no trouble.

CHAPTER XC.

Sini tafularangge sain gisun, waka-o? Damu minde enchu emu gunire ba-bi.	Your advice is very well expressed, eh? But I am of a different way of thinking.
Unenggi okto-omichi achachi, bi geli moo sholon waka	If it is really a case for drug-drinking, no more am I a wooden-post (blockhead)
jikha-menggun-be khairame beye-be dasaraku doro bi-o?	(to the degree of not reflecting:) to spare money by not curing oneself, is there any sense in that?
Adarame sechi? Chara aniya, bi okto-be tasharame jefi,	So what do I mean? (Well) A year or two ago, I swallowed the wrong medicine by mistake,
elekei ergen jochibukha. Tetele gunikha-deri silkhi meijembi.	and nearly lost (destroyed) my life. Even now, whenever I think of it, my gall feels gone to pieces.

Silkhi, the gall, gall-bladder,—Russian *zhelch',*—in Chinese, *tan,* in Chinese belief is the seat of courage; *tan-ta* "big-galled," "brave"; *tan-siao,* "small-galled," "timorous."

Te bichibe, oktosi-sai dorgi-de, sainingge fukhali aku sechi,	Well, amongst doctors, if one were to say that there were none good at all,
chi inu sui mangga; bichi bi-dere; damu musei tengkime sarangge tongga.	one would, indeed, be unjust to them; there may be some; but those we know to be such, are few.
Tere anggala, nikedechi ojorongge, inu damu emke, juwe bisire, dabala!	Moreover those we can just manage to get, there exist only one or two of such!

The verb *nikedembi* means "to just manage to scrape through with what one can get."

Tere-i funchekhengge, gemu jikha-menggun-be bodoro-be sambi.	The rest of them, all know (sambi) how to make (scheme for) money.
Sini banjire b u c h e r e - b e, ai bodombi-o? Akdaraku ochi,	But your living or dying, what care have they for that? If you do not believe me,
si chendeme-fonjire tuwa! Okto-i banin-be saka-o unde-o, utkhai	just try and see! Whether they know the nature of medicines or not, they just
ambarame silkhi niyalma-i nimeku-be dasambi. Eksheme khudalame	make bold to treat people's illnesses. With all haste and speed,

L

sini boo-de jio, sudala-be jafambi seme; galai simkhun-be	they come to your house, say they will feel your pulse; with the fingers of their hand
mayan-de balai emu jergi bishume, ainame ainame emu dasara argan ilibufi,	they perfunctorily feel your fore-arm (*mayan*) once, draw up a prescription anyhow,
"morin-i jikha"-be gaifi, jabukha. Yebe ochi, ini gungge;	ask for their "horse-money," and depart. If you get better, they get the credit;
tasharachi, sini khesebun seme, in-de fukhali daljaku.	if they make a mistake, you lose your life, a matter of entire indifference to them.
Beye beye-i nimeku endembi-o? Khachingga okto-i baitalabure anggala,	Does not a man himself know his own sickness? Rather than employing all sorts of drugs,
beye ekisaka ujirengge wesikhun?	is not it better (*wesikhun?*) quietly to take good care of oneself (one's body)?

CHAPTER XCI.

Simbe tuwachi *arki-nure*-de umesi haji. (Arki, rice spirit, "arrack").

Looking at you (one would say) you were very fond of *arrack*.

Dartai andan-de seme aljabuchi ojoraku. Omikha-dari, urui

Even for a minute you cannot separate yourself from it. Whenever you drink, for sure

lalanji kheperefi, ilime toktoraku okho manggi, teni nakambi.

you get sodden-drunk, dead-drunk; after you cannot stand, then at last you stop.

Sain baita waka. Majige targa-kha-de sain kai. Sarin-*yensi ochi*

There is no good in this. A little self-restraint would be better. When there is a feast,

Yen-sih, an elegant Chinese term for a feast, equivalent to the Manchu word *sarin*, used in conjunction with it here.

ai khendure? Baita-sita bichi, ainara?

what is to be said (against drinking)? On business occasions, what is wrong with it?

Saligan-i majige o m i k h a - d e khwanggiyaraku.

There is no harm in drinking a little modicum of it then.

Baita aku-de, baita o b u m e, khuntakhan jafashakha-i

But when there is none, to fabricate business (occasions), to keep constantly grasping the wine-cup,

Jafashambi, frequentative of *jafambi* "to hold," "to take"; the final *i* indicates continued action.

angga-chi khokoburaku omichi, ai sain-ba bi-o?

to drink with the cup never quitting your mouth, what good points are there about this?

Ungga-dangga-de waka bakha, amba jobolon nechikhe,

It is to offend in the eyes of one's elders (parents), to draw down great afflictions

oyonggo baita-be tookabukhangge-be sabukha dabala!

to impede important business; these are what one has seen it effect!

Omikha turgun-de, tenteke bengse tachikha, erdemu nonggibukha

Because of drinking, in that way, to learn accomplishments, to increase virtue,

niyalma-de kundulebukha, jingkini baita-be mutebukhangge-be, yala donjikha inu aku.

to become respected by mankind, to be able to achieve anything serious, these all are, indeed, things that one has never heard of happening!

Banin fachukhurare, b e y e - b e kokirabure, sain okto waka kai!	That can be no good medicine (*okto*) that flurries the disposition and injures the physique!
Chingkai omichi ombio? Akdaraku ochi, si bulekusheme tuwa!	How can you keep on drinking so enormously? If you do not believe, look at yourself in a mirror!
Oforo gemu ibteneckhe-bi! Ubu waliyabure niyalma waka;	Your nose is all pimply! You are not a man who has not his share (of good things);
ineggi dobori aku, uttu besheme omichi, beye-de beye khudularangge waka-o?	To soak in drink thus, day and night alike, is not that you yourself harrying yourself.

CHAPTER XCII.

Age, si tuwa! ai sui geli bikhe-ni? Niyalma uttu tuttu seme, sinde	Sir, consider this! What has involved you in wrong-doing? When men are speaking this and that, when it is you that
jomburengge, inu simbe sain okini, ekhe tachirakhu sere gunin.	they are criticising, it is that they wish you well, fearful lest you take up evil courses.

Sui, the Chinese *tsui*, guilt, and its punishment; the underlying idea appears to be the Buddhistic one of inherited guilt to be worked off by counterbalancing good *karma*, actions; *tachirakhu*, afraid lest you should learn, unwilling that you learn,—the *rakhu* termination expresses the reverse of the Optative termination in *ki*.

Khulakha bitkhe-be majige urebuchi bakhanara-de gelembio?	Is there any fear (*gelembi*) from your knowing the books you have studied a little more thoroughly?
Jingkini *bengse*be tachire-de umesi mangga bime	To acquire solid accomplishments (*bengse*, a Chinese word) is extremely difficult
ekhe-demun sinde nokai ja.	bad irregular habits are very easy for you.
Ai khachin-i angga khuwajatala gisurekhe seme, i donjichi ai baire?	No matter how I spoke, to the point of splitting my mouth, what did he care about listening?
Neneme, ebi khabi aku, angga mongniokhon-i, dere waliyatambi,	On the contrary, with unintelligent air, with speechless mouth, he put on an impudent look,
tede bi tuwakhai, dolo dosoraku, fanchafi khiyang-seme emgeri asuki de,	as I watched him, I felt inwardly so impatient, I grew incensed, and gave a shout,
i dere fulakha, fudarame mini baru: "Si mimbe baifi ainambi seme?"	his face reddened, and now it was he who addressed me: "Why are you trying to find fault with me?"
yasai-muke gelerjembi; — fukhali khulkhi kesi-aku dabala.	he broke into a flood of tears—most ignorant unlucky creature that he is!
Khendume "sain okto angga-de gosikhon; tondo gisun shan-de ichaku"	It is said "Good medicine, bitter to the mouth: straight talk, unpleasing to the ears,"
sekhe-bi. Aika giranggi yali waka ochi, bi damu	so the saying runs. If he were not of my flesh and blood, I (should) only

Giranggi-yali, "bones-and-flesh," a Chinese idiom for near relationship, "same flesh and blood."

ainame khoshshome urgunjebuchi wajikha kai! Urunaku	be probably encouraging him to amuse himself, and that is all! To do what must
inde eimeburengge, ainambi?	inevitably annoy him, why should I act so?

CHAPTER XCIII.

A. Bi Age-be tafularangge, simbe sain oki-ni	*A*. My lecturing you, Sir (or, Friend!), is because I wish well to you,
ekhe tachirakhu sere gunin. Mini gisun	and am loth to think of your learning evilly. (If) my words

Oki, optative form of verb *ombi*; *tachirakhu*, deprecative form of verb *tachimbi*.

giyan-de achanara gese ochi, utkhai donjire!	are of a kind consistent with reason, then you will listen to them!
giyan-de achanaraku ochi, utkhai naka!	if they are not consistent with reason, then do not! (Literally "stop!")
Simbe ofi, bi teni uttu gisurekhe; guwa niyalma sechi	It is because it is you that I speak thus; if it were an outsider
bi inu ere gese gisureraku bikhe *B*. Age, mini gosime ofi	I would not be using such language. *B*. It is because of your regard for me, Sir,
teni tuttu tafulakha. Arsari guchu ochi, niyalmai endebuku ufaran-be	that you exhorted me so. As for the common run of friends, (and) a man's lapses into error,
sabukha manggi, tafularaku sere anggala, khono basumbi.	after they have seen them, they not only do not admonish him, but laugh at them.
Donjichi "tondo gisun shan-de ichaku, yabun-de tusa; sain	We have heard: "straight talk is not pleasing to the ear, but beneficial for the conduct, good
okto angga-de gosikhun, nimeku-de tusa" sekhe-bi.	medicine is bitter for the mouth, but good for the illness," so the proverb says.
Gemu Age-i adali guchu-de sain ningge, giyanaku udu bi?	If all friends were as good ones as you, Sir! But how many of such can there be?

CHAPTER XCIV.

Ere jergi gisun gemu sini gunin-chi tuchikangge-o?	Does all this sort of talk express your own opinion?
Si bai bukhiyeme gisurekhengge-o? Ere gese	Or were you merely speaking conjecturally? This sort of
"shan-be gidafi khonggo-be khulkhara" baita, yaya bade yabume bakharaku.	"stopping your ears and stealing a bell," you cannot go (that way) everywhere.
Simbe alime muteraku sechi, i sinchi geli alime muteraku kai!	If you declare yourself unable to accept the responsibilitv others are still less able, indeed!
Chananggi getuke-saka alime takasu, enenggi jio utkhai angga ubaliyakangge.	A few days ago, quite distinctly you assumed it, now you come and change your tune (mouth).
Ere be niyalma-i waka sembi-o? beye-i waka sembio?	When you say this, do you impute blame to others, or to yourself?
Khakha niyalma, beyei yabukha baita ochi, beye alime takarangge,	A sterling man, when he himself has done anything, owns to the responsibility,
ainchi inu dere; ubade tubade jailatarangge ainambi? Absi ochibe,	what is so, he says is so; how should he be looking here and there for excuses? In whatever case,

Jailatambi, "to be constantly evading, escaping," a frequentative form of *jailambi*, "to dodge out of the way."

beye alifi yaburengge wesikhun. Ere gese niyalma-de ten gairengge baitaku.	to accept one's own responsibilitv is the superior course. It is hopeless to get at the truth from such men.

CHAPTER XCV.

A. Si sini tere baita-be majige fashshachina. Ere gese sain naskhun-be,	*A*. You should be more energetic in this business of yours. Such a fine opportunity!
ufarabukha manggi, jai ere ucharan-be bakhambi-o?	after you have missed that, will you ever again get such a chance?
"Bodorongge niyalma, muteburengge Abka," sekhe-bi.	"It is man who makes the schemes, but Heaven that makes then succeed," says the proverb.

Mutembi, "to be able,"—Causative form, ***mutebumbi***, "to make possible."

Ere erin forgon udu oyonggo bichibe, bodorongge inu oyonggo.	Though the revolutions of fate are important, forming one's plans is also important.
Bi simbe tuwachi, emu fon-de khan khakhi, emu fonde khon	When I look at you, I see you sometimes very hasty, sometimes very
elkhe dabakha-bi. *B*. Sini gisun udu inu bichibe,	slow, (in both) going to extremes (excess). *B*. Though you speak truly,
si emke-be sakha gojime, juwe-be sara unde.	you only know one part, (the first), you do not know the second part yet.
Ini chisui emu banjinara-ba bi. Bakhara giyan ochi,	There is a way of things coming right of themselves. If it is what is due to succeed,
gunin-aku bade, ucharabumbi. Bakhara giyan *waka* ochi	when one does not expect it, one finds the opportunity. If it is *not* due to succeed,
udu khusun moktolo (mokho-tolo) fashshakha seme, inu baitaku.	though you exert your utmost efforts, still they will be fruitless.

CHAPTER XCVI.

A. Ini boo-de banjirengge antaka? We-i mukun, we-i khunchikhin?	*A.* What means of existence has their family. Whose clansman, whose relation is he?
Boigon khetkhe bi-o? Boo-de udu anggala bi? Aika	Has he a house and land? How many members of his household? Any

Anggala, corresponding exactly to the Chinese *jin-kou* ("mouths" of persons), seems connected with the word *angga*, "mouth."

bekdun sindambi-o? Madagan bakhara-ba bi-o? Jai,	sums lent out by him? Can he get a profit (interest) on them? Again,

Placements de fonds:—*Sindambi*, "to place, lay down," corresponds to the Chinese verb *fang*, the Latin *locare*, meaning, in this connection, "to lend."

aika boo-i turikhen, khudashara niyalma *puseli* neikhengge bi-o?	what house-rent? are there any tradesmen with *shops*?
B. Arkan-seme inenggi banjichi ojoro dabala! Ai	*B.* Indeed, he is but barely able to live from day to day! What
elgiyen fulu sere ba bi? Amba mukun, buye mukun waka,	superfluity of wealth can he have? A great clan, by no means a petty clan,
Fe fujuri boo, akhun-te deo-te, umesi labdu. Jalan-sirara	An ancient distinguished family, elder brothers, younger—very many. Hereditary
khafan inu bi. Te nenekhe-chi, majige ebereke.	rank there is in it, too. Now, compared with past times, they have rather declined!
Neneme, geli sain bikhe. Akhun-deo udu ofi boo faksalafi	Formerly, it went well with them. (When) the brothers, a good many, divided the patrimony,
meni meni enchu tere jakade, ere udu aniya teni suilaskhun okho-bi.	and each took to settling separately, it is then that they have been, (now for a few years) in difficulties.
Tere anggala, yaya inenggi banjire doro, malkhusharangge umesi oyonggo	Besides all that, for a system of daily life, economy is of the first necessity.
mamgiyachi ojoraku. Malkhushachi, goro golmin-de isinachi ombi.	With extravagance, one cannot live. With economy, one can go far and long.
Mamgiyachi, yasai juleri simenggi bichibe,	If one is extravagant, although for a short time one may be leading a merry life,

For a short time, *yasai juleri*, "before the eyes,"—exactly translates the Chinese phrase *yen tsien*, "before the eyes," for "momentarily."

fayafi wajikha manggi, inu simachuka dere!	yet after one has squandered everything away, one is left, truly, alone and dreary!

CHAPTER XCVII.

A. Si naranggi mimbe aikade gene sembi? Kholkon-de uttu, kholkhon-de tuttu,	*A.* Once for all (*naranggi*) how are you bidding me go? Suddenly this way, suddenly that way,
absi toktokhon aku dere. Emu akdan gisun bichi, niyalma	how undecided (are your indications)! With one word on which he could rely, a man
inu dakhame yabure ja sechi-na. *B.* Si geneki sekhe, dabala.	might easily conform to (a request). *B.* You wanted to go, you said!
We simbe gene sekhe? Te bichibe tutafi generaku,	Who said to you "go"? Now as you have stayed behind and not gone,
niyalma-be ergeleme gene sechi ombio? Genembi-sere gisun	can a man be persecuted with being told to go? The talk about going—
we nenekhe khendekhe? Gemu sini angga-chi tuchikangge kai.	who said it first? It all came out of your own mouth.
Sini gisun-be, si onggoraku, neneme niyalma-be laidame deribukhengge,	Your own words, you forget, then turn round and begin to get people into trouble.
yala niyalma-i khendukhe, "niyalma-be sara-de getuken, beye-be sara-de khulkhi,"	Truly, as people say, "clever at knowing other people, a fool at knowing oneself,"
sekhe-bi. Yaya baita-be gemu beye-de dakhuchi, ojoraku sere ba aka.	proverbially. If one acted for one-self, there is nothing one could not do.

CHAPTER XCVIII.

A. Age-i sain gunin-be, bi wachikhiyame sakha. Ere gese-i	*A*. Sir, your good wishes I thoroughly recognise. (For) such
gunin akumbukha, bi khuksheme guniraku doro bio?	great exertion of thought for me, how can I be otherwise than profoundly grateful?

Here the Manchu uses one word, *gunin*, for "wishes," and for "thought," whereas the more cultured Chinese has *i* for "wishes," or intentions, and *sin* (heart) for "thought." *Khukshcme*, means "carrying on the head"—raising a gift respectfully,—the Chinese *ting-tai*, which has become, in Japanese, *chō-dai*.

Ne udu karulame muteraku bichibe, amaga (amagan) inenggi	Though now I can do nothing to reciprocate, on some later day
urunaku kicheme fashshame karulaki. Ai seme?	I will, assuredly, try hard and do my utmost to make you the return I wish. What do I mean?
Damu mujilen-de khadakhai ejeki. Age-i gunin-be	Only that I keep it fixed in my heart, resolved to remember it. Your thoughtfulness, Sir,

Khadakha, or *khadakhan*, "a tent-peg"; *khadambi*, "I hammer in"; *khadakhai*, "fixedly."

ainakha-seme urgederaku.	can never by any means leave me unmoved.

Urgetu, a wooden statue of the dead, anciently buried in the grave with the deceased; hence, a doll; a stock, an idiot. *Urgedembi*, "to receive a favour with a doll's insensibility."

B. Age, ainu, uttu gisurembi? Ya gemu guchu waka?	*B*. Sir, why do you speak so? Who of us all is not a friend?
"Inenggi moo-i abdakha-chi fulu kai; niyalma banjifi ya ba-de ucharaburaku?"	"Days are more numerous than the leaves of a tree," what men born will not meet somewhere?
Seri-seme ba-chi aname yooni karulara-be ereme, gunichi ombio?	Even such a poor service, to expect a return for it—could I think of that?

Ba, a place, means metaphorically an occasion or opportunity, like the Greek *topos*. *Ba-chi anome*, counting a series from this,—including even this.

Age si jachi gunin fulu, jachi guweleke dere!	Sir, you take too much thought, you are too punctilious! (meticulous).

Mr. Burlingame's Letters of Credence

(31st December, 1867.)

Amba Dai-ching Gurun-i Amba Huwang-di fonjime Amba Ing Gurin-	The great *Hwang-ti* of the Great Tai-t'sing Empire enquires about The Great English (British) Empire's
Amba Ejen-de saiyun. Bi gingguleme ABKA'i khese-be alifi,	Great Sovereign's health. I, reverentially receiving the gracious commands of HEAVEN.
dorgi tulergingge-be emu adali obukha, guchulere gurun-be gingseme gunime.	regard native and foreign as alike, and of friendly countries I think with affection,
Entekheme khuwaliyasun sain-be jiramilakha. Uttu ofi, chokhome,	and prize the blessings of a lasting peace with them. Therefore, with that special desire,
sain mutere mergen saisa-be sonchokhobi. Onggolo Gemun-de tekhe	I have chosen the good, capable, ingenious and worthy gentleman; the former resident in the Capital,
Ho-jung Gurun-i Elchin *Bu-an-chen*, dorgi tulergi-i. arbun-dursun-be ureme safi,	United States Envoy *Burlingame*, well-versed in native and foreign affairs and manners,

An-chen is for Anson, his "Christian name." The Chinese, like the Magyars, put the surname first, e.g., "*Wei Toma*," Sir Thomas Wade, "*Kiralfy Imre*," James Kiralfy.

jue Gurun-i iskhun-de kholbobukha baita-khachin-be ichikhiyara-de	who, in managing matters affecting the mutual relations of the two States,
mujilen-i jakanjakha ba-be fun-de tuchibure-de isibuchi ombime,	I feel sure will fully express on my behalf my most cordial sentiments,
kemuni jai jergi jingse khadabukha *Jigang* Sun Gia-gu be	also the officials of the Second Rank (2nd "Button") *Jigang* (Chi-kang) and *Sun Kia-kuh*
tuchibufi sasa Amba Ing Gurun de genefi, gemu chokhoto-i	whom I have ordered to proceed all together to England, all specially
takurakha ujen tusa-i Amban ofi. Yargiyan mujilen	deputed high officials for their important duties. My true and heartfelt
khuwaliyasun sain-i temgetu obukha.	wish for the blessings of concord thus receives the seal (*temgetu*).

Bi ere ilan Amban gemu tondo, kichebe, gulu, ginggun,	I [know] these three high officials to be all loyal, zealous, incorruptible and careful,
urunaku giyan-fiyan-i ichikhiyame mutere-be sambi.	that they will accurately and certainly discharge their functions I feel assured.
Damu ererengge unenggi-be badarabume iskhun-de akdabume,	My sole desire is to give effect to our aspirations for a mutual confidence,
entekheme khuwaliyasun sain de isibuchi, ukhei	which will accomplish the establishment of a good and lasting peace, by which, together,
taifin nechin-be aliki sembi. Gunichi, urunaku,	we may receive rest and tranquillity. I think that, without doubt,
umesi urgunjembi kai.	this would be the greatest boon (or, source of the greatest rejoicing).

In this interesting State Document Johannes von Gumpach ("The Burlingame Mission,—1872") found a "*Kolossal*" mare's-nest in the shape of an assumption of a claim to world-dominion by the Emperor of China. The Book referred to gives the Manchu and the Chinese in the Oriental scripts, and many translations, of which Gumpach's is the only incorrect one. From the name given to Burlingame, "Bu An-chen," the Manchu may have been translated from the Chinese, which was in that case first composed. The above is probably the first translation made from the Manchu into English.

KHAN-I ARAKHA MANJU GISUN-I BULEKU BITKHE-I SHUTUCHIN.

Preface to the "Imperial Mirror-Book of the Manchu Language" (Manchu-Chinese Dictionary).

Bi gunichi, julgei Enduringge Niyalma, futa mampire-me	I reflect, how the Sages of antiquite, from tying knots in cords,
khalifi, bitkhe-chagan banjibukha-chi. Abka-i fejergi jurgan-giyan-be	by transformation (evolution) composed books. From these origins the principles of the whole Empire
gemu shu-khergen-de baktambukha, Abkai fejergi	all in written characters were enshrined (inclosed). In the whole Empire
shu-khergen-be, gemu ninggun khachin-i bitkhe-de baktambukha.	the written characters were all included in books in six scripts.
Ninggun khachin-i bitkhe yongkofi, jurgan-giyan	The books of six scripts being ours completed, their principles of conduct
akumbukhakhungge aku. (lit. none that should be not carried out.)	should all be carried out without omission, with all our hearts.
Aikabade giyangname urebume tuwakhiyame getukeleku ochi	If we are without ripe (skilled) explanation and careful observance of them,
arbun, mudan, tongki, jijun-i doron tutara gojime	form, sound, dots, lines, their rules may be preserved, but after all
ere-i jurgan elei, burubure-de isinambi.	we shall only attain to obscure conceptions of their significance.
Tai-tsu dergi *Hwang-ti*, fukjin doro tachikhiyan-be ilibume	The August (deceased) Emperor Tai-tsu, first established (our) Government and Laws

This ruler, *Nurkhatzi*,—1616 to 1627,—united the divided Manchurian tribes, laying the foundation of the Manchu Empire, and gave them the name Manchu; and abandoning the modest title of Beile (*Beg*) called himself by the Chinese title Hwang-ti, and introduced the Manchu writing, which is an improvement of the Mongolian; and that is derived from the Syriac.—Zakharoff.

The Manchu Empire of China did not really begin till 1644.

yendebufi. Ten-i gosin Abkà Na-de achanakha	and built them up. His extreme bounty resembled that of Heaven and Earth.

Meaning simply that he conferred benefits on his people, that made him seem like a beneficent Deity.

Manju bitkhe-be deribume banjibufi. Amba *shu*,

Manchu writing he initiated. With his great *culture*,

Shun Biya-i gese eldeke.

he shone forth like the Sun and Moon.

Tai-tsung genggiyen *shu* Hwang-ti, banitai umesi

Tai-tsung, the Learned Emperor, was by nature extremely

Abakhai, successor of *Nurkhatzi*—Genggiyen, "bright." Shu, cultured; perhaps from Chinese *shu*, "a book." This Emperor is called in Chinese *Tai-tsung Wên;* the meaning of Wen is "Literature."

Enduringge ofi, Abkai forgon-be badarambume neikhe,

sage, opened and spread the grace of Heaven (*i.e.*, beneficent Government).

Gunin-be sirame, erdemu-be fisembume, shu-i dasan-be

continuing the same ideas, giving wider scope to their excellence, the rule of Culture

ambula selgiyekhe.

he gave in fullest measure to the people.

Selgiyembi, Chinese *süan* 宣 "I promulgate."

Shï-tsu Eldembukhe Hwangti ferguwechuke genggiyen

Shï-tsu, the Enlightened, with his extraordinary intelligence

cholgorome tuchike, mergen baturu Abka-chi khesebukhe

distinguished above his contemporaries, with talents, and bravery graced by Heaven,

This Emperor, whose Dynastic Title or "Temple-name" is given above, is better known by the title of his Reign, which is *Shun Chi* (or *Shun-che*). He reigned from 1644 to 1662, being the first of the Dynasty who really ruled China as well as Manchuria,—and was the immediate predecessor of the Emperor Kang Hi (1662—1723), in whose name this Preface was composed—*Baturu* "brave." This word in varying forms is used over most of Asia and much of Europe. In Russian it is *bogatyr*, in India *Báhadur*, in Mongol *Bagadur*,—whence the Indian *bahádur*,—in Arabic *behádir*, in Persian *Baháder*, in Turkish *behádir*, in Hungarian *bátor*.

dachun kengse banitai salgabukha bime

prompt and daring by nature, dowered with such gifts as he was,

gungnechuke kemungge-i tuwakiyakha,

exercised control with zealous respect for established customs,

oncho gosin-i funiyagan-be badarambukha bime;

and with liberal kindness extended the sway of moderation;

kichere joboro be akumbukha. Mini erdemu nekeliyen beye,

he carried care and labour to the furthest. I myself, of scanty merits,

Mafari-i amba doro-be alifi, soorinde tefi aniya goidakha

inherited from my Ancestors the charge of their mighty system; long years I have sat on the throne,

Or, since I was enthroned, long years have passed:—the illustrious Emperor known to Europeans as Kang Hi,—really the name of the reign,—ascended the throne in 1662, and died in 1723, after one of the longest reigns in history; this Preface was written in 1708, when he had reigned for 46 years.

nu erin seme, Mafari-be alkhudere-e gunin-de tebukhekungge aku,	all the time alike, allowing my mind no repose from the imitation of my Ancestors;
ittu geleme olkhome beye-be awakhiyame, yamji chimari,	therefore with fearful apprehension keeping watch over myself, late and early,
rgen-be bairaku. Tumen baita hikhiyakha sholo-de,	I have not sought for rest. In the intervals of managing the myriad affairs,
iamu bitkhe-be khulame, giyan-be ichime, mini gunin-be	only in reading books, and studying reason, my mind
kumbukha. Geli Sunja Nomun, Duin Bitkhe be aifini	I have exerted to the utmost. Moreover, the Five Canonical Works, and the Four Books, long ago

The five *King*,—Yih King, or Book of Changes, She King, or Book of Odes; Shu King, or Book of History; Li Ki, or Canon of Rites; Ch'un Ts'iu, or Annals of Confucius. (—Mayers.)

The four Books,—The Ta Hüoh, or Great Learning; the Chung Yung, or Doctrine of the Mean; the Lun Yü, or Conversations of Confucius; Meng Tsze, the (Sayings of) Mencius. (—Mayers.)

ubaliyambukha-chi tulgiyen, kheshen khergin-i bitkhe.	I caused to be translated (into Manchu) and besides these, Annals and Memoirs.
Jai, jurgan-be sukhe jergi, dasan-i doro-de kholbobukha,	In addition, in the class of commentaries on Government, affecting the art of ruling,
ele bitkhe-be wachikhiyame ubaliyambukhakungge aku.	hardly can there be books which I have not had completely translated.
Te fe sakdasa sengge urse wajime khamire jaka-de	Now all long-lived venerable patriarchs, very near the end (of their lives),

Fe and *sakda* both mean old, the latter term especially of longlived people, *fe* meaning rather old in the sense of an old system, thus *fe Manju*, old Manchus, *iche* (new) Manju,—much as we speak of "young Turks." *Sengge*, like the Chinese *chang*, means the oldest members of a household.

narkhun gisun somiskhun gunin, ulkhiyen iletu-aku ombi	these have refined words of deep meaning, which would gradually become unknown;
tasharabukha-be dakhalame waka-be songkolofi, tachin	to search out the mistakes made by them, to trace the errors, the habit
banjiname, kimchiraku ofi. Ememu gisun khergen	had never established itself, they passed without scrutiny. Sometimes words and writing
waliyabukhengge bimbime, mudan gairengge tob-aku-de isinakhabi.	were lost and remained so; the search for sounds had ended in inaccuracies.

M

Gurun-i bitkhe kholbobukhangge umesi oyonggo. Dasan i baita

The national literature involves the most important considerations. The art of Government

"The national literature" was really all translated from the Chinese. In Manchuria, Mongolia, Tibet, Corea, Japan, Annam, Tonquin, the Chinese literature and culture became and are supreme.

shu-yang-se gemu ere-chi tuchire-be, dakhame, narkhushame kimchime

and *culture* all issue from this, and accordingly, (unless) precise investigations

getuleken toktoburaku ochi, aibe dakhame yabumbi?

secure clear results, what have we to act upon?

Shanggabume bargiyame b i t k h e banjiburaku ochi

Unless we can succeed in bringing our labours to maturity and fruition by completing these writings,

ai-be durun obombi? Tuttu, bitkhei khafasa-de khese wasimbufi,

what criterion can we establish? Therefore, an Imperial Edict was sent down to civilian officials,

khachin-be f a k s a l a m e, meyen banjibume, inenggidari jiseleme arabufi

that, dividing them into categories, and arranging into sections, they should every day write out fair

tuwabume wesimbubufi. Mini beye, Fulgiyan Fi-i, emke emken-i

and have submitted (words) for my inspection. I myself, with the Red Pencil, to one after the other

kimchime dasakha. Sukhe gisun-de, kenekhunchuken jelen ba bichi,

gave attention and revision. In case of any doubt or ambiguity about the commentaries,

urunaku adali enchu be funiyekhe ichikhi-chi ilgame.

it was made indispensable to collate them and distinguish their resemblances and differencies, without a particle of error.

Yarukha gisun-de melebukhe eden ba bichi urunaku

In case of omissions or discrepancies in the quotations, it was insisted upon, that

Nomon Suturi-de nikebufi, temgetu obume.

reliance should be placed on the Sacred Classical Books and Histories, when fixing a standard.

Temgetu, lit. "a seal"; a proof, a criterion.

Eichi fe sakdasa-de aname fonjime, eichi julgei dangse

Sometimes the old people were asked questions, sometimes the ancient *archives*

Dangse, Chinese word,—*tan-tse* 單子

de kimchime, baichame. Amba ochi, Abkai Shun

were explored into, and examined. Of great things, the Sun in the Heavens,

Na-i giyan; ajige ochi, gebu, jaka, arbun, ton	the laws of the Earth; (geography) of small things, names, objects, forms, numbers,
jai juwan-juwe uju, Sunja jilgan, esheme achabukha mudan-be,	further, the 12 Initials, the 5 Notes of Music, the figuring of Sounds in writing,

Here "great things" obviously means large and striking *external* objects; small things, abstract notions as well as concrete things.—The 12 Initials: the Manchus regarded their writing as syllabic, (in the same low state of development as the lamentable Japanese syllabary), though it is really alphabetic. "Twelve Headings" is what is really meant. —The 5 Notes of the Musical Scale: the Chinese have the Pentatonic scale, thus the scale of C major is played without E, the major third,—or B, the leading note. The Chinese scale is neither major nor minor, but participates of the two. This information is from the fine work by J. A. Van Aalst, of the Chinese Customs Service, published by Order of the Inspector-General of Customs, Sir Robert Hart, at Shanghai in 1884.

gemu yongkiame dosimbume arafi, "MANJU GISUN-I BULEKU BITKHE"	were all completely entered, "THE MIRROR OF THE MANCHU LANGUAGE"
seme gebulekhe. Jilgan mudan-i fulekhe sekiyen-be baime,	was the name given (to the book). The root and source of tones and sounds were sought out,
khergen jijun-i fere da-be khecheme. Ukheri, Shoshokhon	characters and their strokes were sounded to the depths. The total figures; Departments,
gusin-ninggun; Khachin,	36; Categories (or Classes)
juwe tanggu jakunju; deptelin, orin-emu-be banjibufi.	218; Volumes (or Divisions) 21; such is the production.
Manju gisun-be ere-chi melebure burubure-de isinaraku obokho.	From henceforth, the Manchu language has been placed beyond the reach of extinction.

Melebure, "to make to leak away freely," *burebure,* to become lost, extinct. The Active construction, idiomatic to Manchu and to Japanese, is translated by the Passive mode in English.

Ere chokhome Mafari erdemu-i sekiyen-eyen-be iletulere,	Thus especially that the spring and source of Ancestral virtue be shown forth,
fulekhe-be ginggulere shumin gunin kai.	that the root and origin be reverenced, that is my profound desire.
Jijunge Nomon-de khendukhengge. "Niyalma-i	There is a saying in the Book of Changes (*Yih King*): "By men's
shu-be tuwame, Abkai-fejergi-be wembume huwashabumbi"	studying books, the whole Empire is transformed and civilised."
sekhebi.	That is the saying.

Bi Mafari fukjin toktobukha amba bodokon-de gingguleme achabume,

I have with reverence conformed with the great design of my ancestors who founded the Dynasty,

***Fukjin,* at the beginning, *toktobukha,* fixed, established.**

Gurun-boo de *khergen*-be emu obure wesikhun kooli-be sitkhufi kicheme,

to place *letters* on a level better, to identify) with our Realm and lineage, to diligently study their lofty ruling.

Ududu aniya ofi, teni gulkhun yokhi obume shangabukha!

How many years have been, before the entire compilation was brought to a conclusion!

Ere bitkhe-be, tachire urse mini utala aniya kichekhe jobokho-de achabume,

Let students of this book, to second my laborious efforts for so many years,

jilgan mudan-chi khergen jijun-be baire.

seek out characters and strokes from their tones and sounds.

As Manchu has no tones, this surely applies more to the Chinese part of the Dictionary.

khergen jijun-chi *shu-yangse*-be baire ochi, achambi.

Let them from characters (words) and strokes seek *culture*, as it is right to do.

Literally, *if* they do these things (*ochi*), it is right. The Chinese reverence written paper (Chinese writing) so much that to burn it, to keep it from pollution, is a pious act, and little stoves are put up for that purpose, like receptacles for rubbish in a European park.

Ere-chi amasi, yaya khese-be selgiyere, bitkhe we simbume,

From this time forward, every Edict promulgated, or report submitted to the Throne,

jai goroki ba-de khafumbure, eldengge wekhe-de fol oro,

or communication sent to distant places, or monumental inscription engraved on stone

China abounds with such tablets, some being very striking and handsome. *Eldengge wekhe* means literally "glorious stone."

amba doro, amba kooli-de gemu songgoloro temgetu-be bakhara,

will have a criterion in their conforming to a great system, a great canon,

emu gisun, emu gunin, seme, yooni doron tuwaku bisire-be dakhame.

of one speech, of one mind, as there will be an authentic model for all to follow.

Gurun-i bitkhe minggan tanggu jalan-de entekheme tutafi,

The writing of the nation will be preserved and will be left safe for a thousand hundred ages,

Shun, Usikha, Sunggari Bira-i gese, Abka-Na-i siden-de

like Sun, Stars, the Milky Way, between Heaven and Earth

entekheme tutambi dere!

long will it endure!

Elkhe Taifin-i dekhi-nadachi aniya, *Kang Hi*, 47th year, 6th month, ninggun biya-i orin juwe. 22nd (day) (1708).

Sunggari Bira, or *Sunggari Ula*, "the Milky Way;" also the name of a large River in Manchuria, flowing from the South and falling into the River Amur, in Chinese called Sung-hwa Kiang, Hun-tung Kiang, or Ya-tse-Ho.—Zakharoff.

The Milky Way is called in Chinese by the poetical names of "Heavenly River," and "Silver River," and there is a pretty Chinese legend about it.

PREFACE TO THE SECOND EDITION OF THE GREAT MANCHU-CHINESE DICTIONARY, 1771.

The preceding is in Manchu alone, without Chinese; this piece is in both languages, therefore easier to translate.

Julge-be kimchichi, gisun leolen bitkhe khergen-i ulakhangge,	If one examines into antiquity (one finds that) what is handed down of speech and writing,
ba-be tuwame, erin-be dakhame, jalan jalan-de	with regard to the place, in accord with the period, generation after generation,
kubulime khalaraku ome muteraku. Terei	cannot be without change (and) transformation. Their
achanara khafunara-be tuwaki sechi, damu mudan	meeting and coalescing,—if one would have a clear view of these, then only sounds
jurgan juwe khachin-be oyonggo obukha-bi.	and meanings, these two categories, must be made one's main study.
Ubaliyambure-de ochi, khergen-i mudan-be bakharaku ofi;	Yet in translating, people have failed to get the sound of the written word;
tasharabumbime. Inu khergen-i jurgan-be murime	thus mistakes have been caused. Also, the meanings of the written word have been wrested
baikhai, ele tasharabukhangge bi. Ere-i onggolo	in the search for it, and thus caused still greater errors. On a former occasion,
"*tonggime arakha khafa buleku bitkhe*"- be leorere-de, nenekhe jalan-i	when critical discussion was going on about the *T'ung-Kien Ts'ih-lan*, a former generation's

Wylie says this revision of an earlier historical work is by a man who lived towards the beginning of the Ming Dynasty (1368-1647) so learned that he was called the "Walking Book-case" (*Liang küoh shu-ch'u*, "two legged library"). His name was *Ch'en Tsi*— Wylie, Notes on Chinese Literature, 1867, page 21.

ubaliyambukha suduri bitkhe yargiyan-be ufarakha turgun-de,	translation of historical works was found to be deficient in accuracy, and therefore,

Aisin Gurun Yuyan Gurun-i gisun-i sukhen-be kimchime toktobu seme,

that the commentaries in the language of the Kin and Yuan States might be definitely examined

The Aisin,—Kin in Chinese—both words meaning "gold." This dynasty, of Churchen (vulgarly called *Nü-chen*). Tatars reigned from 1115 to 1234, in Manchuria, Mongolia, and *North* China. If not the ancestors of the Manchus, they were a kindred Tungusian race. Contemporaneously, the Sung, a purely Chinese dynasty, ruled over *South* China, with Hangchow as their Capital. Both Aisin and Kin were subverted by the Mongol race of the *Yüan*, (1206-1368) whose best-known rulers are Jengiz (Chinggiz) Khan and Kublai-Khan. "Churchens and Tatars assumed the general name of Mongols in the year 1211."—(History of the Yüan, in Chinese, Book II.). The Manchu writing is elaborated and improved from the Mongol, which comes from the Syriac through Nestorian Missionaries. These had acquired great power, and even used it against Roman Catholic envoys from the Pope.

khese wasimbukhabi. Jai Wargi Ba-i khergen-be emu obukha

an Edict from the Throne was granted. Also the "Unification (or identifying, or standardising) of Western Written Words

Ejetun-i jergi bitkhei Shutuchin arara de, geli khachin aname

Notes on," the prefaces to such works, were also, subject by subject,

yarume fisembukhe-bi.

adduced and enlarged on.

The Chinese is *t'ung wen* 同文 *assimilation* is meant by *t'ung*, which means "with"; *unification* is meant by *emu obukha*, "one-making." The Western countries referred to are Turkestan, etc., not Europe.

Te, "Nonggime toktobukha Manju gisun-i Buleku Bitkhe"

Now, "The Revised Enlarged Mirror of the Manchu Language"

weilere shangakha-be dakhame, tere-i gunin-be getukeleme

has been completed; accordingly, its design is carefully (here)

tuchibufi, amagan jalan-de ulkhibumbi. Khergen-de

set forth, for the information of future ages. The words for which

mudan-be bakharakungge: utkhai Manju Khergen-i

the sounds have not been provided: as for instance, in Manchu written words,

minggan-be, Nikan "*meng-gan*"; *mukun*-be "*mu-ke*" seme

minggan ("a thousand"), in Chinese made "*meng-gan*," "mu-ke" for *mukun*

arakha gesengge inu. Ere khono khergen achabure-de

(a clan), such ways of writing there are. This, indeed, is matching words

lak-seme aku be. Geli dabanakhangge, cheni

unfittingly. (It is) acting still more improperly when they (their)

Nikan Khergen sindara ildun-de, saishara darire-be

allocate Chinese characters, on occasion, in which praise or satire

baktambukhangge bi. Utkhai Aisin Gurun-i Suduri-de

lurk concealed. As in the History of the State under the Kin Dynasty

Manju Khergen-i *uju*-be "*uh-chu.*" *Beile*-be *peh-gi-liyei*

the Manchu word *uju* (head, chief) as *uh-chu* ("steady root"), *beile* as "peh-*gi-liyei*"

"*Beile,*" says Zakharoff, was written in old Chinese books *bo-gi-le;* it meant *Velikyi Knias,*—Grand Duke, First Class Prince or Prince Royal,—Crown Prince,—"until the Emperor's brothers and cousins took the Chinese titles *T'sin Wang* (Imperial or Royal Highness) and *Kün Wang,*—whereupon it was relegated to the third place, after these."

H. Giles gives, in his "Chinese Dictionary," 1892, these very characters condemned by the Emperor, *uh-chu* 兀朮 as meaning "*head or chief.* Manchu *ushuh!*"

geli "*peh-kin*" sere, ichaku khergen arakha gesengge inu.

and as "peh-kin"; these are examples of the writing of inappropriate characters.

Tere anggala adali Monggu niyalma-i gebu bime,

Also, similarly, of the names current among the Mongol people,

khafan tekhe niyalma ochi, lob tsang-be,

a person of official position, (called by the Mongols) *lob-tsang,*

Nikan sain-i *tsang*-sere khergen arakhabi

is written with the good (polite) Chinese word *tsang* 藏 "treasury."

weile bakha niyalma ochi, "Lobtsang"-be

but if the person has offended against the law, in "Lobtsang"

Niken Dao-si *tsang* sere khergen arakhabi.

the word "*tsang,*" plunder, "entrails," used by Chinese Taoists, is the word written;

I have taken the liberty of altering 贓 to 臟, as Taoists speak of "*the Five Viscera,*" but not of "*Body,*" or "*Plunder.*" But even then, there seems little derogatory in the term. The Japanese *Ji-zo,* from the Chinese *Ti-tsang,* "earth-treasury," is a literal translation of the Sanscrit *Kshiti-garbha, Kshiti* meaning "earth," and *garbha* "the womb," and also "shrine for a god"; and *Jizo* is the patron Saint of *pregnant women. Jizo* is a Buddhist Saint; but the Taoists borrowed from Buddhism, and probably *vice versa.* The Manchu alone mentions Taoists (*Dao-si*), the Chinese does not.

Ere-be songkolome dakhachame umai khalakhakungge.

This practice has continued till now without having been changed.

Jachi fiyokorokhaku sembi?

Is it not most nonsensical?

Jai bitkhe khergen-de jurgan-be murime bairengge ochi,

As regards the other practice, of wresting a meaning for a written word,

Monggu gisun-i *obo* serengge, utkhai "mukhaliyame" "baktalimbi" sere

the *obo* of Mongol, is just "to heap up," "to pile up" (a mound)

gulkhun gisun; balai giyangnara Nikan urse

a general term; but Chinese people explain it, foolishly,

o-be den cholgoroko (*tsié-o*) sere khergen, *bo*-be

as the *o* of *tsié-o*, ("lofty and grand"), and the *bo*

geteremburc wechen-i *bo* sere khergen obumbine.

they make the *bo* of *bo* (*poh*)-*tsi* ("Victory Sacrifices").

These efforts at etymology remind one of the English "*Leg-horn*" for the Italian Livorno,—perhaps once called Ligorno as it stood on the *Ligusticus Sinas*,—and "cock-roach" for the Spanish *cucaracha*.

geli kuwasadame, ere-be Nomon Ulabun-chi tuchike gisun sembi.

Again baseless talk, remote from Classical tradition!

Naranggi, jurgan-be baiki sekhe-i bakharaku sere anggala, nememe

In short, not only to fail to get at the meanings one would fain find, but, in addition,

t e r e-i m u d a n-c h i a n a m e ufarabukhangge, ele murtaskhun-aku sembi-o?

to come to losing even their sounds, is not that still more perverse stupidity?

Ainchi, mudan achabure-de da-chi jurgan gaikhaku:—

Indeed, the matching of *sounds* essentially involves no question of *meanings*:—

te-bichi Nikan i "*Tiyan*" sere gisun-be, Manju gisun ochi

take, for instance, the Chinese word *T'ien*, (天, "Heaven"), if you say it in Manchu,

Abka; M o n g g u g i s u n ochi, *Tenggeri;* Tanggut gisun ochi,

is *Abka;* in Mongol, *Tenggeri;* in Tanggutan (*i.e.*, in Tibetan)

Namke; Hui-se gisun ochi, *Asman* sembi. Ere-be

Namke; in the *Hui-tse's* (Moslems, *i.e.*, Turk's) talk, *Asman*. For these (sounds),

Nikan khergen-de baichi, gemu sibkichi achara *jurgan* aku kai.

if one searches for their Chinese transcription, there is no *meaning* to fit theirs that can be found.

Terei anggala: Nikan bitkhe-i "*Tiyan*" seme khergen-be

A further point:—the Chinese written word (c h a r a c t e r) *T'ien* (Heaven),

aikabade Manju gisun-i mudan achabure arachi, "Tiyan" seme

should one write it, with the proper sound in Manchu, *T'i-yen* ("*ladder-smoke*")

arachi achambi; "*Ti-yan*" sere khergen-de aika *jurgan*-bi seme-o?

would be the proper transcription; but how can there be a *meaning* to these characters *t'i-yen?*

Ti sere khergen, ainakhai urunaku wan-tafuku *ti* sere khergen,

the character *T'i*, why should it necessarily be the written presentation of *t'i*, a "ladder with rungs"

yan sere khergen, ainakhai urunaku shanggiyan tugi-i *yan* sere khergen ni?

the character *yen*, why should it necessarily be the character *yen* meaning "vapour" or "smoke"?

Shanggiyan **once meant "white" (as well as "smoke"); it has since been softened to** ***shanyan***. **The old form** ***shanggiyan*** **was nearer to the Mongol** ***chagan***, **Turkish** ***ak***, **Chinese** ***peh***, **or** ***pak***, **"white."**

Shudeme gamame urse, geli shanggiyan-deri tafame wesire-be	People so clever and imaginative, that climbing as on a ladder, up through the smoke,
Abka-i jurgan bi seme,—fiyokorome suchi ombi-o?	is the meaning of Heaven, they say, —are such wild explanations by such men possible?
Ereni badarambume leolechi, nenekhe jalan i Ejete,	If I say more on this subject (enlarge on it), it is that former Sovereigns
Nikan bitkhe-be suwaliyame dasame jabdukhakungge,	had no time left from the cares of Government, for regulating Chinese books at the same time,

Suwaliyame, in addition.

chikhai tasharakha-be songgolome jurchejekhe-be dakhame,	so folk went on making errors as they liked and continued obstinately in them,
umai tuwanchikhiyame mutekheku bime.	there was no possible means of bringing them to order.
Nikan bitkhe-be suwaliyame dasakhangge ochi,	If, in addition to their other tasks, these (Sovereigns) had controlled Chinese books,
elemangge Nikan bitkhe-de gochimbime khusibufi,	then, indeed, they would have been so hampered and involved in these
meimeni ba-i gisun-i enchu-be aname ilgame	that the systematic collation of words differing in various regions
jilgan mudan-i fulekhe-be narkhushame kimchime mutekheku bi.	and the minute study of the origins of tones and sounds, would have been impossible for them.
Duibulechi, "*muke-de muke achabukha, adali*, we	As one might say, parabolically, it is "*like putting water to water, who*
jembi-ni" sere gisun, yala tashan aku kai.	*can eat it?*"—and that is no empty saying.
Gingguleme gunichi Khan Mafa *Sheng-tsu Gosin Hwang-ti*	With reverence my thoughts turn to my Imperial Ancestor, *Sheng-tsu Jen Hwang-ti*

This was the Emperor whose reign was known as K'ang Hi, 1662-1723. *Gosin*, the equivalent of the Chinese word Jen 仁—Benevolent.

Enduringge ferguwechuke Abka-chi salgabufi;	gifted by Heaven with rare intelligence, like that of the Sages;
kemun-be toktobufi. khergen-be dasame, Mafari fukjin	he decided on a standard (rule), and regulated the written word, Ancestors had founded,

tutabukha Gurun i bitkhei, oncho amba narkhun semiskhun be	and had handed down the books of our Nation, vast in range, filled with obscure difficulties,
bireme khafumbume kimchime achabume.	those (through him) were examined throughout and after elaborate scrutiny reduced to order.
Beye "Manchu Gisun-i Buleku" emu yokhi bitkhe-be toktobufi.	I have had consolidated into one work the Mirror of the Manchu Language.

The Chinese, instead of *Beye,* "I" gives *yü* (御) Imperial, or Imperially, a word much used in Japan, there called *Go,* as in *Go-sho,* "the Mikado's Palace," and even *go-zen,* your (Imperial) rice, meaning your rice, or simply the rice cooked for a meal.

This word *yü* appears in the title of the Dictionary as *Khan,—Khan-i Arakha,* written by order of the Khan, *i.e.,* the Emperor, the "Bogdo-Khan" of Russian diplomatic writers, *i.e.,* "the Divine Khan," or "Son of Heaven," *T'ien-tse* in Chinese.

Dulimba be gaime, banjibukhangge umesi akunakhabi.	By the impartial critical spirit of the writers, very good results have been obtained.

This long line, in Manuchu, is represented in Chinese by four syllables (*cheh chung ta pei*) 折衷大備 as against nineteen syllables of Manchu.

Damu tere fon-i banjibume arakha ambasa khafasa, Manju gisun-be dakhame	But by the then *ambans* engaged in composing the work, the Manchu words, as each occurred,
khachin faksulame banjibume arakha gojime, esheme achabure ilan	had indeed been classed in their several categories, but the sideways-fitted three
achangge Nikan khergen-be dosimbukhaku. Sukhen-de	suitable Chinese characters had not been entered. (So) in the Commentaries

To teach *Manchu* to the Chinese, the Manchu syllable *sing* was written with three Chinese words *si-i-ing* 西伊英 There is the same vowel in all three monosyllablic words; of course the first *i* and the third *i* were not pronounced.

To teach uncommon *Chinese* words, the Chinese adopt the same system, often with only two words.

Nomun Ulabun-i toktokho gisun-be folkolome yarufi, sume giyangnarade	words established by *Classical tradition* were picked out, by which scholarly exegesis
tusa bichibe. Inenggi goidakha manggi, ichishame achabure,	was the gainer. But with the lapse of time, in accordance with the (general) tendency,
shudeme gamara tachin ja-i banjibumbi. Mini	a false endeavour to display learning came easily into vogue. My
mujin khing-seme Mafari-be songkolome ofi;	mind was steadfastly set on following the example of my Ancestors.

Dorgi bitkhe ubaliyambure boo-i ambasa-de afabufi	I therefore charged the higher officials of the Translation department of the *Chung Shu*

Dorgi bitkhe, (in Chinese *chung shu*) 書中 Mayers calls "the Imperial Patents Office," Zakharoff, the Chancery of the Palace (*pridvornaya kantzelariya*).

narkhushame kimchime achabume, khachin aname uju-de Manju gisun arafi,	to make the most minute investigation of this matter, to write a heading in Manchu for each subject,
dalba-de mudan-be achabure Nikan khergen kamchibume,	at the side to add Chinese characters corresponding to the (Manchu) sound,
eichi emu k h e r g e n, eichi juwe achangga, ilan achangga khergen-i,	by means of either one character, two, or three, characters connected,
esheme mudan achabume, kholbume khulara-de	to adjust the phonetic accompaniment, so that to those who read them jointly,

Esheme mudan achabume, "adapting of sounds diverted from their prime position," in Manchu, is the Chinese *fan tsieh,* "opposing to each other, and truncating," (反切), by the system above explained.

kheni majige tasharara ba aku obure, jakade	it is made impossible to be led into the slightest error, therefore
khergen-de farfabufi, tere-i mudan-be bakharakungge	those who (or which) miss getting their sound through confusion caused by the written characters used
khomso okhobi. Sukhe khergen sindara-de	must be few. In placing the explanatory words,
niyalma tome gemu ulkhiki-ni seme chokhome inenggidari	with the wish that each and all may understand them, purposely daily-
baitalara an-i gisun-be baitalabukha. Tenteke seskheri	used (in daily use) common words have been utilized. Such as ordinary
sukhen achamjame gaikha bitkhe fiyelen-i fe gisun	commentaries rake together in the way of old ready-made phraseology
jai sula baitaku untukhun khergen-be yooni meitere, jakade	with vain useless empty words are all suppressed, therefore

The Chinese version specifies as "empty words" the words *chĕ, hu, che, ye* 者之也乎 which are really not expletives merely, but particles useful in literary composition, especially in Oriental writing, which does not supply the aids of an elaborate system of punctuation, and division into paragraphs, nor help from Capital letters, Italics, and inverted commas—(quotation marks)—by which European languages are made easy,—particularly Spanish, which goes so far as to place the interrogative and the exclamatory symbols both at the beginning, and at the end, of the sentence affected.

khergen-de lifabufi, tere-i jurgan-be murime bairengge	those who (which), confused by the written words, wrest the meaning that they seek,
ele khomso okhobi. Ukheri bodochi, *Nonggime dosimbukha iche toktobukha*	must be still fewer. Reckoning in all, "Additionally entered new fixed
Manju gisun, sunja minggan funchembi. Jai, julge-i khafan-i	Manchu words" are more than 5,000. Further, about ancient officials'
gebu, etuku makhala tetun baitalan, gurgu gaskha, ilkha	designations, clothes and caps, vessels and utensils, beasts and birds, flowers
tubikhe-i jergi khachin. achabume kimchire-de tusa bisirengge-be,	and fruits, whatever is of assistance for research regarding these classes;
enchu niyecheme arakha banjibun obofi,	has been made to constitute a separate additional composition,
bitkhe-i wajime-de sindakha. Ere-be mini juse omosi,	placed at the end of the book. This (announcement) my sons and grandsons,
khafan irgen-de selgiyebukhe-de.	officials and people will receive with satisfaction.
Khergen-be emu obuchi ombi-ni, amaga jalan-de ulebufi,	The unification of the system for written words is now achieved, will be handed down to future generations,
goidatala tutabuchi ombikai. Utkhai ofi, shutuchin arakha.	and can be long preserved. Therefore, this preface has been written.
Abka-i wekhiyekhe gusin ningguchi aniya, jorgon biya-i	*Kien Lung* thirty-sixth year, twelfth month's
orin-duin.	twenty-four (24th day).

Kien-lung, (in Manchu *Abka-i wekhiye khe* "the Heaven-sustained," name of the reign of the 4th Emperor of the *Ts'ing,* or Manchu Dynasty 1736-1796; like his predecessor, whose reign was known as Kang Hi, he ruled a long time, 60 years. The Preface to the new and enlarged edition of the Dictionary was written in 1771. Its Chinese style is formal and stately, and very concise.

The matching of Manchu sounds need not include the search for appropriate meanings of Chinese characters used, says the Emperor. I have discovered two words, Chinese names for jewels, really Persian words transcribed, which show sound ingeniously united to meaning. (1) *Yang-hung,* "ruby," Arabic *yakut* (from the Persian). The second syllable means "red" (hung). (2) *Tsu-mu-luh,* "emerald," Arabic *zumrud* (from the Persian, which again from the Sanscrit *marakata*). The last syllable means "green" (*luh*). The *yanghung,* or *yakout,* was brought by Arab traders from Ceylon, known as the Isle of Rubies (or sapphires,—*jezirat al-yakut,* for the *jacinthus* was a blue "Oriental sapphire," and in Malay *batu yakut* is crystal,—or white sapphire) as early as the 9th Century A.D., and emeralds from the same place. There is no letter R in Chinese, no letter L in Japanese. Manchu has both.

The Manchu Part of a Monumental Inscription in Corea in Chinese, Manchu, and Mongol.

The numbering, 1 to 20, refers to the twenty lines, or rather, perpendicular columns, of Manchu script. This numbering is quoted in the Notes which follow this Translation.

I.

Dai-tsing Gurun-i Enduringge Khan-i gung erdemu-i Bei.

Stone Tablet of the honours and virtues of the August Emperor of the *Ta-t'sing* State.

II.

Dai-tsing Gurun-i "*Wesikhun Erdemungge*" suchungga aniya tuweri

In the winter (*tuweri*) of the First Year of the Ta-t'sing State's reign "*T'sung-teh*"

jorgon biya-de

in the 12th month (1636)

III.

Gosin Oncho Khuwaliyasun Enduringge Khan, achakha-be efulekhengge

The Bogdo-Khan *Khwan Wen Jen*, the breaking of the Peace

men-chi deribukhe seme, ambula jili banjifi, chookkha khoron

having originated with us, became greatly incensed, and (sent) an armed force

enggelenjifi. Dergi baru ching-seme jichi, yaya, geleme, alikhaku.

to visit us. Eastwards straight on it came, every one, afraid, made no resistance.

Tere fon-de meni sitakhun ejen, Nan Khan-de tomofi, geleme

At that time our insignificant Ruler, cowering in Nan Khan, in fear,

olkhome, niyengniyeri jukhe-de fekhufi, gerendere-be aliyara *gese*,

was cautious, like to (*gese*) one who walks on spring-time ice, waiting for the dawn to come,

susai-chi ineggi. Dergi Julergi geren jugun-i chookha siran-siran-i

the 50th day. East and West, on all roads, (his) armies (were) continually

gidabukha, Wargi Amargi *jiyanggiyun-se*, alin kholo-de jailafi

routed, West and North his *generals*, taking refuge in mountain ravines,

bederechere goroki amasi, emgeri

retreating far back, once (one step)

IV.

oksome mutekheku. Khechen-i dorgi jeku geli wajikha. Tere-fonde	could not move a step. And in the City the food was exhausted. Then
amba chooka khechen-be gaijarangge,—shakhurun edun	the great army's taking of the City, —the frosty wind
bolori erin-i moo-i abdakha-be sikhabure,—tuwai gurgin-de	driving the tree leaves of autumn-time,—in the flames of fire
gaskhai funggala-be dejire,—*gese* bikhe. Enduringge Khan	the goose's feathers burning up,—it was *like that*. The August Emperor
"waraku!"-be dele *erdemu* selgiyere-be oyonggo obufi,	said "slay not!" above all he made the chief thing the manifestation of *virtue*,
Khese wasimbufi ulkhibume, "jikhe-de, simbe *yooni* obure,	he sent down an Edict announcing, "come! I will make you unmolested (*integral*),
jideraku okho-de, suntebumbi," sekhe. Tere-chi Inggültei	if you should not come, I destroy you!" he said. Thereafter (when) Inggültei
Mafuta geren *jiyanggun*-se	and Mafuta the *Generals*

V.

Enduringge khan-i khese-be alifi amasi julesi gisureme jabure jaka-de,	Were conveying backwards and forwards the Bogdo-Khan's behests and answers, then
Meni sitakhun ejen bitkhe-chookhai geren ambasa-be isabufi, khendume:—	Our humble Prince assembled all his high officials, civil and military, and said:—
"Bi *Amba Gurun-i* baru achafi juwan aniya okho. Mini farkhun miyeliyekhun-de	"I was on good terms with *the Great Nation* during 10 years. Through my blind self-deception
"Abkai dailara-be khudulabufi, tumen khala-i irgen jobolon tushakha.	"I brought down swift punishment from Heaven, and the 10,000 families of my people incurred troubles.
"Ere weile mini emkhun beye-de bi.	"The guilt for this is on me alone.

VI.

"Enduringge khan nememe wame jenderaku, uttu ulkhibure-ba-de	"When the Divine Emperor cannot endure to slay, but notifies his will in this manner,
"Bi ai gelkhun-aku mini dergi mafari doro-be yooni obume,	"How could I, by audacity, above me, keep safe the altars of my ancestors,

"Mini fejergi irgen-be karmame, khese-be alime gaijaraku?" sekhe,

below me, protect the people, by not receiving and accepting the Edict?" he said,

manggi, geren *ambasa* saishame dakhafi, utkhai,

after which, all the *ambans* applauded and concurred, and so,

emu udu juwan moringga-be gaifi, chookha-i juleri jifi

taking with him a few tens of horsemen, he came to meet the army,

weile-be alire, jakade.

to acknowledge his guilt, and then

VII.

Enduringge khan dorolome gosime, kesi-i bilume. Achame, jaka-de

The Bogdo-Khan, courteously, graciously, soothed him with favour. By this meeting, straightway

mujilen niyamen-be tuchibume gisurekhe. Shangname bukhe *Kesi*

he opened his heart and soul to him as he spoke. The Favours he conferred

dakhara *ambasa*-de birime *isinakha*. Dorolome wajikha manggi,

he distributed *even to* the attendant (Corean) *ambans*. When the ceremony was ended,

utkhai meni sitakhun Wang-be amasi Du Khechen-de bederebufi.

he then sent back our humble (petty) prince to his capital city.

Ilikhai andan-de Julesi genekhe chookha-be bargiyafi, Wasikhun

Immediately he gathered in his troops who had gone Southwards, and Westward

bedereme; irgen-be bilure, usin-i weilen-be khuwekiyebure,

returned in triumph; he pacified (soothed) the people, exhorting to the labours of the fields,

jakade, goroki hanchiki samsikha irgen gemu dasame jifi tekhengge;

and so, the population, scattered far and near he made come and settle where they had lived;

amba kesi wakao?

was not this great grace?

VIII.

achige gurun Dergi Gurun-de weile bahkafi goidakha. *Sokhon*

Our small country offended against the Suzerain State long ago. *Yellow*

Khonin, aniya, *Du-yuwan Shuwai*, *Jiang Hung-li*-be

Sheep year (1619), *General* (Army Commander) *Jiang Hung-li*

takurafi, *Ming* gurun-de chookha aisileme genekhengge

was appointed, whose army having gone to assist the *Ming* State,

gidabufi jafabukha manggi

was beaten; he was taken prisoner after which (by)

IX.

Dai-dzu "*Khoronggo*" Khan, damu *Jiang Hung-li* jergi udu	*Dai-dzu* (*Tai Tsu*) "*the Warlike*" Emperor only *Jiang Hung-li* and a few with him
niyalma-be bibufi, guwa-be gemu amasi bederebukhe.	of men, were retained, the rest were all sent off back home.
Kesi ere-chi amban ningge aku. Tuttu ochibe, ajige	For mercy (grace) than this exists none greater. Nevertheless, the petty
gurun geli liyeliyefi ulkhiraku ojoro, jaka-de, *Fulakhun*	country grew giddy again and void of understanding, on which, in the *Red*
Gulmakhun aniya,	*Hare* year, (1627)

X.

Enduringge Khan *giyanggiyun*-be takurafi, Dergi ba-be	The Divine Emperor despatched his *Generals* to the Eastern country
dailanjikha manggi, meni gurun-i ejen *amban*	to carry war (to us), whereupon our country's ruler and *ambans*
gemu mederi tun-de jailame dosifi, *elchin* takurafi *achaki* seme baikha.	all retreated to the islands of the sea, and sent *envoys* entreating *for peace.*
Enduringge Khan gisun-be gaifi, *akhun-deo* i gurun obufi.	The Bogdo-Khan accepted their words, and made the countries *elder and younger brothers.*
Ba-na be yooni obukha, *Jiang Hung-li* be nememe amasi bederebukhe.	Our frontiers restored as of yore, and even sent back *Jiang Hung-li.*
Ere-chi *amasi*, dorolokhongge ebereke-aku, *Elchin* takurakhangge	From then on (*after*), courteous treatment was not wanting, the sending of *Envoys*
lakchakha-aku bikhe. Kesi-aku, *oilori* Khebe	uninterruptedly went on. Unfortunately, *floating* (futile; careless) counsels

XI.

dekdefi fachukhun-i tangkan baninafi:—	were uttered, which led to steps being taken which embroiled affairs:—
Ajige gurun jechen-i *ambasa*-de gochiskhun-aku gisun-i bitkhe arafi unggikhe,	*The small nation* wrote and sent orders devoid of humility to its frontier *ambans*,
tere bitkhe-be elchin jikhe ambasa bakhafi gamakha.	these letters the envoys who came hither succeeded in taking away.

N

Enduringge Khan khono *oncho-i* gamame; *utkhai* chookha jikhaku,

The August Emperor still took this *magnanimously;* his army did not come *at once,*

n e n e m e genggiyen Kheso-be wasimbume chookhalara erin-be boljome,

before (*préalablement*) he sent down a clear Ukase fixing his time to resort to arms,

dakhun dakhun-i ulkhibukhangge, shan-be jafafi tachikhiyara-chi, khono

again and again impressing his instructions, holding our ears and teaching us, and yet

dabali kai! Tuttu ochibe, geli urgunjeme

it was superfluous! And yet, notwithstanding, joyfully

XII.

dakhakhakungge. Ajige gurun-i geren ambasa-i weile ele,

obey we would not. The small state's officials' guilt, all the more,

guwechi ojoraku okho. Enduringge Khan-i amba chookha

became impossible to forgive. The Divine Emperor's great army

Nan Khan-be kafi, geli Khese wasimbufi, neneme,

laid siege to Nan Khan, and yet sent down an Edict, first of all,

emu gargan-i chookha unggifi, *Giang-du* be gaifi. Wang-ni,

sent a branch of the army, captured *Giang Du, (Kiang Tu).* The King's

juse sargan, *ambasai* khekhe juse, gemu, jafabukha manggi,

children and wife, the *ambans'* women and children, all, were captured. Then

XIII.

E n d u r i n g g e K h a n geren *jiyanggiyun*-be " ume nechire! "

the Divine Khan (ordered) his Generals, " molest (them) not! "

nonggere-seme fafulafi. M e n i *khafasa Taigiyasa* tuwakiyabukha

with warning words he restrained them. Our own *mandarins* (and) *Taigiyens* (Eunuchs) he set to guard them.

tuttu amba kesi-be isibure jakade, ajige gurun i ejen *amban,*

So great favours he extended to us, then the small state's sovereign and ambans,

jafabukha juse sargan, gemu fe an-i ofi; gechen nimanggi

the captured children and spouses, were all as before; frost (and) snow

kubulufi niyengniyeri okho, olkhon khiya forgoshofi erin aga okho,

were changed to springtime, arid drought was transformed into seasonable rain,

gese. Ajige gurun-i gukukhe-be dasame bibukhe. Mafari doro

like (as it were). The perished small state was set right and preserved. Ancestral worship,

lakchakha-be dakhume

interrupted, was renewed (restored)

XIV.

sirakha. *Dergi Ba*-i shurdeme ududu minggan *ba*-i niyalma	and continued. The people of the Eastern Land, for how many thousands of *li* around
gemu banjibukha, khuwashabukha. Kesi-de khoribukha.	all were given life and better civilization;— with such favours were they surrounded.
Yargiyan-i julgei kooli-de sabukhakungge kai! *Khan-Sui* mukei	Truly, of ancient precededents none has been seen like this! (To) the River Han's water's
wesikhun *San Tiyen Du* ba-i julergi, utkhai *Enduringge*	upper (course) to the South of *San Thien Tu*, thither it was that the *Sacred*
Khan-i isinjikha ba. *Tan* soorin bi. Meni sitakhun	Emperor arrived (that was the) place. The site of the *altar* is (there). Our petty
ejen *Jurgan-i* niyalma-de khendufi, *Tan* soorin-be nonggime	ruler spoke to the men of the *Board*, ordered the enlarging the *Altar* site (to
den *amban* bederebufi, geli *wekhe*-be gajifi	be) lofty and *great*, and they took *stone* thither

XV.

Bei ilibufu entekheme bibume, Enduringge Khan-i Kung	(and) set up a *Stone Monument* to preserve for ever, that the Sacred Emperor's exploits
Erdemu-be, *Abka Na*-i sasa okini seme temgetulekhe!	and Virtues, may last together with the *heavens* and *the earth*, thus borne witness to!
Ere mini ajige gurin-i teile jalan khalame entekheme *akdafi*,	This is our little country's *reliance* during long succeeding generations,
banjire *anggala*, Amba Gurun-i gosin algin, Khoron-i yabun-de	for its life, *and not only so, but* the Great State's bounty, fame, deeds of valour, by (these)
goroki-chi aname gemu dakharangge inu erechi deribumbi kai.	even distant nations all giving submission, that will also indeed commence from this.
Udu Abka Na-i amban-de arakha, Shun Biya-i genggiyen-be	Although one imagined the greatness of Heaven and Earth (figured) the lustre of Sun and Moon,
nirukha-seme, tere-i tumen-de emken ini duibuechi	in depicting them, even to compare with one ten-thousandth part

XVI.

ojoraku. Kheni muwashime folome temgetulerengge.

is impossible. Inadequately, in a rough way, by graving on stone they are signalized.

Abka gechen silenggi-be wasimbufi, fundekhun obumbi banjibumbi.

Heaven makes frosty dew descend, causes cloudy gloom and makes things be produced.

Enduringge Khan, ede achabume, khoron erdemu-be sasa selgiyembi.

The Divine Emperor, conforming to this (example), manifests his power and his kindness together.

XVII.

Enduringge Khan Dergi Ba-be dailakha, juwan tumen, chookha,

The Divine Khan waged punitive war in the Eastern Land, ten myriads, the army,

Kungur-seme geren, Taskha *Pi* gurgu-i gese.

thunder-like (the noise of) the host, like Tigers and Panthers, fierce wild beasts.

Wargi Amargi Gurun gemu agura-be jafafi, juleri o j o r o - b e temsherengge,

The nations of the West and North all grasped their weapons, to be the first they vied together,

khoron ambula gelechuke kai! Enduringge Khan umesi *gosin* ofi,

a martial power greatly fear-inspiring! The Divine Emperor, with the vast *humanity* he had,

gosime wasimbukha khese gisun, *juwan jurgan*-i wasimbukha bitkhe,

mercifully vouchsafed to issue a gracious Edict, in *ten lines* of writing it was sent down,

khoronggo bime, khuwaliyasun. Da-de, liyeliyefi saraku ofi,

albeit stern, yet gentle. At first, because we were misled and ignorant,

beye jobolon-be baikha;

we ourselves sought for trouble;

XVIII.

Enduringge Khan-i genggiyen Khese isinjire, jakade,

The Divine Emperor's clear Edict reached us, and then

amkhafi teni getekhe gese, meni *Wang* gaifi dakhakhangge

as if just awake *after sleep*, our *King*, accepting and submitting to it,

khoron-de gelere teile waka, erdemu-de dakhakhangge kai!

was not only made afraid by power, but made submissive to virtue!

Enduringge Khan gosifi Kesi isibume, dorolome sayin chira

The Divine Khan in bounty extended his grace (to him), courteously, with happy (good) face

injere arbun-i, agura-be bargiyafi,— sayin morin

(and) smiling mien, gathered away the arms of war,—and fine horses

weikhuken dakhu sangnara *jakade* Khechen-i Khakha khekhe	and light fur robes were given as presents; *then* the men and women of the Capital
uchuleme maktarangge, meni Wang-ni bakhafi bederekhengge	were singing and praising, for our Prince was obtaining his return home
Enduringge Khan-i bukhengge Kai.	as a gift conferred by the Sacred Emperor.

XIX.

Enduringge Khan meni irgen-be banjikini-seme,	The Sacred Emperor desired that our population should live,
chookha-be bederebukhe. Meni fachukhun okho samsikha-be	so sent his armies back. Our (people) confused and scattered,
gosime. Meni usin-weile-be khuwekiyebukhe. Efunjekhe	he compassionated. The tilling our fields he encouraged. The defeated
gurun da-an-i okhongge, ere iche an-i turgun kai!	nation he made be as before; by this cause our altars are renewed!
olkhokho giranggi-de dasame yali banjibukha. Tuweri orkho-i	On the dry bones, flesh, restored by him, was made to grow. Winter grass's
fulekhe, geli niyengniyeri erin-be acharakha gese okho.	roots, again, were as if they had met with the spring-season.
Amba *Giyang*-ni da jakade den amba Wekhe ilibufi,	Right by the head of the great *River*, high and great, this Stone has been erected,
San Khan-i ba tumen aniya jorongge. Enduringge Khan-i sain-le Kai!	in the *San Khan* land to exist for 10,000 years. It is by the goodness of the Holy Emperor!

XX.

Wesikhun Erdemungge-i Duichi Aniya. jorgon biya-i iche-jakun-de, ili-bu-kha (1639).	(In) *Thsung-teh's* Fourth Year, on the eighth of the twelfth month, erected (1639).

NOTES. (The numbers refer to the columns of Manchu writing, as explained above.)

(4). . . . "*Inggultai* and *Mafuta*, the *Generals*."

For "Generals," the Manchu adopts the Chinese term *Jiyanggun* (*Tsiang Kün*) a word better known in Europe by its Japanese pronunciation, "*the Shōgun*."

In the Journal of the China Branch of the R. Asiatic Society, Vol. XXIII, New Series, No. 1, 1888 (35 years ago) will be found the three oriental scripts of this interesting *stèle*, accompanied by an English rendering of the Chinese, by far the most elegantly worded, but naturally the most difficult, of the three to translate. In this, made by Mr. W. R. Carles, I had the honour of collaborating. In this, alas! by a blunder for which I acknowledge my share of blame, the Emperor is made to boast of having "slain" these two faithful servants of his, whose names are curtailed in the Chinese way, into "Ing-" and "Ma-." In palliation be it said that there appears no punctuation at all in the Chinese, though the Manchu and the Mongol both have punctuation-marks.

Now there is a fine history, by V. Gorski, of the rise of the Manchu power, in the Reports by the Members of the Russian Ecclesiastical Mission at Peking, a German translation of which, by Dr. Carl Abel and Prof. Mecklenburg (Berlin, F. Heinicke 1858) is in my possession. Gorski gives the story of how *Maruta*, an especially daring Manchu officer, led a brilliant raid with 300 men right to the Corean Capital,—a superb "bluff,—while *Inggultai* was the Manchu Envoy into whose hands came the written proofs that the Corean King was bent on breaking the peace for which he had agreed with the Manchus.

Even the learned may make mistakes sometimes, or, as the Japanese say: *saru-mo ki-kara ochiru*," even a monkey falls from a tree sometimes." If the above instance is not enough to exemplify this, I may add that these German scholars, though acquainted with Russian, could not have known Manchu, or they would not have rendered *Mukden-i Fujurun* as "*Mukden und Futschurun*," mistaking the *i*, Manchu for "of," for the *i*, Russian for "and" (*und* in German). The meaning is "Poem *of* Mukden," not "Mukden *and* Poem." In the excellent Manchu grammar by their countryman, Gabelentz, written about 1832, in the French language, on p. 149, are to be found 14 lines of this imperial poem, with translations into Latin and French.

(7) "The *Bogdo-Khan*" . . . This rendering of "the Emperor" (Chinese *Hwang-ti*), is really Mongol, and appears more correctly as *Bogda* (Khakan) in the Mongol version on this *Stèle*, whenever the Manchu gives Enduringge Khan, "*The Bogdo-Khan*," the Russian variation of it, is met with frequently meaning "*the Emperor of China*" in Russian books and in official despatches. It means "the Divine Emperor." Schmidt's Mongol-Russian-German Dictionary, 1835, does not give *Bogda-Khakan* (Bogda Khan), but gives *Bogdâ Ejen*, and renders it "der Kaiser,"—"Imperator." The term seems vain-glorious; but *Enduringge Ejen*, and *Enduringge Khan*, the Manchu for the Chinese *sheng chu* 聖主, perhaps mean little more than *Dei gratiâ*, and imply an acknowledgment of the responsibility of so high a position, and an aspiration to occupy it worthily. *Enduri* is the Chinese *shin* 神 the Japanese *Kami*,—the Spirit (Spirits), Power (Powers) that rule all nature.

(8) (9). "*Yellow Sheep*" *Year.* "*Red Hare*" *Year.* Cyclical terms. In the Chinese version the terms used are the names of the *Ten Stems* and *Twelve Branches* which combine to form the Cycle of 60 Combinations. In the Manchu and Mongol versions, the terms used are the names of the colours of the 5 elements to which the 10 Stems correspond, and of the 12 animals to which the 12 Branches correspond. In Tibet, each of the 5 Elements, or Primordial Essences, (Water, Fire, Wood, Metal, Earth) is taken, both in the masculine and in the feminine; thus 10 elements are made up, to correspond with the 10 Stems. Rev. Perè Des-

godius (from whose *Essai de Grammaire Thibétaine* I take this information about Tibet) calls the Tibetan cycle *ce cycle, imité des Indiens.* The 12 animals, in the Tibetan Cycle, are the same animals as in the Chinese; but in Sikkim, the Falcon takes the place of the Hare (4th animal). In Annam, the Buffalo takes the place of the Horse (7th animal). See the great work by W. F. Mayers, "The Chinese Readers' Manual." There are in the publications of the Asiatic Society (China Branch) numerous interesting Essays by T. W. Kingsmill bearing on the subject.

According to V. Gorski, one of the conditions imposed on the Corean King, after his surrender, was the adoption of the Manchu Calendar instead of the Chinese. The difference does not seem to be great.

(18) "Light fur robes." In Chinese, the classic phrase *khing khiu* (*king kiu*). In Manchu this is, strictly, *weikhuken furdekhe.* But on this *stèle* is no word *furdekhe* (fur robes), but a word I assume to be formed on *dakhu*, Manchu for "a fur cloak," which is called, in Russian, a *shuba*. The Mongol version, also, uses the word *dakhu.*

GENERAL NOTES ON TANGGU MEYEN.

NOTE ON CHAPTER 44 OF THE TANGGU MEYEN.— In the Chow Li is the origin of the Chinese appellations here reproduced by the author in Manchu script representing the Chinese sounds, but not translated into Manchu by him; for instance, the appellation "Spring Officials" for officers of the Board of Rites, "Autumn Official" (reference to autumnal assizes) for Minister of Crime. "In the 6 sections of the Chow Li (Ritual of Chow),"—says the learned A. Wylie, writing in 1867,—"may be seen the type of the present 6 Administrative Boards at Peking. It is believed to have been written early in the time of the Chow Dynasty, and consists of an elaborate detail of the various officers under that Dynasty (B.C. 1122—255), with their respective duties."

This long period Mayers divides into the *semi-historical*, till about 770 B.C., and the *historical*, later, during which lived the revered Sage Confucius (B.C. 551—479). E. H. Parker, in his interesting book "China," concurs with Mayers in regard to the worthlessness of records before the time of Confucius,—and does not attach much value to them until some time later than that.

NOTE ON CHAPTER 81 OF THE TANGGU MEYEN.—*Erikhe*, "rosary." Schmidt's Mongol Dictionary gives *erike*, for this or a wreath; it gives additional Mongol words formed from it, *erikelekü*, "to string pearls, etc., or to wear them," and the causative verb *erikelkülekü*, "*to make a* person) wear them."

NOTE ON WADE'S SPELLING BY MAYERS, from "Notes and Queries on China and Japan," Vol. I., Hongkong, 1867:—". . . It was doubtless never (Wade's) intention to obliterate the recognized syllabic classes of the standard pronunciation, but rather to provide a scholastic index to the pronunciation of one special dialect" . . . "A person using the Peking colloquial would do right to *pronounce* the name of the capital as Pei-ching, but to *write* the sound thus, for general acceptation, is equivalent to opening a needless gulf between the Northern dialect and all other forms of Chinese." Those are weighty words!

In English, the *Northern* forms are the harsher; the *Southern*, the softer, have become our "Mandarin dialect," the speech of the best educated. Yet we rightly retain the spelling of, *e.g.*, "might," "right," "enough," etc., though it is only far from the Capital that the harsh gutturals are pronunced. In English, as in romanized Chinese, the adoption of the phonetic system would tend to dire confusion and ignorance.

TRANSLITERATION.

There is another and older guide than the Arabic to this subject:—the *Sanscrit*. Since more than 200 years before the "Hegira" (Hejra) started a new era, the Chinese have used a system of representing the Sanscrit Alphabet by about 30 characters (words) used as phonetics. From these we learn that *si* (Western) is used to represent a Sanscrit *sibilant* in combination with a final *i*; the character *sing* (star) similarly; while the character *sin* (heart) is used to represent an initial *s*. These figured sounds are quite clearly recorded as distinct from the aspirates. Under the aspirates we find *hiung* (a bear), which the system known as "Wade's" writes *hsiung*, writing *sin* (heart) as *hsin*. These Tables, made and adhered to for many centuries by learned Orientals, mark out *sien* (thread) and *hien* (now) as perfectly distinct from one another; so that, (although no doubt easier) it is quite wrong to lump them together as *hsien*.

See the interesting work of Stanislas Julien on this subject.

大清滿州
太祖實錄合訂本

大清滿州實錄
（全）

台灣華文書局總發行

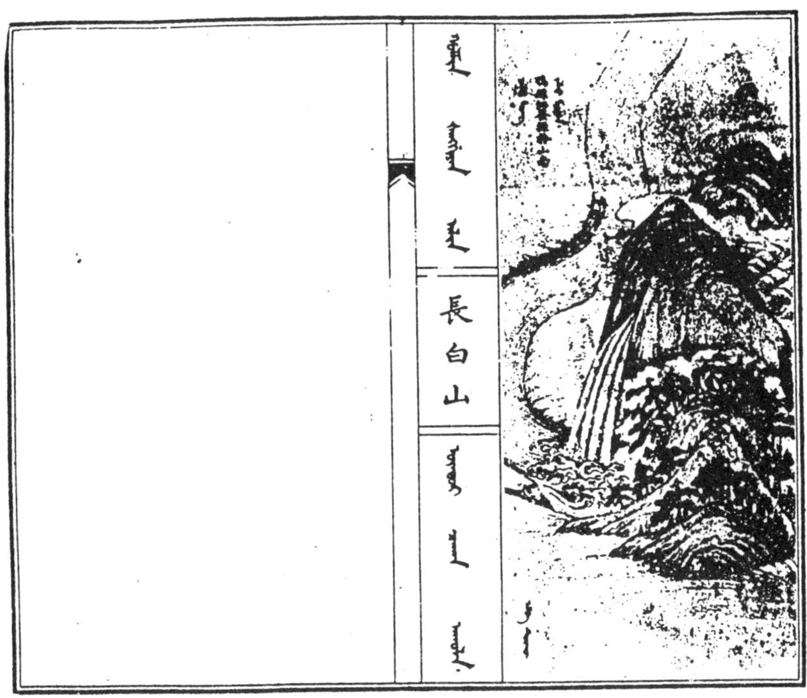

長白山

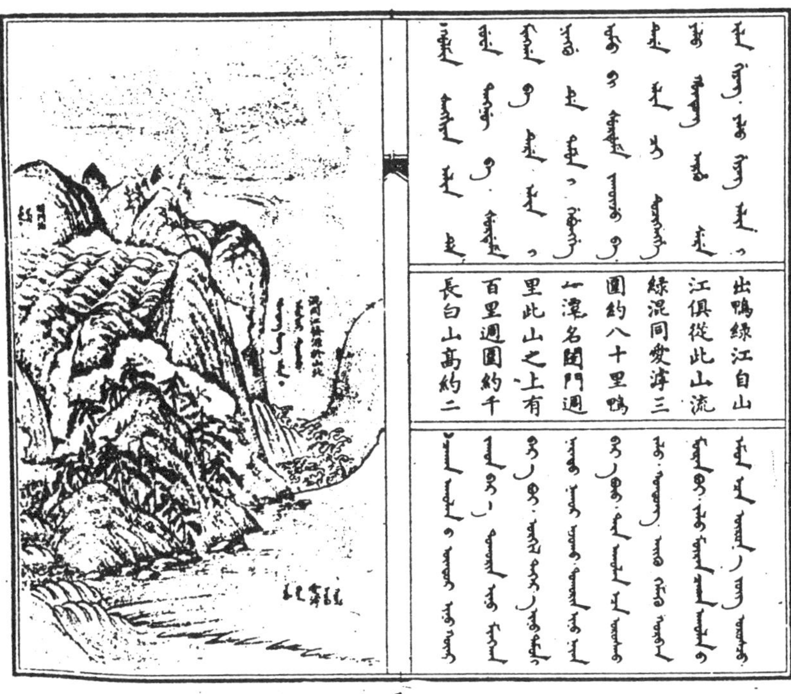

長白山高約二百里週圍約千里此山之上有一潭名闥門週圍約八十里鴨綠混同愛滹三江俱從此山流出鴨綠江白山

낙

장

원본누락

낙

장

원본누락

國可往彼處將所生緣由一一詳說乃與一舟順水去卽其地也言訖忽不見其子乘舟順流而下至於人居之處登岸折柳條爲坐具似椅形獨

踞其上彼時長白山東南鄂謨輝地名鄂多理城名內有三姓爭爲雄長終日互相殺傷適一人來取水見其子擧止奇異相貌非常回至爭鬪之

處告衆曰汝等無爭我於取水處遇一奇男子非凡人也想天不虛生此人盡往觀之三姓人聞言罷戰同衆往觀及見果非常

人異而詰之荅曰我乃天女佛庫倫所生姓愛新漢語金也覺羅姓也名布庫哩雍順天降我定汝等之亂因

낙

장

원본누락

낙 장

원본누락

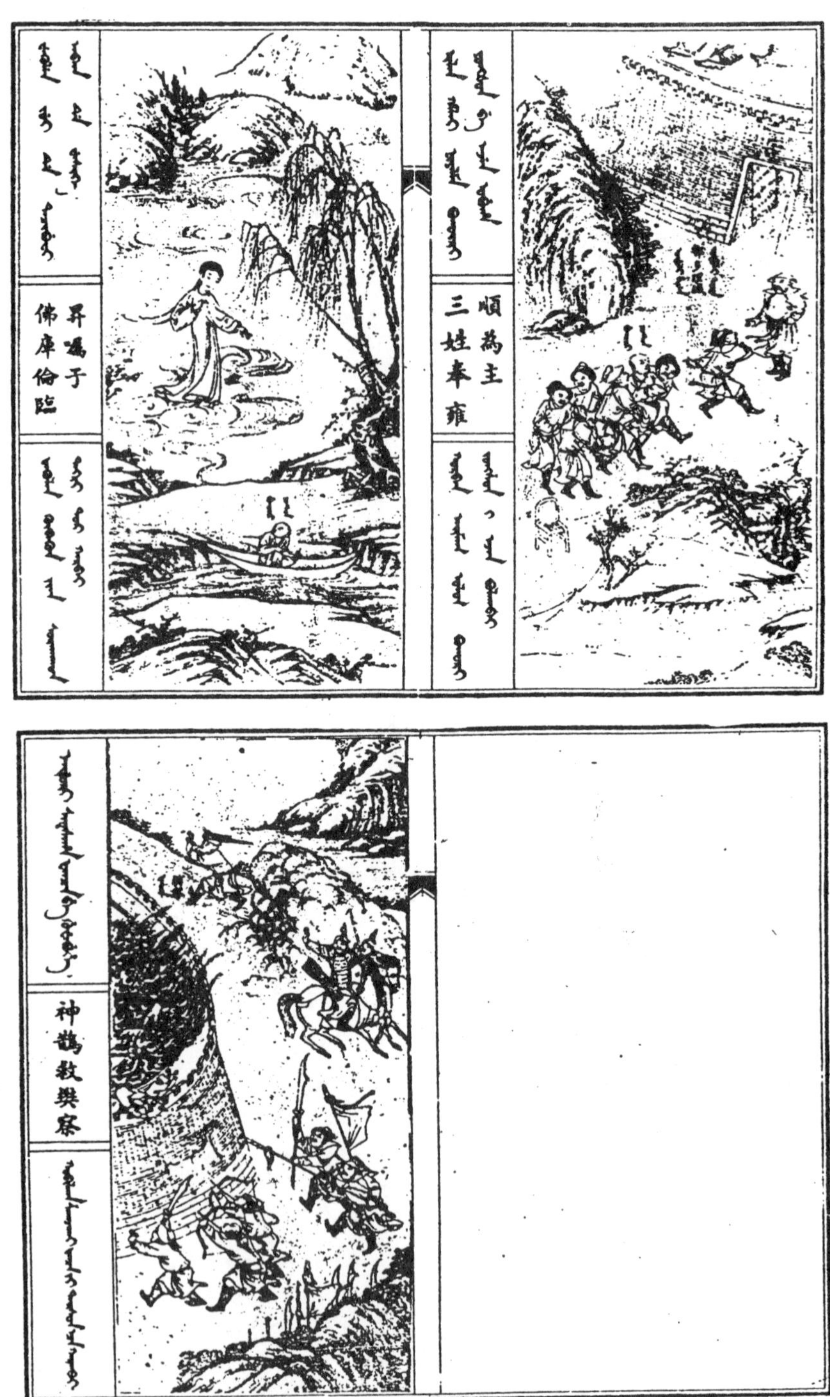
佛庫倫臨昇囑子
三姓奉雍順為主
神鵲救樊察

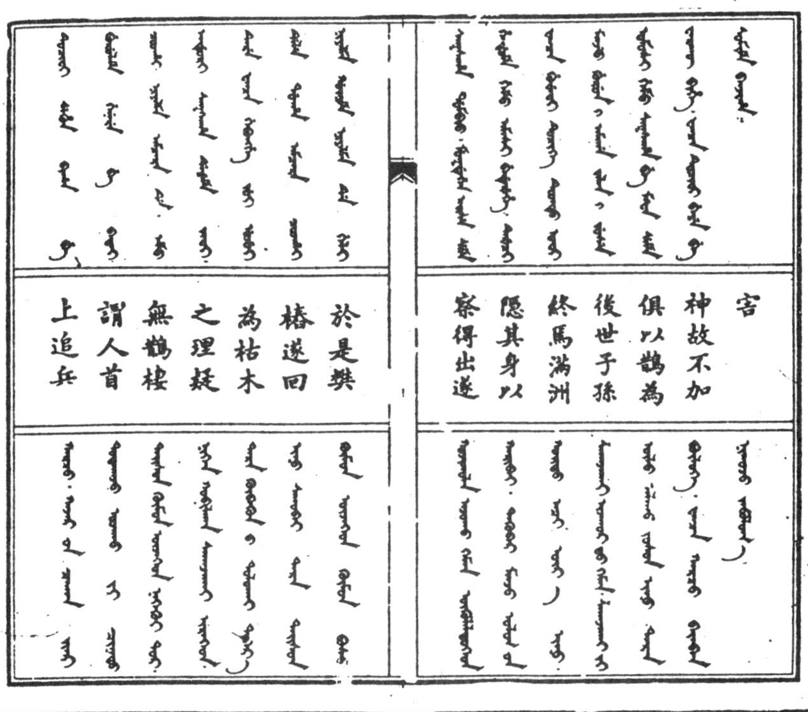

上追兵謂人首無鵲棲之理疑為枯木椿遂回於是樊察得出遂隱其身以終焉滿洲後世子孫俱以鵲為神故不加害

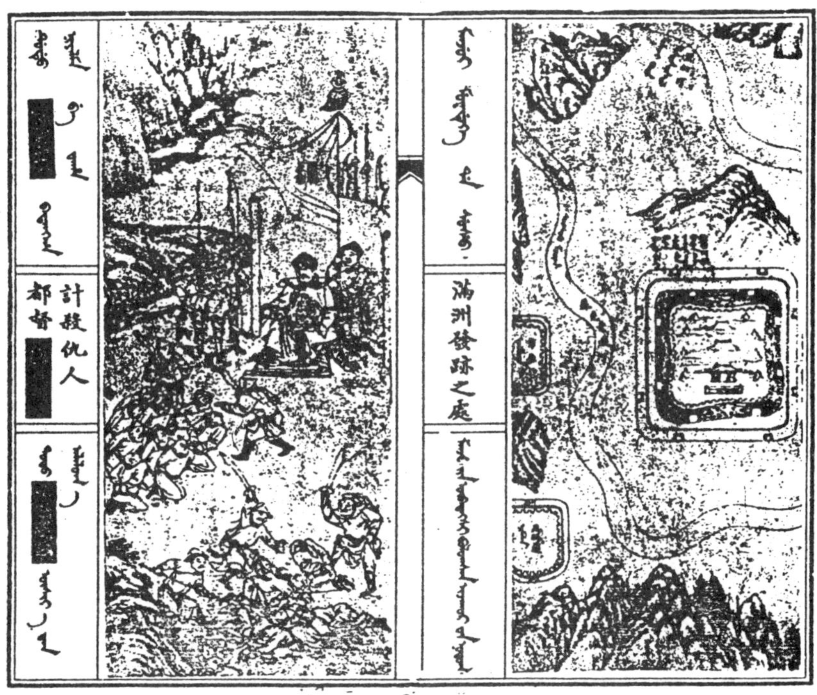

計殺仇人

都督

滿洲發跡之處

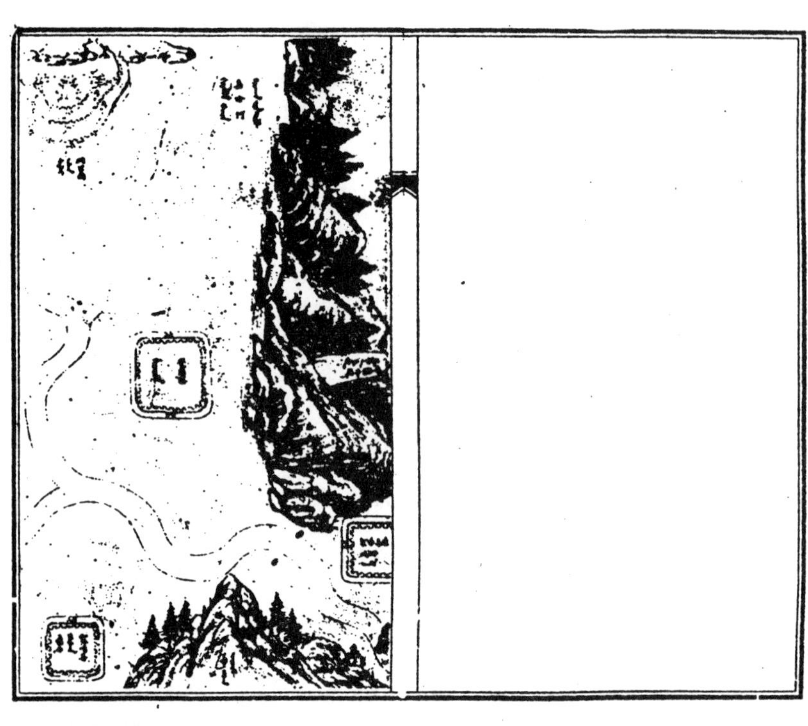

鄂多理西拉國也距語横也阿拉赫圖漢下赫圖阿哈達山名謨河呼蘭

於蘇克素十餘計誘之子孫四殺祖仇人有智畧将[illegible]生其孫都督

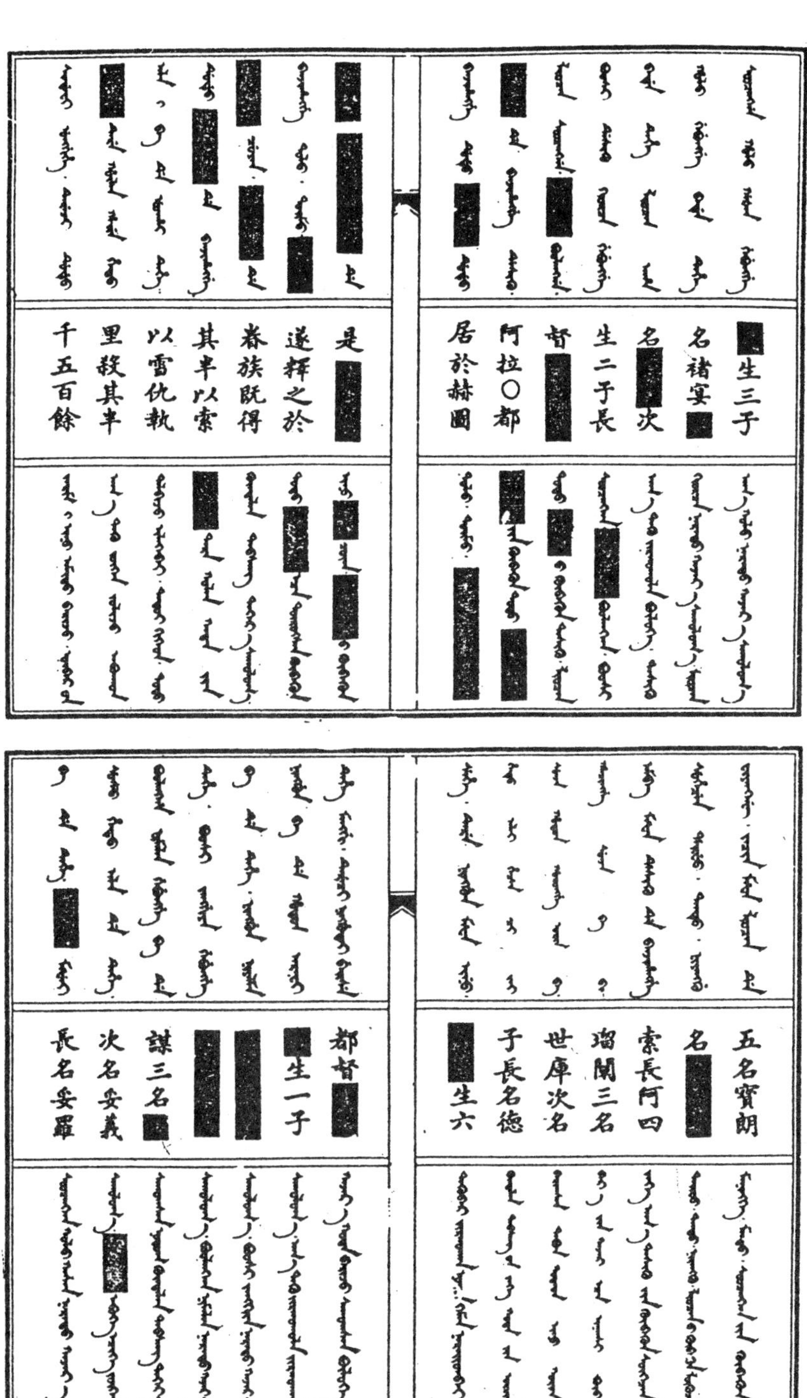

■生三子
名褚宴■
名■次
生二子長
哲■
阿拉〇都
居於赫圖

是■
遂擇之於
春族既得
其半以索
以雷仇執
里敍其半
千五百餘

五名寶朗
名■
索長阿四
瑠闡三名
世庫次名
子長名德
■生六

都哲■
■生一子
■
■
謀三名■
次名安義
長名妥羅

蘭地方寶阿住尼瑪地方寶朗赫圖阿拉住其祖居方[illegible]洛噶善地

長阿住和洛地方索住阿哈和地方瑠闌住覺爾察寶德世庫阿六名寶

名蘇赫臣生三子長祖德世庫五六里長近者不過過二十里拉遠者不

距赫圖阿祖也五城六王乃六城池稱爲六處各立地方六子寶住章佳

名龍敦五名
奇阿珠庫四
武泰三名鉡
名禮泰次名
阿生五子長
圖三祖索長
寧格三名們

臣次名瑪
長名祿瑚
闌生三子
古二祖瑠
尼揚古篇
譚圖三名
代夫次名

子長名康嘉
祖寶寶生四
次名綾敦六
子長名對泰
寶朗阿生二
名塔察五祖
名■五

三名齋堪四
次名額爾袞
魯漢語勇也
巴圖魯巴圖
子長名禮敦
■生五
斐揚敦四祖

[illegible]有才各處擾害時恃其強勇每躍九牛二姓身披重鎧連子俱驍勇常名加呼生七

強悍又一人納生九子皆一人名碩色齊○彼時有四名多爾和三名阿篤齊次名阿哈納

長巴斯翰巴達部欲聘部哈納至薩克寶實次子阿自此強盛初皆賓服六王里內諸部盡

河迤西二百東蘇克素護之自五嶺迤將二姓盡滅其本族六王又英勇遂率智其子禮敦

額爾機自巳子額爾機後遂以妹妻其長克徹殷富翰愛棟鄂部撇而去巴斯心遂割髮留

兄吾汝不甘納曰汝雖不不妻汝阿哈家貧吾妹必雖六王子孫巴斯翰曰爾圖魯妹為妻

兒婦其兄不哈納欲聘吾寶實之子阿徹聞之曰先哈納之名克路人悉傳阿者群賊相呼

阿哈納同名之賊中有與下九賊截殺額圖阿嚕部被托漠河處阿布達里嶺斯翰家回至

吾兒被殺何
順我克儆曰
賊與爾爾當
之我擒此九
部下九賊殺
乃額圖阿嚕
賓之子所殺

曰汝子非賓
使往告克儆
爲聞其言遣
哈達國汗名
必此人也時
令殺吾兒者
允吾兒遂娶

有索長阿部
吾當倍償時
殺吾子金帛
而質若係賊
此九賊與我
饋哈達汗擒
何不以金帛

子未殺吾兒
若果賓賓之
等地屬同族
嚕爲辭耳吾
遠之額圖阿
此不過以路
故又令我降

賊殺之閧又
阿嚕部下九
達汗言額圖
人克徹曰哈
我當殺此二
以金帛遣我
青格謀殺若

翎格與額克
我部下額爾
徹曰汝于是
遣人往詛克
主索長阿私
之即往告其
落額克沁聞

衆議皆定獨
居共相保守
渙散何不聚
十二處甚是
所生令分居
曰我等同祖
不能文相謀

屬二處六王
六王東南所
因引兵攻克
是遂成仇敵
設計誑我於
之此必汝等
云爾部人殺

肩自借兵後
結親兵勢比
建國汗互相
先六王與哈
初未借兵之
處獲其數寨
往攻克徹二

於是遂借兵
處借兵報復
妾父哈達汗
生息吾今詣
處牲畜雖以
我等同住一
武泰不從曰

哈齊號達爾
也次名舒爾
漢話聰睿王
勒淑勒貝勒
祖號淑勒貝
[illegible]即 太
子長名[illegible]

[illegible]生三
姓喜塔剌名
古都督長女
嫡福金乃阿
四子[illegible]
[illegible]第
六王之勢漸

月生 太祖時
[illegible]孕十三
號青巴圖魯初
子名穆爾哈齊
爺也側室生一
里克圖漢語能
號卓里克圖卓

子名巴雅喇
名[illegible]哲生一
族女姓納喇
建國汗所養
側福金乃哈
名雅爾哈齊
漢巴圖魯三

忘一見即識龍
音響亮一聽不
偉言詞明爽聲
體高聳骨格雄
耳面如冠玉身
太祖生鳳眼大
皆妄自期許

常此言傳聞人
治服諸國而為
聖人出勘亂致
者言滿洲必有
時有識見之長
三十八年也是
己未大明嘉靖

行虎步舉止威
嚴其心性忠實
剛果任賢不二
去邪無疑武藝
超羣英勇蓋世
深謀遠畧用兵
如神因此號為
明汗十歲時
喪母繼母妒之
父惑於繼母言
遂分居年已十
九矣家産所予
獨薄後見 太
祖有才智復厚

與之 太祖終
不受時各部環
滿洲國擾亂者
有蘇克素護河
部渾河部完顔
部棟鄂部哲陳
部長白山訥殷
部鴨綠江部東
海窩集部瓦爾
喀部庫爾喀部
呼倫國中烏拉
部哈達部葉赫
部輝發部各部
烽起皆稱王爭

長互相戰殺甚且骨肉相殘强凌弱衆暴寡
太祖能恩威並行順者以德服逆者以兵臨於是削平諸部後攻克明國遼東諸城

諸部世系

〇烏拉國本名呼倫姓納喇後因居烏拉河岸故名烏拉始祖

名納齊卜祿生商堅多爾和齊商堅多爾和齊生嘉瑪喀碩珠古嘉瑪喀碩珠古生綏屯綏屯生都爾機都爾機生二子長名克錫納都督次名古對珠延克錫納都督生徹徹木徹徹木生萬後爲哈達國汗古對珠延生

太蘭太蘭生布顏盡收烏拉諸部率衆於烏拉河洪尼處築城稱王布顏卒其子布干繼之布干卒其子滿泰繼之

○哈達國汗姓納喇名萬本呼倫族也後因住哈達處故名哈達乃烏拉部徹徹木之子納齊卜祿第七代孫也其祖克錫納都督被族人巴岱達爾漢所殺萬遂逃住錫伯部綏哈城其叔旺住外蘭逃至哈達部為部長後哈達部叛旺住外蘭被殺其子博爾坤殺父仇人請兄萬為部長萬於是遠者招徠近者攻

取得之即於萬
可意者莫不索
諸部但見鷹犬
差遣人役侵漁
婪下亦效尤凡
曲為直上既貪
行是非顛倒反

聽處分賄賂公
之凡有詞訟惡
渾河部盡皆服
發及滿洲所屬
時葉赫烏拉輝
自稱哈達汗彼
取其勢愈盛遂

○葉赫國始祖
格布祿襲之
康古嚕卒弟棠
弟康古嚕襲之
位八月而卒其
卒子扈爾漢襲
國勢漸弱萬汗

先附諸部盡叛
往叛投葉赫並
言民不堪命往
察民隱惟聽諂
前鼓之萬汗不
如意即於萬汗
汗前譽之稍不

蒙古人姓土默特所居地名曰璋滅呼倫國內納喇姓部遂居其地因姓納喇後移居葉赫河故名葉赫始祖星根達爾漢生席爾克明噶圖席爾克明噶圖生齊爾噶尼齊爾噶尼生楚孔格楚孔格生台楚台楚生二子

長名清佳努次名楊吉努兄弟征服諸部各居一城始建人多歸之兄弟遂皆稱王甲申歲明萬曆十二年寧遼伯李成梁交哈達國賄以賜勅書為由誘清佳努楊吉努至開原關王廟並所帶兵三百皆殺之清佳努子

尼馬察六人陣
薩哈連烏拉江
益克得哩原係
○輝發國本姓
利而回
林布祿東城失
子歲率兵攻納

多成梁又於戊
漢兵亦損傷甚
喀尼雅罕二寨
復率兵攻克都
父位後李成梁
納林布祿各繼
布齋揚吉努子

長名瑠臣次名
星古禮生二子
瑋亦呼倫國人
國所居地名曰
喇嘛揚噶圖墨
祭天遂改姓納
圖二人殺七牛

姓噶揚噶圖墨
扎嚕後投納喇
祖星古禮移居
長白山發出始
江是也此源從
同江一說黑龍
哈達烏拉即混

名煇發彼時衆
山築城居之故
發河邊呼爾奇
服煇發部於煇
吉努旺吉努征
根達爾漢生旺
根達爾漢齊訥
禪都督生齊訥
哈禪都督嗤哈
拉哈都督生嗤
嗤生拉哈都督
次名䫈党納領
子長名紐領嗤
貝臣貝臣生二

哎攜寧遠伯李
嵗萬曆十一年
外蘭者於癸未
圖倫城有尼堪
克素護河部内
○滿洲國初蘇
國王
七人自為煇發
音達哩殺其叔
旺吉努卒孫拜
攻不能克遂回
自將來圍其城
門扎薩克圖汗
古察哈爾國土

殺阿亥復與成
截困遂克其城
中得脫出中被
兵至遂棄城遁
阿亥城城中包
命達什哈將圍
梁親圍阿太城

記二路進攻成
蘭約以號帶為
寧兵與尼堪外
二月率遼陽廣
主阿亥成梁於
主阿太沙濟城
成梁攻古哷城

有輝汝班師之
朝大兵既來豈
城邊瞭之曰天
願往招撫即至
之尼堪外蘭懼
折兵之罪欲縛
外蘭讒搆以致

成梁因數尼堪
甚多不能攻克
衡殺圍兵折傷
屢屢親出遠城
阿太禦守甚堅
城其城倚山險
梁合兵圍古埒

孫女被陷同于
閩古埒被圍恐
之女祖■
太祖伯父禮敦
之阿太妻係
男婦老幼盡屠
城内人出不分

太而降成梁誘
信其言遂殺阿
城之主城中人
太者即令為此
有令若能殺阿
阿太歸順太師
理汝等不如殺

無罪何故殺之
告明國曰祖父
父子後 太祖
兵併殺■
堪外蘭唆使明
視及城陷被尼
良久亦進城探

不從■候
孫女以歸阿太
獨身進城欲携
■候於城外
城甚急遂令■
既至見大兵攻
■往救之

與汝又賜以都
故以勅書馬匹
死因我兵誤殺
臣曰爾祖父之
我即甘心焉邉
也但執此人與
堪外蘭唆使之

我祖父者實尼
書 太祖曰殺
匹復給都督勅
三十道馬三十
屍還仍與勅書
實是誤殺遂以
明覆曰汝祖父

太祖曰爾乃
太祖往附
外蘭又迫
以歸之尼堪
欲殺 太祖
對神立誓亦
其五祖子孫

皆歸尼堪外蘭
於是國人信之
為爾滿洲國主
築城於嘉班令
即助尼堪外蘭
矣令復如是吾
督勅書事已畢

木湖寨主噶
與本部内嘉
其弟諾密納
官前責治之
譖於撫順將
被尼堪外蘭
滸部長卦喇

河部内薩爾
又蘇克素護
終懷恨不服
歲不死之人
爾世豈有百
人反令我順
吾父部下之

歸毋視為
等先衆來
祖曰念吾
長七 太
立誓四部
殺牛祭天
定遂來附

六王子孫議
投愛新覺羅
此等人不如
曰與其仰望
俱忿恨相議
主常書楊書
哈善沾河寨

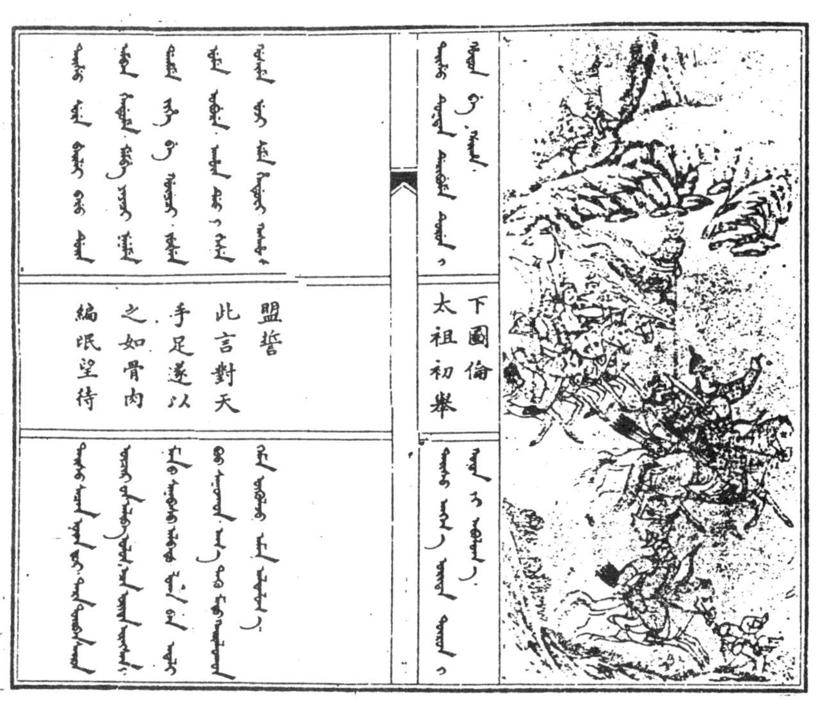

太祖初舉
下圖倫

編氓望待之如骨肉手足遂以此言對天盟誓

癸未歲夏五

太祖欲報祖父之仇止有遺甲十三副遂結諾密納共起兵攻尼堪外蘭時

往告其兄諾密
貝勒耶爲喀達
爾何故順叔勒
達萬汗又助之
爲滿洲主況哈
築城於嘉班令
欲助尼堪外蘭

曰令明國尚
之弟爲喀達
殺唆諾密納
阿第四子龍
有三祖索長
年二十五矣
月也 太祖

喀達賠遣人
密納與弟爲
嘉班不意諾
祖復率兵攻
秋八月 太
克圖倫而回
甲俈三十副

太祖兵不滿百
妻子走嘉班
知遂遣軍民携
蘭在圖倫城預
往攻之尼堪外
 太祖乃起兵
納遂背約不赴

部下一人投
有尼堪外蘭
兵扎營是夜
蘭來戰遂退
兵助尼堪外
之故疑為明
至不料攔阻

時　太祖退
進邊正攔阻
守邊軍不容
南河口臺其
至撫順所東
蘭復棄城逃
往鄂尼堪外

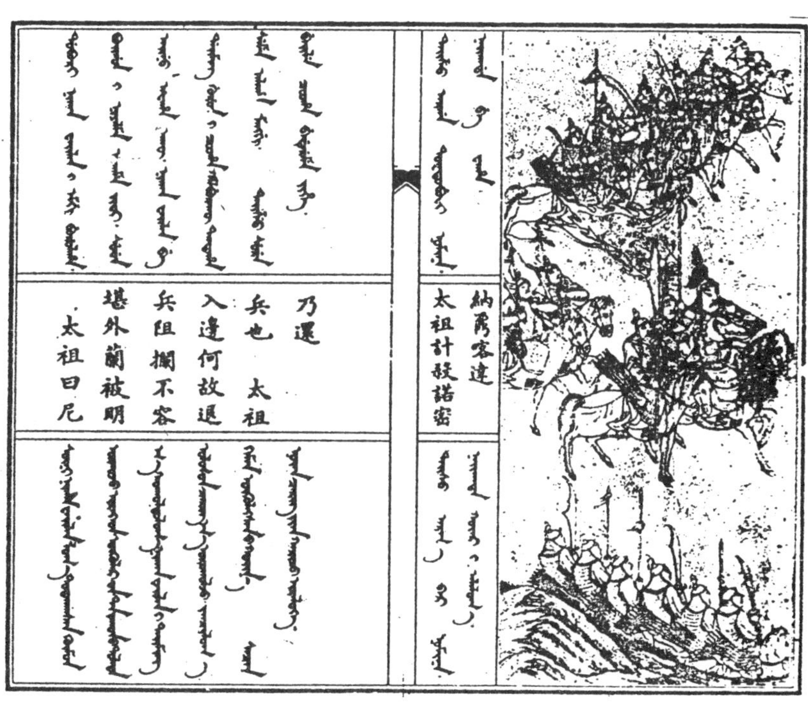

太祖計殺諾密納噶客達

乃還
兵也　太祖
入邊何故退
兵阻攔不容
堪外蘭被明
太祖曰尼

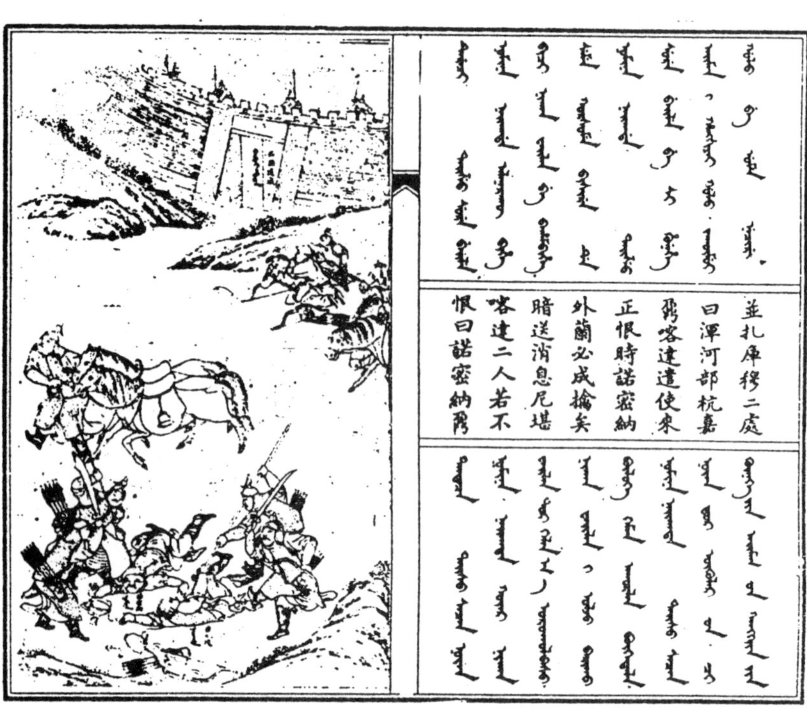

並扎庫穆二處曰渾河部杭嘉鼐喀達遣使來正恨時諾密納外蘭必成擒矣暗送消息尼堪喀達二人若不恨曰諾密納鼐

密納之計陽與言遂陰定破諾納矣 太祖從吾等必附諾密不先破諾密納謂 太祖曰若書三人亦忿甚哈善與常書揚

言愈恨之時嘗行兵 太祖聞其邊路不容爾已不然吾當阻若攻破與我則處乃吾仇敵爾嘉與巴爾達二不許侵犯其棟

其迯散之衆有
薩爾滸城而回
喀達殺之遂取
祖執諾密納鼐
兵器既得 太
将器械盡付之
密納不識其計

與我兵攻之諾
可将盔甲器械
祖曰爾既不攻
密納不從 太
爾兵可先攻諾
祖謂諾密納曰
巴爾達城 太
諾密納合兵攻

言皆誑吾輩耳
洲主耶足証前
於嘉班令為滿
不容況肯築城
往奔明邊尚爾
逼值垂亡之際
蘭前為敵兵所

相謂曰尼堪外
族并先附之人
○尼堪外蘭部
修整其城復叛
令居薩爾滸衆
盡還其妻孥仍
復歸者 太祖

碩翁科羅巴遜
敗哈達兵

遂叛之尼堪外蘭懼携妻孥親屬逃於法納哈所屬鄂勒琿築城居住 太祖以同母妹妻噶哈善

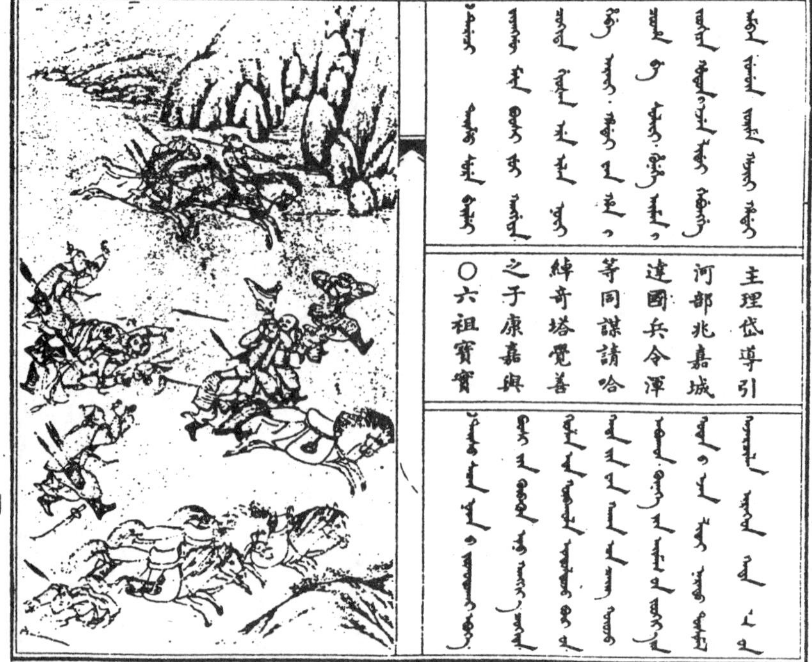

〇六祖寶實之子康嘉與綽奇塔覺善等同謀請哈達國兵令渾河部兆嘉城主理岱導引

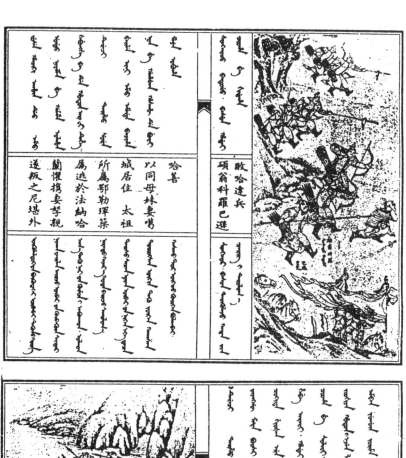

碩翁科羅初
獲所掠而回
四十餘人盡
敵兵遂敗殺
處突然而入
二人追至其
魯巴遂領十

翁科羅巴圖
太祖部將碩
甫分人畜
而去至中途
屬之瑚濟寨
叔 太祖所
理岱亦宗人

祖心神不
登城 太
時方竖梯
瞑之夜亥
夏六月晦
太祖至
廟欲謀殺

子孫同誓於
三祖六祖之
有長祖次祖
科羅巴圖魯
衆故名碩翁
因其英勇超
名諱班偪格

寧因起著
衣帶弓矢
持刀登城
觀之賊見
太祖立
城上皆墜
城而遁九

月内賊乘
夜陰晦拔
太祖住
宅柵木潛
入時有犬
名湯古哈
四顧驚吠

太祖覺
之將二男
一女匿於
櫃下乃執
刀大呼曰
何處賊敢
來相犯汝

不入我即
出毋得退
縮故將刀
柄擊窗有
聲作由窗
而出之勢
仍由户出

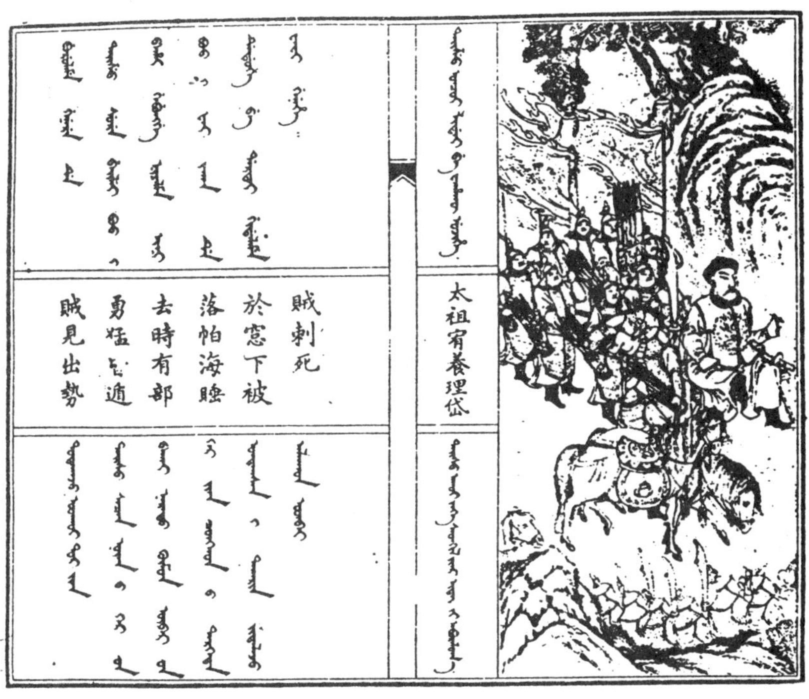

太祖宥養理岱

賊見出勢勇猛乃遁去時有部落帕海睡於窓下被賊刺死

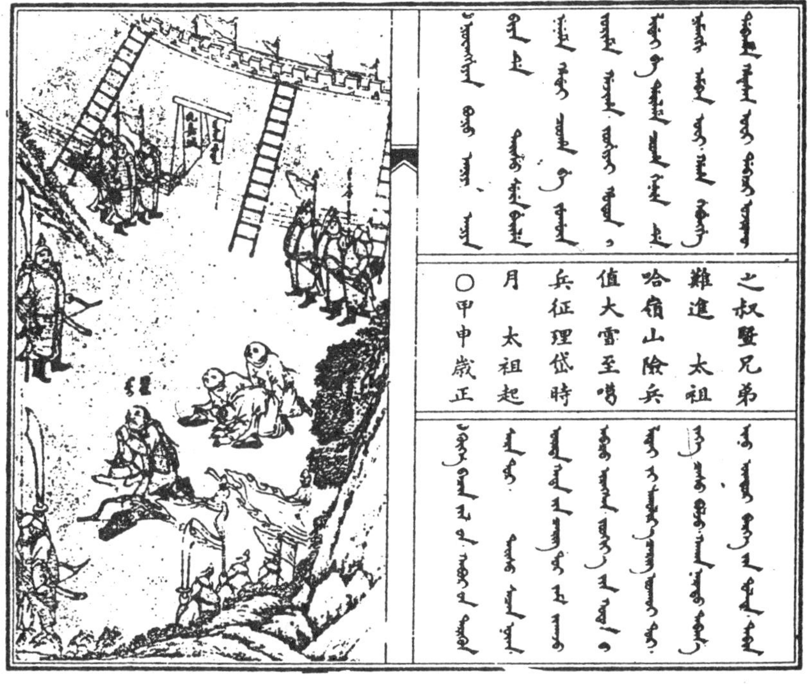

〇甲申歲正月 太祖起兵征理岱時值大雪至噶哈嶺山險兵難進 太祖之叔暨兄弟

輩同勸回兵 太祖曰理岱係我同姓乃忍引他八害我我豈甘心遂鑿山為磴魚貫而上將馬以索縶拽上嶺至理岱城下有三祖之子龍敦預差人報與理岱理岱遂聚兵登城張

號侍敵 太祖部衆曰城內有備何以攻之不如回兵 太祖曰我明知其有備必無還理督兵攻城即時克之宥理岱之死而眷之遂回兵〇龍敦唆薩木占曰薩木占乃 太祖庶

者 太祖聞
謀竟無同住
皆與龍敦同
其兩兄弟中
之聚衆往尋
路 太祖聞
族人遂殺於

聰其言聯領
妹夫薩木占
哈善 太祖
殺噶哈善哈
可與我同謀
見在我家汝
母之弟爾妹

城內大呼
盤旋復回
横闘彎弓
馬登城南
遂按甲躍
太祖大怒
被人害。

汝且勿往恐
皆殺汝妹夫
若不怨汝馬
止之曰族人
蘭城主稜敦
○族叔尼瑪
數人往尋之

曰有敵吾者可速出族人皆惧無敢出者太祖取其屍竟内入室中解

衣服靴帽厚葬之○四月内太祖睡至夜半聞門外有步履聲即起佩

刀執弓將子女藏於僻處令后故意如厠太祖緊隨く后體敵己身潛

伏於煙突側后即回室是夜陰晦忽電光一爍見一賊將近太祖以刀背擊仆喝令家人

意洛漢又言
是實並無他
賊答以偷牛
必來偷牛其
乃佯言曰爾
料兵少難敵
加兵於我自

以殺人爲名
殺之其主必
賊必有主若
　太祖暗思
何用當殺之
漢等言縛之
縛之家人洛

　而疑之乃
　太祖見
忽燃忽滅
在竈燃燈
侍婢不寐
祖夜宿有
五月　太

意遂釋之○
偷牛諒無别
曰此賊實係
後人　太祖
可殺之以戒
主詐言偷牛
此賊實害我

逼近遂發
光見賊已
晦忽有電
時天色甚
之則無矣
不真詳視
其首恍惚

有人形露
空處隱隱
側見排柵
狀至煙突
刀作外便
服內挿弓
着短甲於

祖曰我若
殺之 太
無益不如
至言拉之
兄親族俱
縛之有弟
絰於地遂

擊其首昏
足以刀背
矢穿賊兩
復追射一
肩衣而走
躲過中其
一矢故賊

禦敵又恐
不足何以
弓箭器械
來攻我等
彼必乘虛
則孤立矣
散部落散

食必至叛
掠部屬缺
石糧石被
兵掠我糧
名必來加
假殺人為
殺之其主

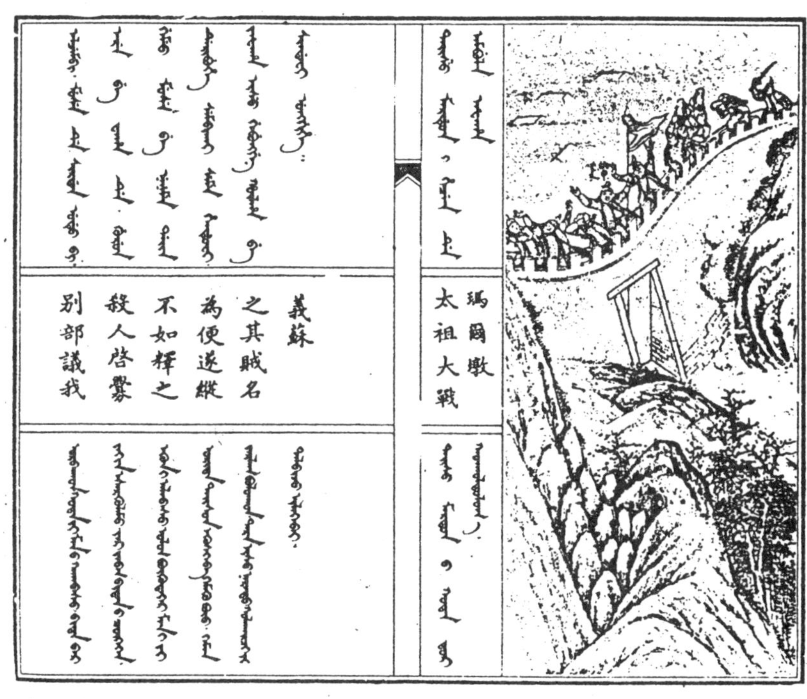

瑪爾墩
太祖大戰

義蘇
之其賊名
為便遂縱
不如釋之
殺人啓釁
別部議我

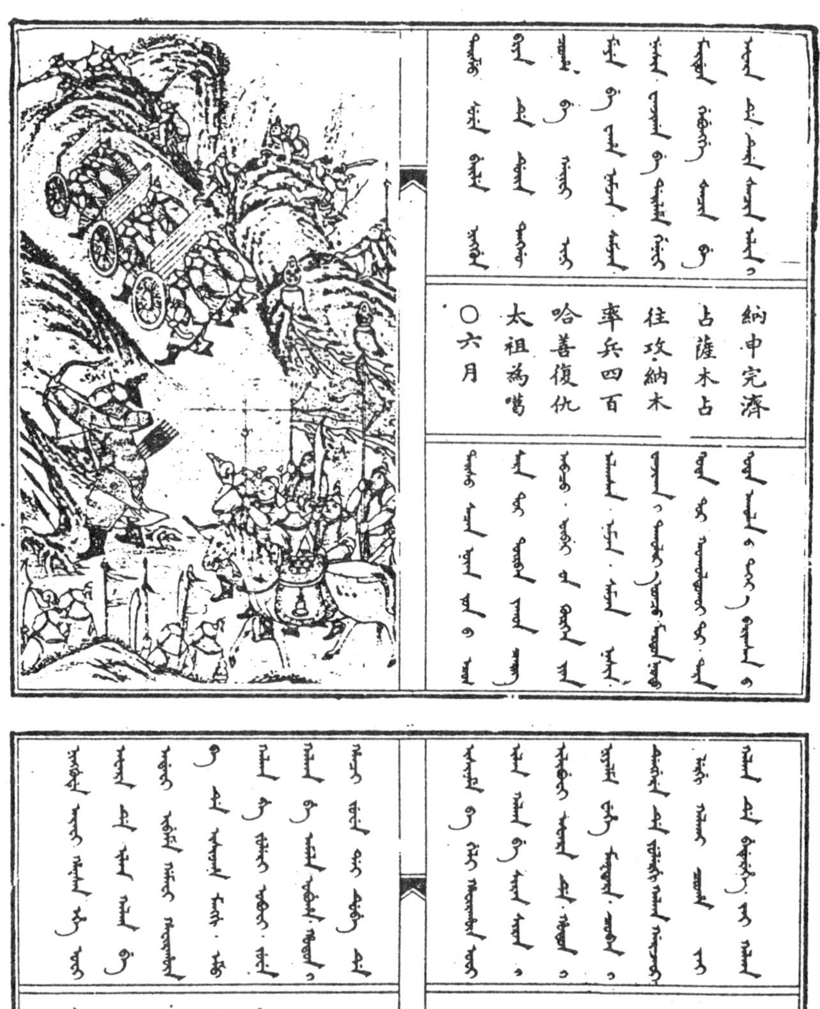

〇六月太祖為噶哈善復仇率兵四百往攻納木占薩木占納申完濟

漢直抵瑪爾墩山下見山勢陡峻乃以戰車三輛並進路漸隘一車前進二車隨之將近城〻路愈隘令三車前後聯絡上攻城上飛石弩之復用

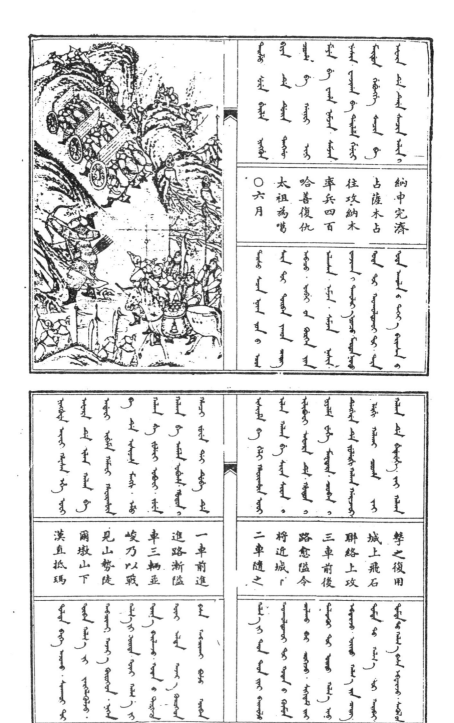

貫其耳復射
納中之面直
射一矢正中
敵於木椿後
距城丈許乃
祖奮勇當前
能上攻 太

後縮首不
於一車之
衆皆斂身
二車俱壞
後車相繼
前車被摧
來撞其車

相議曰昔六
鄂部衆部長
而四○時棟
藩遂取其城
漢棄城走界
之納中完濟
足登山襲破

夜密令兵跣
三日至四日
其汲路連攻
退遂圍之絶
太祖令兵稍
上兵皆却
四人俱仆城

宜乘時往攻
部自亂我輩
諸将曰棟鄂
太祖聞之謂
自相擾亂
用其後部中
血淬箭以備

報仇遂以姘
此機會宜往
仇隙我等乘
哈達國已成
數寨今彼與
達國兵掠我
王族衆借哈

阿海聚兵四
鄂部長阿海
五百往攻棟
太祖率兵
之於九月内
我矣衆皆從
睦必加兵於

備彼重相和
曰我不先發
奈何 太祖
可備有踈失
人之境勝則
不可軽入他
諸将諫曰兵

逞乃遣軍出
城内以為兵
煙籠罩之處
二人伏於火
太祖帶十
攻令兵先行
會大雪遂罷

焚之城將陷
城外房屋盡
城上懸樓井
齊吉達城將
圖阿海所居
太祖兵至
百閉城以待

默思吾既興
太祖聞其言
為我雪仇
助一旅之師
所擒乞貝勒
翁鄂洛處人
祖曰吾曾被

光衆謂 太
人名遜扎秦
完顏部內一
副而四時有
四人獲甲二
出破其衆斬
城 太祖突

太祖登房
並週城房屋
之焚其懸樓
兵臨城下攻
於城 太祖
知之遂斂兵
息翁鄂洛人

令人往送消
兄子岱度墨
前進有兇衮
泰光衮星夜
方遂與遜扎
旅以戳定一
兵至此當乘

太祖箭傷
腿應弦而倒
箭射之穿兩
即以所拔之
僻處 太祖
奔走於煙突
見城內一人

太祖拔箭
傷肉深指許
太祖首透盔
一箭正中
內鄂爾果尼
內之人被城
跨脊上射城

被傷俱登
見太祖
如雙鈎衆
有聲鏃分
圍領矢中
下有鎖子
肉兩塊項

如鈎拔出帶
太祖項鏁卷
一矢正中
乘火煙暗發
一人名洛科
彎射不已時
血流至足猶

悔不已及
地諸將懊
上登仆於
伏二人肩
拄弓下屋
手摀箭眼
太祖以

項血湧出
從容自下
知覺待我
近前恐敵
爾等勿得
太祖曰
屋欲扶回

回
之城而
棄將得
止於是
其血方
日未時

飲水至次
每起時輙
昏迷累次
血猶不止
數寸晝夜
痕纍束厚
復起將箭

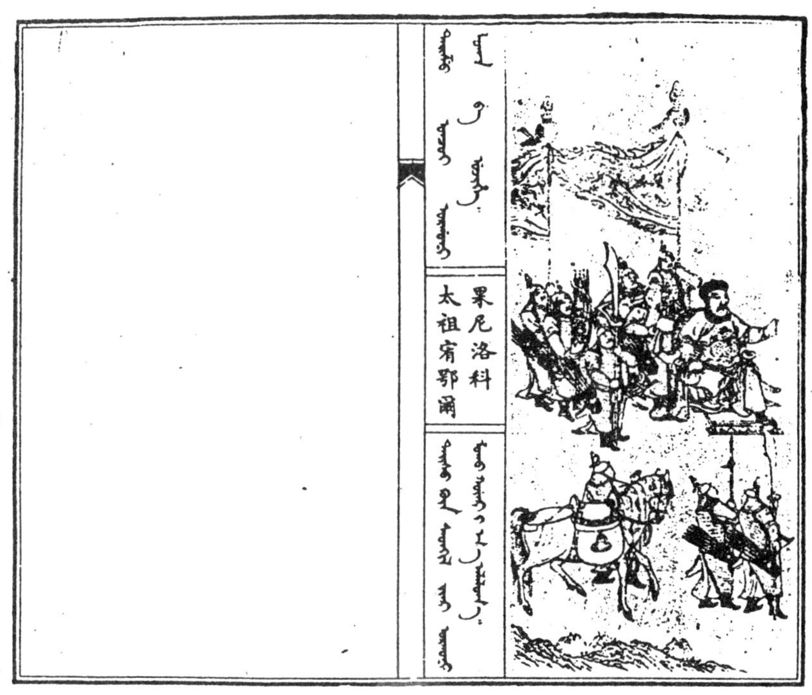
太祖宥鄂爾果尼洛科

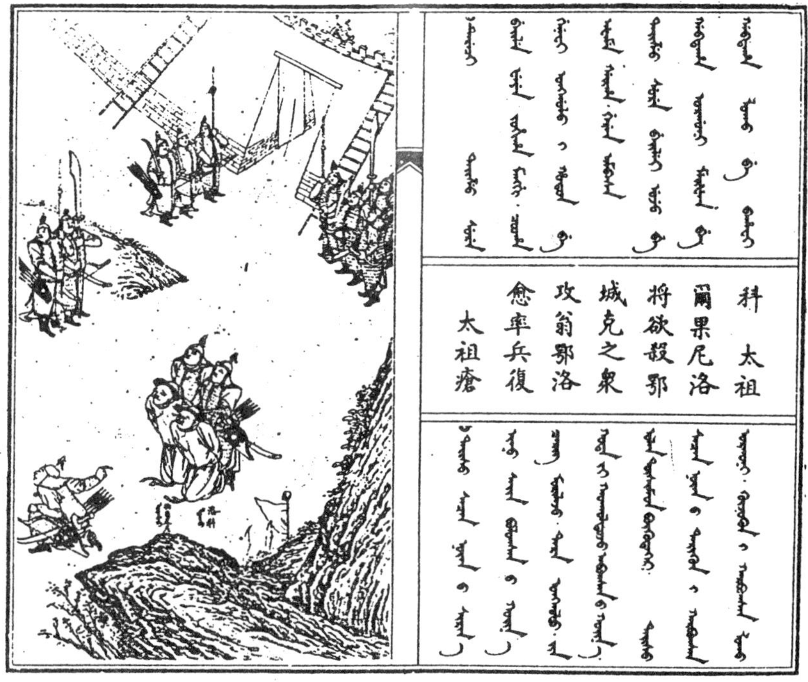
太祖瘡愈率兵復攻翁鄂洛城克之衆将欲殺鄂爾果尼洛科 太祖

曰二人射我乃鋒鏑之下各為其主孰不欲勝吾今釋而用之後或遇敵彼豈不為我用命哉此等之人死於鋒鏑者尤當惜之何忍因傷我而殺之也賜以牛彔之爵屬三百人厚養之

太祖戰殺訥申巴穆尼

乙酉年二月 太祖率五十人甲二十五副畧界藩寨不意界藩寨預知已有備竟無所獲回兵時有界藩薩爾滸棟佳巴爾達四城部長會兵四百追射至界藩南太蘭之野太蘭尚名訥申巴穆尼二人當先追至 太祖一見即單身撥馬欲斬訥申訥申先以刀斷 太

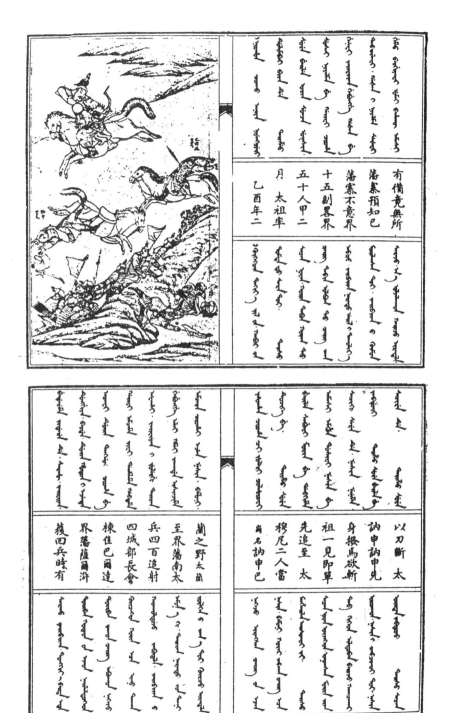

箭肰徐徐引
梢拂雪作拾
下馬佯以弓
太祖曰衆可
為之奈何
曰馬俱疲弱
却而立我軍

二人死俱退
馬下衆兵見
射巴穆尼於
兩段隨轉身
訥申肩背為
奮力一刀揮
祖鞭 太祖

太祖言訥申
欲收主屍
耶汝回我輩
去欲食其肉
人已死何不
中部衆呼曰
斬訥申處訥

太祖立於
畢令兵先行
為疑兵計言
疲我自殿後
麵飲馬解其
嶺以鹽水炒
馬而退待過

係我仇幸得
殺之肉亦可
食言詭送回
欲令疲弱之
兵遠行乃率
七人將身隱
併處露其盔

似伏兵之
勢訥申部
衆又呼曰
汝有伏兵
我等知之
矣二主已
被殺猶欲

盡殺我等
耶於是
太祖全其
羸馬而回

太祖四騎
敗八百兵

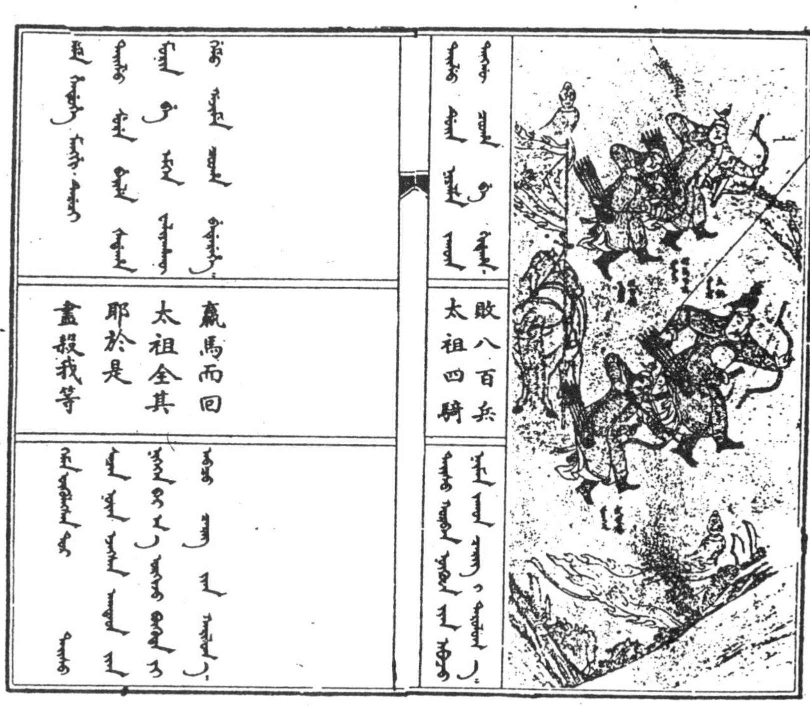

四月 太祖率馬步兵五百征哲陳部時大水令衆兵回止帯綿甲五十人鐵甲三十人

進畧有嘉哈部長蘇庫賚呼密令人報與托漢河章佳巴爾達薩爾滸界藩五城知之遂合

兵一處有後哨章京能古德一見敵兵即飛報不意誤失 太祖處 太祖恃有後哨亦不

被殺猶欲
矣二主已
我等知之
汝有伏兵
衆又呼曰
勢訥申部
似伏兵之

併處露其盔
七人將身隱
兵遠行乃車
欲令疲弱之
食言訖送回
殺之肉亦可
係我仇幸得

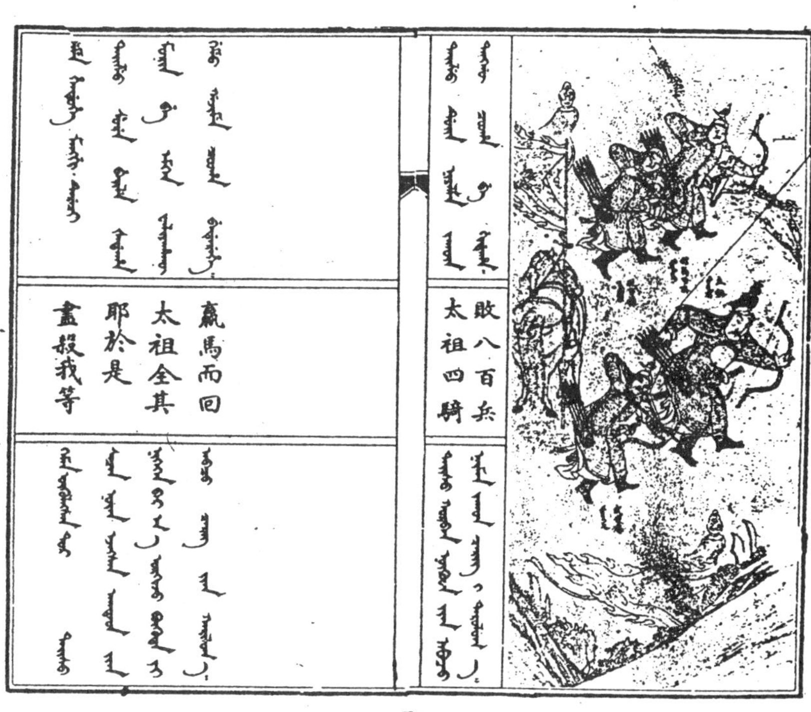

敗八百兵
太祖四騎

羸馬而回
太祖全其
耶於是
盡殺我等

四月　太
祖率馬步兵
五百征哲陳
部時大水令
衆兵回止帶
綿甲五十人
鐵甲三十人

進畧有嘉哈
部長蘇庫脊
呼密令人報
與托漠河章
佳巴爾達薩
爾滸界藩五
城知之遂合

兵一處有後
哨章京能古
德一見敵兵
即飛報不意
誤失　太祖
處　太祖恃
有後哨亦不

稱雄於族中
昔在家毎自
怒曰汝等平
與人 太祖
大恐觧其甲
孫也見敵兵
人宵剌河之

親桑古哩二
八百餘有扎
直至南山約
於界藩渾河
祖見其兵陣
兵忽至 太
深備不期敵

敗其兵八百
兵二十人遂
重圍混殺敵
勇步射直入
淩噶四人奮
人延布祿武
哈齊並二家

回率弟穆爾
下馬將馬逐
敵兵不動遂
執旗先進見
與人言訖自
故心怯觧甲
今見敵兵何

渡渾河 太
不應敵兵已
太祖怒而
勢可追殺之
至衆曰衆此
後之兵將方
共扣正憩時

不及以手斷
兜鍪遂解甲
息不定卸其
戰酣甚疲喘
走時 太祖
皆涉渾河而
人不能抵當

而待先射
盔纓隱身
見之去其
太祖恐敵
奔此山
十五人來
上見敗兵

吉林立於其
一險隘山名
追至界藩有
與穆爾哈齊
殺四十五人
盔甲率兵追
祖稍息重整

為首一人中其腰仆地穆爾哈齋又射死一人餘皆墜崖而死太祖收兵曰今以四人敗八百衆實天助之也全勝而回○九月內太祖率兵往攻安圖瓜爾佳寨蘇克素護河部所屬破之殺其寨主諾謨琿而回○丙戌年五月內太祖攻克貝歡寨渾河部所屬七月內太祖率兵環

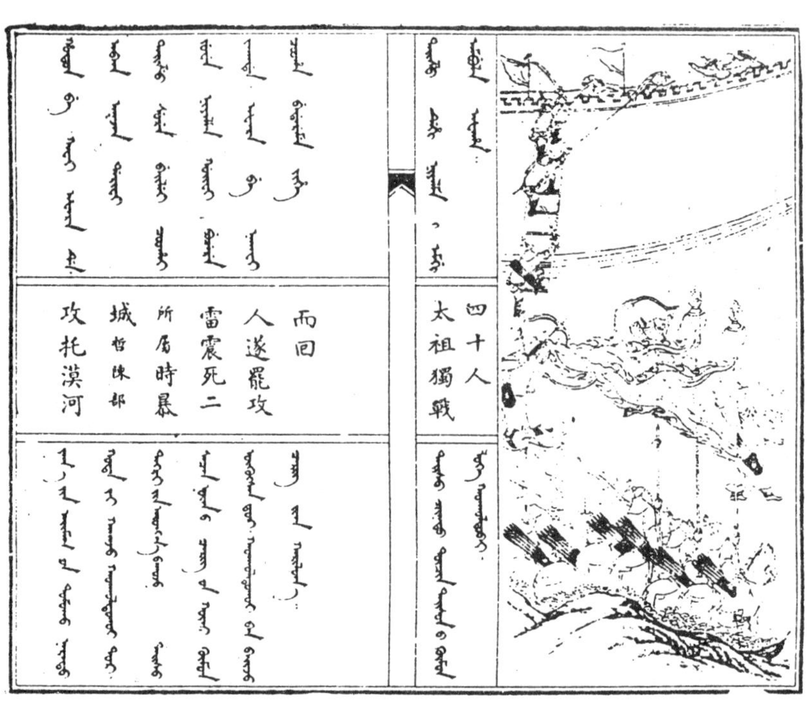
四十人
太祖獨戰

而回
人遂罷攻
雷震死二
所屬時暴
城哲陳部
攻托漠河

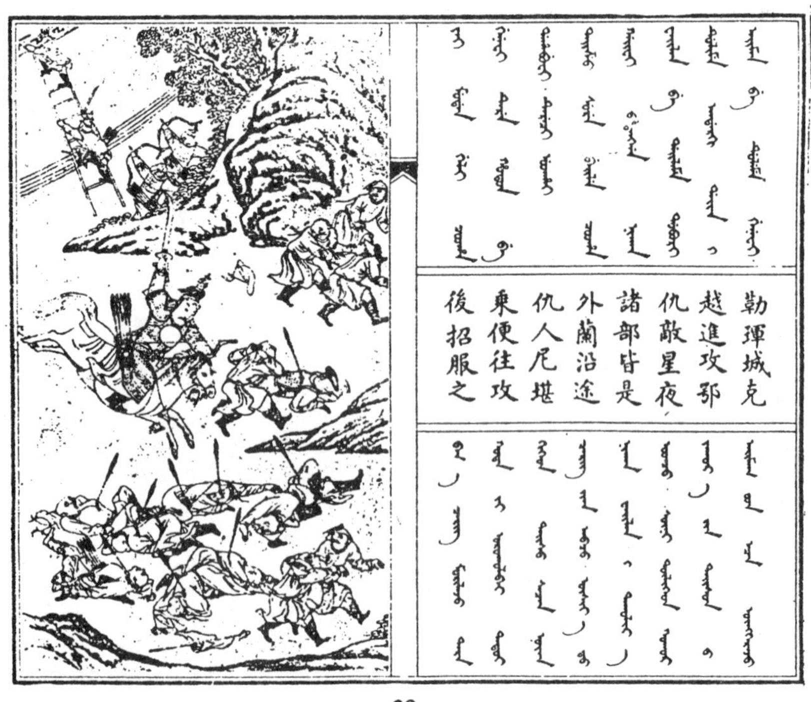
勒琿城克
越進攻鄂
仇敵星夜
諸部皆是
外蘭沿途
仇人尼堪
乘便往攻
後招服之

箭射 太
中内一人
入四十人
蘭單身直
是尼堪外
祖見之疑
氈帽 太
青綿甲戴

首一人穿
子逃走為
進城帶妻
餘人不及
外有四十
城中初城
外蘭不在
之時尼堪

深入其箭
太祖復
傷者六人
又捉中箭
名亦殺之
漢人十九
渾城內有
皆散鄂勒

一人餘衆
八人復斬
奮勇射死
祖不怯猶
十處 太
共中傷三
肩後露鏃
祖胸旁從

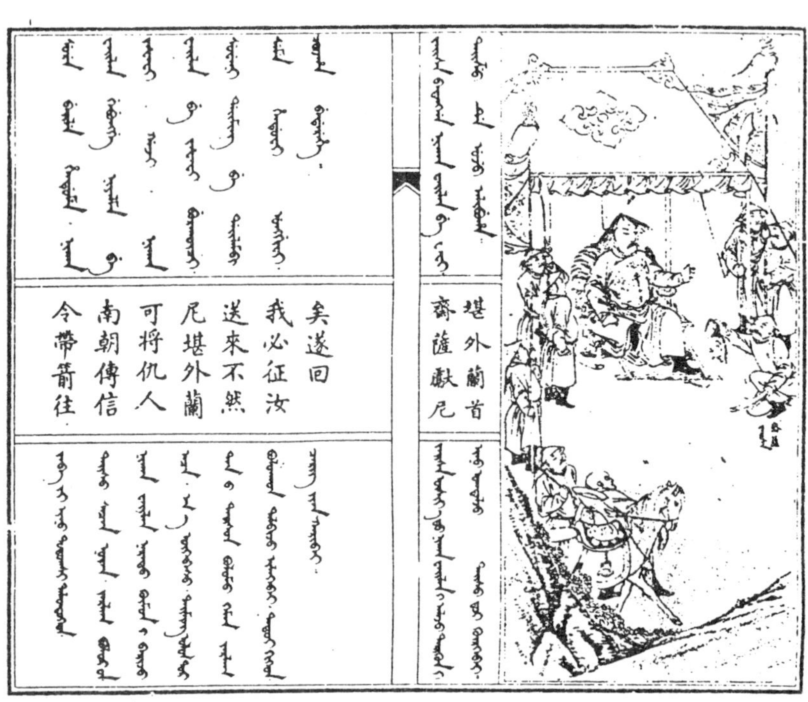

齋薩獻尼堪外蘭首
令帶箭往南朝傳信可将仇人尼堪外蘭送來不然我必征汝矣遂回

明邊吏遣使言尼堪外蘭既入中國豈有送出之理爾可自來殺之 太祖曰汝言不足信莫非誘我入

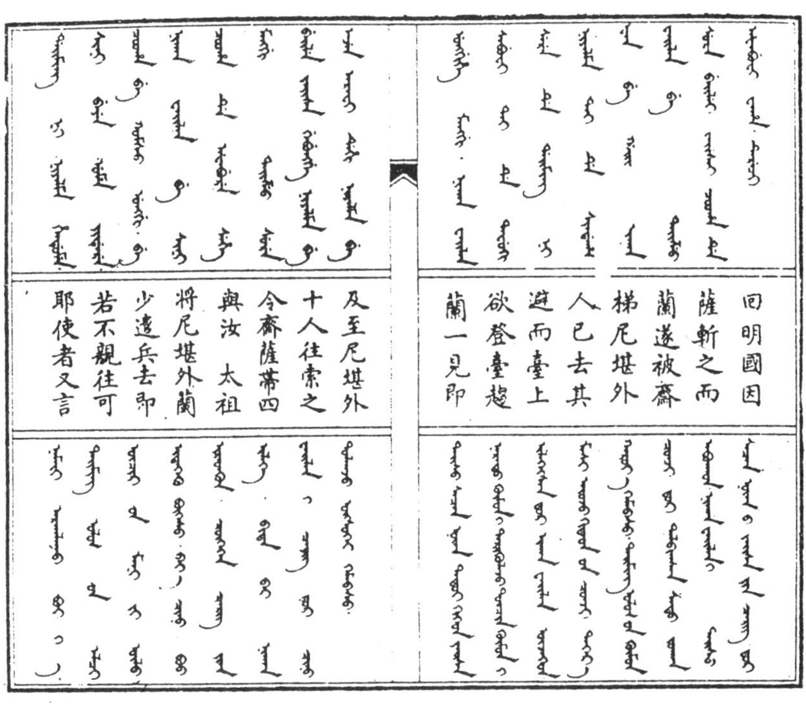

回明國因
薩斬之而
蘭遂被齋
梯尼堪外
人已去其
避而臺上
欲登臺趨
蘭一見即

及至尼堪外
十人往索之
今齋薩帶四
與汝 太祖
將尼堪外蘭
少遣兵去耶
若不親往可
耶使者又言

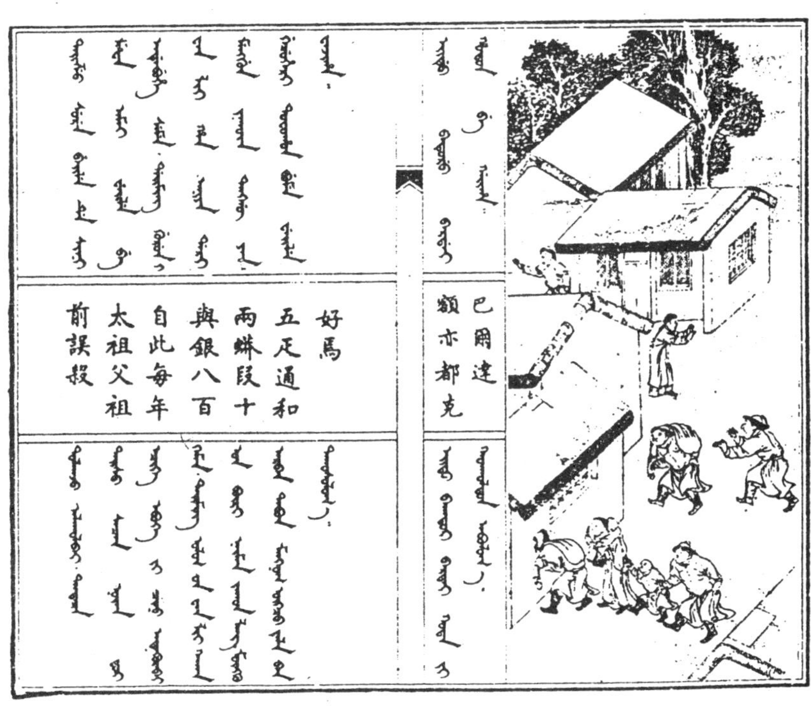

巴爾達
額亦都克

好馬
五疋通和
兩蟒段十
與銀八百
自此每年
太祖父祖
前誤殺

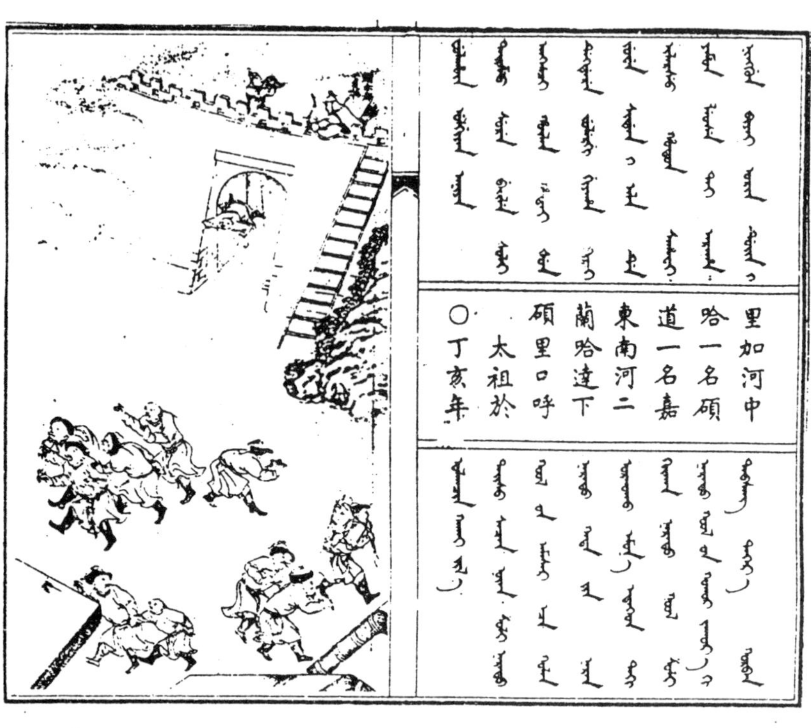

○丁亥年太祖於碩里口呼蘭哈達下東南河二道一名嘉哈一名碩里加河中

一平山築城三層啟建樓臺○六月二十四日定國政凡作亂竊盜欺詐悉行嚴禁

又率兵征哲陳部阿爾泰克其山城殺之○八月內令額亦都巴圖魯領兵取巴爾

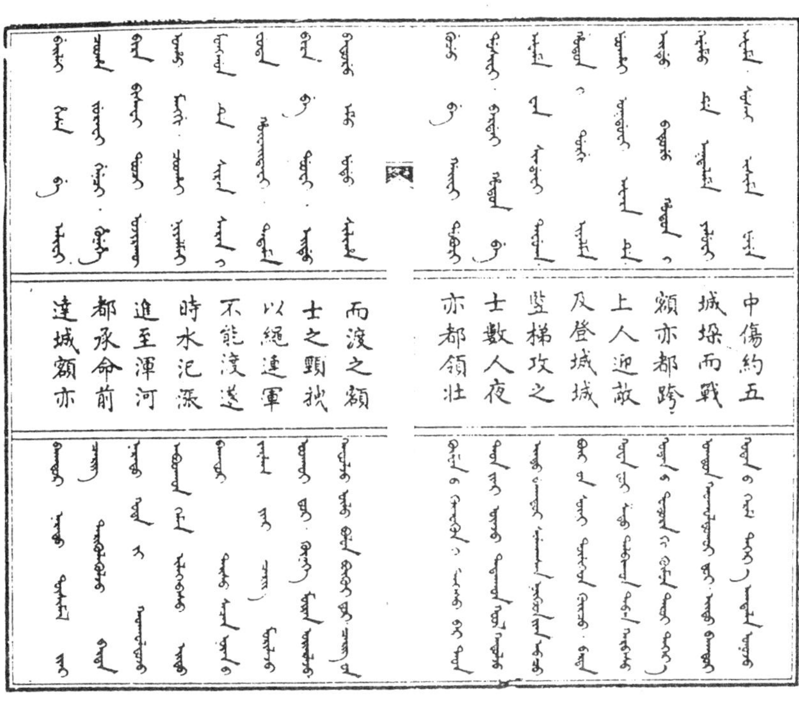
達城額亦
都承命前
進至渾河
時水汜漲
不能渡遂
以繩連軍
士之頸拽
而渡之額
亦都領壯
士數人夜
竪梯攻之
及登城城
上人迎敵
額亦都跨
城垛而戰
中傷約五

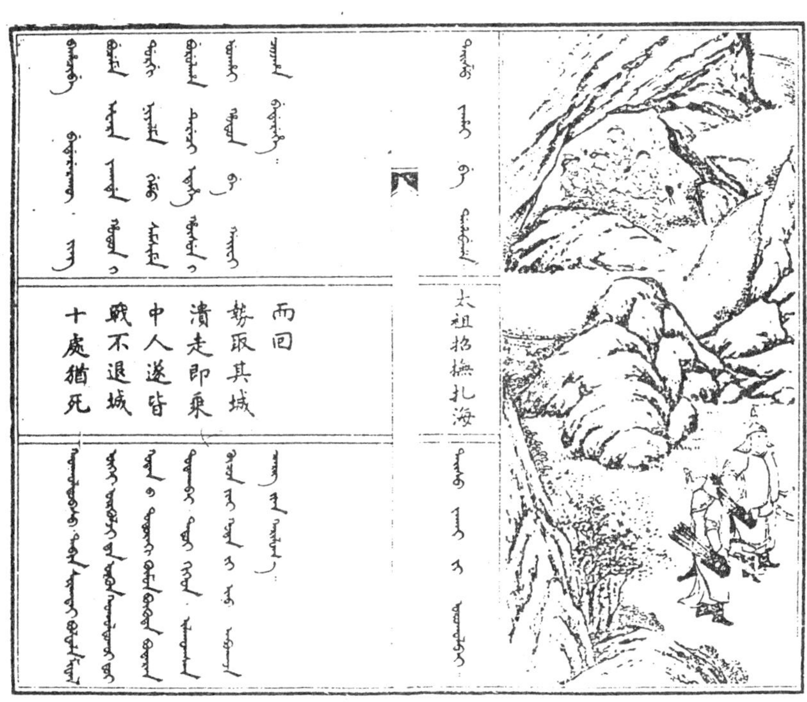
十處猶死
戰不退城
中人遂皆
潰走即乘
勢取其城
而回

太祖招撫扎海

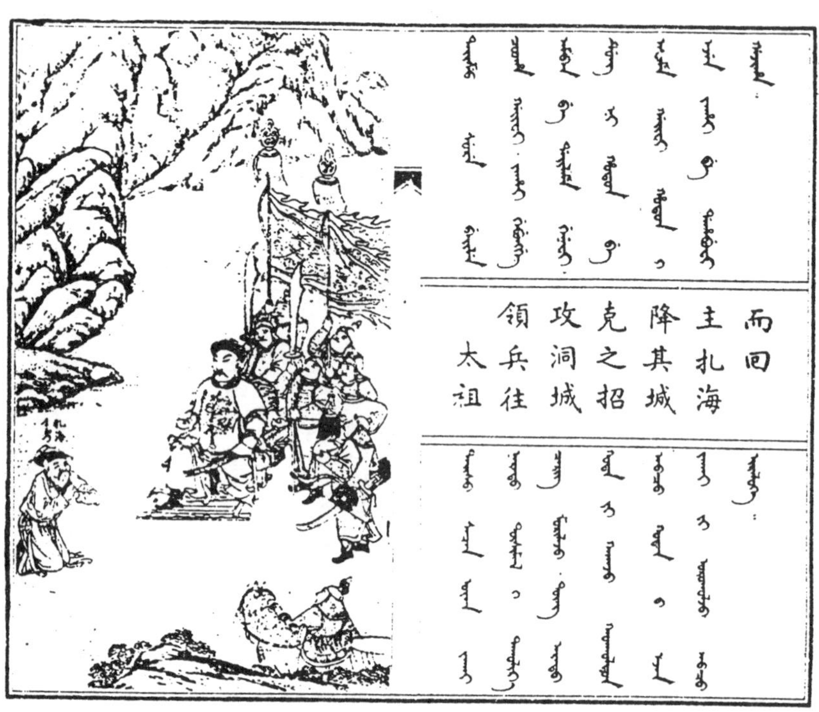

而回
主扎海
降其城
克之招
攻洞城
領兵往
太祖

太祖射柳於洞野

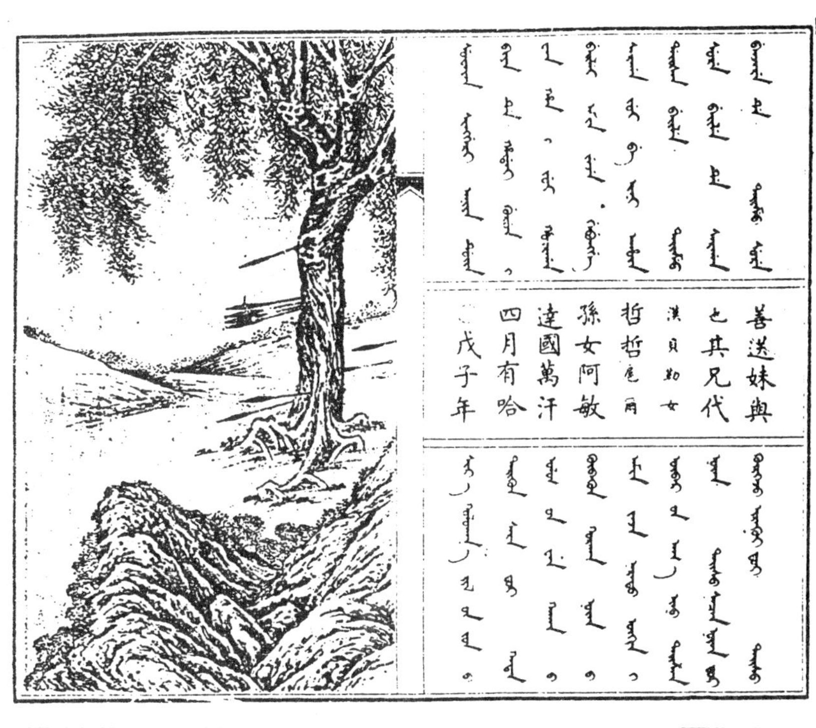

戊子年四月有哈達國萬汗孫女阿敏哲哲扈爾漢貝勒女也其兄代善送妹與

太祖為妃親迎之至於洞地名坐曠野以待時一人乘馬帶弓矢過於前 太祖

訊左右為誰左右對曰棟鄂部人名鈕翁錦善射本部無出其右者 太祖遂令人

喚至時對面一柳相距百餘步令射之鈕翁錦即下馬挽弓射五矢止中三矢上下不一太祖連發五矢皆中矣視之五矢攢於一處相去不過五寸鑿落埋木而五

矢始出代善同妹至太祖設宴成禮遂納之

三部長率眾歸降

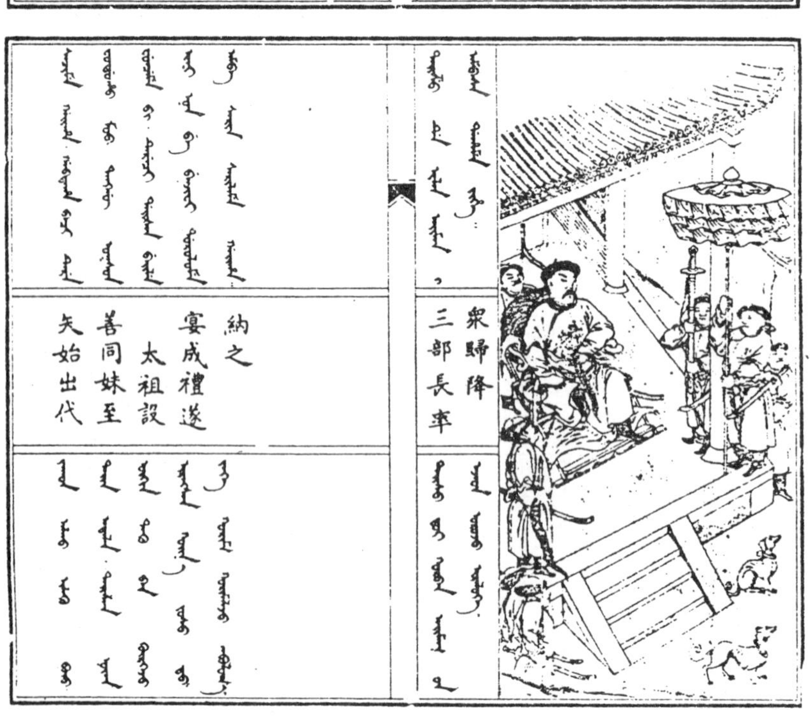

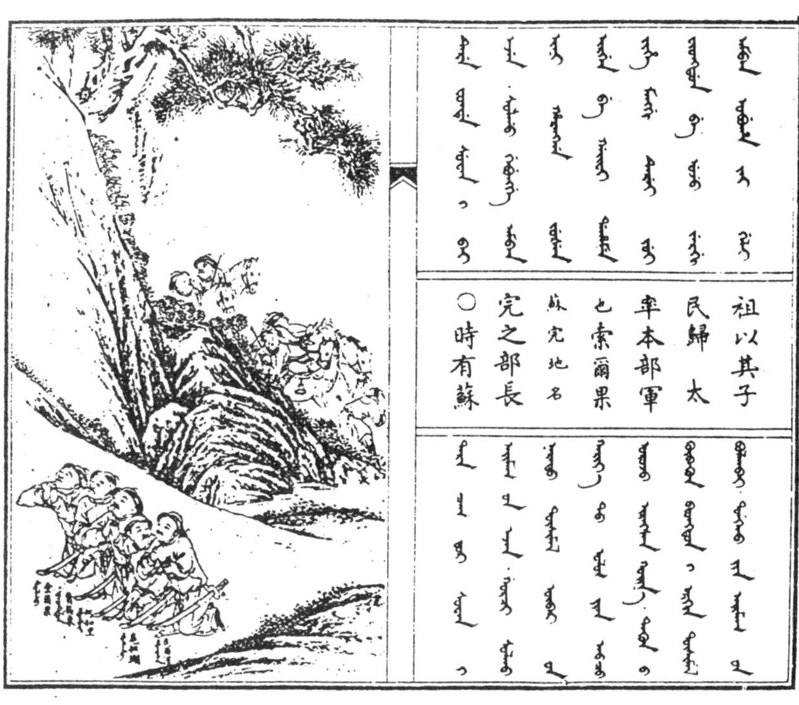

○時有蘇完之部長蘇完地名也索爾果率本部軍民歸 太祖以其子

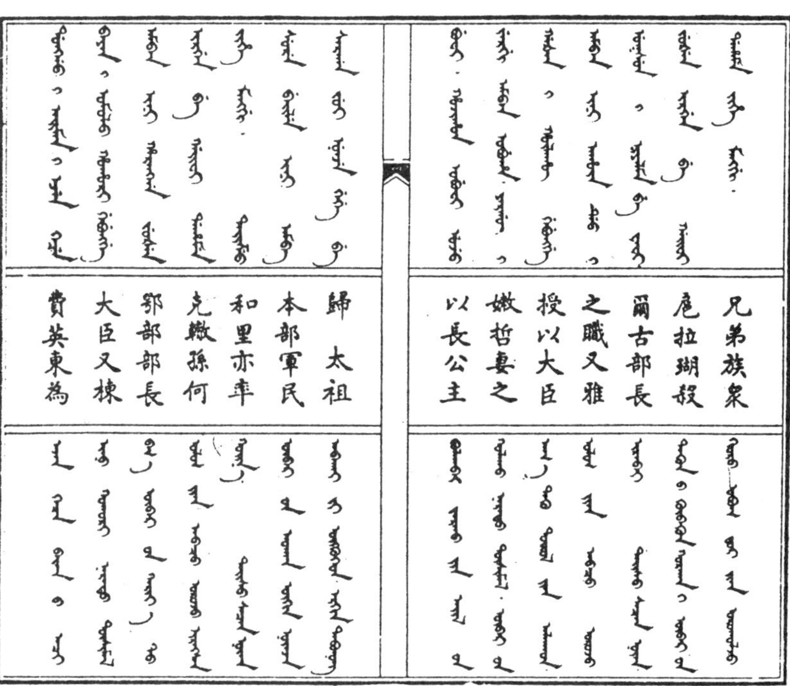

費英東為大臣又棟鄂部部長克徹孫何和里亦率本部軍民歸 太祖以長公主嫩哲妻之授以大臣之職又雅爾古部長扈拉瑚殺兄弟族衆

率軍民來
歸將其子
扈爾漢賜
姓覺羅為
養子亦授
大臣之職
太祖遂

招徠各部
環滿洲而
居者皆為
削平國勢
日盛與明
國通好遣
使往來執

五百道勅
書受年例
金幣本地
所産有明
珠人參黑
狐元狐紅
狐貂鼠猞

狸猻虎豹
海獺水獺
青鼠黃鼠
等皮以備
國用撫順
清河寬甸
靉陽四處

太祖曰若
長締姻
為君配待
有小女堪
非常言我
見其相貌
主揚吉努

葉赫其國
太祖如
國富○初
滿洲民殷
商賈因此
交易以通
關口互市

祿於是年
子納林布
吉努故後
遂聘之揚
耳 太祖
者稱佳偶
貌奇異或

意小女容
恐不可君
長女不與
云我非惜
揚吉努答
聘汝長女
締姻吾願

其大如斗
天隕一星
輿阿地忽
城夕過棟
兵攻完顏
太祖率
母也是年

聰　皇帝
成婚即天
迎之大宴
諸王大臣
太祖率
送妹于歸
九月内親

城大戰
太祖兆佳

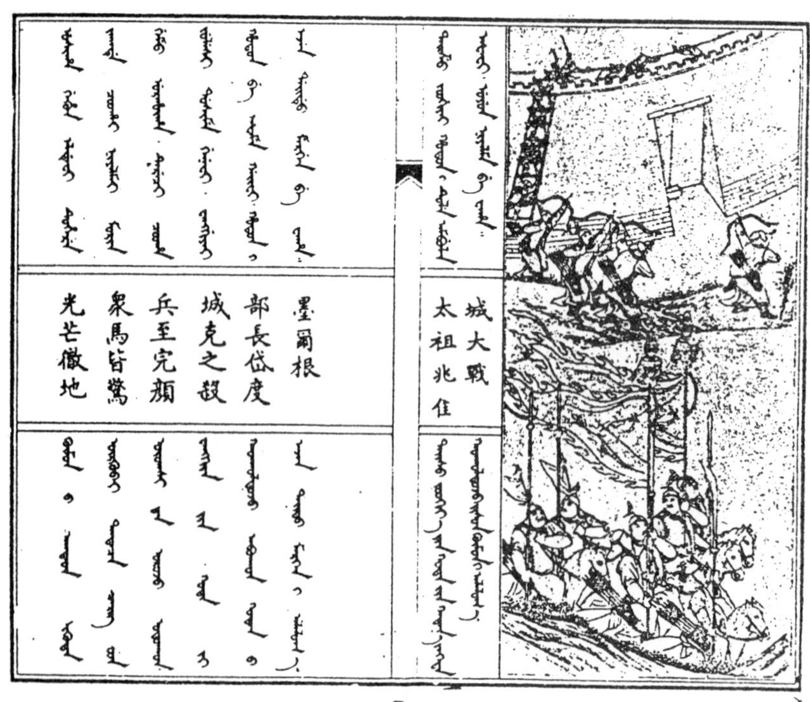

墨爾根
部長岱度
城克之敵
兵至完顏
衆馬皆驚
光芒徹地

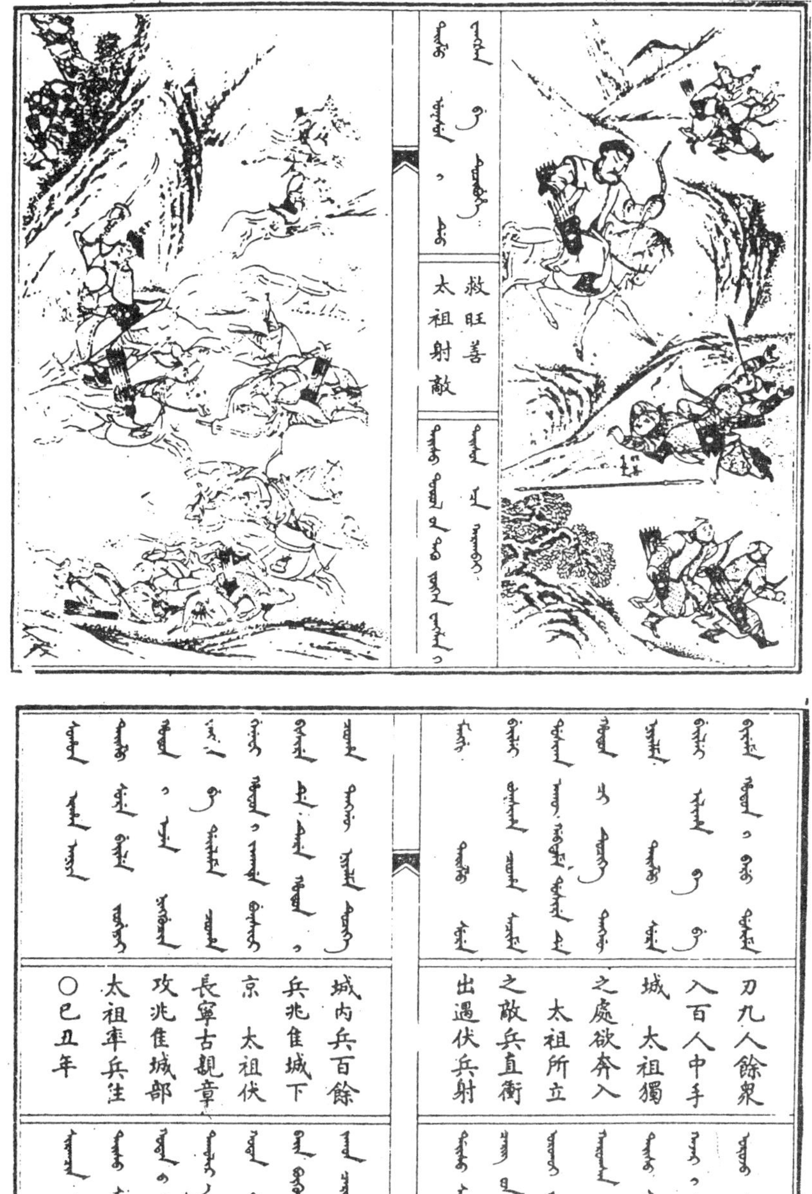

救旺善太祖射敵

○己丑年太祖率兵往攻兆佳城部長寧古親章京太祖伏兵兆佳城下城內兵百餘出遇伏兵射之敵兵直衝太祖所立之處欲奔入城太祖獨入百人中手刀九人餘衆

擄掠亦隨衆
至不禁人之
諭禁之鴉護
相殘害爾往
此微物恐自
護曰我兵爭
甲與大將衆

太祖見之觧
喧嘩爭奪
掠往畜財物
少懈四出擄
城將陷我兵
城圍四日其
四散未得進

一見身無甲
刺之 太祖
其身將以鎗
壓倒於地跨
弟旺善被敵
人突出有族
掠忽城內十

太復隨衆擄
內衝突巴爾
甲來以備城
往取衆護鐵
與巴爾太令
將巴綿甲復
掠之 太祖

勒當阿拜斯祿遣部下伊國主納林布回○時葉赫部盡克之而白山鴨緑江祖遣兵攻長

辛卯年 太古親而回○克其城殺寧死救起旺善面額應弦而發一矢中敵胄涎身馳往

國雖大我不爾乃呼倫爾云我乃滿洲我 太祖答二處擇一讓勒敏扎庫木人寡可將額

國人衆我國五王之理爾一國也豈有輝發滿洲總拉哈達葉赫 太祖曰烏漢二人來謂

赫主納林布
各遣使來葉
發三國會議
葉赫哈達輝
言畢令囘○
顏來相告耶
諫主柰何覥
臣不能竭力
等皆執政之
分給之理爾
畜可比馬有
取況國非牲
大爾亦不得
得取我國雖

太祖曰爾
恐觸怒見責
來言欲言又
主有命遣我
太祖曰我
圖爾德起向
太祖宴之內
拉敏比至
音達哩差阿
輝發國主拜
祿差岱穆布
國主蒙格布
圖爾德哈達
祿差尼喀哩

怒掣刀斷案
太祖聞言大
厲我地耶
境諒爾兵敢
我兵能踐爾
成仇隙只有
不從兩國若
不與今投順
德曰昔索地
惡言往圖爾
言來我亦以
汝如彼以惡
無干何為責
主之言與爾

之易也爾地
故視我如彼
乘亂襲取何
故云云爾等
每擲骨為戲
骨滿洲兒童
亂如二童爭
叔姪自相擾
格布祿代善
一戰耶昔蒙
擱甲冑經此
交馬接刃碎
何嘗覩與人
曰爾主弟兄

四周果有邊垣之阻耶吾即晝不能往夜亦能至彼處爾其奈我何徒張大言胡為乎昔我

父被明國誤殺與我勅書三十道馬三十匹送還靈覲坐受左都督勅書

續封龍虎将軍大勅一道每年輸銀八百兩蟒段十五疋汝父亦被明國

所殺其屍骸汝得收取否遂書前言遣阿林察復之諭之曰爾到彼處當

之何必送書我已知布齋曰此當面朗誦林察將書視其書阿接至家欲

貝勒預知行時布齋我囑畢今處勿復見即住於彼懼而不誦面誦之若

收其書阿也言畢乃書怒責汝但恐見此恨之誠是不避汝主吾弟出言

命布齋曰勒難復主若止見貝二主面誦主曾命對林察曰我與吾弟阿

太祖曰任
而告之
上諸将聞
祖正坐樓
刦去太
所居洞寨
東界葉臣
兵将滿洲
同引葉赫
訥殷二路
屬珠舍哩
長白山所
○時滿洲
林察遂回

有宾
部終為我
哩訥殷二
下流珠舍
寨盖水必
赫刦掠我
異國之葉
乃敢遠附
是我同國
舍里訥殷
河之理珠
山火能踰
有水能透
伊刦去豈

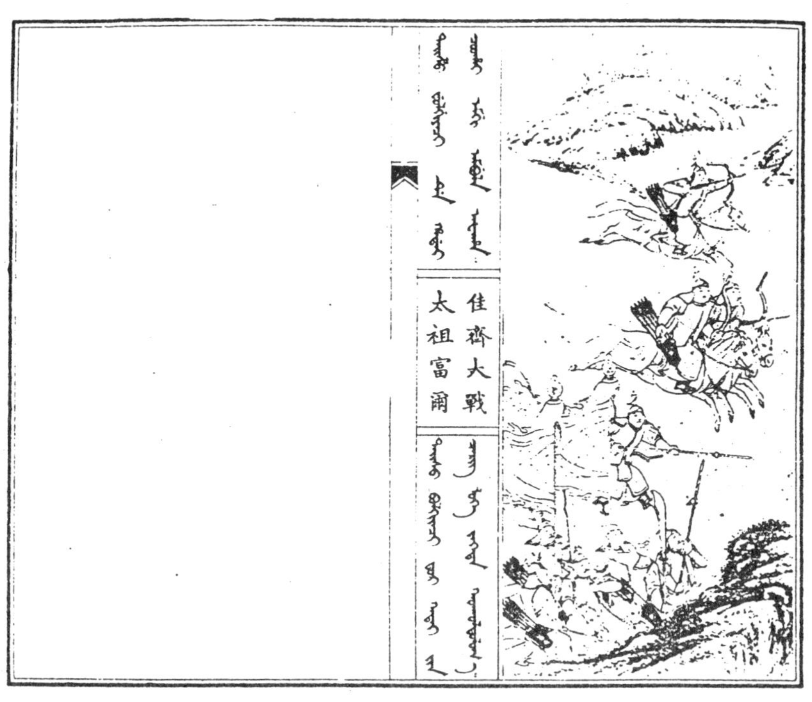

太祖富爾佳齊大戰

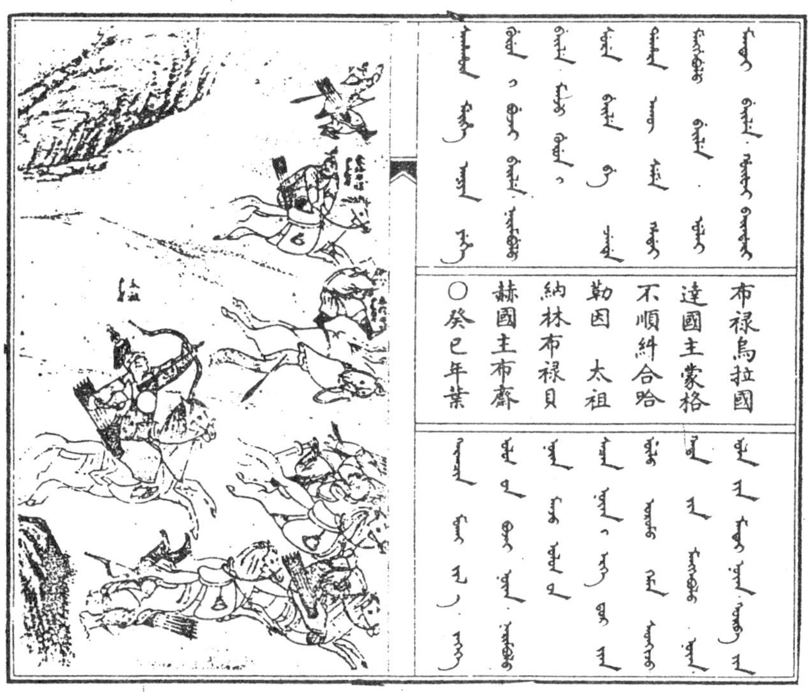

○癸巳年葉赫國主布齋納林布祿貝勒因太祖不順糾合哈達國主蒙格布祿烏拉國

兵從亦取
中途少帶
步兵伏於
太祖以
其國是夜
我兵直抵
達兵已歸

兵追之時哈
太祖即率
去瑚卜察寨
於六月内劫
哩四國兵馬
國主拜音達
主滿泰輝發

兵追至前
之於是敵
為殿以誘
前行獨身
回乃令兵
恐追兵復
至伏兵處

祖欲誘敵
齊寨　太
至富爾佳
達國追兵
而回時哈
爾佳齊寨
哈達國富

馬首射中
因轉弓過
不便於射
時敵在右
目欲射之
來恐傷面
人迎面劈

妨若前一
者三人無
自思後追
戰 太祖
人併馬來
迎之後三
一人舉刀

人泰穆布
什地其家
格布祿馬
一矢射蒙
得復騎發
足振鞍僅
幾墜幸右

太祖馬驚
齊殺來
矢之會一
太祖發
後三人乘
其馬驚躍
敵人馬腹

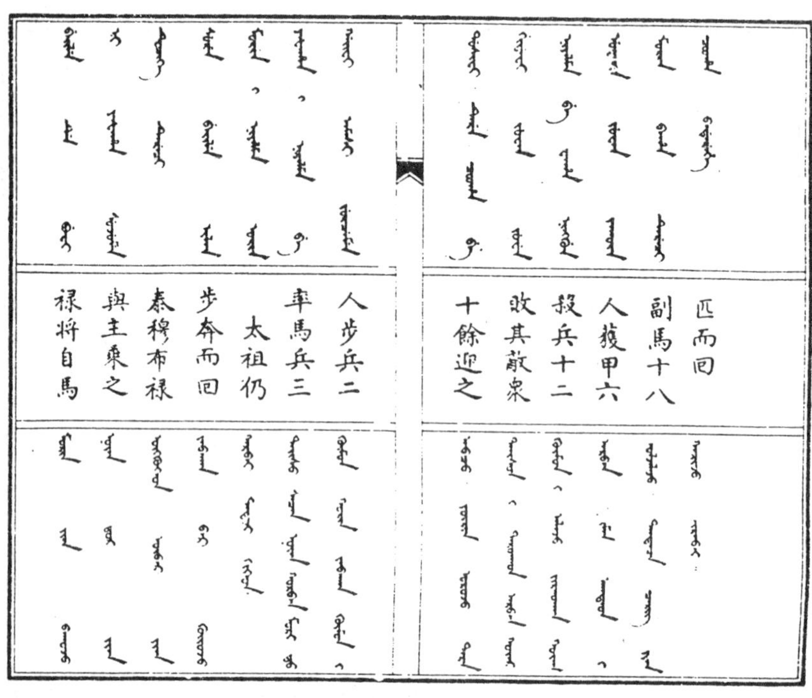

祿將自馬與主乘之泰穆布祿步奔而回太祖仍牽馬兵三人步兵二十餘迎之敗其敵衆殺兵十二人獲甲六副馬十八匹而回

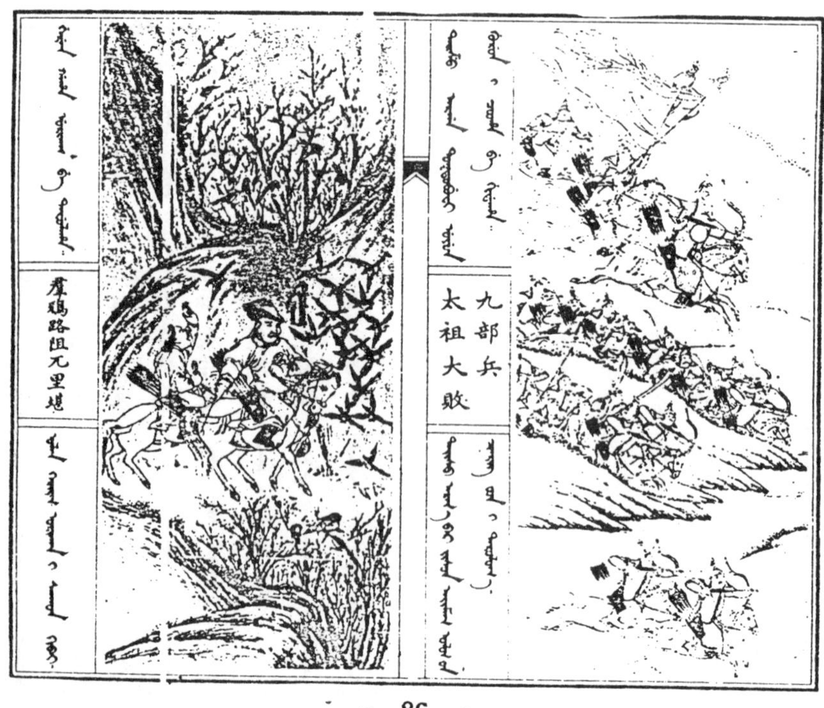

烏鴉路阻兀里堪

太祖大敗九部兵

布占泰
太祖恩養

卦勒察部
安錫伯部
俉莽古明
國主翁阿
古科爾沁
哩嫩河蒙
主拜音達

非也輝發國
布占泰滿泰
布祿烏拉國
達國主蒙格
納林布祿哈
赫國主布齋
○九月内葉

噪不容前
嶺烏鴉羣
里至一山
探約行百
兀里堪東
祖聞之遣
而來 太

處分三路
馬會聚一
什九國兵
搜穩塞克
訥殷路主
主裕楞額
珠舍哩路

行過沙濟
飯罷卽起
火如星密
岸敵兵營
兀渾河北
之及至夕
向渾河探

可從扎喀
 太祖曰
備述前事
里堪遂回
鴉撲面兀
散再往羣
往回時則

嶺兀里堪
探的飛報
太祖言
敵國大兵
將至時近
五更矣
太祖曰人

言業赫國
不日兵來
今果然也
我兵夜出
恐城中人
驚待天明
出兵傳諭

諸將言畢
復寢袞代
皇后推醒
太祖曰
今九國兵
馬來攻何
故此睡是

昏昧耶抑
畏懼耶
太祖曰畏
敵者必不
安枕我不
畏彼故熟
睡耳前聞

無故糾合
我安分反
土彼不樂
命各守國
之我承天
我我當畏
處天必罪

若有欺騙
心始定我
日已到我
心不安今
期未的我
路侵我來
葉赫兵三

赫本無事
[illegible]與葉
祇我[illegible]
光萬靈神
曰天地三
廟再拜祝
王大臣謁

飯畢率諸
精神天明
復睡以息
佑之言訖
之人天豈
欺害無辜
九部之兵

等可盡解
諭之曰爾
於津渡處
克索寨立
率兵至拖
蹬叩祝畢
鞭馬無顛

揚兵不遺
首祐我奮
天令敵垂
拜祝曰願
天鑒察又
兵攻我惟
故令彼引

坦來告曰
守鴉護山
喀處有城
之行至扎
遵令盡解
全勝矣衆
輕便必獲

勝敵我兵
拘束難以
不然身受
唯命是聽
傷肱傷頸
留於此若
臂手頸項

何言訖登
兵見有幾
勒何在我
至呼曰貝
郎塔哩後
喀一人名
失色有扎

甚多衆皆
格城敵兵
往攻赫濟
勢不能克
扎喀關見
時已到圍
葉赫兵辰

此兵若不
驍勇必敗
兵有膽氣
其衆令我
三百尚敗
野我兵二
兵漫山遍

國交戰彼
少昔與明
我兵亦不
來兵為多
祖曰若以
勢向 太
山望敵形

安營是晚
太祖亦
搬運糧草
扎立營寨
探報敵兵
日再戰哨
之否則明

今晚即擊
兵若欲回
往探曰來
太祖遣人
心稍安
法於是衆
勝我甘軍

科爾沁翁
一萬蒙古
哩貝勒兵
發拜音達
泰貝勒輝
烏拉布占
布祿貝勒

哈達蒙格
勒兵一萬
林布祿貝
齋貝勒納
曰葉赫布
一人逃來
葉赫營中

立險要之
於苦戰吾
使汝等至
無憂我不
祖曰爾衆
失色 太
聞之又皆

三萬我兵
一萬共兵
卦勒察兵
勒錫伯部
勒明安貝
莽古斯貝
阿岱貝勒

前進者必
不前領兵
之衆退縮
諒此烏合
雜亂不一
部長甚多
進攻來兵

分列徐徐
步行四面
不來吾等
敵之誘而
時吾迎而
戰彼若來
處誘彼來

攻時太
下是日又
潞格城未
兵先攻赫
起兵葉赫
次日平明
可必勝矣

併力一戰
我兵雖少
彼兵自走
一二頭目
之但傷其
等即接戰
頭目也吾

之遂不攻
戰葉赫見
兵一百挑
額亦都領
陣已完遣
頭預備布
固山兵分

臣等各率
令諸王大
格城相對
處與赫潞
山險要之
陣於古埒
祖兵到立

洲一卒名
撞倒有滿
之馬被木
先入所騎
處時布齋
兵合攻一
三貝勒領

及科爾沁
齋錦台什
稍退有布
人葉赫兵
一戰殺九
敵滿洲兵
城收兵來

棄鞍赤身
安馬被陷
散而走明
顧其兵四
喪膽各不
大懼並皆
來自勒等

痛哭其同
齋被殺皆
勒等見布
敗葉赫貝
之其兵大
前騎而殺
武談即向

占泰跪見
人生擒布
衆次日一
殺敗兵甚
結繩攔路
之處是夜
南渥黑運

國栄河寨
殺至哈達
屍滿溝渠
縱兵掩殺
出 太祖
騎騾馬脫
體無片衣

泰之弟布
烏拉國滿
明言我乃
畏殺未敢
首答曰我
也其人叩
曰爾何人

太祖問
因此縛來
許與贖背
自呼毋殺
欲殺之彼
我得此人
太祖曰

肯殺汝語
既來見豈
必殺矣今
若得汝亦
殺死彼時
布齋已經
汝等昨日

無辜天厭
之兵欺害
等會九部
太祖曰汝
在目勒
擒生死只
占泰今被

初珠舍哩
名大震○
洲自此威
甲千副滿
三千匹盔
四千獲馬
也殺其兵

養之是戰
捨狸猻裘
釋其縛賜
勝於取遂
與人之名
名勝於殺
云生人之

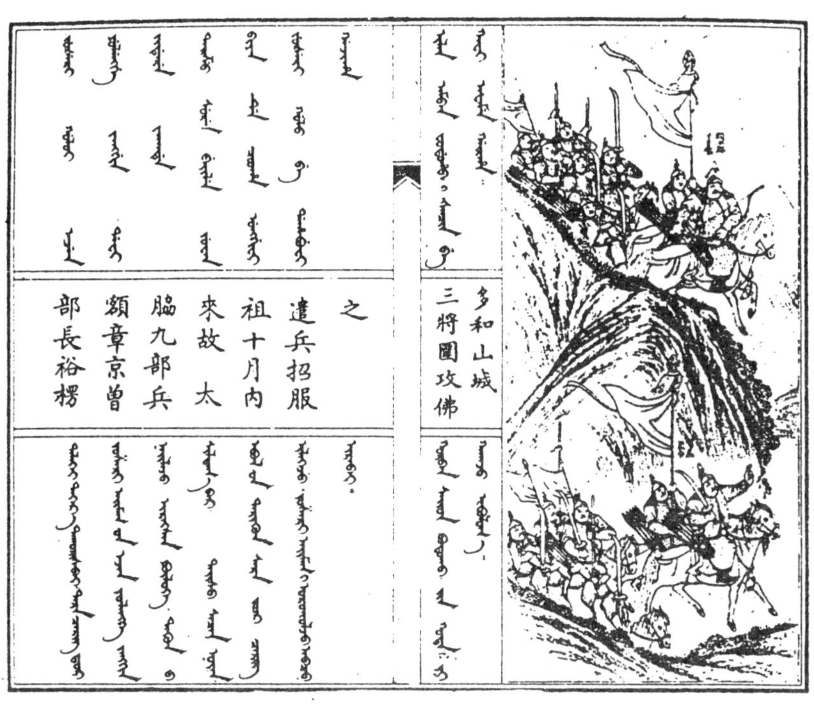

三將圍攻佛多和山城

部長裕楞額章京曾腦九部兵來故太祖十月內遣兵招服之

〇又訥殷部
搜穩塞克什
二人眾七村
人據佛多和
山而居 太
祖於閏十一
月命額亦都
噶蓋扎爾
固齊碩翁
科羅三人
領兵一千
圍佛多和
山日往攻
擊三月丙

下斬搜穩
塞克什即
日回兵〇
甲午年蒙
古科爾沁
部明安貝
勒喀爾喀
部勞薩貝
勒始遣使
往來於是
蒙古各部
長遣使往
來不絕

人來 太祖
從者共二百
亦遣官二員
一員高麗國
内明國遣官
丙申年二月
二人而回○

充格蘇蒙格
城斬守將克
勒克取多壁
拜晋達哩貝
兵伐輝發部
月 太祖領
○乙未年六

護送未至其
斐揚古二人
煌占博爾坤
歸令圖爾坤
太祖欲放
載至是七月
占泰恩養四

陣中所擒布
別而去○先
待公事畢辭
大城以禮相
科地界接入
親迎至妙洪
令部兵盡甲

奪其位其護
殺布占泰欲
尼雅貝勒謀
滿泰叔父興
布占泰至日
父子殺之及
夜入將滿泰

內二婦其夫
父子淫其村
處修邊鑿壞
蘇斡延錫蘭
二人往所屬
兄滿泰父子
國時布占泰

太祖弟舒
將妹滹奈送
生恩猶父子
太祖二次再
布占泰感
辭回十二月
主護送二人

位為烏拉國
占泰遂繼兄
業赫而去布
是興尼雅投
不能加害於
守門戶甚嚴
送二大臣保

太祖為妃錦
古妹欲與
是葉赫布揚
互相結親於
等更守前好
名今以後吾
至於敗兵損

吾等不道以
同遣使曰因
拉哈達輝發
酉年葉赫烏
宴成配○丁
為妻即日設
爾哈齊貝勒

此以後若不
繼而誓曰自
會盟四國相
各一碗歃血
肉一碗血土
骨設酒一盃
宴宰白馬削

禮更殺牛設
等物以為聘
備鞍馬盔甲
妻 太祖乃
代善貝勒為
太祖次子
台什女欲與

結親和好似此屠牲之血蹂踏之土剮削之骨而死如踐盟和好食此肉飲此血福壽永昌

誓畢 太祖亦誓曰汝等應此盟言則已不然吾待三年果不相好必統兵伐之後蒙古得

罷 太祖命穆哈連伐之獲馬四十匹時納林布祿背盟将所獲盡奪之仍擒穆哈連送與

蒙古又将錦台什之女與蒙古喀爾喀部齋賽貝勒結親其布占泰亦因

努三人許什屯旺吉長羅屯噶河二處路楚拉庫内喀部内安所屬瓦爾

又將滿洲納林布祿遣使送與所珍銅鎚都都祜氏將滿泰妻與葉赫通

庫星夜馳征安楚拉領兵一千爾固齊等費英東扎吉與噶蓋子褚英台

喇台吉長幼弟巴雅 太祖命戊年正月服之〇戊其使而招獻葉赫請

貝勒所居
蒙格布祿
是年哈達
禮克圖〇
台吉名卓
魯巴雅喇
名洪巴圖

褚英台吉
回於是賜
畜萬餘而
服之獲人
其餘盡招
寨二十處
至取其屯

往送
十道以禮
十副勅書
之盔甲五
額實泰妻
齊貝勒女
弟舒爾哈

太祖以
三百來謁
恩帶從者
泰不忘其
二月布占
自渓流十
城北有血

王格張格來貢

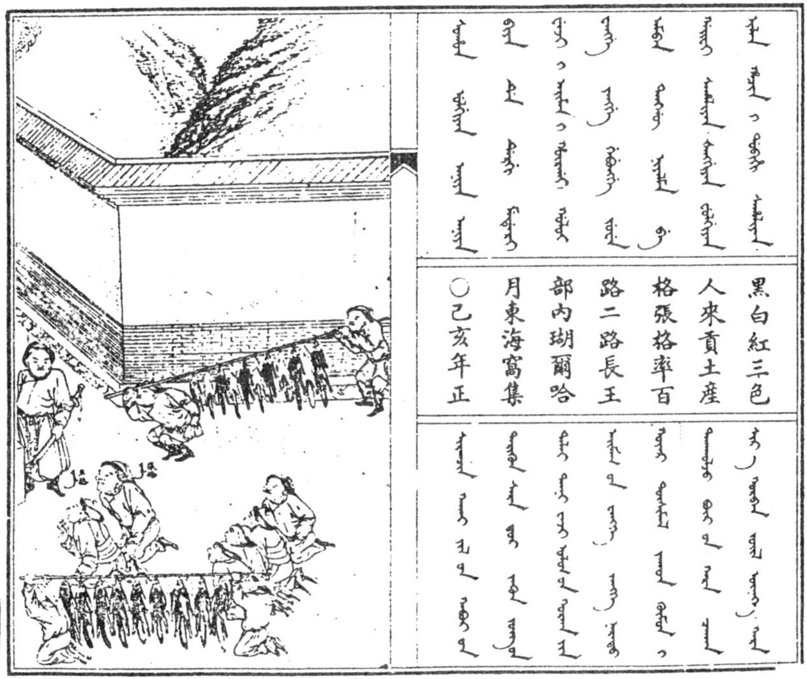

○己亥年正月東海窩集部內瑚爾哈路二路長王格張格率百人來貢土產黑白紅三色

習蒙古書譯
移往來必須
未有文字文
其心時滿洲
女配之以撫
以六大臣之
乞婚 太祖

濟哩等六人
其中路長博
人每歲入貢
部内所居之
寫集瑚爾哈
色貂皮自此
狐皮黑白二

與不學者皆
人念漢字學
太祖曰漢
我等實不能
語編創譯書
語若以我國
字始知蒙古

我等習蒙古
尼嚕蓋對曰
克什額爾德
編成國語巴
欲以蒙古字
二月 太祖
蒙古語通之

知蒙古之人念蒙古字學與不學者亦皆知我國之言寫蒙古之字則不習蒙古語者不能知矣何汝等以本國言語編字為難以習他國之言為易耶噶蓋額爾德尼對曰以我國之言編成文字最善但因翻編成句吾等不能故難耳太祖曰寫阿字下合一瑪字此非阿瑪乎阿瑪父也額字下合一默字此非額默乎額默母也吾意決矣爾等試寫可也於是自

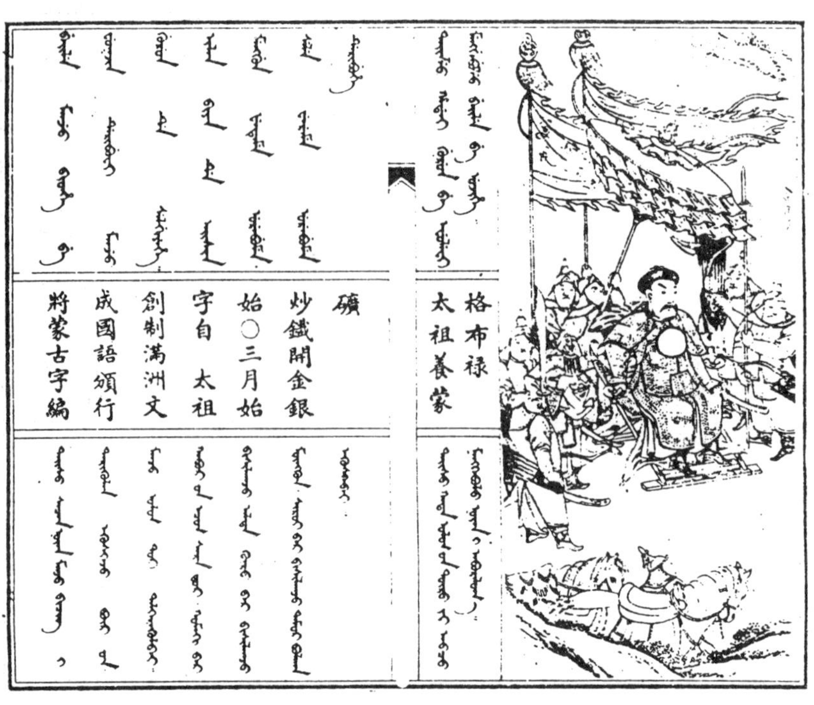

將蒙古字編
成國語頒行
創制滿洲文
字自 太祖
始〇三月始
炒鐵開金銀
礦

太祖養蒙
格布祿

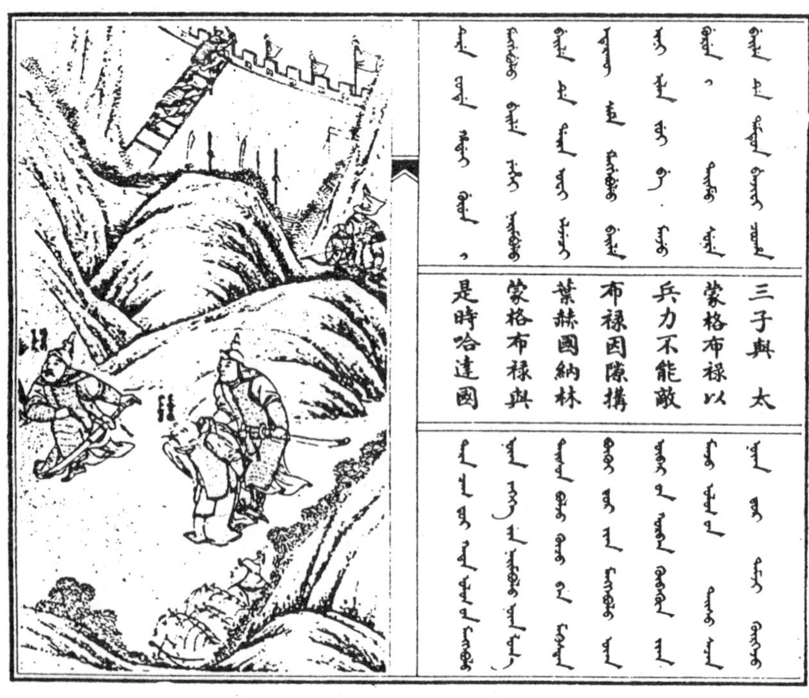

是時哈達國
蒙格布祿與
葉赫國納林
布祿因隙搆
兵力不能敵
蒙格布祿以
三子與 太

所欲之女吾
如此汝昔日
子盡殺其兵
之將挟贖質
執滿洲來援
格布祿曰汝
事齋書與蒙

明之開原通
祿聞之遂令
往助納林布
人領兵二千
英東噶蓋二
太祖命費
祖為質乞援

命領兵一千
若何 太祖
為先鋒試看
勒曰可令我
舒爾哈齊貝
達 太祖弟
月發兵征哈

太祖聞之九
二妻往議
人於開原令
依言約葉赫
好蒙格布祿
二國仍舊和
即與之為妻

爾哈齊貝勒
欲前進時舒
汝兵向後即
哈齊貝勒曰
耶怒叱舒爾
為城中無備
祖曰此來豈
城迎敵 太
祖曰有兵出
不戰向 太
爾哈齊按兵
出城拒之舒
達國哈達兵
前進行至哈

養之哈達國
及豹裘賜而
以己之貂帽
見畢 太祖
殺召至前跪
太祖曰勿
格布祿來報
揚古利擒蒙
其城有大臣
初七日攻得
傷者甚多至
上發矢軍中
遶城而行城
兵尚阻路遂

所屬之城盡
招服之其軍
士跪械民間
財物父母妻
子俱秋毫無
犯盡收其國
而回自此哈
達國遂亡後
太祖欲以
女與蒙格布
禄為妻放還
其國適蒙格
布禄淫惡不
法又與嗜盖
通謀欲篡位
事洩蒙格布
禄嗜盖與通
姦女俱伏誅
○辛丑年正
月 太祖將
莽古吉公主
與蒙格布禄
子武爾古岱
為妻明萬歷
帝不喜使人
來告曰汝何
故破哈達擄
其人民令可

侬還國矣
令武爾古
吾已從命
萬歷帝曰
太祖告明
侵哈達
蒙古兵頻

納林布禄率
而還後葉赫
侬帶其人民
仍令武爾古
乃勉從其言
復國 太祖
令武爾古侬

奴僕牲畜
各以妻子
祈糧不與
之開原城
無食向明
國饑人皆
聽時哈達

萬歷帝不
於葉赫明
之國受制
以吾所獲
侵掠何故
率兵屢次
令葉赫國

易而食之
太祖見
此流離仍
復收回〇
是年 太
祖將所聚
之衆每三
百人内立
一牛录額
真管屬前
此凡遇行
師出獵不
論人之多
寡照依族

寨而行滿
洲人出獵
開圍之際
各出箭一
枝十人中
立一總領
屬九人而
行各照方
向不許錯
亂此總領
呼為牛录
漢語大箭
額真額真
漢語主也

聘葉赫布
布占泰先
宴成婚(一)
禮迎之大
太祖以
太祖為妃
巴海與
之女名阿
泰送滿泰
拉國布占
一月內烏
宮名〇十
录額真為
於是以牛

明安受其
備為聘禮
匹鞍韂俱
六隻馬十
十兩駱駝
領金銀各
領羊裘十
猻裘共十
貂裘猞狸
盔甲十副
安之女以
科爾沁明
又聘蒙古
齋之女後

曾以幣物
經岳太知
妻我前未
國主以女
令為烏拉
中留養之
擒我於陣

太祖曰昔
使求於
之女送遣
聘 太祖
耻之仍欲
與布占泰
禮食言不

哲至癸卯
勒女娥恩
爾哈齊貝
又以弟舒
太祖允之
相往來
結一親遇

告之罪再
若宥我不
丈既恩我
而悔親岳
蒙古受禮
蒙古之女
聘葉赫并

牢牛羊三
築城居住
乃祖居也
二河之間
素護加哈
拉在撫克
處赫圖阿
赫圖阿拉
南崗移於
呼蘭哈達
太祖從
為婚○後
以禮往送
年遣大臣

舅前掠我
未獲罪於
太祖曰我
南太來
止令家人
布祿阻之
后兄納林
葉赫往請
祖遣人至
一會 太
疾篤思母
中宮皇后
役○是年
次犒賞夫

前盟將我
汝葉赫背
天盟誓今
白馬已當
相結親牢
非各許互
曾自任其

加兵侵我
輝發因前
哈達烏拉
我汝葉赫
國兵來侵
後復率九
户布察寨

城汝地曰
國我將築
家已成敵
自今後兩
何必諱言
既如此我
我斷好矣

相會是與
見汝不容
際欲毋一
篤永訣之
今爾妹病
另與蒙古
所聘之女

為仇殺言諡令南太回〇九月内中宮皇后薨后姓納喇名孟古哲哲乃

葉赫國揚吉努貝勒之女年十四適太祖其面如滿月儀範端淑器量

寬洪莊重恭儉聰穎柔順見逆迎而心不喜聞惡言而色不變口無惡言

耳無妄聽不悅委曲讒佞輩適合太祖之心始終如一毫無過失太

祖深為悼惜將四婢殉之宰牛馬各一百致祭齋戒月餘日夜思念痛泣不已將靈停於院内三載方葬於尼雅滿山於是太祖恨葉赫不令母

子相會之仇遂於甲辰年正月初八日率兵往攻十一日至葉赫國二城一曰璋一曰阿奇蘭俱克之收二城七寨人畜二千餘即班師○乙巳年

太祖欲煑
又甚廉
急售之價
難以耐久
人恐水參
濕推延國
潤明人嫌
國以水浸
責參與明
五次曩時
犒賞夫役
郭窜牛羊
外復築大
三月於城

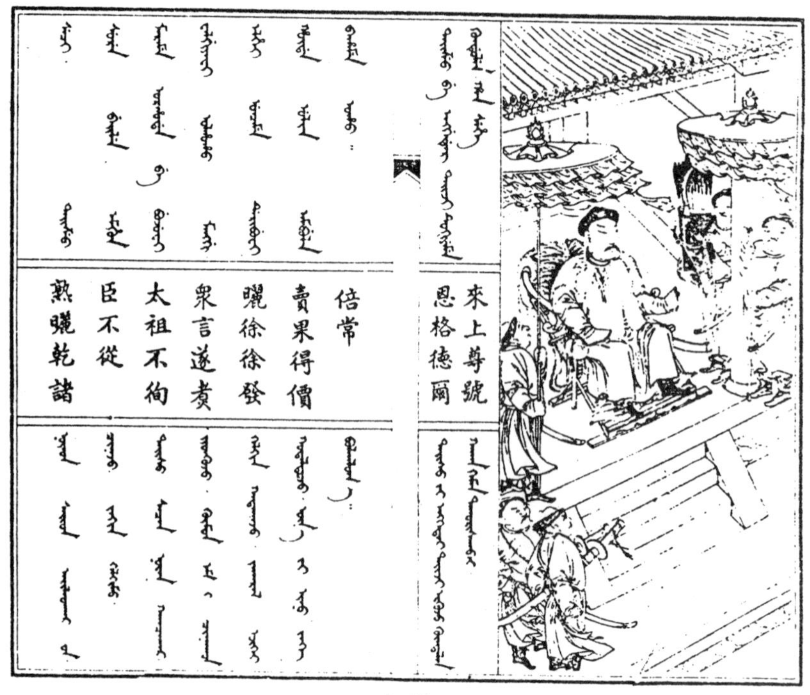

來上尊號
恩格德爾
倍常
責果得價
曬徐徐發
衆言遂煑
太祖不徇
臣不從
熟曬乾諸

〇是年蒙古喀爾喀巴約特部達爾漢貝勒之子恩格德爾台吉進馬二十四來謁 太祖

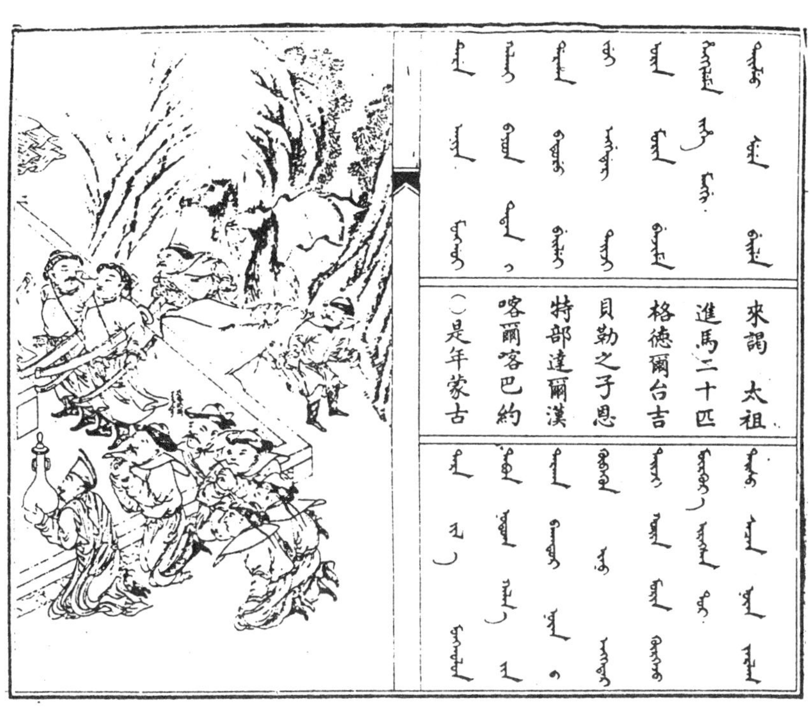

曰越敵國而來者不過有所希圖而巳遂厚賞之〇丙午年十二月恩格德爾又引蒙古喀

爾喀部五貝勒之使進駝馬來謁尊 太祖為崑都侖汗即漢語恭敬之

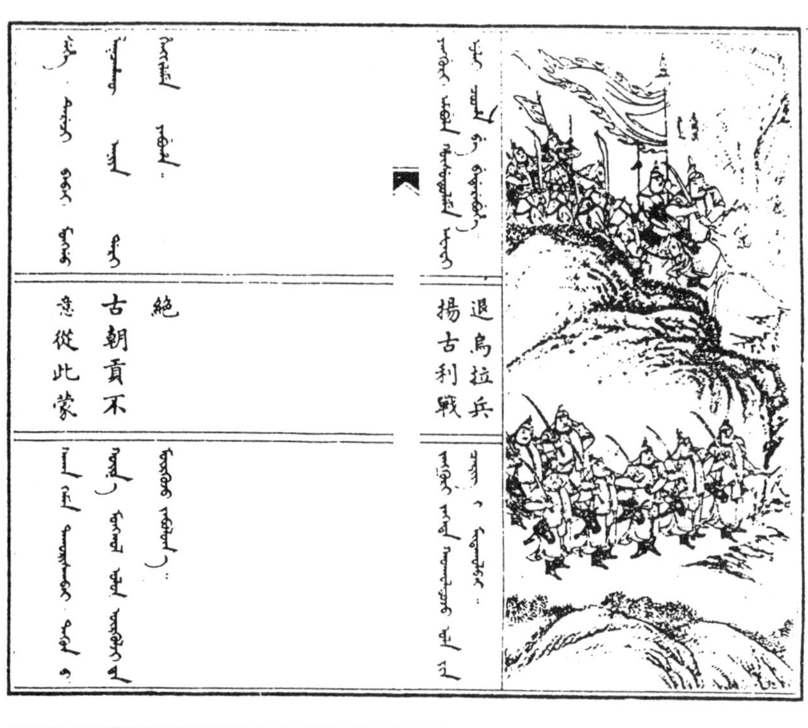

退烏拉兵
揚古利戰

絶
古朝貢不
意從此蒙

貝勒敗烏拉兵
洪巴圖魯代善

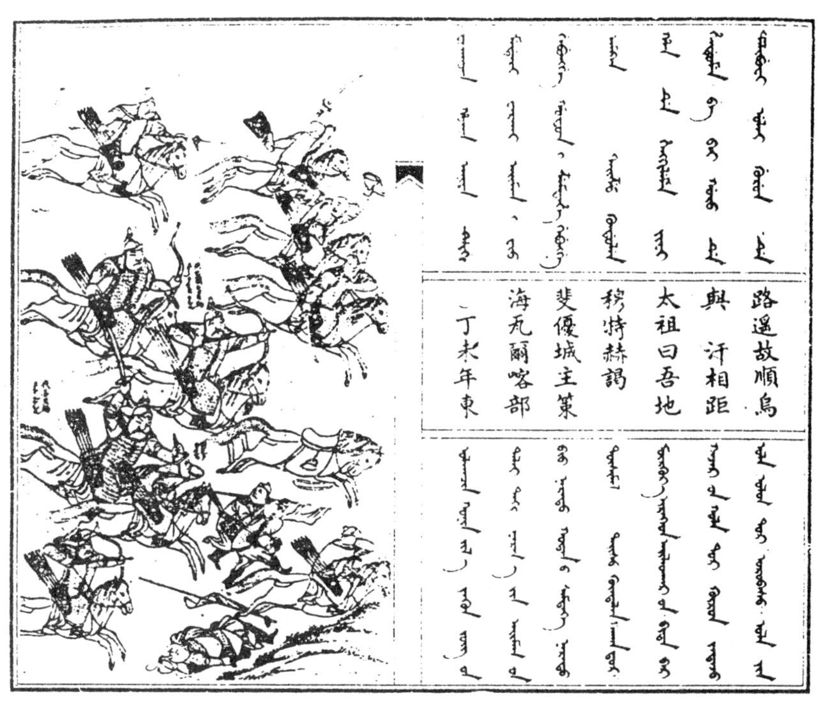

丁未年東海瓦爾喀部斐優城主策穆特赫謂太祖曰吾地與汗相距路遥故順烏

拉國主布占泰貝勒彼甚苦虐吾輩望往接吾等眷屬以便來歸太祖令弟舒爾哈齊與長子洪巴圖魯貝勒次子代善貝勒與大將費英東扈爾漢等率兵三千往斐優城搬接是

夜陰晦忽見旗有白光一耀衆王大臣盡皆驚異以手摩之竟無所有駐之復然舒爾哈齊貝勒曰吾自幼隨征無處不到從未見此奇怪之事想必凶兆也欲班師洪巴圖魯代善二

王曰或吉或凶兆已見矣果何據而遂欲回兵此兵一回吾父以後勿復用爾我矣言訖率兵強進至斐優城收四周屯寨約五百戶先令費英東扈爾漢領兵三百護送不意烏拉國

布占泰發兵
一萬截於路
扈爾漢見之
將五百戶眷
屬扎營於山
巔以兵百名
看守一面馳
報衆貝勒一
面整兵二百
占山列營與
敵兵相持經
一夜次日烏
拉兵來戰大
將揚古利率

衆奮力交鋒
殺烏拉兵七
人我兵止傷
一人敵兵退
回渡河登山
畏懼無復敢
來兩軍扎營
相持是日未
時三王率兵
齊至見之洪
巴圖魯代善
二王策馬奮
怒曰吾父素
善征討今雖

多天助我國勿以此兵為天釋之耶爾手中釋出豈其性命從吾豢猶然是人時未久布占

而主其國年索繫頸免死我國擒捉鐵布占泰曾被衆母得疑懼領兵到此爾在家吾二人

手捉其盔頂被代善王左博克多貝勒拉兵遂敢有直衝入營烏路登山而戰領兵五百二

代善二王各河洪巴圖魯力遂奮勇渡吾等願効死必勝衆皆曰名夙著此戰之威吾父英

所阻及繞山
追又被大山
是方驅兵前
立於山下至
五百兵落後
齊貝勒原率
之際舒爾哈

時追殺敗兵
匹甲三千副
千獲馬五千
里布殺兵三
住父子并胡
被殺生擒常
殺之其子亦

兄併力進戰
圖們代善與
為阿爾哈圖
勇當先賜名
圖魯褚英奮
為達爾漢巴
舒爾哈齊名

太祖賜弟
甚多及班師
傷敵兵凍死
雲大雪其被
晴明霎然陰
殺大敵是日
而來未得掩

即殺我也
曰若殺二將
漢巴圖魯懇
以死罪達爾
於一處因定
爾漢貝勒立
兵百名與達

進戰破敵領
不隨兩貝勒
太祖所托
齊布二將負
圖魯常書納
名為古英巴
殺博克多賜

和穰噶佛訥
赫席赫鄂謨
海窩集部取
一千往征東
漢轄等率兵
費英東扈爾
大將額亦都

禮克圖貝勒
祖令幼弟卓
〇五月　太
布所屬人民
百兩奪納齊
死罰常書銀
太祖乃宥其

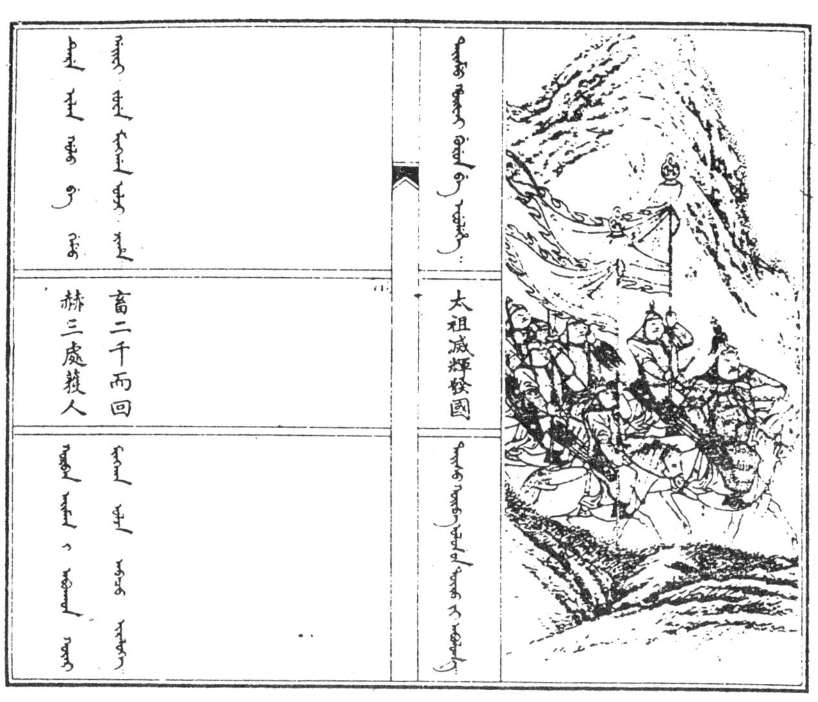

太祖威輝發國

畜二千而回
赫三處獲人

有氣自西
夜方沒又
發國七八
東直冲輝
從星出向
日夜有氣
○九月六

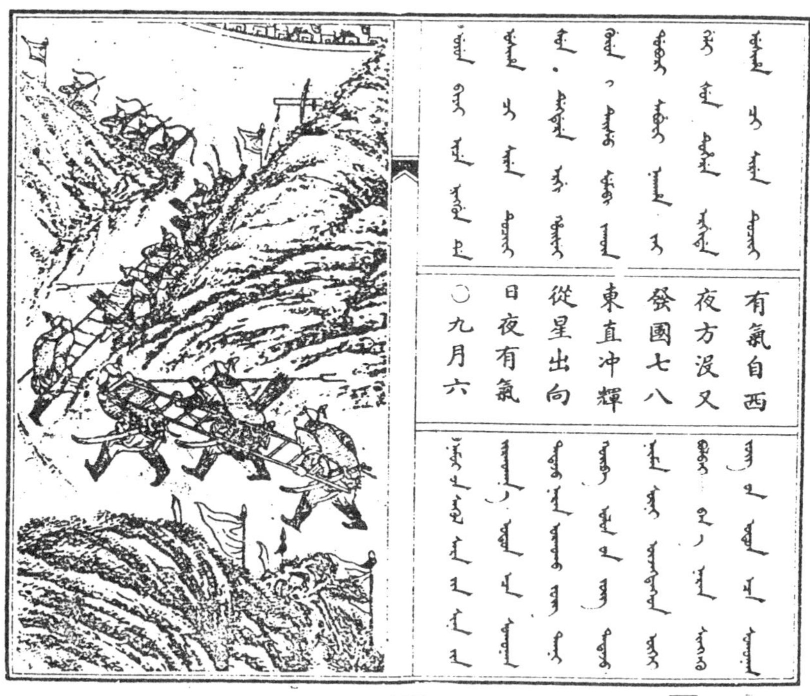

方從星出
月餘方沒
時輝發國
拜音達里
貝勒族衆
多投赴葉
赫其部屬
亦有叛謀
拜音達里
聞之以七
臣之子為
質借兵於
太祖
太祖以兵

一千助之
有納林布
祿賺拜音
達里曰爾
若撤回所
質之人吾
即反爾投
來族衆拜
音達里信
其言乃曰
吾將安居
於滿洲葉
赫之間矣
遂撤回七

生乞將
倚　汗為
言今仍欲
林布祿聯
者誤信納
太祖曰曩
其臣告

達里復遣
族衆拜音
竟不反其
納林布祿
布祿為質
子與納林
臣子復以

於我今又
二次加兵
曾助葉赫
謂之曰汝
太祖遣使
盟不娶
音達里背

許之後拜
書之議而
祖遂息常
為婚　太
子者賜我
許常書之
汗女先欲

聘吾女而不娶何也拜音達里飾詞以對曰吾曾質子於葉赫俟質子歸吾即往娶與爾合謀矣隨將城垣修築三層以自固質於葉赫之子亦撤

回於是太祖復遣使曰今質子已歸汝意又何如也拜音達里恃城垣已固遂絕親 太祖即於九月九日率兵往伐其國十四日兵到即時克

之殺拜音達里父子屠其兵招服其民遂班師輝發國從此滅矣

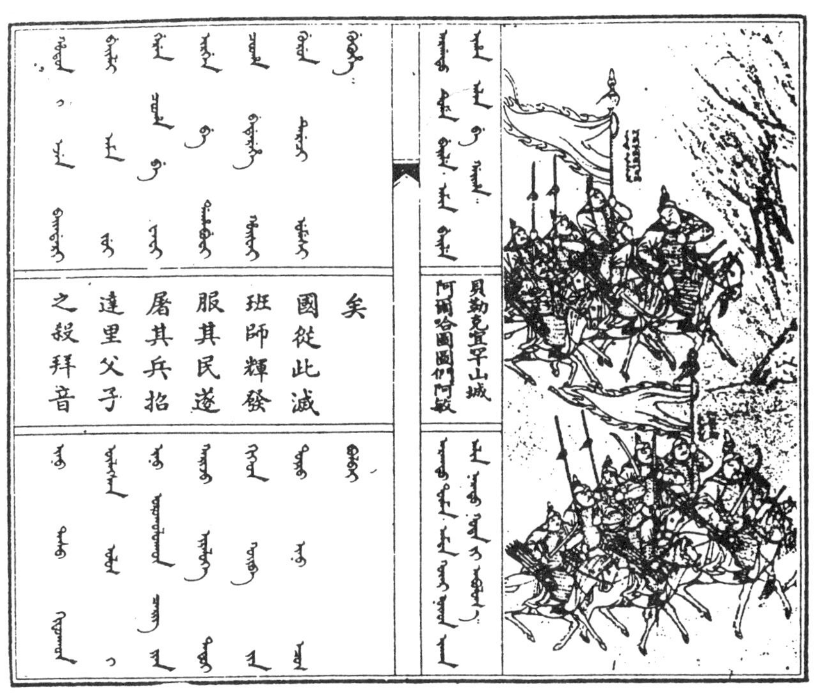

阿爾哈圖圖們阿敏貝勒克宜罕山城

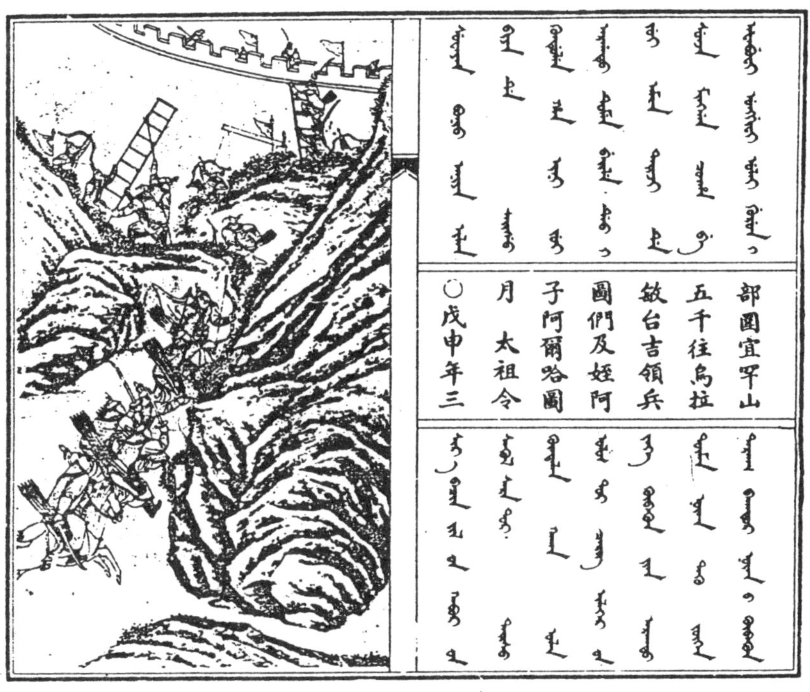

〇戊申年三月 太祖令子阿爾哈圖圖們及姪阿敏台吉領兵五千往烏拉部圍宜罕山

城克之殺千餘人獲甲三百副盡收人畜而回時烏拉布占泰與蒙古科爾沁翁阿岱貝勒合兵出烏拉城約二十里遥見我兵之勢難敵遂回 是年 太祖欲與明國和好謂羣臣曰

俗言一朝為惡而有餘終身為善而不足今欲與明國昭告天地以通和好言畢遂會遼陽副將撫順所備禦宰白馬祭天刻誓辭於碑曰各守兩國邊境敢有竊踰者無論滿洲與漢

畢沿邊立
受其殃誓
盟滿洲必
洲國負此
其殃若滿
等官必受
原道叅將

陽道副將開
巡撫總兵遼
負此盟廣寧
之人明國若
殃及於不殺
若見而不殺
人見之即殺

求曰吾累
遣其臣來
此布占泰
使殺之自
　太祖之
五十人付
月擒葉赫

前好於九
往來欲守
大懼遣使
山城被克
見其宜罕
○布占泰
碑以為記

二月　太
○己酉年
禮儀往送
遣侍臣以
公主妻之
女穆庫什
祖復將生

賴之　太
爲妻吾永
之女與我
若得恩父
誠無顏面
罪於恩父
次背盟獲

月　太祖
歸之十二
查千餘戶
諭朝鮮國
歷帝遣使
於是明萬
傳諭查與

朝鮮者可
所屬有入
部衆皆吾
境瓦爾喀
曰隣朝鮮
書於明國
祖遣使致

命扈爾漢轄領兵一千征東海窩集部所屬瑚葉路克之獲人畜二千而還因有功賞扈爾漢轄盔甲馬匹仍賜名達爾漢轄

額亦都招九路長見 太祖

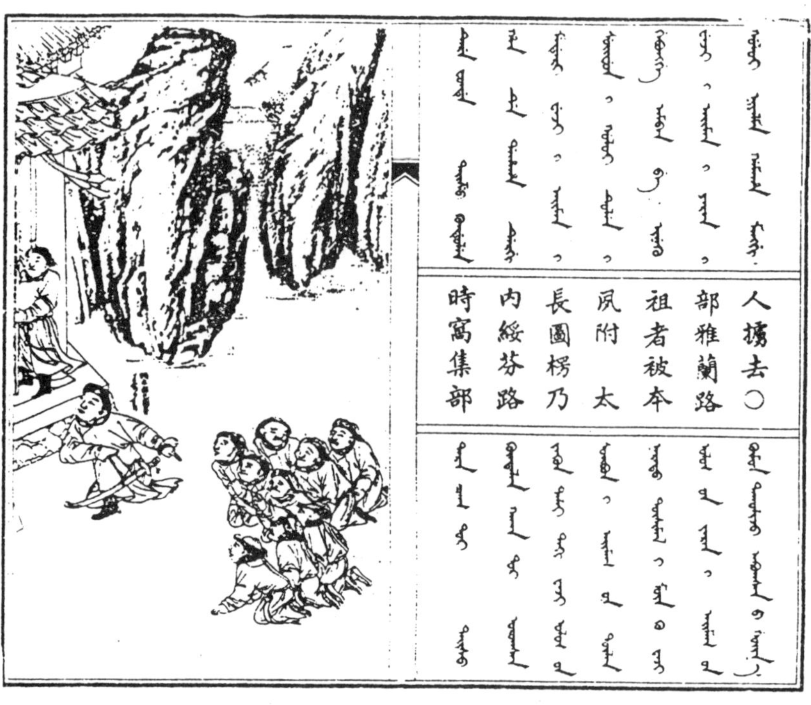

時窩集部內綏芬路長圖楞乃夙附太祖者被本部雅蘭路人擄去○

庚戌歲十一月太祖命額亦都領兵一千往窩集部內那木都魯綏芬寧古塔尼馬察四路將其路長康古禮喀克篤禮昂古明噶圖烏魯喀僧

夫千餘皆
國寒苦曠
太祖查本
年二月
回○辛亥
畜萬餘而
蘭路獲人

領兵擊雅
赴滿洲復
其舉家先
招服之令
克書等盡
瑺松噶葉
格尼喀里

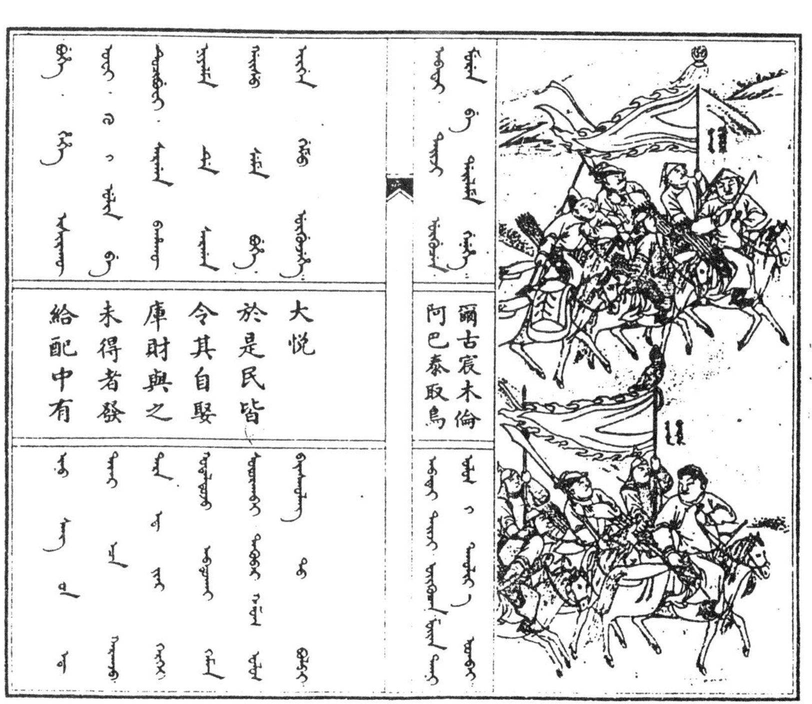

爾古宸木倫
阿巴泰取烏

大悅
於是民皆
令其自娶
庫財與之
未得者發
給配中有

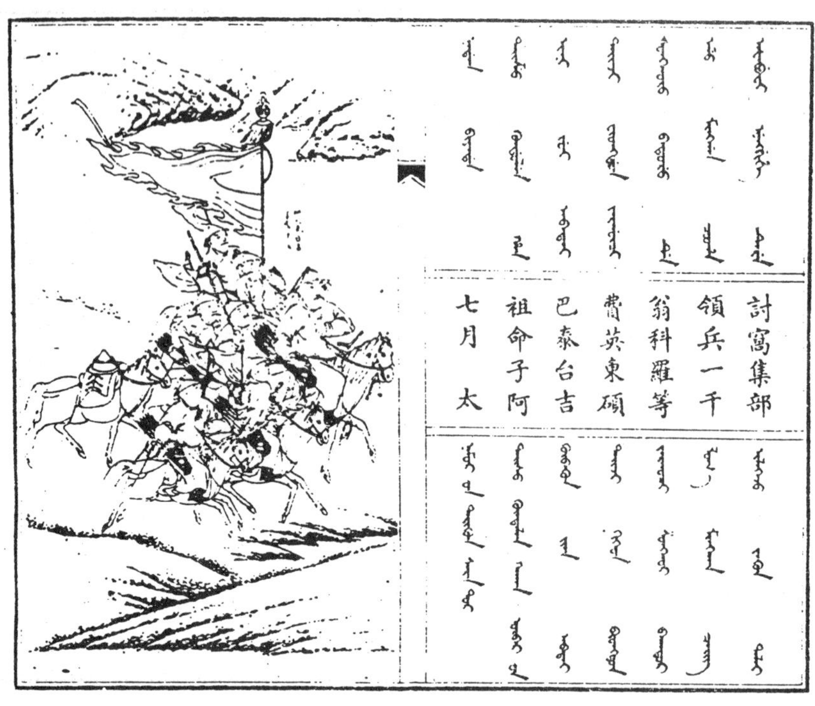

七月太祖命子阿巴泰台吉費英東碩翁科羅等領兵一千討窩集部

內烏爾古宸木倫二路皆取之〇八月十九日太祖同胞弟達爾漢巴

圖魯薨年四十八歲生六子長曰阿敏次曰扎薩克圖三曰圖倫四曰齊

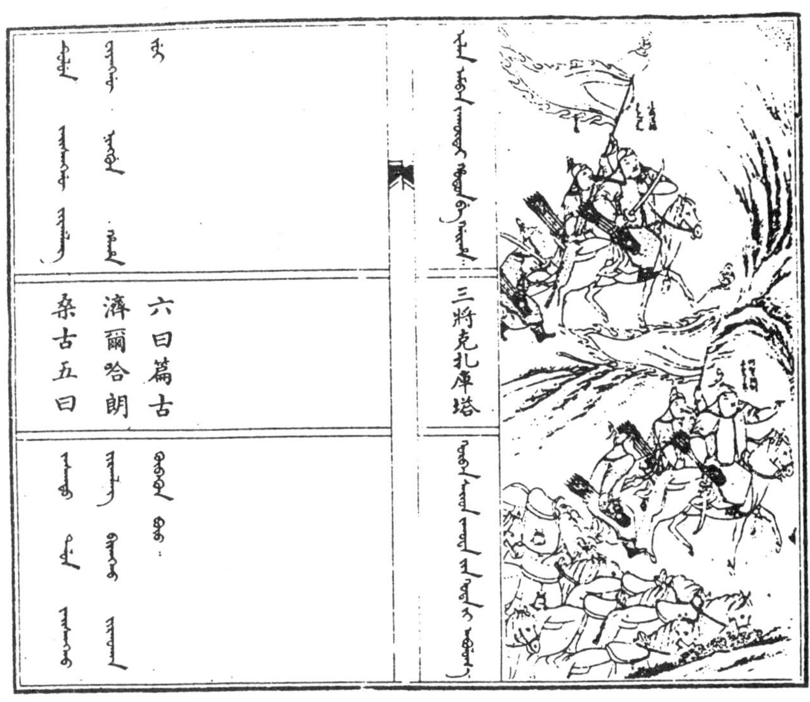

三將克扎庫塔

六曰篇古濟爾哈朗桑古五曰

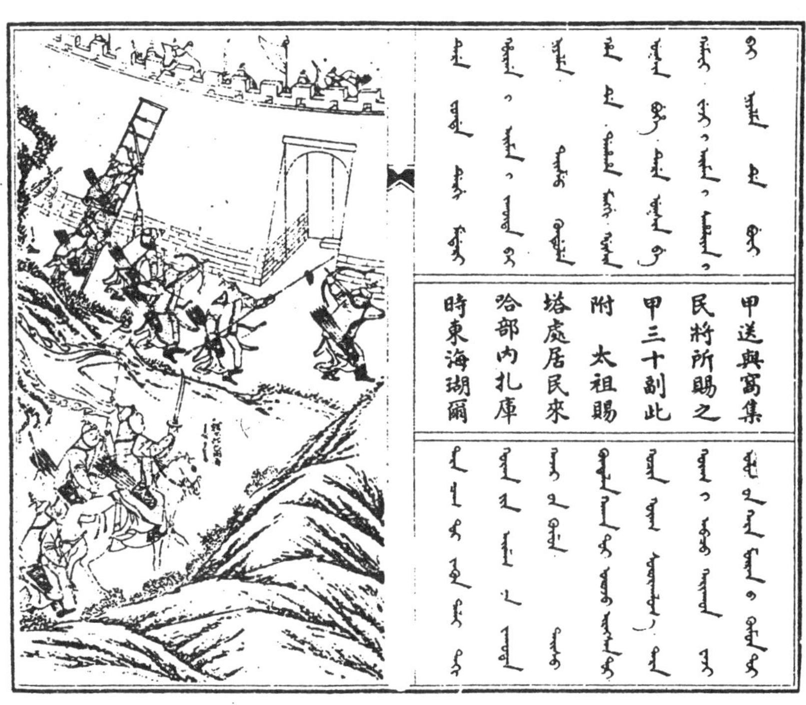

甲送與窩集民將所賜之甲三十副此附 太祖賜塔處居民來哈部内扎庫時東海瑚爾

遂拔其城殺
招之而不服
庫塔城三日
爾哈路圖扎
兵二千征瑚
漢貉三人領
額亦都達爾

何和里額駙
延十二月命
占泰招撫布
受烏拉國布
木上射之又
處居人披於
部內隨哈達

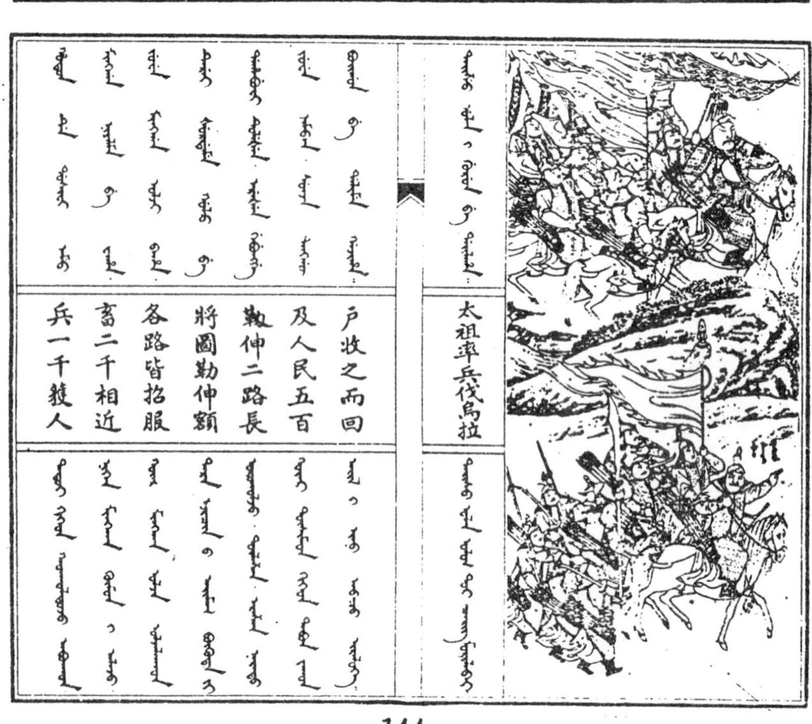

太祖率兵伐烏拉

戶收之而回
及人民五百
敕伸二路長
將圖勒伸額
各路皆招服
畜二千相近
兵一千殺人

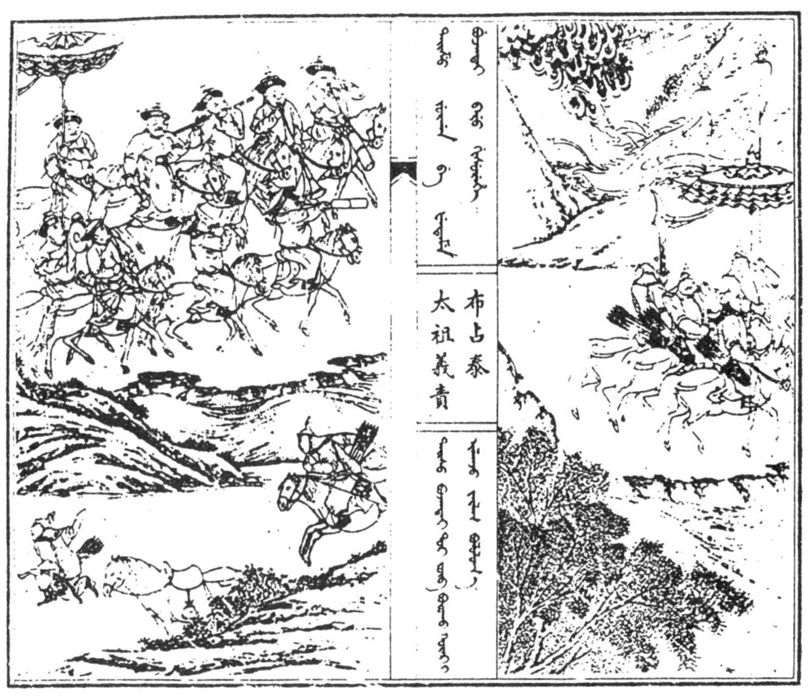
太祖義責
布占泰

壬子年昔
蒙古科爾沁
部明安貝勒
嘗從葉赫九
部兵來戰敗
乘驏馬逃回
至是巳二十

年矣 太祖
聞其女頗有
淑範遣使欲
娶之明安貝
勒送拒他部
之請送其女
來 太祖以
禮親迎大宴
成婚時布占
泰復背盟掠
太祖所屬
寓集部內瑚
爾哈路二次
及欲娶 太

祖所定葉赫
國布齋貝勒
之女又以骲
箭射 太祖
姪女娥恩哲
太祖聞之
大怒遂於九
月二十二日
領大兵往征
之二十九日
至烏拉國
太祖張黃蓋
鳴鼓樂沿烏
拉河岸而行

布占泰領兵出城迎敵至河邊見滿洲兵盔甲鮮明兵馬雄壯衆皆失色無鬪志 太祖遂沿岸而下克其五城直抵於河西岸距布占泰居城二里克其金州城安營十月初一日

太祖出營以太牢告天祭旗忽見東南有氣青白二色直冲烏拉城北我兵屯留三日遣兵四出盡焚其糧烏拉兵晝則出城對壘於河邊夜則入城歇息 太祖二子莽古爾泰貝勒

貝勒
欲渡河擊之
太祖曰不
然汝等出言
毋若浮面取
水之易也須
採其底裏耳

欲伐大木豈
能驟折必以
斧斤伐之漸
至微細然後
能折相等之
國欲一舉取
之豈能盡滅

乎且將所屬
城郭盡削平
之獨存其都
城如此則無
僕何以為主
無民何以為
君遂燬所得

六城焚其房
殺回至富爾
哈河安營布
占泰令吳巴
海巴圖魯乘
舟而來立於
舟上呼曰恩

父汗興兵無非乘怒而來今恩父之怒已息可留一言而去如此遣使三次布占泰八親率六將乘舟來至河中於舟上頓首呼曰烏拉國即恩父之國也焚糧之火可息乎 太祖披

明甲乘白馬率諸王大臣直出衆軍前至河中水及馬腹厲聲曰布占泰先擒汝於陣中已死之身吾養之釋爲烏拉國主仍以三女妻之今欺茂皇天后土背七次盟言擄吾所屬瑚

辱汝試言之
人曾被誰責
生愛新覺羅
當來告我天
女所為不善
射之乎若吾
令汝以骲箭

原為匹偶曾
女嫁汝異國
射吾女吾將
女又以骲箭
已聘葉赫之
又欲强娶吾
爾哈路二次

其骨莫燬其
乎語云穿鎖
徒抱於九泉
於心乎抑將
名我將匿之
女此受辱之
爾何故射吾

非若其無之
我兵之來誠
汝射之為是
知脫有之則
以來汝豈不
或不知十世
百世以前汝

名吾非樂於舉兵聞射吾女故親舉兵來布占泰對曰或者人以讒言令吾父子不睦若果射汝女欲娶汝婚上有天在吾今在水上龍神亦鑒之似此讒言皆虛妄耳布占泰部將拉

布太扎爾固齋繼言曰汗有此怒盍遣一使來問太祖曰拉布太我部下豈無似汝之人汝尚以射吾女為無此事娶吾婚為妄言耶若事有不實須再問事已

哀懇曰
喀爾喀瑪
布占泰弟
布太勿言
大驚止拉
乎布占泰
當吾之刀

彼時汝能
復臨之理
兵豈有不
氷之日吾
安有不結
問為此河
的矣何以

烏拉國存
遂回營在
信也言畢
不然吾不
方見其真
之子為質
子並大臣

婚何將汝
吾女娶吾
爾果未射
太祖曰
一言而行
其度請決
汗若寬大

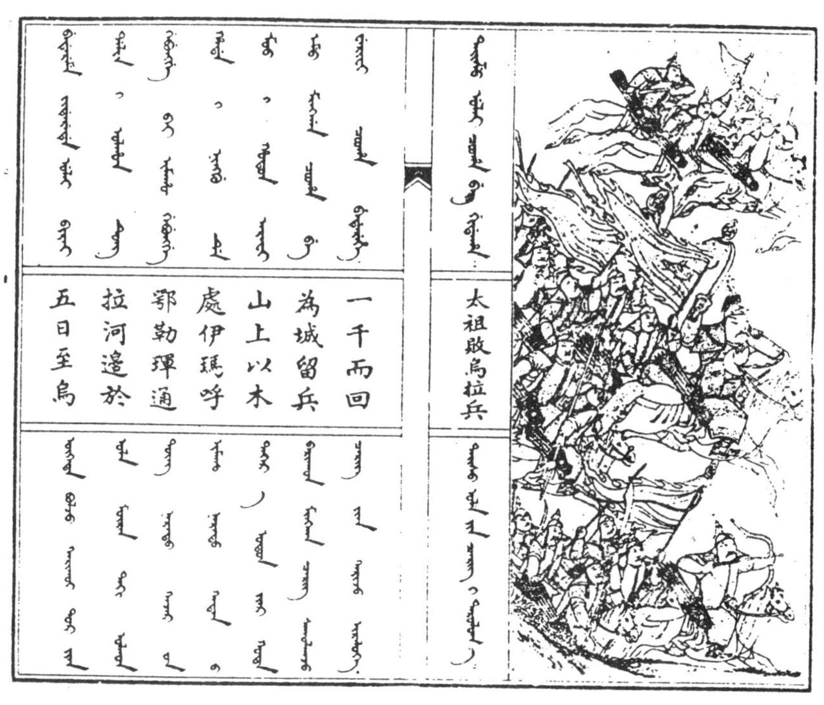

一千而回
為城留兵
山上以木
處伊瑪呼
鄂勒琿通
拉河邊於
五日至烏

太祖敗烏拉兵

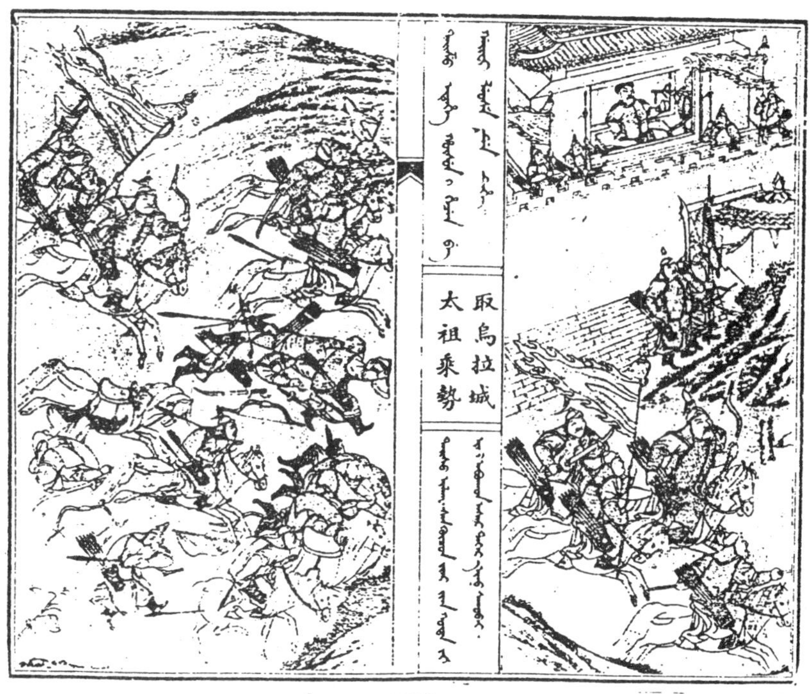
太祖乘勢取烏拉城

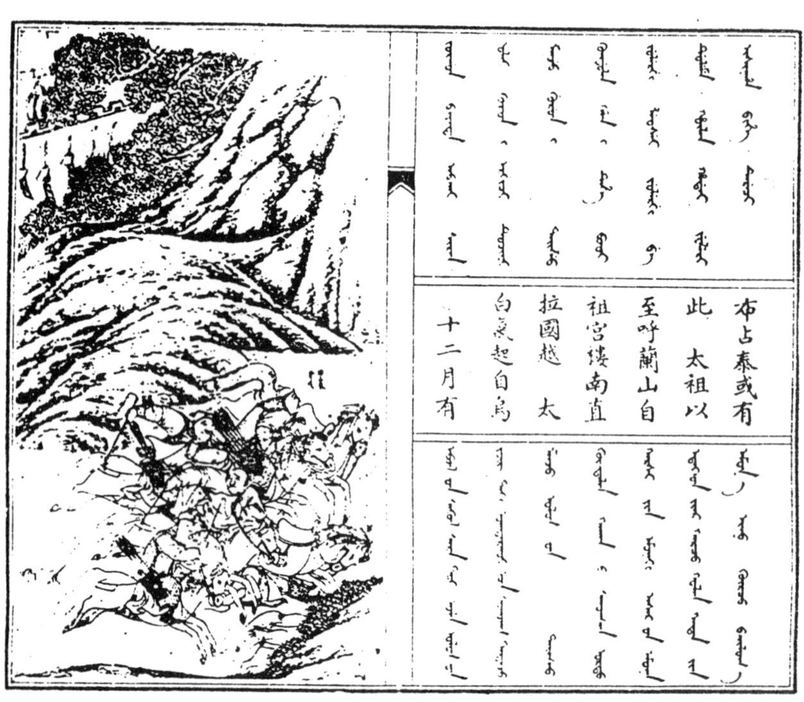

十二月有白氣起自烏拉國越太祖宮樓南直至呼蘭山自此太祖以布占泰或有

和好之意延及一年又聞布占泰欲將女薩哈簾男綽啓鼐及十七臣之子送葉赫為質娶

太祖所聘之女又欲囚太祖二女癸丑年正月親率大兵往征之布占泰擬十八日送

王大臣欲
下領兵諸
太祖部
哈城迎敵
萬越富爾
泰率兵三
次日布占

諜二城屯兵
進克郭多鄂
泰城領兵前
至攻取孫扎
兵十七日巳
質 太祖大
子與葉赫為

爾漢轄顏
里額駙達
英東何和
阿敏及費
巴圖魯姪
祖子古英
申之 太

諭之言復
乎仍將前
之無子遺
國能遠使
豈有伐大
祖止之曰
抵敵 太

耻辱當何
葉赫女其
占泰倘娶
馬何用布
為厲兵秣
戰興兵何
出捨此不

令彼兵既
設計賺之
出城尚議
布占泰不
然曰初恐
科羅等奮
亦都碩翁

傷非為吾
有一二見
大臣等恐
但惜諸王
臣身先之
王及五大
必吾與諸

兩國兵連
太祖曰
可與一戰
壯既至此
今人強馬
之無益矣
如後雖征

遂披甲進
當戰言畢
既欲戰即
經鏖戰今
接不知幾
交兵及相
入弓矢相

中狐身突
於千百軍
助吾自幼
蒙皇天眷
怒而言曰
止之也乃
身怯懼而

祐能敗敵
曰倘蒙天
策諭軍士
敵下城之
太祖決破
士盡甲
動天地軍

聲如雷震
皆欣躍懽
及聞進戰
正疑慮間
惟恐不戰
大臣軍士
戰其諸王

兵可乘勢
奪門取城
遂前進布
占泰率三
萬兵步行
列陣以待
兩軍相距
百步滿洲
兵亦下馬
進戰 太
祖見兩軍
之矢如風
發雪落聲
如羣蜂殺

氣衝天心
中奮甚遂
殺入諸王
大臣軍士
皆奮勇衝
擊烏拉兵
遂敗十損
六七其餘
抛戈棄甲
四散而逃
滿洲兵乘
勢飛奔奪
門遂取其
城 太祖

登城坐西門樓上時布占泰領敗兵不滿百奔城而來其城早巳被克上

豎 太祖旗幟遂大驚及奔回被古英巴圖魯領一旅精兵截之布占泰

見勢不能敵遂衝突而走折兵大半餘皆潰散布占泰僅以身免投葉赫

國去獲馬匹盔甲器械無筭烏拉國所屬城邑皆歸附存兵十日陞賞有

矣
國自此滅
回兵烏拉
與衆軍即
餘人畜散
約萬家其
還其眷屬
投來者盡
有見妻子
拉兵敗後
功將士烏

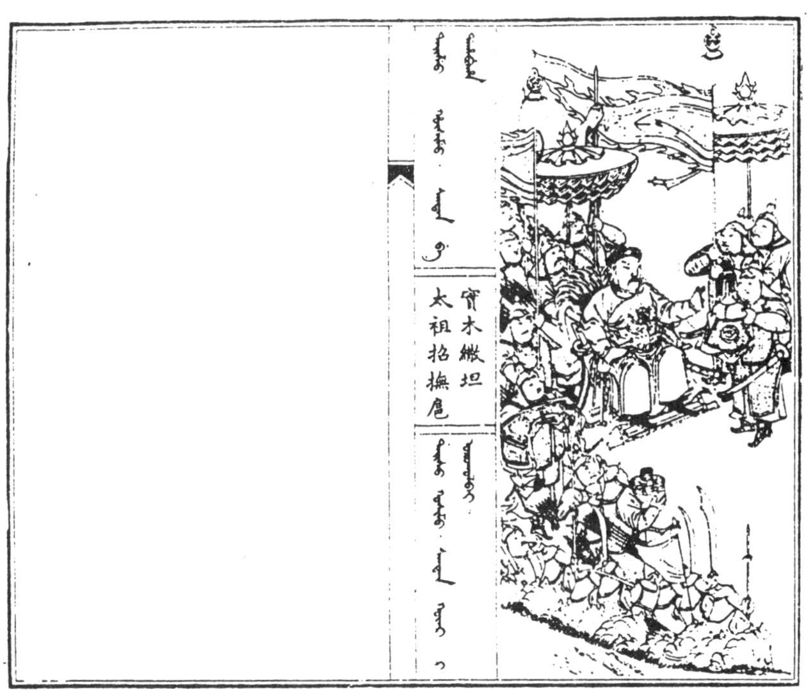

太祖招撫扈實木繖坦

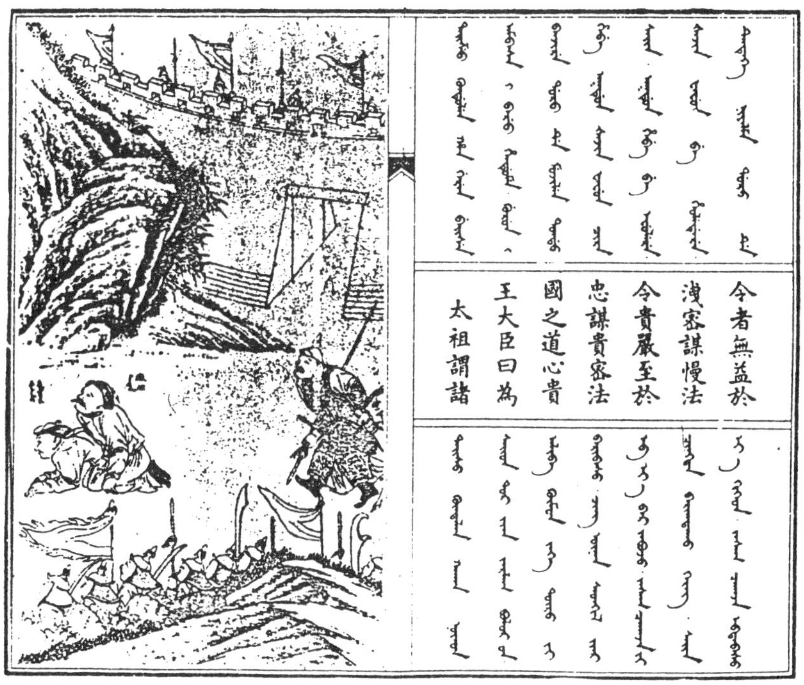

太祖謂諸王大臣曰為國之道心貴忠謀貴密法令貴嚴至於洩密謀慢法令者無益於

誅吾養之連
中被擒應伏
言布占泰陣
使如葉赫國
知 太祖遣
宜各書言所
主無切當處

何汝等之言
人之智慮幾
等勿面從一
有拂戾處汝
果皆是歟若
崇也吾所言
至道乃國之

將賢息預門
赫時有逃者
兵四萬征葉
月初六日領
太祖於九
古貝勒不與
錦台什布揚

三次葉赫國
我如此遣使
汝地當獻與
破其國身投
怒而征之乃
與我為仇故
妻以三女因

於葉赫葉赫遂收璋吉當阿二處部衆獨烏蘇城有痘疾未曾收去 太祖兵至圍烏蘇城

招諭之曰城中軍民降則已不然必攻取之城中人曰若養之則降況大國師衆如林不絶

如流盔甲鮮明如三冬氷雪吾等焉敢抗拒言訖守將織坦扈賓木二人開門出降叩見

太祖以金盃賜酒將所戴東珠金佛帽併衣賜之其璋城吉當阿城烏蘇城雅哈城赫爾蘇

取矣今復侵
烏拉已被盡
曰哈達輝發
於明萬歷帝
臣諳 太祖
布揚古使其
是時錦台什

三百戶而回
收烏蘇降民
焚其房穀遂
共十九處盡
吉岱城大小
布齊呑城鄂
城和敦城喀

有侵我之日
從吾言後必
我和好若不
從吾言是存
葉赫國若肯
自今汝勿侵
謂 太祖曰

信之遣使來
地明萬歷帝
原鐵嶺為牧
陽為都城開
汝明國取遼
諸部然後侵
吾地欲削平

遂遣遊擊馬
時檎周大岐
帶鎗砲手一
千衛葉赫二
城 太祖聞
之修書曰吾
國與兵原為

葉赫哈達烏
拉輝發蒙古
錫伯卦勒察
九國於癸巳
年會兵侵我
上天罪彼故
令我勝于時

殺葉赫布齋
生擒烏拉布
占泰至丁酉
年復盟宰馬
歃血互結婚
姻以通前好
後葉赫負盟

拚原許之女
悔親不與布
占泰乃吾所
恩養者因與
我為仇伐之
殺其兵得其
國彼身投葉

行不已
光垂照隨
赤二色祥
傍如門青
時日出兩
名古呼卯
一曠野處

二十五日至
詣撫順所於
爭書畢親齎
何故乃侵犯
吾與大國有
發故欲征之
赫又留而不

○甲寅年
移時即還
書與之不
教軍場將
拱揖接入
迎之馬上
出三里外

擊李永芳
撫順所遊
日辰時至
止二十六
之其光乃
遂率衆拜
太祖一見

四月明萬歷帝遺守備蕭伯芝來詐稱大臣乘八擡輪作威勢强令拜旨

述書中古令與廢之故種種不善之言太祖曰虛言恐嚇何為下拜善

言善對惡言惡對竟不覽其書今之回四月十五日蒙古扎嚕特部鐘

嫩貝勒送女與太祖次子古英巴圖魯貝勒為婚貝勒親迎大宴以禮

女與太
思貝勒送
爾沁莽古
之蒙古科
仍以禮受
親迎大宴
為婚貝勒

爾泰貝勒
三子莽古
與 太祖
齊汗送妹
嗋特部內
日蒙古扎
受之二十

降民二百
林二路收
部雅蘭西
之南窩集
百征東海
月遣兵五
之○十一

宴以禮受
山城處大
國扈爾奇
迎至輝發
為婚貝勒
■貝勒
祖四子■

月蒙古科
乙卯年正
禮受之〇
迎設宴以
婚台吉親
顒台吉為
祖子德格

女與　太
格貝勒送
部額爾濟
古扎嚕特
十二月蒙
千而回〇
戶人畜一

方明〇四
殿至辰時
太祖升
映之皆黃
黃色人面
寅時天有
二十八日

之〇三月
宴以禮受
迎接設大
太祖為妃
送女與
果爾貝勒
爾沁部孔

月於城東阜上建佛寺玉皇廟十王殿共七大廟三年乃成○是時明萬

歷帝命廣寧總兵張承蔭巡邊承蔭奉命巡邊回遣通事董國蔭曰今欲

更立石碑以汝居處為吾地其柴河撫安三岔三處所種之田勿穫可收

汝人民退居　太祖曰吾世世祖居耕種之地令令棄之想爾心變故出

起恐念吾
治平而頻
違然不願
言自不可
令退居帝
容妝穫而
之田又不

吾國所種
獲助葉赫
帝令反常
王心不變
海水不溢
聞古人云
此言也吾

大國成小
淩我也然
衆國大欺
患汝以兵
吾一身之
成仇敵非
以妝拾若

汝大國何
即退試看
大國欲退
害矣吾非
國自受大
小害汝大
小國若受

外甚多
立石碑於邊
遂侵占疆土
去自此明國
言太過矣遂
董國蔭曰此
俘物矣通事
軍民皆為吾

一千城中
若止屯兵
城自傾擾
屯兵一萬
汝若一城
皆出於天
小國成大

速起兵若已
未與之先可
過於是當此
所可恨者莫
女欲與蒙古
將．汗聘之
臣曰聞葉赫
十七諸王大

巴哈達爾漢
爾岱台吉乃
爾喀部莽古
欲與蒙古喀
受其聘禮又
妹許 太祖
赫布揚古以
○六月初葉

破壞哈達輝
無意也因而
天生此女非
兵則不可蓋
違婚之事與
加兵於彼以
或有大事可
已 太祖曰

力諫興兵不
坐視他適皆
既聞之安得
非諸王可比
汗所聘者
奪之況此女
時攻其城而
與之乘未嫁

能久啓釁流
與何人亦不
災患無論聘
久而亡反成
得其女諒不
盡力征之雖
故如是也今
事激我忿怒

大變欲以此
破壞葉赫釀
而與蒙古是
其女不與我
國助葉赫令
擾攘至此明
國不睦干戈
發烏拉使各

禍已極死期將至矣諸王大臣反覆諫之必欲興兵太祖曰吾以怒而興師汝等猶當諫之況吾所聘之女為他人娶豈有不憾之理予尚釋然於中置諸度外勸以息兵汝等反苦為堅請令吾生怒何也聘

女者不憾汝等深憾何為豈因此遂從汝等之言乎汝等且止言畢令調到人馬皆回其女聘與蒙古未及一年果亡諸王大臣奏曰此女迄今三十三歲已受聘二十年矣被明國遣兵為葉赫防衆葉赫遂倚

如逆天然葉勢橫加侵奪不審是非恃我滿洲一國共主何獨於天下是天下自以為君臨一國也明國

洲與葉赫均任彼悠久滿自有天鑒之以兵衛葉赫不允曰明國明國 太祖蒙古今可征其勢轉嫁與

之矣及是時國之民且置得人畜即本不足以養所以為生無論得其人畜何素無積儲雖得矣但我國

天既佑則可天天自佑之征明國合乎急何為也若且聽之汝等兵為之衛吾之國也既遣赫乃天不祐

傍有青赤色
日卯時日兩
宿於穆奇次
初四日出獵
出入）十月
吏八員執掌
倉官十六員
積糧於是設

處屯田造倉
四隻於曠野
每十人出牛
乃諭各牛彔
貯遂不動兵
務農事裕積
疆圉修邊關
先治其國固

層壕攻取其
拆其柵越三
遂吹螺布兵
倫招之不服
至固納喀庫
倫城本城名
部東額赫庫
二千征窩集

太祖遣兵
遂止十一月
衆拜之其光
行 太祖率
隨 太祖而
道統日似門
有青白光三
祥光又對日

仕族之多輙
者薦之莫因
擇心術正大
切莫拘根基
者反踰親也
吾何故使疎
等薦人勿曰
於正大也卿

所貴者莫過
嘗思之心之
心貴正大予
羣臣曰語云
回　太祖謂
降五百戶而
俘獲萬餘收
城殺人八百

私謂曰何所
二人見之乃
古轄雅喀木
太祖者布陽
之時有随
濡衣捋衣擷
草木之浮雪
降雪已霽恐

祖出獵時天
之可也　太
政之人即薦
難但可以資
一材一藝猶
位凡為政得
才者衆之在
為援引擇有

天作之為君
祖謂羣臣曰
等惜也　太
所惜者為汝
何美之有吾
雪之衣賜汝
不美哉以濡
者賜汝等豈

雪曷若以新
耳與其濡於
但霑濡無益
無衣而惜之
笑曰吾非為
太祖聞之
衣盡進獵也
不有而惜此

用以佐理
國忠良者
治軍有幹
勇者用以
有臨陣英
事幾何苦
者少則濟
治國統軍

任之以事倘
多得賢人各
國事殷繁須
之則勿隱今
理國政者知
任之職有能
卿等當念所
君命之為臣

而懲汝等
肖者何由
不退則不
進不肖者
者何由而
不舉則賢
王曰賢者
太祖訓諸

羅可也
客各處搜
用以宴賓
宴賓客者
令有才堪
用以講古
通古今者
國政有博

者於理國
臨陣之勇
有工拙有
短處事亦
才技有長
一人之身
者有幾夫
又曰全才

等當留心
来未慊汝
好忠直從
忠直吾夙
道莫過於
均平之大
切勿貪婪
宜秉忠直

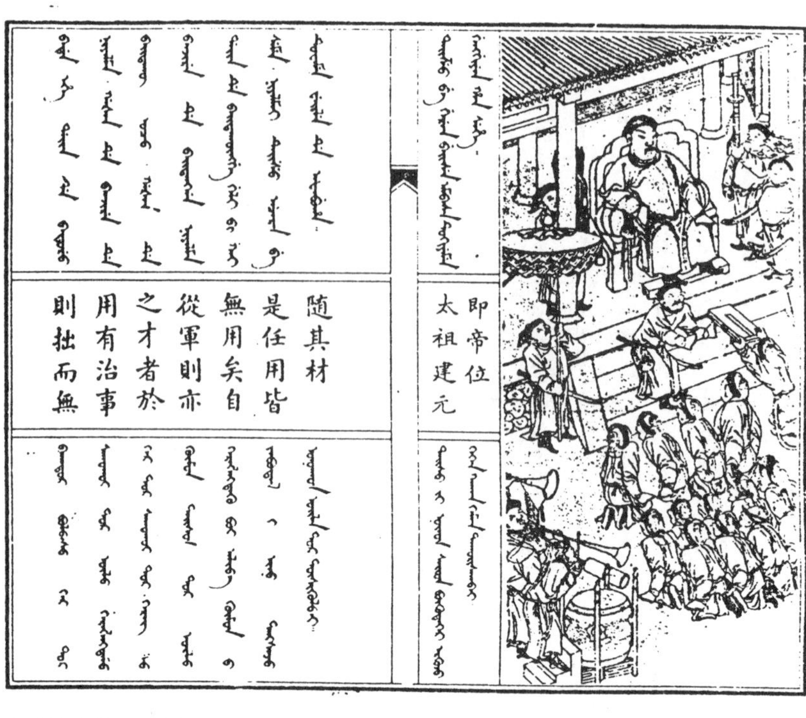
太祖建元即帝位

則拙而無用有治事之才者於從軍則亦無用矣自是任用皆隨其材

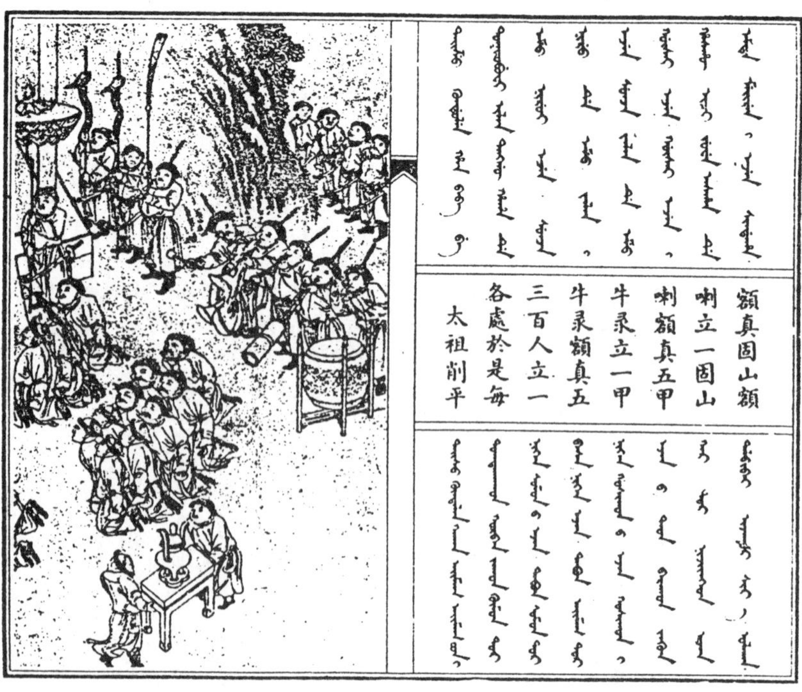
太祖削平各處於是每三百人立一牛录額真五牛录立一甲喇額真五甲喇立一固山額真固山額

九九

真左右立梅
勒額真原旗
有黃白藍紅
四色將此四
色鑲之為八
色成八固山
行軍時若地
廣則八固山
並列隊伍整
齊中有節次
地狹則八固
山合一路而
行節次不亂
軍士禁諠譁
行伍禁紛雜
當兵刃相接

六一

之際披重鎧
執利刃者令
為前鋒披短
甲·即兩截甲
之善射者自
後衝擊精兵
立於別地相
機勿令下馬
勢有不及處
即接應之預
畫勝負謀畧
戰無不勝克
城破敵之後
功罪皆當其
實有罪者即
至親不貰必

太祖五日一
固齊十員
臣五員扎爾
國政聽訟大
而勝又立理
遇戰陣一鼓
勢如風發凡
勇威如雷霆

爭先戰則奮
不忻然攻則
一鬨攻戰無
士各欲建功
用兵如神將
遺必加陞賞
者即仇怨不
以法治有功

之將是非剖
抑者更詳問
言猶恐有冤
聞聽訟者之
太祖前先
今訟者跪於
此循序問達
再達諸王如

五大臣鞫問
次達五大臣
固齊先審理
語凡事扎爾
上古成敗之
曉諭國人宣
焚香以善言
朝當天設桌

析明白以直究問故臣下不敢欺隱民情皆得上達矣 太祖聰明睿智法度精詳敬老尊賢黜讒遠佞恩及無告於國事日夜憂勤上體天意下合人心於是滿洲大治欺詐不生拾物不匿必歸其主若不得其主懸於公署令認識之五穀收穫畢縱牲畜於山野莫有敢竊害者因是諸王大臣會議恭上 尊號遂表聞於 太祖丙辰歲正月朔甲申八固山諸王率衆臣聚於殿前排班 太祖

陛殿諸王大臣皆跪八大臣出班進御前跪呈表章太祖侍臣阿敦轄額爾德尼巴克什接表額爾德尼立於太祖左宣表頌為列國沾恩英明皇帝建元天命

帝於是離座當天焚香率諸王大臣三叩首畢陞殿諸王大臣各率固山叩賀正旦時帝年五十八矣〇明國邊民每年越邊竊採滿洲參礦果木等物擾害無已

一日 帝曰昔與明國立碑宰馬結盟原為杜其混擾令明之邊民累擾吾地吾殺潛越禁邊者亦不為過遂於六月遣達爾漢轄將越邊竊物之人遇則殺之約有五

十餘時 帝聞廣寧新任巡撫至乃遣綱古里方吉納二人往見之巡撫李維翰將綱古里方吉納并從者九人各以鐵索繫之仍差人至滿洲謂 帝曰吾民出邊汝

與抵罪則
爾漢轄執
吾民者違
但將首殺
者曰不然
為之說使
而如是强
何負前盟

殺之人令
殃及於不
邊者不殺
若見越禁
竪碑盟言
帝曰昔
得遽殺之
當鮮還安

所拘十一
欲圖明國
遂息帝
示衆此事
邊上殺以
等人獻之
乎盡將此
豈無罪人

隐者汝國
上乃不容
事已聞於
使者曰此
帝不從
以言挾之
事難寢甚
已不然此

人還即於獄中取自葉赫所擄十人解至撫順所殺之明國遂将所拘十一人放歸

天助冰橋

帝遣達爾漢轄碩翁科羅二将領兵二千征東海薩哈連部二将承命於七月十九日起兵行至兀爾

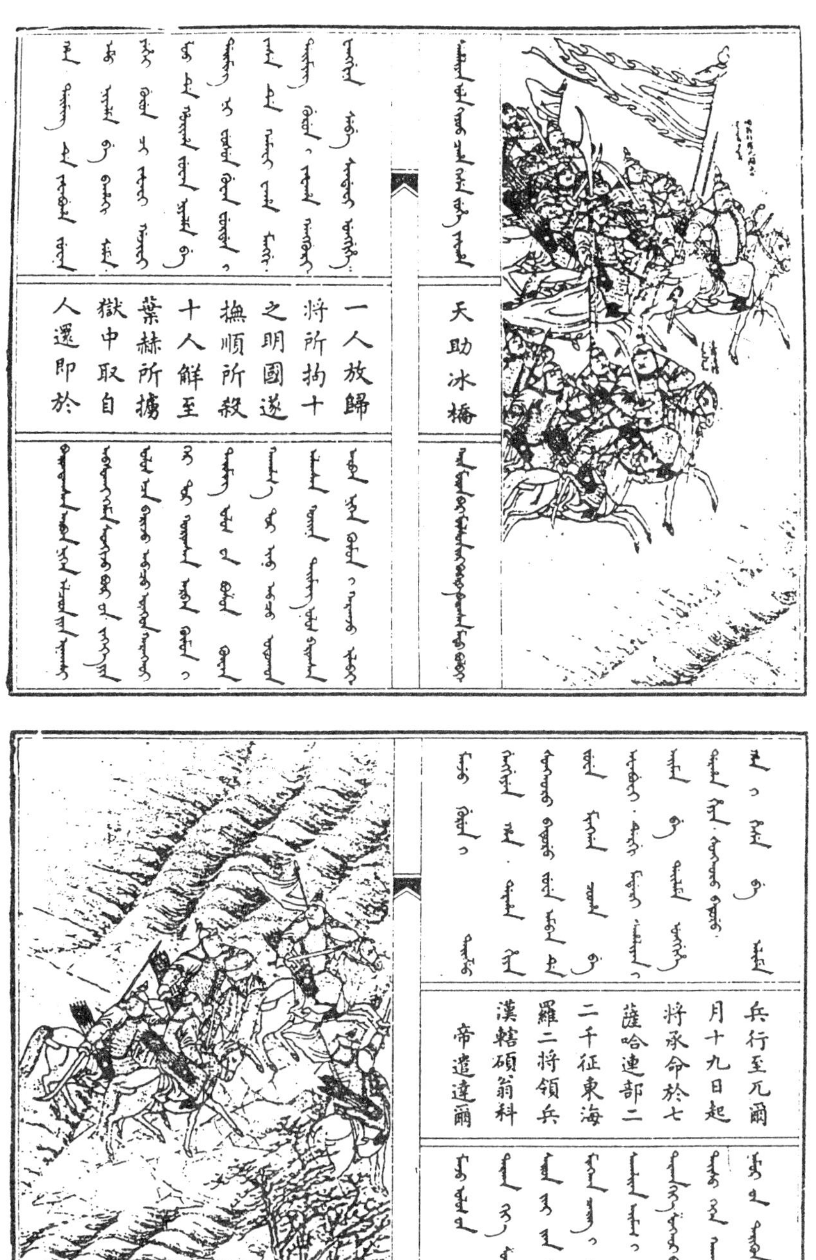

一日達爾漢
是年十月初
中間方結冰
月初十十五
阿里河十一
間方結冰松
十五二十中
每年十一月

初薩哈連江
羅衮寨安營
江南岸佛多
六至薩哈連
北寨三十有
追取沿河南
百隻水陸並
簡河造船二

已解矣廼西
兵復回其冰
寨十一處及
薩哈連部內
領兵渡之取
天助一橋也
相謂曰此實
皆奇之忻然

六十步將士
冰橋一道約
寛二里横結
對寨之處河
江水未結獨
處見薩哈連
二人兵至其
轄碩翁科羅

明安貝勒女
帝納蒙古
二年正月初
〇丁巳天命
初七日入城
兵至十一月
四十人遂回
忻三處路長

之諾壘賽喇
喇 卽役大處
達琿塔庫喇
結又招服陰
一月應時始
復解後至十
一道已渡氷
又如前結氷

二

越一日大宴
城每日小宴
至十一日入
各一百奉獻
駝十隻馬牛
安貝勒以駱
上隨宴訖明

之接見於馬
拉處 卽松內
外富爾簡阿
臣迎至百里
后率諸王大
初八日與皇
間其來見於
巳六年至是

爾台吉為部恩格德喀巴約特蒙古喀爾主遜戴與巴圖魯郡弟達爾漢

、二月以皇外一宿而還物送三十里副及段疋財十戸甲四十至厚與人四留一月贈禮

午天命三而回、戊舟進取之服者乘小負島險不盡取之其散居之民

將東海岸部至日遂居未服諸界妝取散沿東海地遣兵四百妻、是年

已決今歲
勿疑吾意
臣曰汝等
謂諸王大
帝見之
下約丈餘
三丈月之

之上約長
寬二尺月
中此光約
氣直貫月
青黄二色
六日晨有
年正月十

之二月内
令来官乘
以馬百匹
糧往迎復
遣人以餼
来歸 帝
約百餘戸

家屬部衆
四十人率
三處路長
塔庫喇喇
服陰達琿
時間原
必征明國

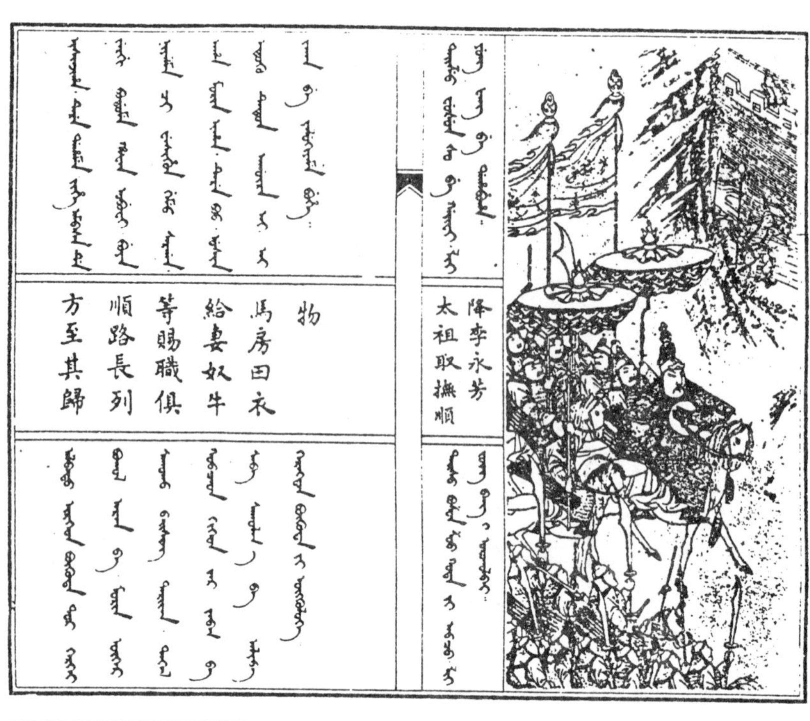
太祖取撫順
降李永芳
物
馬房田衣
給妻奴牛
等賜職俱
順路長列
方至其歸

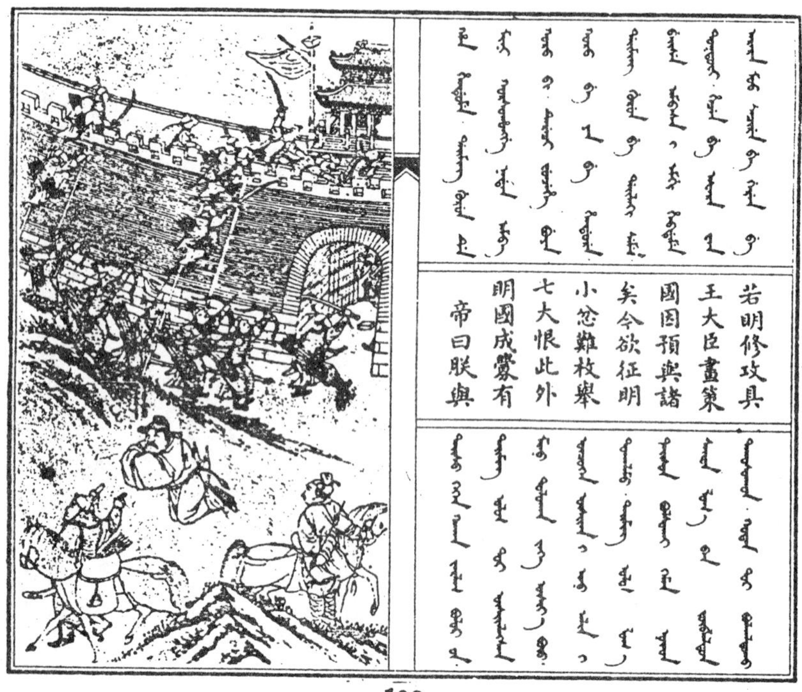
若明修攻具
王大臣畫策
國因預與諸
矣今欲征明
小忿難枚舉
七大恨此外
明國成釁有
帝曰朕與

領兵諸王大
攻戰之策諭
四月　帝頒
以蓋馬房
洩其機遂用
有事來見恐
明之通事或
攻具之木處

盔甲器械其
餧馬匹整頓
三月傳諭催
攻具之木
遣人七百伐
馬院為名遂
乃以蓋諸王
恐洩機於衆

則直抵城門
盡力追襲近
相距若遠即
城邑之遠近
不來詳察其
吾計若誘而
誘而來是中
少遣兵誘之

伏於隱僻處
不合之見須
衆敵寡我兵
兵為上若我
不勞已不頓
以智巧謀畧
正為上軍中
臣曰平時以

使自擁塞而掩殺之倘我兵止一二固山遇敵兵之衆勿令近我即退待大兵然後尋敵所在若止二三處兵須酌量之此乃遇敵野戰之法也至於攻城當觀其勢勢可下則令兵攻之否則勿攻倘攻之不拔

而回反損名矣夫不勞兵力而克敵者是擅智巧謀畧誠爲三軍之主帥若勞兵力雖勝何益當征戰之際最上者莫過於不損己兵而能勝敵者也每牛彔作二雲梯派甲兵二十名以備攻克自出兵日至班

受委托若不能勝其任則委托之事若牛彔等凡所五牛彔主與殺梗令之人諭之不聽即馬各一匹若

主及本牛彔衆罰五牛彔不申法令於五牛彔之主詳問其由若旗違者執之得離本牛彔師日各軍勿

者雖見傷不必致傷如此若一二先之進者不足取邑有一二先至於攻克城國之大事也須知此事乃

悞千人之事事率千人則則悞百人之身若率百人關係非止一强為之者其不能勝任而能勝則勿受

天曰吾父祖
書七大恨告
征明國臨行
將步騎二萬
寅巳時 帝
四月十三壬
並進此諭(
螺令各處兵

圍山額真吹
俱拆畢然後
待環攻之人
山額真錄之
首功可報固
拆城者即為
不為功其首
行賞即殞身

於不殺之人
而不殺殃及
之即殺若見
敢有越者見
皆勿越禁邊
明國與滿洲
立石碑盟曰
欲修和好曾

祖父之誓尚
其一也雖有
殺吾父祖此
生事於邊外
未犯彼無故
草不折秋毫
寸土不擾一
於明國禁邊

人挾令吾獻
里方吉納二
擄使者綱古
拘我往謂巡
盟責以擅殺
之人彼負前
言殺其出邊
侵奪我以盟

出邊入吾地
國人每年竊
江岸之北明
自清河之南
赫此其二也
兵出邊衛葉
國背之反令
如此盟言明

五也邊外葉
兵逐之此其
不容收穫遣
堡耕種田穀
哈卯撫安三
卯三岔法納
柴河山齊拉
邊之敘哈卯

將吾世守禁
古此其四也
之女轉嫁蒙
致使我已聘
為葉赫防禦
也遣兵出邊
殺之此其三
十人於邊上

達擄掠數次
吾所釋之哈
國後葉赫將
哈達必令反
也明國又助
有此天與之
哈達遂為我
吾返兵征之

赫侵吾二次
也哈達助葉
辱我此其六
不善之語以
責備書種種
聽其言遣人
天之國乃偏
赫是獲罪於

侵我我始興
前九部會兵
國呼倫部即
怨於我國先
共主何獨搆
君宜為天下
天降大國之
理果有之乎

畜今復返此
生既得之人
鋒刃者使更
敗而亡死於
存逆天意者
天心者勝而
互相征伐合
夫天下之國

兵因合天意天遂厭呼倫而佑我也明國助天罪之葉赫如逆天然以是為非以非為是妄為剖斷此其七也欺凌至極實難容忍故以此七恨興兵祝畢拜天焚表帝又謂諸王大臣曰此兵吾非樂舉首因

七大恨餘難盡言矣凌迫已極故興此兵然陣中所得之人勿剥其衣勿淫其婦勿離其夫妻拒敵者殺之不拒敵者勿妄殺諭訖遂與諸王暨領兵諸将等鳴鼓樂謁玉帝廟而行營古哷處宿之次日分二路

進兵令左翼四固山兵取東州瑪根丹二處親與諸王率右翼四固山兵及八固山拜雅喇卯時起行至也取撫順行至斡琿鄂謨之野安營而宿是晚 帝将先朝金史講與恩格德爾額駙原係蒙古薩哈連

額駙原係察哈爾國臣乃曰朕觀自古為君者身經征戰之苦皆未得永享其尊令與此兵非欲圖大位而永享之但因明國累搆怨於朕雖再容忍故不得已而興師也是夜忽晴忽雨 帝謂諸王大臣曰陰

雨之時不便
前進可回兵
大王曰與明
國和好久矣
今因其不道
故成仇隙與
師已至其境
若回兵吾等
更與明國和
好乎抑為敵
乎且興兵之
名誰能隐之
天雖雨吾軍
有雨衣弓矢
各有備雨之
具更慮何物

沾濡乎且天
降之雨乃懈
明國之人使
不意吾進兵
此雨有利於
我不利於彼
帝善其言
於夜亥時傳
令軍士方
起行雲開
月霽衆兵
分隊連夜
進撫順邊
兵布百里
旌旗蔽空
至十五日

晨往圍撫順城執一人齋書與遊擊李永芳令之降◯書曰因爾明國兵助葉赫故来征客量爾撫順遊擊戰亦不勝今欲服汝輒深向南下汝設不降誤我前進若不

戰而降必不擾爾所屬軍民仍以原禮優之況爾乃多識見人也不特汝然縱至微之人猶超拔之結為婚姻豈有不超陞爾職與吾大臣相齊之理乎汝勿戰若戰則

吾兵所發之矢豈有目能識汝乎倘中則必死矣力既不支雖戰死亦無益若出降吾兵亦不入城汝所屬軍民皆得保全假使吾兵攻、入城中老幼必致驚散爾之祿

位亦卑薄矣勿以吾言為不足信汝一城若不能拔朕何以興兵為失此機會後悔無及其城中大小官員軍民等果舉城納降父母妻子親族俱不使離散是亦汝等

之福也降與不降汝等熟思慎勿以一朝之忿而不信遂失此機也○李永芳覽畢衣冠立南城上言納降事又令城上備守具滿洲兵見之遂豎雲梯以攻不移時即

登城永芳衣冠乘馬方出城降固山額真阿敦引之永芳下馬跪見帝於馬上拱手答禮其攻城相敵時死者死城已克乃傳令勿殺皆撫之此衆下撫順東州瑪根

賞將所得
營諭功行
至嘉班安
營兵出邊
野處會各
順城東曠
兵回至撫
撫順城大

兵四千拆
十六日留
帝駐撫順
處安歇
於所進之
乃收兵各
堡五百餘
丹三城臺

四千亦至
其拆城兵
付之令歸
七恨之言
給路費書
十六人皆
等處商賈

河東河西
杭州易州
山西涿州
戶有山東
編為一千
軍其降民
萬散給衆
人畜三十

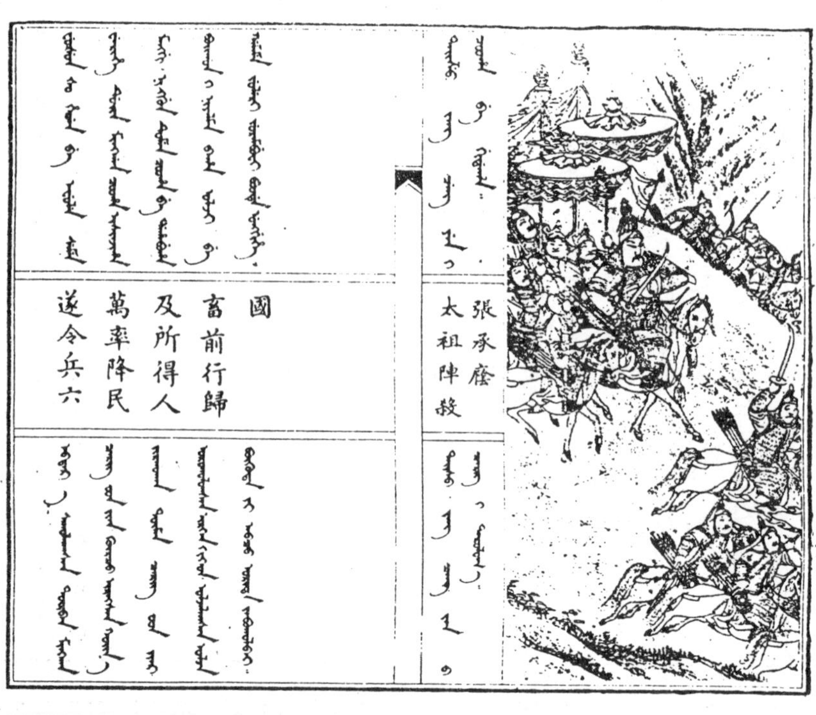
張承廕
太祖陣殺
國
畜前行歸
及所得人
萬率降民
遂令兵六

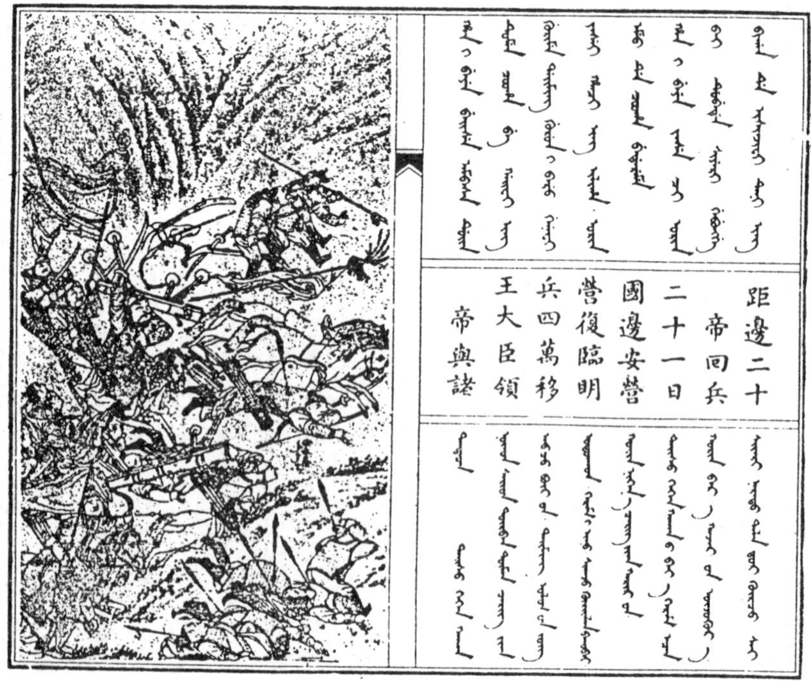
距邊二十
帝回兵
二十一日
國邊安營
營復臨明
兵四萬移
王大臣領
帝與諸

近但躡後兵不敢逼出邊明國滿洲兵已萬急追時處領兵一取撫順等洲大兵盡

世芳聞滿州条将蒲順廷相海遼陽副将守張承廕營廣寧鎮旬方欲安里至謝哩

德尼巴克乃遣額爾待我兵也君耳必不邊以誑其追吾兵出盖欲詐稱與我為敵

彼兵非来帝　帝曰邊隨報盡甲迎至聞之令兵四王二王飛報大王覘視偵探

帝然之遂
敢戰也
我為怯不
回彼必以
兵默默而
後不然我
乘勢襲其
走矣吾欲

不待必自
兵則戰若
兵若待我
回報曰彼
於邊上復
奉命屯兵
停兵二王
什令二王

營銳不可
之殺入其
兵奮勇射
放火砲我
明國兵連
轉向敵營
時其風驟
起及兵臨

初風自西
列陣衝擊
營八固山
列火器安
山險掘壕
分三處據
進明國兵
帥大兵前

器械無算
甲七千副
馬九千匹
損七八獲
絶敵兵十
尸絡繹不
四十里死
餘員追殺

官共五十
千把總等
将叅遊及
殺總兵副
伏屍相枕
皆破死者
遂敗三營
當明國兵

氣二道横
東有青黑
晩自西向
謝哩甸是
日兵宿於
之二十三
輕重以賞
軍被傷之

陞之稽三
進者列等
臣奮勇前
論諸王大
至邊安營
卒二名回
洲止折小
是陣中滿

照明國設
皿等物仍
食牲畜器
田牛馬衣
主又與房
者查歸本
奴僕失散
查給伊親

親失散者
散至於六
婦俱無離
子兄弟夫
民千戶父
國所得降
十六日還
亘天上二

總兵
妻之陞為
貝勒郡主
子阿巴泰
統管将皇
令李永芳
大小官屬

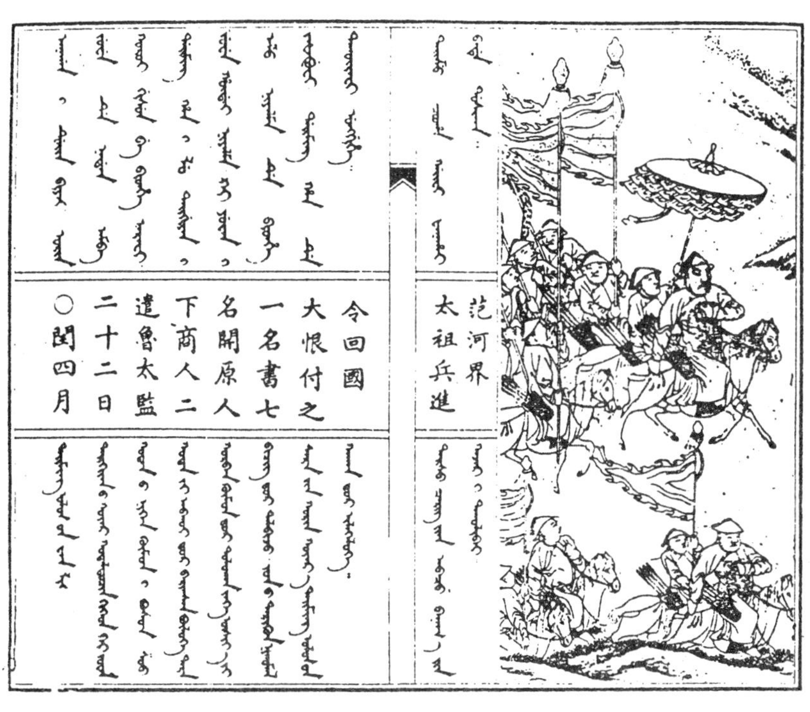

太祖兵進范河界

○閏四月二十二日遣魯太監下商人二名開原人一名書七大恨付之令回國

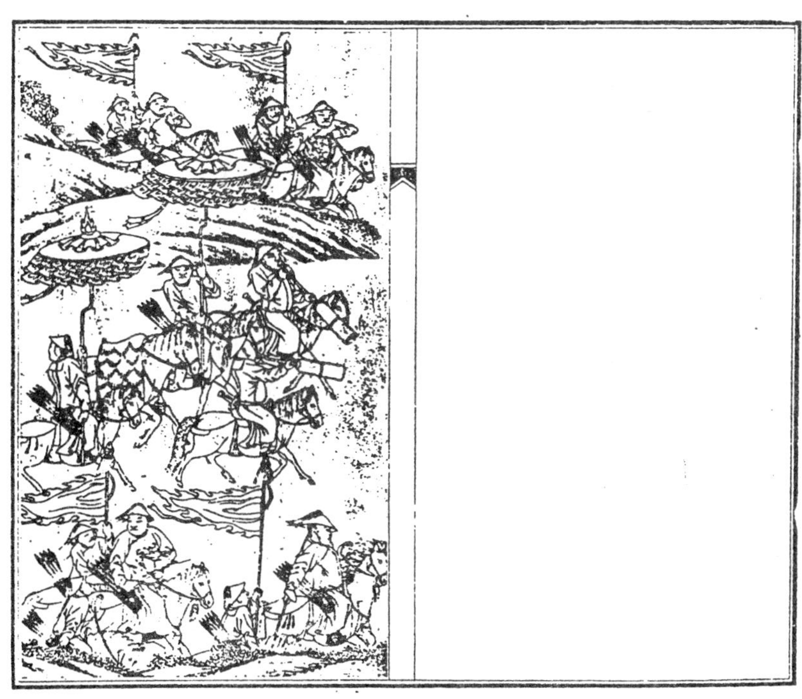

○五月十七日 帝率諸王大臣統軍征明國至十九日進邉克撫安堡及花豹衛三岔兒六小共十一堡二十日招服崔三屯其周圍有四堡民招之不服遂攻取之大兵營於三岔兒堡留六日犒賞三軍均分所得人畜先令兵送人畜歸國又傳令衆軍沿屯搜掘糧窖運畢安營二十八日晨大霧卯時有青赤白三色氣自天垂於營之兩旁上圓似門及起營時氣之兩頭墜於軍之前後相隨

還哉若以
一人何可
所得者雖
曰吾征戰
之人　帝
送還所擄
國修好令
人來言兩
書者共七
名及前送
名從者五
遣通事一
廣寧巡撫
二十二日
敬○六月
十五里方

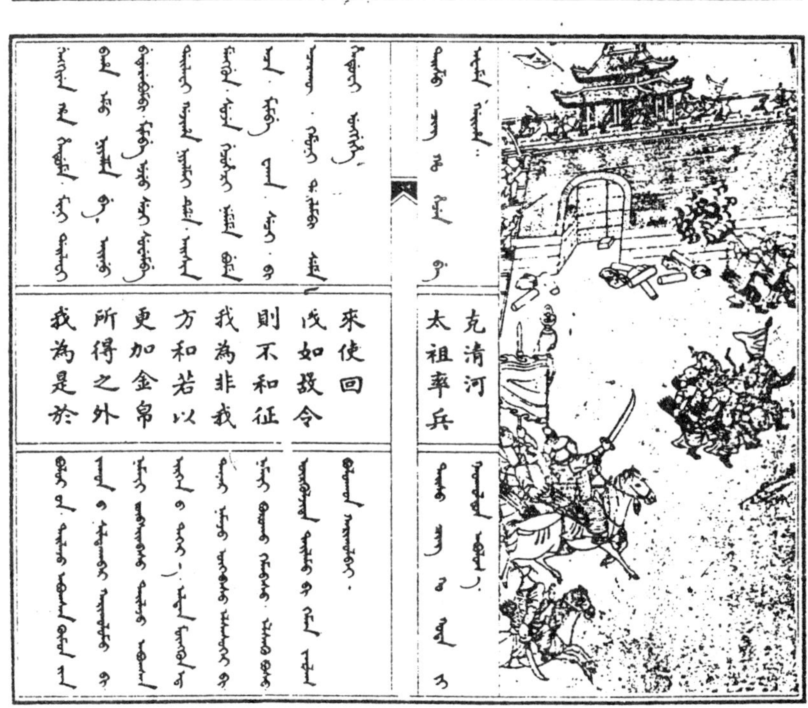

克清河
太祖率兵
來使回
戍如設令
則不和征
我為非我
方和若以
更加金帛
所得之外
我為是於

○七月二十日帝率諸王大臣統大兵征明國入鴉鶻關環攻清河其城守副將鄒儲賢領兵一萬固

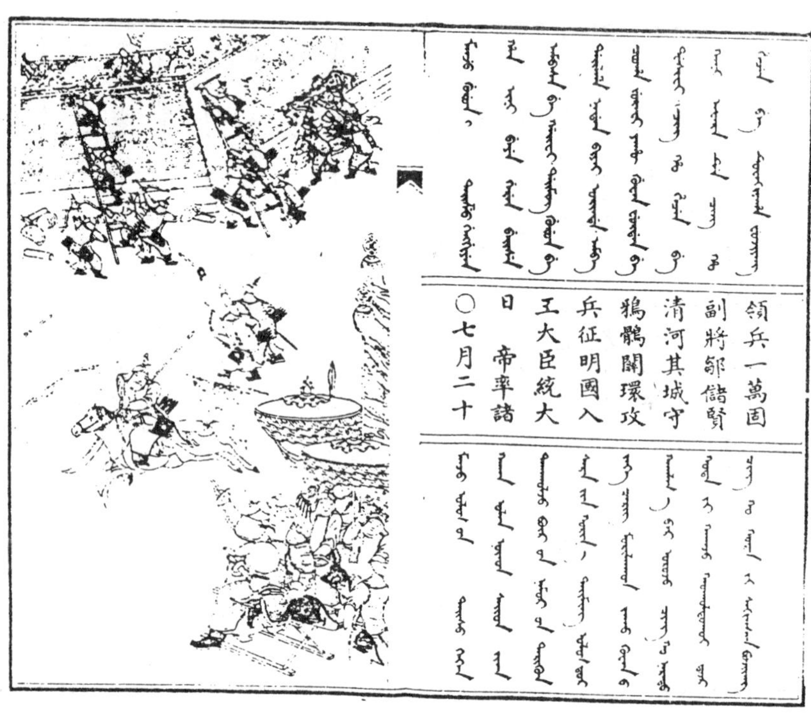

守其中砲手約千餘萬滚木矢石齊下滿洲兵拆城豎梯攻之不避鋒刃躍入四面兵皆潰其城遂拔將

鄒儲賢及兵衆俱殺之一堵墻隳塌二城官民棄城走遂論功行賞畢起兵向遼陽行二日復撤回拆一

百衆往嘉木
德二人率四
帝命納隣音
時秋成
約百餘而去
人及妻子共
棟鄂寨殺七
山林所居新

瀋陽擄滿洲
領兵五千出
副將賀世賢
之日有明國
師當克清河
糧運盡方班
城將周圍之
堵墻鏁場二

窺數次至九
明之偵探潛
運 帝命被
矣納隣音德
慎者斯為貴
之處而能謹
西山於受敵
宿東山明宿

明宿北山令
當令宿南山
避於山險處
農收刈夜則
之曰晝則督
湝河之間戒
湖在渾河界
湖收穫嘉木

與諸王大臣
分之一 帝
明籍其家三
古德偵探不
入官又以葉
德家産半没
納隣之家音
違命之罪籍

帝定二人
三十人得脱
回其餘三百
十人未曙而
收殺處殺七
兵乘夜直抵
兵李如栢遣
月初四日總

遣兵畧會安
月二十五日
寒且止〇九
木石因天漸
營基址收聚
城議定遂經
於界藩處築
地西近明國

馬牧於近邊
匹瘦苦可將
行兵之時馬
士途路更遥
遠其東邊軍
居處與敵相
國為敵我國
議曰今與明

乃行竊盜襲
息事爾大國
納金帛以圖
我為合理可
城決戰若以
日或半月攻
期出邊或十
理可約定戰

若以我為非
書回其書曰
割雙耳令執
順闕留一人
三百斬於撫
其中有屯民
得人畜一千
堡斬殺甚衆

約寬五尺直
白氣自星出
時東南更有
十一日五更
丈餘〇十月
長十五丈寬
形如大刀約
氣自地衝天

南有一道白
九日寅時東
回兵至二十
内業農乎遂
汝國能於城
農夫一千且
百吾將殺汝
殺吾農夫一

至 上陛
之二十日
二百人迎
户來降命
達率民百
部長納喀
海瑚爾哈
二日聞東

後不見二十
斗柄自此以
九日直越北
漸移至二十
每夜向北斗
其出氣之星
四日後不見
衛明國至十

褂四季衣
衣蟒袍小
裘大褂秋
衣蟒段皮
牛十隻冬
口馬十匹
男婦二十
八人各賜

處其為首
者另立一
來欲還家
有遺業而
者列一處
舉家來歸
畢設宴將
殿降衆見

至此吾土
不意施恩
收為臣僕
人民為念
汗以撫聚
畜財物
等圖我人
士欲殺吾

曰滿洲軍
與還家者
多乃附信
不去者甚
見之留而
其欲還者
房田等物
服俱備及

令大王率
日征葉赫
正月初二
四十七年
年明萬歷
未天命四
人至〇己
放還者二

繼學同前
遣承差李
經畧楊鎬
二日遼東
十二月初
率之來〇
眷屬可皆
所居弟兄

十里外所
皆截取之
投城人畜
東十里將
至葉赫城
雅罕寨略
伊特城尼
赫界自克

日深入葉
起行初七
臣統大軍
將諸王大
傑明國自
扎喀關防
兵五千於
將十六員

兵來助與
急林遂領
馬林處告
開原總兵
赫遣使往
兵之日葉
安營當進
城六十里

乃收兵離
附葉赫者
此蒙古乃
所收生畜
又取蒙古
處盡焚之
小二十餘
居屯寨大

之兵以我
罪撤出邊
聲遼人之
曰皇帝若
書回其書
及通事齋
者李繼學
令明國使

二十二日
亦班師〇
而退 帝
懼不能敵
我兵勢重
四十里見
一處出城
葉赫合兵

百兩銀三
千疋金三
再加段三
我與大臣
吾軍士至
千道皆給
所有勅書
道并開原

勅書五百
順所原有
歲幣及撫
理再將我
不罷兵之
王位宣有
七恨崇以
為是解其

千兩兵乃罷〇二十六日令穆哈連領兵一千收東海瑚爾哈部遺民〇二月十五日遣人夫一萬五千赴界藩處運築城之石令騎兵四百衛之

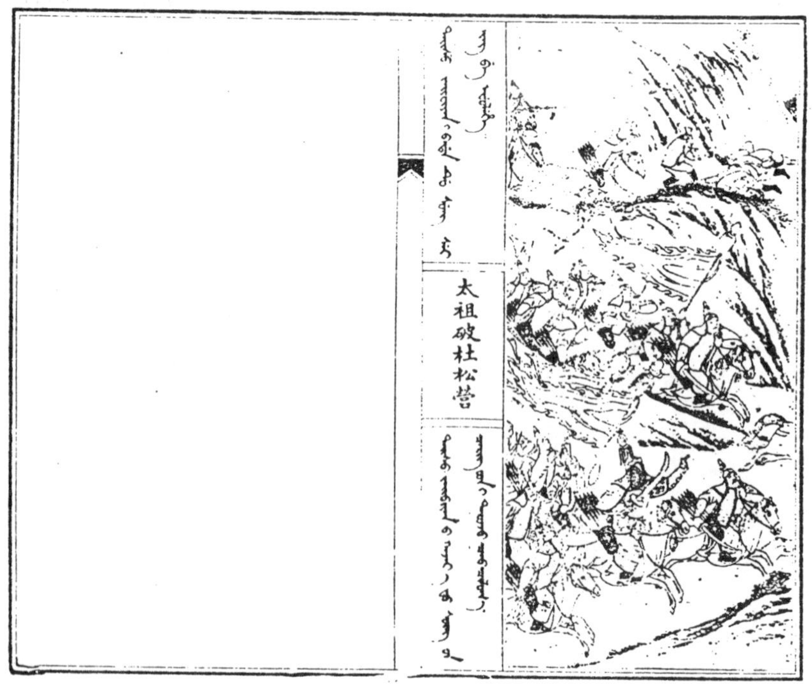

太祖破杜松營

○是月明國
命總兵杜松
榆林人王宣
保定總兵榆
林人趙夢麟
陝西人劉綎
江西人李如
栢遼東總兵

鐵嶺人馬林
宣府人賀世
賢榆林人副
將麻岩大同
人監軍廣寧
分巡道張銓
大名府人海
蓋道康應乾

十四日齋書
叛投者於二
係取撫順時
滿洲人一名
四十七萬遣
二十萬兵號
經畧楊鎬以
起兵至遼陽

洲諸臣曰
十萬侵我滿
臣等統兵二
宣府人文武
原道潘宗顏
泰保定人開
分守道閻鳴
河南人遼陽

路總兵杜：
乃分左翼
遂起兵進發
洲都城約定
合兵攻取滿
日齊出邊境
約三月初一
陽分為四路

兵果會於瀋
路前進後明
月明之時分
月十五日乘
文臣齊至三
將帥及監軍
取滿洲領兵
至言大兵征

王宣趙夢麟監軍道張銓領兵六萬順渾河出撫順關右翼中路總兵李如栢賀世賢監軍道閻鳴泰領

兵六萬往清河出鴉鶻關左翼北路總兵馬林副將麻岩監軍道潘宗顏領兵四萬往開原合葉赫兵出

三岔口右翼南路總兵劉綎監軍道康應乾領兵四萬合朝鮮兵出寬甸口三月初一日諸王聚於朝內

辰時哨探飛報曰昨二十九夜見明國兵執燈火出撫順關此報猶未奏聞其南方哨探又來報曰昨日

兵即時令大
令當先戰此
從撫順關來
敵其大兵必
是誘吾兵南
預見其兵者
故令吾南方
禦之然明國
即將此兵捍
已有兵五百
是實吾南方
曰明國兵來
於 帝 帝
諸王遂奏聞
自棟鄂而進
未時明國兵

祀神後至曰
帝四王因
漢輅按兵候
喀關與達爾
迎敵遂過扎
先往撫順關
且聽之吾等
不能遽至姑
兵其地狹險
清河路雖有
兵來大王曰
曰見清河路
哨探又來報
出正行之際
臣領城中兵
王與諸王大

令兵盡甲善其言即大臣等皆大王與衆心自慰矣夫一見而往其地人令吾兵急

被陷將奈何之吾之人夫兵必竭力攻明將不惜其雖然險固倘罷械界藩山之人夫俱無吾築城運石

勒之言誠亦都曰貝而戰矣額至亦奮勇夫見我兵陣運石人處擺兵布處當於顯

兵立於僻曰何故令四王不悅兵俟　帝漢轄欲掩王與達爾太蘭崗大未時行至

是也吾等當向前立於顯處衆皆從之遂前進與明兵對壘布陣我兵未至之先杜松王宣趙夢麟領兵前來時滿洲護衛人夫騎兵四百伏於薩爾滸山谷口伺敵大

兵過半擊其尾殺至界藩河合運石人夫據於界藩之吉林山險杜松兵圍而攻之山上騎兵率衆人夫一戰折明兵約百人正攻守之際諸王俱至見明兵二萬攻吉

四固山兵之其左翼山兵夾攻右翼四固下衛救以山協助往兵一千登四百更令

內有衛兵曰吾人夫王謂衆臣王三王四上大王二薩爾滸山枝兵立於林山又一

右二固山可也令令照此指揮天將晩即之 帝曰將前議告何諸王遂敵之策若

等所議破諸王曰汝 帝至問往吉林山令兵一千兵言畢遂爾滸山敵可瞭防薩

我兵離城力以戰時衝之際協吉林山下俟吾兵自界藩敵兵固山瞭望右二白旗膽矣再令敵兵自衆敗其界藩兵此兵一山所立之破薩爾滸四固山先兵益於左

唯其助吉衆屍覆成不移時敵直破其營仰射衝殺接戰我兵布陣發砲滸山敵兵進攻薩爾六固山兵兵皆未至進其遠方者陸續而先至疲馬內壯馬者三十里以

陣中明兵
等皆死於
宣趙夢麟
兵杜松王
屍堆積總
遂破之橫
奮勇衝殺
接戰我兵

連發火砲
攻之明兵
河前進夾
旗固山渡
際右二白
正衝擊之
自山而下
林山之兵

逃竄之兵
沿途截殺
已晚令兵
欽山天色
聯絡至碩
十里仆屍

明國兵二
而下追殺
解冰旋轉
渾河者如
與屍衝於
成渠軍器
遍野血流
死者漫山

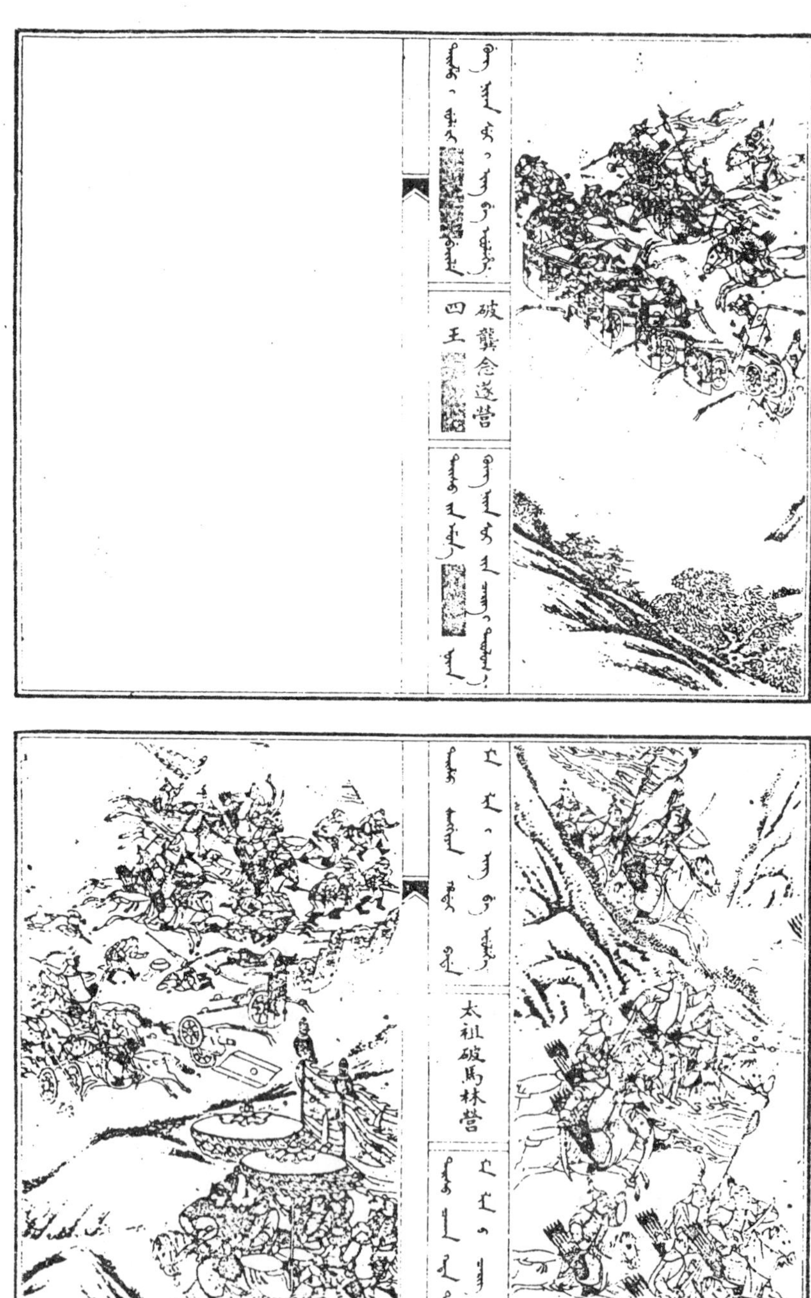
破龔念遂營
四王
太祖破馬林營

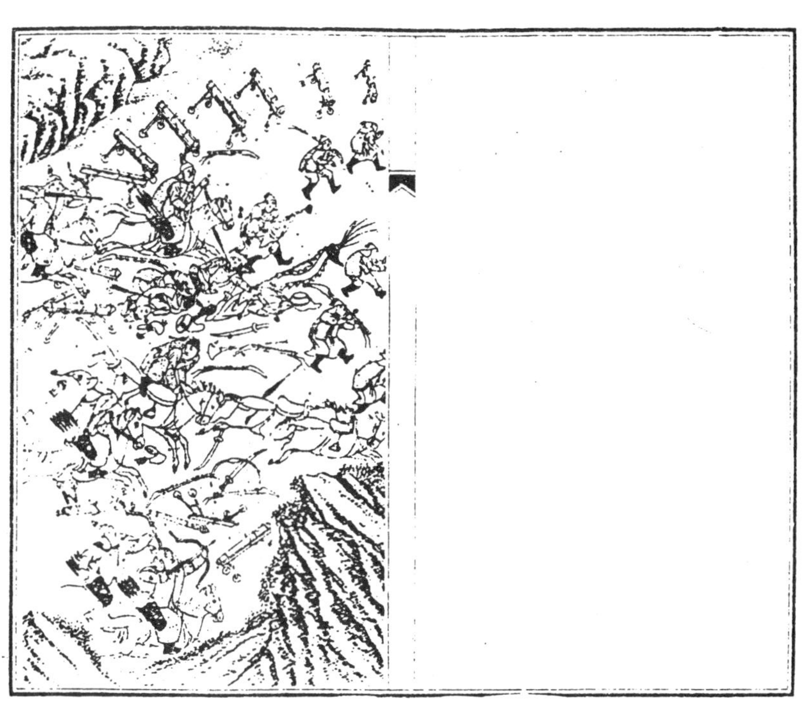

明國左翼北路總兵馬林兵是夜至尚間崖安營鑿壕擊鼓傳鈴周軸巡邏我兵見之遂星夜來報大王次日大王領兵三百餘先往馬林方起營見大王兵至遂傳兵布陣四面而立遶營鑿壕三道壕外列

明國左翼中
大王營不絕
至兵陸續赴
馳報滿洲後
之三次遣人
汾山大王見
營兵立於斐
距三里又一
陣此營西相
三層壕內布
兵皆下馬於
鎗砲其餘衆
兵一層前列
外又容布騎
步立大砲之
大砲砲手皆

兵四王領兵
戰車大敗其
步兵遂推覆
率騎兵突入
齊發砲四王
戰明營兵一
一半下馬步
不滿千人令
率四王領兵
壕列砲 帝
安營遶營鑿
斡琿鄂謨處
步兵一萬至
泌領車營騎
龔念遂李希
路後營遊擊

衝擊其兵必據山上向下曰吾兵當先陣而立 帝兵四萬已布至其處見敵四五人午時兵急領隨從不待四王之崖 帝聞之敵已至尚間大王報到言方立馬眺望於陣中 帝念遂等皆歿盡力追擊

領兵前進即 帝曰吾當來戰大王謂營西面兵遂四五十人明時下馬者方令衆兵下馬往左二固山步戰大王遂登山可下馬戰我也不必曰是兵欲來外兵合 帝營內兵與壕登山見敵衆敗矣衆兵將

衝擊明兵
我兵發矢
發砲接戰
營營中兵
奔明之大
不暇整飛
後行伍亦
之前不待

六固山兵見
勦殺大半其
戰敵兵遂敗
殺入兩兵混
台吉等併力
王三王與諸
入其營後二
策馬迎敵直

皆赤
崖下河水
釋雪尚間
流如陽春
免血水分
林僅以身

陣總兵馬
等皆斬於
副將麻岩
漫山遍野
追殺死者
我兵乘勢
大敗而走
勢不能敵

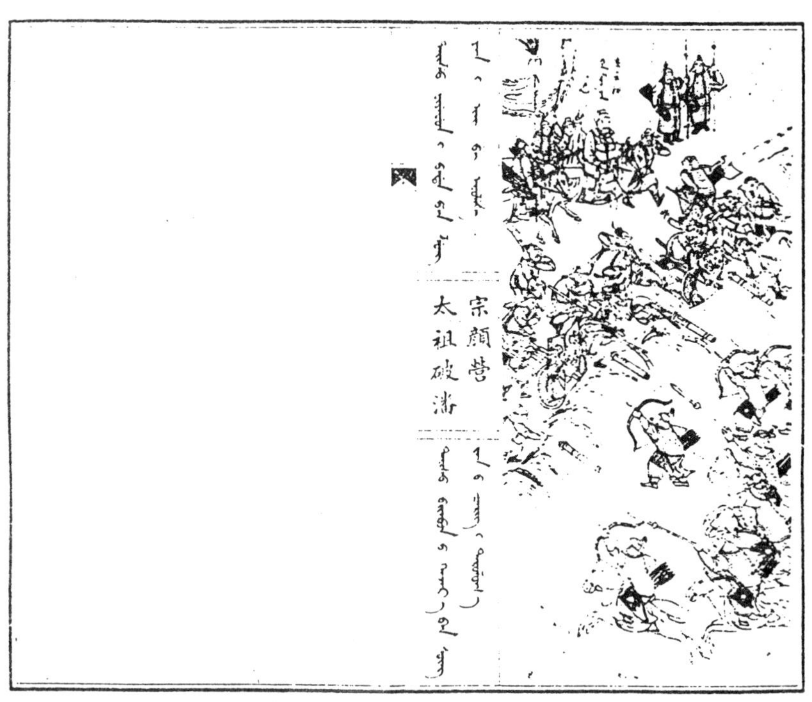
太祖破渤
宗顏營

○乃收兵攻斐芬山潘宗顏之營令兵一半下馬向上攻之宗顏兵一萬以戰車為衛鎗砲連發我兵突入摧其戰車遂破其營宗顏并全軍覆没時葉赫錦台什布揚

古領兵來助明國至中固城聞明國兵敗大驚遂回

四王敗劉綎前鋒

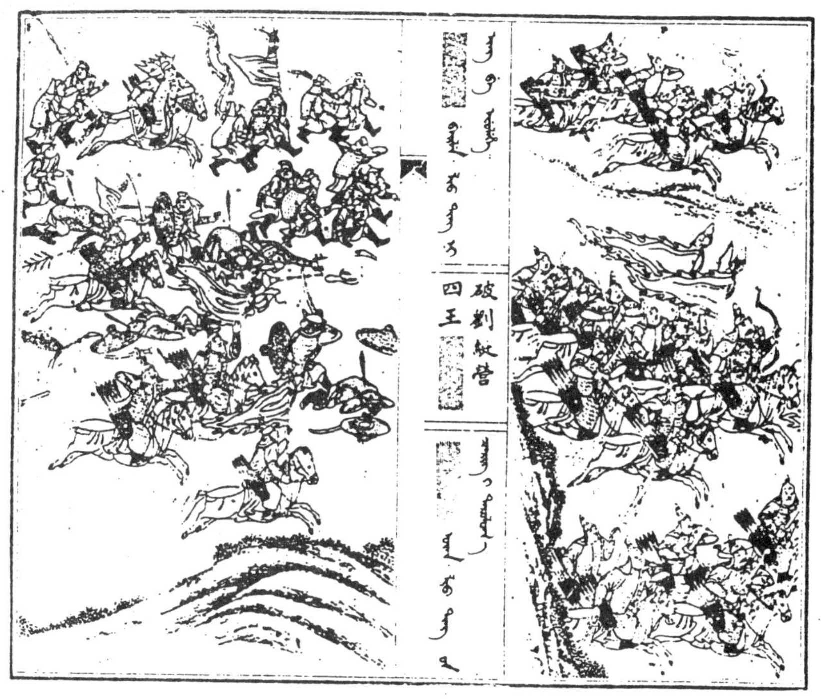
四王
破劉紋營

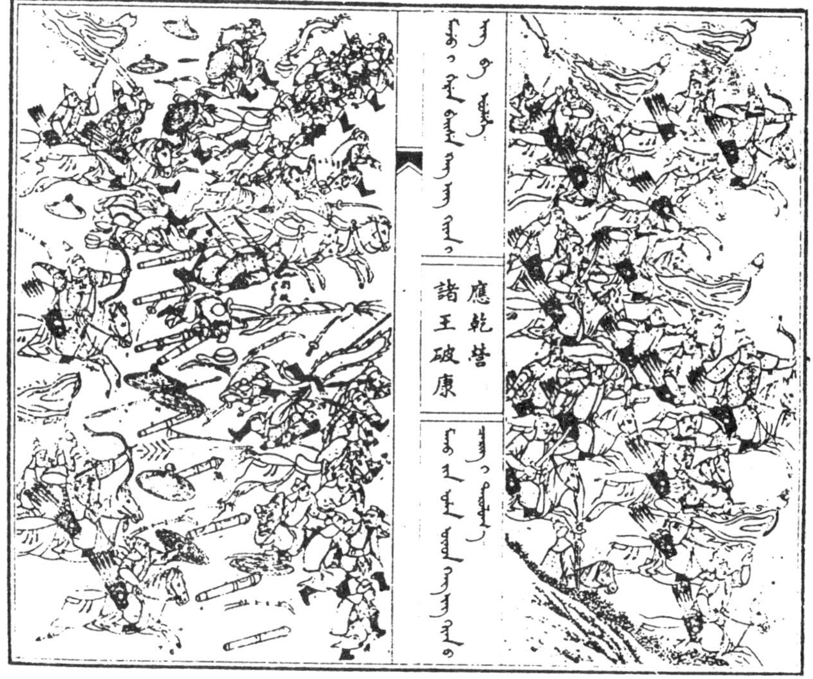
諸王破康
應乾營

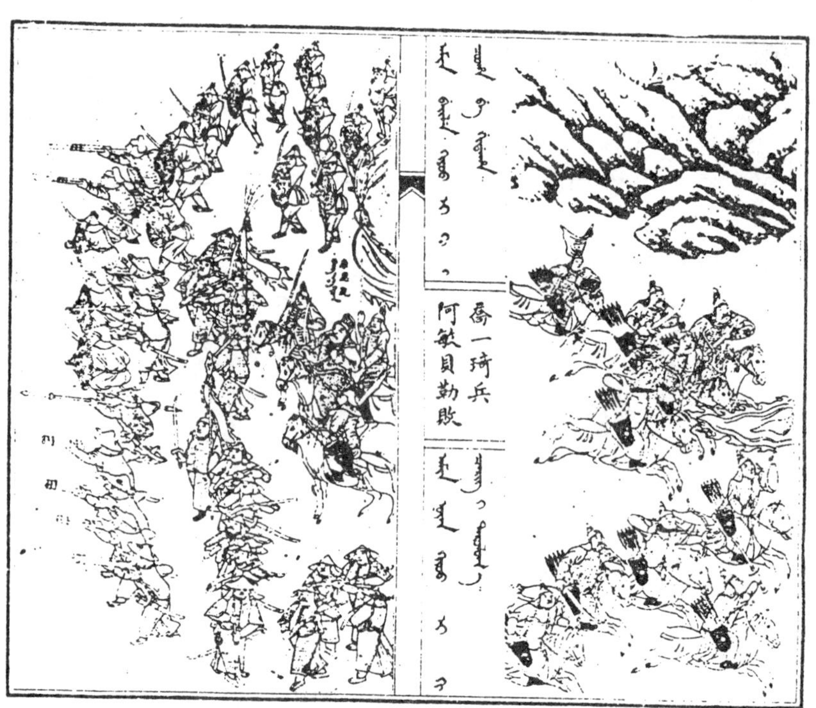
阿敏貝勒敗
喬一琦兵

諸王等領大
之 帝隨率
領兵一千繼
令二王阿敏
是處翼晨又
往 帝駐於
領兵一千先
令達爾漢轄

部城而進遂
二路之兵向
清河路呼蘭
南方棟鄂與
偵探來報曰
本方安營有
申時至古爾
帝收大兵

果前去吾欲
前問曰大王
乘馬至 帝
王亦行四王
起行繼而三
允之大王遂
而徐進 帝
汗可率衆兵

待祭旗後
卒前探消息
十人扮作小
吾領從者二
祭旗大王曰
牛八隻謝天
因破敵乃殺
兵行至界藩

聞有二路兵王至曰今又聚於此見大及公主等正門內時后妃都城徑往宮更大王乃至起行夜近初

留後言畢亦往吾等何故大兄既已獨同行四王曰息汝可隨我哨探前聽消曰汝兄扮作與同之 帝

城天明令諸二王四王八五更遇大王界藩起行至旗畢申時自屯候 帝祭十五里至大大王夜出城

命前去接戰能至吾待父兵迎敵且不來兵吾已有盡被殺矣此二路兵已敗曰撫順關原來柰何大王

納額赫三人真托保額爾而進牛彔額能移者向前寨叔跛額不劉綎兵焚遺皆避於山林時棟鄂路民

綎兵出寬甸賢之兵當劉李如栢賀世以防清河路城留兵四千兵　帝於都甸路劉綎之王領兵敵寬

喀什正行之大兵出瓦爾三王四王率處巴時大王兵於山谷隘爾漢轄遂伏爾漢轄兵達人逃出會達

四百五十餘托保領殘兵中折兵五十額赫死於陣圍住額爾納被劉綎大兵百迎敵搏戰率守衛兵五

西汝令右翼
吾行於山之
曰此言最善
下擊之大王
領兵上山向
後相機吾當
兄領大兵在
擊之四王曰
自山上向下
大王領兵欲
達哩岡布陣
兵遂登阿布
野掠見我大
來令一萬兵
精兵二萬前
際劉綎部下

大潰遂走四
西而進明兵
左翼兵自山
進大王亦率
亦至衝擊而
戰之際後兵
刃相接正搏
從上下擊兵
出衆軍之先
精兵三十起
翼兵前進領
也四王率右
親入負吾言
後觀之愼勿
衝擊汝可在
兵登山向下

部下兵皆執
前戰見應乾
皆至遂列陣
駐兵諸王隨
曠野處四王
兵營於富察
步兵合朝鮮
軍道康應乾

乃安營見監
軍覆沒我兵
死於陣中全
殺入劉綎戰
未布陣之先
營兵來乘其
又見劉綎二
王隨掩殺之

二萬兵掩
衝入破其
兵遂發矢
無所見我
漫昏黑竟
向本營迷
煙塵皆返
風驟起其

砲連發適大
際明營中鎗
列當進戰之
鎗砲層層布
紙甲柳條盔
朝鮮兵皆披
鎗技藤皮甲
筤筅竹扞長

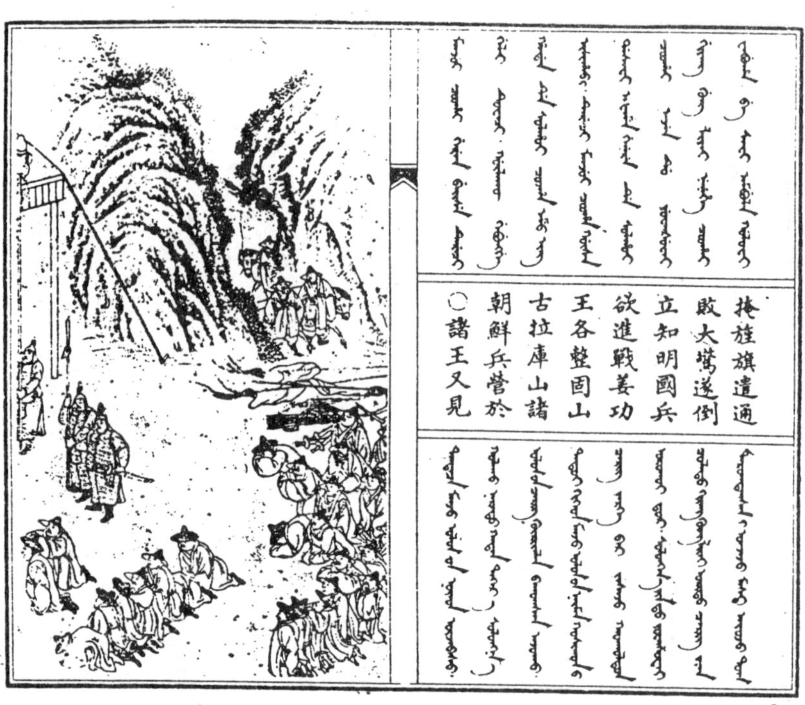

○諸王又見朝鮮兵營於古拉庫山諸王各整固山欲進戰姜功立知明國兵敗大營遂倒掩旌旗遣通

事執旗來曰此來非吾願也昔日倭侵我國據我城郭奪我土地當此急難賴明助之得退倭兵此恩當

報今調吾國兵馬敢不來若宥吾罪願往納降且吾兵有在明國兵營者汝已殺矣

殺殆盡風塵遂止康應乾僅以身免　帝前遣二王與達爾漢轄擊明遊擊喬一琦營破之一琦率殘兵奔入朝鮮都元帥姜功立營

姜功立率兵歸降

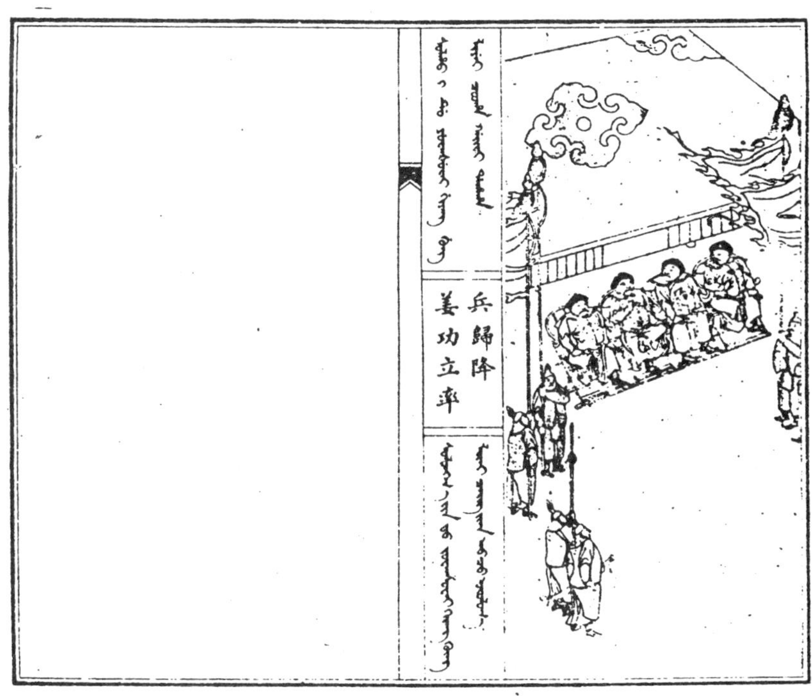

宿於此若
令領兵且
功立曰吾
回告之姜
戰令通事
來不然必
主將可先
爾等若降

議定乃曰
獻之諸王
而已吾即
相從兵丁
擊一員并
有明之遊
我國兵惟
令營中盡

功立率五
王次日姜
帥來見諸
於是副元
急遂自縊
一琦見勢
擲於山下
盡捉明兵

即降言訖
率衆翼日
宿於營吾
見諸王即
副元帥先
逃走令令
衆軍混亂
身先往恐

日收人畜
綖兵駐三
既殺盡劉
大宴諸王
小宴十日
賓禮五日
帝待以
衆官叩見

副元帥率
殿都元帥
城 帝陞
兵先往都
令朝鮮官
設宴相待
來降諸王
千兵下山

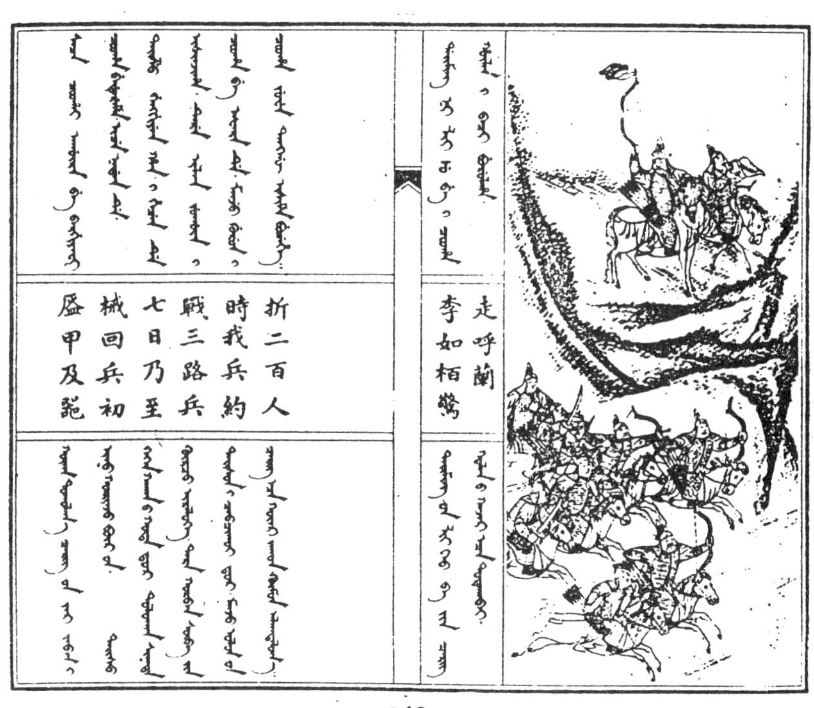

走呼蘭
李如栢驚

折二百人
時我兵約
戰三路兵
七日乃至
械回兵初
盔甲及器

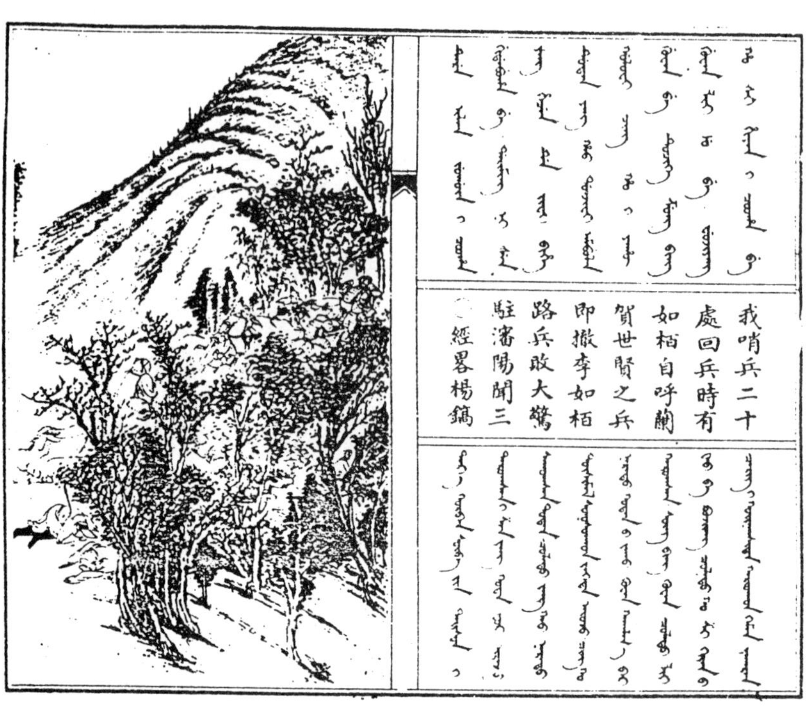

我哨兵二十
處回兵時有
如栢自呼蘭
賀世賢之兵
即撤李如栢
路兵敢大驚
駐瀋陽聞三
經畧楊鎬

兵聲言四十
臣以二十萬
王曰明國君
帝笑謂諸
三路兵已破
死者約千餘
走自相踩踏
大潰奪路而

匹於是明兵
十獲馬五十
而入殺兵四
梢揮之喊噪
狀將帽繫弓
作後有大兵
於山上吹螺
人見之乃立

大恨之事遣
事一人書七
及官三員通
降將張應京
一日令朝鮮
〔〕三月二十
不稱善者也
於四方無有

强究言之間
殺必謂我兵
為我往來勦
吾兵衆若以
兵破敵必謂
若以為我分
來戰各國聞
七萬分四路

鑒之令天之
國結怨穹蒼
若有意與明
此兵吾自來
凌巳甚故興
舉因明國欺
干戈非吾樂
亦知之令動

享國長久吾
如此亦未得
歸於一統雖
主併三四國
金元二國之
往書曰昔者
使者與之俱
書一封遣二

有朝鮮官趙
金大定帝時
不然耳昔者
答前情不得
曾救之故報
倭難時明國
乃因爾國有
其非本心也

助明國吾料
明國爾兵來
故祐我而罪
非以直斷之
是者是非者
國耶亦不過
私我而薄明
眷顧我者豈

間國不一也
王矣且天地
往結局惟在
留之繼此以
特念爾王故
擒爾官十員
無仇陳今陣
之吾二國原

不納由此觀
中立國也遂
亦不助金是
鮮王不助宋
二帝時爾朝
曰吾征徽欽
餘城叛附帝
惟忠以四十

抑以爲既助
同仇明國耶
國原無釁隙
意以爲吾二
太甚今王之
吾二國辱人
欲令子姪主
知又聞明國

極矣王豈不
凌我國橫逆
違天背理欺
奉行天道今
明朝大國必
皆亡耶吾意
獨存今小國
豈有使大國

一千於初
繼選騎兵
野處牧馬
城又擇曠
住卜基築
内遂親西
得耕於境
衛令農夫

築城屯兵防
吾欲據界藩
趂春草餧養
戰馬羸弱當
三日　帝曰
詳○四月初
之耶願聞其
明國不忍背

馬法足下滿洲國主化致書於觀察使朴國平安道書曰朝鮮齎書至其併前使者者十三人官一員從日朝鮮遣月二十八一千〇五俘獲人畜明鐵嶺境九日道入

明國與我之善事也亦非貴邦動干戈矣即四方皆不特隣邦生民塗炭因而征戰明國為仇今貴國與毫無怨惡二百餘載國至今經國與吾二土相連明吾二國地

書云吾有
交道也來
國亦自有
方知然隣
四人來言
張應京等
事原委聞
不必言此
屬已往今
不從何事
此舉其如
吾亦不願
蓋大義也
子豈敢拒
子父之言
國猶如父

也〇六月
好乃為善
疆復乎前
國各守邊
至矣吾二
言不久而
之必喜善
道明朝聞
果行合大
無疆以後
天眷受福
便可常享
即此一念
穹蒼鑒之
之君結怨
心與明國

初八日遣穆哈連收東海瑚爾哈部遺民千戶丁男二千而回帝出城接款降者置酒二百席宰牛二十隻大宴賜所降路長每男婦各十人馬十匹牛十隻衣五件次者賜男婦各五人馬牛各五匹隻衣三件房田等物皆給之

太祖克開原

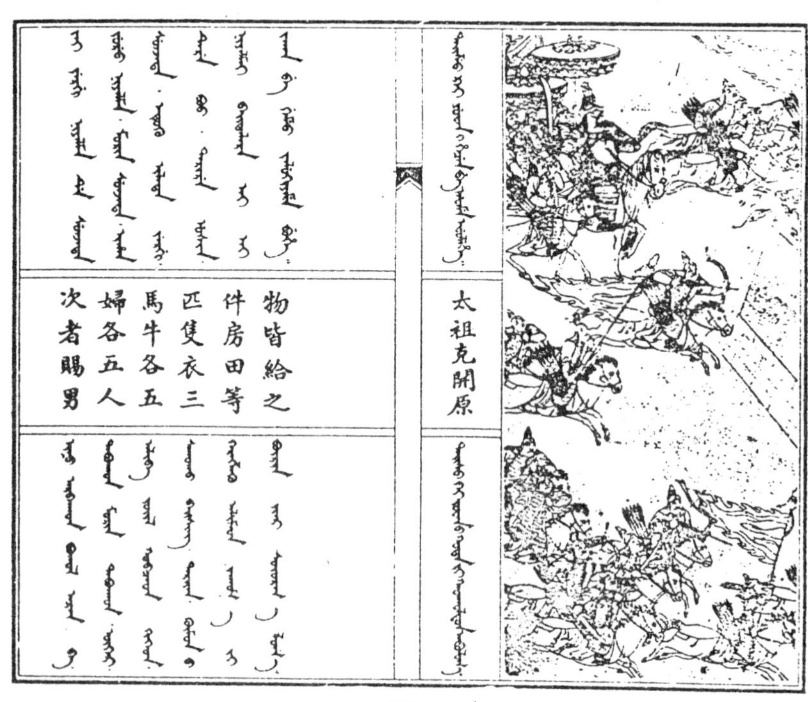

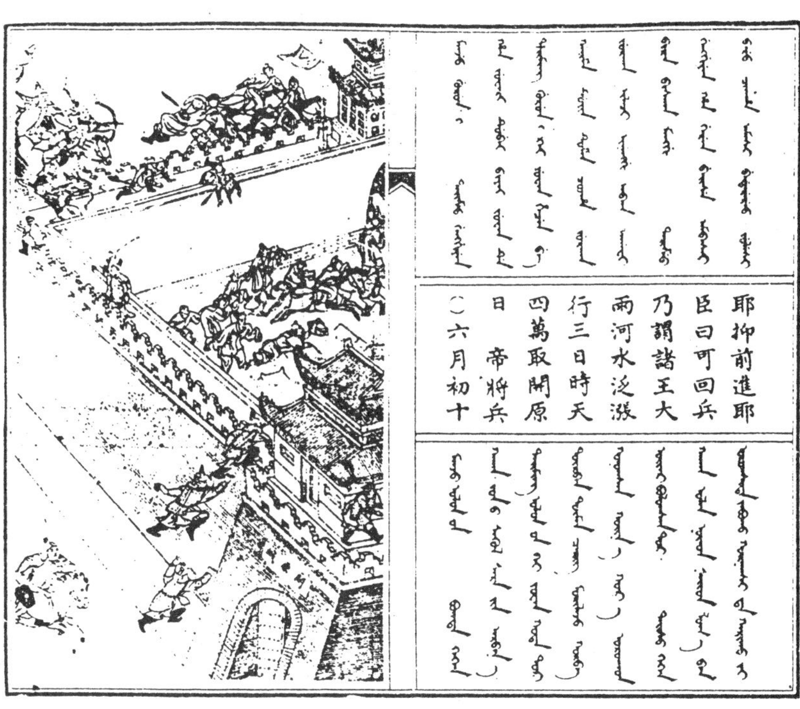

(一)六月初十日帝將兵四萬取開原行三日時天雨河水泛溢乃謂諸王大臣曰可回兵耶抑前進耶

倘路塗泥淖河水難濟何以行之會議屯留二日待水落地乾恐此際有逃者洩機於明知取開原故令

兵進瀋陽地界遂遣兵一百畧瀋陽殺人三十餘生擒二十而回令人視開原路河水可濟否來報曰開

車雲梯進攻
我兵遂布戰
外四門屯兵
布兵防守城
㦬官等城上
守志備禦何
高貞遊擊于
鄭之範叅將
軍道事推官
于化龍署監
兵馬林副將
開原守城總
兵十六日至
聞言遂起大
路不泥 帝
原處無兩道

官等並城中
于守志何㦬
于化龍高貞
範預遁馬林
於壕内鄭之
之兵盡截殺
而走被抵門
破大驚衝突
三面兵見城
皆潰其城外
城上四面兵
遂踰城而入
者雲梯未豎
奪門時攻城
塞門掩殺正
欲先破東面

開原受守備
先投於明居
布圖巴圖魯
盡有蒙古阿
物三日猶未
回收人畜財
四十餘人而
二十人追殺
見即走我兵
之鐵嶺兵一
諸王領兵迎
三千兵來援
探來報鐵嶺
棲而坐有哨
帝登城南
士卒盡殲之

濟渾河牧於
之令兵馬不
築城治屋居
都城於界藩
曰吾等不回
帝謂王大臣
屋遂回兵
廨并民間房
其城郭焚公
功行賞畢毀
與之將士論
子家業盡查
餘來降將妻
總及兵二百
執遂帶二千
職因妻子被

大臣軍士房
帝行宮及王
宴之是月
諸王妃至大
遣人迎后幷
之牧馬於邊
遂至界藩居
月興師言訖
早令之壯八
馬牧於此地
欲居界藩令
何日得肥吾
暑路遥馬匹
方至者今天
之東三四日
或有居都城
二三日至者
近不等或有
自此歸家遠
已經二十日
月炎暑行兵
知也當此六
曰是非汝所
損跑具 帝
歸家以便整
肥壯也士卒
水洗拭方得
採草牧養以
都各修馬廐
奏曰不如還
王大臣議定
邊境可也諸

一百羊一百
人一百牛馬
是賜阿布圖
故來投耳於
彼聞吾養人
天意祐我矣
此來降者知
降 帝曰觀

人覓妻子來
共帶二十餘
守堡戴一位
王和白奇策
屏戴集賓金
原千總王一
月有原居闕
屋皆成(二)七

十疋從者皆
段八疋布八
銀四十兩紬
四十駝一隻
牛馬四十羊
各賜人四十
堡百總等官
疋布百疋守

十兩紬段十
駝二隻銀五
五十羊五十
人五十牛馬
六千總各賜
疋布二百疋
兩紬段二十
駝五隻銀百

賽為人如飛
妃后妃曰爾
將此夢語后
之故夢中云
有隙常思擒
之長與 帝
覺爾賽家古
賽矣隨呼而

言吾擒得爾
鵜鶘執之聲
翔羅得一白
群鳥往來翱
天鵝鵜鶘及
舍 帝夜夢
牛馬財物田
列等賜妻奴

之兆也

國所獲故為
名之人為吾
將以大有聲
夢主吉蓋天
大臣對曰此
王大臣諸王
次日復語諸
禽何以擒之

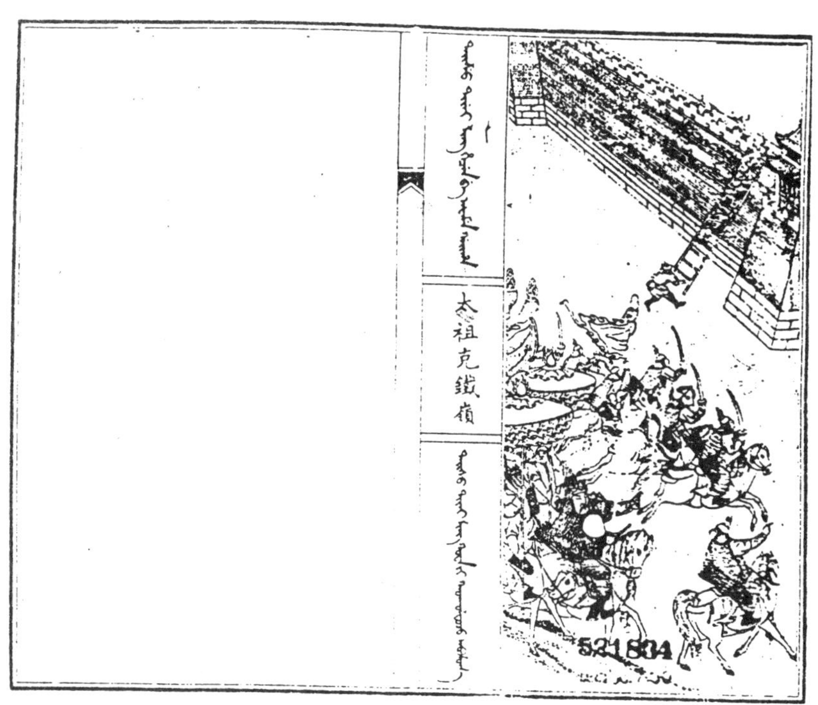
太祖克鐵嶺
521804

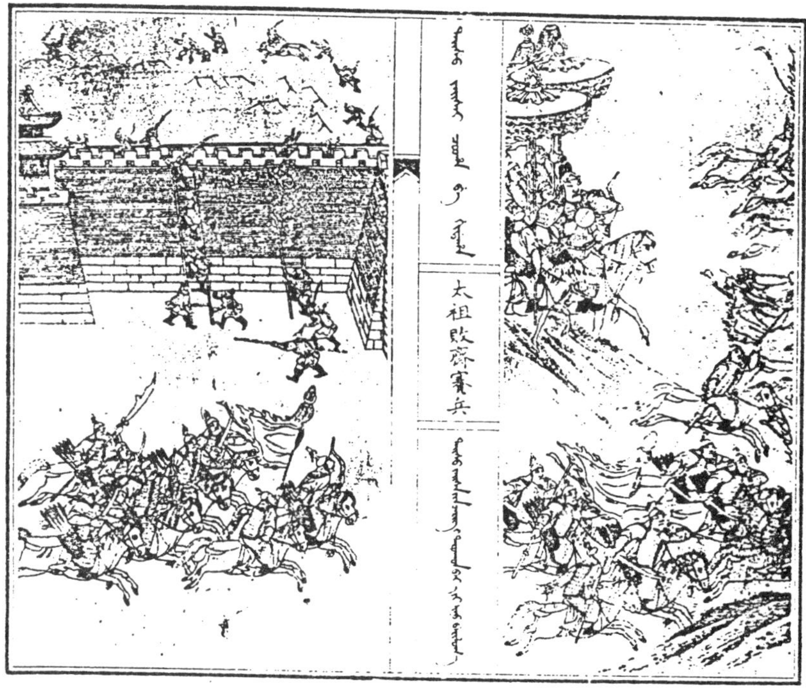
太祖敗齋賽兵

見太祖
陣擒齋賽

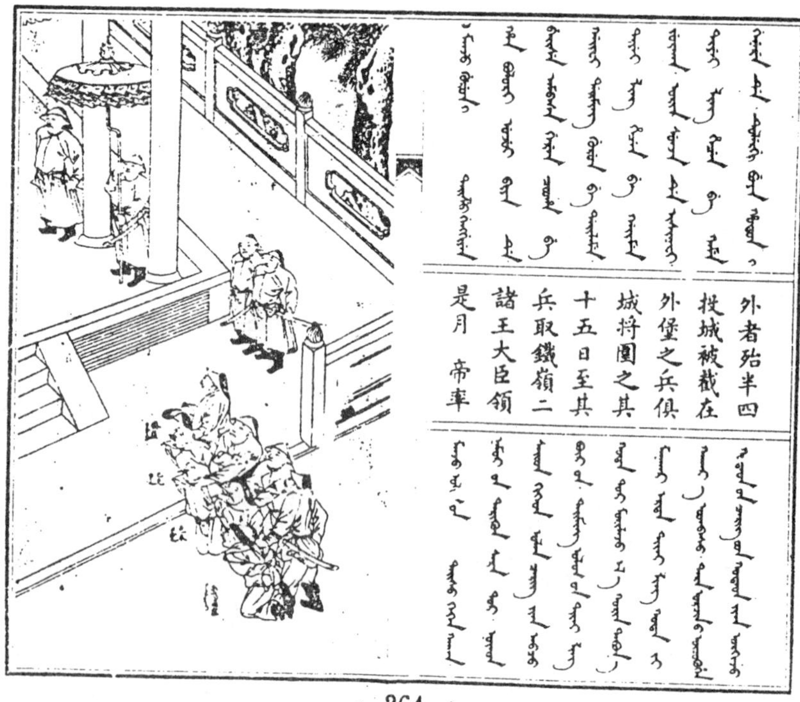
外者殆半四
投城被截在
外堡之兵俱
城將圍之其
十五日至其
兵取鐵嶺二
諸王大臣領
是月 帝率

散遁走我兵
布戰車雲梯
攻城北面城
中游擊喻成
名史鳳鳴李
克泰令衆軍
連放銃砲薛
發矢石我兵
豎梯拆城垛
摧鋒突入四
面皆潰將喻
成名史鳳鳴
李克泰及士
辛盡殺之
帝入城駐於
兵備道官廨

是夜蒙古喀
爾喀部齋賽
扎嚕特部巴
克與巴雅爾
圖岱青色本
諸台吉等約
二十人共領
兵萬餘星夜
而來伏於秫
田內及天明
有出城牧馬
者約十人齋
賽兵見之發
矢追殺我兵
一見即出城
知是蒙古欲

諸王大臣遂
此何悔之有
先殺吾人如
恨有五今又
吾與齋賽之
乃齋賽兵也
帝曰此兵
戰恐貽後悔

大王曰今一
戰可急擊之
見曰何為不
行 帝出城
但躡其後而
吾人已被殺
上命不戰而
進戰又無

於鐘樓內諸
五十餘盡囚
十餘人兵百
布囊又其臣
夫岱噶爾塔
子也齋賽妹
賽明安貝勒
爾沁桑噶爾

克色本併科
賓克圖及巴
色特希爾克
齋賽并二子
者甚衆生擒
河溺死及殺
其兵追至遼
領兵衝殺敗

者餘皆無人破頭顱厮有十數軍中之僕側答曰吾時四王在皆無恙否與王大臣

瑚齋曰汗其部下人爲齋賽等叩見設宴張鼓樂吉夢也次日寨正應 汗之曰得擒齋王大臣俱奇

二子并兵賽兵敗及國寄言齋十一人還博羅齋等齋賽部臣三軍先放人畜盡散

功行賞將兵三日論無以對屯然垂首竟古等皆報保全否蒙等鞍馬俱恙不知汝

令回
也諭畢遂
人放還可
擒百四十
不如將所
所掠奈何
畜為他人
屬軍民生

被殺恐所
其兵已盡
既留齋賽
大臣曰令
帝謂諸王
乃班師
被擒之事
百五十餘

太祖滅葉赫

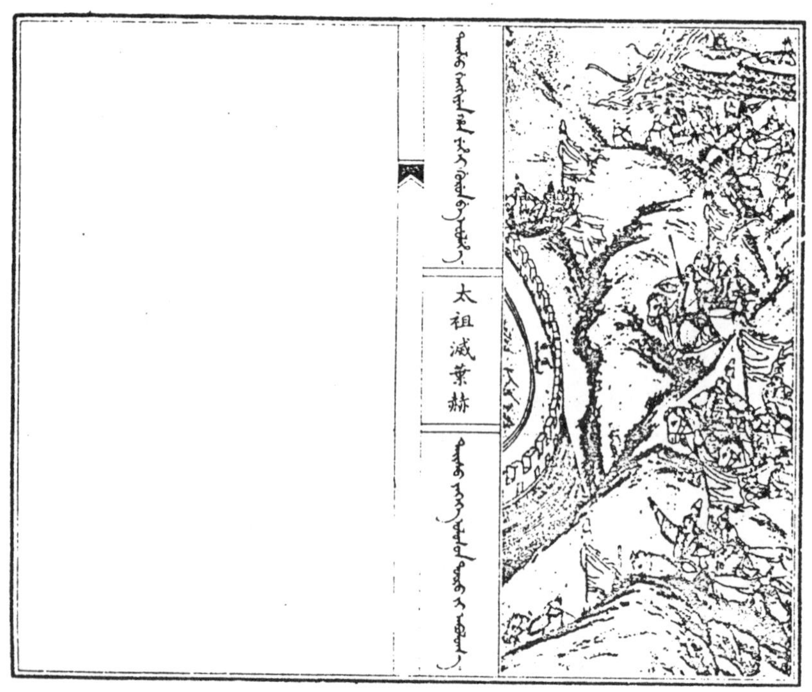

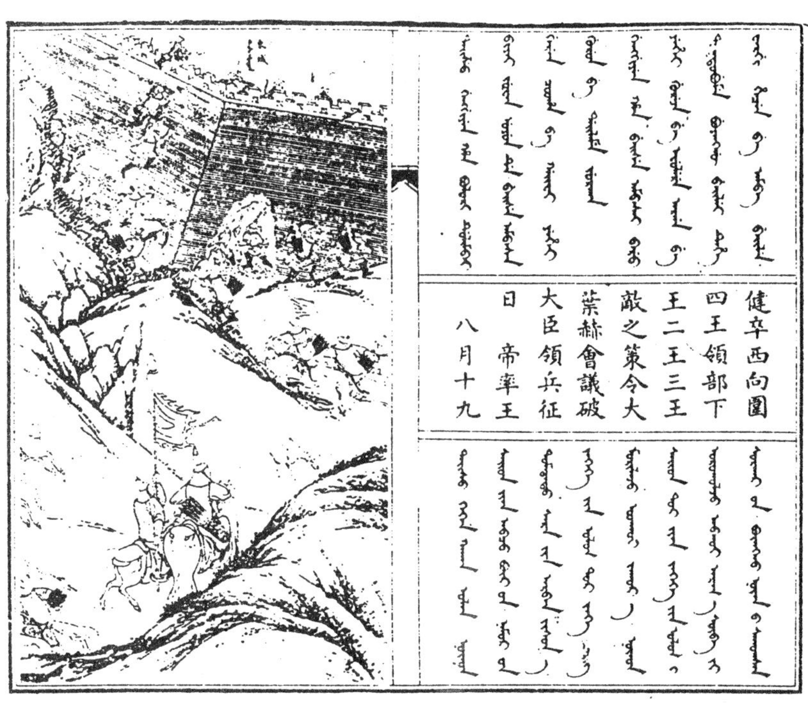

八月十九日帝率王大臣領兵征葉赫會議破敵之策令大王二王三王四王領部下健卒西向圍

布揚古城親率八固山額真并大兵東向取錦台什城議定大、星夜前進、赫哨探見、即飛報於布

揚古曰滿洲大兵至矣於是葉赫國民皆驚惶其屯寨之民近者入城遠者避於山谷二十二日天明大

兵至布揚古布爾杭古領兵出城西立於閭上吹螺吶喊見滿洲兵盔甲明如冰雪旌旗斂戟如林大兵壓境漫山遍野前後不絶如流威勢可畏布揚古大驚急入城諸王領健卒遂圍其城日方昇 帝率大

兵至錦台什城四面圍之遂分隊破其外郭軍士登竪雲梯戰車已備令錦台什降錦台什不從答曰吾非明兵比均男子也吾亦有手豈肯降汝惟有死戰而已遂令兵攻之兩軍矢發如雨我兵即推戰車登

山擁至折其城城上滾放巨石藥礶檑木我兵不退遂折城而入城上兵迎戰復又敗走於是四面皆潰軍民俱降錦者於是城中傳諭勿殺降遣人執黃蓋城中軍民又令衆兵勿殺帝遣人執旗各入其家

台什携妻子登其所居之臺我兵圍之招曰汝降則下不然必攻之錦台什答曰吾不能戰城已被克令困於家雖戰亦不能致勝若得吾妹所生子[illegible]来此一見得聞確實言吾即下矣聞者將此言奏之

曰人之相貌
漢額駙二人
費英東達爾
能辨其真僞
從来未識馬
吾甥
至錦台什曰
領命而去既

兵析臺四王
不然可令吾
之彼降則已
即降汝盍往
言但得汝到
至曰爾男有
西城召四王
常令人往

我之善言是
未得其父活
觀此子顏色
老嫗為也吾
台什曰何用
今来認之錦
往議和好可
格勒之乳媪

遣汝子德爾
最者吾國曾
乎若不深信
汝豈未之聞
使者必嘗告
偉者耶汝國
人中有比奇
汝豈不識常

敵人并命巳
意不過誘取
此臺何為汝
被克今居於
是之固尚且
築其城郭如
已勞民多年
天險之山皆

四王曰汝於
居願死於此
此地是吾祖
戰豈能勝然
今困於此臺
城鐵門已失
殺之耳吾石
欲賺吾下臺

而血可飲耶
者豈肉可食
親屠戮欲盡
汝等征伐六
宥之則生昔
皇考之則死
臺即引見父
已在此若下

實之言歟吾
勝汝而出確
下豈戰不能
確實之言方
何故曰得吾
中汝計耶乃
以名臣攻戰
耳不知執肯

来即下故来
王曰男言吾
前言不下四
慰再三仍執
則生之矣勸
我故而不究
則戮之若以
父若念此恐

之禍已至吾
爲令汝喪身
殺者殺爲者
和乃將吾使
能勝而欲求
好似爭戰不
十次欲相和
吾遣人二三

而誰若念此
四十萬非爾
致明人舉兵
什誰間吾親
怒曰阿爾塔
什往見帝
遂令阿爾塔
回時吾方下

汗察言覩色
什先去見
近臣阿爾塔
爾勿去待吾
矣錦台什曰
皇否則吾去
疾下引見父
耳若願降可

吾等戰不能格勒謂父曰與之見德爾德爾格勒来下矣四王召来相見吾即存彼處當召格勒被傷猶聞吾子德爾錦台什又曰曰我主宜降爾塔什往招其主於是阿追究今回招但前愆何必忍殺之宜也

勒於家以其王留德爾格勿縛我也四日欲殺即殺六矣死於今勒曰年三十縛之德爾格勒回欲殺遂王執德爾格不從於是四言之再三竟則死留則生盍下臺若殺上更欲何為令居此臺之勝城已陷矣

急趨而下錦
降遂携穉子
什妻見夫不
遇之其錦台
之兄也當善
同食曰此爾
與德爾格勒
與之今四王

帝　帝推食
爾格勒見
殺四王引德
當誅其子勿
之罪也其父
而不從是父
曰子招父降
言奏之　帝

揚古布爾杭
不從既而布
圍西城招而
縊之諸王正
自下遂執而
身被火炙乃
殆盡錦台什
其房舍火焚

撤毀臺之兵
台什已死遂
焚諸將疑錦
台什縱火自
斧毀其臺錦
甲我兵遂執
從者重整盔
台什執弓與

過死於吾小
汝等之身不
得生也戰則
過欲恩之使
撫之意予不
妻兄弟也招
去乎汝主吾
肯舍汝等而

兵既至此豈
而不從料吾
王曰初令降
之何顧降大
雖戰亦無如
使曰令吾等
破大驚乃遣
古間東城已

出此言既破
曰汝等再勿
本城大王恕
将吾等仍居
一確實誓言
願降汝可出
又来曰吾等
者以言回告

婦人之理使
来吾豈有殺
岳母可令先
其母乃吾之
或懼而不來
彼弟兄二人
得生果納降
卒之手降則

確言吾二子
愛母曰汝無
互抱以示親
別久相見必
畢滿洲俗凡
大王抱見禮
將母送出城
布爾杭古遂

死矣布揚古
來攻汝等必
已破　汗駕
降不然東城
去乎汝可速
力不能拔而
等居此豈吾
一城復留汝

可去見父皇
出降大王曰
飲之遂開門
古布爾杭古
半送與布揚
將此酒飲半
後殺無赦遂
不從克城之

及汝等倘必
而猶不降殃
我若我誓後
降後殃及於
若殺汝等於
劃酒而誓曰
大王乃以刀
不信故懼耳

布揚古駐馬終不答大王挽其轡曰汝非男子乃婦人耶一言已定立此更欲何為可隨吾往見遂引見

帝布揚古膝不並屈惟屈一膝不拜而起 帝以金杯賜酒布揚古屈膝不端酒亦不飲沾唇而已仍

不拜而起 帝謂大王曰可引汝男仍往彼城 帝默思謂吾既不念舊惡欲豢養之當以為死而幸生

可也反如此漫無喜意仍若仇讐於叩首起拜之間尚不肯屈此人將何以養養之也是夜命縊之以其

毫無犯俱遷
亦無離散秋
夫婦諸親等
戮父子兄弟
民等一無殺
降其諸臣軍
葉赫城郭皆
殺之於是凡

及兵一千俱
遊擊馬時楠
助此二城者
也將明國來
長子留之可
可姑宥念吾
雖有過惡尚
弟布爾杭古

哈爾林丹汗
二日蒙古察
○十月二十
部始合為一
征服是年諸
一語音者俱
鮮鴨綠江同
嫩江南至朝

邊北自蒙古
自東海至遼
滅矣滿洲國
匹葉赫自此
千餘賜以馬
查其無馬者
田糧穀等物
徙而來給房

撫其城取其貢
巳親往廣寧招
於汝國令夏吾
來明人數受兵
吾聞自戊午年
二國乃仇讐也
主安否明於吾
水濱三萬人英

統攠之致問
九姓祖之號
青吉斯汗乃
主青吉斯汗
四十萬衆英
曰蒙古國統
拜瑚齋書來
遣使康喀勒

今復來滿洲王
是汝將前使可
耳若以吾言為
善之言故相絶
驕慢告汝以不
汝使捏言吾之
者常相往來因
先時吾二國使

是非穹蒼鑒之
從吾言二人之
吾名安在設不
之城為汝所得
交惡若吾所服
汝吾二人原無
之吾將不利於
賦倘汝兵往圖

等致書曰齋賽
會合五部貝勒
禮克圖洪巴圖
日求爾喀部卓
送爲其使()是
之言相荅諭畢
回時亦書不善
也可久留之侍

是遣使者之罪
然於來使無與
然即吾亦怒矣
曰汝等之怒誠
則之放歸 帝
可殺有謂可剁
皆怒有謂來使
大臣等見此書

初一日 帝令
善乎○十一月
名聞遠近不亦
不交能發此言
厚吾海汝吾亦
汝海吾汝毋受
國所輸財物厚
亦同議定若明

鑒之倘與之和
負此言者天神
謀直抵山海關
征之必同心合
國乃敵國也如
在乎 汗但明
有罪其處此惟
屢啟釁端誠為

額克星額綽瑚
爾雅希禪庫爾
禪希福五臣齎
誓書與喀爾喀
五部貝勒等共
謀速和同來使
至剛干塞忒勒
黑狐树處遇五
部貝勒宰白馬
烏牛設酒肉血
骨土各一碗對
天地誓曰蒙皇
天后土祐我二
國同心故滿洲
國主併十固山
執政王等今與

喀爾喀五部貝
勒等會盟與明
國修怨務同心
合謀倘與之和
亦必同議若毀
盟而不通五部
貝勒知輒與之
和或明國欲敗
我二國之好密
遣人離間而不
告則皇天不祐
奪吾滿洲國十
固山執政王之
算即如此血出
土埋暴骨而死
若明國欲與五

恩格德爾桑噶
達爾漢巴圖魯
葉爾登綽瑚爾
岱岱青畢登圖
達爾漢莽古勒
稜古爾布什岱
台吉烏巴什都
岱額布格德依

索特音莽古勒
青額森巴拜阿
巴圖魯鄂巴岱
政貝勒都稜洪
者喀爾喀部杭
貝勒不告滿洲
人離間而五部
部貝勒和寀遣

如一永享太平
昌盛二國始終
延長子孫百世
酒食此肉壽得
天地祐之飲此
二國若踐此盟
暴骨亦如之吾
紀算血出土埋

皇天不祐奪其
濟格等衆貝勒
哈圖額滕額爾
勒哲依圖布爾
內齊漢魏徵[illegible]
雅爾圖多爾濟
稜桑噶爾寨巴
爾寨布塔齊都

衣帶鞍馬今還
俗但除一靴帽
輕裘三領徐二
其子克實克圖
再籌之於是賜
明國得廣寧後
五部貝勒同征
賽之歸期須待

在此侍父若齋
保守人畜一子
往来一子在彼
令其二子更番
為旗人侵奪可
恐其所屬人畜
二子俱被擒但
帝曰齋賽與

一萬阿索特雍
萬十二土默特
汝鄂爾多斯一
有六萬不盡屬
幾盡奔逃者僅
十萬蒙古推折
武取大都時四
乎聞昔明之洪

其衆以驕吾國
萬人主何故恃
主吾為水濱三
為四十萬蒙古
汗曰閱来書汝
修書復察哈爾
年正月十七日
○庚申天命五

得天地垂祐哈
不似汝之强但
之衆吾力雖弱
國雖小不似汝
豈不知之然吾
三萬人乎天地
萬而輕吾國為
言驕語為四十

乃以昔日之陳
耶三萬且不足
亦豈盡屬於汝
即左三萬之衆
縱横於汝無與
據汝之右任意
萬此三萬之衆
謝布喀喇沁一

言恣行不道
主而出此惡
地所祐之人
之明遂欺天
何故為異姓
也本無仇隙
隙出此言宜
爾我從来有

有不利於我若
征也若圖之将
寧吾取貢處毋
我有汝且言廣
嶺等八處俱為
順清河開原鐵
赫暨明國之撫
達輝發烏拉葉

愛之何為汝
之錙銖之利
如其愛而與
愛而與之耶
抑以親視汝
畏而與之耶
破彼之城郭
得之物謂能

汝於廣寧所
利於我哉且
聞乎馬能不
獨隆亦未之
智其眷顧也
天乃錫吾勇
惟至誠格天
如逆天然吾

處人畜所克
次所得者何
而回不知二
中一無所獲
人被斬於陣
從臣并十餘
格根岱青之
及再與搆兵

馬脫身敗北
兵棄盔甲駝
汝初與之搆
未受吾兵時
是也昔明國
而出此言誠
四萬之大都
果能復三十

國尚結為同
衣冠相類二
也言雖殊而
與朝鮮異國
誘汝耳且明
畏吾故以利
其孤孽明人
鋒鏑婦女守

震男子亡於
以我兵威所
之厚今不過
來未有如此
明之賞汝從
大兵獨不思
所敗者何處
者何處名城

乃欲貪得有
名以祈天眷
合理不務今
乎今且不求
如此不亦善
國有仇之明
同心協力共
城敗其衆頗

天垂祐破其
日之仇國蒙
皇兄征我舊
者來書當云
汝果有知識
服髮亦相類
也言雖殊而
心爾我異國

前所羈內有
吾使恐未確
四王諫曰殺
殺欲殺彼使
風聞去使見
居之城　帝
囚於拜星所
將去使杻械

林丹汗覽書
什為使齋往
令碩色武巴
鑒之書畢乃
者神祇豈不
怨之國若此
怨於素無嫌
盡之財貨搆

屢言碩色武
五部落使者
還又喀爾喀
去後過期不
吾必殺之矣
勒拜瑚不然
吾亦斥康喀
云若還吾使

遣其人齋書
帝從其言遂
戮之未晚
若踰期不至
歸吾使之期
持書往約以
瑚同來者令
與康喀勒拜

喀爾喀巴約
貝勒盟後有
帝與五部
出徒步逃回
其杻械同潛
察通監者去
碩色武巴什
喀勒拜瑚後
疑也遂誅康
去使被殺無
期己有月餘
大臣曰令過
月餘謂諸王
矣 帝猶待
汗斬之尒旗
巴什被林丹

初一日放扎
今還◯三月
帽靴帯鞍馬
希爾蟒衣裘
齊賽子色特
◯二月內賜
納各還其主
不可背遂不
前日之盟尤
誠為可矜但
曰降者之情
人來投 帝
桑扣肯下一
扎嚕特部宰
吉下一人及
特部索寧台

吾之算若此
殃及其身奪
天后土鑒之
泰懷仇者皇
報而如布占
還國若不思
養今又放吾
子賜衣食豢

蒙恩視吾猶
賽同來被擒
與有罪之齋
滿洲無隙因
兄二人素與
吾與巴克弟
色本立誓曰
嚕特色本回

千總四員○
每牛录下設
真俱為備禦
之其牛录額
副叅遊亦如
之品為三等
序爵列總兵
還帝論功

鞍馬之類令
衣輕裘靴帶
帝仍賜蟒
畢告天焚之
子孫昌盛書
之俾壽延長
恩報神祇佑
心不易常思

以輔國政臨
之盡心竭力
失處極言爭
几　上有闕
之秉心正直
們貝勒女妻
阿爾哈圖圖
總兵以皇子

帝授一品
初率衆來歸
蘇完地名也
七蘇完人也
東辛年五十
總兵官費英
左固山一品
初八日申時

往哭之慟悼
久矣堅執以
喪者吾亦不
漸有一二凋
吾創業大臣
忌　帝曰與
此喪恐有所
王諫曰親臨

喪后妃及諸
也　帝欲臨
滿洲之良臣
而霽遂卒誠
雹霽降靈時
驚雷擊雹雨
朗忽起片雲
終時天色明

帳良久漏下三更始回◯

六月初四日樹二木於門外令曰凡有下情不得上達者可書訴詞懸於木上吾據訴詞顛末以便審問◯

滿洲使者扈壘往扎嚕特達雅台吉處齎来馬八四牛四十四羊一百並所騎之馬衣服器械等物被本部鍾嫩昂阿珠徹特扣肯等棄盟言使兵要於路俱刼之惟放扈壘而已◯

滿洲往五部使者還曰五部貝勒等已負盟矣謁鄂巴岱青二次不容相見諸部之使不来惟二部使者

十一匹牛六
路將齋來馬
洛輝二人於
者錫喇納碩
復截滿洲使
部貝勒領兵
徹特扣肯三

鍾嫩昂阿珠
也○扎嚕特
絕不負 汗
能制然吾身
心俱變而不
曰吾子孫之
巴圖魯之言
至述都稜洪

河懿路
太祖畧蒲

百十二
二十八隻羊
來馬二匹牛
者伊沙穆齋
特色本處使
又奪往扎嚕
十二隻奪之

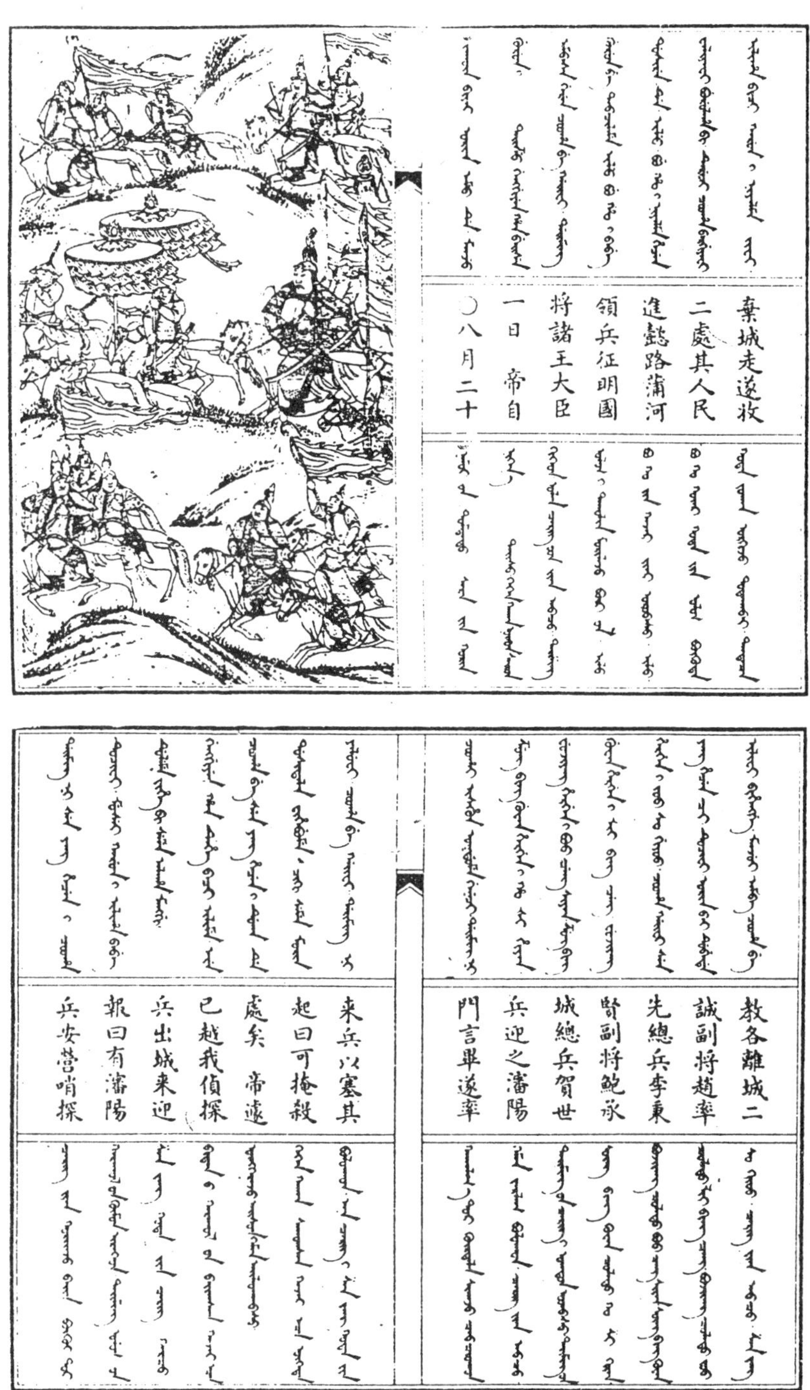

○八月二十一日帝自將諸王大臣領兵征明國進懿路蒲河二處其人民棄城走遂收

兵安營哨探報曰有瀋陽兵出城來迎已越我偵探處矣帝遽起曰可掩殺來兵以塞其門言畢遂率兵迎之瀋陽城總兵賀世賢副將鮑承先總兵李秉誠副將趙率教各離城二

賀世賢鮑承
一固山兵追
河始回其左
陽城東抵渾
率敎兵越濬
殺李秉誠趙
健卒百人追

之三王遂率
可領本部追
敵兵不多汝
王曰近汝之
回 帝謂三
我兵至遂追
十里下寨見

之七日 帝
舒爾哈赤葬
母所生庶名
巴圖魯覺庶
九月皇弟青
軍士乃還○
畜論功賞賜

所獲八千人
勸止之遂將
與達爾漢轄
欲殺入大王
餘回四王復
北門殺人百
先直抵瀋陽

成〇辛酉天
至十一月乃
建軍民房舍
還於薩爾滸
十月自界藩
勞素著者〇
均係近臣勤

之而回二人
墓令從臣奠
吉木巴遜二
畢又至拉哈
泣下三奠酒
至費英東墓
親往奠之因

同一語音者
拉哈達葉赫
衛將輝發烏
吾與強敵爭
父地母垂祐
香祝曰蒙天
王等對天焚

濟格岳託諸
濟爾哈朗阿
[illegible]德格類
莽古爾泰[illegible]
與代善阿敏
十二日帝
命六年正月

俱為我有旣
而征明又得
其撫順清河
開原鐵嶺等
城又破其四
路大兵皆天
地之黙助也
今禱上下神
祇吾子孫中
縱有不善者
天可滅之勿
令殘害以開
殺戮之端如
有殘忍之人

不待天誅遽
興操戈之念
天地豈不知
之若此者亦
當奪其算昆
弟中若有作
亂者雖知之
不忍傷殘
惟懷理義
之心以化
導其愚頑
似此者天
地祐之俾
子孫百世

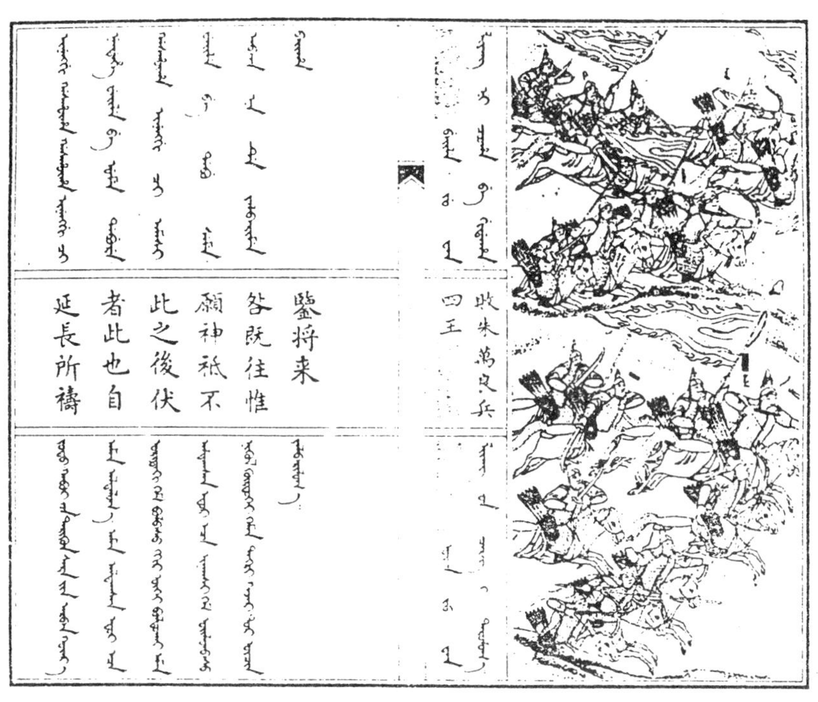
敗朱萬良兵
四王
鑒将来
咎既往惟
願神祇不
此之後伏
者此也自
延長所禱

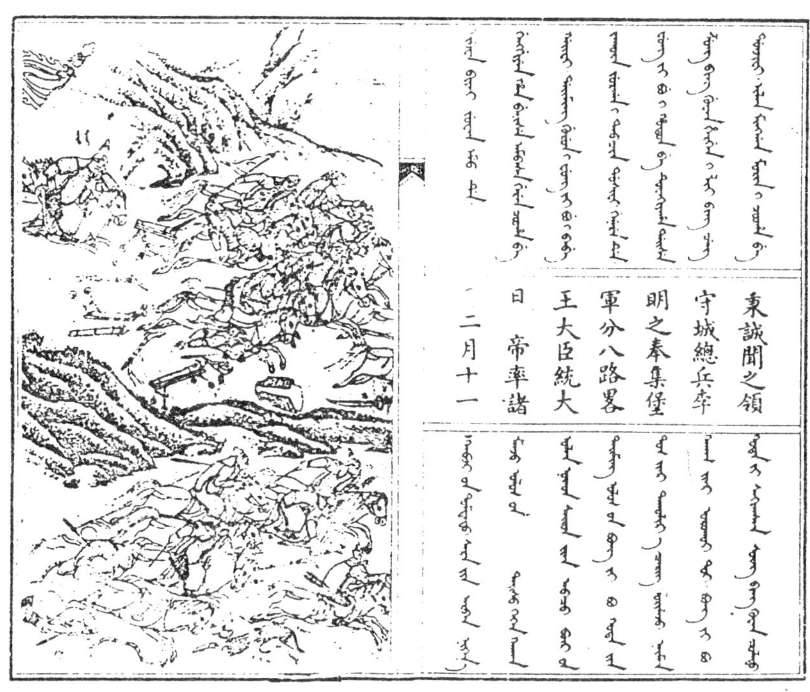
東誠聞之領
守城總兵李
明之奉集堡
軍分八路畧
王大臣統大
日　帝率諸
二月十一

争進殺至壕
兩路擁二門
明國兵敗走
兵随後擊之
拔營奔城我
見我兵至即
國兵結陣一

其山下有明
追殺至山上
兵遇之二路
採左四固山
兵二百為前
六里安營令
三千騎出城

二百被殺其
人過明國兵
曰吾同行三
有小卒來報
午時將回兵
右翼兵亦至
里方立岡上

大兵離城三
擊死 帝率
被城上巨礮
克達及一卒
有糸將吉巴
門掩殺之時
邊方回當擁

兵見之驚走
所立之處敵
殺至二千兵
追二百兵遂
尋敵所在困
吉碩託台吉
台吉岳託台

於是德格類
左翼兵駐此
兵追殺吾率
王可領本部
大臣曰右翼
帝謂諸王
二其兵不遠

行賞畢乃旋
歸大營論功
相遇收兵同
破敵之諸王
回適與分路
至武靖營而
走四王追擊

抵敵亦遂驚
兵勢重不能
營之兵見我
朱萬良率大
時署總兵事
健卒至黃山
四王領部下

處露宿之理
曰人君無野
聚諸王大臣
帝乃陞殿
驢而給食之
俟征明穫牛
國中之牛盡
臣曰與其用
牛以勞之羣
夫最苦可賜
帝曰築城之
爾濟城畢
十一日築薩
師〇閏二月

僕所事之農
僕宜爲其主
主者宜憐僕
民宜尊王爲
於王宜愛民
敬君禮也至
君君恩臣臣
安故天作之
安民安卽王
王王安卽民
於君之下有
治乃成君至
明乃成國國
故築城也君

既已勞矣而
林轉運之造
於山採木於
之地耶鑿石
豈出於築城
築城之木石
成豫慶哉如

人和豈不共
下相親天悅
共之如是上
物亦當與僕
財及所畋之
而主所獲之
業與主共食

步來耶博爾
是喘息想徒
曰自何來如
後至 帝問
副將博爾晉
可也時適有
而掠之最不
犒築城之夫

義舉之如為
朗國當以大
故耳不知征
欲出已之財
等之意實不
更苦乎令爾
築壘之工不

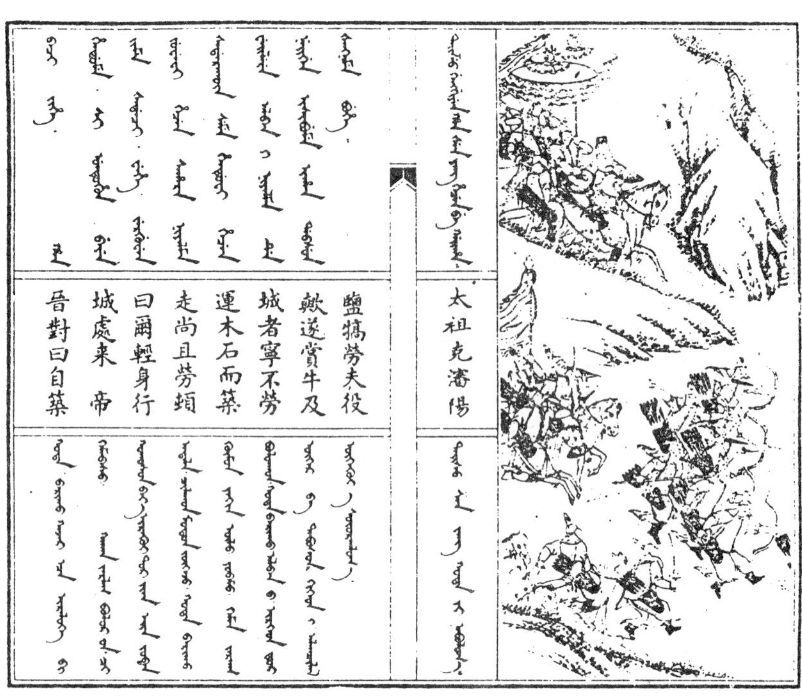
太祖克瀋陽
盬犒勞夫役
敕遂賞牛及
城者寧不勞
運木石而築
走尚且勞頓
曰爾輕身行
城處來 帝
晉對曰自築

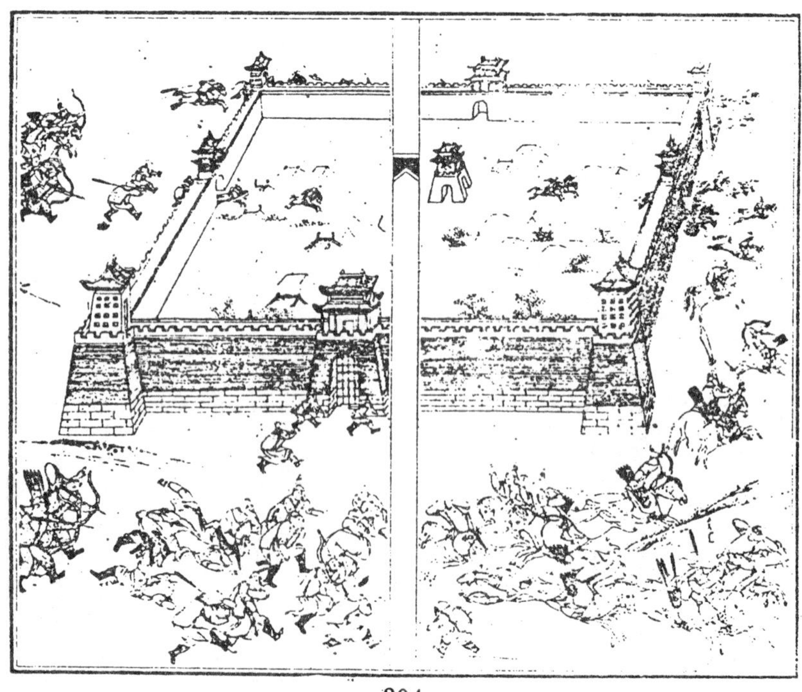

月暈之北
西向東迻
白二氣自
夜行見青
至十一日
水陸並進
渾河而下

梯戰車順
將柵木雲
兵取瀋陽
大臣領大
自將諸王
十日　帝
○三月初

板為營次
東七里柵
大兵至城
二日辰時
於城上十
遂分兵布
二人大驚

賢尤世功
總兵賀世
二更飛報
火哨探至
國沿臺舉
止是夜明
至南面而

丈深二丈
二道濶五
城復有壕
樹栅木近
道於內邊
之又壕一
稭以土掩

椿上覆黍
塹內插尖
城外有深
人其東面
雲梯戰車
攻城兵布
日辰時令

兵賀世賢
屍纍積總
城掩殺覆
兵俱敗逃
入其七萬
守我兵衛
亦登陴堅
嚴城上兵

城衛守甚
砲衆兵繞
列戰車鎗
留砲眼排
墻一道間
內築攔馬
皆有尖椿

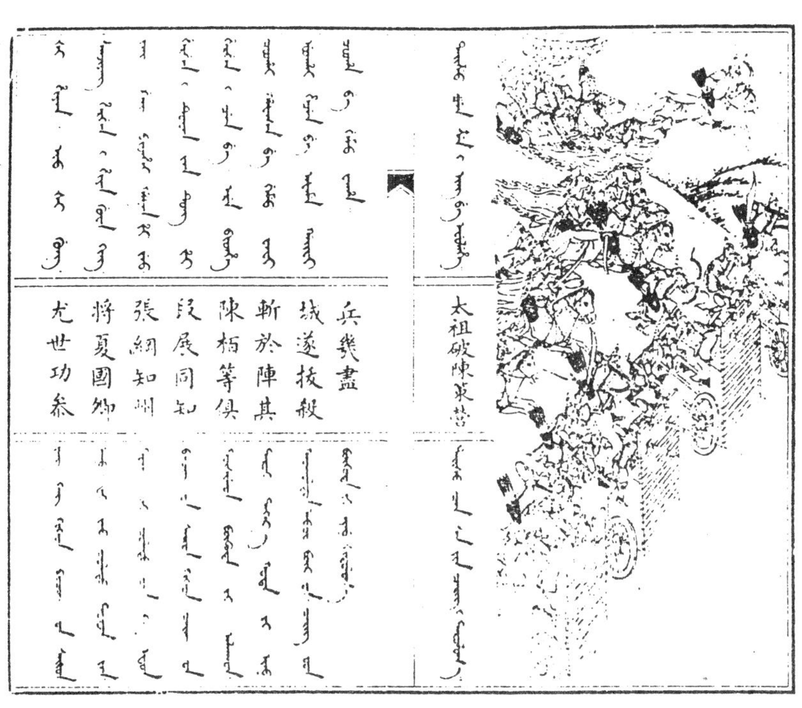

太祖破陳策營

兵幾盡城遂按殺斬於陣其陳栢等俱段展同知張綱知州將夏國卿尤世功叅

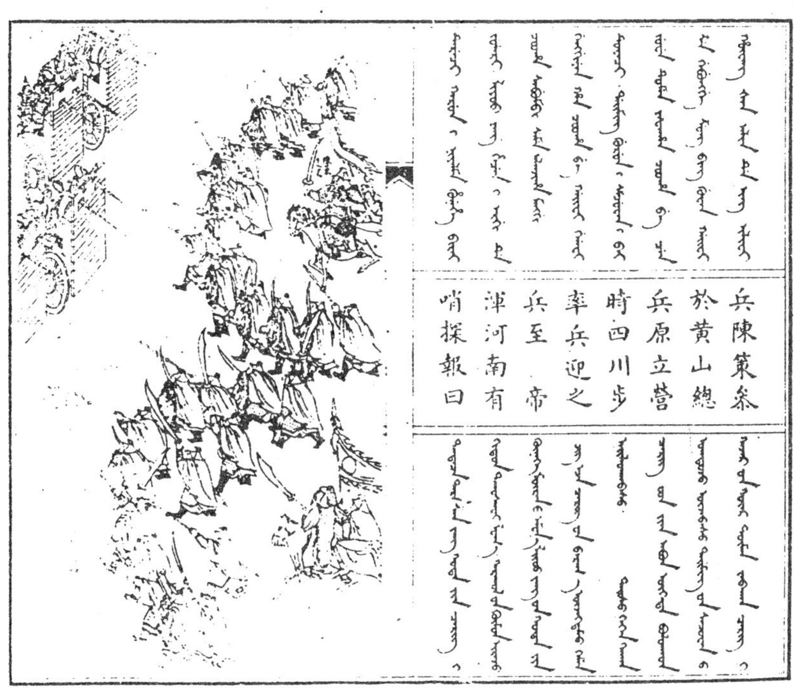

兵陳策叅於黃山總兵原立營時四川步率兵迎之兵至　帝渾河南有哨探報曰

取綿甲戰
右固山兵
帝見之令
有綿甲
鐵甲之外
外有綿盔
劍鐵盔之

鎗大刀利
執竹杆長
二處安營
離城七里
渡河來援
瀋陽領兵
聞我兵至
將張名世

陳策張名
溺死陣斬
至渾河盡
其兵追殺
遂衝入敗
後兵助之
負未分令

軍鏖戰勝
帝見二
至即進戰
綿甲戰車
雅喇不待
之紅甲拜
車徐進擊

大敗三總兵四王

死於陣中實爾泰戰遊擊朗格叅将布哈有先進戰世而我國

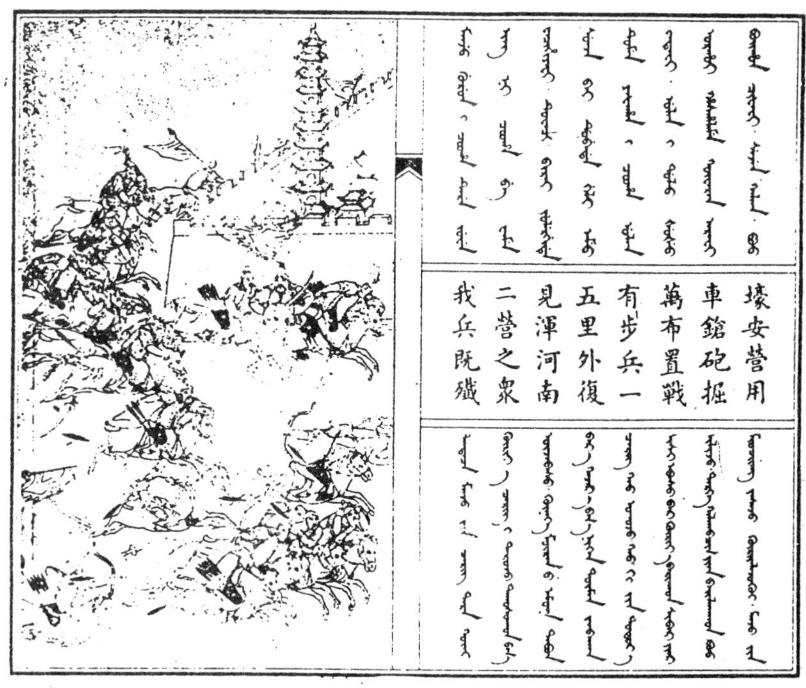

壕安營用車鎗砲掘萬布置戰有步兵一五里外復見渾河南二營之衆我兵既殲

百健兵探
雅遜領二
前探滿洲
兵一千為
鋪安營遣
援至白塔
萬騎兵来
姜弼領三

兵朱萬良
武靖營總
李秉誠守
集堡總兵
戰有守奉
我兵將往
以泥塗之
泰稽為障

敵 帝遂
爾領兵前
須親往吾
曰父皇何
奔 帝前
馬領健騎
四王急上
之遂前進

四王營告
迎敵因至
怒親率兵
帝聞報大
鎗追之
隨後放烏
走明國兵
之一見遂

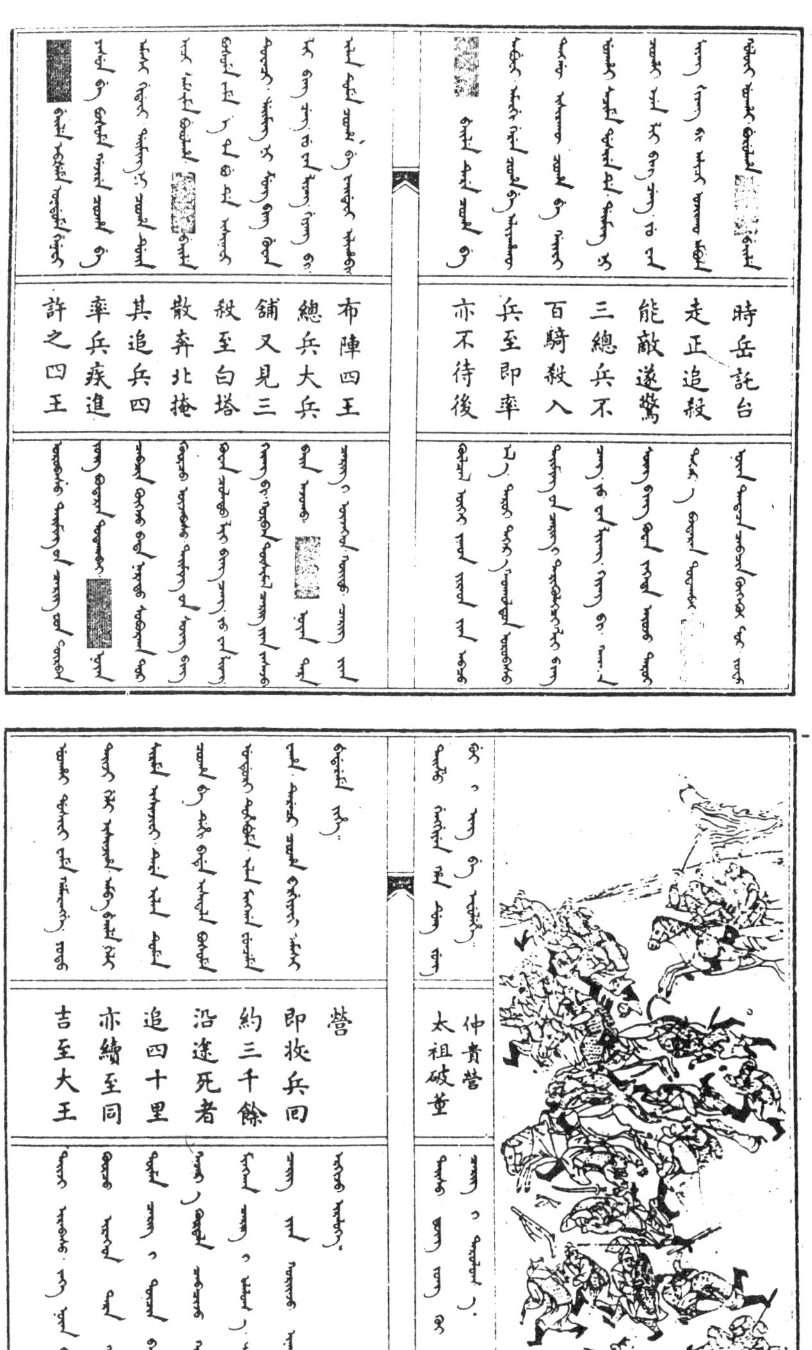

時岳託台走正追殺能敵遂驚三總兵不百騎殺入兵至即率亦不待後

布陣四王總兵大兵鋪又見三殺至白塔散奔北掩其追兵四率兵疾進許之四王

太祖破董仲貴營

營即收兵回約三千餘沿途死者追四十里亦續至同吉至大王

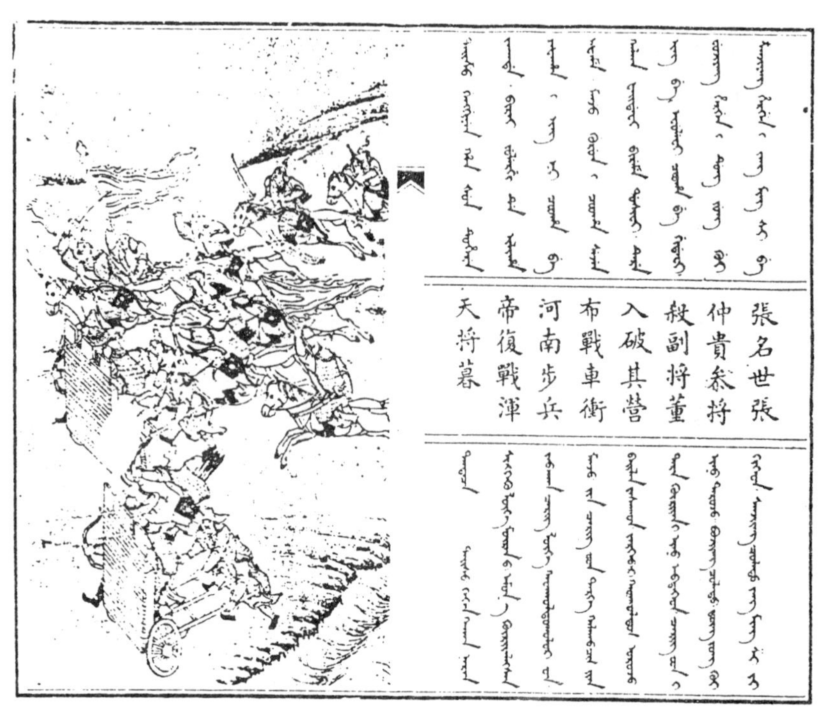

張名世張仲貴叅將殺副將董入破其營布戰車衝河南步兵帝復戰渾天將暮

因汝敗走身之有目兄依賴如　父遜曰吾子帝責雅城內次日大兵屯於

令衆將率教場安營於東門外各領健卒收兵諸王已暮　帝兵殆盡天大斗及衆

還國〇十
三軍令先
人畜分於
賞將所獲
日論功行
職屯兵五
定罪削其
加叱詈遂

失銳氣嚴
風而走以
勝之軍望
故率吾常
寸磔汝何
有失罪應
軍中萬一
而殺入衆

報遼陽城
探見之飛
營明國哨
逃走遂安
民俱棄城
虎皮驛軍
即前進至

遼陽議定
長驅以取
大兵乘勢
大敗可率
已抜敵兵
臣曰瀋陽
聚諸王大
八日 帝

河水於壕
遂放太子
閘之大驚
下寨衆官
至虎皮驛
見其前後
山塞野不

旗蔽日漫
攻遼陽旌
敗令又来
陽援兵盡
兵已取瀋
曰滿洲大
守文武官

禦甚嚴
兵四面守
於城上排
内列火器
塞其西閘

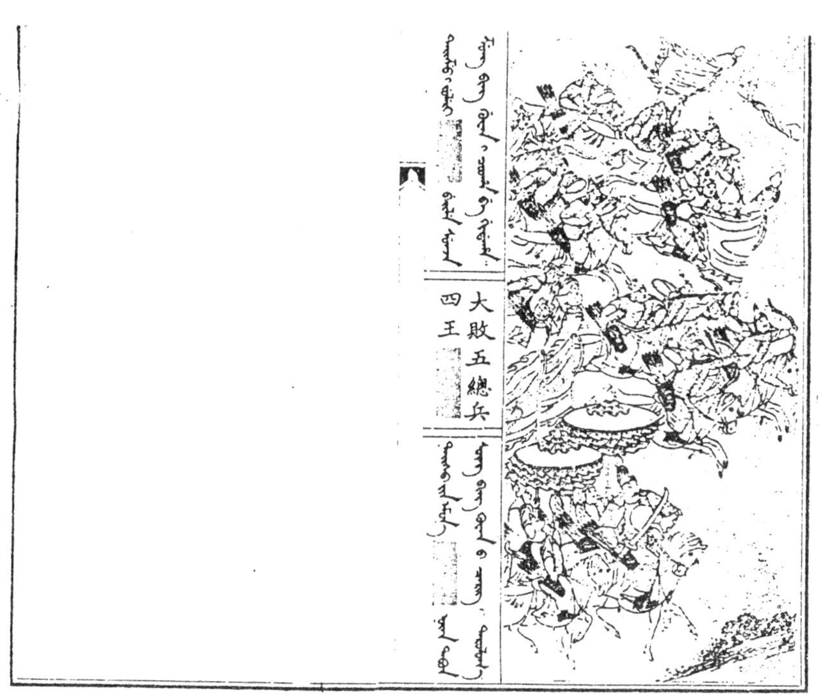

大敗五總兵四王

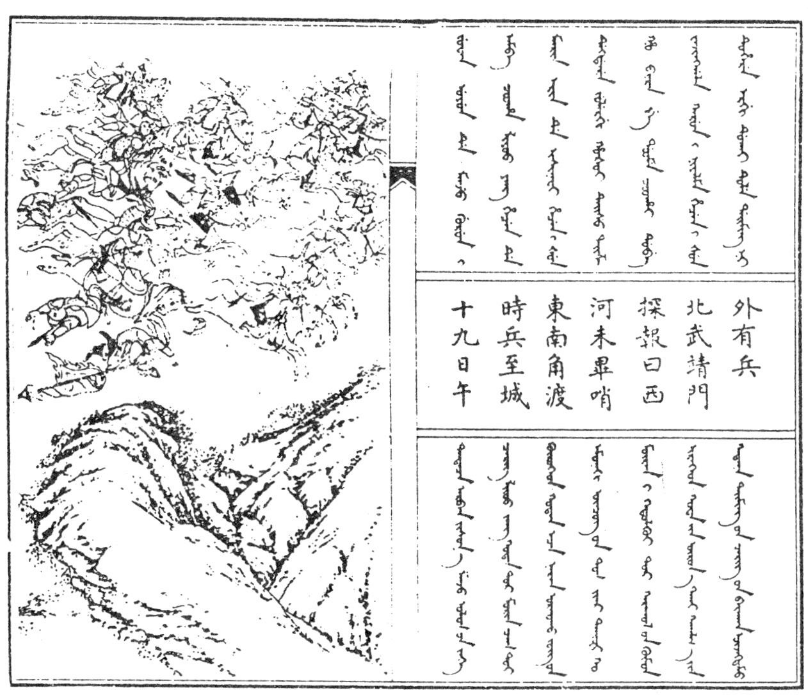

外有兵北武靖門探報曰西河未畢哨東南角渡時兵至城十九日午

帝率左翼兵先往有總兵李懷信侯世祿柴國柱姜弼童仲魁等率兵五萬出城五里布陣帝一見令兵擊其營之左四王領部下健卒隨至亦

欲進戰帝止之曰吾已令兵往擊汝勿前進可領右翼兵駐於城邊瞭望之四王曰令後至二紅旗固山兵瞭望可也遂前進帝又令阿濟格

亦殺入兩
四固山兵
破其營左
四王殺入
放砲接戰
左明營兵
擊其營之

奮力衝殺
助之四王
二黃旗兵
即令扈從
意行 帝
之四王堅
台吉往勸

蹂踐積屍
人馬自相
爭入門者
旗兵擊退
也遇二紅
即武靖門
從西門出

有一營兵
山始回又
十里至鞍
勢追殺六
走四王乘
兵大潰而
相夾攻明

不可勝計
乃收兵是
晚回至城
南七里安
營

太祖率兵
克遼陽

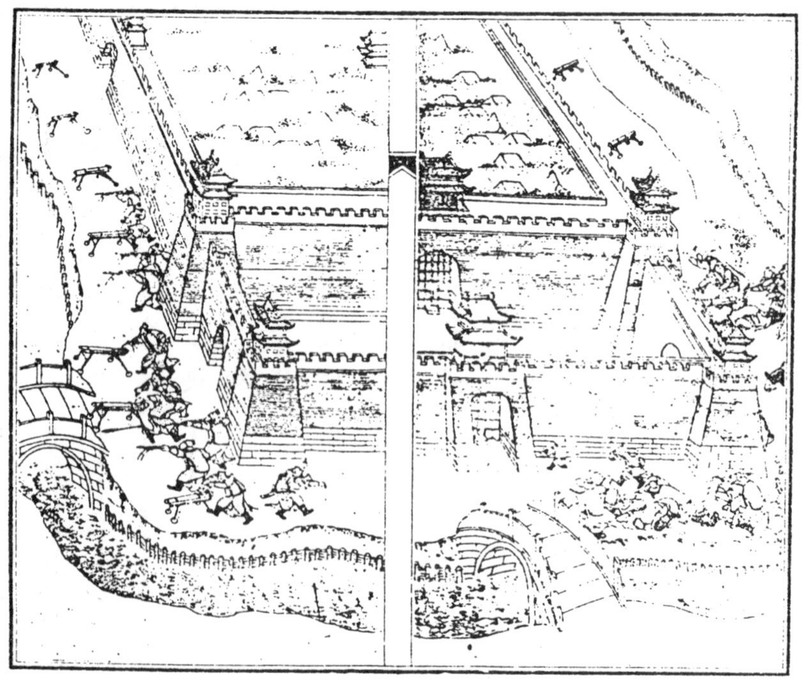

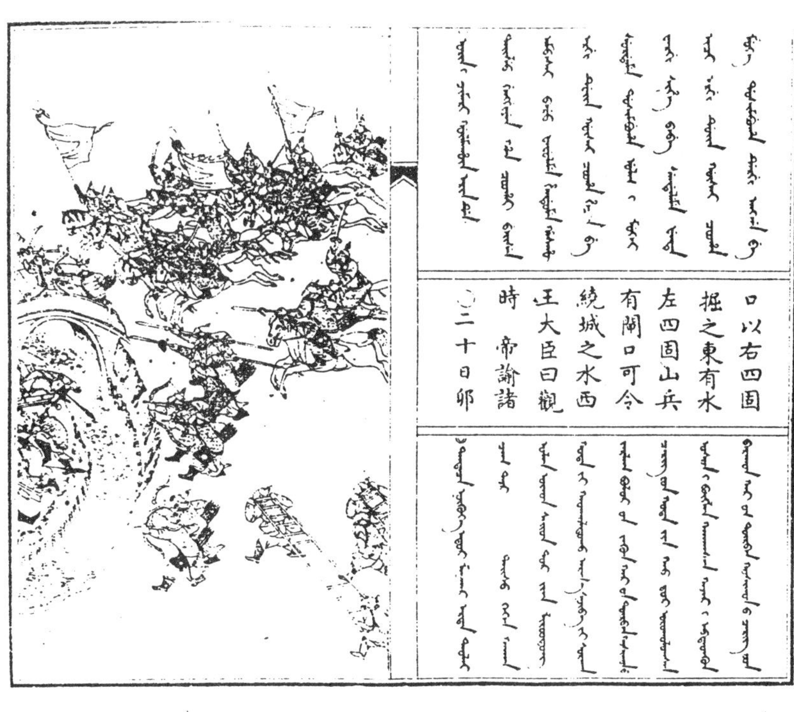

二十日卯
時　帝諭諸
王大臣曰觀
繞城之水西
有閘口可令
左四固山兵
掘之東有水
口以右四固

山兵塞之親
率右四固山
兵布戰車於
城邊以防衛
令衆軍負土
運石壅其水
口明國又有
三萬兵出東

門外安營卯
甲戌門也列
鎗砲三層連
發不已左四
固山遣人來
曰西閘口難
掘若奪其橋
可得也　帝

曰橋可奪試奪之若得之急來告我吾當進攻此門即令來人速往水口壅塞既畢遂令綿甲軍排車進

擊東門敵兵其營中連放鎗砲我兵遂出戰車外渡壕水吶喊而進兩軍鏖戰不退有紅甲拜雅喇二百

殺入又二白旗兵一千亦殺入明之騎兵遂敗諸王部下白甲拜雅喇俱殺入央攻之其步兵亦敗投城

而走我兵乘勢驅殺溺水而死者滿積壕水盡赤時左四固山兵亦奪西門橋分殺守壕之兵明營兵隱

下馬步行兩
時右固山兵
於城內而已
亂往來奔走
喪膽驚擾潰
官員軍民皆
兩角樓城中
城一面據其

其兵遂奪西
梯登城驅殺
勇衝突即監
火礮我兵奮
火箭火砲擲
斷城上亦放
發矢聯綿不
於屋垣放砲

併軍民等多
棟戶部傅國
邢慎言胡嘉
牛維曜高出
旦有監軍道
我兵拒戰達
兵舉燈火與
處是夜城內

兵以益登城
帝即撤攻城
登西城矣
報曰酉時已
四固山兵來
攻城北面左
蔔填內壕正
壕之間運薪

軍崔儒秀自
子投井死藍
何廷魁攜妻
而死分守道
遂縱火焚樓
戰見城被克
北鎮遠樓監
應泰在城東
殺時經略袁
一處沿城追
八固山合為
山兵亦登城
又敗右四固
復布車大戰
日黎明明兵
墜城而逃次

迎 帝午時
萬歲牌肩輿
香以黃紙書
闔城結綵焚
民皆薙髮降
張銓其餘官
中生擒御史
俱死於亂軍
傑李廷幹等
全王宗盛偹
武都司徐國
李尚義張繩
房承勲遊擊
善參將王豸
良副將梁仲
謚總兵朱萬

大張鼓吹入城官民俯伏央道皆呼萬歲乃駐於經畧衙門安撫已畢令張銓來叩見許以高爵厚祿待

之銓曰吾受朝廷寵渥若降順是遺臭於後世汝雖欲生我我惟知一死而已生我固汝國之善事死則

吾之芳名留照汗青矣終不見 帝聞其言曰若不戰而降理當優待被擒之人既不欲生夫欲死之人

豈能養耶宜斬之四王憐之而不忍殺乃援古曉之曰昔宋之徽欽二帝為金太宗皇帝所擒尚爾屈膝

體統耶即留
而失大國之
吾豈肯屈膝
統天下之尊
當今皇帝一
之小朝廷吾
徼欽乃亂世
死亦不忘但
生全我也雖
誠是無非欲
曰王之所教
而不屈乎銓
導耳何執迷
故以此言開
侯吾欲生汝
叩見受封公

欲具本奏知
徒傷生耳故
雖與戰無益
吾觀滿洲兵
其幾千萬矣
靈塗炭不知
不諳時務生
將吏俱愚昧
耳前者當事
後日蒼生應
一時者蓋為
之所以稍存
生之理然吾
期而已無復
十日不死之
我十日但遲

河東勝長幹

其河東之三
之遼陽既下
服遂縊而瘞
帝知其不
外無他願也
矣故一死之
宗祀亦覆絶

吾若偷生併
死俱可保全
五子在家我
吾之母妻及
名於後世且
炭以成我令
和免生靈塗
我朝二國相

站鳳凰鎮東
長甸鎮江湯
甸大甸永甸
新安新甸寬
洒馬吉靉陽
遼靜安孤山
清陽鎮北底
城永寧鎮夷

定遼慶雲古
殺家庄平定
泊曽通鎮西
丁家泊宋家
榆林十方寺
長營靜遠上
安長勝長勇
長寧長定長

鎮夷甜水站柴河威、寧營奉集穆家武靖營平虜虎皮蒲河懿路范河中固鞍山海州東昌耀州蓋州熊岳五十寨復州永寧監欒古石河金州鹽場望海堝紅嘴歸服黃骨島岫巖青台峪等大小七十餘城官

民俱薙髮降○十九日蒙古國喀爾喀部卓禮克圖達爾漢巴圖魯巴哈達爾漢賓爾呼納克等四貝勒部下二千餘騎聞大兵已拔瀋陽乘殘破之餘來寇取瀋陽財粟時有滿洲之遊牧蒙古在城、中遂出城

驅殺獲牛馬
甚多生擒三
十人以獻
帝命斬其二
十四留六人
持書歸責其
侵擾之故○
二十一日遣
朝鮮國王書
曰滿洲國
汗致書於朝
鮮國王如仍
助明國則已
不然有逃人
濟江而竄者
可盡反之今

遼東官民已
薙髮歸降其
降官俱復原
職汝若納我
已附之遼民
而不還異日
勿我怨矣
帝聚諸王大
臣議曰遼陽
乃天賜我者
可還居於此
耶抑仍還本
國耶諸王大
臣俱以還國
對 帝曰若
我兵一還則

征討且此處
國後必復煩
之疆土而還
有矣棄所得
山谷不為我
民必逃散於
守凡城堡之
遼陽必復固

乃明國朝鮮
蒙古三國接
壤要地天既
與我即宜居
之諸王大臣
對曰此言誠
然議定遂遣
人迎后妃皇

子〇二十四
日釋遼陽獄
中官民查削
職閑住者復
其原職設遊
擊八員都司
二員委之以
事　帝論拔

城破敵將士攻
戰之功行賞畢
因得遼東又發
庫銀布帛重賞
總兵以下官員
及士卒等有差
移遼陽官民於
北城其南城則

城而宿勿入民
刼奪財物可登
不許擾害居民
鑾傳令曰軍士
迎之二台吉攬
張鼓樂以肩輿
城中官民富戶
吉領兵至海州

岔河浮橋二台
撫人民併閱三
將領兵一千安
桑古台吉率八
子德格類姪齋
二十九日命皇
臣及將士居之
帝與諸王大

總兵窮亦都卒
日左固山一等
姓〇六月十四
安撫各城堡百
悉至於是下詔
王及諸臣眷屬
初五日后妃諸
民而回〇四月

舟揖遂安撫人
彼已折毀亦無
之人來曰其橋
視三岔河浮橋
於城上次日遣
公廨三軍俱屯
城二台吉宿於
室傳令畢遂入

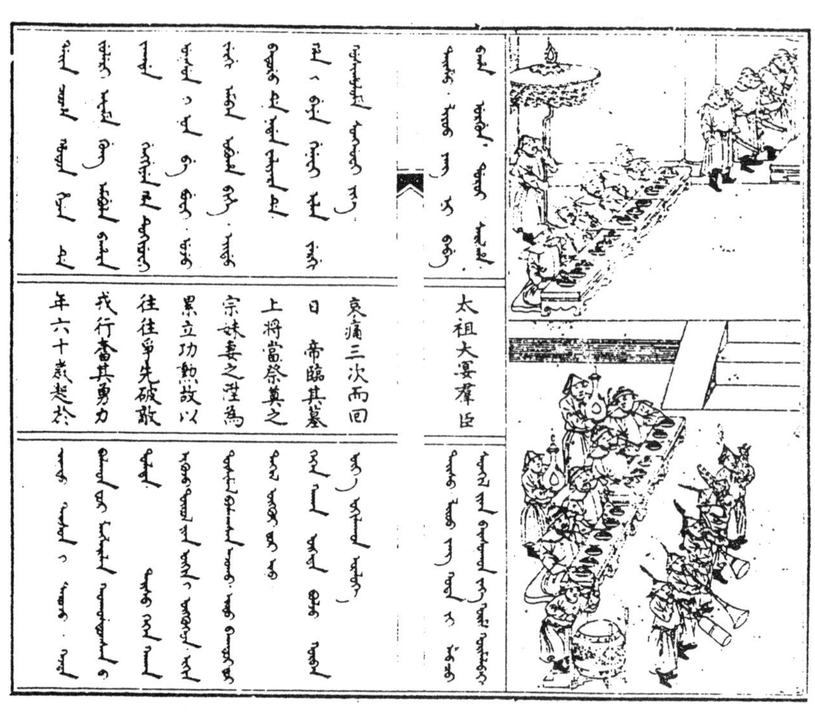

年六十歲卒於戎行奮其勇力往往爭先破敵累立功勳故以宗妹妻之陞爲上將當祭奠之日帝臨其墓哀痛三次而回

太祖大宴羣臣

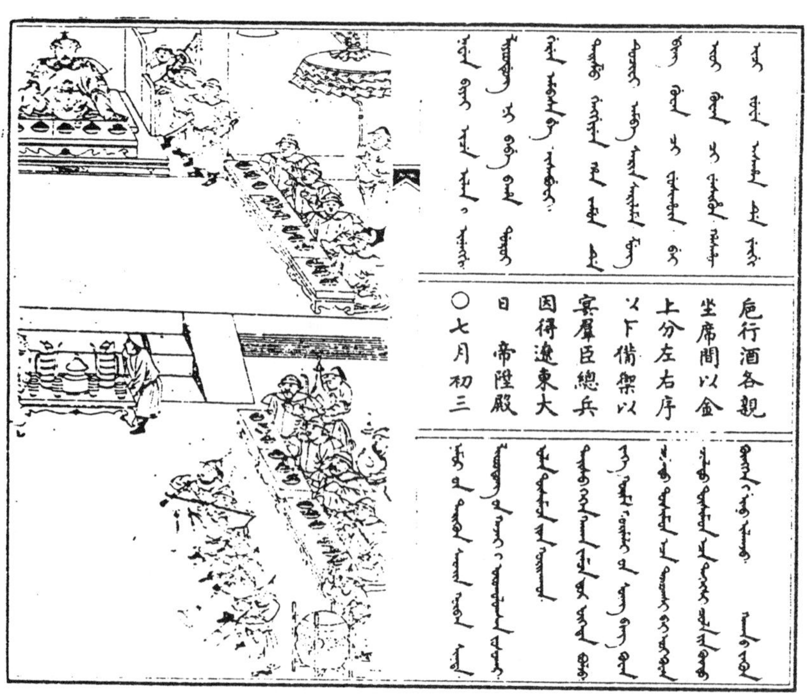

○七月初三日帝陞殿因得遼東大賓羣臣總兵以下備禦以上分左右序坐席間以金卮行酒各覲

庇護亦爾諸
者雖賴上天
等得至於此
祐我也然吾
天厭明國而
失其疆土此
其將士而又
之地故致喪

而侵奪尺寸
反虐害小邦
衆不知自足
歷帝土廣民
曰明國之萬
臣謝恩 帝
賜衣一襲犀
賜之宴畢各

皆潰良策乘
城中人聞之
喊詐言敵來
令堡外民吶
大將毛文龍
通於明海島
良策與民潛
鎮江中軍陳

巳○二十日
心之嘉悅而
勞以此表吾
爾等攻戰之
酬功哉但念
物耳豈足以
酒襲衣乃微
臣之力此盃

海居民於內
千逢鎮江沿
等官領兵三
齋總兵副叅
王率扎爾固
之命四王二
以叛 帝聞
九階李世科

執守堡官陳
山二堡民亦
龍其湯站險
人叛投毛文
并從者六十
其子佟豊年
擊佟養真殺
亂執城守遊

馬一匹甲百
并弓矢雕鞍
靴帽玲瓏帶
猻裘各一領
賜貂裘猞狸
令齋賽誓之
用白馬祭天
女為質 帝

送其二子一
一萬賄齋賽
喀部以牲畜
初九日喀爾
復州○八月
移金州民於
王領兵二千
地命大王三

副十五日諸王送齋賽至十里外設宴餞別將所質之女與大王為妃○十一月十八日命二王領兵五千渡鎮江入朝鮮地攻勦毛文龍兵至鎮江連夜入朝鮮境斬遊擊劉姓者及兵一千五百文龍僅以身免乃還○蒙古喀爾喀部内古爾布什台吉莽果爾台吉率民六百四十五戶并牲畜來歸

帝陞殿二台吉拜見畢設大宴各賜貂裘三領猞狸猻裘二領虎裘二領貉裘二領狐裘一領鑲邊貂裘五領鑲邊

物皆備以聰
田凡應用之
奴僕牛馬房
全盔甲十副
八副弓矢俱
一副又撒袋
副鍍金撒袋
沙魚皮鞍七
兩雕鞍一副
十兩銀五百
布五百疋金
段三十五疋
蟒段六疋紬
領蟒衣九件
迻青鼠裘三
獺裘二領鑲

月扎魯特
命七年正
（）壬戌天
授為總兵
女妻之亦
哩都濟呼
宗弟濟伯
莽果爾以
授為總兵其
彔共二牛彔
並蒙古一牛
牛彔三百人
圖給滿洲一
名青卓禮克
古爾布什賜
古圖公主妻

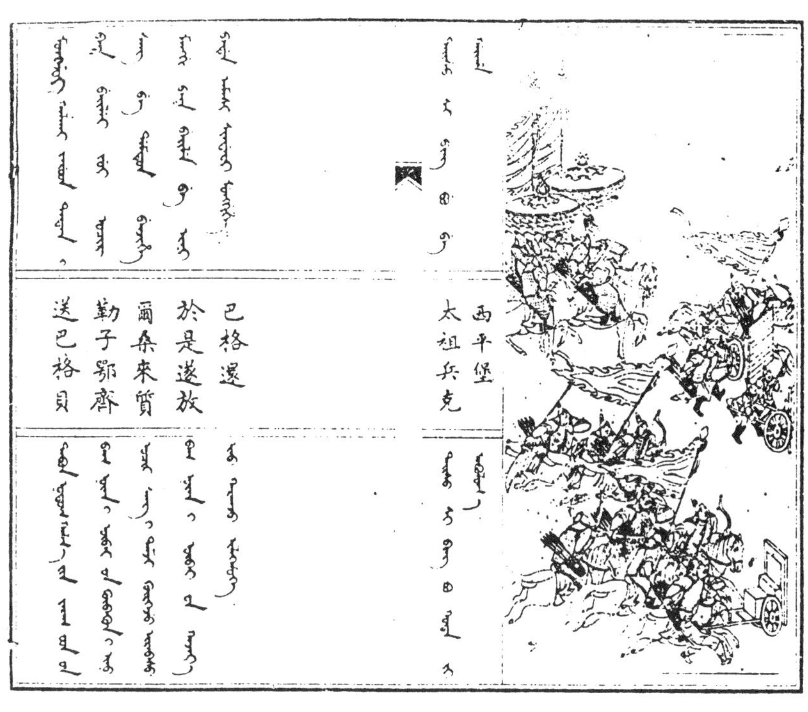

太祖兵克西平堡

送巴格貝勒子鄂齊爾桑來質於是遂放巴格還

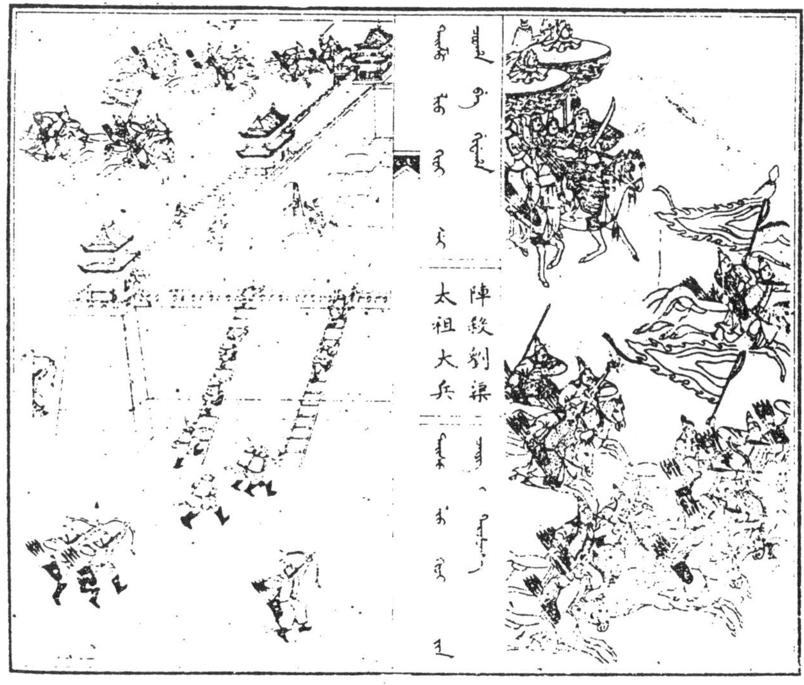

太祖大兵陣殺劉渠

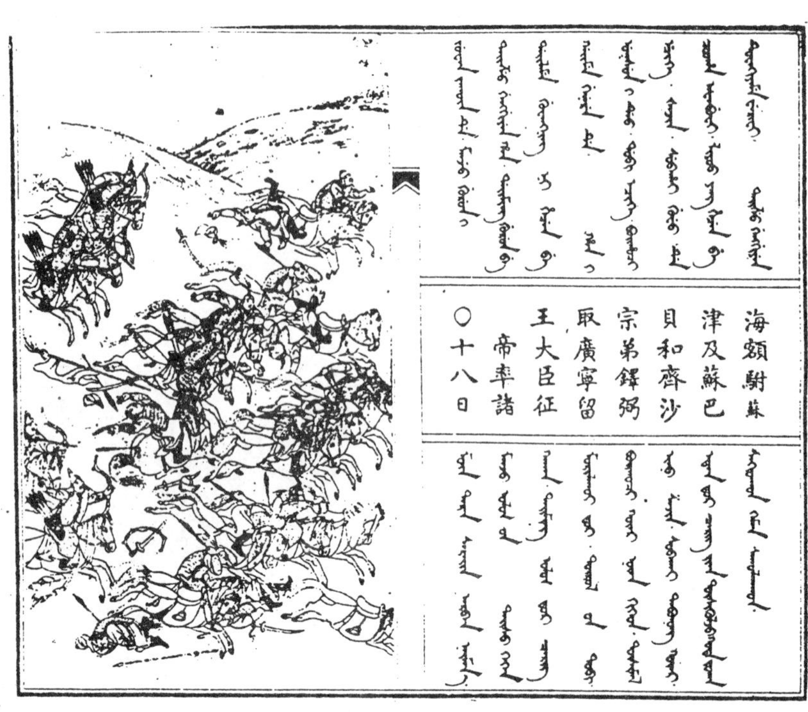

○十八日帝率諸王大臣征取廣寧留宗弟鐸弼貝和齊沙津及蘇巴海額駙蘇

巴海哈達國萬汗之孫帝以宗弟濟伯哩都濟呼之妹妻之故稱額駙沙津等統

兵守遼陽即日起程次日宿東昌堡二十日寅時起營辰時至遼河防河兵見勢不

可當遂逭走前哨健卒追殺二十里外至西平堡乃止申時大兵至遂圍之二十一日招城守副將羅一貴不降辰時布戰車雲梯攻之四面兵皆潰午時乃下一貴及

兵一萬俱殲之尚未收兵哨卒來報曰廣寧城東有兵至我兵迎之尚未成列明總兵劉渠祁秉忠李秉誠副將劉徵鮑承先叅將黑雲鶴麻承宗祖大壽遊擊羅萬言

李茂春等領兵三萬乘機急戰我兵亦不暇布陣卽分投殺入明國兵勢不能支遂潰走我兵乘勝追殺五十里至平洋橋總兵官劉渠祁秉忠及副叅等官全軍覆沒

惟李秉誠鮑承先祖大壽羅萬言適去時天已暮帝收兵回駐西平堡廣寧官生出城納降

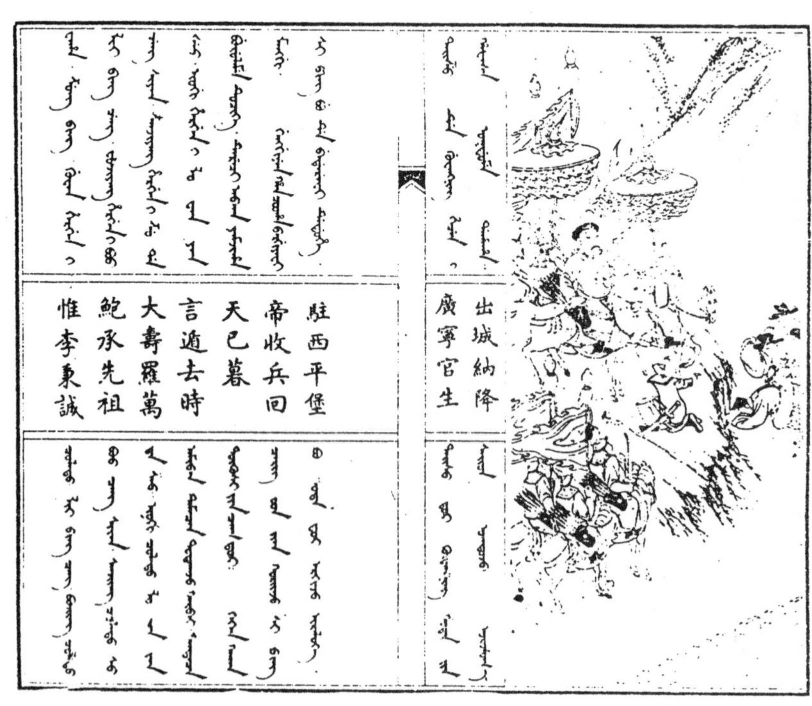

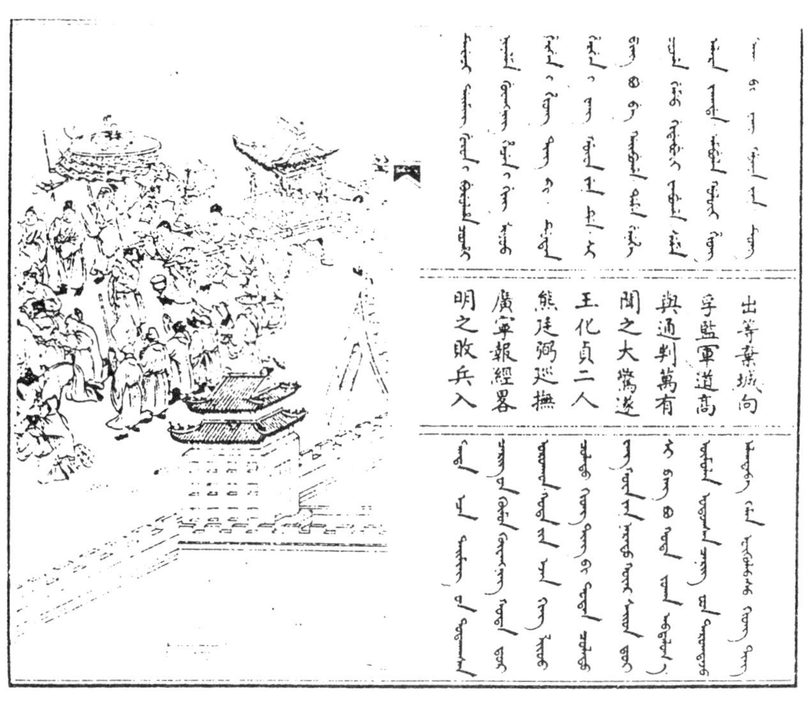

明之敗兵入廣寧報經畧熊廷弼巡撫王化貞二人聞之大驚遂與通判萬有孚監軍道高出等棄城向山海關而逃分巡道高邦佐走至杏山驛自縊有遊擊孫得功千總郎紹貞陸國志守備黃進等把守城門遣七人請降帝賞以銀兩給信牌而去二十二日西興堡備傑朱世勳差中軍王志高請降帝亦

以所乘之鞍
門矣 帝賜
吾等已禁域
二人來降曰
秀才郭攀基
之石天柱及
投明為千總
寧有我國人

兵起行赴廣
二十三日大
畜散與三軍
賞畢其餘人
人畜論功行
日將所得之
信牌而去是
賞以銀兩給

叩首迎謁未
龍亭用鼓樂
執旗張蓋撻
香官生居民
城內各家焚
外望昌崗處
寧城東三里
大兵行至廣

降賜旗而去
將劉世勲來
日鎮靜堡叅
二面二十四
帝賜信牌
堡千總來降
而去又正安
馬幷旗一杆

屯衛備禦
堡鄭登右
延錦安守
遊擊何世
漸大凌河
守堡俞鴻
尚智鐵場
州中軍陳

禦朱世勳錦
龍西興堡備
橋守堡閻雲
投降其平洋
遊擊羅萬言
潛逃入山之
巡撫公廨有
時入城駐於

堡王國泰
印大康守
堡遊擊閻
元勳大清
邊守堡周
滅國祚鎮
世勳守堡
堡叅將劉

維翰鎮靜
安守堡鄭
徐鎮靜鎮
鎮遠守堡
守堡李詩
盡忠鎮寧
山守堡崔
黃宗魯圍

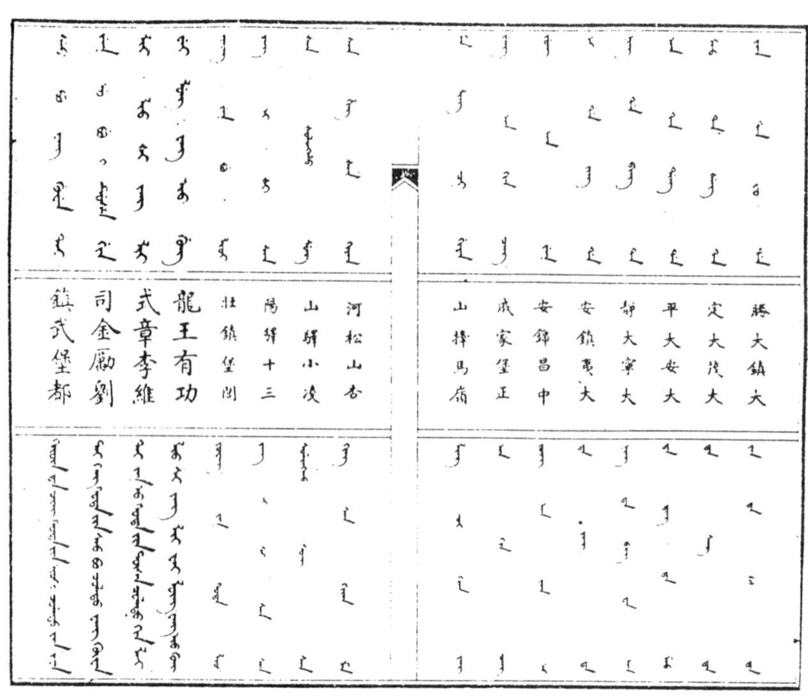
勝大鎮大
定大茂大
平大安大
靜大寧大
安鎮夷大
安錦昌中
威家堡正
山撑馬崗
河松山杏
山解小凌
陽驛十三
壯鎮堡閭
龍王有功
式章李維
司金勵劉
鎮武堡都

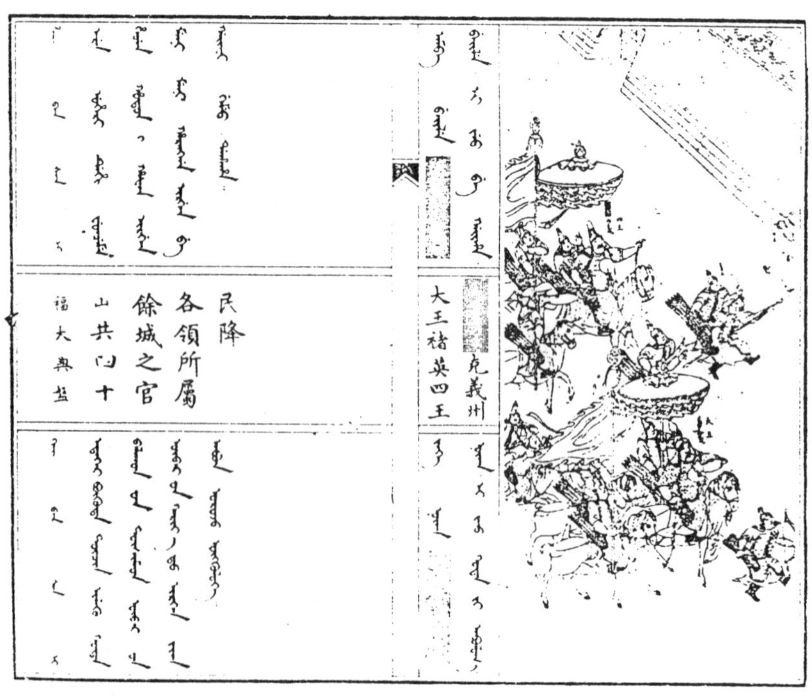
克義州
大王諸英四王
民降
各領所屬
餘城之官
山共四十
福大與盤

王領兵至義州
錦州命大王四
至中左所復回
房屋而走大兵
盡焚沿路屯堡
海闌時熊廷弼
乃移兵欲進山
帝駐兵十日

齊奇卜塔爾布
爾濟固祿綽爾
噶爾瑪昂坤多
賴客賽拜音岱
木吹爾扎勒達
勒哲依圖索諾
魯特部明安諤
十六日蒙古兀

至設慶賀之宴
起行十四日乃
十一日自遼陽
接后妃等二月
回至廣寧遣官
殺兵三千大兵
門不服遂克城
移其民城中閒

頑暴亂是以賊詐僞無兇之不貸無盜遺横逆者懲能者舉之不信持法度賢之風俗主忠諭之曰吾國

陞殿賜宴畢乃牲畜歸附 帝民三千餘戶並吉共率所屬軍喀爾喀等部台等十七貝勒并靈賓爾呼納克彦岱伊林齊特

有才德者固有來降之功今旣歸我俱殃及於國矣變亂爲害而諸貝勒之心天不祐使汝不息是以上

賊欺僞之行珠念佛而盜蒙古人持素風俗如此爾顧蓋因吾國皇天所以眷物必還其主道不拾遺拾

給之〇喀爾
用之物俱賞
馬糧粟凡所
房田奴婢牛
叚布疋銀器
蟒衣金銀紬
皮虎皮等爽
狸猻狐狸貉

賜以貂鼠猞
畀列等授職
國法治之諭
惡不悛即以
善之念若舊
之切毋萌不
能者亦撫育
優待之無才

之規模何以
曰上天所予
固山王等問
月初三日八
民歸降〇三
鮑承先亦隨
時西平敗將
民移於河東

帶所降之官
陽將河西一
廣寧駕還遼
諸王統兵守
七日 帝命
戶並來歸十
有一千二百
喀五部落民

可無失矣爾
幾同心幹國
固山之王庶
八人可為八
之智慮耶爾
見能及衆人
且一人之識
獲罪於天也

恐倚強自恣
人一為國君
人為之此等
毋令強梁之
我而為君者
承　帝曰繼
福祉何以永
底定所錫之

所言有益於
王有得於心
國政時或一
至於八王理
難任彼恋也
此不善之人
有難色者似
心悅誠服而

立之時如不
者立之倘擇
可更擇有德
納諫不遵道
我之位若不
受諫者可繼
中有才德能
等八固山王

衆人畢集共
若面君時當
衆不可私往
適當告知於
或有故而他
彼意也八王
色亦不可任
置時如有難

賢者易之易
當選子弟中
但緘默坐視
賛他人之能
無能又不能
發明之如已
當會其意而
國家者七王

國難免内顧
釋此而征明
國俱来服若
北有蒙古二
南有朝鮮西
多年傾圮東
遼陽城大且
付與我等然

將遼東地方
曰皇天見祐
諸王大臣議
是月 帝集
二人至君前
諂佞不可一
事舉賢良退
議國政商國

之憂必另築城郭派兵堅守庶得坦然前驅而無後慮矣諸王大臣諫曰若舍已得之城郭棄所居之房屋而更為建立毋乃勞民乎帝曰既征明國豈容中止汝等惜一時之勞我惟遠大是圖若以一時之勞為勞前途大事何由而成可令降民築城至於房屋各自建之可也諸王大臣俱敬服帝言遂於城東五里太子河邊築城遷居之名其城曰東京〇七月大臣碩翁科羅巴圖魯辛年六十四歲〇癸亥天

論孰於一已
而俱持以公
事不分人已
其心孰能於
輔之以覩察
王設八大臣
諭曰八固山
○初七日傳

桑與之俱歸
質子鄂齊爾
帝悅遂釋其
復來朝見
是已期年矣
巴格貝勒至
前遣歸蒙古
命八年正月

則曰此人不
不堪任事者
政即衆之有
此人可使從
輔政者則曰
為籌畫有堪
何以敗當深
國事何以成

知一也大凡
所諍即奏上
為非如不從
論非者即以
臣當共持公
於辭色八大
任其非而形
之非不肯自

無以勸善不
蓋賢不舉則
曰不能三也
有不能者即
曰可治軍旅
堪軍旅者則
預備之有才
利於用者當

戰用何器有
凡攻用何具
負當深計之
何以勝何以
凡行軍之事
以下為將者
之二也總兵
堪任事即退

各牢所屬軍
達賴台吉等
博和塔布囊
古塔布囊鄂
諾木台吉莽
布卜台吉索
鄂之拉巴賓
乎喀爾喀五

心寧不愉快
臣僚有益此
有益所設之
所生之子孫
理感宜則吾
能於國事經
無以懲惡果
肖者不錯則

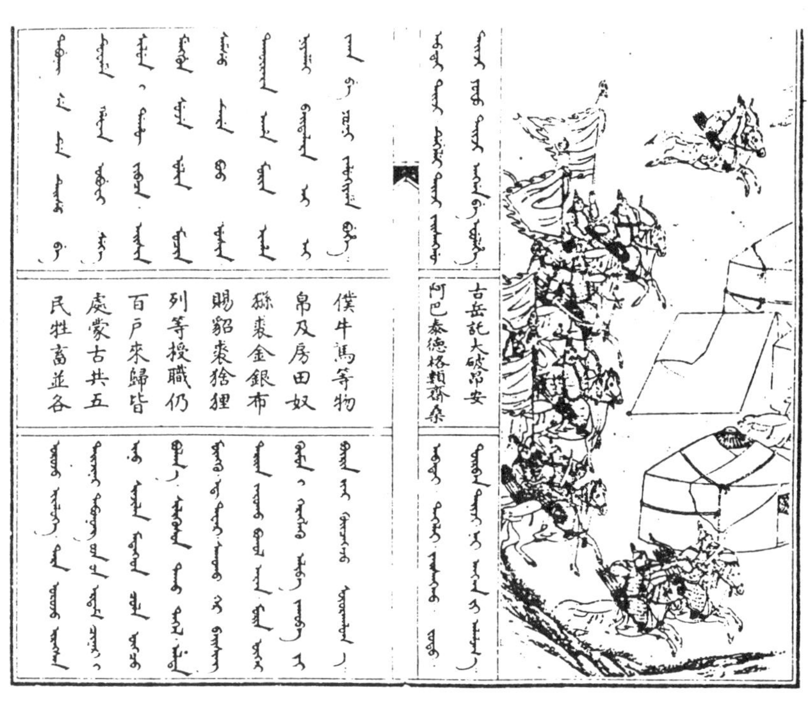

古岳託大破昂安
阿巴泰德格類齋桑

僕牛馬等物
帛及房田奴
猻裘金銀布
賜貂裘猞狸
列等授職仍
百戶來歸皆
處蒙古共五
民牲畜並各

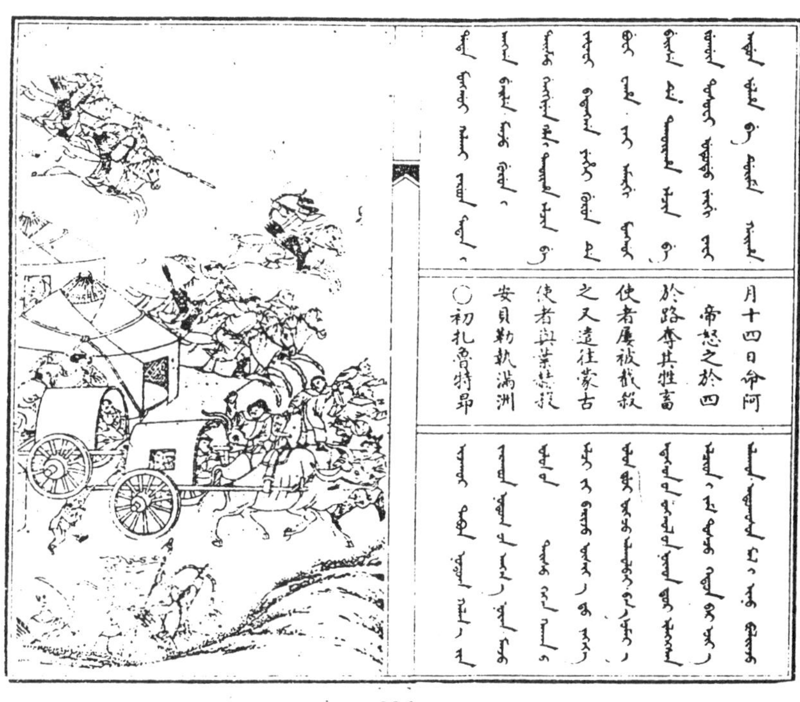

月十四日命阿
帝怒之於四
於路奪其牲畜
使者屢被截殺
之又遣往蒙古
使者與葉赫殺
安貝勒執滿洲
○初扎魯特昂

轄至昂安居處
雅希禪博爾晉
百里乃與泰將
安所屬遂畧地
爾格勒地為昂
兵五十先至額
兵岱務布領精
急趨有前鋒總

地渡遼河縱兵
二日方曙過羅
達夜疾行二十
之至二十一日
領兵三千往討
台吉岳託台吉
類台吉薺桑古
巴泰台吉德格

昂安父子併從
死我兵衝入殺
遂墜馬傷重而
刺中岱務布口
下一人擧小鎗
先射之昂安部
岱務布迎戰當
兵直衝岱務布

昂安避下馬之
餘騎勒馬而立
馬岱務布領十
領三十餘騎下
布禪博爾晉轄
東牛車而奔雅
子併二十餘人
攻之昂安率妻

者於一處盡獲其妻子軍民牲畜及擒桑圖台吉妻子而回乃鍾故貝勒之子而安頓也五月初六日帝出城迎之至四十里古城堡南相見因克敵乃監旗八桿吹螺拜天畢歷帳共出征王大臣叩見乃設宴勞之次日將所得人畜先賞出征將士

其餘列等以賜各官是日天雨帝曰蒙古之國猶此雲然雲合則致雨蒙古部合則成兵其散猶如雲收而雨止也俟其散時吾當亟取之言畢乃還〇時桑圖因妻子軍民既被擒乃致書哀懇曰桑圖書奏於主衆國明汗臣自來無罪故父在日

來叩見即還
無恙桑圖遂
曾叛俘俱存
告以妻子不
帝於是遣使
遣一使來
若果垂憐望
中慎毋懼怯

圖爾即於血戰
者 汗曾云桑
有故還意乎爽
怨鰲臣徵爽武
俘獲以 汗明
得脫妻子俱成
兵下臨惟孤身
罪誠有之今大

格福金及衆
召御妹阿吉
帝御八角殿
月初九日
吉為妃()六
與阿濟格台
城復設大宴
里外宴迎入

台吉至六十
古台吉杜度
上命齋桑
貝勒送女來
沁部孔果爾
日蒙古科爾
俱歸()十七
其妻子與之

耳即執政諸
常法所不容
因其紊亂綱
有怨哉不過
責者豈於我
中亦有被貶
如我國諸王
懲創其惡者

善者誅惡以
善以感發其
體之莫若舉
然天心何以
可不體天心
制禮作樂豈
天作之君凡
公主訓之曰

臣者原酌其
汝等妻諸大
吾之所以將
事成何婦道
法行背理之
居家婦女違
身殉國耳爾
心之盟故以

蓋因不背同
共歿於陣者
子披堅執銳
敗綱常乎男
豈肯縱恕以
苟犯吾法吾
法爾等婦女
王尚不令枉

帝諭諸王曰
汝母阻我
倘犯事之後
不預訓諸女
御妹曰姑若
分可也又謂
之光各安其
爾等當依我

賴日光而生
魅如萬物俱
其惡甚於魑
勢淩逼其夫
毋若爾等倚
令受制於汝
匹配之也豈
才論其功而

之死今還其
有當誅無致
王視之倘罪
當以八固山
等凡有罪過
歸也此降王
故慕我而來
因其君不仁

貝勒來附是
也兀魯特部
而更求其逸
更圖其榮逸
之來歸蒙而
無所約束今
原任意獨行
喀爾喀貝勒

[illegible]
古八也因來
扈爾漢姓佟爾
爾漢額駙原名
臨痛哭之適
十八 帝親
漢額駙卒年四
日大臣達爾

〇十月二十
何以為報耶
養之恩更將
供職則吾祿
等不敬謹以
既得之而汝
倉業最難今
等竟何益哉

月與郡主同
天命九年正
地至是甲子
妻之往送其
女遜岱郡主
巴圖魯貝勒
御弟達爾漢
帝嘉之將

來叩見求婚
台吉先諸部
子恩格德爾
圖魯貝勒之
部達爾漢巴
爾喀巴約特
之藏〇初喀
子賜以大臣

不祐殃及吾待之則穹蒼依歸若不厚而以我國為兄棄其故土之弟兄為弟親弟兄以妻為父遠離其

其父而以我格德爾遠離天岳祐使恩與之誓曰皇意欲厚待之京　帝嘉其請命求往東來欲率部衆

恩格德爾台哈廉台吉及碩託台吉薩吉岳託台吉台吉杜度台台吉阿濟格吉濟爾哈朗吉齋桑古台

吉德格類台王阿巴泰台二王三王四吾子孫大王天自保祐俾恩撫無間則合之子壻而身吾於天作

人若吾女有
而虐害其國
者多侮其夫
妻左右近臣
諸貝勒以女
聞喀爾喀部
吾女乎吾嘗
今汝受制於

故妻以女豈
念汝等遠附
女為畏朕原
女者勿以吾
立家而娶吾
在我國結婚
爾等降王凡
地可也又曰

之〇二十八
隱衆當盡告
毋自諱各有
艱苦之情切
予之過凡有
不責其非是
之過告之而
告朕是汝等

有不賢而不
别女妻爲或
即廢之另以
之罪不至死
罪當誅則誅
論即告朕知
汝等毋與較
似此不賢者

日諭曰總兵
以下備禦以
上凡有官職
者果恪守乃
職夙夜匪懈
盡心以為國
者吾視之如
子誠為有益
若懐窓惰安
佚之心而怠
慢天職則視
之如子竟何
益耶爾等各
宜竭力為國
今漢人蒙古
并各國雜處

國中其逃叛
盗賊詐偽橫
逆者當細察
之爾等若嚴
加察訪則惡
者不敢於為
惡國有不治
者乎國治則
吾心安方見
恭恭汝等之
益也若俱沈
安佚而不稽
查之惡者竊
發而為國亂
國亂則吾心
不安恭恭汝

世食 汗禄
眷顧俾子孫
共意則皇天
其身若同心
蒼不祐殃及
懷二心者穹
故國兄弟而
為好惡猶念

汗之喜怒
回本國不以
忠其厚恩恩
汗撫育若
誓曰蒙恩父
恩格德爾亦
長永享榮昌
吉等命得延

而慢其夫者
女或侍父母
賴吾女然吾
至此爾則倚
於汝令移居
吾女固仰望
但昔居汝國
犯俱不加罪

其餘一切過
惟篡逆不赦
爾後若有罪
文曰恩格德
爾暨郡主其
誥賜恩格德
畢 上以制
永享榮昌誓

吉領兵往移
朗杜度等台
桑古濟爾哈
託阿濟格齋
并阿巴泰岳
王三王四王
日命大王二
庇之也初六

不溺愛以曲
女雖至死必
惟汝是庇吾
而不得舒吾
受吾女之制
女也爾心或
有何事苦吾
或有之諒爾

搭狸猻衆送
珠寶哩各賜
果爾代子滿
都達哈并莽
子囊努克門
衆恩格德爾
雕鞍良馬貂
弟兄各賜以

之恩格德爾
張義站大宴
出東京迎至
部衆回 帝
王即奉命移
部下人民諸
弟莽古爾代
恩格德爾并

還京復賜恩
格德爾等田
卒耕牛金銀
蟒段布帛貂
鼠猞狸猻皮
及房田應用
之物仍以平
虜堡人民賜

之〇二月十
六日皇弟卓
禮克圖貝勒
薨年四十三
歲〇初與科
爾沁部遣使
往來者數年
至是復遣使

詰其處約固
和好其部長
遂遣使齎書
來書曰鄂巴
洪台吉等致
書於明掩衆
光威震列國
睿主陛下吾

嫩江台吉等
聞　汗諭莫
不欣服然主
持其大事裁
之自　汗吾
等莫有敢違
命者但察哈
爾汗及喀爾

而誓曰滿洲
各一碗焚香
骨血土酒肉
宰牛馬置白
台吉等會盟
偕青蒙果各
都齊達爾漢
往與鄂巴阿

庫爾禪希福
遂遣巴克什
之而已 帝
也惟 汗籌
何以為我謀
必來征伐將
與大國同謀
喀部知吾等

死若科爾沁
血出土埋而
殃如此骨暴
不祐降以災
之和者穹蒼
沁知而先與
計不令科爾
所誘中其巧

察哈爾餽贈
後滿洲若為
合意既盟之
天地顧同心
以盟言昭告
欺凌之憤故
因有察哈爾
科爾沁二國

來帝命大
科與沁使者
爾禪希福與
榮昌誓畢庫
孫萬禩永享
壽得延長子
則天地祐之
死果能踐盟

血出土埋而
殃亦如骨暴
不祐降以災
之和者穹蒼
洲知而先與
巧計不令滿
贈所誘中其
為察哈爾餽

鍔弼旺善貝
月內命宗弟
而焚之〇四
同前立誓書
烏牛對來使
等亦宰白馬
薩哈廉台吉
吉碩託台吉

台吉岳託台
格台吉杜度
朗台吉阿濟
台吉濟爾哈
台吉齋桑古
台吉德格類
四王阿巴泰
王二王三王

皇伯父禮敦
皇后用黃其
紅幪中宮
皇祖考用
紅各有其等
以行幪分黃
諸靈櫬肩輿
牢祭畢乃移

諸陵前用太
妣及 皇后
至 皇祖考
陵三人承命
處同名移先
名赫圖阿拉
呼蘭哈達山
和齋往祖居

吶喊斬草人
漢人形放砲
亭命東草為
里迎至接官
出東京二十
令衆軍披掛
率諸王大臣
間將至 帝

祭奠沿途無
紅逐日宰牛
篇古之子用
奇皇叔塔察
宗弟祜爾哈
魯青巴圖魯
達爾漢巴圖
巴圖魯皇弟

吾征明國以
前跪奠祝曰
諸 祖考靈
以祭諸靈躬
焚金銀紙張
儀宰牛羊多
之乃歲陳祭
立寢殿奉安

四里崗上建
東京城東北
靈過乃起至
考及 皇后
旁候 皇祖
士俱俯伏道
帝暨諸王軍
以奪其地

拏三員領兵
毛文龍令遊
〇五月明國
亦同移於此
圖圖們靈櫬
皇子阿爾哈
亥代皇后及
而起其繼娶

也祝畢再拜
寅中默祐可
達天地神祇
地乞祖父上
葬於所獲之
陽令迎先靈
遂得廣寧遼
復祖父之仇

順鴨綠江越
長白山寇滿
洲東界所屬
輝發地時有
滿洲守將蘇
爾東安擊破
之追殺三日
其兵無一人
得脫〇二十
八日科爾沁
部桑噶爾寨
台吉送女來
帝設宴與
皇子多爾袞
台吉為妃〇
八月初十日

額駙總兵官
何和哩卒年
六十四命皇
后等往弔之
帝於宮中
大慟曰佐吾
創業諸臣何
不遺一人以
送我之終也
〇是月 帝
聞毛文龍兵
渡朝鮮義州
城西鴨綠江
入島中屯田
命正白旗固
山副將楞額

已渡江遂縱
天明料明兵
進遂隱伏至
於山僻處前
連夜領兵潛
西岸楞額禮
江宿於義州
夜則斂兵過
江入島收穫
告曰晝則渡
一諜者詰之
之於途中獲
兵一千往襲
将事武善領
山遊擊萬副
禮鑲紅旗固

其糧而回
禮等盡焚
溺死楞額
舟墮水皆
其餘爭入
五百餘人
陸地掩殺
楞額禮等於
俱拋戈潰走
國將士大驚
突至其島明
禮即渡夾江
砲傳烽楞額
偵探未及來
兵前進明之

與姪義脫走
之明廉子澗
軍執二人殺
李國詳下中
領兵入城有
城而走二人
等所敗遂棄
迎戰為明康

京國王遣兵
纂起兵攻王
兵官李國謀
韓明廉與總
義來降澗父
鮮國韓潤韓
十年正月朝
○乙丑天命

滿泰貝勒妻
烏拉國岳母
稗益我也又
我之憂毫無
昔日惟知貽
星阿二兄者
有拜珠扈祜
曰吾宗室中

帝謂諸王
切應用之物
財帛衣服一
奴房田牛馬
之職仍給妻
職韓義備禦
韓潤遊擊之
來歸 帝賜

座賀正旦行
延二兄於上
人妻入中宮
齋錦台什二
及葉赫國布
往日納妻也
皇后之姊長
并岳母皇姨

令人請二兄
亦不可廢遂
然愛敬之禮
有何益哉雖
夫與我為難
母等皆構其
及葉赫國岳
皇后之母也

至旅順口其
一萬由海上
聞明國遣兵
衣送還帝
賜二兄補服
勸飲宴畢仍
還跪令宮婢
之后妃等亦

酌酒令人奉
宴帝跪而
行婦禮畢設
后妃三人亦
下鋪氈而坐
媼回至東榻
二兄後拜四
家人禮先拜

十里大宴入
后妃等出迎
帝與諸王及
宴之將至
至瀋陽北岡
為妃四王迎
妹來與四王
善台吉送其

貝勒子武克
科爾沁宰桑
而回○二月
殺其兵毀城
六千克之盡
命三王領兵
正月十四日
城駐兵乃於

恐食用不足
備令欲遷移
民之居室未
築宮廨方成
曰東京城新
諸王大臣諫
欲遷都瀋陽
諸王大臣議

三月 帝聚
等物令之還
帛盔甲銀器
金銀蟒段布
之賜以人口
送婚遂優待
禮成配因其
城復設宴以

力役繁興民
不堪苦矣
帝不允曰瀋
陽四通八達
之處西征明
國從都爾弼
渡遼河路直
且近北征蒙
古二三日可
至南征朝鮮
自清河路可
進瀋陽渾河
通蘇克素護
河於蘇克素
護河上流處
伐木順流而

下材木·可
勝用出遊打
獵山近獸多
且河中水族
亦可捕取矣
吾籌慮已定
故欲遷都汝
等何故不從
乃於初三日
出東京駐虎
皮驛初四日
至瀋陽○是
日有前遣去
喀爾達富喀
納塔裕三人
招瓦爾喀部

八旦祭旗畢
羅會之宰牛
日至穆瑚覺
必音行獵四
城初三日至
月初二日出
而迎之於四
獲甚衆乃畋

至是聞其俘
討凡爾喀部
兵一千五百
瑚徹爾格領
善副將達珠
上命宗弟旺
而至○初
三百三十人

宰牛羊四十
瀋陽北岡復
四十三日至
及降民等而
百餘犒三軍
併所獲之欵
以酒二百埕
臣抱見畢乃

首 帝與三
處俱利遂叩
洪福所到之
對曰仗 汗
俱利否旺善
曰爾等所向
軍叩見 帝
旺善等率衆

酒四百埕設四百席大宴勞之未時入城賞旺善達珠瑚徹爾格從征軍士每名銀五兩○二十三日

帝設大宴聚諸王訓之曰語云其為人也孝弟而好犯上作亂者未之有也吾後代子孫當世守孝弟之

道不可違也其為長上者居恒當和洽其子弟為子弟者亦宜承順親愛方可至於上待下下事上務以

真心實意愛敬之慎勿懷虛假之念且我滿洲原與漢人蒙古國別俗殊今共處一城如同室而居若遇

未及准備有
越墻時屯中
至官屯方欲
州南薔參衙
百兵夜入耀
明毛文龍三
月二十七日
言可也○六

汝等毋負朕
指示者此耳
和好吾之所
當聚宴以聯
薄少飲食亦
得所之時雖
卑幼者必無
畢幼過嚴則

總之職以金
職遊圖妻千
人妻備禦之
加努納岱二
乃宣至賜青
帝聞而奇之
盡追殺之
揚古利領兵

守耀州總兵
墜墻驚走有
其兵敵人遂
首登墻截殺
內豎車轅為
遊圖二人妻
執刀與納岱
青加努妻先

河上人馬溺
将追殺直抵
來攻守城諸
宫渡河夜半
處兵自天妃
寧遠山海二
修城将半有
城四人奉命

糧州重修其
實等率兵守
剛岱茂海光
命屯布嚕阿
國中〇八月
自此播揚於
重賞之其名
帛牛馬列等

樂衛齋扎努
博爾晋轄備
代管副将事
〇初命遊擊
匹散與衆軍
一面其餘馬
将各賜銀牌
等賞破敵諸

所獲馬匹列
隻祭旗畢将
十里宰牛八
功 帝出迎
屯布嚕等獻
甲器械無算
馬七百匹盔
死者甚衆獲

二千而來
察部時獲人
東汚北出勤
二人領兵討
謨喀木達尼
還〇初命雅
見畢大宴乃
招來頭目叩

出征諸將並
之迎至渾河
而來　帝聞
部招五百户
海南瑚爾哈
兵二千討東
通貴尼堪領
塞紐克衷諾

爾與北阿祿
令聞南察哈
必互相救援
一遇有敵兵
結盟願合為
對天地歃血
宰白馬烏牛
者我二國曾

於　帝曰向
乃遣使馳書
汗興兵來侵
哈爾國林丹
沁鄂巴聞察
初九日科爾
大宴而回〇
帝出城迎之

乞助千人五
其砲手火器
惟　汗裁之
賫助兵多寡
今聞舉兵已
馬先來告我
伊沙穆乘二
已預聞急遣

告不意　汗
兵之確實往
年欲探其與
夾攻我自去
結草未枯來
五日乘河氷
兵於九月十
會林丹汗舉

帝覽畢遂修
在　汗也
後其齋賽惟
而來乘虛襲
意彼若連兵
加兵於我之
有附察哈爾
哈達爾漢皆

已其齋賽巴
巴林二人而
者洪巴圖魯
我合吾所恃
刈其禾欲與
洪巴圖魯急
不能盡知獨
部貝勒中吾

若折兵敗能抜必退城上彼不郭守禦於當堅備城豈容之但衆害寡天立者也以

凡國皆天所寡惟在乎天蓋兵不在衆不必過慮也寡吾皆應之用兵或多或巴洪台吉汝書荅之曰鄂

以後無復不勝而回人與之戰甲僅五十兵五百帶發時輝發也曾征輝林丹之祖

薩克圖汗昔圖們扎自無虞矣敢復侵汝難取亦不而退彼知危即不敗走彼國且

者也汝設識為英勇以致勝者乘機一戰不拔而退伺其攻城據城待戰勿從之若

於走也慎敵欲其便人必是怯出戰者此兵寡而欲負難必有軍交戰勝敢侵凡兩

明國朝鮮遂能已耶曰無罪彼意侵汝即事彼果有和以圖無之有即與汝等何罪

屢屢來侵和好至今扎薩克圖曾與圖們沁貝勒等昔汝科爾而圖無事欲與之和

卒孫林丹
爾車臣汗
○初祭哈
書往送之
遣四使賫
砲手八人
初十日發
城池也於

國所恃惟
因我等諸
得安居哉
豈令我等
城郭蒙古
滿洲苟無
葉赫哈達
烏拉輝發

沁來謁
稜從科爾
扎爾布色
是岱青子
洪台吉至
叛歸鄂巴
瑪武爾占
達達噶爾

稜公格賓
扎爾布色
妻并六子
岱青率其
弟也人民
岱青車臣
納明安部
立盡奪賓

張屯漢人
海州所屬
甘泉鋪南
令之回〇
段帛等物
厚賜銀器
皮二張又
千張海獺

張青鼠皮
領貂皮百
狸猻裘二
刀二口鎗
甲十二副
金帶二束
四件玲瓏
帝賜蟒衣

百七十人
追之殺兵
聲即領兵
爾坤聞砲
將齋沙武
防海州遏
遂敗走時
其四人敵

與之戰殺
身無甲冑
中滿洲人
襲其屯屯
兵三百夜
龍文龍遣
人通毛文
謀叛密以

○十七日帝因臣民有嗜酒者遂降旨諭之曰自來曾聞飲酒之人於飲中得何物於飲中增何藝如是裨益者有耶飲酒者與人爭鬭以刀傷人反自害其身者有之或墜馬傷其手足折其頸項而死或為鬼魅所壓而死或縱酒成疾而死或仆於途路而失衣冠或得罪於父母兄弟或恃酒力而毀敗其器具消落其家業者有之

也愚者飲傷人之酒者而飲此食其飽人飽人何不傷人食能所造酒能同是五穀

夫酒與食餺飥可食炊桑可食不能飽也飢時飲酒聞之矣况無益吾嘗似此種種

利於行佞忠言逆耳口利於病云良藥苦之賢者有何美哉古亡飲酒有因之而逃

夫惡奴僕妻飲而為而為妻憎至於夫飲罪於君上德更且見者飲之敗之喪身毀

至帝出
初四日乃
五百十月
其衆一千
路進兵俘
爾哈部二
征東海瑚
領兵一千

拜巴布泰
子阿拜塔
鰲〇初命
德可勿戒
之口必敗
旨酒美人
聽必壞道
言聳人之

開原鎮北
往助之至
臣領大兵
率諸王大
於初十日
各路軍士
帝遂調
其勢已迫

舉兵來侵
曰林丹汗
五使告急
洪台吉遣
五日鄂巴
十一月初
宴而回〇
城迎之大

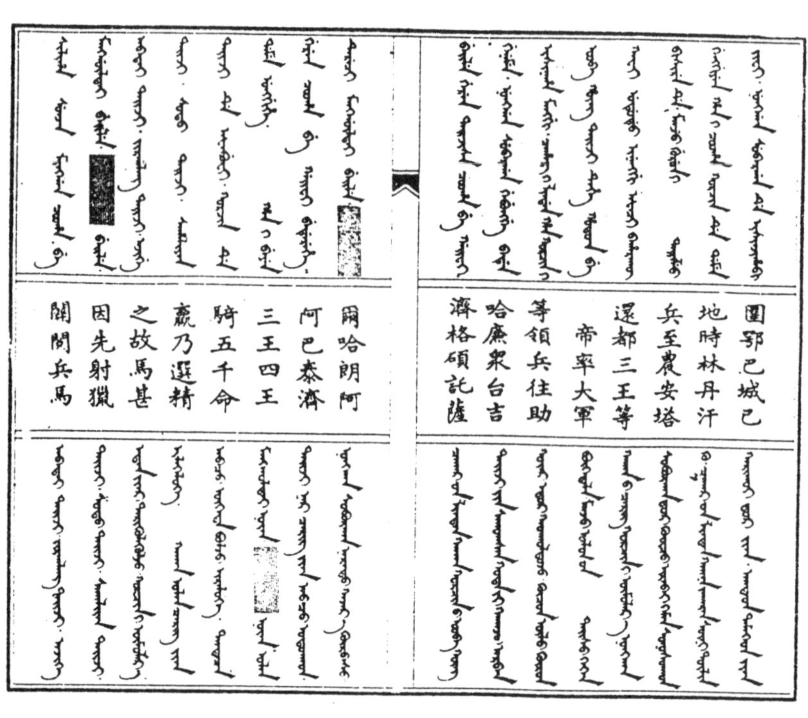

閱閱兵馬因先射獵之故馬甚羸乃選精騎五千命三王四王阿巴泰濟爾哈朗阿濟格碩託薩哈廉衆台吉等領兵往助

帝率大軍還都三王等兵至農安塔地時林丹汗圍鄂巴城巴

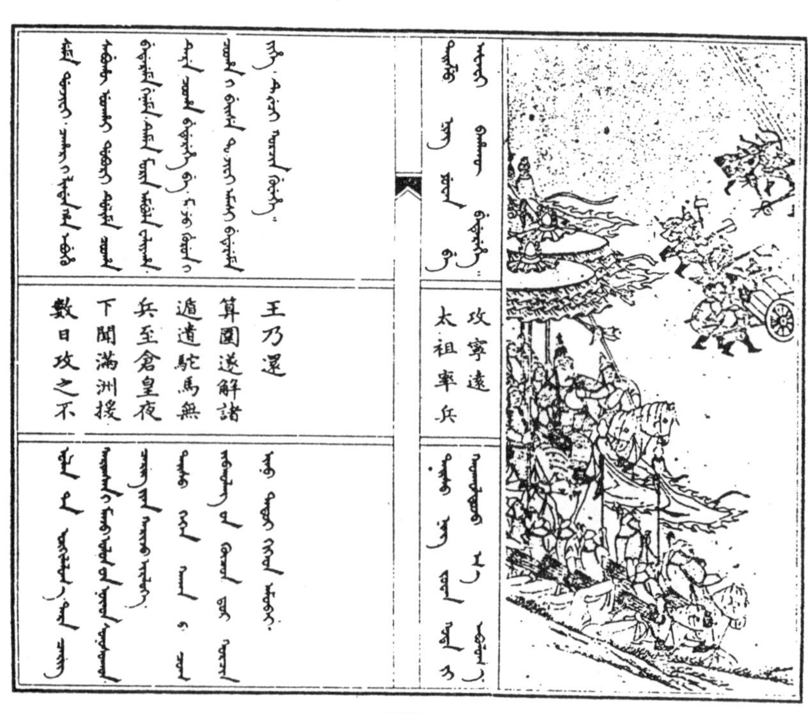

太祖率兵攻寧遠

數日攻之不下聞滿洲援兵至倉皇夜遁遺駝馬無算圍遂解諸王乃還

車覆城下
四日以戰
具於二十
軍中備攻
帝即令
爾爲寡也
萬亦不以
約有十三

萬虛也吾
來兵二十
降理且稱
死守豈有
治之義當
之地吾修
汗所棄
錦二城乃

日復攻之
進少卻次
洲兵不能
戰不退滿
石齊下死
砲藥礮雷
城固守鎗
祖大壽嬰

滿桂參將
崇煥總兵
寧遠道袁
奮力攻打
不墮軍士
城已穿而
寒土凍鑿
進攻時天

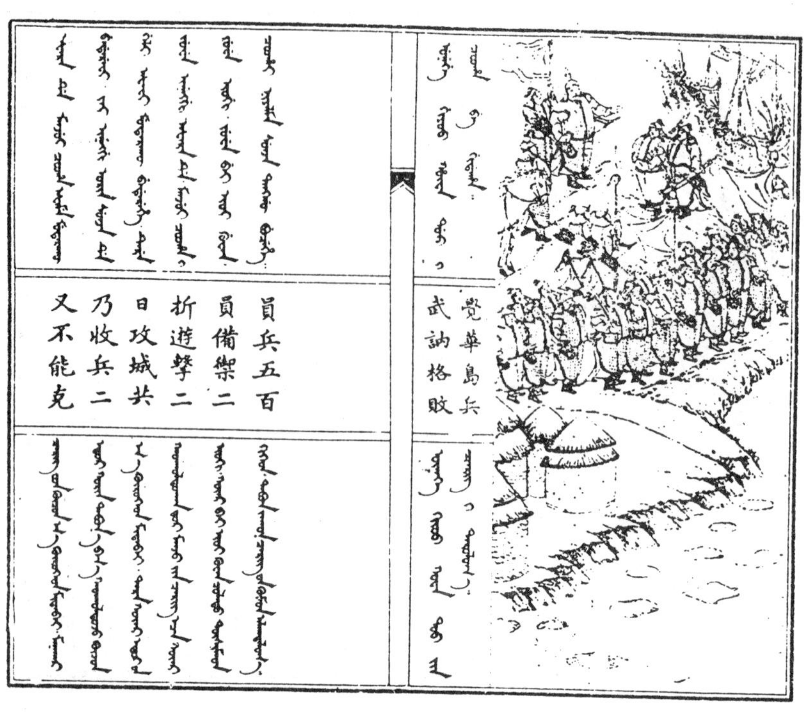
覺華島兵
武訥格敗
員兵五百
員備禦二
折遊擊二
日攻城共
乃收兵二
又不能克

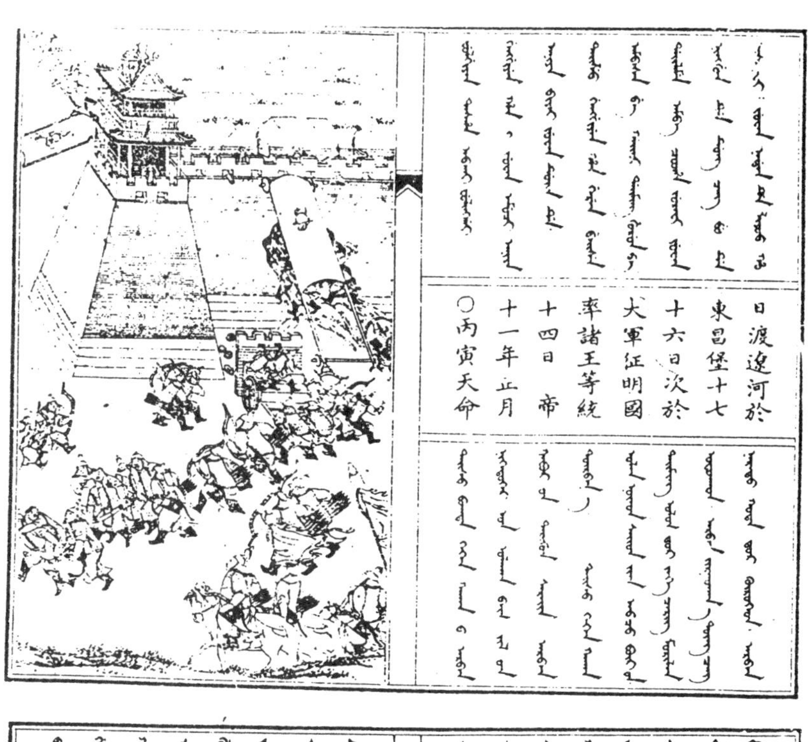

○丙寅天命十一年正月十四日帝率諸王等統大軍征明國十六日次於東昌堡十七日渡遼河於

曠野布兵南至海岸北越廣寧大路前後絡繹首尾莫測旌旗劍戟如林有前鋒至西平堡獲哨探問之

告曰明之兵右屯衛一千大凌河五百錦州三千此外人民隨處而居大兵將至右屯衛守城恭將周守

懼焚房殺而
七城軍民大
山連山塔山
河小凌河杏
鳳翼並大凌
左輔中軍毛
忠松山參將
張賢都司呂
孳蕭聖中軍
前進錦州進
右屯衛大兵
積糧俱運貯
四萬將海岸
八人領步兵
適 帝遣將
廉率軍民已

加兵耶寧
汗何故遽
煥答曰
遠道袁崇
以高爵寧
若降即封
矣爾衆官
城破之必
十萬兵攻此
告曰吾以二
漢人入寧遠
安營縱所俘
截山海大路
越城五里橫
大兵至寧遠
走二十三日

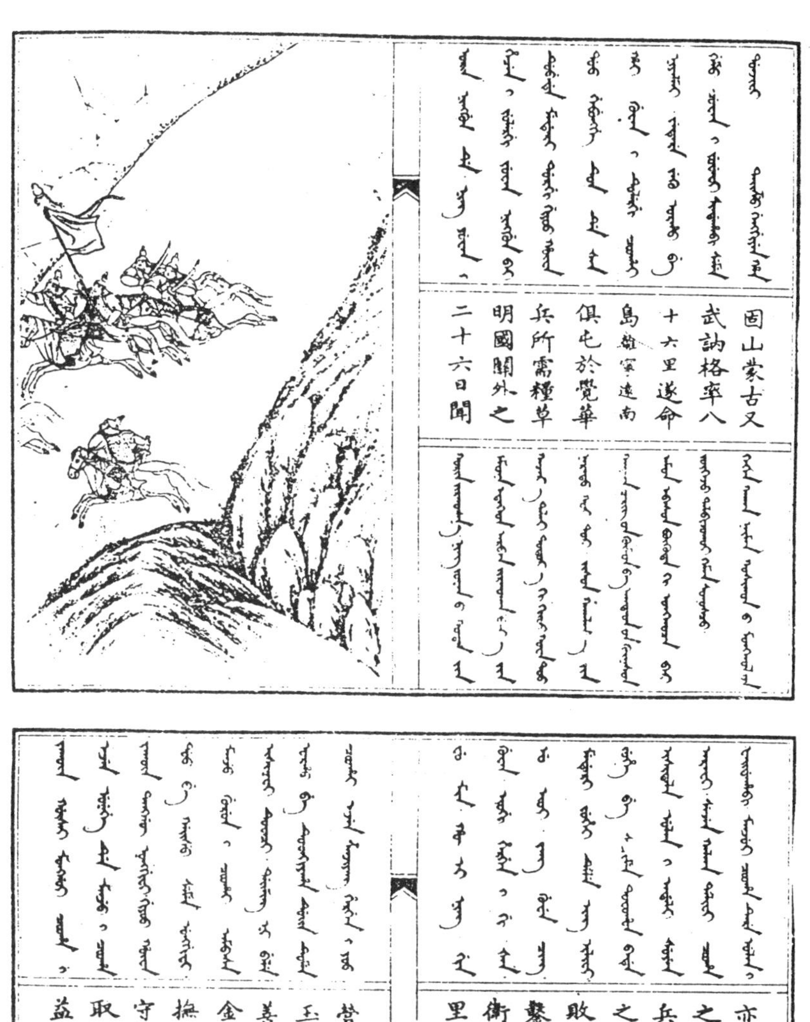

二十六日聞
明國關外之
兵所需糧草
俱屯於覺華
島離寧遠南
十六里遂命
武訥格率八
固山蒙古又
益兵八百往
取之見明國
守糧參將姚
撫民胡一寧
金冠遊擊季
善張國青吳
玉於冰上安
營鑿冰十五
里以戰車為
衛我兵從未
鑿處進擊遂
敗其兵盡殺
之又有二營
兵立於島山
之上遂衝入
亦盡殺之焚

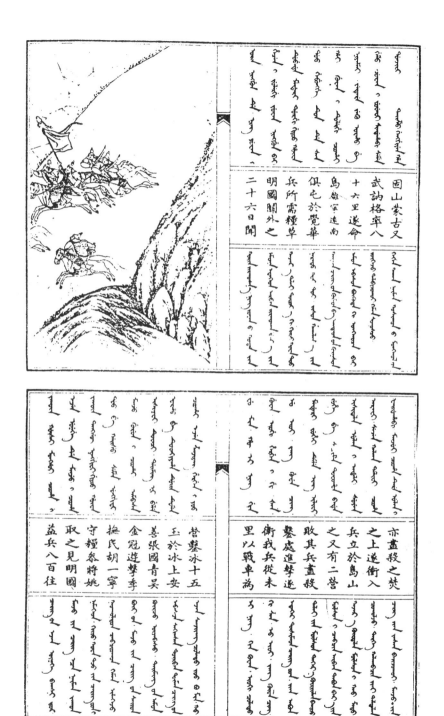

其船二千餘及糧草千餘堆乃還大營二十七日帝還至右屯衛將糧草盡焚之二月初九日至瀋陽

帝自二十五歲征伐以來戰無不勝攻無不克惟寧遠一城不下遂不懌而歸〇三月初三日帝曰

吾籌慮之事甚多意者朕或倦勤而不留心於治道歟國勢安危民情甘苦而不省察歟功黜正直之人

有所顛倒歟再思吾子嗣中果有效吾盡心為國者否大臣等果俱勤謹於政事否又每常詳察敵國之

可喻於精者
有粗言之而
切於理者亦
閒論之而深
大凡語言有
俾從而識之
勇者聞朕言
所見以對其

意俾伊亦抒
言者告以朕
可也若可與
者入而盡言
暨精練行陣
有啓沃朕心
夜籌畫之際
情形當此晝

生享之勇者
治之國而彼
分內賢人理
射十拙隨而
有云一人善
出諸口也諺
其難堪故不
靦面斥之恐

知之矣將欲
具器局吾已
問耶彼之才
豈不令人鬱
而坐聽吾言
勇敢仰視吾
不能言又無
或有其人既

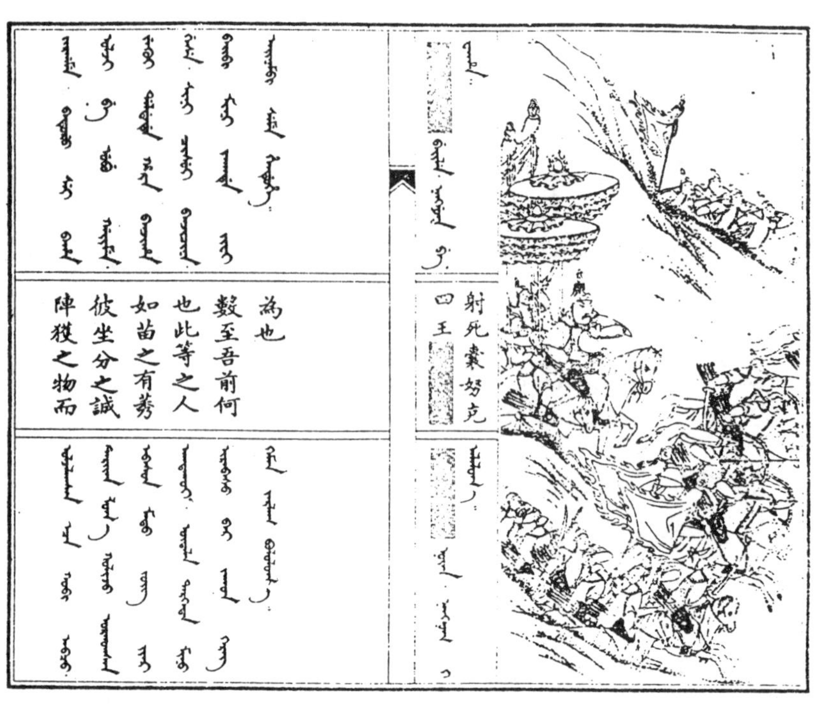
射死囊努克
四王
為也
數至吾前何
也此等之人
如苗之有莠
彼坐分之誠
陣獲之物而

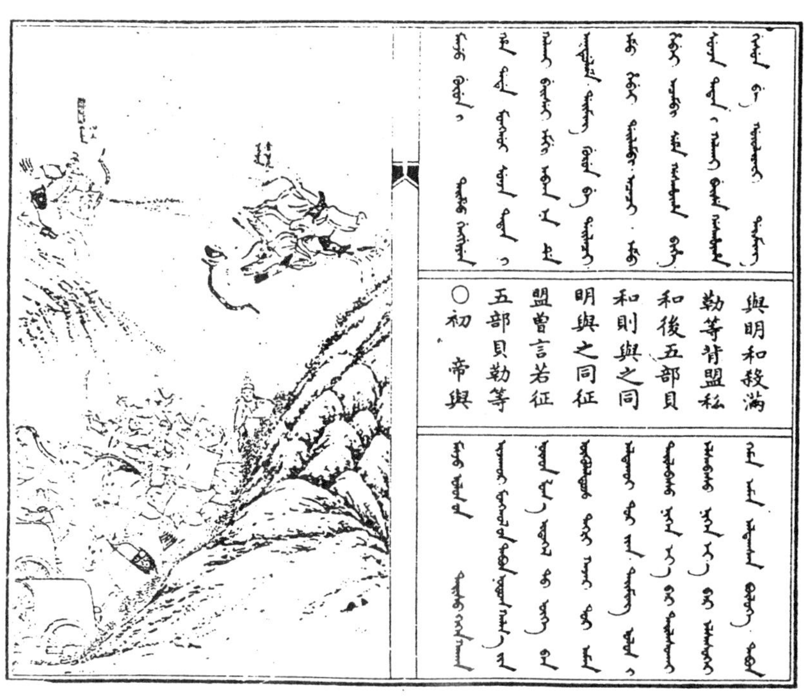

與明和殺滿
勒等背盟私
和後五部貝
和則與之同
明與之同征
盟曾言若征
五部貝勒等
○初 帝與

衆軍繼之於
其居處親率
率之急進尋
精騎令諸王
遼河安營選
十方寺邊渡
之初五日出
臣統大軍征

日率諸王大
於四月初四
是與之爲惡
財物牲畜由
刼滿洲使者
受其賞又屢
首於明國多
洲斥堠軍馘

初六日大兵星夜前驅次日天明分兵八路並進前鋒四王二王阿濟格台吉碩託台吉先至囊努克寨

囊努克乃喀爾喀巴林部落葉赫巴國之幼子囊努克領從者數人棄寨而走滿洲諸王隨後追之囊努

克且戰且走忽背後一王突至囊努克未及避被射死於馬下射之者乃四王也後大兵續至取環近屯

寨收其牲畜初九日令大王二王四王暨濟爾哈朗阿濟格岳託碩託薩哈廉衆台吉等領精兵一萬往

實喇木倫
相左遂渡
回兵之路
夜續進與
返三王乘
至其地而
進不能未
王馬乏欲
諸王而進諸
二千繼前去
山諸將率兵
三王及八固
及則回復令
之如馬力不
有人民即收
實喇木倫過

來降拉班
率百户人
得爾格爾
布囊與弟
落拉班塔
喀巴林部
二日喀爾
祭旗畢初
宰牛八隻
月初一日
邊安營五
至瑚琿河
帝率兵回
還大營
畜無筭乃
河收獲牲

帝聞鞍
擊李良美
餘生擒遊
之殺兵千
巴布泰敗
山驛城守
遣兵襲鞍
将毛文龍
将士〇明
列等賞給
千五百俱
畜五萬六
将所獲人
所屬是日
古爾布什
兄弟原係

總兵官巴篤
少却而我國
砲齊下明兵
南門城中矢
滸初更攻城
遣兵襲薩爾
〇十二日明
将毛文龍復
乃回
敵兵已敗
至途中聞
鞍山進發
諸王俱向
夜入瀋陽
山有警即

宴畢至范河
行接見禮大
遇於中固城
迎之行三日
衆台吉等遠
三王四王并
勒之兵卽令
巴乃一闊貝

來叩見以鄂
鄂巴洪台吉
聞科爾沁部
十六日 帝
兵二百餘○
遂敗追殺其
吶喊而入敵
禮自山向下

拜抱見 帝
帝膝下再
首鄂巴復詣
台吉進見叩
拜思噶爾二
同和爾和岱
屬列於帳前
帳鄂巴率部

郭迎十里陛
帝謁廟乃出
鄂巴將至
之二十一日
王復設宴荅
諸王次日諸
宰牛羊以宴
郊外鄂巴亦

離坐荅之和爾和岱拜思噶爾二人隨之亦各如此見畢復位而跪 帝問台吉等安否後諸王亦依次行接見禮鄂巴等獻貂皮貂裘駝馬曰我等之物俱被察哈爾喀爾喀兩處之兵掠去竟無堪獻者 帝

曰彼二部兵原為貪得而來掠其所有不待言也今爾我無恙得相會足矣遂大宴畢各賜雕鞍馬匹金頂帽錦衣金帶鄂巴大喜曰今蒙賜大重吾等恐明日仍當取還是以且喜且訝而未敢深信也 帝曰

拜思噶爾二
令和爾和岱
之甚厚鄂巴
每日設宴待
巴等同入城
靳也遂與鄂
索取當不爾
之佳者即向

中衣服器具
等若見諸王
未必甚佳爾
而已其物恐
或隨意持贈
後賜與之物
足為意但以
此微物耳何

巴結盟誓曰
馬烏牛與鄂
初六日宰白
姪也〇六月
貝勒子 帝
爾漢巴圖魯
之圖倫乃達
吉女敖哲妻

賚以圖倫台
大設宴具奩
帝乃擇定
諸王轉奏之
之吾可娶也
以女若果允
汗曾許我
人問諸王曰

之人蓋天俾
此俱受困厄
共議國事彼
二部來與我
今鄂巴積怨
巴亦蒙天祐
科爾沁部鄂
爾喀速兵侵
又察哈爾喀
天天遂祐之
忍乃昭告於
欺凌難於隱
爾喀爾喀部
明國并察哈
命之人因被
我本順天安

疆土公正
復前代帝王
俾鄂巴得與
鄂巴誓曰天
自永為眷顧
克敦盟好天
危咎其人如
者天亦以災
子孫有敗盟
災危和好後
必咎之降以
之不然則天
誑者天必眷
不替而無欺
體天心相好
相合也如能

賴台吉後裔
韋而殺我達
殺幾盡又無
部諸貝勒虜
將我科爾沁
知劫殺不已
而不得彼惟
悠今欲相好

未有纖微過
哈爾喀爾喀
來効忠於察
薩克圖汗以
勒等自事扎
吾科爾沁貝
以盟言告天
明汗契合今

恩仍與察哈
好若渝盟忘
汗祝天地盟
故來此謂
祐　汗所助
不敢忘天所
　汗協助吾
免又得滿洲

皇天默佑獲
合兵相加韋
我敢於相抗
敵也彼又謂
好吾等故成
劫害不圖和
貝勒因優故
賽又殺我六

率鄂巴三跪
香獻牲 帝
河岸當天焚
牛馬盟於渾
之眷顧時宰
誓天自永為
盟言世好不
罪其人如守

天亦以災危
有敗盟者皇
後之子孫倘
恩天必眷之
言不忘 汗
災危如踐盟
和者天降以
爾喀爾喀相

當時昆仲奔
賴皇天祐之
兵侵害鄂巴
天察哈爾起
總之主宰在
而國乃興矣
必佑之為君
敗為善者天

致令國勢衰
者天必咎之
帝曰為惡
巴賜以汗號
七日大宴鄂
衆焚之○初
二誓書宣於
九叩首畢將

○初十日土
謝賜號之恩
布帛鄂巴等
器雕鞍蟒緞
衣服各種銀
盔甲并四季
禮克圖復賜
和岱為青卓

圖都稜和爾
齊為扎薩克
爾漢弟布塔
圖梅為岱達
謝圖汗其兄
天道賜名土
抵敵吾故順
北鄂巴獨力

婢錢蒙古俱
達葉赫烏拉
棟鄂完顏哈
塔諸貝勒及
曰昔我寧古
帝訓諸王
○二十四日
鐵嶺駕遂還

王二王送至
南崗處令大
大宴至蒲河
路経一宿設
王大臣送之
國 帝率諸
敦哲自回本
謝圖汗留妻

馬者須加厚美女及購良取若聘民間毋得私有所八家均分之但得一物令鑒預定八家吾以彼為前

當見聞之矣豈無耳目亦待我言汝等至於敗亡不爭奪戕害以昆弟中自相曲不尚公直貪財貨尚私

也昔衛鞅云同心共事人諫其過誠為息心若能力規諫而存姑不可不極力昆弟中有過之事至諸王

忘而行貪曲訓誡慎毋遺此言朕嘗為忠而輕財貨於衆當重公隱匿必分給所獲之物毋賞之凡軍中

貽悞於汝等就汝等豈欲訓言無非成者多也凡我大有害於國不知由小及謂小而無患忠臣凡事勿

而不諫則非形者下也違上也諫於既諫於未形者也又忠經云藥也甘言疾言實也苦言飾言華也至

内不得安勞遍慮事物而苦心志使之於是人必先天將降大任任大任也故對曰君相之意何居羣臣

里奚食牛天禹舉魚鹽百說舉版築膠舜發畎畝傅皆由困而亨古明君賢相謂羣臣曰自耶昔宋劉裕

受其福以享
為君致令國
以歷艱苦者
識天意者也
之言誠為善
此而已若人
民隱天意如
為相必能恭

國事是人而
為君必能達
不能是人而
性增益其所
所以動心忍
使食不得充
得逸餓體膚
筋骨使外不

稱也吾昔日
則君王何以
為君為王否
有德政方可
吾民也不知
知艱苦致勞
多享安逸未
民恐爾諸王

艱苦所聚之
已以及民吾
艱辛使之推
降吾身歷盡
之民甚苦故
苦天見我國
致令國受其
安逸者為君

若亡我我或
而有此訓天
令　汗愛我
者不愛之也
人令其悅怡
也以甘言誨
流涕者愛之
言誨人令其

圖對曰以苦
諄復也土謝
無心何爲此
得毋以人孰
曰恐汝介意
謝圖畢既而
之言明訓土
曾將所慮及

貫積貨農夫
以罰示威商
當以賞示信
勿憂也國家
謂太子曰汝
在白山之東
故都會寧府
帝自汴京幸

也昔金大定
而篤行之可
訓承我基業
如此心領所
言爾諸王亦
謝圖曾有此
決不敢忘土
忘之矣吾心

積粟爾八固山四大王四小王繼我之後亦效彼之嚴守法度信賞必罰使我不與國事得坐觀爾等措置以舒其懷可也言畢書訓詞與諸王〇七月二十三日帝不豫詣清河溫泉坐湯十三日大漸欲還

京遂乘舟順太子河而下遣人召后迎之於渾河相遇至艾家堡離瀋陽四十里八月十一日庚戌未時崩在位十一年壽六十八國政及子孫遺命預有告誡臨終遂不言及羣臣更番昇

奉夜初更至瀋陽入宮中諸王大臣并官民號慟不絕 帝后原係葉赫國主揚機努貝勒女為後復立烏拉國滿泰貝勒女為后然心懷嫉妒每致 帝不懌雖有機

智終為 帝之明所制留之恐後為亂階預遺言於諸王曰俟吾終必令殉之諸王以 帝遺言告后后初遲疑未決諸王曰 先帝有命雖欲不從不可得也后遂服

禮衣盡以
珠寶飾之
泣謂諸王
曰吾自十
二歲事
先帝錦衣
玉食已二
十六年吾

不忍離故
相從於地
下吾二幼
子多爾袞
多鐸當善
撫之諸王
泣而對曰
二幼弟吾

等若不友
愛是忘父
也豈有不
善撫之理
於是后於
十二日辛
亥辰時自
盡壽三十

七乃與
帝同殮已
時出宮安
厝於瀋陽
城内西北
角又有二
妃阿吉根
代因扎亦

殉之 帝
自幼不飲
酒心懷中
正之德深
於謀畧善
於用兵騎
步二射絕
倫勇力出
衆睿知如
神不思而
得聞微言
創國書順
者以恩撫
之逆者以
兵討之賞
不計仇罰

不避親如
是明功賞
嚴法令推
己愛人鋤
强扶弱敬
老慈幼恤
孤煢寡人
皆悅服自
二十五歲
奮跡崛起
帶甲僅十
三人然侵
伐從不施
無罪者天
故祐之削
平諸部及

征明國得遼陽廣寧地又征蒙古威名大震有光於祖考興國開疆以創王基

太祖未即位時先娶之后生長子褚英賜號阿爾哈圖圖們次子代善號古英巴圖魯繼娶后所生莽古

爾泰德格類中宮皇后生[illegible]即天聰皇帝也繼立之后生阿濟格多爾袞號墨爾根岱青多鐸號

額爾克楚虎爾皇妃生阿巴泰又三妃生五子阿拜湯古代塔拜巴布泰巴布海

敬題重繪
太祖實錄戰圖
八韻

昊天有成命長
白發嘉徵
實錄內古載長
白山約高二百
里週圍約千里
鴨綠混同愛滸
三江所出初天
降仙女於長白
山東北布庫哩
山下有神鵲銜
朱果吞之成孕
生子生而能言
長成母告子曰
天生汝令汝定
亂可往彼成將
所生緣由一一
詳說乃與一舟
順流而下言訖
不見時長白山
東南鄂謨輝三
姓爭雄聞之往
見果非常人異
而詰之答曰我
乃天女所生姓
愛新覺羅天降
我定汝等之亂
衆皆驚異遂擁
回三姓人息爭
共奉為主以女

妥之定號滿洲
實我朝發祥之
始也草創大東
始規模方夏肇
旅猶五百闕甲
未十三增
實錄內載我
太祖龍行虎
步舉止威嚴心
性忠實剛果武
勇蓋世用兵如
神初起止遺甲
十三副兵不滿
百克圖倫城後
攻納申完濟漢
亦僅率兵四百

恩威並行
順者以德服逆
者以兵臨於是
剿平諸部後攻
克明國遼東諸
城建都盛京
帝業遂定圖
遼先靖近捫創
更鼓升 實
錄內載攻翁鄂
洛城時 太
祖升屋射敵被
賊箭中首透盔
即以所拔之箭
射賊應弦而倒
又被他賊射中

躬冒矢石
吉　天興兵
仇乃書七大恨
傾　先世之
張　太祖欲
心其後兵力漸
未嘗不流涕動
皆錄至此

容下屋每欲請
拔箭眼拄弓從
太祖以手
近前項血湧出
恐敵知覺勿令
拔回　太祖
出衆見被傷欲
項鐵卷如鉤拔

重繪二本以一
盡見因命依式
宮恐子孫不能
清本敬貯乾清
乃內家盛京時
守錄八冊
承重繪傳奕世
祖德繼續勳孫

思
仁是用興艱難
戰無不克惟
乘有
七恨便以進千
國斗山遂困書
師二十萬於薩
彼方甚大破明

也毋忘凜日兢
開創之艱難
年子孫毋忘
示我大清億萬
藏傳之奕世以
本恭送盛京尊
本貯上書房一

한국학에 대한 저자의 변

필자가 <한국학과 우랄·알타이학>이라는 제목으로 책을 내놓게 된 목적은 한국 문화의 원류적 입장에서 한국 문화의 전체적 상황을 서술하여 '거시적 한국학' 혹은 '우랄·알타이 지역을 포용하는 한국학'을 한국 학계와 세계 학계에 알리자는데 그 의의가 있겠다.

해방된 지 벌써 63년이나 흘렀다. 그리고 '한국학'도 많은 발전을 하였다. 그러나 대체적으로 역사의 분야에서는 삼국시대(고구려, 백제, 신라, 가야), 발해, 고려, 조선을 거쳐 현대에 이르는 과정만을 연구 대상으로 삼았거나 또는 여기에 한정된 연구와 분석을 통한 논문과 저서를 남겼을 뿐이다. 또한 역사에서 주로 '고대사' 부분에서는 상고사의 영토 문제 및 중국 대륙에서 과연 고구려와 백제, 그리고 신라가 어떤 역할과 기능을 하였으며 또한 백제와 신라의 영토가 중국에 존재하였는가이다. 그리고 고구려의 영토가 중국에서 어디서부터 어디까지 걸쳐 있었느냐의 초점도 역사학계에서는 늘 언쟁의 소지를 안고 있었다. 특히 고구려와 수나라 그리고 당나라와의 관계에서 전쟁이 가지고 있는 역사적 의미는 과연 무엇이었으며 을지문덕 장군의 살수대첩 승리는 수나라에게 어떤 영향을 끼쳤으며, 안시성 성주 양만춘 장군의 당나라에 대한 승전 역시 중국과 우리와의 관계사적인 측면에서 볼 때 득과 실은 지금쯤은 객관적으로 바라볼 시각이 필요하다.

또한 백제와 신라의 경우도 일본과의 문화 전수 관계만을 생각하지 말고 그 자체를 연구, 분석한 다음에 비교, 검토가 필요할 것이다. 만약 이러한 절차 없는 연구는 사상누각이 될 것은 정한 이치이기 때문이다. 그리고 발해의 역사 연구도 오늘날 너무나 매스컴 위주로 현장 답사적 연구가 진행되는 듯해서 북방 연구에 뜻이 있는 학자들에게 있어서는 매우 안타깝다. 왜냐하면 매스컴이란 짧은 시간에 많은 효과를 연출하기는 하지만 시청자의 입맛에 맞추어야 하기 때문에 편집자의 의도가 숨어 있고 또한 인기 위주의 편성도 배

제할 수 없기도 하기 때문이다. 더구나 방송은 차분히 연구하고 분석해서 결과를 기다리기보다는 결과를 빨리 시청자들에게 알리려는 방송의 본연의 임무, 성급함 때문에 잘못 전달될 가능성이 많다.

앞으로 발해의 연구는 언어학・민속학・고고학 등 종합적인 연구가 처음부터 결합하여 시도되어야 할 것은 물론이다. 또한 고려와 조선시대의 역사연구에 있어서는 고려사를 중심으로 하는 문헌 연구와 현지답사적 성격을 띤 민속 사학적인 입장도 전혀 무시해서는 안 되리라 생각한다. 그리고 고려는 주변 외적과의 관계가 끊임없이 있었다. 특히 거란과 몽고의 침입에 대한 교섭사적인 측면에서의 역사 연구는 무엇보다도 절실히 필요한 때이다.

또한 현대사의 연구도 이데올로기적인 차원에서만 볼 것이 아니라 한민족사적인 맥락에서 현대사 역시도 조명을 하여야 하며 무엇보다도 거시적인 관점과 더불어서 미래 지향적인 목표를 내걸고 문제를 해결해야 할 것이다. 또한 우리는 몽고의 침입과 임진왜란 그리고 일제 시대를 조명함에 있어서 너무나 피해의식적인 관점에서 역사를 기술하여 왔다. 그리하여 지금도 일본과의 관계는 순탄치 못하다. 이유야 어떻게 되었든지 앞으로 우리의 관계 개선이 무엇보다도 절실히 필요하다. 이것이 앞으로의 객관성을 유지할 기초의 초석이 될 것이리라.

그리고 남과 북이 갈라져 있는 현실적인 상황에서 이데올로기적인 측면에서 현대사 고찰은 가급적 피해야 한다. 우리는 애국적 입장에서 이러한 남북의 문제를 접근하기보다는 애족적인 관점에서 기술하는 것이 오히려 남북통일 이전까지 필요할 것이리라. 왜냐하면 국가를 위하는 관점에서는 상호간 안목이 학자들과 정치가들 사이에서도 다를 수 있을 것이며 같은 학자들끼리도 시대적・역사적 맥락에서 다루는 방법도 그렇게 동일할 수는 없을 것이다. 따라서 통일이 되는 그날까지는 남북이나 또는 남은 남대로, 북은 북대로 서로 감정을 아끼고 아껴 극도의 이성적인 면모를 갖추어 현대사를 조명해야 할 것이다. 자기감정에 치우치지도 말아야 할 것이며, 서양이나 동양의 어느 사상적 사조나 시대적 흐름을 통한 한 시대의 사조에 의해서 얻은 결과에 의한 것으로의 잣대로 한국의 현대사를 기술해서는 자손대대로 씻지 못할 오점을 남기게 될 것이니 감히 누가 섣부르게 이러한 행동을 자행할 것인가. 그런데도 오늘날 생각보다는 많은 지식인들이 시대에 영합하고 마치 시대의 양심인 양하면서 현대사의 흐름을 단순히 양극적 대립 양상으로 묘사한다면 그것은 민족의 아픔을 빙자로 그 속에서 자기주장과 그림만 교묘하게 그리려는 속셈은 아닌지 반문도 해보는 것은 필자만의 억측은 아닐 것이리라.

동서고금을 막론하고 어떤 상황 속에서라도 자기 민족사를 외면할 수는 없을 것이다. 그것이 영광스러운 역사이건 수치스러웠던 지난날의 과거일지라도 말이다. 그리고 이러한 사실들을 학자들이 기술할 때에도 아무리 객관적인 사실이나 실증적 토대 위에서 사건을 전개한다고 하더라도 성실한 태도를 바탕으로 서술해야 할 것은 두 말할 필요가 없을 것이나 작금의 여러 정황을 판단해 볼 때 매우 유감스럽기 짝이 없다. 왜냐하면 자기의 민족사를 서구적인 시각에서만 논의하려고 한다든지 또는 너무나 실증적 위주로 역사를 보려고 애를 쓰는 학자 중에서는 한국의 신화나 고대 상고사의 중요한 핵심에 대한 부정적 견해를 보이는 것이 이러한 범주에 속해 있다고 보겠다. 그리고 또한 방심해선 안 될 것은 무조건 어떤 신빙성 없는 몇몇 문헌이나 문중의 어떤 개별적 서한문과 기행문 등 기타 널리 산재해 있는 여러 기록, 말하자면 비 객관적 자료에 의거한 역사의 기술은 더더욱 경계해야 할 것이다.

그리고 대체적으로 언어 분야에서의 지금까지는 일본 학자들이 중심이 되어 연구되었던 국어사와 국어학사 부분과 부분적으로 방언학 관계 연구가 해방 이후에 있어서도 계속적으로 연구되었다. 또한 국어학의 큰 범주에서 볼 때는 일반적으로 다음과 같이 말할 수 있을 것이다.

경성제대를 중심으로 소창진평 교수의 업적인 '조선어학사 연구'와 '향가 및 이두 연구' 그리고 '조선 방언 연구' 또한 하야육랑 교수의 '조선 방언학 시고', 이 밖에 소창진평의 작은 방언학 관계 논문인 '함경도 및 평안도 지방의 방언 연구' 등은 해방 이후에도 서울대학을 중심으로 계속적으로 이 방면의 연구를 낳게 하였다. 또한 경성제대 학파들은 해방 이후에 중세 국어에 대한 연구를 적극적으로 하였다. 여기에 대표가 될 만한 것은 중세 국어 문법이며 'ㆍ'연구와 같은 소실문자 연구, 방점, 훈민정음, 향가 및 만엽집, 어두자음군, 계림유사 연구는 괄목할만하다고 할 수 있을 것이다. 그리고 해방 이후 서울대 後世代들은 국어사에 대한 안목을 갖게 된 것 같다. 아마도 이러한 이유 중의 하나는 적어도 Gustaf John Ramstedt(핀란드 Helsinki 대학 교수, 작고)의 여러 저서의 영향이 아닌가 하며 또한 Nicholaus Poppe(미국 Washinton 대학 교수, 작고)의 우랄·알타이어 입문서와 그 밖의 수많은 두 분의 논문들이 해방 이후에 우리 한국 학계에 소개되었기 때문인데 더더욱 서울대를 선두로 연구되었기 때문일 것이다. 그리하여 국어사에 대한 논의가 거의 40여 년 간 끊임없이 있어 왔던 것도 사실이다.

그리고 방언학의 경우에 있어서도 이제는 현지답사를 통한 자료집인 '방언사전'류는 그런대로 몇 종류가 시판되어 나온 셈이 되었다. 그리고 최근에 이르러서는 각 지방을 중심으로 지역 방언 연구가 상당히 활발하게 이루어지고 있는 셈이다. 그리고 이러한 언어 분야를 제외하고라도 70년대 들어와서는 변형 생성 언어학을 중심으로 많은 미국 및 유럽의 공시적 언어학 방법이 구조주의 언어학의 뒤를 이러 도입되어 우리 한국어 학계를 풍미하였고 이러한 영향은 현재까지도 이어지고 있는 실정이다. 그리하여 젊은 층의 경우에 있어서 언어습관을 보면 이러한 영향의 증거를 볼 수 있겠는데 예를 들면 "나는 하늘을 본다"라는 문장 대신에 "하늘이 보여진다"라고 거침없이 말하고 있고 세칭 영어의 수동태적인 표현 방법이 우리 한국에도 자연스럽게 자리를 잡아가고 있는 형편이다. 말하자면 고유의 언어적 습관을 저버리고 미국적 언어습관에 네이티브 스피커가 되어간다고 하여도 크게 무리한 말이 아닐 것이다. 쉽게 말하면 한국어를 영어화하여 실생활에 사용하고 있다는 말일 것이다.

또한 문화와 민속적인 분야를 간단하게 살펴보면 다음과 같다.

해방 전에는 조선 총독부의 답사 자료집(특히 역사, 민속, 고고학…)등이 한국의 기초 인문과학을 거의 대변해 주었다고 하여도 과언이 아닐 것이다. 또한 경성제대의 연구팀들이 지금의 몽고, 서장, 시베리아의 연해주와 만주 일대를 어떤 침략적 목적을 가지고 현지답사를 한 자료집 및 사진첩과 연구 결과물이 이 시대에 있어서는 청구논총이나 경제제대 논문집 그리고 조선 총독부를 통해서 많이 출간되었다. 그리고 현재 서울대학교의 '규장각'이나 '경성제대 도서관' 등에도 방대한 양의 이런 도서들이 꽂아 있다. 아마도 침략 조성의 일환으로 이루어졌다고는 하지만 조선 총독부와 경성제대에서는 동아세아 그리고 북방학에 적어도 1세기 전부터 관심과 연구가 진행되었다고 필자는 믿으며 이러한 증거에 경성제대 서고에서 우리는 그 엄청난 분량의 도서에 감탄 받게 된다. 어떤 의미에 있어서는 일본이 한국을 침략했던 기나긴 세월 속에서 최대한 한국의 기초 인문과학 분야를 닦았다고 한다면 지나친 억측은 아닐 것이다. 바로 이러한 점이 우리로서는 분통하고 자존심이 상하지만 어쩔 수 없는 노릇이다. 단지 필자로서는 지금부터라도 늦지는 않았다고 생각한다. 사실 해방 전후를 맞아 우리 학계에서는 몇몇 선각자들에 의해서 문화와 민족 그리고 민속적 접근이 시도되었다.

특히 일본학자 중에서 秋葉 隆은 '만몽의 민족과 종교'라는 공저를 내놓음으로써 어느 의미에서는 '북방학'의 학문적 계기를 뚜렷하게 세상에 알리게 하였으며, 또한 '조선 무속의 현지 연구'라는 책을 통해서는 한국의 전통적 무속 신앙을 현지를 통해 연구해 냈다는 사실에 우리는 많은 것을 생각하게 한다. 비록 정치적 목적이 전혀 없지는 아니했겠지만 그래도 조선 무속을 연구했다는 것은 어떤 의미에서는 당시 천하고 누구 하나 학문적 위치에서 보려고 하지 않은 하찮은 집단을 애정을 가지고 관찰하고 현지 무속인을 찾아 굿의 장면 뿐만 아니라 여러 소도구에도 관심을 가졌다는 것은 매우 놀라운 일이기도 하다. 또한 秋葉 隆은 그의 약력에서 볼 수 있듯이 동경 외국어 대학에서는 사회학을 전공하였고, 졸업 논문으로 '무속의 연구'를 학위 논문으로 제출하였다. 아마도 그가 '조선 무속의 현지 연구'라는 책을 쓴 것도 결코 위의 사실을 통해서 보면 우연만은 아닌 것이다. 또한 그는 동경 제국대학 대학원에 입학하여 '가족 제도 연구'를 연구 테마로 삼았다. 그리고 한 때는 東洋文庫(舊 모리손 文庫)에서 일을 하였고, 민족학 연구를 위하여 佛, 獨, 英, 美國에 체류하면서 많은 공부와 견문을 넓혔다는 사실이 지금부터 거의 1세기 전이라는 것에 필자는 자못 놀라웠다. 그리고 秋葉 隆은 그 후 일제 강점기에 있어서는 경성 제국대학에서 '朝鮮 巫俗 の 現地硏究'로 문학박사 학위를 취득하였다. 그 후 그는 일본의 민족학회 이사와 더불어서 'The Area Files committee of the Japanese Society of Ethnology(朝鮮部長)'을 역임한 것을 보더라도 여러 이유가 있었음에도 불구하고 한국을 연구한 선구자였던 것만은 틀림없는 사실이며 여기에 머무르지 않고 秋葉 隆은 경성 제국대학에 大陸資源科學硏究所를 만든 창설 위원임을 생각할 때 그의 꿈은 역시 동북 아시아를 연구의 전체 대상으로 삼았던 것으로 추측된다면 지나친 필자의 억측만은 아닐 것이리라.

아마도 이러한 일본의 지식인 생각은 미루어 짐작해 보건대 이 당시 전반적인 흐름으로 볼 수밖에 없을 것이다. 따라서 이러한 무드 조성이 결국 대동아 전쟁이라는 세계 제2차 대전의 싹으로 발전하였을 것은 정한 이치일 것이다. 그러길래 그의 저서 중에는 '満蒙 の民族と 宗教'가 있지 않은가 생각된다.

결국 일본 지식인은 학문과 국가가 상호보완적으로 조화 있게 균형을 절묘하게 맞추었다는 사실에 우리는 유념할 필요가 있을 것이다.

물론 이 당시 모든 일본 지식인이 황국사관에 젖어 있었다고는 볼 수 없겠지만 적어도 상당수의 최고 엘리트 집단인 지식인과 정치인들은 일본의 대동아 정책 즉 동북 아시아에 널리 산재되어 있는 민속학, 인류학, 역사학적 측면에서 체계를 정리한 것도 어느 측면에서 볼 때는 일본이 지향했던 동북아 정책과 지식인과 학자 사이에 상호간에 이해 관계가 맞았기 때문일 것이다. 말하자면 일본의 학자들은 이러한 사실을 역사성을 통해서 볼 때 결과론적이기는 하지만 국가적 시책과 정치적 목적에 수반되는 연구를 적어도 상당히, 기꺼이 응했다는 것이다. 즉 학자들의 연구가 국가의 공통적 시책에 부합되었으며 어느 면에서는 국가적 목적에 오히려 앞장서서 주도면밀하게 이루어졌다는 사실에 우리 한국 학자들은 많은 생각을 하게 될 것이다.

생각해 보면 학자들의 연구라는 것도 국가와 민족을 위해서 좋은 의미에서 사용되어야 할 것이다. 그것이 철학이든 사회학이든 기타 민족학이든 구분되지 말고 국가관과 일치되었을 때 그 학문이 더욱 더 빛날 것이다. 말하자면 국학으로서 민족학이 되어야 할 것이며 그 민족학은 국학으로서 그 민족의 대표적 학문으로 발전되어야 할 것은 두 말할 필요가 없을 것이며 또한 그 나라의 상징적 학문이 바로 국학으로 표상되어야 할 것이다.

적어도 우리는 이러한 경우를 동양에서는 일본에서 쉽게 찾아 볼 수 있었다. 말하자면 일본의 경우는 국가관의 목표 내지 목적에 순응하고 오히려 앞장서서 국가관의 지향적 성격에 수많은 학자들이 보조를 맞춘다는 사실이다. 그리고 이러한 사실에 많은 일본 학자들은 무비판적으로 국가를 상대한다는 것이다. 그래서 우리는 일제시대에 경성제대나 조선총독부나 동경제대와 같은 국가 기관에 소속된 학자나 여기에서 연구비를 받아 실제로 현지답사를 하였던 연구위원들의 업적을 보게 되는 것이 아닌가 한다. 특히 이 시대에 지금의 러시아, 우즈벡, 카자흐스탄, 키르키스, 만주 지역 중에서도 Orochi, Orcha, Goldi, Solon, Nanai, Hezhen(赫哲), Gilyak, Chuckhee, Kamchakadal, Orochon, Tungus 족에 관한 언어와 민속(특히 민간 신앙적인 무속과 신화, 전설과 민요)그리고 역사, 고고, 인류학 등의 학문이 현지 중심적 연구가 진행되었었고 여기에 국한하지 않고 몽고지역 중에서도 외몽고와 내몽고 그 밖의 길림, 요녕, 흑룡강 등 무수한 지역에서 수많은 현지답사를 하였던 것을 보더라도 이것이 단순히 학자들의 자신에 개인적인 학문이라고만 생각할 수는 없을 것 같다. 여기에 학문적 특징 중의 하나는 분명히 국가와 민족과 학문의 상호 지향이 동일할 수도 있다는 사실을 말해 주는 것이며 또한 상호 보완적 특징임도 암시해 준다고 볼 수 있을 것이다.

이러하기 때문에 어떤 의미에서는 흥할 때는 엄청난 위력을 국가가 발휘할 수 있겠지만 이와 반대로 망할 때는 전체가 온전하지 못함도 우리는 세계 제2차 대전을 통해서 역력히 알 수 있었다.

그리고 중국의 경우에 있어서도 대체적으로 어느 의미에서는 일본과 상당히 흡사함을 엿볼 수 있을 것이다. 말하자면 중국의 대표적인 철학자라고 볼 수 있는 공자·맹자·노자·장자의 경우에 있어서도 선대로부터 내려오던 인간과 세상에 대한 관점을 참고로 하여 자신의 세계관과 인생관을 여기에 결부시켜 하나의 시대적 철학으로 승화시켰다고 본다면 지나친 필자의 억측만은 아닐 것이다. 즉 이러한 철학자들의 당시의 철학관은 역사적인 측면과 연결되어 오늘날 중국의 거대한 사상으로 발전하여 하나의 국가관과 우주관으로 자리를 잡게 되었을 뿐만 아니라 중국 민족의 영혼도 이러한 사상에 의해서 모든 활동 생활이 영향을 받기 때문에 지극히 중국적으로 삶을 영유한다는 사실이다. 따라서 철학과 사상과 신앙적인 삶이 쪼개져 있는 것 같지는 않다. 말하자면 철학관이 바로 사상에 의해 형성되었으며, 이 사상이 또한 종교와 연결될 수 있다는 것이며, 이 관계에서 중국 역사와 중국인의 삶이 함께 했다는 사실에 우리는 주목할 필요가 있을 것이다. 이러한 사실 속에서 우리는 중국 민족이 자기들의 선대에서 이룩한 철학과 사상, 그리고 신앙적 사고에 깊이 심취해 있음을 알 수 있었다. 즉 국가와 사상과 신앙 그리고 생활이

늘 함께 공존해 있음은 우리는 중국에 대해서 부인할 수 없을 것이다라고 필자는 굳게 믿는 바이다.

이러한 사실들이 일본의 경우와 매우 흡사함은 우리는 하루 빨리 인지하여야만 우리 한국도 새로운 천년을 맞아 우리의 확고한 세계관과 민족관을 가질 수 있을 것이다. 그것이 바로 <거시적 한국관> <광의의 한국관>인 것이다.

이러한 일본과 중국의 경우를 통해서 새삼스럽게 느껴야 할 필요성은 두 가지로 간단하게 요약할 수 있겠는데 다음과 같이 요약할 수 있을 것이다.

첫째로는, 그 민족의 개인은 국가를 뛰어 넘어서게 된다면 매우 불행해질 수 있다는 사실이다. 즉 개인의 위대성 역시도 그 민족관과 결부가 되어야 할 것이며 또한 개인의 위치도 결국 국가 내에서 존재해야 할 것이다. 말하자면 국가는 개인을 포용하며 개인은 국가나 민족과 더불어 가야 한다는 것이다. 이러한 사실들이 중국이나 일본의 경우에 있어서는 매우 자연스럽게 형성되고 있고 그들의 생활 속에서도 자리를 잡고 있다는 사실이다.

둘째로는, 국가가 어떤 목표를 설정했으면 일본이나 중국의 경우에 있어서는 대체적으로 민중들은 상당히 적극적으로 추종하든지 또는 묵묵하게 뒤따르는 경향을 볼 수 있었으며 또한 지식인의 경우에 있어서도 일부의 경우에서는 오히려 적극성을 갖고 체계적으로 그 국가관에 조화된 이론과 논리를 펴는 경향을 보았으며 또는 적극적인 모습은 결코 아니다 하더라도 여기에 순응하고 협조하는 자세를 보인 지식인이 퍽이나 많았다고 생각된다. 이러한 경우를 우리는 가깝게는 일제 시대에 많은 우파적 지식인과 중도적 입장을 취했던 지식인을 통해서 관찰할 수 있었을 것이다. 말하자면 아마도 한국의 경우에 있어서의 지식인이나 학자, 교수들이 우파적 성향을 띄고 있다고 한다면 그것은 말할 필요도 없이 대학사회에 있어서는 '어용 교수' 등으로 몰려서 무수한 수난이 80년대에 있었음을 우리는 기억할 수 있을 것이리라. 이러한 한국적 상황에서 본다면 일본과 중국의 경우에서는 개인적, 개별적 세계관과 인생관보다는 국가적인 어떤 이념과 지향적 목표가 더욱 중요시되고 있음을 알 수 있었으며 특히 중국의 경우 그들의 북경에 있는 '혁명역사박물관'에서도 '실사구시'라는 현관입구의 모택동의 대자보를 통해 알 수 있음직도 하다.

그러나 반면에 지금까지 한국의 경우에서는 대체적으로 개인의 각자 의견을 매우 중요시하였으며 또는 개별적인 감정을 무엇보다도 높이 평하여 '솔직하다', '진솔하다', '감정을 숨김 없이 묘사하였다', '노골적인 감정을 여과 없이 숨김없이 반영하였다' 등의 평가를 받기를 원하였다고 하겠다. 말하자면 국가나 시대가 때로는 인물이나 상황을 요구할 수도 있는데 여기에는 별로 크게 달갑게 받아들이는 수용 태세는 아니었다고 볼 수 있을 것이다. 그래서 우리는 흔히 대학 사회에서나 일반 시민사회에 있어서도 지금까지는 '전유' 아니면 '전무' 또는 '생' 아니면 '사' 중의 택일적인 상황이 있었으면 있었지 중간적인 입장은 전혀 인정받지도 못할 뿐만 아니라 오히려 '어용적'이니 '무능적'이니 하는 말로써 상대방에게 입장을 난처하게 만들었던 예가 어디 한두 번 뿐이었겠는가. 또한 아예 어느 의미에 있어서는 국가관이나 시대의 요구 그 자체를 인정하지 않고 무조건 반대적인 입장에서 보려고 하였으며 그것이 어떤 원칙인 것처럼 표방하여 왔던 것도 어찌 부정만 할 수 있겠는가.

그러기 때문에 우리는 중국이나 일본에게서 배울 수 있었던 것과 배워서는 안 될 것을 하루 빨리 구분하여 새로운 길을 모색하여야 할 것이다. 왜냐하면 역사적으로 보나 지리적인 여건으로 보아도 중국과 러시아는 북쪽에 붙어 자리 잡고 있으며 우리 한국과의 성격과 그들의 성격이 너무나도 판이하게 다르기 때문이다. 또한 일본 역시도 역사적・지리적 여건으로 보아 남쪽에 자리 잡고 있는데다가 또한 성격과 기질 면이 너무나 다르기 때문에 상호간에 좋지 않은 감정에 휘말릴 수 있기 때문이다. 늘 우리는 이러한 상황 속에서 그들에게 주권을 빼앗기거나 수많은 전란을 통해서 얼마나 많은 고통과 수난을 '임진왜란', '병자호란', '삼별초의 항쟁', '거란족의 침입', '여진족과의 전쟁', '대마도 정벌'이라는 이름으로 치렀던가 생각하면 한스럽기 짝이 없다. 아마도 이러한 때는 우리는 앞에서 언급했던 '실사구시' 내지 '냉철하고 냉엄한 현실'을 제대로 인식하지 못했던 데에서 오는 결과임을 스스로 자인하여야 할 것이다.

그렇기 때문에 오늘날도 중국인을 대체적으로 '대륙적 기질', '만만디', '왕서방 기질', '속을 알 수 없는 민족'이라고 하면서 일본인은 '약은 민족', '손해는 보지 않는 민족', '섬기질 족', '셈이 정확하고 빠른 민족', '깔끔한 민족'

이라고 하며 한국인을 '기마족의 북방 기질과 섬의 기질이 결합한 반도 기질 민족', '체념의 민족', '사치스러운 민족', '形式을 좋아하는 민족', '겉과 속이 다른 민족', '名分을 앞세운 실리파', '되는 일도 없고 안 되는 일도 없는 나라', '실속이 없는 껍데기 같은 나라'라고 하는 것도 어느 면에서는 우리가 인정하여야 앞의 미래가 보일 수 있을 것이다. 우리 한국 사람은 형식에 약하고 내용에는 눈을 쏟지 않는다고 한다는 말 자체가 비판에는 익숙지 못하고 칭찬에는 약하다는 뜻이고 먼저 칭찬을 해주면 모든 것이 쉽게 해결된다는 의미로 받아들일 수 있을 것이다.

이상의 첫째와 둘째를 통해서 우리 민족은 우리나라와 가장 접근해 있는 러시아를 비롯하여 중국과 일본을 정확하게 알아야 할 필요성은 충분히 이야기한 셈이다. 그래야 앞으로도 우리 민족이 나아가야 할 지표를 정하고 그 정한 예정표에 의해 정진할 것이 아닌가 한다. 아무리 우리의 목표가 확고하고 무지개를 껴안은 세계라 할지라도 주변의 국가가 방해하고 이러한 사실을 먼저 알고 장애물을 친다면 소용이 없을 것은 뻔한 이치이기 때문이다.

우리는 秋葉 隆의 저서를 통해서 많은 점을 시사받았으며 그의 약력을 통해서도 충분히 배운 바 있었다. 또한 이러한 상황 등을 통해서 일본을 알게 되었으며 그 당시 조선은 무엇을 하였으며 어떤 국가관과 민족관이 있었길래 이렇게 무수한 한을 얻게 되었는가를 곰곰이 다시금 생각할 기회를 갖게 되었다고 할 수 있을 것이리라.

해방 전후를 하여 우리 민족에도 몇몇 선각자들에 의해 역사, 민속, 문화 분야에도 어느 정도 성과는 있었다. 단재 신채호의 '조선상고사'는 본래 1930년대 '조선일보'에 연재되었던 '조선사'인데 1948년 단행본으로 간행되면서 그 내용적인 여러 사항 등을 고려하여 '조선상고사'라고 개제되었다고 볼 수 있다. 저자 자신이 말했던 것처럼 '조선상고사'에 대하여 '…… 그것은 미정고이니 아직 추고를 가할 여지 있는 것이다.'라고 한 점을 보면 그가 '한국사'에 대한 애착이 얼마나 강했는가를 엿볼 수 있을 것이다. 아마도 필자의 생각으로는 그가 그토록 한국의 상고사에 집필을 집중한 것은 일제하에서 민족적인 사상을 고취시키기 위함이 아닌가 생각한다. 그렇게 말할 수 있음은 그의 저서 '조선상고사'를 보면 '총론'에서 역사에 대한 정의를 말할 때 '아'와 '비아'

로 나눠서 생각한 점에서 우리를 우리답게, 새롭게 인식할 수 있을 것이다. 또한 그는 '아의 성장발달의 상태……'에서 '여진・선비・몽고・흉노' 등이 본디 '아의 동족으로 ……'에 관한 그의 견해와 또한 '아와의 상대자인 사린 각족의 관계를……'에서 '아에서 분리한 흉노・선비・몽고며 아의 문화의 강보에서 자라온 일본이……'와 '오늘 이후는 서구의 문화와 북구의 사상이 세계사의 중심이 된 바 아 조선은 그 문화사상의 노예가 되어 소멸하고 말 것인가……' 그리고 '북벌진취의 사상이 시대를 따라 진퇴된 것이며' 또한 '흉노・여진 등의 일차 아와 분리한 뒤에 다시 합하지 못한 의문이며' 종교 문화상 등의 창작이 불소하나, 매양 독립적・단편적이 되고 계속적이 되고 계속적이 되지 못한 괴인'의 열거에서 우리는 정말 새로운 재인식이 필요할 때가 왔다고 필자는 생각하는 바이다. 어느 의미에서 볼 때 신채호 선생의 위와 같은 생각은 대륙적이고 기마 민족적 생각의 발상에서 비롯되었을 것을 생각하면 지금 우리에게 좋은 본보기가 될 것임은 자명한 사실일 것이다. 말하자면 신채호 선생의 탁견은 오늘날 우리에게 비록 시사하는 바가 컸으나 결국 우리 후배들이 행동적으로, 학문적으로 여기에 크게 동조 내지 동참하지 못함은 참으로 후회스러운 일이다. 물론 이런 필자의 생각은 결과를 통한 식견인 셈이다.

우리는 지금이라도 신채호의 생각한 바대로 한국과 과거 흉노・선비・몽고・여진과의 관계를 새롭게 재인식하여야만이 대륙적인 기마적 민족으로 태어날 것이다. 그리고 이러한 사실이 왜 중요한 이유는 한국적 세계화에는 이런 기질과 민족성이 꼭 기저에 수반되어야 할 것이기 때문이다.

신채호는 역시 '제2편 수두시대'의 '조선 고대 총론'에서도 '고대 아시아의 동부 종족이 ① 우랄 어족, ② 지나 어족 양자로 나뉘었으니 …… 조선족, 흉노족 등은 전자에 속한 자니, 조선족이 분화하여 조선, 선비, 여진, 몽고, 퉁구스 등 족이 되고, 흉노족이 천산하여 돌궐(今 新疆族), 흉아리, 토이기, 분란 등 족이 되었으니 지금 몽고, 만주, 토이기, 조선 사족 사이에 왕왕 동일한 어사와 물명이 있음은 몽고(大元)제국 시대에 피차 관계가 많으므로 받은 영향도 있으려니와, 고사를 참고하면 조선이나 흉노의 사이에도 관명・인명이 같은 자가 많으니 상고에 있어서 동일한 어족인 명증이니라'라고 하였으니 여기에서도 조선, 선비, 여진, 몽고, Tungus, 돌궐, 토이기, 만주 간의 관계를 충분히 간략하게나마 밝혔다. 이러한 사실을 통해서 볼 때 역시 신채호는 조선의 선각자임은 자명한 사실이다.

또한 이 시대에 몇몇 민족적인 차원에서 역사 분야 이외에도 이능화, 최남선, 손진태, 송석하, 김재철, 김소운, 정노식, 고정옥, 이여성 등 많으나 먼저 손진태의 '민속학논고'를 생각해 볼 수 있겠다. 손진태는 그의 저서를 통해서 한국의 민속과 전통을 밝혀 보려고 하였는데 그러한 이유는 그가 아마도 일제 시대에 역사학을 자유롭게 연구할 수 없었기 때문에 민속학에 주력하였을 것으로 볼 수 있을 것이며 또한 손진태는 3・1운동을 통해서 '민중'이라는 존재가 결코 무시될 수 없는 귀중한 민족적 차원에서 부각되어야 한다는 사실에 스스로 공감한 듯하다. 또한 그는 한국의 민족문화에 대한 연구는 한자에 만연되어진 양반 계급에서 찾기보다는 오히려 하층의 민중들에게서 발견하여야 한다는 생각이 들었을 것 같다. 그리고 결정적으로 민속학에 대한 영향은 그가 일본 와세다 대학의 사학과에 입학하여 1920년대 바람이 일기 시작한 사회주의 영향을 받아 '민중', '민족'에 대한 관심으로 전향하여 민중문화의 기저를 알아야 하겠다는 생각이었기에 이러한 학문에 몰입하였을 것이다. 또한 津田左右吉을 비롯 前間恭作, 西村眞次의 영향도 자못 컸던 것으로도 보인다.

또한 손진태는 민속의 방법론에 있어서도 '민속 조사론', '역사 연구 방법론', '비교 연구론'을 선택하여 연구하였다. 그러기 때문에 그는 연구의 성과에 있어서도 '민속학적 관심을 다른 분야 학문을 위한 보조적 입장에서가 아니라 독자적인 과학으로 인식하고 있었다'라고 말할 수 있을 것이리라. 특히 손진태는 그의 '민속학논고'에서 '조선 Dolmen에 관한 조사연구'에서도 볼 수 있었듯이 '고인돌'에 대한 고문헌과 본인이 직접 발견한 '돌멘'이며 또한 전국적 규모의 분포, 형식, 그리고 그 원형과 민족학적 의의를 기술한 것은 당시로서는 대단한 탁견임은 분명하다. 또한 '고인돌의 명칭 및 이에 관한 신앙과 전설'에서 '고인돌'에 대한 명칭이 W.G.Aston에 의해 '고인(支, 장)', '돌' 두 단어의 합성어임을 밝혔다. 그리고 손진태는 고려시대의 이규보 역시도 '고인돌'을 '지석'이라고 한 점을 지적하였다. 그리고 평안도에서 부르는 '괴엔돌'

역시 같은 것으로 해석되며 또한 '되무덤', '도무덤' 역시도 동류로 지적한 것이다. 그리고 손진태는 '장생 고'에서 '장생'의 명칭을 나열하면서 그것의 다양한 기능도 밝혔는데 하나는 물질상으로 보아 목장승, 석장승이고, 또 성질상으로 보아 이정표와 수호신으로서의 장승, 또한 소재 장소상으로 보아 사원의 장승, 읍촌동구(입구)의 장승, 경계의 장승, 노방의 장승으로 구별한 점은 오늘날의 민속학의 영향에도 지대하게 끼쳤다고 할 수 있을 것이다.

그리고 우리는 이 시대에 이능화의 업적을 생각해 볼 수 있을 것이다. 그는 (1896~1943) 종교 연구에 업적을 낸 인물이다. 그가 대상으로 삼은 종교는 무속·불교·도교·기독교 그리고 신흥 종교이었다. 그러기 때문에 이능화는 조선 종교의 통사 체계를 수립하려고 노력하였으며 또한 조선의 여성에 관한 습속과 기녀의 풍속도 함께 관심을 가졌다. 특히 그의 '조선 무속 고'는 방대한 문헌을 기초로 한 조선 무속 통사 체계라고 할 수 있을 것이다. 특히 그가 '한글자료(문헌) 89종', '중국문헌 32종', '일본문헌 1종', '출처 불확실 2종'을 합한 124종의 여러 문헌을 통해 '조선 무속 고'를 집필한 점에 우리는 놀라지 않을 수 없다. 결국 이능화의 학문은 그 방법론에서 전통적인 학문의 방법을 존중하였고 실학의 문헌 고증학적 방법도 덧붙여서 당시의 학자로서 놀라운 점을 엿볼 수 있겠으나 개체적 사실과 현상에 너무나 치우쳤기 때문에 총체적 원리나 역사성을 규명하는 데 있어서는 여전히 문제점으로 남겨 두었다고 보겠다. 말하자면 이능화는 개체들의 현상을 통해서 민족적인 문화유산인 '무속'을 보려고 한 것으로 생각된다.

또한 당시의 김재철은 1933년 '조선연극사'를 간행하여 최초로 연극사를 체계화하였다. 그는 1907년 충북 괴산에서 출생하녀 1926년 경성 제일 고등 보통학교를 졸업하고, 1931년 경성제대 본과 조선문학과를 졸업하고 평양 사범학교에서 교편을 잡고 1932년 사망하였다. 그의 연극사는 차례에서 말해 주듯이 '가면극'과 '인형극', '구극'과 '신극' 그리고 결론 다음으로 부록으로 '조선 인형극(꼭두각시 극각본)'을 첨가하였다. 특히 가면극에서 삼국시대 이전의 가면극과 신라의 가면극, 고려시대 가면극 등으로 구분지어서 생각한 점과 인형극에서도 그 어의에 대한 제반 사실들을 다루었다는 것이 당시의 나이와 시대로 보아서 매우 탁견이 아닐 수 없다. 이러한 그의 생각은 후에 김일출의

'조선 민속 탈놀이 연구'에서도 읽을 수 있으며 이두현에게도 큰 영향을 주었다고 볼 수 있을 것이다. 말하자면 김재철은 한국의 연극사를 '고대제의', '신라의 가면무', '고려의 나례나 산대도감극', '조선의 산대극', '구극과 신극'으로 구분한 점이 바로 김일출의 '원시적 탈놀이의 유습', '처용무', '가면', '검무', '향약' 5기, '나례와 나희', '사자놀이, 산대놀이(산대잡극과 산대놀이), 황해도 탈놀이'에도 영향을 끼쳤으며 또한 이두현의 '고대 제천의식', '고대의 연극(고구려악, 백제악, 신라 향약과 가면희)', '중세의 연극', '근세의 연극(산대, 나례, 광대, 소학지희, 판소리)', '가면극과 인형극의 전승 : 농경의례와 가면호희(입춘굿과 소놀이굿), 하회 별신굿 탈놀이, 산대도감 계통극', '현대연극'의 구분을 짓게 하는데 있어서도 영향이 컸음을 엿볼 수 있을 것이다.

그리고 사상적인 문제점은 여전히 남아 있겠지만 정노식의 '조선창극사', 고정옥의 '조선민요 연구', 이여성의 '조선복식사'에서는 삼국시대의 복식을 중심으로 하는 '상대 조선 복식의 전모'를 규명하고자 노력하였다. 그리고 연구 방법론도 역사고고학을 선택하여 복식 유물자료에 의해 유물 자체 연구방법인 복식의 구조를 명확히 하려고 노력하였다. 이여성은 배화여고 배지를 도안하였다고 하기도 하며, '독서회'를 이끌고 있었는데 이 회원 모두가 이여성을 따라 월북하였다고 한다. 그래서 제자 모두 월북하여 남한에 남아 있는 사람은 하나도 없다고 알려져 있다.

또한 '한국문화사 서설'을 쓴 조지훈이 경우를 보게 되면 해방 이후 '한국문화'에 대한 견해의 저서 중에서는 가장 잘 짜여진 저서라고 할 수 있을 것이다. 특히 내용면에서 볼 때 크게 몇 부분으로 나눠 생각하였는데 '한국문화사 서설'에서는 한국문화의 성격, 한국문화의 위치, 한국문화의 발전, '한국사상사의 기저'에서는 한국 신화의 원형, 한국종교의 배경, 한국사상의 전거, '한국예술의 흐름'에서는 한국미술의 생성, 한국음악의 바탕, 한국문학의 전개, 그리고 '한국문화논의'에서는 민족문화의 주체성, 전통의 현대적 의의, 향토문화 연구의 의의, 또한 '한국정신사의 문제'에서도 민족 신화의 문제, 한국휴머니즘의 정신형성, 개화사상의 모티프와 그 본질, 마지막으로 조지훈은 그의 저서에서 '한국예술의 이해'에서는 한국예술의 원형, 반세기의 가요문화사, 고전 국문학 주해문제를 다루었다. 특히 그의 저서 가운데에서 우리에게 감동을 주는 구절은 '…… 신화는 신의 이야기이다. 따라서 신화의 주인공은 신이요, 신화는 신의 이야기가 아니라 도리어 인간이 터득하고 만든 원초의 인간 이야기인 것이다. 그렇기 때문에 신화는 인간이 발견한 정치와 사회와 과학과 문학과 역사의 원형으로서 의의를 지닌다.'에서 우리는 실증적 역사의 사고나 그밖의 서구적 안목에서 흔히 보는 과학적 사고를 통해서 한국의 신화를 바라보면 안 된다는 것이다. 이렇게 될 때만 우리는 민족적인 사고에서 우리 신화를 바라보며 접근할 수 있을 것이며 그래야만 한국 신화의 원형을 그나마 알 수 있고 따라서 이러한 사고 체계 속에서만 한국의 신화 체계와 사상 그리고 기저 속의 Deep thought를 건져 낼 수 있으리라.

그리고 동시대의 저서 중에서 우리의 눈길을 끄는 것은 김원용의 '한국문화의 기원'이다. 여기에서 그는 '한국민족'과 '한국문화의 원류' 그리고 '한국문화의 기원' 등 다양한 소제목으로 한국문화에 대해 밝혀보려고 노력한 흔적이 역력히 보이며 많은 고민도 엿보인다. 그러한 이유는 확실하게 그가 하나의 획을 긋지는 않고 가능성을 제시하면서 여러 상황을 설명한 점이 오히려 긍정적 평가를 받는다고 볼 수 있을 것이다. 특히 그는 고고학의 원로 학자로서, 작고는 하였지만, 그가 평생을 통해 연구하였던 대상이 한국문화의 원류와 기원 문제인데 이러한 주제를 선사시대에서 삼국시대 말기까지를 통해서 어떤 해답을 얻으려고 고고, 인류, 역사학적인 방법을 도입한 점은 오늘날 우리에게 시사해 주는 바 매우 크다고 할 것이다.

그리고 가장 좁게는 한국의 전통적 민속을 통해 민중의 삶을 알 수 있는 것은 아마도 '세시풍속'이 아닐 수 없을 것이다. 임동권은 그의 '세시풍속'에서 '한국의 세시풍속은 오랫동안 관습에 의하여 농업·어업을 비롯하여 모든 세시풍속은 태음력에 의하였으니'라고 하였다. 그리고 세시풍속을 기록한 문헌으로는 '동국세시기', '형초세시기', '경도잡기'가 있으며 우리의 세시풍속을 알기 위해서는 참고적으로 '농가월령가', '조선의 년 중 행사(오청 저)', '세시풍속집(방종현 저)', '조선민속 고(송석하 저)', '한국의 세시풍속(최상수 저)', '남국의 세시풍속(진성기 지음)' 등이 있다고 하겠으나 가장 좋은 방법 중의 하나로는 '현지답사'이며 '현장'을 중심으로 앞으로 보다 적극적인 방법을 통해서 '세시풍속'은 더 고찰되어 연구되어야 할 여지를 안고 있다. 왜냐하면 가장 그 민족의 살아 숨쉬는 현장적 삶이 바로 '세시풍속'을 통해서 재현되기 때문일 것이다. 말하자면 '세시풍속'이야말로 그 민족의 과거와 현재 그리고 미래를 향한 출발점인 동시에 그 국가의 살아 있는 민족 삶이기도 하며 세시풍속 자체 내에는 민중의 삶과 지배계급뿐 아니라 어쩌면 사농공상 모두가 이 속에 스며 있기 때문일 것이다. 우리가 흔히 역사나 고고학은 기록이나 유품, 유물, 유적 등을 통해서만 연구가 가능하며 또한 꼭 이것이 바탕이 될 때에만 그 정확성을 인정받기 때문에 살아 숨쉬는 현장적 느낌보다는 그렇게 그냥 이해되기 쉬울 뿐이다. 그러나 세시풍속이란 한국적 사고에 의한 한국적 생활 속에서 다져진 '삶 자체'이기 때문에, 모든 분야가 다 이 세시풍속에 녹아 있기 때문에 우리는 한국적 의미에서 원형적 사고 내지 삶의 순환체계로 받아들이며 이것은 연희적 행위에 의한 통과의례로 받아들이는 것이 아닌가 한다.

저자가 본 저서인 '한국학과 우랄·알타이학'을 통해서 말하고 싶은 사항 중에서 몇 가지만 밝히고 <한국학에 대한 저자의 변>을 마치기로 하겠다.

첫째로는 해방 반세기를 맞이하여 이제는 우리 문화에 대한 깊은 통찰을 통한 발전과 변화를 가져야 한다는 사실이다. 이를 위해서는 자기반성이 선행되어야 할 것은 말할 필요가 없을 것이다.

둘째로는 그 민족의 고유한 문화자체를 개발하여 하나의 모델을 만들고 다듬어서 세계화한다는 생각을 지금부터라도 할 줄 알아야 한다는 사실이다.

셋째는 우리 스스로가 우리 문화를 축약, 과장, 왜곡을 전혀 하지는 않았는가에 대한 자기반성을 하여야 할 단계가 왔다는 것이다.

넷째는 이제는 새천년을 맞이하여 우리 고유문화를 세계화하기 위해서는 우리의 고유 모델을 '거시적 한국문화'로 삼아야 한다는 것이며, 이 '거시적 한국문화'란 그냥 탄생되는 것이 아니라 부단한 노력과 개발, 그리고 종합하여 '新種子'로 만들어야 한다는 것이다. 말하자면 지금까지 잊고 살았던 '북방문화'를 잘 결합하여야 한다는 사실에 주의하지 않으면 안 된다는 것을 깨달아야 할 것이다.

다섯째는 지금까지는 '북방문화'라고 그저 막연하게 말로만 하여 왔다고 보겠다. 그리고 추상적 개념을 가지고 '북방문화'를 요리한 셈이다. 그러다 보니 모든 것이 어설프기 짝이 없었으며 또한 정확한 이론 없이 여기 저기에 흩어져 있는 구절들을 모아서 논문이나 저서를 내 놓았기 때문에 일관성 면에서도 부족하지만 문헌적 참고에도 거의 문제점이 노출되기도 하였다. 거기에 전문적 지식을 토대로 하는 현장 답사가 이루어져야 함에도 불구하고 서구나 일본, 중국학자들의 업적을 그냥 모방 내지 번역하여 세상에 내놓기가 다반사이었다고 하여도 지나친 필자만의 생각은 결코 아닐 것이다. '북방'과의 관계는 1990년대부터 개선되어서 다행히도 지금은 러시아, 중국, 몽고 등 여러 북방지역을 현지답사를 할 수 있는 기회가 있어서 퍽이나 다행스러운 일이다. 그러나 이제 기회는 주어져 있지만 이 기회를 제대로 활용하지 못하는 데 문제가 자못 심각한 지경에 왔다고 필자는 감히 말하고 싶은 것이다. 그러한 이유 중의 몇 가지는 다음과 같다.

첫째, 이제는 중국 지역에도 갈 수 있는 기회가 왔기 때문에 우리는 우리와 적어도 同系로 볼 수 있는 지역인 내몽고 자치구라던가 Uigŭr와 더불어서 신강성 그리고 부분적으로 티벳, Santa어(Santa is spoken in the chinese province of Kansu, It is spoken by about 150,000 people), Mongour어(Mongour is spoken in parts of the province Kansu and Chinghai in China), Dagur어(Dagur is spoken by 250,000 people in North-Westsrn Manchuria) 등의 중국지역에서 Altai언어가 사용되고 있지만 현지답사 前에 충분히 문헌적 연구가 검토되어야 함에도 불구하고 우리의 현 실정은 그렇지 못하고 있는 것을 부인할 수 없을 것이다. 말하자면 중국 내의 알타이어족이 살고 있는 분포도를 먼저 작성하고 여기에 준하는 선행 연구가 검토되어야 한다는 것이다.

둘째, 또한 몽고 지역에도 이제는 마음대로 가는 세상이 되었다. 우리는 사실상 지금까지 우리 민족을 알타이계라고 하면서 더욱 더 Mongolian 인종과 가장 가까운 동족이라고 하지 않았는가. 또한 이러한 차원에서 어린아이의 궁둥이에 있는 파란 점을 '몽고 반점'이라고까지 그 동안 말하여 왔다. 사실상 몽골어는 적어도 Mogo어(Mogol is spoken in Afghanistan), Oriat어(Oriat to which Kalmuck also belongs us spread over a Vast territory, Oriat dialects are spoken in the North-Western part of the Mongolian people's Republic(Outer Mogolian)), Buroat어

(Buriat is the Northern most Mongolian Language. It to spread mainly in the Buriat Autonomous Socialist Soviet Republic, East Siberia. Varios groups of Buriats live also in the Irkutsk and Chita regious(in East Siberia) and in the area called Barga in Manchuria. Some Buriats live also in the largest Mongolian in the narrower sense, is the largest language among its immediate relative. It comprises a number of dialects spoken the Mogolian People's Republic and Inner Mongolia, including about 650,000 in Outer Mongolia and 1,465,000 in Inner Mongolia Khalkha어(Khalkha is the most important dialect of Mongolian. It is spoken by almost 650,000 people, I. e, 75% of the total population of the Mongolian People's Republic. …Khalkha compries a number of subdialects. The subdialects spoken in the Eastern and Southern parts of the Mongolian Peopel's Republic display some features common to Mongolian dialects spoken in parts of Inner Mongolia) 그리고 이 밖에도 제어 등이 있다. 그래서 이제는 단순하게 '몽고어'라는 표기보다는 'Buriat Mongo어' 등으로 하여야 할 것이다. 이러한 표기를 주장하는 것은 이제는 그만치 이 분야의 연구가 진행되어야 한다는 뜻이다. 또한 이제는 몽고로 현지답사를 가는 실정이기 때문에 더더욱 이러한 분위기가 필요한 것이리라. 말하자면 이제는 막연하게 'Mongolia'라고 하지 말고 좀 더 구체적이면서 적극적인 방법으로 이 분야를 수용해야 할 것이다. 가까운 러시아나 일본은 이 지역에 대한 연구를 적어도 1세기 전부터 연구를 하지 않았던가.

셋째, 그리고 이제는 신채호 선생이 말했던 것처럼 '흉노 등의 일차적으로 우리와 분리한 뒤에 다시 합하지 못한 의문이며…'라는 차원에서 지금부터라도 이 방면에 노력을 해야 할 것이다. 그리고 이 지역의 언어에 대해서도 다시 거론한다면 이와 같을 것이다.

Juchen or Jurchen is an extinct language which was still spoken in Manchuria at the time of the rise of the Mongols in history(1388-1644)) 그리고 Manchu어(Manchu is the literary language of those Manchu who Conquered China and established there the Ch'ing dynasty(1644-1911).

It was also their colloquial language. At the present time there a few speakers left, although Manchus, Solons and Dagurs). 그리고 Goldi어(Goldi or Nanai, as they call themselves, are a small people of 7.000 in the lower course of the Amur river). Ulcha어(Ulcha is spoken by hardly more than 1,500 people in an area located down-stream of that of the Goldi. Some scholars regard it as independent language but, according to others, it is a dialect of Nanai. At any rate, it does not possess Classification features distinguishing it from Goldi.) Orochi어(Orochi is spoken in the Amur region on the sea-shore. the number of speakers amounts to a few hundred). 그리고 Oroki어(Oroki is spoken by a few hundred people on the island of Sakhalin. It is little explored) 또한 Udehe어는(Udehe or Ude is spoken by a small group hardly exceeding 1,000 speakers along some tributaries of the Amur and Ussuri) 그리고 Negidal어(Negidal is spoken by less than 800 people in the basin of the Amgun river) 그리고 Evenki어(Evenki is spoken in various of Eastern Siberia, mostly in the northern parts of it, roughly between the yenisei river and 85° of northern latitude. The total nomber of speakers approximately amouts to 40,000. Evenki is divided in three groups of dialests, the northern, southern, and eastern. Evenki received its script in 1030. First it wsa based on the Latin alphabet, but since 1038 the Cyrillic alphabet has been used). 또한 Lamut어(Lamut is spoken by 9,000 people in Various parts of the Magadam and Khabarovsk regions(Krai) in Kamchatka, and in the Autonomo Yakut Soviet Ropublic. ……There are three Groops og Lamut dialects : the eastern, western, and central. The Lamut did not have any kind og writing prior to 1931. The present Cyrillic alphabet was introduced in 1937). 그리고 Solon어(Solon is spoken by a few thiusand peopel in North-Western Manchuria, in the citis of Tsisikar, Hailar, Butkha, Mergen, Manchuria along the Russian frdntier. The Solon do not have a system of writing of their own. Those who can write and read use Manchu). 또한 이밖에도 여진의 경우에 있어서도 누구의 언어 채집에 의한 음성표기냐에 따라서 명명 상이할 수 있겠다.

예를 들면, 김광평의 음성표기법이 있을 수 있을 것이며 또한 W. Grube와 L.Legeti의 음성표기방법이 명명 약간씩 상이할 수 있겠는데 가령 여진어에서는 '산'의 의에 해당되는 음을 '아리'라고 하는데 다른 음성표기법에 있어서는 'ali"a-li' 등과 같이 쓰임을 알 수 있을 것이다. 또한 만주어의 경우에 있어서도 표기 체계에 있어서 문헌어적 표기법과 구어적인 방법이 상이한데 가령 만주어에서 '산'의 의에 해당하는 음은 'alin'인데 이는 문헌어적 표기이며 구어적 표기는 'aliN['alin}'이다. 이러한 사실을 통해서도 이제는 막연한 지식과 학문적 모호성에서 탈피하여 구체적 분석적 그리고 현장성을 최대한으로 살려 낸 '북방학 연구'가 절실하게 요구된다고 하겠다. 말하자면 지금까지의 만주, 여진, Tungus에 관한 학문적 체계는 너무나 근시안적이었으며 풍선처럼 뿌리 없는 지식이 난무하였다고 할 수 있을 것이다.

넷째, 또한 '북방학은 위와 같은 현실 속에서 연구가 있어 왔음을 누구도 부인할 수는 없을 것이다. 설상가상으로 알타이어족 중에서 Chuvash-Turkic에 대해서는 더더욱 우리에게 달라진 바도 거의 없는 상태이지만 많은 문헌이나 현지답사를 통해서 이론적, 현장적 토대 위에서 Turkey계를 연구할 필요성이 있다고 할 수 있을 것이다. 그리고 이 지역의 언어에 대해서도 다음과 같음을 알아야할 것이다.

Chuvash어(The only surviving, r-language <'none' versus Turkic toquz> is Chuvash which is spoken by almost 1.5million people in the Chuvash Autonomous Sociallist Soviet Republic in the USSR. to be exact, in the middle course of the Volga River. It comprises two main dialect(spoken up stream).

Chuvash is the descendant of one of the dialects of the ancient Volga Bulgar which was spoken in the Bulgar Kingdom on the banks of the Ⅶcentry AD to the Ⅴcentry) 그리고 Turkic 언어를 보면 다음과 같다.

Yakut어(Yakut is the northernmost Turkic language and is spoken in the Yakut Autonomous Socialist Soviet Republic, in the Northern part of East Siberia. The Yakuts call themselves Sakha(saxa). The name Yakut was given to them by the Turqus who called them. The Yakuts number approximately 240,000. The Yakut language differs considerably from all the orther Turkic language both phonemically and Morphologically, as well as with regard to be vocabulary which is less them 50percent of Turkic orgin. 또한 Tuva-Khakas group에 속한 언어들은 다음과 같다.

Tuvinian어((Thva, Soyot, 또는 UriaKhai)spoken by 100,000people in the Autonomous Tura Region, in Eastern Siberia(prior to 1944 a semi-independent people's republic, a satellite of the USSR since 1921). is an adag-language. 그리고 Karagas어

(Karagas(Tofu). Uselly related to Tuvinian, is spoken by 500-600 people in a locality of the Krasnoyar나 province(Kri). They are belived to be decendants of Samoyeds who adopted a Turkic language). Yellow Uighur어(The Yellow Uighur sari uyrur are a small group living in the chinese province of Kansu.······Some Yellow Uighurs speak a particular Mingolian dialect) 그리고 Shor어(Shor sor is spoken by 105,000 people in the northern part of the Altai range and in the Kuznetsk Alataw mountain range, in the river basins of Kondoma, Mrass, and Tom). 그리고 Chulym어(Chulym cilim is the collective name of the dialects Ketsik, kuarik kuarik, and Chulym proper shich are spoken in the basin of the Chulym has no script. Its speakers use the Russian literary language).

이 밖에 있어서도 Turkey언어에 있어서는, Tuba and related dialect가 있으며 또한 The Kypchak Group 등의 언어와 그리고 Karai어와 Knmyk어 Karachai-balkar 어 Crimean Tatar어 인데 여기에서 Crimean Tatar was spoken, prior to World War II, by the Soviets during World War II,······Crimean Tatar is now 'the language of a small ethnec grdup living mainly in the Uzbeck Republic.' ······They spoke a dialect vary little differing from standard Turkish. The speakers of this dialect numberd(1940) hardly more than 50,000.······The Crimean Tatar language can be regarded as proctically extinct). 그리고 Tatar어(Tatar tatar is spoken by almost five million people mainly on the Autonomous Republic and in the adjacent parts of the Volga region, and in various places in Western Siberia. Their Language comprises seven dialects. The central dialect is spoken by more than 1.5million people in the republic. This dialect is also Called Kazan Tatar(after the name of the capital) or kazan Turkic.

The Western or Mishar misar dialect is spoken in the Gorkii, Tambov, Voronez, Ryazan, Penza, Simbirsk, Samara, Saratov and orenburg regions, in the Autonomous Mordvan Republic, and in the Bashkin Republic······)

또한 Bashkin어는 'Bashkin basqθrt is Spoken by 900,000 in the Autonomous Bashkin Soviet Republic in the Volga region.······Formerly, the Bashkin did not have a literary language of their own but need the same literary and script as the Tarars)이며 이 외에도 Turkey 제어에서는, Nogai어, Kazakh and KaraKalpak어가 있겠는데 여

기에서 Kazakh어는 'Kazakh qazaq is spoken by 3.5 million people in the Kazakh Union Repubilc'에서 사용되고 있으며 또한 Kirghiz어는 'Kirghiz qir ɣ iz (또는 Kara-Kirghiz as it is called sometimes) is spoken by almost one million people in the Kirghiz Union Republic'에서 1만여 명이 현재 사용하고 있다고 보겠다. 또한 알타이어, The Changhatai Group, Uzbek어 East Turki어, Salar어, The Turkmen어가 있다.

그리고 Turkmen group어에 있어서는 'The Turkmen(on Southern) group comprise Turkmenian, Gagauz, Turkish and Azenbaijan Turkic'와 같이 Turkmenian어 Gagauz어 Turkish어 그리고 Azerbaijan어 등으로 구분하여 볼 수 있을 것이다. 또한 Turkey 제어의 경우는 매우 복잡하게 얽혀 있기 때문에 위와 같은 대단위의 다양한 제어와 더불어서 다음과 같은 제어도 있다.

Historical periodezation of Turkic languages는 'The history of the Turkic languages can be followd back into the times much older than the history of the Mongolian or Manch Tungus Languages'의 차원에도 볼 수 있을 것이다. 여기에는 The language of the Huns이 있는데 이는'There is among whom there had been tribes speaking a language which may regarded as the oldest possible from of Turkic and indentified with Proto-Turkic'라는 차원에서 보았기 때문일 것이다. 또한 Historical periodzation of Turkic language에는 'Volga and Danube Bulgarian'이 있으며 그리고 'Ancient Turkic 어'어가 있겠다. 이 Ancient Turkic어는 'The Turks became known, for the first time in history, in the VICentury. Even recorded in Byzantine sources.'와 같이 6C경에야 비로소 알려지기 시작하였다. 또한 Turkey의 문자에 대해서는 일반적으로 다음과 같이 알려져 있다. 첫째는 'Runic script'이라는 문자이다. 이 문자에 대해서는, 'Ancient Turkic includes the language of the so-called Orkhon-Yenisei monuments written in runic script. There monuments, inscriptions on steles, are found in the area around the Upper course of the yenisei river in East Siberia ; in the Valley of the Orkhon river in Outer Mongolia and in the area east from Orkhon, inclouding a Locality situated not far from Ulbaz Bator, the Capital of the Mongolin People Republic, to the exact, some 25-30miles to the east.……Besides inscription on steles, a look of divination, some documents and fragments of Manichean and other manuscripts in runic script have been preserved.'이라고 한 점을 보면 'Runic script'은 고대 Tukey어를 이해하는 데 무엇보다도 중요한 열쇠이기 때문에 '룬 문자'의 해독은 매우 중요하게 받아들일 수 있을 것이다.

둘째는 'Brahmi script'이라는 문자인데 이는 'Somr Ancient Turkey texts are written in Brahmi script. The Brahmi script as was need by the Turks in Centural Asia is shown in the table on p62'에서 보듯이 현재에서는 이 'Indic Alphabet'를 옛 문헌에서만 볼 수 있다.

셋째는 'The Manichean script'인데 이 문자는 'A number of Ancient Turkic texts are written in the so-called Manochean script. Ancient Turkic who professed the Manichean religion used a script which is called the Manichean script. Other Manichean Turkic and also non-Manichean Turkic(Bubbhists) used the so-called script which had devdloped from Sogdian.……

The Manichean script goes back to the Palmyran script which is one of the Varieties of the Middle Aramaic script. Paimyran is aiso regarded as the prototype og Syriac from which Estrongelo developed'에서 보듯이 역시 이 문자도 옛 문헌에서만 볼 수 있다.

넷째는 'The Sogdian script' 문자인데 이 역시도 'A number of Ancient Turkic texts are written in Sogdian script. The Sogdians were an proper who lived in a country which included the present Tadjikistan(In the USSR) and the adjacent areas of Uzbekistan. The Sagdian script was rarely used by the Turkic, and there are only Buddhist manuscripts written in it. Most of the letter probably date from the Ⅷ Century.' 마찬가지이며 또한 'Uighuric script'에 대해서도 역시도 'By far the larger number of Ancient Turkic texts, namely those of later origin(Ⅸ～ⅩCenturies), are written in the so-called Uighur script. The letter developed from the Sogdian alphabet, to be exact, from what the German scholars call "Sogdische Kursivschrift", I. e., Sogdian speed writing. The Uighur alphabet Was, at a later time, probably in the second half of the Century, transmitted to the Mongols.

Works in Uighur script are mostly Buddhistic, Nestorian, and Manichean in content, although there are also fragmento of Calendars, astrological works, and specimens of poetry. …… The Buddhist literature in Uighur script reached its acme in the Ⅸ~Ⅹ Centuries.' 이와 같음을 통해서 볼 때 이제는 거의 고문헌이나 옛 비문을 통해서나 찾아 볼 수 있을 것이다.

이상과 같이 사실상 '북방학'이란 다채롭고 다양하고 방대하면서 그 부분부분이 섬세하여 어디서부터 터치를 해야 할지 그렇게 용이한 일은 아닌 듯하다. 이러한 관점에서 본다면 지금까지 한국에서의 '북방에 대한 연구'는 무계획적이며 기초를 거치지 않고 바로 본론으로 들어와 무엇인가를 열심히는 건드렸지만 그것들이 지금 와서 생각해 보면 매우 무모한 단편적 지식의 종합체였다고 하여도 과언은 아닐 것이다. 아마도 이러한 생각은 필자만의 생각은 아닐 것이다.

이제 우리는 '한국학'을 원본대로 정확하면서도 기초부터 차근차근 고찰할 시기가 왔다고 필자는 생각한다. 말하자면 이제는 자료가 없다느니 또한 북방지역에 갈 수 없다느니 하는 이러한 옛 모습의 논리에 맞춰서 '한국학'을 해서는 안 된다는 것을 명백한 현실로 받아 들여야 한다는 것이다. 이제는 '북방학'도 뚜렷하게 'Ural-Altai학'이라고 구체적으로 칭하면서 바로 이것이 '한국학'이며 이러한 'Ural-Altai학'이 전제되지 않은 '한국학'은 '형식적 한국학' '협의의 한국학' '임시적 한국학'이 자연히 될 수밖에 없을 것이다. 우리는 이러한 의미에서 볼 때 '한국학'이란 그 바탕이 'Ural-Altai학'이어야 하며 또한 이러한 학문적 기초와 바탕이 이루어 졌을 때만 '거시적 한국학' '미래지향적 한국학' '대륙적 한국학'의 면모가 갖춰지게 될 것은 명확한 사실일 것이다. 그리고 우리는 'Ural학'에 대해서는 거의 외면한 채 오랜 세월을 보냈다. 여기에는 몇 가지 이유가 있기는 하다. 몇 예를 들어 보면 다음과 같다.

첫째로는, 한국어가 처음에는 Ural-Altai제어에 속한다고 하다가 나중에 들어와서는 Nikolaus Poppe나 Gustaf John Ramstedt의 학설에 따라서 Altai 제어 쪽으로 기울어졌고 이것이 정통적 학설로 인정됨에 따라서 상대적으로 Ural 제어에 대해서는 외면하기 시작해서 현재에 있어서는 거의 연구의 실정이 전무하다고 하여도 과언이 아니다.

둘째로는, Ural 제어에 속한다고 흔히 말하고 있는 지역은 옛 소련을 비롯하여 스칸디나비아 반도의 Finland와 Hungary등 동구라파에 있는 곳이기 때문에 지역적으로도 멀 뿐만 아니라 연구의 대상으로 하기에는 그 지역 사정이 매우 용이한 일이 아니었기 때문이었다.

셋째로는, 선입견적인 측면에서 볼 때 과연 한국어와 Ural 제어 간에 얼마만큼 유사성이 있을까 하는 막연한 심리에서 연구가 별로 없었던 때문이 아닐까 한다. 이러한 상황이 거의 해방 이후 현재에 이르는 과정에까지 그대로 지속되었기 때문이다.

그러나 우리는 'Ural-Altai학설'이나 'Altai학설'이나 모두 우리 스스로 연구하여 결정해야 할 과제를 안고 있다고 하겠다. 설령 '古Asia학설'이거나 '고Siberia학설' 또는 그 밖에도 '고대 한반도 학설' '북방계 와 남방계의 혼합설'을 주장할 수도 있을 것이리라. 그러나 이 모든 학설 자체를 우리 학계가 스스로 검토하고 검증하여 비교적인 측면에서 연구한 그 결과를 토대로 어떤 학설은 인정해야 할 것이며 또한 그렇지 못한 학설은 인정하지 못할 것이다. 또한 그렇지 못한 학설은 어디가 어떻게 문제점이 있는지를 스스로 밝혀내어 비판을 가해야 할 것인데 해방 이후 외국학설만 일방적으로 무조건 수용하기만 급급하였기 때문에 제대로 제 학설들을 이해하고 여기에 대한 안목이 모자랐기 때문에 어쩔 수 없이 비판을 할 수 없었다. 따라서 외국학설에 의존한 채 무조건 그 이론에 매달릴 수밖에 없었던 것이다.

그러하기 때문에 어떤 학설을 정확하게 따르기보다는 밀려 들어 오는 모든 학설을 우선 알아야 한다는 사실이 보다 시급하였던 것이다. 그러다 보니까, 결과는 학설이 난무하여 학설끼리 경쟁되었던 것도 지난날의 우리 학계의 현실이었던 것이 사실이었다. 그리하여 설상가상으로 독일에서 유학한 학자들은 독일식 사고체계와 학문적인 전통 방법을 고수하려고 하였으며 미국에서 공부하고 온 학자들은 개방적 민주적 사고방식의 학문적 자세를 고집하려고 노력하였으며 또한 그동안 경성제대나 일본에서 공부하여 온 최초의 신세대들은 일본 제국주의식 방법을 통해 엄격하고 권위주의식 생각을 버리지 못했던 점을 우리는 솔직하게 시인하여야 할 것이다.

말하자면 한국식의 방법론이나 '틀'이 없이 짜깁기식 서구의 모자이크식 학문 방법에 우리는 젖어 있었던 것이었다.

이제부터라도 한국식 방법론을 개발하여야 할 단계에 왔다는 것이다. 말하자면 한국학의 개념과 정의 그리고 학문적 성격과 범위까지도 우리 스스로 결정하고 결정한 다음부터는 여기에 스스로 맞추어서 연구하여야 할 것이다. 사실 지금까지는 우리 스스로 결정해서 연구한 바도 거의 없었지만 실제적으로 어느 정도 결정하였다고 하더라도 조금 있으면 곧바로 이러한 결정 사실을 번복하고 또다시 거론해서 다시 원점으로 돌려놓은 경우도 우리는 허다하게 보아 왔던 것이다. 물론 학문이란 국제성을 벗어날 수는 없다고 하더라도 민족의 독자성을 부인할 수만은 없는 것이다.

앞에서 언급한 'Ural학' 역시도 우리 스스로 연구할 단계에 왔다는 것을 강조하고 싶다. 원래 Ural어족은 소련 서북 Siberia, Ural산맥 동쪽과 서쪽 그리고 남쪽 Volga강 중류지역 Estonia 공화국, 까렐리아 자치공화국. Hungary, Rumania, 체코슬라바키아, 유고슬라비아 등지에서 사용되는 어족이며 전체 사용자 수는 약 3000만 명에 이른다.

대체적으로 Ural어족을 간단하게 분류하면 다음과 같다. 크게 보면 Ural어족은 '핀-우그르'어파와 'Samoyed'어파로 구분하여 생각할 수 있겠다.

〔A〕 Samoyed 어파

언어는 Ural어에 속하며 러시아 서북 최 북쪽에 살고 있는 몽고인 들이다. 한때는 싸얀산맥 근처까지 Samoyed족들이 분포하였다. 전체 인구는 약 30,000명 정도이며 순록을 방목하는 유목민족이다.

이 Samoyed 어파에는 다음과 같은 제어들이 있다.

① yurak어가 있는데 자신들은 Nenets라고 하여 '사람'이라는 뜻이다. 인구는 23,000명 정도이다. 이들은 주로 순록을 방목하고 살며 어업 사냥이 주 생업이라고 하였다.

② Enets어가 있는데 일명 '예니세니 Samoyed'라고 칭하며 인구는 300여 명 정도이다. Enets라는 말 역시 '사람'을 뜻한다. 역시 주로 순록을 사육하며 어업이 생업이다.

③ Selkup어가 있는데 인구는 3,000여 명 정도이다. Selkup 또는 solkup이라고 자신들을 말하고 있는데 이 말은 '타이가 출신의 사람들'을 뜻한다. Selkup족의 수사 단위는 과거에 있어서는 '다람쥐 가죽'이었다고 한다. 그리고 Selkup족은 사냥과 어업이 주업이며 순록은 교통수단의 일종이라고 한다.

④ Targi어는 Russia 중부 Siberia의 최 북쪽에 위치, 말하자면 소련 민족 중에서도 가장 북방에 살고 있으며 인구는 약 800여 명 정도이면서 생업은 어업, 사냥 순록을 기른다. 극지에 살고 있기 때문에 아직도 원시성을 갖고 있다고 하겠다.

⑤ Kamassi어는 아직 그 인구수를 모르고 있는 형편이다.

〔B〕 Fenno-Ugric어파

우랄어족에서 Samoyed어파가 분리된 후 Fenno-ugric어파는 '우그르 어계', '핀-페름 어계', '핀-불가 어계', '핀-라프 어계', '발덕-핀 어계' 등으로 나눠 발달하였다.

(가) 우그르 어계

Fenno-ugric의 공동체 어파는 '우그르 어계'와 '핀-페름 어계'로 나누어지며 '핀-페름 어계'는 그 후 계속해서 '핀-불가 어계', '핀-라프 어계', '발덕-핀 어계'로 분리되어진다. 또한, 'Ugric 어계'는 '오브-우그르 어계'로 나눠져 여기에서 'Vogul어', 'Ostyak어'로 구분되며 또 'ugric 어계'에서 'Hungaria어'로 나뉜다. 또한 Ugric 문화의 특징 중의 하나인 몽고족처럼 말(馬)의 문화인 유목문화였다는 것이다.

① Vogul어는 소련 러시아공화국 안의 우랄 산맥 동쪽 시베리아에 있는 Khanty-Mansi민족지역에 살고 있는 민족의 언어이다. 그들은 자신들을 Nansi족이라고 하며 인구는 6,500여 명이다. 5C경 동쪽에서 온 여러 동방 민족의 영향을 받았으며 생업은 사냥이며 특히 웅(熊)을 숭배한다. Mansi족은 Mosh와 Por족으로 나뉜다. Por족은 신화에 따르면 하늘의 아들인 곰의 자손이라 하며 또 다른 신화에 의하면 곰은 여자 곰이었고 이 여자 곰이 여자 아이를 낳아 자

손이 퍼졌다는 이야기가 있다.

② Ostyak어는 Vogul어 사용지역과 큰 차이는 없다. 자신들을 Khanty족이라고 부르는데 이는 Ostyak어로 '콘다 강 근처에서 온 사람'이라는 의미로 'Khandt-Kho'에서 유래되었다고 한다. 이들의 문화 역시 웅(熊)을 숭배하는 민족이다. Khanty의 인구는 약 19,000여 명쯤 된다고 한다.

③ Hungarian어는 Magyar족의 언어이며 헝가리인들은 헝가리에 1,100명 그리고 체코, 유고, 루마니아, 소련 오스트리아에 300여 만 명이 살고 있다고 한다. Magyar족은 문화와 관계를 가졌으며 또한 이란계와도 문화적 교류를 갖게 된다. 이러한 이유는 Magyar족이 반유목 민족이기 때문이다. 또한 Hungary는 Turkey계 Khazar족의 지배도 받게 된다. Hungary라는 말의 유래는 5C경 이동을 할 때 Turkey계 언어로 이름 지어진 'on-Ogur'라 하여 의미는 '열 개의 화살'이라는 뜻이다.

(나) 페름 어계

'핀-페름 어계'는 '페름 어계'와 'Fenno-Volga어계'로 나뉜다.

① Votyak어는 소련의 Kama강변 Udmurt인이라고 하며 인구는 60만 명 정도이다. 17C 이전까지는 Turkey계 민족들의 지배하에 있었다.

② Syrjan어는 소련의 Komi자치 공화국에서 사용되고 있으며 우랄 산맥과 Kama강 사이에 있는 Komi-Permyak민족 지역에서도 사용된다. 자신들은 Kami족이라고 부르며 이 Komi의 의미는 '사람'이라는 뜻이다.

(다) Volga어계

'Fenno-Volga어계'는 다시 'Volga어계'와 'Fenno-Lapp어계'로 나뉜다. Volga어계는 Mordva어와 Cheremis어로 나뉜다.

① Mordva어는 소련 서부 Siberia Volga강 좌우편에 살고 있는 Mordva족의 언어이며 Mordva 자치 공화국을 구성하고 있다. Mordva족은 Moksa족과 Erza족으로 구분된다. 인구는 130만여 명이며 16C 이전까지는 Turkey계 tatar족의 지배하에 있었다.

② Cheremis는 자신들을 'Mari'라 지칭하며 이 의미는 '사람'이라는 뜻이다.

인구수는 50여 만 명에 이르고 있으며 Turkey계 영향을 받았으며 13C-16C까지는 Tatar족의 지배를 받았으며 17C에 들어와서는 러시아의 지배를 받았다.

(라) Lapp어계

Fenno-Lapp어계는 Lapp어와 Baltic-Finn어계로 나뉜다.

① Lapp어는 Norway, Sweden, Finland, Russia 4개국의 북쪽에 위치한 언어이다. 인구는 3만여 명이다. 자신들은 Saame족이라고 부르고 있으며 원래는 몽고계이어서 고대 시베리아 원주민이 후에 핀-우그리아 어계의 영향을 받았던 것으로 추측된다. 이 Saame족들은 현재 러시아의 서북단 Kola반도에 살고 있다고 한다.

(마) Baltic-Finn어계

Baltic-Finn어계는 Finland와 소련 접경지역과 Ladoga호수 근처에서 사용된다. 현재는 Estonia, FinnLiv, Vatja, Vepsa, Karelian어로 나뉜다.

① Estonian어는 소련 내의 15개 공화국 중의 하나이다. Baltic 3국이란 Estonia, Litvia, Lithuania를 말한다. Estonia 인구는 약 100만 명이며 1,200년대부터 여러 지명과 인명이 기록되어 있다. Estonia는 독일 Denmark에게는 13-14C, Poland에게는 16C, Sweden에게는 1645-1710년, 그리고 다시 독일의 지배를 받았으며 1917년 독립되었다가 1940년에는 소련이 합병되었다.

② Finnish어는 Finland와 Karelia자치 공화국과 Leiningrad 부근에서 사용된다.

③ Liv어는 Latvia공화국 수도인 Riga 부근에서 약 150여 명이 사용한다고 한다.

④ Vatja어는 Estonia공화국 동부에서 수십 명이 사용하고 있다.

⑤ Vepsa어는 약 10,000여 명이 사용하고 있다.

⑥ Karelian어는 Karelia자치 공화국과 Kalinin지역에서 사용한다. 인구는 18만 정도이고 Finn어와 매우 가깝다.

이상에서처럼 우랄어족의 제어들을 어계별로 나눠서 생각해 보았다. 참으로 많은 제어들을 우리는 그 동안 잊고 살았다고 할 수 있을 것이다. 생각해 보면 참으로 어처구니없기도 하지만 후손으로 안타깝고 억울하기도 하다. 이토록 거대하고 장엄한 우랄・알타이어족을 왜 우리는 그토록 잊고 살았을까. 선각자였던 신채호님의 예언 따라 우리는 '오늘 이후는 서구의 문화와 북구의 사상이 세계사의 중심이 된 바 아 조선은 그 문화사상의 노예가 되어 소멸하고 말 것인가…' 이와 같이 전락되고 말았지 않았는가 자문해 본다. 또한 신채호님이 말씀하였던 '북 대 진취의 사상이 시대를 따라 진퇴된 것이며'에서 보더라도 우리는 고구려 시대 이러한 북방 기상을 갖고 그 웅지의 뜻을 광개토왕과 장수왕 시대에 펼쳤으나 대륙의 중원 땅을 결코 완전히 차지하지 못했으며 고려시대에 와서도 겨우 한반도만이라도 지키기 위해서 윤관이나 서희 등의 활약도 우리는 이제는 까맣게 잊은 듯하고 조선에 들어 와서도 김종서 등이 세종의 명을 받아 북쪽의 변방을 지키기는 하였으나 결국 고려나 조선은 원과 청의 굴욕적 지배를 받았던 것도 우리는 익히 알고 있을 것이다. 이 모두가 '북방에 대한 진취적 웅지'가 결정적으로 부족하였던 것이 아닌가 생각된다. 또한 북아적 진취의 사고를 가졌던 무인이나 문인들이 오히려 역사적으로 볼 때 환영을 받기는커녕 따돌림이나 수세에 몰려 어려움을 당했던 것으로 우리는 기억하고 있을 것이다. 그래서 결국 수천 년 역사 속에서 단 한 번도 북아를 단행해 보지 못했던 것이 아닌가 생각된다.

또한 신채호 선생님의 '我에서 분리한 흉노, 선비, 몽고며 아의 문화의 강보에서 자라온 일본이……'에서도 오늘날 우리는 신채호님의 대륙적인 기질을 알 수 있을 것이며 여기에다가 신채호님은 한반도가 대륙의 주체적 원근이라고 생각하였던 것처럼 보이며 또한 그 근원적 바탕에서 보면 흉노, 선비, 몽고 등의 북방 제어 등이 한국에서 비롯되었음을 주지하였던 것이다. 이와 같이 우리의 극히 일부 선각자들은 1C 전부터 이 방면에 이론적 생각은 하였던 것 같다. 단지 이러한 사실을 과학적이고도 치밀하며 문헌과 서구적 이론을 배경으로 구체화하지는 못했을망정 감각적 사고는 있었던 것 같다. 오히려 해방 이후에 위와 같은 단편적 지식이나마 이것을 객관적 집대성을 우리가 못했던 것이 부끄러운 뿐이다. 이러한 상황은 지금도 계속되고 있는 실정이다.

그리고 어느 면에서는 강보에서 자라온 일본이 일찍부터 오히려 이 북방

방면에 이론적인 배경과 현장적, 민속적 측면을 통하여 인류·역사·민속·언어적인 성과가 세계적 수준에 있음을 우리는 부인할 수 없는 상황에 현재 도달해 있다고 보겠다. 일본은 명치유신을 통하여 과거 우리의 강보에서 벗어났고 지금은 어쩌면 우리 스스로가 일본의 강보에 있지나 않나 자문자답을 해본다. 아니 확실히 북방학에 대한 학문은 아마도 필자의 견지로서는 그렇다라고 감히 말하고도 싶다. 아마도 이러한 심정은 일본에 대한 패배의식에서 오기보다는 오히려 자책감이나 오기에서 일부러 그런 생각을 해 본다는 것이다.

그리고 신채호님의 '흉노, 여진 등의 일차 아와 분리한 뒤에 다시 합하지 못한 의문이며'에서도 우리는 뼈아픈 고대 우리 민족사를 보는 것 같다. 왜 우리는 고대 동일계 어족이었을 것으로 보이는 흉노와 여진을 잃고 지금까지 살았을까 하는 의문점을 자아내게 한다. 우리는 이 시점에서 이러한 사실에 반성을 해야 할 것이다. 그것이 무엇이냐 하면 다음과 같은 것이로다.

첫째로는 유목적이며 기마적인 생활을 하였던 까마득한 상고대에 있어서는 우리 한민족 자신들도 이러한 기질 속에서 흉노나 여진, 말갈 등의 제족과 동일한 지역에서 혼거하면서 동일한 생활환경을 조성하였을 것이다. 그러다가 Nicolas Poppe의 학설에서처럼 원시 한국어를 사용하였던 부족들은 오늘날 한반도에 제일 먼저 이주하여 정착하면서부터 자연스럽게 한반도에 맞는 농경문화로 생활이 바뀌게 되었다. 이러한 환경적 변화의 계기는 과거 흉노·여진·말갈 등의 제족과의 관계에서 소원해짐은 정한 이치일 수 있을 것이다. 문제는 바로 이러한 점에 우리는 유념해야 할 것이다.

말하자면 농경민족으로 변화되면서 어쩌면 북방이 생활은 잊어버리기 시작하였을 것이며 또한 이로 인하여 과거 동일한 제족이었던 흉노 등 제족과의 관계는 우리 스스로 끊고 살았을 것이다. 그리고는 오히려 우리가 그들을 북적이라고 하여 도둑처럼 여기면서 살았음을 우리는 용비어천가를 통해서 알 수 있었을 것이다. 왜냐하면 아마도 우리 한민족은 동일어계였던 북방계 제족보다는 문화적으로 최상의 漢族을 어느 의미에서는 선택하여 그들과 더불어 또는 영향을 받으면서 살고 싶었다고나 할까. 따라서 한문화의 영향을 받으면서 생존하자니 자연히 동일계라지만 그들과의 관계는 소원해질 수밖에 없었을 것이며 어쩔 수 없이 아마도 북적이라고 호칭한 듯하다. 말하자면 중국의 영향에서 온 듯하다. 이러한 시간이 수천 년 흐르는 동안에 우리는 우리 스스로 분리된 이후 다시는 결합할 수 없었던 것이다.

둘째로는 우리 韓族은 상고대에 있어서는 방목하면서 기마적 생활을 하였을 것이다. 그래서 아마도 이 당시에는 대륙적 기질이었던 性格 역시 반도 기질로 바뀌어 지게 되었으며 이로 인해 기마 방목적 생활권에 속하였던 과거의 북 방족이었던 제족과는 상대적으로 거리감을 느끼게 되었으며 오히려 이제는 동일한 농경 문화권인 중국과 가깝게 지내고자 했던 마음이 설상가상으로 중국에 흠뻑 빠져 이제는 헤어날 수 없는 지경에 이르렀다는 말이며 이로 인하여 고대 동계였던 북방족과는 오랫동안 헤어져서 살 수밖에 없었던 것이 아닌가 한다.

셋째로는 문화 대국인 중국의 영향을 오랜 세월 동안 받다 보니 문화적으로 한족보다 훨씬 못한 동계인 북방족을 우리 스스로 그들을 천대시하고 멸시하지는 않았나 다시금 생각해 본다. 아마도 중국의 영향 그대로 본받아 북방족을 우리도 북적이라고 하였음을 보면 이러한 사실에 부인할 수는 없으리라.

이러한 생각이 어떤 의미에 있어서는 오늘날 우리 한국 민족의 성격적인 측면에서 볼 때 사대정신을 키우지는 않았나 의구심을 갖게 한다. 그래서 역사적으로 보면 결과론적인 측면에서 볼 때 우리 민족은 예로부터 결국 당, 원, 명, 청을 섬기면서도 동계인 흉노, 여진 등은 적대시하고 살아 왔던 것을 보면 사대적 사고가 있었던 것 같다. 이러한 사고는 현대에 들어 와서도 강자에게는 무조건적 복종 내지 무조건적 그들의 문화에 대한 향수 등으로 나타나고 있으며 또한 약자에게는 멸시 천대를 하고 있음을 우리는 동족인 중국의 조선족에게 대하고 있는 예를 통해 알 수 있을 것이다. 또한 지식인의 사회인 대학에서 조차도 문화 대국의 문화권을 중심으로 모든 학문의 초점이 맞춰지고 있으며 논문 역시도 강대국의 논문을 인용하거나 또는 그들의 이론과 그들의 결과를 통해서 우리의 원인을 규명하려고 그동안 많은 시간을 할애하지 않았던가 하는 점에서 우리는 문화사대 지식인이었던 것도 사실이다. 웬만하면 우리 스스로 우리의 문제점에 대한 원인을 규명하고 그것을 치료할 생각은 없고 외국의 이론을 통해서 우리의 문제점을 찾아 치료할 생각이 더 많았던 것을 어찌 부인만 할 수 있겠는가. 아마도 이러한 생각이 결국 신채호님의 지적한 바처럼 우리의 크나큰 고대사에 제사를 잃었던 것으로 생각할 수 있겠다.

필자는 지금까지 스스로 한국학에 대한 여러 사실들을 나름으로 생각한 바를 서술하였다. 물론 필자 자신이 박학하지 못하고 깊은 학문을 못한 탓에 무게 있게 글을 펼치지는 못했지만 본서를 통해 충분히 의사 전달은 하였다고 본다.

결국 지금까지 논의의 초점은 한국에서의 '한국학'에 대한 과제와 전망을 말한 셈이었고 진정한 의미에 있어서 '한국학'이란 무엇이며 왜 이 '한국학'이 우리 민족에게 그토록 필요한 것인가 또한 앞으로 '한국학'의 범위는 결국 '우랄 · 알타이 지역과 제어'까지를 포함해야 한다는 사실에 주목한 셈이었다. 이러한 사실이 실행되면 보다 폭넓고 웅지에 넘친 한민족으로 성장되지 않을까 생각한다.

아무리 세계화시대에 살고 있다고 하더라도 이럴 때일수록 자기 민족에 보다 충실하여야만 보다 열정을 갖고 고대에서 현대까지 연구해야만이 보다 나은 미래가 있을 것이다. 그래서 이제라도 '거시적 한국학', '광의의 한국학'을 되찾아 과거 영광스러웠던 고구려의 기상을 물려받고 백제의 찬란한 문화와 신라의 섬세한 기풍을 기반으로 하면서 흉노, 여진 등 상고대에 같이 동거동락했던 마음의 자세를 잃어서는 안 되겠다. 결국 필자는 '한국학에 대한 저자의 변'에서 이야기하고자 한 것의 가장 핵심적 소견이란 앞으로의 한민족은 필히 북방의 유목적 기마문화와 한반도의 농경문화를 결합하여 새로운 새 문화를 창출해야 할 것이다. 그러자면 더더욱 우랄 · 알타이 문화와 언어에 대한 깊은 지식이 있어야 하겠으며 이것과 더불어 한국 그래서 이것 등의 결국 '한국학'이라는 명칭으로 변화되어 새로운 미래를 창출해야 할 것이다.

무릇 학자의 사명이란, 없었던 사실을 발견하고 여러 사람에게 알려 유익하게 살 수 있도록 하는 마음의 자세가 있는가 하면 지금까지의 여러 사실과 이론들을 종합하여 어떤 결론을 도출해 내려는 마음가짐도 필요할 것이며 여러 곳에 산재해 있는 자료들을 찾고 수집하고 선택하여 문헌 자료를 집대성

하는 것도 후학들에게 또는 후손들에게 매우 중요한 안내자의 역할을 하는 것이다.

그러나 위와 같은 여러 사실들이 학자에게는 무엇하고 바꿀 수 없는 귀중한 작업인 것만은 틀림이 없을 것이다. 그렇지만 필자가 본서에서 밝히거나 번역하거나 모으거나 토를 달아서 내놓는 '한국학과 우랄·알타이학'은 과거 상고대의 거대했던 한민족의 기상과 기개로 본서가 동기가 되어서 '거시적 한국학'이 이 땅에 뿌리 내렸으면 하는 바람이다.

세월은 흘러 한국의 역사도 수천 년이 흘렀다. 이제는 한 번쯤 과거 찬란했던 기상을 되찾을 때가 오지 않았는가 하는 생각은 비단 필자만의 바람은 아닐 것이다. 끝으로 이 장대하고 넓은 저서를 출간하는 데 흔쾌히 허락해 주신 역락출판사의 이대현 사장님과 여러 차례 연구실을 방문해서 본 저서가 출판되어 세상에 나오게 해주신 안현진 부장님에게도 감사드리고 본교 대학원 김희지 박사와 박찬식 박사에게도 필자의 자문에 응해준 것에 고마움을 표하며 이따금 필자의 자료정리에 도움을 준 본교 국어국문학과 김이주, 김정아에게도 고맙다는 인사를 한다. 또한 항상 논문과 저서를 출간할 때면 경원대학교 설립자였던 故 원계 김동석 총장님을 생각하게 된다. 그것은 평소 '우랄·알타이' 연구소를 필자에게 설립하게 해서 '거시적 한국학'을 1990년도부터 문을 열겠다는 약속이 생각나기 때문이다. 이 책을 통해 고인의 명복을 빈다. 또한 역락출판사의 무궁한 발전을 기원하며 이대현 사장님을 비롯 편집 선생님들의 노고에 감사드린다. 아마도 이렇게 'Ural-Altai와 한국학'을 연계해서 24권씩이나 한 번에 출판한다는 사실은 필자가 아는 바에 의하면 세계에서 처음 있는 일이라고 감히 말하고 싶다. 이런 점을 통해서 본다면 본 작업은 실로 방대하고 장대한 작업이 아닐 수 없는 것이다.

2007년 12월 5일
어린이 함성이 들려오는 복정골 K동 405호에서 필자
一山 박상규 삼가 올려드림

저자 一山, 박상규(朴相圭)

一山, 박상규는 올해 회갑 나이이며 이리 남성중, 대구 능인고, 고려대·경희대 수학. 1987 "한국어의 복수 접미사 비교 연구"로 문학박사학위취득. 현재, 경원대학교 국어국문학과 교수. 전공은 '우랄·알타이 언어·민속학'으로 논문 100여 편, 역·편·저서 50여 권.
북경대학에서 '한·중 무속고' 100주년에서는 '대청황제 숭덕 비문의 언어학적 비교연구' 발표. 울란바토르 대학, 이스탄불 대학, 일본 동지사 대학, 동경 역사 민속박물관, 쓰쿠바 대학 등 세계 많은 대학에서 논문 발표.
학회는 '세계샤만학회' '동Asia 고대학회' '국어국문학회' '제주학회' '한국민속학회' '한국무속학회' '한국민요학회' '한국몽골학회' '한국방언학회' '우랄·알타이 연구회' '국제비교한국학회' '한민족학회'에서 회장, 이사, 감사, 총무이사, 평의원을 지냄.
중국 남경대학 특별 초빙교수 역임.
詩集으로 '마음의 풍경'(글누림, 2007. 11. 간행)이 있음.
호 一山은 故 양주동 교수님, 법명一道는 어느 女僧으로부터 받음.

한국학과 우랄·알타이학 2
관련자료·연구총서

만주어 관계 문헌의 『百排』에 관한 고찰 (상)–고찰편

인 쇄 2007년 12월 13일
발 행 2007년 12월 20일
저 자 박상규
발행인 이대현

발행처 도서출판 역락
등 록 1999년 4월 19일 제303-2002-0014호
주 소 서울 서초구 반포4동 577-25 문창빌딩 2층
전 화 02-3409-2058, 2060
팩 스 02-3409-2059

정 가 70,000원
ISBN 978-89-5556-588-1 93700

잘못된 책은 바꿔드립니다.